D. Ew. Harrison
from H. E. H. Probyn
2. 9. 33.

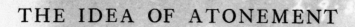

THE IDEA OF ATONEMENT

BY THE SAME AUTHOR

THE UNIVERSITIES OF THE MIDDLE AGES. 1895.
DOCTRINE AND DEVELOPMENT. 1898.
CHRISTUS IN ECCLESIA. 1904.
THE THEORY OF GOOD AND EVIL. 1907.
PHILOSOPHY AND RELIGION. 1909.
IS CONSCIENCE AN EMOTION? 1914.
CONSCIENCE AND CHRIST. 1916.

THE
IDEA OF ATONEMENT

IN

CHRISTIAN THEOLOGY

BEING THE

BAMPTON LECTURES FOR 1915

BY

HASTINGS RASHDALL

D.Litt. (Oxon.), D.C.L. (Dunelm.), LL.D. (St. Andrews)

DEAN OF CARLISLE
FELLOW OF THE BRITISH ACADEMY
FORMERLY FELLOW AND TUTOR OF NEW COLLEGE, OXFORD

MACMILLAN AND CO., LIMITED
ST. MARTIN'S STREET, LONDON
1919.

MACMILLAN AND CO., Limited
LONDON · BOMBAY · CALCUTTA · MADRAS
MELBOURNE

THE MACMILLAN COMPANY
NEW YORK · BOSTON · CHICAGO
DALLAS · SAN FRANCISCO

THE MACMILLAN CO. OF CANADA, Ltd.
TORONTO

EXTRACT FROM THE LAST WILL AND STATEMENT

OF

The Late Rev. JOHN BAMPTON

CANON OF SALISBURY

. . . " I give and bequeath my Lands and Estates to the
Chancellor, Masters, and Scholars of the University of Oxford for
ever, to have and to hold all and singular the said Lands or
Estates upon trust, and to the intents and purposes hereinafter
mentioned ; that is to say, I will and appoint that the Vice-
Chancellor of the University of Oxford for the time being shall
take and receive all the rents, issues, and profits thereof, and
(after all taxes, reparations, and necessary deductions made) that
he pay all the remainder to the endowment of eight Divinity
Lecture Sermons, to be established for ever in the said University,
and to be performed in the manner following :

" I direct and appoint, that, upon the first Tuesday in Easter
Term, a Lecturer may be yearly chosen by the Heads of Colleges
only, and by no others, in the room adjoining to the Printing-
House, between the hours of ten in the morning and two in the
afternoon, to preach eight Divinity Lecture Sermons, the year
following, at St. Mary's in Oxford, between the commencement
of the last month in Lent Term, and the end of the third week
in Act Term.

" Also I direct and appoint, that the eight Divinity Lecture
Sermons shall be preached upon either of the following subjects—
to confirm and establish the Christian Faith, and to confute all
heretics and schismatics—upon the divine authority of the holy
Scriptures—upon the authority of the writings of the primitive
Fathers, as to the faith and practice of the primitive Church—
upon the Divinity of our Lord and Saviour Jesus Christ—upon
the Divinity of the Holy Ghost — upon the Articles of the
Christian Faith, as comprehended in the Apostles' and Nicene
Creed.

v

" Also I direct, that thirty copies of the eight Divinity Lecture Sermons shall be always printed, within two months after they are preached ; and one copy shall be given to the Chancellor of the University, and one copy to the Head of every College, and one copy to the Mayor of the city of Oxford, and one copy to be put into the Bodleian Library ; and the expense of printing them shall be paid out of the revenue of the Land or Estates given for establishing the Divinity Lecture Sermons ; and the Preacher shall not be paid, nor be entitled to the revenue, before they are printed.

" Also I direct and appoint, that no person shall be qualified to preach the Divinity Lecture Sermons, unless he hath taken the degree of Master of Arts at least, in one of the two Universities of Oxford or Cambridge ; and that the same person shall never preach the Divinity Lecture Sermons twice."

PREFACE

ONE of the most crying needs of the Church at the present moment is a serious attempt at re-thinking its traditional Theology. A large part of that theology has obviously become more or less unintelligible to modern men who do not possess technical knowledge of its history and contents. It needs to be re-examined, and (where necessary) reconstructed, in the light of modern philosophy, modern science, and modern criticism. How far the ancient formulae should be frankly abandoned, or how far they admit of re-interpretation in terms of modern thought and experience, is a question on which for the present there are likely to be considerable differences of opinion : but there ought, I think, to be no dissent from the proposition that we should, as little as possible, go on using ancient formulae without knowing —perchance without caring—what was their original meaning, or how far that is a meaning which we at the present day can really appropriate. Personally, I am heartily in favour of the more conservative course of preserving (as far as possible) the continuity of Christian thought and expression. I believe that in very many cases the traditional language, when once its true meaning is known, will be found to be far more patient of a reasonable and a modern interpretation than is often supposed. It is, indeed, impossible that any educated person at the present day can really think of God and the universe exactly as was done by the men of the fourth century or of the thirteenth or of the sixteenth. The most conservative theologian's conception

of God and the universe has been altered by Copernicus
and Newton, by Lyell and Darwin, by modern conceptions of history and modern biblical studies, even when
what is technically called "the higher criticism" and
its results are abjured or ignored. For all or most educated
clergymen and laymen, in our own Church at least, a
fundamental revolution has been effected by the abandonment of the older theories of biblical inspiration and an
entirely altered attitude towards the biblical account of
creation and the early history of the Jewish people.
These changes cannot be without their influence upon
our interpretation of dogmas and doctrines which grew
up under the influence of the earlier conceptions. And
yet it is quite possible that the old formulae may be re-
interpreted without more violence to their original
meaning than they have suffered over and over again
during the past history of doctrinal development. Indeed
in many cases, the kind of re-interpretation that is
needed is simply a return to some earlier stage in the
development of the traditional theology, though in others
it will involve a continuation of some line of development to which the Church is already more or less deeply
committed.

The present work deals only with one department,
or (better) one aspect, of the traditional theology—with
what is technically known as the doctrine of the work
of Christ as distinct from the doctrine of His Person.
My object has been to examine the traditional doctrine
of "salvation" through Christ—in particular of salvation through the sufferings and death of Christ—and
the closely connected theories as to the way in which
the salvation brought into the world by Christ is to be
appropriated by the individual soul. This has involved
some treatment of the "doctrine of grace," and, indeed,
has occasionally led me into various other departments
of theology; but I have tried to confine myself as much
as possible to the questions which centre round the
doctrine of the atonement. Logically, no doubt, any
enquiry into the "office" of Christ should pre-suppose
a much fuller treatment of the doctrine of His Person

than will be found in these pages. But there are some advantages in beginning with an enquiry into the former subject. The need for further study and bolder expression is here peculiarly pressing, and is perhaps more widely felt than in any other region. On the one hand, the idea that we are to be saved through Christ, and in some sense through His Cross, is much dearer to the hearts of most religious people than any technical presentation of the incarnation : it is, indeed, very largely through its bearing upon the practical question, " How am I to be saved ? " that the doctrine of Christ's divinity interests them at all. On the other hand, there has been far more that is definitely irrational, repellent, and immoral in many theories of the atonement than there has been in any accepted theory of the incarnation. The revolt against these theories is, indeed, already pretty general ; but the way to a healthier and more modern presenta ion of the subject is blocked by the surviving débris of shattered systems. Moreover, there has been far more variation in the Church's teaching on this subject than there has been as regards the doctrines of the Holy Trinity or of the incarnation. The doctrine of the atonement has never been defined by any Creed or " general " Council of the Church. The Creeds indeed decide no question connected with the subject which has ever been matter of dispute among Christians. The Apostles' Creed says literally nothing about it ; the Creed commonly called "Nicene" or "Constantinopolitan" confines itself to the bare statements that the Son of God " for us men and for our salvation came down from heaven," and that He was crucified " for us." No Council that can possibly claim ecumenical authority has ever gone beyond such simple statements ; and, if we look at the whole course of development from the New Testament to the end of the scholastic period, there is no subject upon which less of a *consensus patrum* can be alleged than on the question, " In what sense and for what reason can Christ be said to have died for us ? " In these circumstances there is perhaps some hope of getting a hearing even in conservative circles for a theological enquiry which is directed rather to the question "What is true?" than to the question "What has been decided?"

Some will perhaps be disposed to complain that I have not confined myself more strictly to questions of present truth and meaning, instead of devoting so large a space to the history and development of the traditional doctrines. My reason for adopting the historical method of treatment is that it is not possible to enquire into the truth of any particular presentation of such a doctrine as that of the atonement till we know whence that presentation comes to us, what authority it can claim, and what reason there is, or ever was, for believing it to be true. Theologians, and even philosophers, who have approached the subject without such a preliminary enquiry have too often assumed that there is some one doctrine on the subject which can somehow claim to be *the* doctrine of the atonement, which has come down to us from the teaching of Christ or at least from the very earliest days of Christianity, which has always borne the same meaning, which has always been accepted and always must be accepted as the central doctrine, if not as the whole, of Christianity. Writers who adopt this method often occupy themselves with finding ingenious apologies and explanations for precisely those features of the traditional theories which can least claim to represent any reasonable process of thought, any profound religious conviction, or any compelling weight of authority. When philosophers, often personally quite unattached to traditional Christianity, have supposed themselves bound to find profound metaphysical explanations of what they take to be "*the* Christian doctrine of the atonement," the result has often been some theory not particularly rational in itself, something which presents hardly any resemblance to the belief which it is supposed to interpret, and which has, almost avowedly, no real relation to the historical Personality in connexion with whose work all Christian theories of the atonement actually grew up. A due appreciation of the historical origin, and subsequent variations, of the doctrine is the essential pre-requisite of any attempt to interpret or

re-interpret it in terms of modern thought.   It is not
worth while to find philosophical justifications for theories
which originally rested upon some misinterpretation of
Hebrew prophecy, or which represent some comparatively
modern perversion or exaggeration of an earlier and more
reasonable belief.

I am aware, of course, that the historical enquiry has
been very imperfectly carried out in these pages.   I have
been obliged, especially in the later periods, merely to
examine the views of a few great typical writers without
attempting a continuous history of opinion, and the
historical enquiry stops altogether with the first phase
of the Reformation.   It would have been quite easy to fill
another volume as large as the present with accounts
and criticisms of later views ;   but this would have
carried me far beyond the limits permissible to a Bampton
Lecturer, even when he avails himself to the full of his
accustomed licence to print much more than was actually
delivered in the pulpit.   The development of the more
or less authoritative dogma practically ends with the
age of Luther and Calvin :   the history of modern
speculation on this subject I have deliberately regarded
as lying beyond my province.   I have consequently
been able to take very little notice of modern, and especially of contemporary, writers.   But I hope it will not
be supposed that I have failed to acquaint myself with
their work or that I underrate its importance.   I have,
I believe, examined all the main lines of thought on the
subject which find defenders at the present day, but I
have only occasionally and by way of illustration mentioned the theologians by whom they have been maintained.   I have not attempted to enter in detail
into the particular forms which each type of theory
assumes in the hands of particular writers.   In the case
of most of those writers with whom I seriously disagree it
would, I believe, be possible to show that their views
are only reproductions, sometimes in more or less disguised and attenuated forms, of some one or more of
the older theories which have been fully dealt with in
these pages.   With regard to the writers with whose

general position I am in sympathy, I have usually ab-
stained from mentioning even their names, not because
I under-estimate their work, but simply because I have
so often found it impossible to indicate in any short and
summary way the extent to which I could appeal to them
in support of my own views.   I should be so far from
claiming any particular originality for the general position
taken up in these pages that I should claim on the
contrary that it represents substantially the view which
is now held not only by a consensus of the more " liberal "
theologians, but by a large and increasing number of
those who would not care to be so described.   If there
is any originality in my treatment of the subject, it lies
rather in my view as to the origin of the traditional
doctrine than in the statement of my own belief upon
this supremely important subject.

The question of the way in which human souls may
be saved—that is to say, may attain to the highest ideal
or true end of their being—is obviously one which leads
the enquirer at every turn into the profoundest questions
of Moral Philosophy, of Psychology, and of Metaphysic.
A full and complete philosophy of salvation would involve
nothing less than a philosophy of the universe.   It would
involve a discussion of all those questions about the
ultimate nature of the universe, about its ultimate goal
and destiny, about the relations between mind and matter,
between subject and object, body and soul, the universal
and the particular, God and man, the human will and the
divine, necessity and contingence, time and eternity,
which it is the business of philosophy and philosophical
theology to answer.   Into these ultimate questions I
have rarely attempted to enter in the present work.
I need hardly say that I have advanced nothing which I
do not believe to be capable of philosophical defence,
but I do not profess in these lectures to be writing philosophy for philosophers.   In some cases I have been able
to refer to other works in which I have discussed such
questions more or less fully : in others I hope I may
be able to deal with them hereafter somewhat less inadequately.   In these pages I am content to assume

the general truth of the Christian attitude towards the universe, and to ask in what way, upon that assumption, the modern thinker is to interpret, in the language of ordinary theology and of ordinary life, the particular aspect of the traditional creed with which this book is concerned.

My obligations to Professor Harnack's great work on the history of dogma will everywhere be obvious, in spite of my profound dissent from his attitude towards attempts, ancient and modern, to construct a Christian philosophy of the universe. On the historical side I should probably have been still more indebted than I am to the extraordinarily learned work, *Le Dogme de la Rédemption*, by the Abbé Rivière, Professor at the Grand Séminaire of Albi, had it fallen into my hands earlier. As it is, I did not know of the book until the lectures were almost finished ; but I have freely used his help in discovering treatises or particular passages where the subject is dealt with by some of those later Fathers whom I do not pretend to have read from cover to cover,— especially in the additional chapter or long note which I have inserted between Lectures IV. and V. I must also acknowledge obligations of the same kind to *The Doctrine of the Atonement* by the Rev. J. K. Mozley—a brief but thoughtful and independent treatment of the subject. I regret that the very learned *History of the Doctrine of the Work of Christ* by the Rev. R. S. Franks, Principal of Western College, Bristol, came into my hands only when most of the book was in type. Perhaps it may be well to add that, except as regards a few authors to whom I have referred in quite an incidental manner, the account I have given of patristic and other writers rests upon an independent study of their works. Except in the case of St. Augustine I have read through all the writings of the Fathers whom I have dealt with at any length in the lectures : in his case I have read, I believe, all that was at all relevant to my subject.

At various stages in its composition, the present work owes much to the advice and assistance of the Ven. A. L. Lilley, Archdeacon of Ludlow ; the Rev. B. H. Streeter,

Canon Residentiary of Hereford; the Rev. J. R. Wilkinson, Rector of Winford; and the Rev. C. W. Emmet, B.D., Vicar of West Hendred. I am under especial obligations to Mr. Emmet, who has been good enough to read the whole of my first proofs, and to Archdeacon Lilley, who has performed a similar kind office for the final revise. I must also express my warm thanks to Professor Cooke, Canon of Christ Church, who has taken much pains in answering enquiries of mine on points of Hebrew learning. If I have escaped some of the pitfalls which await the student incidentally straying from the paths with which his own reading has made him tolerably familiar into those with which his acquaintance is very imperfect, I owe it largely to the kindness of these and other friends.

H. RASHDALL.

THE DEANERY,
CARLISLE, 7th October 1919.

CONTENTS

LECTURE I

THE TEACHING OF CHRIST CONCERNING FORGIVENESS

LECTURE II

THE PRE-PAULINE AND THE PAULINE DOCTRINE OF ATONEMENT

I. *The Origin of the Atonement Doctrine*

LECTURE III

THE TEACHING OF PRIMITIVE CHRISTIANITY

LECTURE IV

PATRISTIC THEORIES

CONTENTS

CONTINUATION OF LECTURE IV

LATER GREEK FATHERS

LECTURE V

LATIN THEOLOGY—AUGUSTINE, ANSELM, ABELARD

LECTURE VI
SCHOLASTIC THEORIES

LECTURE VII
LUTHER AND THE REFORMATION

LECTURE VIII
THE TRUTH OF THE ATONEMENT

CONTENTS

APPENDICES

ERRATA

Page 130, Note C, line 21, *for* Dillman *read* Deissmann.
Page 345, line 11, *for* "Wedgewood" *read* "Wedgwood."

LECTURE I

THE TEACHING OF CHRIST CONCERNING FORGIVENESS

But the publican, standing afar off, would not lift up so much as his eyes unto heaven, but smote his breast, saying, God, be merciful to me a sinner.   I say unto you, This man went down to his house justified rather than the other.—LUKE xviii. 13, 14.

LECTURE I

THE TEACHING OF CHRIST CONCERNING FORGIVENESS

FOR a large proportion of those who have professed the Christian religion, that religion has included the doctrine that salvation is to be won in some sense through the death of its Founder and through belief in the saving efficacy of that death. At times, though by no means always, that doctrine has been regarded as the central truth or even as the whole of that religion. To enquire into the origin, the history, the meaning, the truth of that doctrine is the principal aim of the present lectures. A full and exhaustive treatment of the subject would involve a preliminary enquiry into the history of Jewish ideas about sin and its forgiveness, about the origin and meaning of sacrifice, and a number of other cognate matters. But such an enquiry would lie far beyond the scope of these lectures. For my present purpose it will be best to take as our starting-point the teaching of Jesus Himself, and only at a later stage to ask what light previous Jewish beliefs may throw either upon our Lord's own teaching or upon the later doctrine of the Church.[1]

[1] It may be well to state briefly the critical principles presupposed in the present lecture. I accept the usual " two-document theory," *i.e.* the view that the authors of the first and third Gospels had before them (1) Mark in its present form or a form closely resembling it, and (2) a document (consisting perhaps chiefly of sayings and possibly at some stage of its composition connected with the Apostle St. Matthew) which used to be known as " the Logia," but is now commonly spoken of as Q (*i.e.* Quelle)—a document containing at least the matter common to Matthew and Luke which is not found in Mark, and probably some sayings or narratives only preserved by one of them. There were doubtless other documents, especially a Judaeo-Christian Apocalypse used in Mark xiii and the parallel passages in the two other Gospels, and a source peculiar to Luke. On the much debated question about the priority of Q or Mark, I believe in the priority of Q, and I am strongly inclined to the view of Prof. Bacon (*The Beginnings of the Gospel History*) that Mark can be broken up into a document which he calls P—a body of teaching, oral or written, based on the teaching of St. Peter, extracts from Q and other

3

The first question before us is, then, "What did Jesus Himself teach about the forgiveness of sins? Did He teach the doctrine that sin can only be forgiven through the atoning efficacy of His death, or anything like that doctrine?" It should by no means be assumed that a doctrine is not true because it is not to be found in the teaching of Christ. More and more generally it is coming to be recognized that all Christian doctrine has arisen from the reflection of the Christian Church upon the life and work of its Founder, from its experience of what He has been and may be to the religious life of His followers, from the application of His teaching to the solution of problems which He did not Himself explicitly raise. But it is obvious that the authority which is claimed for a traditional doctrine and the interpretation which we put upon it may be profoundly affected by the relation in which it stands to the actual teaching of the Master. And in particular, if it should be found that the interpretation which is given to a doctrine and its comparative prominence as compared with other elements or aspects of the Christian religion have varied very widely, it is clear that our freedom to choose between these different interpretations may be greatly enhanced by the discovery that none of the conflicting views can claim to represent in any direct or exclusive manner the explicit teaching of its Founder. Still more will our attitude towards such interpretations be affected if it should be found that some of them are positively inconsistent with the teaching of Him whose mind they purport to represent. In this as in other spheres of

---

sources, and the additions of an Editor. At the same time I am sceptical as to the possibility of definitely delimiting these elements with certainty, and I regard Prof. Bacon's distrust of Mark as exaggerated. I believe the third Gospel to have been written by Luke, the companion of St. Paul. On such minute questions as the precise limits of Q, as to whether the Mark used by the two Evangelists differed sufficiently from our text of Mark as to be properly designated a Proto-Mark or " Ur-Markus," as to whether Luke's special source was already combined with Q before it was used by him, and the like, I have not found it necessary to form a definite opinion. Decided opinions on such subjects must be left to those who have spent years of study upon the Synoptic problem. On points which can be affected by the solution of such questions, it is wisest for those who have only a general acquaintance with the problem to keep their minds open to alternative possibilities. Fortunately it is often possible to form a judgement as to which version of a saying or an incident is the more primitive without committing oneself to a particular critical hypothesis.

thought questions of origin must be carefully distinguished from questions of validity, but the question of
validity cannot always be decided without a clear view
on the question of origin.   A doctrine of the atonement
may be true although it has little starting-point, or no
starting-point at all, in the actual teaching of Christ.
But the very fact of the possibility makes it all the more
imperative that we should discuss the question of Christ's
own attitude on the matter without presuppositions, and
without assuming that we are bound to discover in it,
even in a rudimentary form, the later doctrine of the
Church, or rather any one of the numerous doctrines
of the atonement which have at various times been taught
as the doctrine of the Church.   It may be well to state
at once that I hope to show you that there is a possible
doctrine of the atonement which has as much authority
behind it as any other, and the truth of which is quite
unaffected by any conclusion that we can reasonably come
to on the question of origin.

What, then, was our Lord's teaching about sin, its
punishment, and its forgiveness ?   The question cannot
be answered without a glance (it must necessarily be but
a hurried glance) at His teaching about certain other
subjects.   The substance of His very earliest teaching
is contained in the words : " Repent ye, for the kingdom
of heaven is at hand " ; and all His discourses presuppose
in the background, where they are not in the foreground,
the closely connected ideas—the Messianic Parousia or
manifestation, the Messianic judgement, the Messianic
kingdom.   He announced the near approach of the
great judgement which had been foretold by the prophets
of His nation, and which occupied a still more prominent
position in the popular apocalyptic literature of the two
centuries preceding His ministry.   If I were to embark
upon an enquiry into the exact nature of that judgement,
I should almost inevitably become involved in the discussion of questions foreign to my present purpose.   No
subject connected with theology is at the present moment
more hotly debated than the question what our Lord
actually taught about the kingdom of God, about His

own future coming, about the judgement which was to follow that coming, and about the real meaning of the language which he used in this connexion. It is not necessary for my present purpose that I should discuss these questions in detail. It will be enough for me to indicate very briefly the general position which will be presupposed in these lectures. I believe that—probably not from the earliest days of His teaching,[1] yet before the close of it—Jesus had become convinced that He was in some sense, though it may be in a much altered sense, the promised Messiah of His race. At Caesarea Philippi He accepted St. Peter's confession : " Thou art the Christ." [2] Even before that memorable moment in His career He had felt moved to preach that the promised kingdom of God was at hand. It is not impossible that He began to announce the near approach of a personal Messiah before it had become clear to His own mind whether He or another were the promised Messiah or Son of God or Son of Man. But eventually He accepted—if somewhat passively and almost

---

[1] That this was so is suggested (a) by the form of the earliest teaching—simply that the kingdom was at hand, (b) by our Lord's frequent habit of speaking of the " Son of man " in the third person and in reference to the future, (c) by the fact that, if we accept as historical the scene at Caesarea Philippi, He cannot have definitely taught His own Messiahship up to that moment. If this view is accepted, the account of the voice at the baptism (according to Mark only heard by our Lord Himself) must be coloured by later ideas. The account of the temptation hardly implies a consciousness of Messiahship. It does seem to imply a mental struggle as to whether He would proclaim Himself a Messiah in the sense of popular expectation, and this question was answered in the negative. All the evidence goes to show that Jesus only accepted His own identification with the Messiah at a late date, not without reluctance, and in a greatly transfigured and spiritualized sense.

I feel much in sympathy with the treatment of this subject in Prof. Bacon's *The Beginnings of the Gospel Story*. Prof. Bacon points out (p. 106 *sq.*) " that ' the Christ ' is never Jesus' title for Himself, and on the sole occasion outside the present [Peter's confession at Caesarea Philippi] when it seems to be admitted, the admission in both parallels, and even as it would seem in Mark's own model, is, as it were, under protest." He calls attention to the significance of the words " thou sayest " before Pilate. The question is, of course, closely connected with the exceedingly difficult problems : (1) What was the original meaning of " the Son of man " ? (2) Did Jesus apply this title to Himself ? And (3) if so, in what sense ? Even if He did apply the title to Himself, and if we admit that the title was Messianic, the very obscurity and comparative unusualness of the expression seem to indicate that He shrank from a more open and definite avowal. But the whole problem is immensely complicated and difficult. We cannot point to any definite consensus among the experts. Perhaps we may say that probably the title " Son of Man " was sometimes (not so early or perhaps so frequently as the Evangelists represent) used by Jesus, and that it was used messianically, though the probability is far from a certainty, and this probability is one of the strongest pieces of evidence that Jesus did claim in some sense to be the Messiah.

[2] Mk. viii. 29 (= Matt. xvi. 16 ; Lk. ix. 20).

reluctantly—the position of the Messiah. The sense which He gave to the idea of Messiahship had something in common with the current ideas, or at least with the higher of those ideas, but something also that was peculiar to Himself. The ideas of the age on the subject were, indeed, many and various. Out of these various and conflicting ideas about the kingdom of God He selected the most ethical and the most spiritual, and in His own teaching they were still further spiritualized. For Him the idea of the kingdom of Heaven was a spiritual and an ethical conception. Whether He thought of earth or heaven as the scene of the kingdom, whatever the means by which He supposed that His heavenly Father was about to inaugurate it, whatever was to be His personal position in it, it is clear that for Him the kingdom of God was not a political institution to be realized by any effort of revolutionary violence,[1] nor was it *primarily* a cosmic catastrophe which should bring to an end the present social and physical world-order. It was essentially a state of society in which God's will should be perfectly done—done as it is in heaven.

The political Messiahship of the prophets, which still had its adherents in contemporary Judaism, Jesus decidedly rejected. His mission was certainly not to overthrow the Roman power, to restore the ancient glories of the independent Jewish monarchy, and to punish the enemies of Israel. His conception had much more affinity with the apocalyptic idea of a purely supernatural Being, who should descend from heaven, bring to an end the existing order of society, conduct a great judgement of the living and the risen dead, and set up—whether on earth or in heaven—an ideal kingdom of an entirely superhuman character.[2] But in one respect

---

[1] This notion was not absent from the Apocalyptists, nor was it extinct in the days of Jesus. The New Testament by itself would prove the contrary, even apart from passages in many Apocalyptists, especially in the Psalms of Solomon. It is extremely important to remember that " it is indubitable that He developed His own ideas in regard to the sovereignty of God in conscious opposition to the Zealot movement " (Dalman, *The Words of Jesus*, p. 138).

[2] On the history of these apocalyptic ideas the literature is enormous ; they are, in fact, largely dealt with in all recent works upon Jesus and the origins of Christianity. The leading English books are Charles, *Eschatology, Hebrew, Jewish and Christian* ;

His conception of the Messianic office was fundamentally different from that of any Apocalyptist. It was
differentiated from it by the very fact that He claimed
to be Himself that Messiah—He, a human Being, born
in the humblest station, leading a thoroughly human
life of teaching and preaching, ministering and suffering,
" a man of sorrows and acquainted with grief." In so
far, then, as He applied to Himself the apocalyptic
language, this could only refer to a future manifestation
of Himself as Messiah—a manifestation to be brought
about by the interposition of God and (as He came
ultimately to expect) after His own bodily death. To
this future manifestation of Himself as Messiah He did,
it is probable, apply more or less of the current apocalyptic
language about the celestial glory and exaltation of the
Messiah. Much, indeed, of the eschatological language
attributed to our Lord in the Gospels is, I believe, of very
doubtful authenticity. The various attempts to fix the date
of the coming more or less definitely are too conflicting
and too doubtfully attested to be relied upon with any
confidence. They may well represent so many successive
attempts to reassure the minds of disciples whose hopes
of the longed-for Parousia were constantly disappointed.[1]

Stanton, *The Jewish and the Christian Messiah* ; Latimer Jackson, *The Eschatology of
Jesus.*

The recent tendency to emphasize the apocalyptic character of Jesus' own ideas, to
make " Eschatology " the essence of His teaching, and to disparage or explain away the
ethical and spiritual side of it culminated in Schweitzer's brilliant but extravagant book,
The Quest of the Historical Jesus (E.T. by W. Montgomery), to which the reader may
be referred for information as to other writers and theories on the subject. For a discussion of Schweitzer's ideas and their bearing upon the religious estimation of Christ,
I may especially refer to Emmet, *The Eschatological Question in the Gospels* ; von Dobschütz, *The Eschatology of the Gospels* ; Bacon, *The Beginnings of the Gospel Story*—
all very valuable books. An extremely sane estimate of the real place of Eschatology in
the teaching of Jesus is to be found in a book on *The Synoptic Gospels* by Mr. Claude
Montefiore, who writes from the standpoint of Liberal Judaism. Prof. Percy
Gardner (in *Exploratio Evangelica*) may also be noticed as a writer who, while recognizing
the element of truth in the recent theories, has refused to let himself be carried away by
the ultra-eschatological view of Christ's teaching. In my *Conscience and Christ*, Lect.
II., I have briefly discussed the eschatological question chiefly in its bearing upon the
ethical teaching of our Lord, which Schweitzer and his disciples treat as a mere "interims-
ethik "—an ethic adapted to regulate the lives of His followers during the few months
which would elapse before the end, of no great significance even then and almost destitute
of value for modern men. I may refer to this book for further justification of the view
I have taken in the text.

[1] In Matt. x. 23 it will be before the disciples have time to go through the cities of
Israel ; in another saying, " there be some here of them that stand by, which shall in no

The long discourse contained in the thirteenth chapter of St. Mark and its parallels represents, by very general admission, a " little Apocalypse," which may contain some genuine sayings of our Lord, but is far too much coloured by the ideas and experiences of the disciples during their " Judean mission " to be relied upon as an accurate record of the Master's teaching. The details of this eschatological language cannot be trusted. That the eschatology has in some cases been developed and exaggerated by tradition or by the Evangelists can be asserted with considerable confidence : [1] most of it *may* be due to them. But, when all deductions have been made, enough remains to make it probable that our Lord did Himself look forward to some kind of catastrophic judgement of the world and visible setting up of the Kingdom of God in the more or less near future, and that He expected that at that moment He would Himself be recognized as the Messiah or divinely appointed King of Israel. It is doubtful whether He thought of Himself as the actual Judge. In the oldest form of the sayings it would appear rather that He con-

---

wise taste of death till they see the kingdom of God come with power " (Mk. ix. 1). Matt. xvi. 28 has " the Son of man coming in his kingdom " ; Luke ix. 27 the still more indefinite " till they see the kingdom of God." Elsewhere (in the " little Apocalypse," Mk. xiii. 30 = Matt. xxiv. 34 ; Lk. xxi. 32) " this generation shall not pass away until all these things be accomplished." And yet the Evangelists have preserved the statement that He did not know the date of the judgement (Matt. xxiv. 36 = Mk. xiii. 32). The apocalyptic discourse (Mk. xiii and parallels) assumes a considerable interval between the departure of the Messiah and His glorious reappearing in judgement. It is highly improbable that Jesus can have said *all* these things, and it is impossible to get back to a representation of His words which can be absolutely trusted. The author of the fourth Gospel has spiritualized the whole idea of the " second coming " ; the coming of the Kingdom is interpreted to mean the coming of the Holy Spirit and His dwelling in the hearts of the disciples and of the collective Church, any more literal "coming again" or Parousia being thrown quite into the background. These Johannine discourses cannot be relied upon as giving an historically true account of the words of Jesus or His own interpretation of them ; but they represent, nevertheless, the eternal meaning of His words—the meaning which they must bear for us, and what was really essential in the meaning they bore for Him, whatever was the exact extent of the eschatological background to His thought.

[1] See Canon Streeter's Appendix on " Synoptic Criticism and the Eschatological Problem " in *Oxford Studies in the Synoptic Problem*. He concludes that " in the series Q, Mark, Matthew, there is a steady development in the direction of emphasizing, making more definite, and even creating sayings of our Lord of the catastrophic Apocalyptic type, and of thrusting more and more into the background the sayings of a contrary tenor " (p. 433). This does not, of course, exclude the possibility that Luke may here and there have diminished the eschatological element to render the teaching of Jesus more intelligible and acceptable to the Greek mind. This possibility is recognized by Canon Streeter in a later article (*Foundations*, p. 112).

ceived of Himself as a witness, or perhaps an assessor, at that great inquest. But still the judgement was in some way connected with His Parousia or appearance as the Messiah, and the definite establishment of the kingdom was thought of as closely following upon that judgement. It is difficult to avoid this conclusion without questioning the historical character of our texts to an extent which would at least leave it doubtful whether our Lord ever claimed to be the Messiah at all.

The Parousia, the judgement, the kingdom all belong to the future, and to the near future. But side by side with these passages which treat the coming of the kingdom as an event in the future, there are others which speak of it as something taking place now in the present. " If I, by the finger of God, cast out devils, then is the kingdom of God come upon you ($\ddot{\epsilon}\phi\theta\alpha\sigma\epsilon\nu$).[1] It is here already. " Thou art not far from the kingdom of God," [2] our Lord said to the scribe. It is implied that, if his spiritual condition were just a little higher, he would already be within the kingdom. " From the days of John the Baptist until now the kingdom of heaven suffereth violence, and men of violence take it by force." [3] And there are parables—notably those of the sower, the mustard-seed, the leaven, the tares, the seed growing secretly—which, interpreted with any naturalness, seem to imply that the kingdom of God was beginning to be set up here, now, in this world, as the teaching of Jesus began to sink into human hearts, and the little society of His disciples widened the circle of its membership and its influence. In the light of these sayings and parables there is no reason whatever for denying the historical character of the memorable words, " The kingdom of God is within you," or (as some would interpret the probable Aramaic), " in your midst," [4] although they rest upon the authority

---

[1] Lk. xi. 20 (=Matt. xii. 28).

[2] Mk. xii. 34.

[3] Matt. xi. 12 (=Lk. xvi. 16). The allusion is doubtless to the Zealots.

[4] Lk. xvii. 21. The fact that the words are addressed to the Pharisees is a difficulty in the way of supposing that the saying, if its context has been preserved, bore for our Lord Himself the meaning " within you," though the Greek $\dot{\epsilon}\nu\tau\dot{o}s$ $\dot{\upsilon}\mu\hat{\omega}\nu$ must certainly have this meaning : but the difficulty is not insuperable, and contexts of sayings are less trustworthy than the sayings themselves. Dalman favours the view that the original Aramaic meant " within." See Dalman, *The Words of Jesus*, pp. 145-6.

of St. Luke alone.[1]   In all such passages it would only
be a germinal or potential kingdom of Heaven that
Jesus would have seen about Him in the little society
of His followers : the true kingdom itself He no doubt
regarded as future.   But the very fact that the conception
of the future kingdom could pass so easily into the idea
of a present, ethical kingdom — that the eschatology
could so easily become a " transmuted eschatology " [2]—
shows that at bottom even the future and " eschatological " kingdom represents a spiritual and ethical ideal.
Whenever, wherever, however it was to be set up, the
essence of it was that it was a society in which the will
of God should be perfectly done—a " reign of God "
among men.

It is, however, unnecessary for our present purpose
to enquire how many of what are usually called the eschatological sayings of Christ are genuine, and with what
degree of literalness (so far as they are genuine) our
Lord Himself understood the traditional apocalyptic
language.   For us—at least for our present purpose—
all this eschatological language must be treated as the
accidental historical dress in which the ethical and
religious ideas of Jesus would appear to have clothed
themselves ; and it is with those ideas themselves, and
not with their historical setting, that we are now concerned.   Little or nothing in the conclusions to which
I shall hope to lead you will depend upon the acceptance
or upon the rejection of any particular view as to the
eschatological problem.   They will remain but little
affected if every eschatological utterance of Christ be
accepted and interpreted with the utmost possible
literalness ; they will be quite unaffected if the whole
of them be set down as the aftermath of Judaeo-Christian
imagination.   Only one possible view of the eschatological question will be irreconcilable with the position
here taken up, and that is the view which regards eschatology as the real substance of Christ's message, and

---

[1] Canon Streeter gives good reasons for supposing that the saying was contained in
Q (*Oxford Studies in the Synoptic Problem*, p. 201).   It may have been omitted by Matthew
simply because it was not understood.
[2] von Dobschütz, *The Eschatology of the Gospels*, p. 150.

systematically minimizes the importance of His religious and ethical teaching. That is a position with which I must not now attempt to deal. I would only remind you in passing that that question is not primarily one of criticism or history, but a question of moral and spiritual values on which we can all judge for ourselves without pretending to be experts in synoptic criticism or apocalyptic literature. What concerns us here is not so much the nature of the kingdom as the conditions under which it could be entered. There was, indeed, in our Lord's teaching very little eschatological detail.[1] His teaching related almost entirely to the conditions of entering the kingdom. And here there can be no doubt about what He taught. The clear, unmistakable, invariable teaching of Jesus was that men were to be judged according to their works, including in the conception of works the state of the heart and intentions as scrutinized by an all-seeing God. The righteous were to be rewarded, the unrighteous were to be punished. All that is said about the nature of the rewards and of the punishments is vague and clothed in the language of metaphor—metaphor for the most part already elaborated and appropriated to this use by Jewish tradition. The wicked were to be shut out from the brilliantly lighted banqueting-hall when the duly qualified guests were taking their places at the Messianic banquet—to be left in the darkness outside, where there should be wailing and gnashing of teeth, and so on.[2] Or the judgement is likened to a harvest in which the tares are thrown into the furnace and burned.[3] In some of the recorded sayings we are told that the punishment of sin will be "aeonian." We need not linger over the meaning of the word. Its fundamental meaning in the Gospels would seem to be " belonging to the aeon, the age," that is to say, the coming age, the Messianic age. It certainly does not *mean* " everlasting," though sometimes no doubt it is applied to things which are everlasting. But it is

---

[1] If we put aside the " little Apocalypse " and other sayings which seem to me of more than doubtful authenticity.

[2] Matt. viii. 12 (=Lk. xiii. 28); Matt. xxii. 13, xxv. 30.

[3] Matt. xiii. 40-43.

highly probable after all that the use of this term and of others which suggest the same idea is due to the Evangelists (especially to the first Evangelist) rather than to our Lord Himself.   There is little reason for supposing that Jesus thought of the punishment of the wicked as of everlasting duration.   We have no means of deciding with absolute certainty which of the conflicting Jewish opinions on the subject our Lord adopted, even if, indeed, it was a question on which He had any definite pronouncement to make.   Neither the nature nor the duration of the punishment is defined.   It is probable that His thoughts did not commonly travel much beyond the judgement and its immediate consequences.   He certainly thought of condemnation at the judgement as involving terrible consequences, whether the fate of the wicked were immediate destruction or destruction after a period of punishment or (though this is improbable) permanent exclusion from the joys of the heavenly kingdom and from the light of God's presence.[1]   And the question, who were to suffer such penalties and who were to be acquitted and admitted to that state of blessedness which He called the kingdom of God, was to be determined by their conduct and character.   The wicked were to be punished, the good were to be rewarded. And the goodness which was to be demanded for admission to the kingdom represents a higher, more spiritual, more universalistic morality than had ever been taught before.

---

[1] I have discussed this subject more fully in an appendix to my *Conscience and Christ*, and will here content myself with summing up the conclusions there arrived at. (See also a scholarly article by the Rev. H. D. A. Major upon " Aἰώνιos: Its Use and Meaning especially in the New Testament," in the *Journal of Theological Studies*, No. 69, 1916.)

(1) Our Lord did not commonly look beyond the judgement and gave no definite teaching as to the fate of those then rejected, though there are a few passages which might suggest a possibility of future amendment.

(2) It is doubtful whether the passages which speak of an " eternal punishment " (αἰώνιos κόλασιs), all of them (if the revised reading be accepted in Mk. iii. 29), found only in the first Gospel, represent a genuine word of Jesus.

(3) Even if that expression was used by Jesus, it probably meant simply " Messianic," the punishment of the future Messianic Age.

(4) It certainly cannot be proved that our Lord taught the doctrine of everlasting punishment, and, at least for those who think it improbable that He should have taught a doctrine so clearly inconsistent with the spirit of His own teaching about the love of God, it is probable that He did not.

It will be impossible here to examine at length the ways in which our Lord deepened, transcended, and spiritualized the ethical ideas of Judaism. But there are one or two points on which it will be desirable to say a word, as they have a close bearing upon the question "What was the doctrine of salvation taught by Jesus Himself?"

(1) In the first place He deepened morality by the emphasis which He laid upon the intention, the motive, the state of the heart and the will. The lascivious thought, prevented from passing into act by fear of the consequences, was as bad as adultery. The angry word *might be* as bad as murder if it expressed as much hatred. If He did not quite explicitly declare that all morality was summed up in the commandments of love to God and one's neighbour, He did explicitly teach that these were the two *chief* commandments ; and so much emphasis was laid upon them that, even if it be an editor who has added the words, " On these two commandments hang all the law and the prophets," [1] he has done no more than develope the logical implication of his Master's teaching. In proclaiming, therefore, that men are justified by their works, Jesus must not be supposed to have laid stress upon acts to the exclusion of thought and intention. This insistence upon the importance of the state of the heart was not, indeed, absolutely new, but it represents a truth which had never been insisted upon with equal emphasis. Matthew Arnold was not wrong in making its "inwardness" a characteristic feature, if it was not *the* characteristic feature, of the morality of Jesus. If He taught justification by works, that meant for Him justification by the state of the heart as judged by an all-seeing God, and the right state of the heart was one of fervent love towards God and one's neighbour. Works were interpreted to mean that state of the heart and the will from which external good acts

---

[1] Matt. xxii. 40. Cf. Matt. vii. 12 : " All things therefore whatsoever ye would that men should do unto you, even so do ye also to them : for this is the law and the prophets." The very reduplication makes it probable that in one, if not both, of the passages the Evangelist was dependent upon a source. Mark may have omitted the words from dislike of legalism or indifference to all that concerned the Jewish law.

resulted as necessarily and naturally as the character of the tree reveals itself in its fruit. " By their fruits ye shall know them. Do men gather grapes of thorns, or figs of thistles ? Even so every good tree bringeth forth good fruit, but the corrupt tree bringeth forth evil fruit." [1]

(2) What was the relation of Jesus to the Mosaic Law ? The problem is a difficult one, and its solution may be appreciably affected by the answer we give to various critical questions, by the estimate we form as to the genuineness of certain expressions of respect for the law on the one hand and certain " universalistic " sayings on the other. But, on the whole, it does not seem difficult to arrive at a tolerably decided answer which will not be much affected by the view we take of isolated sayings. It is certain that He disregarded altogether the elaborate extensions or developments of the law which were due to extra-biblical tradition or to the ingenuity of Pharisaic scribes. On the other hand He never expressly denied the binding authority of the Mosaic Law, except in so far as such a rejection was implied in that development of its strictly moral requirements which has already been mentioned. When the letter of the Mosaic Law seemed to Him to stand in the way of some higher, more strictly ethical, more universal principle, he brushed it aside. Thus he disallowed the freedom of divorce which the law had (" to them of old time ") permitted. " It was said also, ' Whosoever shall put away his wife, let him give her a writing of divorcement,' but I say unto you. . . ." [2] He would not let the duty of Sabbath observance stand in the way of mercy, humanity, or, indeed, of human well-being in general. " The Sabbath was made for man and not man for the Sabbath " is a maxim of very far-reaching application.[3] And still more so, " The son of man is Lord even of the Sabbath." [4]

---

[1] Matt. vii. 16, 17.

[2] Matt. v. 31. (" To them of old time " is from the beginning of the passage, v. 21.) It is true that the emphasis " I say unto you " may be due to the Evangelist (being peculiar to Matthew), but the contradiction is implied in the saying itself.

[3] Mk. ii. 27.

[4] Especially if we understand " Son of man " to mean here " Man," *i.e.* " Humanity in general " (Mk. ii. 28 = Lk. vi. 5).

Above all, He laid down the principle that that which went into the mouth could not defile a man, but only that which came out of the mouth. " Perceive ye not, that whatsoever from without goeth into the man, it cannot defile him ; . . . That which proceedeth out of the man, that defileth the man. For from within, out of the heart of men, evil thoughts proceed, fornications, thefts, murders, adulteries, covetings, wickednesses, deceit, lasciviousness, an evil eye, railing, pride, foolishness : all these evil things proceed from within, and defile the man." [1] These words cut away at a stroke the whole principle of Jewish legalism. The distinction between clean and unclean meats was, in a sense, the most important feature of the Mosaic Law considered as a code of ritual observances. The sacrificial system had little practical importance out of Jerusalem. The food restrictions and the idea of ceremonial pollution, on the other hand, affected the daily life of every Jew throughout the world, and were the main root of that social exclusiveness which constituted the great defect of Jewish morality from the point of view of a more universalistic Ethic. St. Mark is not wrong in adding to the words of Jesus the comment, " This he said, making all meats clean." [2] In uttering those memorable words our Lord was practically cancelling the whole system of the Mosaic Law and its ancient taboos as a matter of eternal moral obligation ; and He could not have been altogether unconscious of this tendency. He did not explicitly distinguish between the moral part of the law and its ceremonial injunctions ; but practically, when He speaks with respect of the law, it is the moral part that is emphasized, and even this required the filling out or completion which He gave it. The ceremonial part is never insisted on, and often disparaged. He had (so far as His thought is disclosed) no desire to induce his countrymen actually to give up the observance of the law when it did not conflict with a higher law. But it is clear that

[1] Mk. vii. 18-23 (=Matt. xv. 17-20). Some critics look with suspicion upon this and other recorded explanations of our Lord's sayings, but in any case there can be no reason to doubt the saying itself.
[2] Mk. vii. 19 (reading with R.V. καθαρίζων).

He no longer regarded those ceremonial rules as a part of the eternal law of God in the same sense as the moral part of it and the two supreme commands in which He summed it up. In the words of Loisy, " The emancipation of Paul, much more apparent, was not more real." [1]

(3) The third question which it is relevant to my main subject to raise is this, Was Christ's moral teaching universalistic ? In principle that question is answered by what has already been said. If the non-observance of the law had no real tendency to defile, if non-observance of the law interposed no barrier between the soul and God, all ground was taken away for denying that a Gentile as a Gentile might be admitted to the Kingdom of God. For even orthodox Judaism did not regard the mere fact of race as constituting such a barrier. The law itself placed the Gentile fully on a level with the Israelite if only he had become a member of the Israelite Nation-Church by circumcision and submission to the law. Any sayings which seem to militate against this principle may therefore fairly be regarded as belonging, if genuine, to a period in which our Lord had not yet fully developed the implications of His own teaching. Doubtless He regarded His own personal mission as being a mission to Israel : He thought of Himself as the Messiah of His nation, although it was part of the Messianic mission to prepare for a universal world-judgement. There is no critically unassailable evidence that He ever spoke of actually converting the world to His Gospel or making Gentiles into members of a world-wide Church—at least before that divine recognition of His Messiahship to which He probably looked forward. But, in the light of His explicit rejection of the food distinctions and His general attitude towards the law, we have a right to infer that, when He based human morality upon the law of love of God and one's neighbour, He meant by one's neighbour not the fellow-Jew but the fellow-man. And this interpretation is borne out by the explicit teaching of the parable of the Good

[1] *Évangiles Synoptiques*, i. p. 569.

C

Samaritan,[1] by His words to the Centurion,[2] the story
of the ten lepers of whom only the Samaritan returned
to give glory to God,[3] and a number of passages in
which the Messianic salvation is made to depend upon a
goodness which cannot with any naturalness be supposed
to include submission to circumcision and observance of
the ceremonial law.[4]

The very heart of the mission of Jesus, as He conceived it even at the beginning of His ministry, was to
preach the possibility of entrance into the Kingdom for
the " spiritually disinherited masses " in Israel [5]—the
tax-gatherers, " the sinners," the poor, the ignorant,
probably the Samaritans. In this He was simply continuing the work of the Baptist. These classes must have

[1] Lk. x. 30-37. As to a suggestion by M. Halévy (adopted by Mr. Claude Montefiore) that the original form of the parable was "Israelite, Priest, Levite," see my *Conscience and Christ*, p. 112.

[2] Lk. vii. 9 (=Matt. viii. 10).

[3] Lk. xvii. 16. Cf. also the visit to Samaria and the rebuke to the sons of Zebedee
in Lk. ix. 52-55.

[4] " I say unto you that many shall come from the east and the west, and shall sit
down with Abraham, and Isaac, and Jacob, in the kingdom of heaven : but the sons of the
kingdom shall be cast forth into the outer darkness " (Matt. viii. 11). These words in
Matthew are certainly universalistic, since they are suggested by the faith of the Centurion. It is true that in Luke (xiii. 28) they are addressed to the people, and it may
be that by the excluded are meant the Jews of the Dispersion. But (a) the saying itself
comes from Q and the context cannot be relied upon ; and (b), if we take the saying by
itself, it is extremely improbable that " the sons of the kingdom " meant the inner circle
of Pharisees or the Jews of Jerusalem as opposed to the Dispersion. Dalman says :
" The sons of the theocracy are thus those who belong to it in virtue of their birth, who
thereby have a natural right to the possession of it " (*The Words of Jesus*, p. 115) : it
is difficult to suppose that any Jews, least of all Galileans, would think of the Jews of
Jerusalem as having this superior claim. There is the less reason for attempting to deny
the universalistic character of Jesus' teaching, inasmuch as a certain kind of Universalism
was already believed in by many Jews. Parts of the book of Enoch are so far universalistic that the Messianic judgement extends to Gentiles, and it is implied that some
Gentiles would be acquitted at the judgement. In the Similitudes it is only the sinners
who are punished, and it is especially " the kings and the mighty and the exalted and those
who rule the earth" who will "go forth from His presence and their faces will be filled with
shame, and darkness will be piled upon their faces " (cap. lxii. ed. Charles). In a later
section, Gentiles who have taken no part in the oppression of Israel are admitted to the New
Jerusalem, after falling down and doing homage to Israel (xc. 30-33) : "And the Lord of the
sheep rejoiced with great joy because they were all good, and had returned to His house."
Unwilling as he is to attribute any high ethical value to the teaching of Jesus, Schweitzer
admits that " Universalism is provided for in the eschatology of late Judaism and in that
preached by Jesus, since it is assumed that among those elected to the Kingdom of God
others will be revealed who do not belong to the people of Israel. Universalism is therefore involved in the Jewish conception of the Messiah. Whereas, however, late
Judaism and Jesus only represent it as realized in the coming Supernatural Age, Paul
antedates it and affirms that distinctions were already abolished in consequence of the
death and resurrection of Jesus " (*Paul and his Interpreters*, p. 108).

[5] See the extremely important Introduction to Prof. B. W. Bacon's *The Beginnings
of the Gospel Story*, p. xxxvi *sq*.

been but lax observers of the law, even when they observed
it at all.   Jesus was not an enemy of Judaism ; He *was*
the declared enemy of Pharisaism as Pharisaism was
understood by the Jerusalem scribes.   The very notion
that those who did not observe the law might be morally
better than those who devoted their whole energies to
observing it strictly, carried with it a latent Universalism.
It is never suggested in His teaching to these classes
that what was needed by them was a more rigorous
observance of the Law, more sacrifice, more fasting,
more avoidance of ceremonial uncleanness, more separation from the Gentiles.   Always and invariably the emphasis is on moral righteousness, love of God and one's
neighbour, the state of the heart.   This being the general
tone of Jesus' teaching, we need have no difficulty in supposing that He made the explicit declaration : " Many
shall come from the east and from the west, and shall
sit down . . . in the kingdom of heaven : but the sons of
the kingdom shall be cast forth into the outer darkness,"[1]
nor need we assume that He was thinking merely of the
Jewish " Dispersion " in contrast to the innermost circle
of Judaism—the " sons of the kingdom "—in Jerusalem.
But it will not matter very much how we settle these
disputed critical details.   The spirit of Christ's teaching
is universalistic—so completely so that no one could drink
at all deeply of that spirit without becoming universalistic
also.   St. Peter[2] was a Universalist no less than St.
Paul, and Jewish Christianity soon became so no less
than the Gentile Churches more directly under the influence of St. Paul.

Such in its general character was the righteousness
which was to be rewarded at the judgement, and it was
the corresponding kind of wickedness which was to be

---

[1] Matt. viii. 11 (= Lk. xiii. 29).

[2] And this quite independently of the story of Acts x.   The whole point of St.
Paul's attitude in Gal. ii. 11 is that Peter had admitted the principle of Gentile Christianity without submission to the law, though he inconsistently shrank from acting up
to his convictions in the presence of Jews.   This admission (now generally made) under-
mines the whole basis of the theory held by Baur and the Tübingen school, according
to which the earlier history of the Church represents a bitter and internecine warfare
between a Pauline and a Petrine Christianity.   Of course there is a germ of truth in
that theory, but it represents an enormous exaggeration : it was to James, not to Peter,
that the Judaizing section appealed.

punished. Goodness thus understood was the one
condition of entrance into the kingdom—that and not
descent from Abraham, not the performance of any outward rite,[1] not the state of a man's intellectual belief,
except of course in so far as morality itself implies some
measure of belief. Only those whose righteousness
should exceed the righteousness of the scribes and
Pharisees should enter into the kingdom of Heaven.[2]
It is those who are persecuted for righteousness' sake
to whom the kingdom belongs.[3] "The Son of man
shall come in the glory of his Father with his angels;
and then shall he render unto every man according to
his deeds."[4] "Every tree that bringeth not forth
good fruit is hewn down and cast into the fire."[5] "Not
every one that saith unto me, Lord, Lord, shall enter
into the kingdom of heaven; but he that doeth the will
of my Father which is in heaven."[6]

[1] The question may be raised whether Christ commanded baptism. The only evidence that He did so is supplied by (a) Matt. xxviii. 19 and (b) the fourth Gospel.

(a) In Matt. xxviii. 19, the risen Lord says: "Go ye, therefore, and make disciples of all the nations, baptizing them into the name of the Father, and of the Son, and
of the Holy Ghost: teaching them to observe all things whatsoever I commanded you."
Critics have always looked upon these words with some suspicion, because, wherever baptism
is mentioned in the New Testament, it is always baptism "in the name of the Lord Jesus"
(Acts ii. 38, xix. 5; 1 Cor. i. 13; Rom. vi. 3; so in Didache 9, though in cap. 7 the
Trinitarian formula appears). It has recently been contended that Eusebius several times
over quotes the words in the following form: "Go ye, and make disciples of all nations
in my name, teaching them to observe whatsoever I commanded you." (See Mr. F. C.
Conybeare's article on "Three early doctrinal Modifications of the Text of the Gospels"
in the *Hibbert Journal*, vol. i. p. 102.) It is highly probable that this represents the
earliest form of the saying, and in any case the words must be regarded as extremely
doubtful. For an important reply to Mr. Conybeare, see the Bishop of Ely's article
in the *Journal of Theol. Studies*, vol. vi. p. 481 *sq.* I certainly cannot accept Dr.
Chase's conclusion that "the whole evidence . . . establishes without a shadow of doubt
the genuineness of Matt. xxviii. 19." Even if the words should be genuine, they would
not prove that our Lord made salvation depend upon baptism.

(b) In John iv. 1 we read: "The Pharisees had heard that Jesus was making and
baptizing more disciples than John, although Jesus himself baptized not, but his disciples" (cf. iii. 22). There is nothing intrinsically improbable in the statement that Jesus
carried on the work of the Baptist, but nothing is said about any command or any utterance which would make baptism a necessary condition of admission into the kingdom.
Even if we took John iii. 5 ("born of water and the Spirit") as an actual utterance of
Jesus, we need not treat baptism as, in Christ's view, more than a symbol of the moral
change.

[2] Matt. v. 20.

[3] Matt v. 10 (peculiar to Matthew, but the same doctrine is implied in Lk. vi. 22, 23).

[4] Matt. xvi. 27 (cf. Mk. viii. 38).

[5] Matt. vii. 19. The same principle is implied in Lk. vi. 43-45, though here there
is no reference to the burning of the corrupt tree.

[6] Matt. vii. 21. The saying in this form may be suspected of representing the
Church's later view of the Person of Christ, and Dr. Moffat (*The Theology of the Gospels*,
p. 72) is perhaps right in regarding it as an eschatological version of Lk. vi. 46: "Why

Sometimes, it may be suggested, Jesus seems to treat acceptance of His own claims as one of the conditions of salvation or of acquittal in the Messianic judgement. " Every one therefore who shall confess me before men, him will I also confess before my Father which is in heaven." [1] It may be that in such passages the representation of the Evangelists has been more or less coloured by the later belief of Christ's followers and by the later teaching of St. Paul and the whole early Church as to the importance of faith in Christ.[2] It is hardly possible that our Lord can have kept the fact of His Messiahship so close a secret till the very eve of the Passion, and yet have openly taught, at the beginning of His ministry, that non-recognition of His Messianic claims would involve condemnation at the judgement. But if we assume that the words are exactly reported and were spoken before the confession of Peter, after all the confession of Jesus before men does not necessarily imply acceptance of His Messiahship.   Even if we take every such passage in the Synoptists as a faithful reproduction of the Master's teaching, we shall find that invariably it is obedience to the will of God as declared by Him and His disciples that seems to constitute the acceptance which is to be rewarded—obedience to His commands rather than any intellectual belief about Him or His Messianic work.   Everywhere that work— whether definitely thought of as Messianic or not—is presented as primarily that of a prophet or teacher. He had come to call men, to call them into the kingdom,

call ye me Lord, Lord, and do not the things which I say ? "   In either form there is the same stress on doing, as opposed to believing.

[1] Matt. x. 32.   In Lk. xii. 8 the words are " shall the Son of man also confess." The saying in some form comes from Q.   In Matthew it forms part of the charge on sending out the Twelve—a discourse which seems coloured by the circumstances of the later Galilean mission.

[2] That the cures of Jesus were in some cases, if not perhaps in the case of the possessed, dependent upon the existence in the sufferer of some measure of faith in His power to heal is probable.   This is strongly supported by the statement in Mk. vi. 5 that " he could there do no mighty work" because of their unbelief (weakened in Matt. xiii. 58) ; but faith of this kind does not necessarily imply faith in His Messiahship or even in His teaching, still less faith in the atoning efficacy of His blood.   At the same time the emphasis in many passages of St. Mark upon the necessity for faith as a condition of the cure and the passages in which praise is bestowed upon faith may well be due (as is suggested by Prof. Bacon) to the " Paulinism " of that Evangelist, or (as I should prefer to say) to the influence of a later conception which was not at all exclusively Pauline.

to sow the seed of the word, to proclaim glad tidings. The only sign which He would give is the sign of Jonah —that is, He would preach repentance without any sign at all.[1] He had come to seek and to save that which was lost : He did that by teaching the poor and the ignorant, the men and women of ill-repute, whom no one had troubled to teach before. He came as a Physician of souls : like the bodily physician, He effected His cures by advice, by warning, by prescribing a remedy ; and the remedy was to repent, to sin no more,[2] and to obey the will of God as He declared it. It was in giving commands that He most definitely claimed exceptional authority for Himself : " It was said to them of old time, but I say unto you." [3] He called upon men to come unto Him, but it was just that they might learn of Him. He called upon men to follow Him, but it was in order that they might imitate Him—particularly in the case of those whom He called upon to follow Him most closely by becoming, like Him, preachers of His message to other men. Acceptance of Jesus meant acceptance of His message. If He ever spoke of His Messianic glory or dignity, it was always with reference to that future manifestation of His Messiahship to which He looked forward ; and at that manifestation the question would be not what men had believed about Him, but whether they had obeyed Him. " Every one therefore which heareth these words of mine, and doeth them, shall be likened unto a wise man, which built his house upon the rock : and the rain descended, and the floods came, and the winds blew, and beat upon that house ; and it fell not : for it was founded upon the rock." [4]

[1] Matt. xii. 39, xvi. 4 ; Mk. viii. 12 ; Lk. xi. 29. The explanation in Matt. xii. 40 (the parallel between Jonah's three days in the whale's belly and the Son of Man's three days in the heart of the earth) is no doubt (as the context and the parallels suggest) a later addition.

[2] An important element is no doubt omitted in the statement of " remedies "—His sympathy, but (a) the sympathy was expressed in the teaching, and (b) it could not well be insisted upon, though it was practically manifested, by Jesus Himself. Cf., however, " Come unto me, all ye that labour," etc.

[3] Some critics would ascribe these words to the Matthean Editor, but this will hardly be done by those who claim that Christ taught the Pauline doctrine of justification by faith.

[4] Matt. vii. 24, 25 (=Lk. vi. 47-49).

Nor does it appear that the teaching must necessarily be obeyed from conscious respect for the Teacher.   Words spoken against the Son of Man might be forgiven, but not conscious resistance to the voice of conscience. Those who were rewarded for having given meat to Christ when He was an hungred, and drink when He was thirsty, are not the people who acknowledged His claims, but those who had fed and clothed the least of His brethren.[1]

Such is one side of our Lord's doctrine about salvation. It differed from the common Jewish theory of justification by works merely in the fact that for Him " works " had a different signification.   But side by side with this teaching about a judgement according to works, we meet with teaching equally explicit and equally simple about the possibility and the need for repentance, and the certainty of forgiveness when there was such repentance. There is no inconsistency between the two doctrines, for (as we have seen) our Lord always regards the works as indicative of the state of the heart.   For Him judgement according to works meant judgement according to the present state of the heart, not the striking of a balance between the whole of a man's good deeds and the sum of his bad deeds in the past.   And therefore it followed that, where there was sincere repentance, the man would be pronounced good at the judgement ; external good works would necessarily follow, so far as opportunity was given.   The need for repentance formed the very essence of the appeal which Jesus made from the first days of His ministry, as indeed it had formed a part of the teaching of His forerunner, the Baptist.   " From that time began Jesus to preach and to say, ' Repent ye ; for the kingdom of heaven is at hand.' "[2]   This was, indeed, from first to last Jesus' conception of His own mission—to proclaim that the kingdom of Heaven was open not merely to the respectable and law-observing scribe or the learned rabbi, but to the poor and outcast, those who knew not the law and those who had broken it, if only they would repent.   " I came not to call the

---

[1] Matt. xxv. 34-40.   [2] Matt. iv. 17 (=Mk. i. 15).

righteous but sinners." [1]   " It is not the will of your
Father which is in heaven that one of these little ones
should perish." [2]   There is no notion at all that He had
brought with Him into the world any new way of procuring forgiveness of sins but this—the way of repentance.
True, the same message had been delivered by the
prophets and by the Baptist ; only Jesus' conception of
the repentance demanded by God was deeper than theirs
and His conviction of God's willingness to pardon more
profound.   And the purity of His doctrine was not
marred by inconsistent additions.   To Jesus, as is implied by the etymology of the Greek word μετάνοια as
well as by the whole current and spirit of His teaching,
repentance meant, not the mere offer of an apology to
God or the desire to escape the threatened punishment,
but a radical change of heart or character, or (if we think
of the probable Aramaic original) a " return "—" a
return to God."   When and in so far as the man's
will was rightly directed now, when and in so far as he
condemned and abhorred the evil of his past, God would
not reckon against him, or punish, the sins of the past.

And that truth about the forgiveness of sins was simply
an element or particular application of a much wider
and still more prominent element of our Lord's teaching.
He taught men to look upon God as a Father who loved
impartially all human beings, and who in all His dealings
with them would be guided by a desire for their true
and highest good, now and hereafter.   Such a view of
the character of God is by no means incompatible with
the idea of divine justice, with belief in the divine anger
against transgression, or in future punishment for un-
repented sin.   But it does imply that punishment must
be threatened and inflicted in love, with the view of
making the sinner better.   And when the change of
character was already complete, there could be no further
need of punishment.   Everywhere in Christ's teaching
the idea of forgiveness is treated as closely associated

---

[1] Mk. ii. 17 (=Matt. ix. 13).   Luke (v. 32) adds " to repentance."   This is clearly
a gloss, but substantially a true gloss.
[2] Matt. xviii. 14.

with, as a necessary corollary of, His fundamental doctrine of God's fatherly love towards all His children. " When ye pray say, ' Our Father . . . forgive us our trespasses.' "

Let us examine a little more in detail some of the passages in which this doctrine is clearly set forth.   The bare call to repentance as the one great pre-requisite of entrance into the Kingdom, which formed the substance of the earliest teaching, implies by itself that God is willing to forgive ; and it implies with almost equal distinctness that forgiveness is dependent upon no condition whatever but repentance, and the amendment which is the necessary consequence of sincere repentance. The proclamation of the divine forgivingness is closely associated with the human duty of forgiving others. " If ye forgive men their trespasses," we are taught in the sermon on the mount, " your heavenly Father will also forgive you." [1]   And the pattern prayer which the Master bequeathed to His disciples asks for forgiveness, as if the asking and the willingness to forgive others were all that was required to secure its fulfilment.[2]   The condition which makes forgiveness dependent upon our forgiving other men may be regarded as a corollary of repentance—a test and pledge of its reality.   If a man does not forgive the wrongs that other men have done him, his repentance, his change of heart cannot be genuine or complete : he must still be wanting in that intense and impartial love to all his brethren which is the essence of the moral ideal—that moral ideal which is perfectly realized in God.   " Ye therefore shall be perfect "—complete, impartial, all-embracing—in your love for others " as your heavenly Father is perfect," or, as St. Luke has it, " Be ye merciful, even as your Father is merciful." [3]

This teaching is further illustrated and developed by many of the parables.   There is the parable of the lost sheep, which illustrates the yearning of God for the repentance of the sinner, and His rejoicing when he

---

[1] Matt. vi. 14 (=Mk. xi. 25).   Cf. Lk. vi. 37.
[2] Matt. vi. 12 (=Lk. xi. 4).   [3] Matt. v. 48 ; Lk. vi. 36.

returns like the recovered sheep to the fold.[1] The
parables of the unmerciful servant [2] and of the two sons,
one of whom refused to work in the vineyard but afterwards repented and went,[3] teach the same lesson.   But
the parables which most definitely emphasize this side
of our Lord's teaching belong to that great section of
St. Luke's Gospel which has no parallel in the other two
Synoptists.   In the two parables of the prodigal son and
of the Pharisee and the publican,[4] we have the fullest
expression of this fundamental idea—that God forgives
the truly penitent freely and without any other condition
than that of true penitence.   In the second of these
parables, and in this place alone in all the four Gospels,
there occurs the word which was hereafter to play so
prominent a part in theological controversy.[5]   The
publican, who smote upon his breast and said, " God, be
merciful to me a sinner," we are told, went down to his
house *justified* rather than the self-complacent Pharisee.
Whatever may be said of later usages of this term, here,
at all events, we need not hesitate to say that justification
means practically the same thing as forgiveness or
acquittal.   Forgiveness, then, according to Jesus, follows
immediately upon repentance.   No other " condition of
salvation," to use the technical term of later theology,
has to be fulfilled.   There is not the slightest suggestion
that anything else but repentance is necessary—the
actual death of a Saviour, belief in the atoning efficacy
of that death or in any other article of faith, baptism,
confession to any but God, absolution, reception of the
holy eucharist, Church membership—not a hint of any
of these.   The truly penitent man who confesses his
sins to God receives instant forgiveness.[6]   Such was the

---

[1] Matt. xviii. 12-13 ; Lk. xv. 4.   To which St. Luke adds the parable of the lost
piece of money (xv. 8-10).

[2] Matt. xviii. 23-35.

[3] Matt. xxi. 28-31 ; cf. Lk. xv. 11.   In some form the parable must be from Q :
this is important as showing that the doctrine is not confined to Luke or his special
source.

[4] Lk. xv. 11-32, xviii. 9-14.

[5] In Matt. xi. 19 (= Lk. vii. 35) it is used in another sense : " The [divine] wisdom
is justified by her works."

[6] The necessity of repentance implies that in our Lord's thought salvation is never
actually " merited."   It cannot be demanded as a matter of right : forgiveness and

only condition of salvation while Christ was yet on earth; and in the whole range of our Lord's other teaching there is not the shadow or shade of a suggestion that the offer of salvation made to man while He was yet on earth was to be withdrawn, or narrowed, or saddled with fresh conditions in consequence of, or subsequently to, His death. Even those who formulated the theology upon which this notion has been based give no hint of such a thing. How far what they taught is reconcilable with what the Master taught will be matter for subsequent consideration. Here I only note that they do not suggest that their teaching on this head rests upon any express word of the Master, nor do they claim to be in any way authorized to contradict that teaching. There may be room—I hope to show that there is room—for a doctrine of the atonement through Christ which is wholly consistent with the teaching of the Master Himself; but, if that is so, it must be a doctrine which does not modify or contradict the simple teaching about the forgiveness of God which is taught by the parable of the prodigal son. It is surely a difficult thing to say—as must be done if some later doctrine of the atonement is treated as the very essence of Christianity—that what was taught by Christ Himself was not Christianity at all.

Before turning from the teaching of the Master to that of His disciples it will be well briefly to examine one or two special passages which have sometimes been supposed to militate against this representation of Christ's teaching, and to justify the attribution to our Lord Himself of the doctrine that forgiveness of sins was dependent upon some objective consequence of His work and particularly of His death. I shall confine myself

---

salvation are gifts. Cf. Lk. xvii. 7-10. So far, no doubt, M. Goguel is right, but when (*L'Apôtre Paul et Jésus Christ*, p. 282) he insists that in the words " her . . . sins are forgiven because she loved much," the love must be taken not as the cause, but as the sign of pardon, he seems to me over-subtle. Jesus would never have pushed the idea that forgiveness cannot be merited to the point of denying that the moral condition of the penitent is a reason for God's forgiveness. This, in fact, can only be denied if it is held that forgiveness is bestowed on one and refused to another quite arbitrarily, and independently of the state of their will, *i.e.* without any repentance at all. The repudiation of such a view does not of course prevent our recognizing that the repentance itself is due to the grace of God.

for this purpose to the Synoptists, reserving the teaching of the fourth Gospel for later discussion. No scholarly defender of the Johannine authorship will contend that we can go to that Gospel for the *ipsissima verba* of the Master uncoloured by the later reflections of the disciples, the Church, and the Evangelist himself.

I shall venture to put aside as irrelevant to the present problem those passages in which our Lord is represented as forgiving sins or declaring their forgiveness by God.[1] In nearly every case this declaration was made in connexion with the healing of disease. Whether Jesus thought of all disease as in some sense a punishment for sin,[2] or whether He thought of the bodily healing as a sort of sign or pledge of God's forgiveness to the sinner, these passages not merely do not favour the idea that He looks upon the forgiveness as in some way dependent on an atonement to be effected by His death ; they are evidence against His having authorized any such notion, and still more explicitly do they negative the idea that the forgiveness was dependent upon belief in this atonement. The man with the palsy knew nothing about the future death of Jesus, nor, if the forgiveness was dependent upon this future event, could the statement, " thy sins have been forgiven," be true. It is not said " they will be forgiven," or even " may they be forgiven," but " they have been forgiven." In the case of the woman who was a sinner,[3] that is even more distinctly the case. It is because she had much love, as was shown by the costliness of her offering, that her sins had been

---

[1] M. Loisy is disposed to think that in Mk. ii. 5 (=Matt. ix. 2 ; Lk. v. 20) the claim to pronounce that sins are forgiven is unhistorical. He points out (*Évang. Synopt.* i. p. 88) how naturally the words, " Arise, take up thy bed," etc. (Mk. ii. 11), will follow the words, " Saith unto the sick of the palsy " in v. 5 ; and how satisfactorily the hypothesis of an insertion in the original source will account for the curiously awkward parenthesis, " He saith to the sick of the palsy, I say unto thee." This hypothesis seems to me not impossible, but I cannot agree with M. Loisy that in " Thy sins be forgiven thee," our Lord " ne dit pas et il n'entend pas dire : ' Tu es guéri ' " (*ibid.* p. 475). Taking the passage as it stands it seems clear to me that the announcement that the man's sins have been forgiven is intended to imply, or at least to be the condition precedent to, the bodily healing.

[2] He certainly did not think of it as implying any particular degree of sinfulness in the particular sinner. Cf. Lk. xiii. 2-4.

[3] Lk. vii. 47 (ἀφέωνται). There is no need to assume that our Lord's knowledge of this woman was confined to this single act. Cf. Goguel, *L'Apôtre Paul et Jésus Christ*, p. 281.

forgiven, and for that reason alone : no other is suggested. These declarations of forgiveness being then put aside, there are two passages, and two only, which can be thought to favour the theory that Jesus Himself taught that forgiveness was in any sense dependent upon His death. The two passages are the words, " and to give his life a ransom for many," and the language used at the Last Supper.

With regard to the first of these passages, two questions arise. (*a*) Is the saying genuine ? and (*b*) what, if genuine, was its original meaning ?

(*a*) The genuineness of the first saying—the passage about the ransom—is very far from being beyond question. The words are found in Matthew and in Mark ; that is, according to the usually received critical theory, they come originally from Mark, and from Mark were introduced into the first Gospel by its author. The whole passage is substantially the same in Matthew ; in the verse which contains the actual words, there is verbal identity.[1] When we turn to the Gospel of St. Luke we find no exact equivalent for them. We find the contention as to who should be the greatest, without, however, the incident about Zebedee's children, and in another context. The dispute is made to take place at the Last Supper. We get the reply about the Kings of the Gentiles, and the words, " He that is the greater among you, let him become as the younger, and he that is chief, as he that doth serve." And then follow the words, " For whether is greater, he that sitteth at meat, or he that serveth ? Is not he that sitteth at meat ? But I am in the midst of you as he that serveth." [2] The additional words in St. Matthew and St. Mark are of exactly the kind which are spoken of by critics as ecclesiastical additions. They suggest a report coloured by the later doctrinal teaching of the Church. The version of the saying given by St. Luke seems to me far more natural, far more suitable to the context, and far more obviously in harmony with the

---

[1] Mk. x. 43-45 (=Matt. xx. 26-28).
[2] Lk. xxii. 27.

rest of our Lord's teaching than the version adopted by St. Mark.[1]

(b) The hypothesis of a doctrinally coloured insertion is to my own mind the most probable account of the words about the ransom. Still, I am far from denying that they may possibly represent a genuine saying of the Lord, and the question arises what, if they are genuine, was their original meaning? In answering this question, it is important to bear in mind the context in which they stand.

The words come just after Jesus had begun to speak of His approaching sufferings and death. It is probable on many grounds that the allusions both to the crucifixion and to the resurrection on the third day must have been, to say the least, much vaguer than the language of the Evangelists might lead us to suppose : otherwise the astonishment and dismay with which His death filled His followers is quite unintelligible ; [2] nor could we explain His afterwards contemplating, even for a passing moment, the possibility that the cup might pass from Him. Still, there is no reason to doubt that Jesus was beginning at this time to feel a growing presentiment or conviction that His career on earth was to end in a violent death, and that it was somehow through death and apparent defeat that His Messianic task was to be fulfilled and the Messianic Kingdom set up.[3] And then follows an incident which (as related by St. Mark)

---

[1] For further discussion of this question, see below, pp. 49-56.

[2] In two of the most definite predictions (Mk. ix. 9, 31 ; Matt. xvii. 9, 22-24) the reference to the resurrection on the third day is omitted by Luke, though he has the prediction of betrayal in the second case (Lk. ix. 44) ; in the third all three Evangelists record the prediction both of death and resurrection (Mk. x. 33-34 ; Matt. xx. 17-19 ; Lk. xviii. 31-33). If the predictions were so explicit, the scattering after the Crucifixion (testified to by Matt. xxvi. 56 ; Mk. xiv. 50 ; Gospel of Peter, 13, which very possibly represents the lost ending of St. Mark) would be as difficult to account for as the surprise which the Resurrection visions seem to have created. St. Luke tells us that they understood not the saying, but (as he puts it) it is too definite for misunderstanding to have been possible. These statements are probably based upon much vaguer and more indefinite anticipations, which assumed the form of definite predictions in the minds of the disciples after the event.

[3] It is possible, but less probable, that He discovered references to the death of the Messiah in the prophets, as He is represented as doing in Lk. xviii. 31, xxiv. 25-27 ; but even in these passages nothing is said of any expiatory effect of the Messiah's death. The prophecies are merely used to show that the violent death of the Messiah was part of the " determinate counsel and foreknowledge of God," and therefore no disproof of the Messiahship of Jesus.

has all that air of characteristic originality which so often carries far more conviction of authenticity than elaborate critical arguments. The sons of Zebedee asked that they might sit the one on the right hand, the other on the left in His kingdom.[1] Our Lord replies by the memorable question whether they were able to drink of His cup, by the assurance that they should drink of that cup, and the declaration that to determine who should sit on His right hand and on His left was not His to give. Then with the view of allaying the indignation of the ten, and exposing those misunderstandings as to the nature of the Messiah's kingdom out of which such ambitious questionings arose, He continues, " Ye know that they which are accounted to rule over the Gentiles lord it over them, and their great ones exercise authority over them. But it is not so among you : but whosoever would become great among you shall be your minister ; and whosoever would be first among you shall be servant of all. For verily the Son of man came not to be ministered unto, but to minister, and to give his life a ransom for many." [2] Now, if we assume that these words are correctly reported, especially if we suppose that their connexion with the incident about the sons of Zebedee is historical, there is something to be said for the view that they were meant to be taken quite literally, that the deliverance spoken of was a physical deliverance from actual, physical death.[3] Jesus may have felt that the ministry to His disciples, which was the object of His whole life, was to be pushed to the point of dying for them, and that in some way this death of His would save their lives—at least for the present. He was to die, but they were to live. The Jewish rulers who were arming themselves against Him and His followers would be satisfied with one life. The surrender of His life would make it unnecessary for them to lay down theirs. Such

[1] Luke's suppression of the incident, if it stood in Q, is easily accounted for by his habitual desire to omit anything which might seem to reflect on the character of an Apostle. St. Matthew tries to save the character of the two sons by putting the blame upon their mother. It is quite possible that the connexion of this incident with the following discourse may be due to the Evangelist.

[2] Mk. x. 42-45 (=Matt. xx. 25-28).

[3] So far as any interpretation of them can be considered to suit it.

a meaning would suit the context well. In that case the death would be spoken of as a kind of service. Just as His life had been a life of service for others, so would His death be. And in this His disciples were to imitate Him. To offer a unique expiatory sacrifice for the sins of the whole world was clearly a kind of service which was wholly beyond their power. To work, to suffer, and, if need be, to die in the service of others was quite within their reach.

The chief reason against limiting the meaning of the saying to the idea of dying physically that others might physically live is that the words are undoubtedly, if not exactly a citation, yet at least an echo, of prophecy. The words " to give his life " recall the words applied by the later Isaiah to the " suffering Servant of Jehovah," " his soul was given over unto death "; and the " for many " still more certainly recalls the immediately following words, " he bare the sins of many." [1] The word ransom is found in the same section of Isaiah, but in a much earlier chapter and in quite a different application. [2] In the passage before us the word may be with much more probability supposed to have been suggested by the passage in Job : " If there be with him an angel, an interpreter, one among a thousand, to shew unto man his uprightness ; and he be gracious unto him, and say, Deliver him from going down to the pit, I have found a ransom." [3]

---

[1] Is. liii. 12 (LXX.).

[2] " I have given Egypt as thy ransom " (Is. xliii. 3).

[3] Job xxxiii. 23-24 (R.V.M.). Cf. also Ps. xlix. 7 : " None of them can by any means redeem his brother, nor give to God a ransom for him." (Cf. Ritschl, *Die christliche Lehre von der Rechtfertigung*, ii. 83 *sq.*) If the passage in Job was the source, it would no doubt imply to an early Christian the whole theory of the *descensus ad inferos*, which the most " eschatological " of interpreters will hardly attribute to Jesus Himself. Jesus nowhere else shows a knowledge of Job. We may think also of Hosea xiii. 14. But in truth the idea of the ransom is so common in the O.T. that it is unnecessary to look for some particular passage to explain its use here. The word λύτρον in the LXX. (τὰ λύτρα plur., 17 times out of 20) is the equivalent for four Hebrew words : (1) *kopher* " ransom " (root, *kaphar, kipper*), Ex. xxi. 30, xxx. 12, usually explained from the Arabic to mean a covering or propitiatory gift ; but the original sense is more probably to be found in the Bab.-Assyr. usage of the verb, " to wipe off " by a ritual act; so in Syriac, " to wipe." Driver (art. " Expiation " in *Ency. of Religion and Ethics*) holds that in Hebrew the idea of purgation was early associated with the word ; hence the thought was of *expiation* rather than of propitiation. God is never the object of " kipper " (or ἱλάσκομαι in LXX.) as is constantly the case in pagan writers. (2) *geʾullah* " redemption " (root *gaʾal*, lit. " to enforce a claim that has lapsed," so " to re-claim," " vindicate "), the act or right of re-claiming, redeeming, a field or

Such a combination of isolated expressions from the Old Testament is much more likely to come from the Evangelists or from tradition than from Jesus Himself. But if our Lord did use these words, and if in using them He had in mind the passage of Isaiah about the suffering Servant, it is improbable that He should have thought of His death as benefiting " many " merely in the literal and prosaic sense of saving them from a similar physical death, though this reference need not be altogether excluded. The " ministry " which would be performed by His death would be thought of as something like that rendered by His life ; the benefit which it would procure for them would be some kind of spiritual service, and a service which would have a liberating, releasing effect. We need not, if they are the words of Jesus, ask for a very definite answer to the question, " From what, or from whom, was His death to release them ? " If Jesus used the words, it might be very much in the sense of the great saying that the man who would save his life should lose it. His death would be the means of procuring an abundant spiritual life—the life of the Messianic kingdom, a life which was none the less thought of by Jesus as spiritual because in its fulness it could not be enjoyed till the kingdom had

---

slave, Lev. xxv. 24, the payment made for redemption, Lev. xxv. 26, 51 *sq.* (3) *pidhyon*, *pᵉdhuyim* " ransom " (root, *padhah*), Ex. xxi. 30, Num. iii. 48 *sq.*, 51, the price paid as a ransom. (4) *mᵉhir* " price," " gain " (verb not used), Is. xlv. 13. If used by our Lord, the most probable **original** appears to be *kopher* in an Aramaic form. If the saying is due to the Evangelist or to tradition, we need not suppose an Aramaic equivalent. The idea of λύτρον might easily be got out of the general idea of redemption (ἀπολύτρωσις). That God had redeemed Israel, *i.e.* bought it and so made it His property, is an idea of which the O.T. is full, and in the N.T. it is transferred to the spiritual Israel (Eph. i. 14 ; Acts xx. 28). The thought thus requires no answer to be given to the question to whom the ransom was paid, nor even a very definite answer to the question from what the people of God were delivered : the main thought is that they were bought *for* God, *i.e.* the Kingdom, salvation, eternal blessedness. The word λύτρον is not found in St. Paul, though we have ἀπολύτρωσις several times, and the idea occurs in 1 Cor. vi. 20, vii. 23 : " Ye were bought with a price." The statement that Christ gave Himself as a ransom is found in 1 Tim. ii. 6, where the right reading is ἀντίλυτρον. M. Rivière (*Le Dogme de la Rédemption*, p. 49) remarks that " in the New Testament— and most often also in the Fathers—we only find the preposition ἀντὶ when it is called for by the word ' ransom.' " It is noticeable that sometimes God is said to " ransom " (λυτροῦν) His people in the sense of " deliver " or " save " in passages where no sort of price or equivalent is paid, *e.g.* Exod. vi. 6 (*ga'al*), Deut. xxi. 8 (*padhah*). So in Jer. xviii. 23, Ps. lxxviii. 38, where *kipper* is used of God's action, " purge away " will represent the idea ; Driver translates " expiate," but the thought at leart comes near to " pardon."

D

been fully set up in the age that was yet to come.[1]   The
main thought suggested by the term "ransom" is the
idea of a price paid to secure benefits for another—
particularly a price paid to secure life or liberty.   If we
must say in black and white what the benefit was which
Christ expected His death to assist in procuring for
many, it would be doubtless admission to the kingdom
of Heaven.   The idea that the sufferings of the righteous
were in some way accepted by God instead of the sufferings of the guilty, had a place in Jewish thought long
before the time of Christ.[2]   Its classical expression is
that very section of the deutero-Isaiah of which these
words are almost certainly an echo.   Later Jewish
tradition did not usually identify the suffering Servant
with the Messiah,[3] though that interpretation was not,

[1] Prof. Wendt (*Teaching of Jesus*, Eng. Trans. ii. 226) understands the words in
the sense of Matt. xi. 28 ("Come unto me, all ye that labour," etc.) ; but it is difficult
to see how Christ's *death* (as distinct from His teaching) could have a liberating effect
upon souls oppressed with the weight of the law, unless we attribute to Jesus the fully
developed theories of St. Paul, which Wendt is of course far from doing.

Another account of their probable meaning given by Prof. Menzies also deserves
consideration (*The Earliest Gospel*, p. 202) : "Now, considering the ideas on which He
was dwelling at this time, the profit He speaks of as accruing to many from His death
must have consisted in their being in the Kingdom which was to be open to believers
afterwards, and not excluded from it and left outside.   Thus we are led to the belief
on His part that His death would have the result of bringing into the Kingdom many
who might otherwise have been left outside it.   In what way precisely He expected this
to come about we cannot determine.   His followers as yet were few ; He had by no
means succeeded in gathering Jerusalem into the fold.   But if He died, a change might
take place in this particular.   The death of the Messiah must have a profound influence
on the chosen people.   It must arrest the national conscience and bring about a general
movement, such as His preaching had failed to produce, towards the Kingdom.   In this
way He might regard His death as a means of blessing to 'many,' His life as a ransom
for many, His blood as shed 'for many.'   As much as this seems plain.   If Jesus
expected, as can easily be shown that He did, that the Kingdom would be visibly erected
the moment after [I should say "not long after"] He died, and if it was to be erected, as
He must have believed it would, on a scale worthy of God and of the chosen people,
with multitudes in it who showed no sign yet of turning towards it, then His death
must have seemed to Him to be the means by which those multitudes were to be saved."
This seems to me rather too modern and elaborate.   I should prefer to substitute the
simpler thought suggested by Prof. Burkitt, that the Messiah's death would end the long-
suffering of God towards Israel, and hasten the Kingdom.   More than this the complete
absence of any parallel in the teaching of Jesus makes it impossible for us to say.

[2] See below, p. 71 *sq.*

[3] Some of the Jewish interpreters (in the Talmud, the Targums, and later) did identify
the Servant of Jehovah with the Messiah, but even some of these, while admitting that
the concluding verses of Is. lii. referred to him, explained Is. liii. in other ways, and in
Is. liii. the verses which seemed to speak of the death (as distinct from the sufferings)
of the Messiah were explained away.   Others identified the Servant with historical
individuals—Jeremiah, David, Hezekiah, etc. ; but the prevailing interpretation (especially after Rashi in the eleventh century) was that which has been generally approved by
modern critics, *i.e.* that which identifies the Servant with Israel or the idealized Israel (as
is distinctly implied by Is. xli. 8, 9, xlix. 3).   There is no evidence to show that in or

indeed, unknown, and may possibly be pre-Christian. It is certainly possible that our Lord may have applied Isaiah's conception of the suffering Servant to the Messiah, and so to Himself; or that, without any such identification, He may have thought of His death as benefiting others, not in any unique or exclusive way, but just as the sufferings of other righteous men had done and might yet do — perhaps, as Prof. Burkitt has suggested in his striking paper on the parable of the wicked husbandmen, by causing the Lord of the Vineyard to hasten the judgement,[1] to take away the vineyard from the sinful generation which had rejected His Son and to give it to others—and so bring about the deliverance of the faithful in Israel. Or, less definitely, it may be supposed that the thought is that His sufferings would be accepted by His Father, and procure benefits for many, just as the prayers and intercessions of the righteous might do. But, in whatever sense Jesus may have expected that the sufferings of the Messiah were to benefit others, the assertion that they would do so is a long way off from the dogma that forgiveness of sins could be purchased in this way and in no other. There is nothing to suggest that the particular benefit which His death would win was the forgiveness of sins, or that the benefit which it would procure was anything *sui generis*—different in kind from the benefit which the sufferings of other righteous men might obtain for them, or that the way in which it was to

---

before the time of our Lord the idea of a Messiah who should suffer and die was known. See the collection of translations in *The Fifty-Third Chapter of Isaiah according to the Jewish Interpreters* by Driver and Neubauer (with Introduction by Pusey, 1877). Some modern writers still hold that in particular places the prophet is thinking specially of some historical individual. Schultz, for instance (*Old Test. Theology*, i. 314), thinks that the prophet speaks of himself in xlviii. 16 *sq.*, l. 4 *sq.* (and elsewhere), but only as "the common mouthpiece of all in Israel who are faithful to their God."

Among the later Jews (apparently not till after A.D. 135) there was a doctrine of a preparatory Messiah, the son of Joseph, who was to suffer and die as a warrior in defending the nation and prepare the way for the true Messiah, the Son of David, but no atoning effect was attributed to His sufferings. See Stevens, *The Theology of the New Testament*, p. 15; Dalman, *Der leidende und der sterbende Messias.* In 4 Esdras vii. we find a human Messiah who is to die after a reign of 400 years; so the Samaritan Messiah (*Taeb* or "Restorer" [?]) dies after reigning 110 years, his death being followed by the judgement. Such conceptions are entirely different from the idea of the "Suffering Messiah," though sometimes confused with it. See Mr. Emmet's article "Messiah," in *Encycl. of Rel. and Ethics*, vol. viii. pp. 577*a*, 579*b*.

[1] *Proceedings of the Third International Congress of Religions*, vol. ii. p. 321 *sq.*

operate was by constituting an expiatory or substitutionary sacrifice. To say that the sufferings or the prayers of Himself and other righteous persons would benefit many is not inconsistent with the teaching of His saying about the forgiven publican. To understand them as meaning that apart from His death there could be no forgiveness would be to make His teaching in this passage wholly and irreconcilably inconsistent with the teaching of that parable and, indeed, with all the rest of His teaching about the love of God and His willingness to forgive the sinner on the one condition of penitence. And even if we ignore that consideration, and insist on reading into this passage the doctrine—hard, literal, fully developed—of an expiatory sacrifice for sins, even so there is not a single trace of the doctrine that the appropriation of the forgiveness is conditional upon the individual's belief in the efficacy of that atoning sacrifice or upon belief of any kind or sort.

Considered as a purely critical question, the probabilities for and against the genuineness of the words, taken as an isolated saying, are nearly equal ; but, when we look at them in the context supplied by the general tenour of Christ's teaching as a whole, I feel that the probabilities are very strongly against them. It is, I admit, not inconceivable that our Lord may have come to identify Himself more or less definitely with the suffering Servant of Isaiah's prophecy, though the use of the words by no means necessarily implies that He did so. He may have applied to His own case the principle which the prophet had applied to the interpretation of the sufferings of the righteous in Israel without thinking of Himself as *the* only suffering Servant of Jehovah. The chief difficulty in the way of believing that He identified Himself in any exclusive way with the suffering Servant and thought of His death as having any vicarious efficacy, is the fact that this solitary sentence of Mark is the only trace of His having done so.[1] If

[1] "The parable of the wicked husbandmen (Mk. xii. 1), while it represents Jesus as predicting His death, is strong evidence against the notion that He attributed any saving efficacy to that death : all that it does is to hasten the judgement. It is not the sin of man, but the unbelief of the Jews which called for the sending of the heir. And the

He did utter the words, they must represent a passing reflection rather than the central idea of His Gospel. Had He really believed that deliverance from sin and its penalty was in any paramount and exclusive way dependent upon the effects of His death, still more had He thought of this dependence as being the vital essence of His message, it is inconceivable that He should not have taught that doctrine in a much more definite and explicit manner than this ; it is inconceivable that He should have taught so much that is inconsistent with it : it is inconceivable that such teaching, had it been given, should have failed to be remembered ; most inconceivable of all is it that a few days or a few hours later He should have prayed that the chief purpose for which He came into the world should remain unfulfilled.   On any view of this passage it teaches nothing at all approaching the traditional doctrine of the atonement ; certainly it does not show that Christ regarded His own death as a vicarious punishment, a substitutionary sacrifice, or even an objectively valid expiation without which sin could not be forgiven.   Thus, even if the words are genuine, the only doctrine of the atonement which can trace itself back to Jesus Himself is the simple doctrine that His death, like His life, was a piece of service or self-sacrifice for His followers, such as they themselves might very well make for one another.   The more the interpretation of the saying is made to involve something nearer to the traditional atonement doctrine than this, the greater becomes the historical improbability that it was ever uttered by our Lord.   We may be quite sure that either the words were not uttered at all, or that their meaning fell very far short of the doctrine of the atonement in the form which eventually obtained currency in the Church.

There is one other Synoptic saying or group of sayings which may be appealed to as a proof that a certain expiatory value was attached by our Lord Himself to

heir was sent, not to die and save, but to deliver the same message.   The death, so far from saving, is the cause of their condemnation.   (See the article referred to above, p. 35 n. 1.)   The notion that the purpose of the death was to increase the guilt of the Jews was held by strongly anti-Jewish Christians," such as the author of the so-called Epistle of Barnabas.   See below, p. 195.

His approaching death. They are to be found in the
narratives of the Last Supper. It is well known that
the four accounts which have come down to us of our
Lord's words on that occasion are not consistent with
each other, and in several of them there are difficult
questions of reading.[1] Not all these reports can be
literal history; for in point of detail they contradict
one another. Even if we put aside minor differences,
it is difficult to suppose that all of them can be genuine;
for they seem to represent different and not easily
reconcilable conceptions of the symbolical acts which
they record. Some of them have certainly more probability of being genuine than others. Only one of the
versions contains any reference to the forgiveness of sins,
and the words which contain this reference are precisely
the words which may most confidently be set aside. In
St. Matthew the words " unto remission of sins "
are added after the words " this is my blood of the
covenant which is shed for many." Matthew's account
is obviously dependent upon Mark's, and the most conservative critic will have no hesitation in treating this
addition as an explanatory gloss by the author or last
editor of the first Gospel. If these words are set aside,
there is no explicit reference to the forgiveness of sins
in any of the narratives; the question remains whether
there is anything to suggest even by implication the idea
of an expiatory or a vicarious efficacy in the death.

Allusions to the blood of the covenant are found in
all the accounts except the shorter text of St. Luke.
There are some difficulties in the way of supposing that
these words come from our Lord Himself. In the first
place, there is the singularity of Mark's expression, " my
blood of the covenant," which looks very much as if it
had arisen from a conflation of two readings—" my
blood " and the " blood of the covenant." [2] And then

---

[1] The four narratives are Matt. xxvi. 26-29; Mk. xiv. 22-25; Lk. xxii. 15-22
(verses 19*b*, 20 being omitted in the best MSS.); 1 Cor. xi. 23-25. I accept the text
of Westcott and Hort, who treat the doubtful words as an interpolation.

[2] Matthew and Mark have the words " This is my blood of the covenant "; St.
Paul has " This cup is the new covenant in my blood." In the shorter text of Luke
there is no suggestion that the cup was symbolical of blood : the cup is given only with
the words " I will no more drink," etc. It is highly probable, therefore, that Luke

the idea which the words imply seems quite different from that suggested by the words which follow with slight variations in all the accounts except St. Paul's : " Verily I say unto you I will no more drink of the fruit of the vine, until that day when I drink it new in the kingdom of God." If our Lord thought of the meal which He was celebrating with His disciples as itself the Messianic banquet, or if the real significance of the giving the cup was that it was simply that this was the last time He would take a meal with them before He sat down with them to the Messianic banquet in the Kingdom of God, it is not very likely that He thought of it also as symbolizing His own blood and of that blood as ratifying a covenant between God and His people.[1] And the argument against their genuineness is strengthened by their omission in the shorter text of Luke.[2] But even

---

represents the earliest tradition, and that the words " this is my blood " were intro-duced later on the analogy of " this is my body." Both expressions—" this is my blood of the covenant " and " this is the covenant in my blood "—are so awkward that they look like an attempt to conciliate two traditions, in one of which the words were " this is my blood," and in the other " this is the blood of the covenant " or " this cup is the covenant." If the first version was really a saying of Christ, it would have to be understood in whatever way we interpret " this is my body " ; if the latter version should be regarded as genuine, it will remain doubtful whether the wine was simply regarded as symbolical of blood in general—the blood such as would be necessary for the ratification of a covenant, or whether the wine was meant to be symbolical of Christ's own blood, and that this was the blood with which the covenant was to be ratified. In any case it is difficult to suppose that, if the words about the covenant were used at all, there was not some reference to His own death, since it is improbable that the symbolism of the cup and of the bread should have nothing in common. If we suppose that the cup was only given with the words " I will not drink," etc., this objection will hardly apply. In that case there was originally *no* symbolism in the cup (except what is implied in the *common* religious meal) but only in the bread.

[1] The impossibility is perhaps not so absolute as it is made by M. Maurice Goguel (*L'Eucharistie des origines à Justin Martyr*, p. 81 *sq.*, who adopts the suggestion of Völter), but the probabilities are against it. M. Goguel (p. 85) insists further (with Baur, Volkmar, Bousset) that to suppose that our Lord thought of Himself as inaugurat-ing a new covenant would be inconsistent with His own view as to His Mission and His relations to Judaism, and that it may therefore be set down as a " Paulinizing addition." But as the new covenant was distinctly foretold by the prophets (especially in Jer. xxxi. 31) in connexion with the Messianic epoch in a way which would naturally be under-stood to make its inauguration the work of the Messiah, the objection does not seem to me fatal. In any case, as M. Goguel admits, the difficulty may be got over by rejecting the word " new," which seems to be the true reading only in St. Paul, and understanding the idea as the renewal of the Old Covenant rather than the making of a new one. At the same time I feel that the other saying (" I will not drink," etc.), in spite of its absence in St. Paul (who may have omitted it as irrelevant to his purpose), is much less likely to have been invented afterwards, and that it is improbable that both are genuine. Prof. Burkitt treats the saying about the covenant as genuine, and understands it in the same way as he understands Mk. x. 45 (in the article referred to above, p. 35 *n*. 1).

[2] I assume that the true text of St. Luke is the shorter version, omitting the words " which is given for you : this do in remembrance of me " in Lk. xxii. 19 and the whole

if this saying be genuine, it will not bear the interpretation which has been put upon it.   The new covenant which is here referred to can hardly be other than that new [1] covenant spoken of by more than one prophet, especially by Jeremiah : " Behold, the days come, saith the Lord, that I will make a new covenant with the house of Israel, and with the house of Judah : not according to the covenant that I made with their fathers in the day that I took them by the hand to bring them out of the land of Egypt. . . . But this is the covenant that I will make with the house of Israel after those days, saith the Lord ; I will put my law in their inward parts, and in their heart will I write it ; and I will be their God, and they shall be my people ; and they shall teach no more every man his neighbour, and every man his brother, saying, Know the Lord : for they shall all know me from the least of them unto the greatest of them, saith the Lord : for I will forgive their iniquity, and their sin will I remember no more." [2]   There is nothing sacrificial about such a covenant as this : there is no suggestion that the forgiveness promised had anything to do with a sacrificial death, or was dependent on any condition whatever.   The covenant was not, indeed, properly speaking, a covenant at all, for it was unilateral : it was a " covenant which is no covenant," [3] because it consisted simply in the announcement of free forgiveness.   It may be said that our Lord's teaching elsewhere suggests that He might have thought of Himself as inaugurating a new covenant-relation between God and His people. There would be no great difficulty in supposing that He may have done so ; and if He did, He might

---

of verse 20.   These verses are pronounced by Westcott and Hort to be a " Western " interpolation, arising, of course, from a desire to accommodate the Lukan narrative to the others.   They are also rejected by Nestle, who says, " It is to be observed that the last discovered Syriac omits the nominative clause τὸ ὑπὲρ ὑμῶν ἐκχυνόμενον after τῷ αἵματί μου, which is the only member that seems to be derived, not from 1 Cor. xi. 24 f., but from Matthew and Mark, and that does not agree in construction with the rest.   This confirms the supposition that these two verses are not part of the original text " (*Textual Criticism of the Greek Testament*, p. 277).   It is strange that M. Goguel should prefer the longer text.

[1] The word new (καινῆς) is found in St. Paul and in some MSS. of Matthew and Mark.

[2] Jer. xxxi. 31-34 (quoted in Heb. viii. 8, x. 16).   It was, of course, thought of as superseding the covenant of Ex. xxiv. 7, 8.   [3] Menzies on Mk. xiv. 23.

quite conceivably have spoken—with a touch of bitter irony—of His blood as supplying that ratification by blood without which in ancient times a covenant was not thought of as complete.[1] But if the blood used in ratifying a covenant—originally the blood of the covenanting parties themselves, afterwards that of an animal victim—may be considered as in a sense sacrificial blood, the sacrifice was in no sense expiatory or propitiatory. The custom points back to that possibly older idea of sacrifice which implies communion rather than expiation or propitiation. Equally little is there any idea of expiation or propitiation in those other words which have more probability of being genuine—the declaration that He would not drink of the fruit of the vine until He should drink it new in the Kingdom of God.   Here the wine is not regarded as in any way symbolical of blood or of death.   If it is treated as symbolical at all, it is as a sort of anticipation of the Messianic feast.

There remain the words " This is my body which is for you " in St. Paul,[2] or, as they stand in St. Mark, " Take ye : this is my body."   Here we can have little difficulty in accepting the last version as the more primitive, especially as the " for you " is absent also from the genuine text of St. Luke. The four words, " This is my body," are the only words which are absolutely identical in all four narratives. The words, " Take ye : this is my body," do not even necessarily involve any definite, or at all events any exclusive, reference to the

---

[1] It is the more difficult to suppose that He thought of the cup as symbolizing that blood because of the different significance which He gives to the blood in the saying, " I will no more drink," etc.   If the saying is genuine, it may be the Evangelist who has put it into close connexion with the giving of the cup.

[2] The longer text of Luke adds " which is given " ($\delta\iota\delta\acute{o}\mu\epsilon\nu o\nu$).   I do not think it necessary to ask whether, when St. Paul says that he received the tradition " from the Lord," he refers to an ecstatic vision or simply to the established tradition of the Church. If he does refer to a vision, the vision may well be supposed to have been influenced by the established usage of the Church, nor does he claim to be adding anything to the Gospel tradition.   The phenomena of the Gospel texts are a sufficient proof that discrepant traditions soon began to circulate in the Church, possibly arising out of differences of local usage in the celebration of the eucharist.   Whether St. Paul is supposed to be recounting a vision or to be repeating his version of the common tradition, his authority cannot be regarded as final ; or, indeed, when it *adds* to the other versions, as superior to what may be supposed to come from Q or St. Mark.   The tradition that was put into writing later may obviously be more primitive than one that was written down earlier. St. Mark may therefore represent an earlier tradition than St. Paul, and St. Luke an earlier tradition than either.

impending death at all. Still it is difficult to believe that the coming parting was altogether absent from the Master's thought. The most natural interpretation of the words is simply this : " As I give you this bread, so I give, I devote myself wholly to you (*to* you rather than *for* you). I desire to identify myself with you in the closest possible manner : take this as a farewell expression of our spiritual union." [1] It has been suggested that the original Aramaic word for body is one which was also used to mean " self." " I give myself to you." [2] But this suggestion must not be taken as certain. Better established is the metaphorical interpretation of bread in the sense of doctrine sometimes found in the Talmud.[3] But we need not assume that there is

[1] The idea afterwards elaborated by St. Paul about the Church being the body of Christ will thus have had a germ in our Lord's own mind, in the suggestion that in giving them the bread His disciples were mystically becoming partakers in the body which was soon to be broken on the Cross ; this supplies, however, no foundation for the theory that sins could only be forgiven through the efficacy of that death. We are told, indeed, that in the apocalyptic and rabbinical conceptions of the Messianic Supper " the good to be enjoyed is the Messiah Himself, and it is to this that Jesus refers when He speaks of the bread and wine as His own body and blood " (Denney, *The Death of Christ*, p. 34, who refers to Spitta, *Die urchristlichen Traditionen und Sinn des Abendmahl*). Jesus may conceivably have been influenced by this conception, but that would not imply either a theory of a vicarious atonement or the doctrine that reception of the eucharist was essential to salvation or admission to the kingdom.

[2] Castellus (*i.e.* Castle) Lex. to Walton's *Bibl. Polygl. sub voce* says that "guph" (lit. " body ") is used in the sense of person or self in later or Rabbinic Hebrew and in the Aramaic of the Talmud, but he does not support this statement by a quotation. In Pirke Aboth iv. 10 (ed. Taylor) there is a saying of R. José (2nd cent. A.D.) : " He will himself (gupho) be honoured by men." There is a somewhat similar usage in Ex. xxi. 3, 4, where the Hebrew "b e gappo," which signifies literally " in his body," is employed in the sense of " by himself." The evidence from Palestinian Aramaic is later, third or fourth century, *e.g.* Talm. B. Beça 3a : " This law is itself (guphah) only a precaution." I owe this suggestion to the Rev. J. R. Wilkinson, and some of the above information is derived from Prof. Cooke, who himself doubts whether our Lord used the word " guphi " and in this sense.

[3] On John vi. 51 (" the bread that I will give is my flesh ") John Lightfoot (*Horae Hebraicae*, 185-9. iii. p. 307) remarks : " He tacitly confutes that foolish conceit of theirs about I know not what dainties the Messiah should treat them with ; and slights those trifles by teaching that all the dainties which Christ had provided were Himself. Let them not look for wonderful messes, rich feasts ; He will give them Himself to eat ; bread beyond all other provision whatever ; food from heaven ; and such as bringeth salvation. . . . There was nothing more common in the schools of the Jews than the phrases of ' eating and drinking ' in a metaphorical sense. . . . *Bread* is very frequently used in the Jewish writers for *doctrine*. So that when Christ speaks of *eating His flesh*, He might perhaps hint to them that He would feed His followers not only with His doctrines, but with *Himself* too."

Lightfoot (*lib. cit.* iii. 308) adds : " There is mention even among the Talmudists themselves of eating the Messiah," and quotes " Rabh " [Abba Arika, third century] as saying, " Israel shall eat the years of the Messiah," and from Hillel the words, " Messiah is not likely to come to Israel, for they have already devoured Him in the days of Hezekiah." The word translated " devoured " may, I believe, mean simply " destroyed."

any reference to such rabbinic notions. Quite apart from any such speculations, it was not only in death but in life that Jesus devoted Himself to His disciples. There is no necessary reference to the death ; still, it is probable that the words were uttered with especial reference to the parting and the death which He regarded at least as probable. But for our Lord to say that He was giving Himself for His disciples involves no idea of atonement—still less of an atonement upon which the forgiveness of the sins of the whole world depended. Even if we retain the words " which is for you " after " body," or if without them we take the giving as having an exclusive reference to the death, the words can at most mean no more than this : " I am going to sacrifice my life for you. I am ready to face death on your behalf—in the fulfilment of the Messianic mission which God has entrusted to me for your sakes." In that case our Lord will be thinking of His death as sacrificial or vicarious only in the sense in which any great leader of men might regard a martyr's death as an act of self-sacrifice on behalf of his followers. Doubtless He may have felt that the death of the Messiah had a significance which the death of no other man could have, but He claims for it no unique expiatory value.

When we come to the giving of the cup, we do indeed find that all the authorities except the shorter Luke see in the cup a symbol of Christ's blood, while St. Matthew and St. Mark add the words, " which is poured out for many " (Mark) or " concerning many " (Matthew); but as these words are not found in St. Paul or in the shorter text of St. Luke, their genuineness becomes doubtful. Without them there is nothing to suggest that the death was thought of as having a vicarious efficacy or even any sort of efficacy. Even if they are retained, they will at most, like the gift of the bread, suggest the idea that our Lord looked upon His approaching death as an act of self-sacrifice for His disciples. In the case both of the bread and the wine, the words " for you " are in all probability a later addition; and in the shorter text of St. Luke there is not even any word to suggest that

Jesus ever thought of the wine as in any way representative or symbolical of blood or of death, or as being
more than the cup of the last Passover which He would
celebrate with them.   The addition of words which
suggest that view seems to have grown out of the desire
to find in the giving of the cup a meaning analogous to
that which Jesus probably did attach to the giving of
the bread.   The shorter text of St. Luke gives us by
far the best attested narrative of the whole incident.   I
will read the words as they stand there, that you may see
how little there is in them to suggest the idea of an
expiatory death :

"With desire I have desired to eat this passover with
you before I suffer : for I say unto you I will not eat it
until it be fulfilled in the kingdom of God.   And he
received a cup, and when he had given thanks, he said,
'Take this, and divide it among yourselves : for I say
unto you, I will not drink from henceforth of the fruit of
the vine until the kingdom of God shall come.'   And he
took bread, and when he had given thanks, he brake it, and
gave to them, saying, 'This is my body.   But behold, the
hand of him that betrayeth me is with me on the table.'"[1]

The Lukan account seems to me the most primitive narrative which has come down to us.   Here
there are no words which can imply that the death was
"instead of" or even "on behalf of" the disciples :
the body is given *to* them as His life had been given to
them.   At the same time I wish to insist upon the point
that our conclusions will not have to be seriously modified,
whatever view we take of the critical points.   If only

---

[1] On the whole this account is the simplest and seems most primitive ; and yet in
two points there is something to be said for the other versions.   (1) If we hold (as is
frequently done) that the Fourth Gospel is right in representing that the Supper took
place on the day before the Passover, we must suppose that the words (peculiar to Luke)
implying that it was a Passover must be a later insertion, unless, indeed, as Prof. Kennett
has suggested, the words mean "I will make this meal a Passover."   (2) It seems probable
that the words "until it be fulfilled in the kingdom of God" represent a modification of
Mark's "until that day when I drink it in the kingdom of God."   The alteration may be
intended to avoid the suggestion of a literal eating and drinking in the kingdom.   None
of the narratives, except St. Paul's and the longer Luke (which is doubtless based upon
St. Paul), imply that our Lord thought of Himself as founding a permanent institution.
St. Paul's words, "Ye do show the Lord's death till he come" (as Mr. J. R. Wilkinson
suggests), may easily have grown out of the words "until it be fulfilled in the kingdom
of God."

we reject Matthew's addition "for the remission of sins," there is nothing in any of the narratives to suggest that the approaching death was in any way whatever to bring about the forgiveness of sins, or that Jesus was dying "for" His followers in any other sense than that in which He had lived for them—in any sense but that in which other martyrs have died for their cause and for their followers. That the death of the Messiah had more significance than the death of other martyrs is true; that the service which in life and in death the Messiah was rendering to the world was a greater service than others could render is equally true. It is true that in actual history the death of Christ has had spiritual effects incomparably greater than those which have flowed from any other death; but the fact remains that there is nothing in the sayings attributed to the Master at the Last Supper which implies any fundamental difference in kind between the service which He was conscious of performing ånd the service to which He was inviting His disciples. Christian experience may afterwards have discovered such a unique significance; but that does not justify our reading back into Christ's own words an idea which there is nothing in His language to suggest.

We have found, then, nothing in either of the two places which we have examined which can compel us to abandon the conclusion that our Lord never taught that His death was necessary for the forgiveness of sins, or that any condition was required for forgiveness but the supreme one of repentance and that amendment which is implied in all sincere repentance.[1] The only doctrine of the atonement which can with any certainty, or even with any probability, be traced back to our Lord Himself is the simple doctrine that His death, like His life, was one of self-sacrifice for His followers, and that such a death of self-sacrifice would be a continuation of that spiritual service of the brethren to which His life had been devoted.[2] That is the doctrine already implied

---

[1] As to the "Sin against the Holy Ghost," which may be thought to be inconsistent with this statement, see Additional Note B, below, p. 56.

[2] Dr. Dale's statement (*The Atonement*, p. 71) that "the same fundamental conception of His death appears in them all" (*i.e.* all the passages in which He alludes to His death)

in the simpler words of St. Luke: "But I am in the midst of you as he that serveth," when read in the light of his approaching death; and even if the Markan addition be genuine, it will not appreciably add to what is implied in them.   Simple as it is, the doctrine which they contain is, indeed, one of profound significance; and it is the basis of all that is true and eternal in later doctrines of the atonement.   The fact that the Messiah should be thought of as dying—and dying by an agonizing and a shameful death —implied a fundamental change in the whole idea of Messiahship and of the Messianic kingdom.   It represents the whole difference between the sense in which Jesus at the end of His ministry accepted the Messianic title, and the sense which it had hitherto borne for the Jewish world.   The thought that it was through suffering, through the death and apparent defeat of His chosen One, that God was going to set up His kingdom, and that those who would participate in the joys and glories of that kingdom must follow Him in the path of self-sacrifice, was no arbitrary appendix or addition to the teaching of the Master.   It only added a crowning illustration of the ethical principle which ran all through that teaching—the principle that love is the highest thing in human life and the highest revelation of the divine nature.   The doctrine that God will forgive the sins of the penitent upon the one condition of sincere repentance and amendment is, as we have seen, simply a consequence and particular application of that prin-

---

seems to me the direct opposite of the fact.   The whole treatment of the subject by Dr. Dale is absolutely pre-critical and unconvincing.   It is based upon the assumption that every word attributed to our Lord by any Evangelist—including the fourth—represents His *ipsissima verba*, even when it is absolutely inconsistent with other alleged sayings. Equally unconvincing are the arguments of Dr. Denney (*The Death of Christ*), and they are only the more illogical inasmuch as he does not share Dr. Dale's uncritical assumptions.   His suggestion that our Lord's submission to a baptism of repentance proves that His *death* had an expiatory effect is a fair specimen of his arguments (*l.c.* 13 *sq.*).

No scholar will now be prepared to defend the view that when our Lord spoke of Himself as coming " to fulfil the law " He meant " to suffer instead of the guilty the death which the law denounced for sin."   Anybody who wants to realize the gulf which divides even conservative theologians from the orthodoxy of two generations ago should read Smeaton's *The Doctrine of the Atonement as taught by Christ Himself* (1871), where this interpretation is defended.   Unfortunately many theologians fail to realize that the older theories which they still defend have no foundation except in a system of exegesis which they have abandoned.

ciple. And that being so, we are already able to find a meaning in the later doctrine which sees in the death of the supreme Revealer a pledge or symbol of the forgiveness which He had preached and promised. In so far as "the doctrine of the cross" means the supreme beauty of loving service, and in particular its efficacy in touching the heart and regenerating the lives of others, the doctrine of the cross may be traced back to the teaching of our Lord, and forms the very centre of it. The germ of all true theories of an atonement through the death of Jesus is to be found in that teaching of His : no one of these theories is actually there.

How far the later doctrine or doctrines of the atonement constituted a legitimate development of the idea which was really involved in the teaching of the Master— how far, in so far as it added to that teaching, what was added was simply based upon the experience of Christians as to the life-giving efficacy of their Master's life and death, and how far the later development of Christian thought involved ideas of a quite different origin and character—these are the problems which we shall be investigating in subsequent lectures. On no account must we rush to the conclusion that, if we find in the later doctrine anything which was not due to the explicit, or even the implicit, teaching of Jesus, it can possess no truth or permanent value. The legitimacy and the necessity of development in Christian doctrine are as indisputable as its actual occurrence. Many things may be true about Christ which Christ Himself never taught. Many things may legitimately be inferred or deduced from Christ's teaching which He never deduced from it Himself. Many things may even be added to it which cannot even be said to be logically deducible from it. Many things which Christ never Himself taught may nevertheless be true, may even be so far absorbed into the teaching of the Christian Church as to become in some sense a permanent and indispensable part of Christianity ; for the doctrine of the Holy Spirit and of His presence in the Church which Christ founded is as important an element in Christianity as the belief

in a supreme revelation of God through the historical
Christ. But some continuity, some consistency, some
congruity there must needs be between the development
and the germ from which the development has sprung,
if the religion which has grown out of Christ's teaching
is to claim any identity with the religion which was
preached by its Founder.

In the following lectures I propose to examine the
later doctrine, or rather doctrines, of the atonement,
and to ask how far they are consistent with the teaching
of Christ on the one hand, and on the other with the
reason and conscience of the present. But I shall
venture from the first to assume two things : (a) That,
though a doctrine of the atonement may add something
to the actual teaching of Jesus, no doctrine of the
atonement can be a legitimate development of our Lord's
teaching, no doctrine of the atonement can be genuinely
Christian, which contradicts a feature of that teaching so
fundamental as the truth that God is a loving Father,
who will pardon sin upon the sole condition of true
repentance. And (b) that there is only one way in which
any more developed doctrine of atonement can possibly
be in harmony with this fundamental element in Christ's
teaching. The only atoning influence that can be
recognized in the death of Christ, or in any other aspect
of His work, is one which operates by actually helping
to produce that repentance and moral regeneration upon
which, and upon which alone, according to the Master's
express teaching, forgiveness depends.

I have not entered upon any formal argument in
favour of the truth or the adequacy of Christ's own
doctrine about the forgiveness of sins. That doctrine
is one which many Christians will be disposed to accept
simply upon the authority of Christ Himself, when
once they are satisfied that it is really His. But for
those who feel that the authority which is attributed to
Christ must in the last resort be based upon the appeal
which His character and teaching make to the moral
consciousness of mankind, there is no necessity to base
the doctrine upon the bare *ipse dixit* of the Master. It

is one that may be trusted to appeal to the reason and conscience of mankind on its own merits. That sin ought to be forgiven when there is sincere repentance is a truth which, like all ultimate ethical truths, must be accepted simply because it is self-evident. Or perhaps it may be better described as a deduction from, or implication of, that doctrine of universal love which is itself an immediate affirmation of the enlightened conscience. For those who believe in a righteous God, God must be supposed to act in the way which the moral consciousness approves. If a man has actually returned to the right moral state—for that is what repentance means—a righteous God must forgive the past, must judge him according to what he is, and not according to anything that he was and has ceased to be. The doctrine is, as we have seen, no arbitrary appendix to Christian theology or to Christian ethics. It is a truth which flows directly from Christ's fundamental doctrine that the most essential element in the moral ideal of man and in the nature of God Himself is love. Christianity is the religion which for the first time proclaimed in all its fulness those twin-truths which are best expressed in the simple phrases—the fatherhood of God and the brotherhood of man ; and the most direct and immediate corollary of that doctrine is the truth that he in whom the sinful will has been changed, and in proportion as it has been changed, is already reconciled to God.

ADDITIONAL NOTES TO LECTURE I

NOTE A

THE RANSOM FOR MANY

(Matt. xx. 28 ; Mk. x. 45)

It seems desirable to support the view of this passage which I have taken in the text by some further critical considerations.

The first gospel notoriously contains many passages which are commonly set down as ecclesiastical additions—passages added by the

E

first Evangelist or his latest editor to the sources which he used in common with the other Evangelists whether on the basis of some later tradition or on his own responsibility, and they are often of a kind suggestive of later ecclesiastical organization or doctrinal development. In this category are commonly placed St. Peter's walking on the water, the words about binding and loosing, the committal of the keys to St. Peter, the injunction to bring quarrels to be settled by the Church, the resurrection of the bodies of the Saints, the allusion to baptism in the name of the Holy Trinity in the parting words of Jesus.[1] All these sayings or narratives are peculiar to St. Matthew. It is certain that, if the words about the ransom were found in St. Matthew's Gospel only, few modern critics would have any hesitation in putting them in the same category, and treating them as an insertion made by the author or editor in the light of later Christian doctrine, or perhaps as a still later gloss or addition which had got into the text. But the words are as a matter of fact found also in St. Mark. Yet, after all, few will be disposed to deny that ecclesiastical or doctrinal additions to the earliest tradition are to be found even in St. Mark, or to contend that St. Luke's Gospel never preserves the original form of sayings better than the other two Synoptists, even when these are agreed. There was no theological reason why the author of the third gospel should have omitted the words if he had found them in his text of Mark: if (as I believe) the author was Luke, St. Paul's companion in travel, he would have welcomed a saying which to him would certainly have suggested something like the doctrine of that Apostle. The fact that he omitted it, therefore, points to one of two things—either (a) that in this case he relied upon some other authority—presumably Q (so Loisy), or his own special source, or (some would say) a special source in which Q had already been more or less embodied ;[2] or (b) that these words were absent from the copy of Mark used by Luke though present in some later copy employed by St. Matthew. To prefer the authority of Q to that of Mark (if that be the alternative adopted) is a critical opinion which needs no apology. There is, I think, a balance of authority for supposing that Q is earlier than Mark, and was more or less used by him. On any view the authority of Q is as good as that of Mark, and a saying that was omitted by Q, when the immediate context is preserved, must be held to be doubtful — much too doubtful to justify our attributing to our Lord with any confidence a doctrine which there is no other satisfactory evidence of His having taught. If we look simply to the attestation, the saying is doubtful : if we look to the character of the words—to the fact that this is just the kind of doctrinal gloss which was so often inserted by transcribers—it seems to me the more probable view that they were never uttered by our Lord : and that probability is increased if we accept the view that St. Mark's Gospel

---

[1] Matt. xxviii. 19. See above, p. 20, n. 1.
[2] See Prof. Vernon Bartlet's article in *Oxford Studies of the Synoptic Problem*, p. 315 *sq.*

is here and there coloured by the influence of St. Paul, or rather, as I should myself be disposed to say, by the later doctrine of the Church which was by no means exclusively Pauline. But perhaps the strongest objection to them is their irrelevance to the context. Our Lord has been speaking of His death as a kind of service—a service which His disciples were to imitate. There is a sudden transition to a different order of ideas—which is then immediately dropped and in no way followed up or explained. As Loisy remarks, "L'idée de la vie donnée en rançon appartient à un autre courant que celle de la service" (*Évan. Syn.* ii. 241). Wellhausen calls it a μετάβασις εἰς ἄλλο γένος. Those who regard the words as genuine can only escape the force of the argument by very strictly interpreting the passage in the light of its context, and understanding the death simply as a continuation of the life of service.

It is much more probable that our Lord may have thought of His death—the death of the Messiah—as foretold in Scripture than that He should actually have taught that it was the means, and the sole means, by which sin could be forgiven. The first belief would not be inconsistent with His general teaching about God and the forgiveness of sins : the latter would be a contradiction of it. He is represented as teaching that His death had been foretold in Scripture in the following places :

(*a*) "The Son of Man goeth even as it is written of Him" (Mk. xiv. 21 ; Matt. xxvi. 24. Cf. Lk. xxii. 22).

(*b*) "For I say unto you, that this that is written must yet be accomplished in me, And he was reckoned among the transgressors." (Lk. xxii. 37). Here He actually quotes Is. liii. 12, but not that part of the chapter which may conceivably be understood as implying the doctrine of an expiatory sacrifice for sin. Because the Messiah had to die, it does not follow that everything said of the suffering Servant was applied by Jesus to Himself in a literal and an exclusive sense.

(*c*) "And Jesus saith unto them, All ye shall be offended because of me this night, for it is written, I will smite the shepherd, and the sheep shall be scattered" (Mk. xiv. 27 ; Zech. xiii. 7).

(*d*) "Behoved it not Christ to have suffered these things, and to enter into his glory ? And beginning from Moses and from all the prophets, he interpreted to them in all the Scriptures the things concerning himself" (Lk. xxiv. 26, 27). In this case the passage rests on the authority of a single Evangelist, and cannot be regarded as much better historical evidence than if the Evangelist had (as is so often the case elsewhere) simply noted the fulfilment of prophecy on his own account. But if all these sayings are correctly reported, no one of them shows that Jesus in any way made the forgiveness of sins dependent on His own death.

It is of course *possible* that our Lord might here Himself have evolved the conception of the suffering Messiah out of Is. liii. ; but it is extremely improbable that He should have done so in view of the facts :

(1) That the passage about the ransom contains the only trace of His having done so.

(2) That such an interpretation of Isaiah was unknown in His time.

(3) That the idea of a suffering Messiah is absent from the book of Enoch and the other apocalyptic literature in which the more eschatological critics find the chief source of His Messianic conceptions.

It is to be noted that in Matt. xii. 18 the Evangelist represents Jesus as fulfilling the prophecy of the suffering Servant not by His death but by His works of mercy, quoting Is. xlii. 1-4. In the sermon in the synagogue at Nazareth, Jesus applies Is. lxi. 1-2 to Himself, but regards Himself as fulfilling it simply by His preaching (Lk. iv. 17-22).

The argument against the words may be strengthened by showing that there are parallel cases where Mark introduces later ecclesiastical or dogmatic language, while one or both of the other Evangelists give a simpler and more historically probable version of Christ's words : [1]

(a) In Mk. i. 1, "The beginning of the gospel of Jesus Christ, the Son of God." No other Evangelist applies the term "gospel" to his book or indeed uses that term at all.

(b) In Mk. i. 13 (Matt. iv. 11) the statement that angels ministered unto Christ after the temptation is omitted by Luke. This is the more significant in view of the frequency of allusions to angels elsewhere in St. Luke's writings.

(c) In Mk. i. 14, Mark speaks of Jesus as preaching "the gospel of God," and in the next verse gives our Lord's words as "Repent ye, and believe in the gospel." These last words are omitted by Matthew and by Luke (but Luke is not here closely parallel).

(d) In the passage about the blasphemy against the Holy Ghost, Luke has preserved the shortest and simplest form of the saying (xii. 10), "Every one who shall speak a word against the Son of man, it shall be forgiven him ; but unto him that blasphemeth against the Holy Spirit, it shall not be forgiven." Here Mark adds, "but is guilty of an aeonian sin," and Matthew, "neither in this aeon nor in that which is to come." Mark and Matthew agree (substantially) in prefixing the words, "All their sins shall be forgiven, etc." (Mk. iii. 28 ; Matt. xii. 31). Matthew is no doubt dependent on Mark, and Luke may preserve the simpler saying as it stood in Q (but see below, p. 57).

(e) All three Synoptists (Mk. viii. 35 ; Matt. xvi. 25 ; Lk. ix. 24) give the saying, "Whosoever would save his life, etc." Mark alone after "for my sake" adds "and the gospel's." There is a similar addition in the saying, "There is no man that hath left house or brethren . . . for my sake" (Mk. x. 29 ; Matt. xix. 29 ; Lk. xviii. 29).

(f) In Mk. x. 39, our Lord is made to say, "The cup that I drink ye shall drink ; and with the baptism that I am baptized withal

---

[1] For a number of minor "editorial touches" in Mark (not reproduced by Matthew or Luke) see Moffat, *Introduction to the Literature of the New Testament*, p. 233.

shall ye be baptized." The last clause referring to baptism is omitted by Matthew.

(g) In the "Little Apocalypse" Mark alone has the words, "The gospel must first be preached unto all the nations" (xiii. 10). This is absent in Matthew, but a little later Matthew varies the saying "ye shall be hated of all for my name's sake" (which is found in all three) by inserting after "all" the word "nations" (Matt. xxiv. 9 ; Mk. x. 13 ; Lk. xxi. 17). Here (xiii. 13) we find Mark alone introducing the technical word "gospel," while Matthew follows Mark in introducing words which make our Lord expressly contemplate the mission to the Gentiles. Luke is free from either addition, and yet nobody will suggest that, had he found them before him either in Mark or in a separate copy of the apocalyptic source used by all three, he would have had any disposition to leave them out. In view of Luke's "universalism" this is a remarkable instance of his tendency to preserve sayings of the Christ in their original form, free from "ecclesiastical" or doctrinal additions.

(h) It is more probable that a Roman centurion would say, "Certainly this was a righteous man" (Lk. xxiii. 47) than "This man was a Son of God" (Mk. xv. 39 ; Matt. xxvii. 54). The agreement of Matthew and Mark against Luke throughout the Passion-narrative is particularly noticeable.

(i) If we accept the "shorter text" of Luke's account of the Last Supper, his narrative is far the simplest and least influenced by later eucharistic ideas. (See above, pp. 43-44.)

It would seem then that Mark, or the last editor of Mark, has a tendency to make slight additions expressed in later ecclesiastical or doctrinal language, where Luke preserves the simpler and more probable form of the saying. Sometimes he is followed by Matthew, sometimes not. What is the explanation of this last fact is a question for the critics. It may be that sometimes Matthew had before him a copy of Mark from which the addition was absent, or he may in these particular passages have been following Q and not Mark. It cannot be too strongly insisted that, when a common source is inferred to account for the resemblances between two or more Gospels, we can never be sure that any two Evangelists had before them the same text of that source except in so far as they actually exhibit verbal identity. All the Gospel sources must have been more or less subject to a process of constant and gradual correction—at least in small details. In the case of the ransom passage, if we adopt the view that Q contained no Passion-narrative or discourses leading up to the Passion, we may suppose that Luke was here using his special source (the existence of which is particularly obvious in the Passion-narratives) ; but in view of the verbal identity of the rest of the verse, it is more probable that Matthew was following a copy of Mark in which the insertion had already been made, while Luke had before him a better text of Mark. Apart from the theory that Q had no Passion-narrative, the simplest supposition would be that the words were absent from Q, and that Luke here followed Q. The hypothesis of later assimilation to

Matthew is also one that cannot be ignored.[1] On any view of the critical question at issue, few will be disposed to deny that, in a particular case where Luke disagrees with Matthew or Mark, Luke may have preserved the more primitive form of the saying.

I will quote two opinions on the general question of Luke's merits as a reporter of our Lord's sayings :

"The general opinion is that the latter's [Luke's] setting of the Logia is in many, perhaps in most cases superior to Matthew's" (Moffat).[2]

"Although the stylistic corrections of St. Luke are so numerous, we cannot say that he has completely obliterated the characteristics of his exemplar. Indeed, in spite of all, we cannot but recognize that his work of revision is ever carried out in a conservative spirit, and that his readers receive from him a just impression of our Lord's style of discourse" (Harnack).[3]

Harnack after quoting and adopting Wernle's conclusion that St. Luke had before him the discourses of the Logia-source in their primary form, not in a secondary edition, adds, "Wernle is also correct in his further remark 'Almost everywhere St. Matthew has preserved a better text than St. Luke' ; yet he ought to have added that in St. Matthew there are to be found many alterations of the text of a very drastic nature—far more drastic than any St. Luke has allowed himself to make."[4]

To the instances above given of Mark's tendency to introduce matter coloured by later ideas we should have to add a whole series of others if we accepted Professor Bacon's view of the second gospel as a whole. According to him the Gospel is based upon Q, a Petrine narrative (P) and other traditions, put together by an editor (R) who used his material with extreme freedom and with a strong Pauline tendency. His object is to exhibit Jesus as the wonder-working Son of God, in the full Pauline sense, to negative what had now come to seem the too legalistic teaching of Q, and to emphasize everywhere the Pauline ideas of salvation through the free gift of God on the condition of faith. The editor wrote at Rome, was decidedly universalistic, and strongly anti-Jewish. Without denying a considerable element of the truth in Prof. Bacon's view of the Gospel, I cannot but feel (1) that *some* of Prof. Bacon's illustrations of a Pauline tendency are somewhat fanciful and far-fetched ; (2) that very often ideas which he calls Pauline should be rather described as the ideas common to the whole later Church ;[5] (3) that the whole construction is highly speculative. It represents what very well may have happened, but what the evidence is scarcely sufficient to show did happen. For this

---

[1] "In some passages (*e.g.* iii. 22 f.) it is even possible that the canonical Mark has been affected by Matthew or Luke" (Moffat, *Introduction to the Literature of the New Testament*, p. 205).

[2] *Introduction to the Literature of the New Testament*, p. 195.

[3] *The Sayings of Jesus*, p. 115.

[4] *Ib.* pp. 116, 117.

[5] For a more moderate estimate of the Paulinism of St. Mark, see Menzies, *The Earliest Gospel*, p. 38. Cf. also Moffat, *l.c.* p. 235.

reason I abstain from adding to the above list a number of cases very similar to the passage about the ransom, and have confined myself to cases where there is demonstrable evidence of the existence of a tradition from which the additions are absent. Prof. Bacon ascribes not merely the words about the ransom but the whole verse (Mark x. 45) to the editor, though he admits that the teaching of the words ("came not to be ministered unto, but to minister") is implied in the context, which he accepts as a genuine saying of Jesus. To my mind the last clause, but not the whole verse, reads like a subsequent gloss. If it stood in Luke's copy of Mark or of Q, I cannot see why he should have omitted it.

It may be well to mention some authorities on both sides of the question. The words are accepted as genuine by Ewald, Renan, Hilgenfeld, O. Holtzmann, Keim, Albert Réville, Beyschlag, Wendt, Goguel, Schweitzer, but most of them would not interpret them in the sense of the later atonement doctrines. Until recently few modern writers who treat the saying as genuine understood them in a strictly expiatory sense. Of late, however, it has been precisely the writers who most definitely treat the expiatory idea as an illusion who are the chief champions of the genuineness of the words, and who most distinctly attribute to Jesus the expiatory meaning, *e.g.* Schweitzer. It is of course useless to add the names of the older theologians for whom all words attributed to Christ in the Gospels are genuine, even when they contradict each other.

The genuineness of the words is denied by Pfleiderer, Wrede, Wellhausen, Schmiedel, Loisy, Bousset, Bacon, Montefiore. Among those who seem doubtful may be mentioned Jo. Weiss and Prof. Menzies.

The authority of some of the writers who reject the words may seem to be discounted by the fact that they deny that Jesus anticipated His death at all, or even (in the case of Wrede) that He claimed to be the Messiah, but this is by no means the case with all of them. Loisy, for instance, can hardly be accused of minimizing the eschatological element in the teaching of Jesus, though he does not (like Schweitzer) make it the whole, or treat the ethics of Jesus with contempt.

There is room for difference of opinion on the subject ; but any one who, in the teeth of this conflict of Gospel-texts and of modern authorities, is really prepared to say that the genuineness of these words is certain, and to make his whole interpretation of the teaching · of Jesus turn upon the assumption of their genuineness, must be a person who has little sense of the nature of historical evidence. If he confines himself to holding that there is a slight probability in their favour, that is an opinion which cannot be positively refuted ; but it becomes less probable the greater the superstructure which the words are made to bear. That it occurred to Jesus as a passing thought that His sufferings were another instance of the prophetic principle that the sufferings of the righteous redound to the benefit of the nation— it may be (since He was the Messiah) a crowning instance of that principle—is a possible view ; but to interpret His whole conception of His mission in the light of this solitary utterance tends to the refutation of the hypothesis which involves such an improbable corollary. If the words are genuine, they must be interpreted in a way which is congruous both with the context of the particular passage and with the ideas of Jesus as revealed by His other reported sayings. If it is insisted that they can only bear the meaning which later dogmatic theology put upon them, they cannot be genuine.

On any view of the historical question it is impossible to rest our whole doctrine of salvation upon a doubtful interpretation of a single doubtfully genuine word of the Saviour. The salvation of mankind cannot depend upon a critical possibility or even a critical probability. The only reasonable course is to arrive at some conception of the general character of Christ's teaching independently of this passage, and then to ask what meaning the words (if genuine) may bear consistently with that general character.

NOTE B

THE SIN AGAINST THE HOLY GHOST

Since *prima facie* the saying about the sin against the Holy Ghost may be regarded as an exception to what has been said about the unrestricted offer of forgiveness on the one condition of penitence, it seems desirable to say a word about it, although the difficulty of the passage is as great for those who suppose our Lord to have taught a doctrine of atonement through His own death as for those who deny it.

The saying occurs in different forms and in different contexts. In Mark and Matthew it is connected with the controversy about casting out devils through Beelzebub; in Lk. xii. 10 it comes after the declaration, "Every one who shall confess me before men, etc." Here it has no connexion with the context. In Mark it is thrust in at the end of the Beelzebub passage in a way which suggests that its place is due to the Evangelist. It is therefore very doubtful whether the context can help us to its meaning.

It may be well to print the three versions side by side :

Mark iii. 28-9	Matthew xii. 31	Luke xii. 10
Verily I say unto you, All their sins shall be forgiven unto the sons of men, and their blasphemies wherewithsoever they shall blaspheme : but whosoever shall blaspheme against the Holy Spirit hath never forgiveness, but is guilty of an eternal sin ($\alpha i\omega\nu i o \upsilon$ $\dot{\alpha}\mu\alpha\rho\tau\dot{\eta}\mu\alpha\tau o\varsigma$); because they said, He hath an unclean spirit.	Therefore I say unto you, Every sin and blasphemy shall be forgiven unto men; but the blasphemy against the Spirit shall not be forgiven. And whosoever shall speak a word against the Son of man, it shall be forgiven him; but whosoever shall speak against the Holy Spirit, it shall not be forgiven him, neither in this world nor in that which is to come.	And every one who shall speak a word against the Son of man, it shall be forgiven him; but unto him that blasphemeth against the Holy Spirit, it shall not be forgiven.

Now it is clear that, if we compare Luke and Mark, there are two ways of interpreting the facts :

(1) We may suppose that Luke's is the earlier, and that Mark has tried to get rid of the suggestion that blasphemy against the Son of man could be forgiven (consistently with his plan of exhibiting Jesus as the wonder-working Son of God) by altering "against the Son of man" into "unto the sons of men" (a strange and unusual expression in the New Testament) ; and the greater simplicity of Luke in the latter part of the saying is a reason for preferring his version, which omits the words "he is guilty of an aeonian sin" (a difficult and unprecedented expression). We may then suppose that both Luke and Mark took the saying from Q ; Mark has distorted it, and also brought it into connexion with the Beelzebub incident ; while Matthew has put together the original Q saying and the secondary Markan version, and substituted "neither in this world nor in that which is to come" for the mysterious "is guilty of an aeonian sin." Or (2) we may admit that Matthew has combined Mark and Q, but may suppose that the variation between Mark and Matthew points to Mark's version as the original reading of Q, and that Matthew altered the unusual "sons of men" into "men," while Luke or Luke's copy of Q altered it to "against the Son of man."

Which interpretation is preferred will depend in part on the view that is taken of the general nature and tendencies of Q. If we accept Prof. Bacon's view of Mark as a writer who systematically altered the simpler teaching of an earlier narrative (based on the teaching of Peter) and that of Q, in order to exhibit Jesus everywhere as the wonder-working Son of God, the critic may be disposed to agree with him in accepting the first explanation.[1] On this view the meaning, if we accept Mark's context, will be : "To speak against the Messiah may be forgiven, but to speak against the Spirit of God, whose work these healings are, shall not be forgiven. To suggest that this work of God is due to the powers of evil is to speak, not against man but against God." If the context is not accepted, it is really hardly worth while to attempt to give possible meanings to the saying, for the exact shade of meaning will depend upon the context. We can only assume that some act which might be regarded as an offence against Himself led Jesus to say that an offence against the Messiah was a less sin than sin against the Holy Ghost, by which no doubt He meant wilful and persistent resistance to the voice of conscience.

The second view has the advantage of giving us a more easily intelligible saying. If Mark's version (apart from the context) be the original one, there will be nothing at all about blasphemy against the Son of Man. The saying will be simply that the one sin which will not be forgiven at the judgement is the sin against the Holy Ghost. The saying will be still simpler if we take the absence from Luke of "but is guilty of an eternal sin" to imply that Mark has added these words (by way of explanation) to the saying which he (like St. Luke)

---

[1] *The Beginnings of the Gospel Story*, p. 38 *sq.*

found in Q. On the whole, this seems to me the most probable explanation. There is some reason for believing that " aeonian " is a technical word, the Aramaic equivalent of which did not belong to the vocabulary of Jesus Himself. That allusions to the " Son of Man " were *sometimes* introduced by the Evangelists into a saying in which it was originally absent, is generally admitted.

In no case has the passage really any bearing upon our Lord's general teaching about forgiveness. It is implied that the sin is one which has not been repented of. Our Lord says that such a sin will not be forgiven at the judgement, and He does not generally look beyond the judgement. Without the addition of Mark and Matthew, nothing is said about the duration of the punishment which will follow the judgement.

On the critical question cf. Streeter, *Oxford Studies in the Synoptic Problem*, p. 171.

NOTE C

THE LAST SUPPER

The view which I have taken as to the genuineness and original meaning of the words attributed to our Lord in the institution of the Eucharist is largely based upon the work of M. Maurice Goguel, *L'Eucharistie*. I will quote the passage in which he expounds his view as to the original meaning of the Saviour's act :

"Le don de soi qu'exprime la cène ne peut être compris que comme un don que Jésus fait à ses disciples. L'idée d'expiation étant écartée, la question de savoir si Jésus pense au passé, au présent ou à l'avenir, perd beaucoup de son importance. Ce que Jésus donne aux siens, c'est lui-même, c'est-à-dire l'essence même de sa pensée, de sa foi, de son cœur, il se dépense sans compter pour allumer en eux la flamme qui le dévore, pour faire naître et pour entretenir en eux et chacun d'eux les aspirations, les énergies, les certitudes qui l'animent. Il se donne, c'est-à-dire, il se communique lui-même à eux, il veut les associer à son œuvre et pour cela rien ne lui coûte, il ne recule ni devant les fatigues, ni devant les souffrances, il ne reculera pas même devant la mort s'il arrive que Dieu dresse la croix sur son chemin. Ainsi compris le don de Jésus ne peut être enfermé ni dans le présent, ni dans le passé, ni dans l'avenir. Rien ne vient limiter ce que Jésus exprime par la distribution du pain comme son corps. La compréhension de cet acte est très large, elle enferme le ministère de Jésus tout entier et ces heures de suprême réunion qu'il passe avec ses disciples dans la chambre haute, les souffrances, la mort, la crise quelle qu'elle soit qui est imminente, mais aussi le triomphe final qui est certain, le retour glorieux, la réunion dans le Royaume de Dieu." [1]

Some of these last expressions seem to be hardly justified, but on the whole I have not seen a better account of the original meaning

[1] *L'Eucharistie*, pp. 100-1.

of our Lord's acts and words. I should differ from him in the following ways :

(1) In accepting the shorter text of Luke as the genuine text of that Evangelist.

(2) I should be disposed to find in them a rather more definite reference to the coming death. A true explanation must give a meaning both (*a*) to the comparison of the bread to the body, and (*b*) to the giving. I do not think the first condition can be satisfied without supposing an implicit reference to the death, though the thought need not be limited to the death. Cf. the very similar view of Prof. Bacon : " At the (ordinary) evening meal—not the passover supper, which would have presented the closer symbol of the slain lamb—Jesus assumed his usual part as dispenser of the food. But on this occasion he made the loaf a symbol of his body. Its destruction should not be dissolution, but a stronger union of the brotherhood by as much as the sacrifice made for its sake was now greater." [1]

The words " This do in remembrance of me " are found only in St. Paul's account (and the longer text of Luke), and may certainly be regarded as a later addition. If we set these words aside, there is nothing to suggest that our Lord had the intention of founding an institution or permanent rite of any kind. Whatever exactly happened at the Last Supper, the idea of perpetually commemorating that supper or of investing with a new significance the Jewish offering of cup and bread at the table was the work of the Church, not of its Founder. Whatever we may regard as the true meaning of the Eucharist for the later Church or for ourselves as a permanent and often repeated rite, no such significance must be read back into our Lord's own words : though I should strongly insist that a true doctrine of the Eucharist for the later Church should at least be based upon the meaning which our Lord's act had for Him, so far as we can discern it.

There can be little doubt that the Eucharistic rite grew out of and added a fresh meaning to some Jewish rite. As to what Jewish rite it was which was invested with that new meaning, there may be some difference of opinion. Many critics not usually disposed to prefer St. John to the Synoptists as an historical authority, admit that he is right in holding that the Last Supper was not a Passover, though the meaning and associations of the Passover may subsequently have been transferred to the Sacrament which grew out of it. There is much to be said for supposing that it was the Kiddûsh, the religious meal still celebrated by strict Jewish families after the lighting of the lamps on the eve of Sabbaths or great Festivals, at which there is a solemn blessing of the cup and the bread by the father of the family.[2]

---

[1] *The Beginnings of the Gospel Story*, p. 204.
[2] See Box, *Journal of Theological Studies*, ii. p. 357, and the more recent work by Drs. Oesterley and Box, *The Religion and Worship of the Synagogue*, pp. 346 *sq.*

LECTURE II

THE PRE-PAULINE AND THE PAULINE
DOCTRINE OF ATONEMENT

Him who knew no sin he made to be sin on our behalf ; that we might become the righteousness of God in him.—2 COR. V. 21.

LECTURE II

I. *The Origin of the Atonement Doctrine*

IN my last lecture I tried to show that our Lord Himself taught the simple doctrine that God is, and (it is implied) always has been, willing to pardon the sins of the truly penitent.

The Church of later times has—no doubt with many degrees of consistency and of emphasis, in a great variety of forms, phrases, and senses, but still almost universally and continuously—taught that forgiveness of sins, and the salvation of which forgiveness may be considered the first step, are to be obtained through the influence of Christ's work; and in that work a conspicuous and sometimes an exclusive place has generally been assigned to His death. Moreover, the appropriation or application of this redemptive and saving efficacy has—in a less uniform and unqualified way, but still pretty generally—been supposed to depend on the individual's belief about Christ, and sometimes even upon his belief in this particular doctrine as to the efficacy of His atonement. When, why, and by what stages did this immensely important evolution of doctrine take place? That will be the main subject of the succeeding lectures. This morning we shall deal with the first beginnings of this great development.

But before we proceed to a consideration of these questions it will be necessary very briefly to glance at some of the Jewish ideas which paved the way for the Christian doctrine of atonement, and provided (so to speak) the medium in which it was developed.

(1) In all early forms of religion there is a tendency to look upon gods as deliverers or saviours. In the earliest forms of it the deliverance is not at all a deliverance from sin, but from national or personal dangers of some quite material kind. The whole history of Israel was such as to strengthen and emphasize this tendency. Long before the Israelites came to regard their national God Jahve as the only God, they were distinguished above other peoples by the intensity and exclusiveness of their loyalty to that national deity. And this solemn and exclusive marriage of Israel to its God (to use the metaphor of the prophets), if it did not begin with the deliverance from Egypt, was at least strengthened and rendered indissoluble by that national rebirth. When the prophets in later times reproached the people for disloyalty to their God, it was always the deliverance from Egypt that was put at the head of Jehovah's claims upon His people's allegiance. The exile brought with it a cry for a fresh deliverance ; and that extraordinary event, almost unparalleled in history—the actual return of the people after seventy years of captivity in a foreign land— still further strengthened the tendency to look upon Jahve as the Deliverer or Saviour.[1]

(2) Time would fail me here to trace the growth of the expectation of a new and still greater deliverance, of a coming establishment of a kingdom of God indefinitely more perfect and more worthy of the name than

[1] Some enquirers would even say that the very earliest conception of God (at least among Semites) is that of Saviour. There is a myth which goes back to an indefinitely remote period of human history, in which the sea is regarded as identical with, or the abode of, a great monster (Tehom, Leviathan, eventually identified with Satan), and which tells of his defeat by a Saviour (" Heilbringer ") who is thought of at first as a semi-divine earthly hero and then as a God in heaven, who has partly vanquished, and will perhaps more completely vanquish, this monster. This myth has assumed all sorts of forms, and has left many traces of itself in much later Jewish literature (Is. xxvii. 1, li. 9-11 ; Ps. lxv. 6, 7 ; Amos ix. 3, etc.). In Judaism the delivering Deity was at a comparatively early period identified with Jahve. The Jewish belief in a Messiah who should eventually complete the conquest of this enemy, and inaugurate a kingdom of God on earth, may be said to be one of the forms in which the much more widely diffused belief in an ultimate deliverance of humanity or a future age of gold has clothed itself. On this subject see Dr. Oesterley's most interesting work, *The Evolution of the Messianic Idea.*

the golden age of David and Solomon, of a great judgement of the heathen who persecuted and oppressed the
people of Jahve (now fully recognized as the only true
God, the Creator of heaven and earth), and (at certain
periods) of an ideal king by whom the deliverance
should be effected, but the Saviour and Judge is always
Jehovah Himself.   The pictures that were constructed
of the ideal king and the ideal kingdom varied widely.
Sometimes the Messiah was thought of as a conqueror
and national emancipator ; at other times, the kingdom
is invested with more supernatural, and in the highest
prophetic teaching more ideal and ethical, attributes.
Even in the greatest of the prophets the kingdom is
still represented as a terrestrial monarchy, with its
capital in the ancient stronghold of Zion ; but still
that kingdom is a kingdom of righteousness and peace,
something much more righteous and more spiritual than
any monarchy the earth had ever seen.   In the later
apocalyptic writings the judgement assumes a more
distinctly supernatural character, and the kingdom
which it inaugurates hovers more doubtfully between
heaven and earth.   The idea of a deliverance from the
Syrian or the Roman tyranny came to be more and more
closely associated with the anticipation of some great
physical catastrophe, an end of the world or of the present
stage in its history.   And before the time of Jesus there
were many apocalyptic writings in which the political
side of the Messiah's work had almost disappeared.
He had become a completely supernatural Being : the
judgement had become a universal judgement, extending
over the whole world ; the kingdom which He was
to inaugurate assumed a more and more transcendental
character, though it never altogether ceased to be a
kingdom in which exceptional privileges were to be
enjoyed by pious Jews.

All this tended to emphasize the idea of a future
salvation—salvation for the nation from its foes, salvation for the individual in the day of the Messiah's judgement.   It was the recognized function of the Messiah
to save pious Israelites at the judgement and to condemn

F

others.[1] In proportion as the idea of the judgement became more universal and more ethical, the nature of salvation became more ethical too, and by consequence more individual. To prepare for the coming judgement, to become fit to meet the Judge, to become worthy of admission to the Messianic kingdom, became the form in which the Jewish mind expressed that desire for emancipation from sin and its consequences which in all peoples and under all conditions is the natural aspiration of the awakened and developed religious consciousness. Jesus, if He accepted the Messianic position, and used some of the traditional language about the Messiah's appearing in glory, did so with many reserves. The very notion that He, a human being, a " man of sorrows and acquainted with grief," was to be the Messiah, implied a profound change in the conception. Jesus completed the spiritualization of the Messianic idea and of the judgement which He foretold. If some of His followers may have been disposed to revert to earlier and lower conceptions of the Messianic dignity, there came a time when the Church accepted or even carried further that spiritualization of the Messianic idea and the Messianic kingdom, and interpreted in a purely spiritual sense the language which prophets and psalmists had used about the Messianic salvation. Even Jewish Christians accepted the principle that salvation was for the whole world and not for Jews only. The Messiah was thought of as one who had brought with Him deliverance from sin, and would secure for those who had accepted Him deliverance at His second coming in judgement—a coming which the early Christians long continued to expect in the near future.

(3) So far there has been nothing to connect the idea of salvation with that of suffering or death. That connexion is supplied by the primitive institution of sacrifice, and in particular animal sacrifice. I will not enter into any elaborate discussion as to the origin of this strange rite. It is probable that there is much truth

---

[1] " When he hath reproved them [the wicked], he shall destroy them. For the rest of my people shall he deliver with mercy " (4 (2) Esdras xii. 33, 34).

in the view that its explanation is closely connected with totemistic ideas. The tribal ancestor-god being supposed to be incarnate in some species of animal and the life of the animal to reside in the blood, the slaying of the animal, the eating of its flesh and the drinking of its blood, were regarded as the means of communion with the tribal God. It is a matter of profound significance for the history of religion that the original idea of sacrifice should be thus shown to be not so much propitiation as communion.[1] At the same time the distinction between the two ideas must not be pushed too far. The propitiatory idea could easily grow out of that of communion. The eating of the sacrificial flesh, and still more the drinking of the sacrificial blood, were the means of renewing or restoring communion with the god when for any reason he was supposed to be angry or displeased with the sacrificers. But, when we remember the extreme fluidity and inconsistency of primitive religious ideas, we must not seek for too much definitiveness and precision in this matter. The idea of communion is always liable to be degraded into that of propitiation ; and in earlier religion the higher idea was perhaps never entirely free from adulteration with the lower. In primitive religion the external rite is the important thing : different explanations might be given of it at different times, by different people at the same time, or even by the same persons at different moments. Perhaps the two interpretations were never sharply distinguished even by the same people at the same moment. The essential point for our purpose is the primitive human belief that gods or spirits could be influenced by the killing of animals. Originally there was nothing particularly ethical about this mode of seeking for divine assistance, except in so far as the god was thought of as friendly to the tribe, and in so far as the common worship of him contributed to the strengthening of the tribal bond. If you wanted the help of a

---

[1] The classical expression of this view is Robertson Smith's great work, *The Religion of the Semites* (new ed. 1894, p. 269). Cf. also Jevons, *Introduction to the History of Religion*, ed. 2, p. 131 *sq.*

king or other potentate, you offered him a present. If
you wanted to establish, or to renew when interrupted,
friendly relations with the tribal god, you offered him
a sacrifice. In proportion as the idea of the god and
the purpose for which his help could be effectually
invoked became more ethical, the idea of sacrifice became
more ethical too.[1]   In primitive Judaism the idea of
sacrifice had very little to do with sin ; or at least sin was
regarded merely in the light of ritual irregularity, the
disastrous effect of which, quite apart from the motives
or intentions of the offender, had to be counteracted by
some other ritual observance. As the conception of
Israel's God Jahve became purer and loftier, the idea of
satisfaction for moral transgression became more prominent : still more so when Jahve came to be thought of as
the one and only true God, the Creator of heaven and
earth. Not all the Jewish sacrifices, but some of them,
were regarded in this light. In particular the ritual of
the great day of atonement emphasized that particular
aspect or explanation of sacrifice according to which
the votive offering was looked upon as a substitute for
the offender. It was not, indeed, so much the goat that
was killed as the goat that was sent forth into the wilderness which was supposed to be the bearer of the nation's
sins : but still the sacrifice of the other goat was an
essential part of the process by which the consequences of
sin could be averted, and possibly (though this is more
doubtful), for the higher religious consciousness of later
Judaism, the actual sinfulness of the heart taken away.
This, I say, is more doubtful ; for that spiritualization
of Jewish religion by the prophets which so largely
paved the way for Christianity, did not, to any great

---

[1] Prof. Kennett (developing previous suggestions) maintains that the earlier prophetic attacks upon sacrifice, and upon the moral abominations connected with it,
both at the "high places" and in the Temple at Jerusalem, were not merely (as commonly
supposed) an assertion of the *comparative* worthlessness of sacrifice, but a deliberate
opposition to the whole institution. Not till the reform of Josiah was a compromise
effected between the prophetic and the priestly religion ; sacrifice was confined to Jerusalem and purified from its immoral associations, after which this minimum of sacrificial
observance was tolerated by the later prophets. See his article on " The Conflict
between Priestly and Prophetic Ideas in the Church of Israel " in *The Interpreter*, vol.
xiv. No. 2 (Jan. 1918). This view assumes that Deut. xii.-xxvi. belongs to the sixth
century B.C.—a later date than is assigned to it by Driver and the older critics.

extent, take the form of investing with symbolical or sacramental meanings the old sacrificial rites. The prophets and the more spiritual psalmists openly disparaged animal sacrifice, and insisted that the blood of bulls and of goats could not really take away sin or procure its forgiveness. What was needed was simply true repentance and amendment. " Thou desirest no sacrifice, else would I give it thee, but thou delightest not in burnt offerings." [1] But, whatever may be thought about the later Jewish ideas concerning sacrifice, the important point for us is not so much the explanations that have been given of the institution as the fact of its existence. Whatever explanation might be given of it, however much it might sometimes be disparaged in comparison with moral righteousness and inward repentance, not the most spiritually-minded Jewish teacher, at least after the reconciliation between the prophetic and the sacerdotal Judaism under Josiah—still less any rabbi of the early Christian period—had any thought of actually doing away with animal sacrifices or denying their necessity, though it was by no means invariably that they were in any very close way connected with the forgiveness of other than ritual transgressions.

And I need hardly remind you that the institution of sacrifice was common to Jew and Gentile. The early Christian writers lived in a world in which on every side the altars reeked with the blood of slain victims, in which the very idea of religion was barely separable from the practice of sacrifice. And, whatever might be the case with the highest religious minds, the popular notions about the remission of sins, whenever and so far as they were thought to be sins against a god, were intimately connected with the idea of slain victims. With the few the sacrifice might be felt to be a mere symbol or expression of penitence or piety ; for the popular imagination the guilt and its consequences were taken away by the actual performance of the rite. In such a world it was almost inevitable that any new remedy for sin should be treated and spoken of as a new

[1] Ps. li. 16.

kind of sacrifice. For men living in such an environment the most spiritual conception of salvation, the
very idea that repentance was the one only condition of
forgiveness with God, could hardly express itself more
simply and intelligibly than by saying that repentance
was the true reality of which animal sacrifices were but
the shadow : " The sacrifice of God is a troubled spirit : a
broken and contrite heart, O God, shalt thou not despise."[1]
When repentance came to be closely associated with
belief in a crucified Messiah, the application of sacrificial
language to His death was, independently of any more
definite cause, an easy and very probable development
of existing ideas. Actual experience of the emancipat-
ing, cleansing, life-giving effects which flowed from the
Messiah's life and death could hardly express itself more
simply and naturally than by calling Him " the Saviour,"
by speaking of His outpoured blood as the symbol
of all the benefits which had resulted from His life and
His death, as the true sacrifice for sin which made all
other sacrifice unnecessary. Belief in salvation through
a Messiah whose blood had been shed upon the cross
wanted very little in the way of definite external suggestion to pass into the idea of salvation through that blood.

(4) But there was another source for the idea, which
connects, in a far deeper and more spiritual way, the
taking away of sins with the suffering of another. According to the creed of primitive Israel Jahve rewarded
loyalty to himself by national success and personal
prosperity, and punished disloyalty by national defeat
and personal misfortune. The great problem for the
devout Jew was to account for the apparent exceptions
to this simple philosophy of history. In particular the
experiences of the exile branded the difficulty upon the
nation's heart, and compelled a fundamental revolution
in its theology. The nation had never been so faithful
to its God ; the law had never been so well observed ;
individual piety had never been so general and so profound. Yet the sanctuary of God was trodden under
foot by the Gentiles : the nation was in captivity : the

[1] Ps. li. 17.

individual Jew—all the more so in proportion as he kept
aloof from heathen religious rites and heathen modes of
life—was an object of persecution, scorn, and derision.
Many were the expedients devised by the religious consciousness of the time for reconciling theology with fact.
Sometimes the sufferings were regarded as a national
expiation for a national guilt, though the expiation fell
upon others, and not upon the actual offenders. At
other times they were a trial or probation, intended to
test, and in testing to deepen and strengthen, national
and individual faithfulness to Jehovah. In this way
suffering might not only expiate the past; it might
regenerate the character for the future, and the benefit
of this regeneration might be experienced by many
besides the sufferers. Thus suffering came to be looked
upon as a mark not of God's wrath, but almost of His
favour : " Blessed is the man whom thou chastenest,
O Lord," we read in the Psalms.[1] The ideal Jew came
to be represented as normally and naturally poor and
afflicted : the righteous nation was a suffering nation ;
and it was the really faithful and religious kernel of the
nation on which the heaviest load of suffering was laid.
All these ideas found their fullest and most perfect
expression in that picture of the suffering Servant of
Jehovah which forms the central core of the second Isaiah's
prophecy. It is the generally accepted view of criticism
that it is the Jewish nation, or perhaps sometimes the
ideal Israelite, the true and spiritual Israel within Israel,
as it were, that is represented as " despised, and rejected
of men ; a man of sorrows, and acquainted with grief."
It was the idealized Israelite who was wounded for the
transgressions of his people; upon whom the chastisement of its peace was laid, and with whose stripes
it was healed, on whom the Lord had laid the iniquity
of all.[2] These chapters paved the way for a doctrine

[1] Ps. xciv. 12.
[2] Is. liii. 3, 5, 6. To ask how far the prophet thought of the saving influence of Israel
upon the heathen world as strictly expiatory, and how far he was thinking of moral and
religious influence, heightened by the example of patient suffering, is too large a question to be entered on here. Cf. J. K. Mozley, *The Doctrine of the Atonement*, p. 26 *sq.*,
and the striking passages from modern writers there quoted.

of atonement by the blood of Christ. They impressed upon the religious consciousness of the Jew, and of Gentile Christians also when they came to know the Jewish scriptures, the undeniable reality of vicarious suffering—that profoundly true and spiritual idea which so easily degenerates into the superstition of vicarious expiation, and even the more immoral notion of vicarious punishment. And the doctrine is prominent in later Judaism—in the Apocalypse of Baruch for instance, whose author was St. Paul's[1] contemporary, in the fourth book of Maccabees, and in the teaching of the rabbis.[2]

In this doctrine there was contained the germ which might easily develope into the doctrine of an innocent Messiah who should suffer and die for his people. It has sometimes been supposed that such a development had already taken place before the time of Jesus, but the evidence is quite insufficient to show that this was so. There is no satisfactory evidence that up to this time the Servant of Jehovah had ever been identified with the Messiah. Certainly this was not the usual interpretation. But once that step was taken, the development of a doctrine of atonement through the Messiah's sufferings was natural,

[1] " Lo ! Thou hast shown me the method of the times, and that which will be after these things, and Thou hast said unto me, that the retribution, which has been spoken of by Thee, will be of advantage to the nations " (Syriac *Apocalypse of Baruch*, ed. Charles, xiv. 1). " And if others did evil, it was due to Zion, that on account of the works of those who wrought good works she should be forgiven, and should not be overwhelmed on account of the works of those who wrought unrighteousness " (*ibid.* xiv. 7). Cf. cap. lxxxv., where the prophets intercede for sinners. So in 4 Macc. vi. 29 the martyr Eleazar prays : " Make my blood a purifying sacrifice ($\kappa\alpha\theta\dot{\alpha}\rho\sigma\iota\nu$), and my soul a substitution for theirs ($\dot{\alpha}\nu\tau\dot{\iota}\psi\upsilon\chi\sigma\nu\ \alpha\dot{\upsilon}\tau\ddot{\omega}\nu$)." Cf. i., ii., ix. 24, xii. 18, xiii. 22, and xviii. 4. Cf. also 2 Macc. vii. 33, 37.

[2] " As a much higher aspect of this solidarity . . . we may regard the suffering of the righteous as an atonement for the sins of their contemporaries. ' When there will be neither Tabernacle nor the Holy Temple,' Moses is said to have asked God, ' what will become of Israel ? ' Whereupon God answers, ' I will take from among them the righteous man whom I shall consider as pledged for them, and will forgive all their sins '; the death of the perfect man, or even his sufferings, being looked upon as an expiation for the shortcoming of his generation " (Schechter, in the *Jewish Quarterly Review*, vol. iii. p. 43 *sq.*).

Mr. Claude Montefiore remarks : " Vicarious atonement was not unknown to them [the Rabbis]. The passages cited by Weber are quite accurate. ' There lies atoning efficacy in the deaths of the righteous.' ' When there are righteous men in a generation, God lets them die (or suffer ?) for the sake of others ; when there are no righteous, then the innocent children are taken ' " (" Rabbinic Judaism and the Epistles of St. Paul " in *Jewish Quarterly Review*, vol. xiii. p. 200).

and indeed, in the then state of human thought, inevitable.

(5) One more possible source of the later theories about the atonement may be briefly noticed. Were we engaged upon a general history of Christian doctrine, we should have to say much about that Jewish-Alexandrian philosophy which is best known to us through the writings of Philo. Here we need do no more than briefly notice the fact that, among the attributes and functions of the Philonian Logos, one was that of mediator —mediator between God and men. The neo-Platonist conception of God tended to remove Him to the utmost possible distance from the material world, and consequently to make Him unknowable, inaccessible, unapproachable by man. Only through a mediator could He be brought even into that degree of contact with matter which was implied in the fact of creation : only through a mediator could He be known by man. For Philo this mediator was the Logos—a spiritual entity of which it is impossible to say whether it should be described as personal or impersonal, a principle or a substance, a creation or an emanation, a being independent of God or an aspect, an activity of God Himself. This conception exercised, I need hardly say, enormous influence over Christian theology from the date of the fourth Gospel onwards. It may have contributed something to the development of St. Paul's conception of the pre-existent Christ. And at a later date—through the Gnostic systems or more directly—the Philonian idea of mediation strengthened the tendency to think of the Son as a mediator. But the mediation of the Philonian Logos was chiefly performed through the bringing of knowledge. The Logos is the Saviour chiefly because he takes away ignorance, which is the cause of sin ; though the Logos is also represented as in some sense atoning for sin and strengthening the sinner against temptation.[1] The high - priest's acts on the great day of atonement are treated as a symbol of this

---

[1] Bigg, *Christian Platonists of Alexandria* (2nd ed. p. 45 *sq.*) and the references given in Dr. Bigg's notes.

atoning function of the Logos. The mediation of the Logos is not brought into connexion with the Messianic idea, still less with the idea of a suffering or dying Messiah. Nevertheless, these Philonian conceptions certainly influenced later theories about the atonement; this influence is particularly evident in the Epistle to the Hebrews.[1] It may conceivably have affected even St. Paul. But the *origin* of the doctrine is not to be sought for in this quarter. There is nothing in the Jewish-Alexandrian philosophy to explain precisely the feature of it which most requires explanation—the idea of an atonement effected by the death and sufferings of an historical Messiah.

(6) There are those who will not be content with a theory which finds the origin of the atonement doctrine in so simple and obvious a cause as the existing beliefs of the Jewish people. They will remind us of the wide diffusion of ancient myths about Osiris, Attis, and other dying gods, and in particular of the " mystery-religions " which had already obtained a considerable hold over the civilized world of the time, one at least of which, the religion known as Mithraism (in which, however, there is no dying Saviour), proved a formidable rival to Christianity in its struggle for ascendency in the Roman Empire. So long as we are concerned merely with the origin of the doctrine in its simplest form, such theories are, as I shall hope to show, wholly gratuitous. If the purely Jewish ideas which have been enumerated are sufficient, when taken in connexion with the actual facts of the life and death of Jesus and the actual experience of Christians, to account for the growth of the atonement doctrine, we need not seek for it a remoter or more recondite origin. These Jewish ideas had of course themselves something in common with the ideas about atonement or expiation which are discoverable in other religions of the ancient world. The Christian

---

[1] Especially in the conception of the great High-priest. In later times the influence is greatest precisely in the theories of the atonement other than those which eventually became the dominant conceptions in the West. The Philonian theory of atonement has much in common with Clement's, something in common with that of Athanasius— little or nothing in common with the theories of Tertullian or Augustine.

doctrine of the atonement, both on its higher and on its lower side, owed its existence to the same spiritual needs and the same psychological tendencies which under other conditions have produced other doctrines of atonement and expiation. And at a somewhat later date, when Christianity was transferred from Jewish to pagan soil, it can hardly be denied that the fully elaborated Christian doctrine of the atonement, and still more the sacramental ideas more or less connected with it, were to an appreciable and an increasing degree coloured by the influence of the mystery-religions, their phraseology and their ritual, by the ideas about sin and salvation, initiation and purification which were connected with these mystery-religions, and by the rituals and organizations to which they had given rise. We may even recognize that, if the origin of the doctrine was Jewish, the atmosphere of the Hellenic world at the same time was eminently suited to its acceptance and its development; and that atmosphere was one which was undoubtedly permeated by the ideas associated with the mystery-religions.[1]

To what extent it is necessary to look beyond the Old Testament for the source of the doctrine is a problem the solution of which must obviously depend upon the answer which is given to the fundamental question: "When and where did this doctrine originate?" To this question a fairly definite answer can be given. Many people sufficiently critical to see that in all probability the theory does not come from Christ Himself vaguely suppose that it must be due to St. Paul.[2] That

---

[1] The question is further discussed in Appendix II. The whole question of the influence exercised by non-Jewish religions upon Christianity has been investigated in an extremely sober and judicial spirit by Clemen in *Primitive Christianity and its non-Jewish Sources* (Eng. trans.), to which work the reader may be referred for further information about the subject and its literature. He does not regard the doctrine of atonement, as distinct from the sacramental beliefs connected with it, as one which owes anything to non-Jewish sources. He should perhaps have emphasized more than he has done the Hellenistic (but not strictly Hellenic) atmosphere in which it probably grew up, or at all events reached its full development.

[2] See for instance Goldwin Smith, *His Life and Opinions*, p. 223. Goldwin Smith is a typical representative of the vague English liberal theology of the last generation. Even Loisy seems to me to attenuate the significance of 1 Cor. xv. 3, and attributes the growth of the doctrine mainly to St. Paul. Cf. also Glover, *The Conflict of Religions in the Early Roman Empire*, p. 154.

view is rendered absolutely impossible by a single sentence in one of the practically undisputed Epistles of St. Paul himself. " I delivered unto you . . . that which also I received, how that Christ died for our sins according to the scriptures." [1]   The belief that in some sense Christ died for sin—in order that sin might be forgiven and removed—was thus quite certainly part of what St. Paul received.   It was already an article of the Church's traditional creed when the Apostle of the Gentiles was baptized into it.   It was due neither to the theorizing nor to the visions of St. Paul.   It resulted from the reflection of the Church in the interval which elapsed between the Crucifixion and St. Paul's conversion—a period which cannot have been more than a very few years.   From the tone in which St. Paul alludes to the recognition of his Gospel by St. Peter it is natural to infer its eventual acceptance by the Church of Jerusalem.[2]   At the same time it is important to notice the complete absence of such a doctrine in the early speeches attributed to St. Peter and to St. Stephen in the Acts of the Apostles.   In so far as these speeches may be supposed to be based on early documents or trustworthy tradition as to the character of the earliest apostolic preaching, they suggest that there may have been a period when the idea of salvation through the death of Christ formed no part of that preaching.   Of the doctrine that salvation is to be attained through the Messiah's work and through belief in Him they are full : and also of the idea that Christ's death had been foretold by the prophets.   But so far salvation is thought of as something due simply to the Messiah's teaching, and to the sentence of acquittal which He will hereafter pronounce at the judgement upon those who have accepted Him as the Messiah and listened to His call for repentance.   The resurrection and not the death of Christ is the central fact of the Gospel message, being regarded as the proof of His Messiahship and the pledge of His power to save at

---

[1] 1 Cor. xv. 3.
[2] Gal. ii. 2-4, 14-16.   But the efficacy of Christ's death is not here in question.

the judgement. If these speeches are not treated as historical testimony to the character of the earliest apostolic preaching, they equally point to the survival in some part of the Church of a type of theology in which the saving efficacy of Christ's death played no part, or at the very least to the existence of Christian circles in which very little stress was laid upon it.

Whatever may be thought of the use I have made of the Petrine speeches, it will hardly be denied that in the speech of St. Stephen we have, reproduced with considerable fidelity, a genuine and most interesting monument of the earliest Christian thought. One of the ideas which run through this closely reasoned historical argument is this—that, so far from the sufferings of Jesus and His rejection by the nation militating against the conception of His Messiahship, they go to establish it. For all through Jewish history their fathers had persecuted the prophets and messengers of Jehovah. But the inference which is drawn from this fact and from other facts in the history of Israel is not that it is through the sufferings of the Messiah that salvation is to be won ; but rather that the special privileges of the Israelite nation are no essential or permanent part of God's self-revelation of Himself, that the law is but an episode in the history of God's dealings with His people, that the worship of God is not limited to Jewish soil, to the Temple area, to any place or any people. The germ of all the Pauline ideas about Gentile liberty, and the uselessness of the law to secure justification or salvation, of all the universalism taught by St. Paul, is to be found in St. Stephen's teaching. We may perhaps say that by implication it is suggested that the justification which the law could not secure was in some way to be obtained through Christ. That idea was, indeed, involved in any possible teaching of Christianity as a universal religion for Gentile as well as Jew, whether the technical phrase " justification " was used or not. But still there is not a word about the remission of sins through the death or sufferings of Jesus. Whatever may be thought of the negative evidence supplied by the earliest speeches

in the Acts, they at all events supply us with no positive
evidence as to the date at which the forgiveness of sins
began to be definitely and specifically connected with the
death of Jesus.   The one certain datum for our enquiry
is the fact that by the date of St. Paul's conversion, which
may have occurred at any time between a year and six
or seven years after the crucifixion, the Church or certain
circles in it had come to believe that Christ died for our
sins.   It is natural to conjecture that it was in the
more Hellenized atmosphere of Antioch or Caesarea or
Damascus that this doctrine had been elaborated, while
the Church of Jerusalem—or those in it who regarded
James as their leader — adhered to the more simple
doctrine that for admission to the kingdom nothing
was required but repentance—a repentance which,
however, some of them at least interpreted as involving
and including obedience to the Jewish law.[1]

By what process was the new conviction reached ?
The same all-important sentence of St. Paul will tell us.
" Christ died for our sins," and it was " according to
the scriptures " that He so died.   Jewish prophecy
then was the source of the idea.   The early Christians
came to believe that Christ had died that sins might be
forgiven because they found it, as they thought, distinctly foretold that He should do so in books which
they regarded as in the most literal and plenary sense

[1] It was certain " men of Cyrene " who, after the dispersion of the Jerusalem Christians caused by the " tribulation that arose about Stephen," preached the Gospel for the
first time to Greeks at Antioch (Acts xi. 19, 20).   It was in this circle perhaps that the
doctrine was first developed.   Stephen had prepared the way for it by his universalistic
preaching, but the special significance attached to the death of Christ is still absent from
his great sermon in Acts vii.   Philip, it will be remembered, was one of the same circle
of Hellenistic Christians.   See Kirsopp Lake, *The Earlier Epistles of St. Paul*, p. 408 sq.
Prof. Lake notices the significance of the fact that it was chiefly in writing to churches
where Palestinian Jews were carrying on a propaganda that St. Paul has to defend his
doctrine.   In addressing Gentile churches such as Corinth he takes it for granted, showing that it was the Gentile churches which found the doctrine most congenial to their
mode of thought.   The doctrine was not " derived " from the " Mysteries," but it
was congenial to people familiar with the " mystery-religions," and perhaps suggested
itself first to them.   St. Peter must have accepted the doctrine independently of St.
Paul or the argument described in Gal. ii. would hardly have been possible, but he may
no doubt have been influenced by St. Paul's emphasis upon it as he certainly was by St.
Paul's Universalism.   St. Luke need not, therefore, be treated as necessarily unhistorical
in putting the doctrine (in a simple form) into St. Peter's later speeches in the Acts.
I may add that Prof. Lake's brief study of the historical situation presupposed by the
Epistle to the Romans is of the utmost value, but it would be out of place to enter further
upon the historical aspect of the Epistle.

inspired writings.   In that fact I believe we can discover the historical origin of the atonement doctrine.

We have seen that the view that the sufferings of the righteous might be in some way accepted on behalf of the nation at large, that they would in some way redound to the benefit of others, was already a familiar Jewish idea.   It is probable that the suffering Servant of Is. liii. had not been identified with the Messiah in any exclusive or pre-eminent fashion ; but in the light of the actual facts—of the fate which had actually befallen Him who was, as His disciples had trusted, to redeem Israel—nothing could be more natural than such an identification.   It is certain that the Servant of Jehovah was explained to mean the Messiah from a very early period in the history of the Church : and, when once the idea was suggested, it was not difficult to discover allusions to the suffering Messiah in all parts of the Old Testament.   But no passage is so frequently quoted in early Christian literature as this great chapter of Isaiah. It was by the 53rd of Isaiah that Philip proved the Messiahship of Jesus to the Eunuch.[1]   And what a solution the Messianic interpretation of this magnificent prophecy must have supplied to the great problem with which the Christians were occupied during the first days after their Master had left them—the stumbling-block, the " scandal," of the cross !   We are told in the Acts how the Jews of Berea searched the scriptures daily whether these things—the teaching of Paul and his companions—were so.   It was doubtless out of similar searchings of the scriptures that the Christians of these earlier days discovered the solution of their enigma.[2]

The most formidable obstacle to the acceptance of Jesus and His religion by Jewish minds, and not (as we see very clearly from the objections of Celsus) by Jewish minds only, was the difficulty presented by the idea of a suffering Messiah.   How could one whose career had ended in the malefactor's cross be the mighty Conqueror of whom the prophets told or the heavenly being of the Apocalypses ?   How could one who was

---

[1] Acts viii. 31-35.   [2] Acts xvii. 11.

despised and rejected of men be a God or the Son of God ? The Resurrection vision and the anticipated second coming in glory were to those who accepted them a partial solution, but it was just the foolishness of the cross that prevented their being accepted. What a clearing-up of all these perplexities must it not have been to find that it had been foretold that the Messiah was to suffer, and that it was precisely by His suffering and death that He was to perform His Messianic task of saving from sin all who believed on Him ? The marvellous applicability of every word of that moving chapter to the events of Christ's life and death when considered in the light of this idea is such that, even in the full light of modern criticism, we find it difficult to part with the notion that it was originally intended to apply to a personal Messiah. Any vague language which Jesus Himself may have used about the necessity of His death, about its being in the counsels of the Father a necessary condition of the coming of God's kingdom, or about His dying " for " His followers, any suggestions which He might have made as to His death not separating Him from those He was leaving but binding them all more closely together,[1] would inevitably be remembered, and interpreted in the light of that and other prophecies. If Jesus had ever, even for a passing moment, applied to Himself the language of Isaiah, still more if He had actually used the metaphor of the ransom or any expression which a Jew familiar with the LXX. could so translate, the rapid development of the doctrine would be all the easier : but the supposition is by no means necessary. It is inconceivable that the followers of Jesus, sharing the common ideas of His time, could read the 53rd chapter of Isaiah in the days after He was taken away from them without the idea occurring to some of them that this was He of whom the prophet had spoken, and to whom might literally be applied the prophet's language about the saving, vicarious efficacy of His sufferings and His death. On the presuppositions of the early Christian—with his ideas about prophecy and inspiration

---

[1] See above, pp. 42, 58, 59.

—it was simply inevitable that the theory, once suggested, should meet with wide acceptance. And when once this interpretation was accepted, he required no further proof for a doctrine of atonement through Christ's death. The belief was accepted on authority. It became part of the Christian's accepted creed that sins were forgiven through the death of Jesus, because God had expressly revealed that by this and by no other means were they to be forgiven. In many and marvellous ways doubtless such a supposition fell in with, and seemed to explain, the actual experience of individual Christians and of the Church at large. Since they had accepted the simple teaching of Jesus about the Fatherhood of God, since they had come to believe that this Jesus who had been crucified was now sitting as the glorified Messiah on the right hand of God, since they had become members of the rapidly growing society of His followers, they had felt the burden of sin lightened, they had experienced a moral transformation and regeneration which they had never known before. And when once they had discovered from Isaiah that Jesus had died to save men from their sins, still more when it had become part of the traditional creed which they accepted at baptism, it would seem natural to believe that it was the death that had caused all these effects—not indeed to the exclusion of other parts of Christ's work (that was never believed by the ancient Church), but as an essential condition of the forgiveness which Christians believed themselves to have obtained. It is not true to say that the *origin* of this belief in the saving effect of Christ's death is to be found in the " experience " of Christians. In the absence of some authoritative statement, no experience could testify, or could well have been believed to testify, to the fact that precisely the death of Christ rather than any other of the things which Christians believed about Him was the cause of what they experienced —the sense of forgiveness, the change of heart, the consciousness of reconciliation. But as soon as this authoritative pronouncement was forthcoming, experience might well be so interpreted as to confirm the doctrine : the transition from the idea of salvation through a Saviour who had been crucified to the idea of salvation through His crucifixion was a natural and easy one, but no experience could by itself prove such a doctrine ; it could hardly even have suggested it.   In fact it may be doubted whether the experience could have existed apart from antecedent belief in the actual, objective fact of forgiveness.[1]   Apart from some authoritative assurance that God had forgiven, and forgiven in consequence of Christ's death, there was nothing to suggest any special connexion between what the Christian experienced and the death of the Messiah.   At all events, if we look to the way in which the doctrine was actually asserted by the early Christians, we shall see reason to believe that in point of fact it was always the language of prophecy which was given as the ground for the belief.   Most commonly the belief was asserted, as we shall see hereafter, in actual quotations from Is. liii. or other prophecies, or in short traditional formulae which were obviously based upon and derived from such passages.   In the first instance, it cannot be too strongly or too confidently asserted, the doctrine was accepted simply and solely on authority.   And this is the clue to the entire absence in the greater part of the early Christian literature of any uniform or definite theory as to why Christ's death was necessary, and how it made possible a forgiveness which would otherwise have been impossible.   The Church accepted the statements of Isaiah : every one was free to interpret them as he pleased.

Simple Christians wanted no further theory about the meaning of Christ's death.   But it was inevitable that minds trained either in the Rabbinic or in the Hellenic schools should not be satisfied to accept the faith of the atonement without some attempt to explain a doctrine of salvation which to the reflecting mind surely required some explanation.   And a long series of theories were

---

[1] At first no doubt this assurance was supplied simply by the statement of Jesus Himself that sin would be forgiven at the judgement.   The language of prophecy would connect this forgiveness with His death.

accordingly constructed : the first, the most famous, ultimately though not immediately the most influential, was that of St. Paul. What was St. Paul's theory? I will try to state it briefly.

II. *St. Paul's Theory of the Atonement.*

There are two ways of setting forth St. Paul's teaching about sin, forgiveness, justification. We may look at his actual words, at his actual theories, in the spirit of the accurate and critical historian of thought, and set them forth in the form in which they presented themselves to his intellect. From this point of view it is all-important to avoid the temptation to which so many historians of thought have yielded—the temptation to read back modern ideas and systems into the great thinkers of antiquity for whom they feel admiration and reverence. Or, on the other hand, we may try to penetrate behind the formulae, sympathetically to realize the religious and moral convictions which expressed themselves in those theories, and to find in them, or translate them into, ideas which shall be of present and eternal significance. The same alternatives present themselves in dealing with any ancient thinker. If we adopt the first method, no ancient thinker (Christian or pagan) has ever proved entirely acceptable to the modern mind : if we adopt the other, we find the most ancient thinkers dominating the highest thought of the present, almost to a greater extent than was the case in any period of modern history since the Renaissance. There are no modern philosophers who actually accept the systems of the universe propounded by Plato or Aristotle ; yet in a very profound sense there are among us many Platonists and many Aristotelians, while there is hardly any serious philosopher who does not acknowledge immense obligations to these and other ancient philosophers. Both methods have their value in dealing with such a writer as St. Paul, as they have in the interpretation of Plato or Aristotle ; but intellectual honesty and clear-sightedness demand that they should not be mixed up

with one another. I shall regard it as a duty pertaining
to intellectual honesty first to exhibit St. Paul's theories
as they must present themselves to the cold, impartial,
critical exegete; and then to ask how far they represent
ideas of permanent value to the Christian Church. It is
chiefly in two epistles—the Epistle to the Galatians and
the Epistle to the Romans—that St. Paul's theories of
atonement and justification receive their fullest elaboration, and the Epistle to the Galatians is probably no
more than an anticipatory sketch of the ideas afterwards
more fully developed in the great doctrinal epistle.
We may therefore in the main confine our attention to
this writing, though we shall constantly have to seek
for further elucidation in other epistles—particularly
in the two Corinthian Epistles which belong in thought
and in date to the same group.[1] I may add that there is
much in these great epistles besides the theories which
we are examining—much teaching the spiritual value of
which is quite independent of the theories enunciated in
their more argumentative parts, but it is with the
theories that we are for the moment more immediately
concerned.

The great problem which St. Paul sets himself to
answer in the Epistle to the Romans is this—how was
it possible for Gentiles to attain through Christ admission
to the kingdom of God, acceptance with God, justification and salvation, without observance of the Mosaic
law? Did not such an attitude towards the law make
the promises of God to the Jews contained in the Old
Testament of none effect? How could the law, which
St. Paul still accepted as the supernaturally revealed
law of God, be really a disclosure of His will, if those who
at least attempted to observe it were to be rejected by
God at the Messianic judgement, while Gentile Christians who made no attempt to do so were, as St. Paul
had proclaimed, in the way of salvation? Such was
the problem which presented itself to Jewish and Judaiz-

---

[1] As to St. Paul's later doctrine of salvation, see Additional Note G at the end of
this lecture (p. 141). It may be convenient to say that I accept the genuineness of all
the Pauline Epistles except the Pastoral Epistles, though I recognize that the genuineness of 2 Thessalonians, Colossians, and Ephesians is not so certain as that of the rest.

ing Christians. Such was the problem which even to St. Paul's own mind presented a real difficulty which he had to put forth all his rabbinical learning and all his dialectical subtlety to meet.

The argument of the epistle divides itself into two halves. The first half is negative, the second positive. The first part of the argument seeks to prove that justification was not obtainable by the works of the law, the second half that it was obtainable through a new " righteousness of God " which Jesus the Messiah had brought into the world. The first part presents little difficulty. When St. Paul speaks of the law, he does not distinguish as sharply as we should do between the moral and the ceremonial parts of it. While it is to the moral part of it that he attaches primary importance, he is very emphatic in asserting that he who is circumcised is bound to observe the whole law, including the most arbitrary of external rites and ceremonies. He appears to regard the Mosaic law as the most perfect expression, prior to the coming of Christ, of that divine law of which the Gentiles also possessed a less perfect knowledge written in their own consciences. And this moral law was the will of God. God had enjoined upon all the observance of the moral law, and upon Jews that of the ceremonial law also, offering rewards to those who should keep it, and threatening punishment in the form of death to those who disobeyed it. Those who kept the law had earned justification : that is to say, such persons would be pronounced just by God, because in fact they would be just, and acquittal was no more than their due. But St. Paul appeals both to the authority of scripture and to universal human experience[1] to show that nobody ever had kept or could keep the whole law of God in all its completeness and exactingness. The universality of sin was simply a fact of the world's experience. Neither Jew nor Gentile had attained to the righteousness of God—righteousness as God conceived it, the righteous-

---

[1] The appeal to well-known facts is the primary foundation of St. Paul's conviction, and occupies the first two chapters. In chapter iii. he introduces a confirmatory appeal to scripture.

ness which would satisfy His requirements. " There is
no distinction; for all have sinned, and fall short of the
glory of God." [1]

We need not dwell on St. Paul's teaching about the
true function of law in creating or deepening the sense
of sin,[2] and even the sin itself, or about the relative and
temporary advantages which the Jew enjoyed over the
Gentile in possession of the oracles of God and other
spiritual privileges. This side of his teaching is very
important for his theology in general, but it is not of
primary importance for our present purpose. All that
we need insist on is the fact that according to St. Paul
the sentence of justification or acquittal, the pronouncement that a man is righteous in God's sight, cannot in
the actual condition of human nature be pronounced
upon any child of man on account of his performance
of the works of the law. How far, and in what sense, this
universal sinfulness was regarded by St. Paul as necessarily resulting from the sin of Adam—how far it was
thought of as inherited guilt or liability to punishment
and how far as an inherited sinfulness, how far the
origin of sin is to be found in the fall of Adam and how
far in the intrinsic weakness and sinfulness of man's
fleshly nature—these are questions upon which there
has been much dispute, and which for our present
purpose we need not discuss elaborately. Innumerable
attempts have been made to get rid of the conceptions of original sin, of predestination, and of the ideas
associated with these conceptions, from St. Paul's teaching. I cannot but think that they all fail. It is true
that the theory that the source of sin is the fall of Adam
is scarcely to be found in the Old Testament,[3] and plays

---

[1] Rom. iii. 23.

[2] " The law came in beside ($\pi\alpha\rho\epsilon\iota\sigma\hat{\eta}\lambda\theta\epsilon\nu$) that the trespass might abound " (Rom.
v. 20). This was one of St. Paul's most original conceptions, and yet there is a suggestion
of it in the Apocalypse of Baruch (ed. Charles, xv. 5, 6) : " Man would not rightly have
understood My judgement, if he had not accepted the law, and if his fear had not been
(rooted) in understanding. But now, because he transgressed, though he knew, yea, on
account of this also, he shall be tormented because he knew."

[3] " The fact remains that the Old Testament supplies no trace of the existence, among
the sacred writers, of any *interpretation* of the fall-story comparable to the later doctrine
of the Fall " (Tennant, *The Fall and Original Sin*, p. 93). " The serpent is not identified, apparently, with Satan " (p. 104).

a smaller part in later Jewish speculation than its prominence in Christian theology might lead us to suppose. It is true, again, that, so far as the origin of sin was sought in an historical event, the fall of the sons of God recounted in Gen. vi. is more often alluded to than the fall of Adam. But there can be no doubt that the idea of the *yezer hara* or inherited tendency towards evil was known to the Jews long before the time of St. Paul, and that the derivation of human sinfulness from the fall of Adam was a fairly prominent conception both with the rabbis, and with the apocalyptic writers who lived just before or during St. Paul's lifetime.[1] There is no reason therefore for attempting to explain away the *prima facie* meaning of St. Paul. He tells us that "through one man sin entered into the world, and death through sin; and so death passed unto all men, for that all sinned."[2] What St. Paul actually states is not that *sin* was transmitted to all men, but *death*; and he emphatically declared that the penalty was endured even by those who had not sinned after the likeness of Adam's transgression. When he says "all sinned," he is probably thinking of a collective or constructive sin:[3] he means that all sinned in Adam in much the same sense as that in which (according to the author of the Epistle to the Hebrews) Levi paid tithes in Abraham.[4] But if we look to the whole drift of his argument, it is impossible to doubt that he does mean to connect the fact of universal sinfulness with the fall of Adam. The whole object of his argument is to establish a universal sinfulness: the introduction of Adam would be irrelevant if this universal sinfulness was not causally connected with Adam's fall; and it is quite clear from his picture of the condition of fallen humanity at the beginning of

---

[1] See Additional Note E at the end of this lecture (p. 135).
[2] Rom. v. 12.
[3] " So soon as we grasp the thought that it was not in truth the first man as an individual who was the subject of the fall, but man as man, we see the historical beginning to be merely the form which expresses the universality of the principle which has no beginning; and thus the substantial agreement of the passage [Rom. v. 12 *sq.*] with the line of thought in Rom. vii. is placed beyond doubt " (Pfleiderer, *Paulinism*, E.T., 2nd ed. i. 46). See Additional Note D on this passage at the end of this lecture (p. 133).
[4] Heb. vii. 9, 10. Cf. 2 Cor. v. 14: " One died for all, therefore all died."

the epistle, as well as from the passage in which he
speaks of his own personal experiences, that this sinfulness was no mere constructive or imputed sinfulness.
It is true that he seems to allow the possibility that some
at least of those between Adam and Moses had not
actually sinned, or at all events that they had not sinned
wilfully in the teeth of an express command like Adam,
and that therefore sin was not imputed to them as it was
to those who had received the law.   But he cannot be
supposed to mean (in Pelagian fashion) that the bulk of
Adam's posterity became actually sinful merely through
following Adam's bad example, or that they just happened of their own free will to sin as Adam had done.
He means undoubtedly that Adam's posterity inherited
a sinful tendency which normally resulted, especially in
those in whom the evil tendency was stirred into activity
by the law, in a sinful heart and actually sinful deeds.

Side by side with this theory, there is, indeed, another
which underlies all St. Paul's thought about the matter :
and that is the theory (so powerfully suggested by obvious
facts of experience, and widely diffused at a certain
stage of religious development) that the flesh is the source
of moral evil : [1] man is necessarily sinful because he has

---

[1] Rom. vii. 14, viii. 3, 7, 10 ; 1 Cor. xv. 44-50. Cf. Weizsäcker, *Apostolic Age*, i.
p. 150. Much controversy has taken place as to what flesh ($\sigma\acute{a}\rho\xi$) means for St. Paul. It
is probable that it practically includes the whole of men's natural desires and inclinations.
Thus St. Paul speaks of " the mind ($\phi\rho\acute{o}\nu\eta\mu a$) of the flesh," Rom. viii. 6, 7, " the
desire of the flesh," (Gal. v. 16, cf. 24), " the will [or volitions, $\theta\epsilon\lambda\acute{\eta}\mu a\tau a$] of the flesh "
(Eph. ii. 3), though the very form of expression shows that there is a certain distinction
between the literal flesh and the psychical activities connected with it. On the other
hand Ménégoz goes too far when (on the strength of Rom. vii. 18) he defines $\sigma\acute{a}\rho\xi$ as
" l'homme tout entier, corps et âme," for St. Paul does not regard the human $\pi\nu\epsilon\hat{v}\mu a$ as
identical with the Spirit of God (" the Spirit itself beareth witness with our spirit," Rom.
viii. 16). There is a human spirit as well as the divine Spirit which acts upon it, and the
human $\pi\nu\epsilon\hat{v}\mu a$ is not part of the $\sigma\acute{a}\rho\xi$. A more measured statement is Weizsäcker's :
" After all this there can hardly be a doubt that for Paul the antithesis of flesh and spirit
ultimately rests on the nature of flesh, *i.e.* on the natural quality of men " (*Apostolic
Age*, i. 152). " This is of course not incompatible with the power to understand the
divine command, or with a secret inclination to it fostered by his own mind before, any
more than after, the fall (Rom. vii. 22). But the power to fulfil the divine will is not
included in this ; it only comes through the Spirit " (*ib.*).

Elsewhere St. Paul speaks of a $\nu o\hat{v}s$—a Greek term which does not seem to stand in
any definite relation to the Hebraic antithesis between spirit and flesh. Sometimes it
appears to mean the intellect as opposed to the spirit in the sense of the higher spiritual
aspirations (1 Cor. xiv. 14, 15 ; cf. Col. ii. 18) : at other times it is practically equivalent
to the spirit as opposed to the flesh (Rom. vii. 25). When used in the sense of intellect,
it may become enslaved to the flesh, so that St. Paul can speak of the " mind ($\nu o\hat{v}s$) of
his flesh " (Col. ii. 18). It is not to be supposed that St. Paul has any absolutely strict
and uniform way of using these terms, any more than most of us (when not writing

a body which creates evil impulses and weighs down the higher part of his nature. This theory played quite as prominent a part in St. Paul's thought as the theory of the fall. But the two are not inconsistent: it is natural to infer that Adam's fall was itself the necessary result of his fleshly nature.[1] If the first man was essentially " earthy " ($\chi o\ddot{\iota}\kappa\acute{o}s$), he could hardly have avoided sinning. I cannot therefore doubt that St. Paul does believe in an hereditary sinfulness (as well as an hereditary penalty) which normally resulted in actual sin. And this consequence was a necessary consequence: it is impossible honestly to understand the ninth chapter of the Romans in any but a strictly predestinarian sense. Man is as clay in the hands of the potter. God has willed to make some vessels to honour and others to dishonour. " So then he hath mercy on whom he will, and whom he will he hardeneth." [2] These words cannot be explained away. It is impossible to deny that on the whole the Augustinian and Calvinistic [3] inter-

---

philosophy or psychology) are consistent in our use of such terms as " mind," " soul," " spirit," " self," " will," " desire."

How far the doctrine that the flesh is the source of sin came to St. Paul from Hellenic sources (directly or through Alexandrian writers such as Philo) is disputed. (Clement holds that it did.) The idea is so natural that it does not require such a hypothesis, though a certain Philonic influence on St. Paul (direct or indirect) is not improbable. It should be observed that it is " the flesh," not specifically (as with dualistic thinkers) " matter," which is for him the source of evil. The logical development of this doctrine would involve something like a docetic view of Christ's person, and St. Paul goes near to such a position when he represents Christ as being merely sent " in the likeness of sinful flesh " (Rom. viii. 3) or coming in the outward form ($\mu o\rho\phi\acute{\eta}$) of a servant (Phil. ii. 7). But fortunately he never did develope the doctrine. His idea probably was that the heavenly and sinless nature of the Messiah's Spirit (identical with the Spirit of God) prevented the flesh from having its usual effect in producing sin, and so made possible the transmutation of His body into an aethereal or " glorious " body—something between matter and spirit.

[1] Weizsäcker is probably right in holding that the universality of sin is for him the consequence of a divine decree, referring to Rom. vii. 23 (*Apostolic Age*, 152-3, cf. 149). The failure of both Jew and Gentile to attain righteousness by the works of the law is part of the providential arrangement by which they are prepared for the righteousness which comes by the free favour of God, so that the ultimate purpose is one of mercy. " God hath shut up all unto disobedience, that he might have mercy upon all " (Rom. xi. 32). I cannot admit with M. Goguel (*L'Apôtre Paul et Jésus-Christ*, p. 184) that the statement of Rom. xi. 32 " goes very clearly (' très nette ') against Predestination. It is only inconsistent with it in the sense in which all statements about human freedom and responsibility made by Determinists appear inconsistent to those who do not hold, and perhaps do not understand, the philosophical doctrine of Determinism.   [2] Rom. ix. 18.

[3] At least that of the sub-lapsarian Calvinists. Whether St. Paul would have accepted the position of the supra-lapsarian Calvinists—that the fall itself was necessary —is not quite so clear, but it is highly probable that he would.

pretation of St. Paul as regards these questions is justified, with the momentous exception that St. Paul knows
nothing of everlasting punishment. The wicked are
punished, but they are punished by annihilation or in
some way which ends in annihilation. The punishment
of sin is literal death. St. Paul knows nothing of a
natural or universal immortality : the redeemed alone
are immortal.[1]

Whatever answer we may give to these much disputed questions, the important point for the understanding of St. Paul's theory of redemption is the fact
that all men are now actually sinful. They have all
sinned, and consequently all have incurred the doom of
death. They are unjust, and cannot therefore be pronounced just on account of anything they have done.
Justification cannot be obtained through the works of
the law : how then can it be obtained? St. Paul's
answer may be considered under two heads, though
in his own argument these are not very sharply distinguished. We may ask what is the objective ground
of justification, or we may ask what is the subjective condition of its appropriation by the sinner.

The objective source or ground of justification is
the death of Christ. The righteousness by which the
Christian attains justification is a righteousness of God :
a righteousness which is not due to the sinner's works
at all—not even to his repentance. It is something
brought into existence by God as a free act of favour or
mercy (the word " grace " has become so technical that
we are apt to forget its original meaning) through the
sending of the Messiah, the pre-existent and sinless Son
of God, into the world. If we ask what it is in Christ's
work which secured this justification, the answer is not,
indeed, as consistent and clearly cut as it is in modern
theological systems. Sometimes reconciliation or justification or salvation [2] is attributed generally to Jesus

---

[1] See Additional Note F at the end of this chapter on "The Eschatology of St.
Paul" (p. 139).

[2] As to the difference in meaning between the terms reconciliation, justification,
salvation, redemption, sanctification, see Additional Note A at the end of this lecture
(p. 124).

the Christ and to the outpouring of the Spirit. Christians are said to be " justified in the name of the Lord Jesus Christ and in the Spirit of our God " : [1] sometimes it is treated as in a special manner the effect of the resurrection,[2] which was, we must remark with St. Paul, not merely the pledge, but in some sense the direct cause, of the transformation of the mortal body into an immortal one.[3] But there can be no doubt whatever as to the prominent place which the death of Christ plays in St. Paul's thought. Christians are " justified freely by his grace through the redemption that is in Christ Jesus : whom God set forth to be a propitiation [or as others translate " propitiatory "] through faith, by his blood, to shew his righteousness, because of the passing over of the sins done aforetime, in the forbearance of God ; for the shewing, I say, of his righteousness at this present season : that he might himself be just, and the justifier of him that hath faith in Jesus." [4] That is the main thesis of the Roman Epistle. The intimate connexion between justification and the death of Christ is stated over and over again. We are " justified by his blood." [5] We were " reconciled to God through the death of his Son." [6] And so on. The justification of sinners was made possible by God through the death of Christ, though the death is not emphasized in such a way as to exclude from any share in the justifying effect all other aspects of His work.

St. Paul does not quite say why God could not remit the penalty of sin without the death of His Son. But it cannot be denied that those theologians who declare that this would be incompatible with God's justice—the justice which requires that somehow sin should be punished—or with the consistency which demands the

---

[1] 1 Cor. vi. 11. So " God was in Christ "—throughout His work—" reconciling the world unto himself " (2 Cor. v. 19).

[2] Rom. iv. 25 ; 1 Cor. xv. 17.

[3] " Always bearing about in the body the dying of Jesus, that the life also of Jesus may be manifested in our body " (2 Cor. iv. 10). Still this transformation is due in our case as in Christ's to the power of God (2 Cor. xiii. 4). In Rom. viii. 11 the transformation is effected through the Spirit of God : " He that raised up Christ Jesus from the dead shall quicken also your mortal bodies through his Spirit that dwelleth in you."

[4] Rom. iii. 24-26.   [5] Rom. v. 9.   [6] Rom. v. 10.

infliction of the particular punishment which God had threatened, namely death—are only bringing out the latent presuppositions of St. Paul's thought.[1] This at least is what his argument requires. It is, indeed, difficult to say in what relation, according to St. Paul, physical death stands to spiritual death—death in a moral and spiritual sense together with all its consequences.[2] He seems to regard them as in some sense convertible terms or as involving each other. If St. Paul believed in immortality only for the saved, the identification is easily explained : physical death involved spiritual as well as physical annihilation, just as physical resurrection was the necessary presupposition of complete and permanent spiritual life, though a sort of foretaste of it was possible here below. At all events it is part of his argument that sin in some way demands death. And it is clearly St. Paul's conception that Christ has paid that penalty in order that man may not have to pay it. It is impossible to get rid of this idea of substitution, or vicarious punishment, from any faithful representation of St. Paul's doctrine. True, the idea of substitution is not so much emphasized as it is by later theologians. St. Paul seems led into it, as it were, against his will by the necessities of his argument. He never uses the

---

[1] It is difficult to find in the Old Testament a distinct enunciation of the principle, though of course particular sins have the penalty of death annexed to them. St. Paul can hardly have thought of Ezek. xviii. 20 (" the soul that sinneth, it shall die ") with its distinct repudiation of the doctrine that one man is punished for another's sin. (The very next verse contains the assurance that the wicked who returns from his sins shall live.) More probably he had in mind the actual infliction of death upon Adam and his posterity, though there is in Gen. iii. no universal threat of death for all sin. And he read these chapters of Genesis, as do Christians, in the light of a kind of Haggada, which is really of other origin.

[2] There is clearly a logical hiatus in St. Paul's scheme here. Was the death threatened for disobedience to God's commandments *physical* death such as Adam suffered ? But others suffer that also, even the redeemed. If the penalty deserved was *spiritual* death, why should the necessity for such a death be removed by the physical death of Jesus? St. Augustine was obviously puzzled to answer this question. M. Ménégoz has insisted on this hiatus (*Le Péché et la Rédemption*, p. 75). The difficulty can best be met if we suppose that St. Paul thought that, though even the redeemed had to undergo the penalty of physical death, they escaped its full severity by their subsequent resurrection, while the spiritual accompaniments of the new life brought into being through Christ were something graciously bestowed by God over and above the mere resurrection or restoration of physical life. It must be remembered that, though Christians occasionally died, St. Paul thinks in his earlier epistles of salvation without any death at all as the normal case. The discovery that some Christians could die before the Parousia had caused serious perplexity at Thessalonica.

preposition ἀντὶ (instead of) but always ὑπὲρ (on behalf of) in this connexion.[1] Christ is always said to have suffered " on behalf of " men, not " instead of " them. And that preposition ὑπὲρ by itself conveys no suggestion of expiation or substitution or equivalence, unless such a force is given to it by the context. But some such notion seems directly to be involved in such passages as the following : " God, sending his own Son in the likeness of sinful flesh and as an offering for sin, condemned sin in the flesh." [2] It is true the word offering is not actually in the Greek, but περὶ ἁμαρτίας ("for sin ") is the usual Septuagint term for the " sin-offering." What can this mean but that in the death of Christ the judgement pronounced against the sin of Adam and his posterity was satisfied ? Again in the Epistle to the Galatians we are told that " Christ redeemed us from the curse of the law, having become a curse for us : for it is written, Cursed is every one that hangeth on a tree." [3] According to this argument, it may be noted

---

[1] In 1 Thess. v. 10 and Gal. i. 4 the MSS. waver between ὑπὲρ and περί.

[2] Rom. viii. 3. Probably St. Paul's idea is that the actual " flesh " which caused the sin and was permanently the source of sin was punished, and in some sense destroyed —and with it the sin—when Christ died. Flesh, like sin, is to St. Paul a sort of half-personal entity. It is obvious that this idea makes it difficult for St. Paul to avoid either (1) a Docetic view of Christ's body or (2) the admission that Christ became sinful. It is certain that he intended neither.

[3] Gal. iii. 13. Dr. Denney notices that St. Paul avoids applying to Christ the precise words of Deut. xxi. 23, " accursed of God." Weinel writes : " So the curse spent itself on Him, the innocent, that knew no sin, and thereby it is done away. All they that were ' under the curse ' have now been redeemed by Him. This is the clearest, the most consequent theory that St. Paul advances of the death of Jesus. But just like the belief in sacrifice, it rests upon a strange idea of primitive man, upon his conception of the curse, upon its objective reality, so to speak. Just as Isaac's blessing works itself out, because it is uttered, and neither God nor Isaac can alter it in anywise, so this curse of the law must also spend itself on some one. Now if it lights on one who was not doomed to die through his own guilt, then it has ' worked itself out,' its force is spent, for it has put itself in the wrong. And so the curse being removed, God's mercy has free play " (St. Paul, Eng. trans. p. 308). This account of the matter may be accepted, except that (1) like all attempts to reduce St. Paul to a theory, it probably errs on the side of over-definiteness and exclusiveness, and (2) though St. Paul's thought is not quite so primitive as Weinel supposes. It could be more fairly stated in terms of that theory about the intrinsic necessity of punishment to wipe out guilt or " vindicate the moral law," which is still held by eminent philosophers. No doubt this notion itself is ultimately derived from the instincts and superstitions of primitive man, but it is always a mistake to suppose that the thought of a reflective and highly civilized age is the same as that of the primitive notions which have contributed to produce them.

In much the same spirit it is insisted by Pfleiderer that Paul understands by sin " not as we might think, a permanent tendency of the will, evil inclination, bias, or the like, but with the usual personifying tendency of antiquity, he makes the sinful principle

parenthetically, it was not merely death that was needed for the forgiveness of sins but this particular kind of death. Nothing but crucifixion or some similar mode of execution could have the required effect. The point is interesting because it illustrates the complete dependence of St. Paul's argument upon the authoritative letter of prophecy. So again, " Him who knew no sin he made to be sin on our behalf ; that we might become the righteousness of God in him." [1] This can hardly mean anything but that God treated the sinless Christ as if He were guilty, and inflicted upon Him the punishment which our sins had deserved ; and that this infliction made it possible to treat the sinful as if they were actually righteous. There are, indeed, only a few passages which necessarily suggest the idea of substituted punishment or substituted sacrifice. But there they are, and St. Paul's argument is unintelligible without them.

Granted that the death of Christ was in some sense a sacrifice or a punishment, why should the endurance of such a penalty by an innocent Being make it just or right for God to forgive those who were really sinful ? To this question there is no clear, definite, and categorical answer to be got out of St. Paul's arguments, elaborate as they are. It is true that Jesus was sinless, and therefore had no penalty to pay on His own account : " him who knew no sin, he made to be sin on our behalf." [2] Again, there is great insistence on the voluntariness of the death. " Ye know the grace [mercy] of our Lord Jesus Christ, that, though he was rich, yet for our sakes he became poor." [3] Another reply might be that Jesus

---

an independent entity, an active subject to which all manner of predicates can be attached " (*Primitive Christianity*, i. 277). But after all the conception of " sin " for St. Paul is primarily ethical, and had best be treated as such in any modern interpretation, though his ethical conceptions are connected with theories of the universe, and particularly of the spiritual world, which are not ours. It is too much to say that " he really saw in sin a demonic spiritual being which takes possession of men," etc., except in so far as he undoubtedly connected the existence of sin with a personal devil and other evil spirits.

[1] 2 Cor. v. 21 ; cf. Col. i. 19-23 ; Eph. ii. 11-16. In this last passage the enmity which is " slain " by the Cross is primarily the enmity between Jew and Gentile, but the context implies that this was effected by the cancelling of an enmity between God and man occasioned by the law which had made the Gentiles " children of wrath."

[2] 2 Cor. v. 21.

[3] 2 Cor. viii. 9. The words clearly imply pre-existence : so in Phil. ii. 6-8.

was for St. Paul not only sinless, but the Messiah, the pre-existent Son of God. If St. Paul never calls Him God, if he habitually distinguishes Him from the Father to whom alone the name God is actually applied, still he does say that "God was in Christ reconciling the world unto himself." [1] God was in Christ in a unique and paramount sense. But these considerations do not answer the question why the voluntary death of such a sinless Son of God should justify or make possible the gratuitous acquittal of the guilty. The later theory that the merit earned by a voluntary death of the divine Son was so transcendent that it could earn the pardon of sinners as of right is not perhaps far off from the thought of St. Paul in some places : [2] but it is not actually elaborated.

St. Paul's general disposition is to explain the arrangement simply by the will of a God who is merciful but none the less arbitrary. God in the plenitude of His power chose this particular way of cancelling the guilt which had been incurred, " having blotted out the bond written in ordinances that was against us, which was contrary to us : and he hath taken it out of the way, nailing it to the cross," [3] and substituting therefor a righteousness which was wholly due to His goodwill and pleasure. At other times some attempt is made to establish a rational connexion between the death of the One and the acquittal of the many. The most definite solution is that supplied by the words : " because we thus judge, that one died for all, therefore all died." [4] It is tempting to treat such passages as the utterance of deep feeling, and to regard them as wholly metaphorical ; but if we do so, we must abandon the hope of presenting St. Paul's doctrine in a theoretical form. Behind all the

---

[1] 2 Cor. v. 19 ; Rom. ix. 5 is ambiguous.

[2] Cf. Phil. ii. 5-9. The notion that deliverance could only be effected by One who was God as well as man, or that the death of a God-man must have infinite value, is not found in St. Paul, though a very easy development of what he does say. For a further discussion of St. Paul's Christology, see Additional Note B at the end of this lecture (p. 127).

[3] Col. ii. 14. Here remission is only connected with death upon the Cross by a metaphor which explains nothing. The death of Christ could only be regarded as a guarantee of forgiveness because God had proclaimed that it was so.

[4] 2 Cor. v. 14.

passionate sense of a new spiritual life springing from Christ and His influence, of which St. Paul was immediately conscious, there is a theory ; and the theory seems to be that, because Christ died, each individual believer may be considered to have really died also, and so satisfied the divine decree that sin shall bring death, and thereby become free also from obedience to the law, which lost its hold on the man when once its extreme penalty had been endured.

"One died for all, therefore all died." It is not easy to put a very precise meaning upon such a statement. As is natural with so difficult a conception, St. Paul's own interpretation of it seems to waver. Sometimes it looks like an arbitrary arrangement on the part of God, a legal fiction by which He agrees to assume that all men died, because of the exceeding worth of Him who did literally die. The arrangement is more or less arbitrary, and yet there is a natural fitness or appropriateness in it on account of the parallel which it affords to that sin of Adam which involved all his posterity in its consequences. "So then as through one trespass the judgement came unto all men to condemnation ; even so through one judgement ($\delta\iota\kappa\alpha\iota\omega\mu\alpha\tau\sigma$)"—one judicial sentence of acquittal [1]—" the free gift came unto all men to justification of life. For as through the one man's disobedience the many were made sinners" [$\kappa\alpha\tau\epsilon\sigma\tau\acute{\alpha}\theta\eta\sigma\alpha\nu$, were constituted, placed in the position of sinners] " even so through the obedience of the one shall the many be made [or constituted] righteous." [2] At other times the notion seems to be more mystical, or (better) metaphysical. The whole human race are, as it were, summed up in Christ—the perfect Man, the Man from heaven, the pattern Man, the crown and realized ideal of the whole human race, the universal of " Humanity," as a modern philosopher might say—in the same sort of rabbinical-mystical way as that in which, according to the author of the Epistle to the Hebrews, Levi paid tithes to Melchizedek in Abraham because " he was yet

1 Not, as A.V., " the righteousness of one," or R.V., " one righteous act."
2 Rom. v. 18, 19.

in the loins of his father, when Melchizedek met him." [1] That is the notion which seems to be most directly suggested by the words, " One died for all, therefore all died." [2]   At other times again the thought becomes more ethical, and consequently more metaphorical or symbolic.   It is through an act of spiritual surrender or emotional unity or identification with Christ at baptism that the Christian may be said to have really died, and so to have suffered the penalty of sin with or in Christ, and with Him to have risen to a new life of righteousness here and of glory hereafter.   Thus we read : "Are ye ignorant that all we who were baptized into Christ Jesus were baptized into his death ?   We were buried therefore with him through baptism into death : that, like as Christ was raised from the dead through the glory of the Father, so we also might walk in newness of life." [3]   And again in the Galatian Epistle : " They that are of Christ Jesus have crucified the flesh with the passions and the lusts thereof." [4]   The death of the fleshly element in man satisfied the judgement that the sinner should die.   It is clear that a metaphor is here passing into a theory.   There is nothing in common between baptism and death except that in both cases there is a going down and a rising up ; while, if we think of the thing signified in the sacrament, the laying aside of sin is not really death.

It is doubtless true that in the deepest religious consciousness of St. Paul the idea of death presents itself less as a penalty than as a necessary stage in the passage to a new and higher life. [5]   But still the formal

---

[1] Heb. vii. 10.   This aspect of the death of Christ will thus be a particular application of the principle of the incarnation in general—" to sum up all things in Christ " (Eph. i. 10).

[2] 2 Cor. v. 14.   [3] Rom. vi. 3, 4.   [4] Gal. v. 24.

[5] Cf. Rom. iii. 25, 26.   On this ground Weizsäcker attempts to get rid of the idea of substitution from St. Paul (*Apostolic Age*, i. 160-63).   But it is obvious that, so far as this is St. Paul's theory, it turns on a metaphor which does not wholly correspond to the facts.   Converted and baptized Christians do sin.   I cannot think that Weizsäcker is successful in his attempt to explain away all punitive or expiatory ideas in the teaching of St. Paul.

St. Paul nowhere actually speaks of baptism or the act of justification as at once trans-forming the natural and mortal body (which included the lower soul or $\psi v\chi\acute{\eta}$) into a spiritual and immortal body, but there is much in his teaching to suggest this idea (*e.g.* 2 Cor. iv. 10).   He was prevented from developing it in a consistent manner by his

H

thesis which St. Paul is trying to establish cannot be established unless the metaphorical or spiritual death to sin is regarded as somehow equivalent to the literal death which had been denounced as the punishment of sin. Doubtless St. Paul in such passages was not unconscious that there was an element of metaphor in his argument; but rabbinical arguments often turn upon an exegesis which takes metaphor for literal fact and literal fact for metaphor, and yet they are quite seriously intended as arguments. And it must be remembered that, though the effect which St. Paul attributes to Christ's resurrection was an ethical effect, it was not to him merely ethical; he thought of the participation in Christ's death as directly killing that fleshly nature which was the source of sin, and beginning that transformation of it into a new and incorruptible body which had taken place in Christ's case already, and which for the redeemed portion of humanity would be completed at the Parousia or second coming.

Such is in barest outline St. Paul's doctrine when coldly dissected by the critical understanding. Honest exegesis will not let us get rid of this idea of expiation or substitution. And yet that is an idea which can be reconciled neither with the demands of the moral consciousness as interpreted by the modern intellect, nor with the plain teaching of St. Paul's Master and ours. It is, indeed, important to note that St. Paul never actually applies the word "punishment" to the death of Christ. He seems instinctively to shrink from it, even when his argument is leading him straight up to it, and only in three or four places does he employ definitely sacrificial language. Generally his thought is juridical rather than sacrificial. Only in three or four passages is the death of Christ actually described as a sacrifice. There is the passage already quoted in

---

Eschatology. The judgement, the resurrection, the transformation of mortal bodies into immortal were in the future. The present transformation could therefore be only a sort of potential transformation, the sowing of a seed which could only be reaped at the resurrection. How St. Paul's suggestions about the transformation of the corruptible body into the incorruptible were developed by the Greek Fathers we shall see hereafter (below, p. 239 *sq.*).

which the traditional word for sin-offering is applied
to it (περὶ ἁμαρτίας). Again, St. Paul tells us that
Christ "gave himself up for us, an offering and a
sacrifice to God for an odour of a sweet smell." [1] Then
there are the words, perhaps used with reference to the
approaching paschal festival, "Our Passover also hath been
sacrificed, even Christ." [2] And finally, and perhaps most
important, there is the statement that God sent Him
forth "to be a propitiation" [3] or "to be propitiatory."
Here it may be observed that, though the word used
must in honesty be so translated, its association with
"mercy" and "mercy-seat," if not its actual derivation,
makes the thought of God's mercy more prominent than
the means by which the mercy was obtained. It was not
as an object of the Father's wrath that the Son effected
the propitiation, but because it enabled the Father to pass
over the sins done aforetime and to provide another way
of making man righteous than by punishing.[4] In all
these passages there is probably a certain amount of
metaphor about the sacrificial language used. And yet
it is difficult without the use of such terms as "vicarious
sacrifice" or else "vicarious punishment" to describe
an arrangement by which the innocent endured a death
which would otherwise have had to be endured by the
guilty, and which had the effect of reconciling the guilty
to God.[5] It is probable that St. Paul was more conscious
of the metaphor in the sacrificial passages than in the
legal. The Jewish sacrifices did not play a large part
in the religious ideas of Rabbinism—least of all probably

---

[1] Eph. v. 2. The metaphorical character of the language is here particularly evident.
Cf. Phil. iv. 18, where he speaks of almsgiving as "an odour of a sweet smell, a sacrifice
acceptable, well-pleasing to God."

[2] 1 Cor. v. 7. The "for us" is omitted in R.V.

[3] Rom. iii. 25 (ἱλαστήριον). Drs. Sanday and Headlam take the word to be an
adjective. For a further discussion of this passage, see Additional Note C at the end of
this lecture (p. 130). Cf. also Rom. v. 9.

[4] And yet "that he might himself be just" as well as "the justifier of him that hath
faith" (Rom. iii. 26) seems to suggest that the forgiveness was possible because Christ
bore the penalty.

[5] "According to biblical ideas, therefore, there is no such thing as a 'vicarious
punishment of Christ,' inasmuch as vicarious suffering is the negation of punishment, is
expiation instead of punishment" (Pfleiderer, Paulinism, i. 96-7). The distinction is not
altogether ungrounded, but it is a fine one. After all it only comes to this—that a
punishment which is borne by the innocent is not strictly a punishment. The same
might be said about any theory of "vicarious punishment."

among the Jews of the Dispersion. It is otherwise with the juridical language. That is vital to his whole doctrine. St. Paul naturally thought in terms of law. At the same time one element—and that the most distressing—of later substitutionary theories is entirely absent. There is no suggestion at all that by the death of Christ an alteration was effected in the attitude of God to man; so that, whereas He had formerly been angry and hostile, He was placated (the very word has often been used in later times) by the death of an innocent victim, and made, as He previously was not, propitious, loving, willing to forgive and to renew. " For St. Paul as for Jesus, it is in the last analysis the love of God which is the true cause of pardon for sins and of salvation."[1]

Amid all the difficulties and ambiguities which we encounter in endeavouring to interpret St. Paul's thought, this at least is clear. All through his epistles the atonement is presented as an arrangement due to the eternal and unchangeable love of God. He constantly speaks of our being reconciled to God through the death of Christ, never (in the unfortunate language of our Articles) of God as being reconciled to us. " We are ambassadors therefore on behalf of Christ, as though God were intreating by us : we beseech you on behalf of Christ, be ye reconciled to God." [2] And still more definitely : " God was in Christ reconciling the world unto himself." [3] It is true that the death of Christ is exhibited as satisfying the anger of God, however unintelligible to us may be the thought of a righteous anger which can nevertheless be satisfied by the death of the innocent : but at all events the anger is in the thought of St. Paul anger against sin, anger not incompatible with love of the sinner. " God commendeth his own love toward us, in that, while we were yet sinners, Christ died for us." [4] The love of Christ is always treated as a revelation of the Father's love, His character as a revelation of God's character ; no opposition or antagonism is ever suggested between the justice of the Father

---

[1] Goguel, *L'Apôtre Paul et Jésus-Christ*, p. 331.
[2] 2 Cor. v. 20, 21.   [3] 2 Cor. v. 19.   [4] Rom. v. 8.

and the lovingkindness of the Son. If he had been pressed with the question why this method rather than another was adopted, St. Paul might very probably have replied by his favourite metaphor of the clay and the potter : he might have said, "God wills it : that is enough." But we should not be going very much beyond the language which St. Paul actually uses if we were to say (with later thinkers), "because this method was the one which showed most love, and was calculated to call forth most love in us, and so best to accomplish God's ultimate purpose of saving many from sin." Such a theory is suggested by many a passage in St. Paul, but actually to represent this as St. Paul's own con- sciously adopted and consistent theory would be to attribute to him what he does not actually say, and to ignore much which he does say. St. Paul certainly does attribute to the death of Christ an actual, objective efficacy, though by far the greater part of what he says may well be explained and justified by the subjective effect which the love of God revealed by Christ produces in the soul of the believer. This side of the matter—the appeal to human love and gratitude made by the amazing love of God shown in the sending and the death of Christ—is the side of the atonement doctrine increasingly insisted on in the later epistles,[1] in which the problem of the law and all the difficulties which it raised are no longer before his eyes.

There is no getting rid of the substitutionary element in the theology of St. Paul, and yet, with all the elabora- tion of the Roman Epistle, there is no quite clearly formulated theory as to why the death of Christ was necessary, or as to what it does for the sinner. Many theories are suggested ; none is deliberately adopted and systematically worked out. And if we bear in mind what we have seen to be the probable origin of the whole doctrine, the absence of any real theory is in- telligible enough. The belief in the efficacy of Christ's

---

[1] Phil. ii. 1-8 ; Col. i. 12, 13 ; Eph. i. 1-10, v. 1, 2. The idea of a transaction in the past which still has an objective effect is not absent from these epistles. But there is a tendency to emphasize (1) Christ's self-sacrifice as an example, (2) the outpouring of knowledge through the Revelation in Christ. See Additional Note G below, p. 141.

death rested for St. Paul, as for the Church in general,
upon the authority of the Old Testament ; and so does
the theory by which St. Paul endeavours to explain or
at all events to justify that belief. At every turn he
appeals to Old Testament authority. It is the Psalmist
who proves that man is universally sinful ; it is the book
of Genesis or the prophecy of Ezekiel which proves that
man must die because he had sinned : it is the book of
Deuteronomy which proves that Christ was accursed
because He was crucified. It is the Jewish doctrine
of the " Man from heaven," derived from the book of
Enoch and elsewhere, which proves that Humanity was
restored to what had been lost by the first Adam through
the action of the second Adam—the Man from heaven.
It is probable that, if St. Paul were distinctly asked how
he knew that Christ's death had procured forgiveness,
he would have said, " God has said so in the Scriptures." [1]
He does attempt to theorize ; but his theories of substitutionary punishment or sacrifice go very little beyond
a statement of what seemed to be implied in the language
of Isaiah liii. when combined with the teaching of the
Old Testament about the necessity of the sinner's death.
By a curious accident that chapter, so universally appealed
to by other early Christian writers, is only once actually
quoted in St. Paul.[2] Yet it is not too much to say that
it is always being paraphrased by him, and even when
the passage was not actually present to his mind, he had
before him the tradition of the Church which was mainly
based upon that section of Isaiah, and in the light of
which he found the same doctrine in other prophecies.

At bottom St. Paul's conception of God was the same
as that of his Master. Directly or indirectly he had
learned it from Him, though doubtless there was much
in later Judaism and in the immediate environment of
St. Paul to pave the way for such a conception. But
that conception of God carried with it the belief that
He must have a gracious purpose towards Gentile as

---

[1] That the will of God was inscrutable, that His commands, *e.g.* as to sacrifice,
were to be obeyed without asking why, was of course a familiar thought in the later
Judaism. Cf. 2 (4) Esdras iv. 11, vii. 19, viii. 2.

[2] " Who was delivered up for our trespasses " (Rom. iv. 25). But cf. Rom. v. 19.

well as Jew. Possibly even before his conversion he
may have striven to reconcile a universalistic conception
of God with the teaching of the Old Testament. And
now he had seen evidences which he could not dispute
of the presence of God's Spirit among Gentiles as well
as Jews. He had felt himself called by God to carry on
that work of Gentile conversion : he had felt the impossibility of observing the law in all its strictness even
for Jews, and the hopelessness of the attempt to impose
it upon Gentiles. But, unlike Jesus, he was a rabbi, a
Pharisee of the Pharisees, and he could not all at once
disencumber himself of all the old traditions and beliefs
of orthodox Judaism—the thought of God as a jealous
God, an exacting Judge, a stern enforcer of the law and
executor of vengeance for disobedience to it, of the
obligations of the ceremonial law, of the plenary inspiration and authority of Scripture in the very letter of it.
He had to find some way of intellectually reconciling
the old conception and the new. Hence he was driven
to discover somehow within the circle of Old Testament
ideas a theory which would explain how it was that God
was at one and the same time the stern promulgator of
the law with all its terrible penalties and the gracious
and merciful Father who would forgive the penitent,
restore him to His favour, and bestow upon him the
holiness which he could never win by means of the law
and his unaided efforts to obey it.[1] He could effect this
reconciliation by his theory of the substituted death of
an innocent Son of God. We who are not encumbered
as he was by the presuppositions of Judaism, who do not
feel bound to see in the Jewish law a direct, complete,

---

[1] Mr. Claude Montefiore has energetically protested in various articles in the *Jewish
Quarterly Review* (" First Impressions of Paul " in vol. vi., " Rabbinic Judaism and
the Epistles of St. Paul " in vol. xiii., " Rabbinic Conceptions of Repentance " in vol. xvi.,
etc.) against the tendency of Christian theologians to assume that St. Paul's feeling about
the burden of the law really represents the whole truth about Rabbinic Judaism, and
has declared himself unable to understand this attitude of St. Paul towards the law.
In his more recent book, *Judaism and St. Paul*, the same writer has suggested that the
law was more felt as a burden among the Jews of the Dispersion who were brought into
more frequent relations with Gentiles. Whether he is equally right in representing the
Judaism of Tarsus as Judaism of a lower type than the strictly " rabbinic Judaism " of
Jerusalem, I will not venture to say. He is no doubt justified in saying that the idea of
the forgivingness of God was a prominent feature of rabbinic teaching, but he hardly denies
that this teaching was not logically reconcilable with the teaching of the Pentateuch.

and unique manifestation of God's will, or in every prophetic phrase an infallible prediction of the future which had to be literally fulfilled, may feel that after all St. Paul was but pouring new wine into old bottles. There is a real contradiction between the spirit of the Old Testament and the spirit of Christ which St. Paul's theories fail to bridge. We can bridge that gulf by methods which were not open to St. Paul, but only on condition of subordinating the older revelation to the new to an extent for which St. Paul was not prepared,[1] and adopting an attitude towards the Old Testament which has only recently been adopted even by Christian theologians.

Before we leave the question of the connexion of Christ's death with the forgiveness of sins, we must notice another aspect of St. Paul's argument. In fact we may almost say that it is the most important point of his argument in the Epistles to the Romans and the Galatians. That God had forgiven sin through Christ, and pre-eminently through His death, was common ground between himself and his opponents. It was part of the common faith of the Church. That connexion is assumed rather than proved. What St. Paul aimed at proving was that not only forgiveness but salvation was possible without the works of the law, that the law had no longer any binding hold upon those who had been so redeemed. He wants to show that the death of Christ was the ground not merely of the individual's forgiveness

---

[1] "Between the fundamental Pharisaic view on the one side—according to which God is the stern Judge who does not forgive without demanding payment or expiation, and the law as an absolute tyrant who inexorably insists upon his rights—and, on the other side, the Christian consciousness for which God as the Father of Jesus Christ is the Will of Love, and the law only a ' paedagogic ' institution of temporary significance—between these two standpoints there is undoubtedly an inconsistency which cannot be logically removed, but only psychologically explained. From the consciousness of Paul, in which the filial spirit of Jesus had to struggle with the legal spirit of the Pharisee, there could only spring a theory of redemption which vacillated between the two. But for this very reason—because, namely, it was a compromise between the two, fighting the legal religion with its own forms in order to open up the way for the freedom of the children of God—for this very reason it was from the first, and ever afterwards, an excellently adapted means of transforming the legal into the evangelical consciousness by elevating the former into the latter " (Pfleiderer, *Primitive Christianity*, i. 336-7). " The Pauline doctrine of the righteousness of God, which, on the ground of the expiation which has been made, justifies the believer, was a compromise between the prophetic and the Pharisaic theories " (*ib.* 364).

for the past, but of the cancelling of the law's claim upon Jew and Gentile alike, the removal of the burden which he had himself found so intolerable. " Christ is the end of the law unto righteousness to every one that believeth." [1] And yet, though this is St. Paul's object throughout, the connexion between this supersession of the Law and the death of Christ is not very easy to trace.

The only formal argument is contained in the comparison of the relation between man and the law to the relation between husband and wife. As the wife is released from the tie that binds her to her husband by the death of the latter, so by union with Christ, implying a participation in His death, the bond that binds the Christian to the law is severed, and he becomes united to Christ.[2] It has been remarked [3] that the parallel really requires that the law should be dead, not the man who was subject to it, and that is precisely the thing to be proved. Putting aside the somewhat unconvincing parallel, what the Apostle really means is no doubt that the constructive death through participation in the actual death of Christ has satisfied the law's claims over the sinner.[4] The penalty for transgression having been paid, that penalty which gives the law the only hold that it has upon the sinner, there is no further duty of obedience.

St. Paul assumes—he does not really prove—that

---

[1] Rom. x. 4. In Gal. ii. 21 he argues that, if justification could be obtained by the law, Christ would have died in vain. If this is regarded as an attempt to prove this point, it must be admitted that it is an attempt to prove the theory by itself, but it may of course be an *argumentum ad hominem*, based on what the opponent had in common with the writer.

[2] Rom. vii. 1-6.   [3] Goguel, *L'Apôtre Paul et Jésus-Christ*, p. 135.

[4] Perhaps St. Paul does not sharply distinguish this theory from the idea that the flesh being killed (constructively in Christ's death), the source of evil inclinations is removed. Cf. Rom. vii. 4, 6, " Ye also were made dead to the law through the body of Christ. . . . For when we were in the flesh, the sinful passions, which were through the law, wrought in our members to bring forth fruit unto death. But now we have been discharged from the law, that being dead in which we were held ; that we should serve in newness of the spirit, and not in oldness of the letter." Here most commentators take " that in which we were held " ($\dot{\epsilon}\nu$ $\dot{\psi}$ $\kappa\alpha\tau\epsilon\iota\chi\acute{o}\mu\epsilon\theta\alpha$) to mean " the law." Drs. Sanday and Headlam hold that the meaning is " the old state," the antecedent being loosely suggested by the context. The revisers read $\dot{\alpha}\pi o\theta\alpha\nu\acute{o}\nu\tau\epsilon s$ instead of $\dot{\alpha}\pi o\theta\alpha\nu\acute{o}\nu\tau o s$ and translate " having died to that wherein we were holden." In any case there is here no real argument. St. Paul does not explain why the removal of sinful inclinations should emancipate from the ceremonial requirements of the law.

the remission of the penalty for past transgression carries with it emancipation from all requirements of the law for the future. The antinomian consequences of such a doctrine would be appalling enough, but for the fact that the Spirit's presence—which was for St. Paul as important an effect of Christ's coming as the forgiveness of past sin—carried with it a disposition, and a capacity, to observe all that was of eternal obligation in the law. Verbally St. Paul is inconsistent in this matter. Side by side with strong assertions as to the total emancipation of Christians from the duty of observing the law, there is the doctrine that the ultimate object of the sentence of acquittal or justification is that "the ordinance of [righteous conduct required by] the law might be fulfilled in us."[1] But if the law is still to be observed, why not, we may ask, the whole law, ceremonial as well as moral? The two sides of his doctrine can only be brought together by the assumption that there are two elements in the law, one temporary, the other eternal. This assumption is really made, but never avowed, by St. Paul. Still less does he discuss the principle upon which the temporary is to be distinguished from the eternal, the ceremonial from the moral. We may suppose that, had the question been put to him, he would have said, "That is one of the secrets which the Spirit directly communicates to believers." We should not be going much beyond St. Paul's real thought if we substituted as a modern equivalent the statement : "The distinction is revealed by the human conscience now purged, stimulated, and enlightened by the teaching and influence of Christ."

And here I may take the opportunity of saying that in my belief the influence of the character, example, and teaching of Jesus—particularly His moral teaching—upon the mind of St. Paul was much more powerful and important than it is at the present moment fashionable to admit. It is true that in St. Paul's theories more is said about the glorified Messiah than about the human Jesus. It is true that the actual words of Jesus are not often formally quoted. But if we ask what were the

---

[1] Rom. viii. 3, 4.

influences which predisposed St. Paul's mind to the
conversion which was completed by the vision on the
road to Damascus, what were the psychological causes
which accounted for the change in his attitude towards
Judaism and the law, the first place must be given to
the influence of Christ's teaching and personality,
whether based upon personal knowledge or upon what
he had learned from Christians. St. Paul's conversion
implied a moral and religious transformation, not merely
a change of opinion. There is nothing in the vision of
a glorified Messiah, taken by itself, to account for such
a moral change, though it may well have confirmed a
conviction arrived at on other grounds or prepared the
way for the subsequent influence of Christ's teaching.
And as a matter of fact the allusions or echoes of the
Master's sayings in his writings are so numerous as to
suggest that some theologians who have written about
St. Paul are not very familiar with the Gospels.[1] Still
more striking is their agreement in ethical ideal. And
this identity between St. Paul's moral teaching and His
Master's, this appreciation of its very essence, cannot
be a mere accident ; it can be accounted for by no theory
so natural as the supposition that, like other Christians, he
knew the traditions about Christ's teaching which were
afterwards embodied in the Gospels. The very existence
of the Gospels is a sufficient proof of the place which
Christ's life and teaching played in the actual consciousness of the Christian community, if not in their formal
statements of doctrine. St. Paul could not have been
ignorant of them, nor could they have failed to influence
him. No Christian need hesitate to admit that the
influence which turned St. Paul from a Pharisee of the
Pharisees into an Apostle was no less the work of God's
Spirit because some of it was due to the teaching of our
Lord, and perhaps not so much to his ecstatic experiences
as he himself supposed. It was from Jesus that he
had learned that the vital essence of the law was all
contained in the two great commandments. It was from

---

[1] See an admirable chapter in M. Goguel's *L'Apôtre Paul et Jésus-Christ* on " Ce
que Paul connaît de la vie et des paroles de Jésus " (Pt. I. chap. iii.).

the teaching of Jesus that he had learned that such a
fulfilment of the law as the Pharisee of the parable could
boast would not satisfy God's demands for absolute
purity of heart, and perfect love towards one's neighbour.
It was from Jesus that he had learned that the penitent
publican would be forgiven, though he had not fulfilled
the law.   It was from Jesus that he had learned that that
which went into the mouth could not really defile either
Jew or Gentile.   All these things he had learned from
Jesus, by whatever channel the influence reached him.
And these truths were really inconsistent with the doctrine
which St. Paul had learned from the Old Testament—
that the soul that sinneth shall die without any hope
of forgiveness, though doubtless there was much in the
prophets and later Jewish writers which was equally
inconsistent with such a doctrine.   To suggest that
Jesus had borne that threatened death for all, and that
that was the reason why a just God could also show
Himself to be a merciful God, seemed to him to meet the
difficulty.   It is because for modern minds it does not
meet the difficulty, that St. Paul's theory of the atonement cannot be our theory of it ; and, in spite of all St.
Paul's authority, it was never really accepted by a great
deal of later Christian thought.

III. *St. Paul's Doctrine of Justification*

And now we must turn to the other side of St. Paul's
doctrine.   The objective source of justification is a free
act of God which operates in some way through Christ's
death : its subjective condition is faith.

But what does faith mean to St. Paul ? Does it
mean belief ? And if so, belief in what ? I think it
cannot be denied that St. Paul does habitually identify
faith with intellectual belief.   That is shown by the
illustrations which he gives to prove that even before
Christ's coming faith had been the root-principle of
goodness in the holy men of old.   Abraham's faith [1]

---

[1] Faith (πίστις) never seems by St. Paul to be used in the sense of trust, except so
far as trust is implied in believing the statements or promises of another.

consisted in believing God—believing the various divine communications made to him, in particular believing that he should beget a child when he was a hundred years old. The verb which corresponds with faith is always " believe." The faith which justifies a Christian is clearly, at least in the argumentative passages, belief of some kind about Jesus. When we come to ask what about Jesus is to be believed, St. Paul's answer is not quite so clear or so consistent. " If thou shalt confess with thy mouth Jesus as Lord, and shalt believe in thy heart that God raised him from the dead, thou shalt be saved." [1] Here the two salient points of the creed which saves are the Messiahship of Jesus and His Resurrection : not a word about any special significance in the death except in so far as that death is presupposed by the Resurrection. More frequently St. Paul's language is even vaguer. He speaks of faith in general, or of faith in Christ.[2] It is doubtful whether there is a single passage in which faith is categorically said to be faith in His blood, though one passage is so translated in the Authorized Version.[3] We should not perhaps be going very far from St. Paul's real meaning if we said that the belief to which St. Paul attributes the justifying effect was belief in the whole revelation of God through Christ, in God's whole scheme of supplying out of His special grace or favour a means of justification to those who had failed to obtain it as of right through the law of Moses or the law of their own consciences. But the variations of his language on this point show how far he is from the stereotyped systems of later times— particularly the Reformation systems. In one passage of the Roman Epistle he actually attributes salvation not to faith at all but to hope.[4]

No doubt, to the deepest religious consciousness of St. Paul faith was much more than belief. If we ask what faith really stood for in St. Paul's inner experience,

---

[1] Rom. x. 9.   [2] Phil. iii. 9.
[3] " Whom God sent forth to be a propitiation, through faith in His blood " (Rom. iii. 25, A.V.) : the R.V. is no doubt right in connecting the words with " propitiation," and placing commas before and after " through faith."
[4] Rom. viii. 24.

we may well say that the "new and significant peculiarity
in St. Paul's conception of faith is the mystical union with
Christ, the self-identification with Christ in a fellowship
of life and death"; or speak of an "unreserved, self-
forgetting surrender of the whole man to the Saviour,"[1]
or of "an intense personal apprehension of Christ as
Master, Redeemer and Lord";[2] or we may even (with
Dorner) speak of faith as "a general expression for subjective religion." But these conceptions have little in
common with Abraham's faith in the promise that he
should have a son when a hundred years old. All such
definitions do quite truly represent what St. Paul means
by faith in his passages of deepest and most personal
religious emotion, but they are not the sense in which
the word is used in his formal argument, and it is with this
that we are immediately concerned. For St. Paul in his
logical moments faith means belief.

How and why does faith procure justification? And
what does justification mean? Does justification mean,
as Protestant theology has held, the declaring righteous
or, as medieval and Roman theology affirm, the actually
making righteous? As to the actual signification of
the Greek word, there cannot be a moment's doubt.
The verb δικαιόω means to "declare righteous," not
to make righteous. Equally little doubt can there be
that the whole trend of St. Paul's thought requires that
God shall be supposed of His own free grace to pronounce men righteous who are *not yet* in point of
fact actually righteous.[3] The idea of justification (in

to acquit :

---

[1] Both these expressions are from Pfleiderer (*Primitive Christianity*, i. 347), and are
quoted with approval by the Dean of St. Paul's (Dr. Inge) in "Faith and its Psychology."

[2] Sanday and Headlam, *Romans*, p. 162. On p. 33 the writers enumerate the
various senses in which the term is used by St. Paul, but they do not ask themselves
how far this variation affects the logical validity of his argument.

[3] The original meaning of δικαιόω is "to treat justly, to do justice to," as a judge
does. This might sometimes be done by condemnation or punishment, just as in Scot-
land a man who is hanged is (or was) said to be "justified"; and this meaning occurs in
Ecclus. xlii. 2; but in practice the word is usually employed in the sense of treating
justly the innocent party, avenging him if he is the accuser, acquitting him if he is the
accused. Cf. 2 Sam. xv. 4, where Absalom wishes that he were "made judge in the
land, that every man which hath any suit or cause might come unto me, and I would do
him justice" (δικαιώσω); here the meaning might cover the rejection of an unjust
plaint, but the emphasis is clearly on the other side, and generally the meaning is to decide
in favour of a cause or person. Thus, when the object is a person (as distinct from a

this connexion) is primarily "acquittal" : but, when
the acquittal has not been earned by the merits of the
accused and is due solely to the undeserved mercy of his
judge, acquittal becomes practically equivalent to forgiveness.   It is definitely a part of St. Paul's thought
that God does, in consequence of or by means of the
work of Christ, forgive those who have done nothing to
deserve forgiveness.   So far the righteousness which is
ascribed to them is (to use the technical term) an "imputed," [1] in other words an unreal righteousness.   But
at the same time there is no idea that God pronounces
some men just, treats them as if they were just, and yet
leaves them exactly as unjust as they were before.   On
the contrary the moral and spiritual effects of justification
are more prominent than its retrospective efficacy.   To
put it in the later technical language, sanctification
necessarily accompanies or follows upon justification.[2]
If justification and sanctification are not in St. Paul
actually identified, the justification is immediately and
necessarily followed or accompanied by sanctification.
The effect of this free forgiveness on God's part, when
it meets with the response of faith in the sinner's heart,
is to make him willing to keep God's commandments,
and to enable him to do what he was not able to do before.
"Now being made free from sin, and become servants
to God, ye have your fruit unto sanctification, and the
end eternal life." [3]   The Holy Spirit was for St. Paul
communicated by or at baptism,[4] and that baptismal

---

cause) it practically means "acquit," *e.g.* in Solomon's prayer : "judge thy servants,
condemning the wicked . . . ; and justifying the righteous, to give him according to
his righteousness " (1 Kings viii. 32).

[1] "Abraham believed God, and it was reckoned unto him for righteousness " (Gen. xv.
6, LXX., quoted in Gal. iii. 6 ; Rom. iv. 3, 22).   In the last passage the A.V. translates
"imputed."   The word (ἐλογίσθη) does not necessarily imply that what is reckoned or
imputed does not correspond with the actual fact.   Cf., *e.g.*, 1 Cor. iv. 1 : " Let a man so
account of us," etc. ; 2 Cor. x. 2, xi. 5 ; but when God is represented as " not imputing
to them their trespasses," it clearly has the meaning of not taking account of trespasses
which really have been committed.   There is, however, no trace of the characteristic
Protestant notion that Christ's righteousness is imputed to us.

[2] "And such were some of you : but ye were washed, but ye were sanctified,
but ye were justified in the name of the Lord Jesus Christ, and in the Spirit of our
God " (1 Cor. vi. 11).

[3] Rom. vi. 22.   And in that way the ordinance (δικαίωμα) of the law was fulfilled
" in us, who walk not after the flesh, but after the spirit " (Rom. viii. 4).

[4] Or the laying on of hands if this already followed immediately after baptism.

profession of repentance and faith, which in those days
followed so immediately upon acceptance of Christianity
that in the earliest Christian thought little distinction
was made between them. And the presence of the
Spirit brings with it a moral change of which the baptized
is immediately conscious, and which shows itself forthwith in his life. Christians know in themselves that
Jesus Christ is within them : those who do not are no
longer in the faith.[1] The presence of the Holy Spirit
is the presence of Christ. "No man can say, Jesus
is Lord but in the Holy Spirit," [2] and "the Lord is the
Spirit." [3] We can hardly even, after the fashion of
later theology, speak of faith and justification as the
conditions precedent of sanctification : if faith is impossible without some measure of the Spirit's presence,
at least the beginnings of sanctification must precede
justification. And the presence of the Spirit must
produce good works. St. Paul assumes that believing
in Christ involves becoming "obedient from the heart
to that form of teaching whereunto ye were delivered." [4]

The death to sin of which St. Paul speaks is thus
something very much more than the fictitious payment
of a penalty, or the passive acceptance of that payment
by the believer : it is only the negative side of a newly
created slavery to righteousness.[5] "We who died
to sin, how shall we any longer live therein ?" [6] It carries
with it the reality, and the consciousness, of sonship.
"Our old man was crucified with him, that the body
of sin might be done away, that so we should no longer

---

[1] "Try your own selves, whether ye be in the faith ; prove your own selves. Or
know ye not as to your own selves, that Jesus Christ is in you ? unless indeed ye be
reprobate " (2 Cor. xiii. 5).
[2] 1 Cor. xii. 3. It does not seem necessary for our present purpose to examine St.
Paul's conception of the Spirit or of the relation with God's Spirit or Christ's Spirit
(which are practically identified) and the human spirit. Possibly " even the Pauline
πνεῦμα is *in itself* a transcendent physical essence, a supersensuous kind of matter, which
is the opposite of the earthly, sensuous materiality of the σάρξ " (Pfleiderer, *Paulinism*,
i. 201). It is extremely important to bear such considerations in mind when the attempt
is made to treat St. Paul's intellectual notions as eternally binding dogmas for all subsequent Christianity ; but they do not affect the nature or the value of his strictly religious
and ethical conceptions, with which we are here mainly concerned. The idea of the
Holy Spirit was of course not unknown to Judaism. " Whatever the righteous do,
they do through the Holy Ghost " (Jewish Prayer-book).
[3] 2 Cor. iii. 17.   [4] Rom. vi. 17.   [5] Rom. vi. 19, 20.
[6] Rom. vi. 2.

be in bondage to sin; for he that hath died is justified from sin." [1] The last argument would have no force if justification meant merely a counting righteous which was not accompanied or followed by a making righteous. The hearing of faith brings with it the presence of the Spirit. [2] The process of sanctification is no doubt thought of as a gradual process—not indeed to be completed till after the judgement—but it begins with conversion or baptism; the measure of the Spirit which is then and there communicated is an earnest or pledge of a fuller outpouring. He that "anointed us is God, who also sealed us [sealing is no doubt associated with the idea of baptism, if it does not actually mean baptism], and gave us the earnest of the Spirit in our hearts." [3] The earnest means of course a part-payment which is the pledge of full payment. "As many of you as were baptized into Christ did put on Christ." [4] Christ here stands for an ideal of life, an ever present influence, not a mere means of escape at the judgement. "God sent forth His Son . . . that he might redeem them which were under the law, that we might receive the adoption of sons." [5] The act of adoption is no doubt treated as a sort of legal sentence on the part of God, an anticipation of the sentence which shall hereafter be pronounced at the judgement, for it takes place once for all when a man becomes a Christian. This idea is forced upon St. Paul in order to make out that God's promises to Israel have been fulfilled: he could only treat the Gentiles as Israelites by applying to them the ideas anciently connected with legal adoption, [6] which made men members of a family into which they were not born. But for St. Paul the idea of this legal adoption is almost swallowed

[1] Rom. vi. 6-7.

[2] "Received ye the Spirit by the works of the law, or by the hearing of faith?" (Gal. iii. 2). "But unto us which are being saved it [the word of the cross] is the power of God" (1 Cor. i. 18).

[3] 2 Cor. i. 22; cf. Eph. i. 14 ("the earnest of our inheritance").
[4] Gal. iii. 27.   [5] Gal. iv. 4, 5.

[6] According to Prof. Ramsay "the legal processes referred to in the Galatian Epistle are Graeco-Asiatic as applied in practical administration by the Romans," rather than distinctively Roman. The Jews had no such ideas about adoption. This is therefore a good instance of the influence upon St. Paul's mind of Graeco-Roman ideas and institutions.

I

up in the thought of the moral regeneration and the consciousness of communion with God in Christ which immediately followed. " Ye received not the spirit of bondage again unto fear ; but ye received the spirit of adoption, whereby we cry, Abba, Father. The Spirit himself beareth witness with our spirit that we are children of God : and if children, then heirs ; heirs of God, and joint-heirs with Christ." [1] " Because ye are sons," because ye have been formally adopted by God, " God sent forth the Spirit of his Son into our hearts, crying, Abba, Father." [2] And the consciousness of sonship must produce actual good works. The most precise statement of the relation between Christ's death and the moral transformation which it produces in Christians is to be found in Rom. viii. 3, 4. We are there told that " God, sending his own Son in the likeness of sinful flesh and as an offering for sin, condemned sin in the flesh : that the ordinance of the law might be fulfilled in us, who walk not after the flesh, but after the spirit."   St. Paul here passes with such swift transition from the idea of a sacrificial or juridical expiation of past sin to that of an actual destruction of sin's power in the believer that he can hardly be supposed to have distinguished very sharply between the two things. At all events it is made perfectly plain that St. Paul did think of the act of justification as destroying the power of sin for the future, and producing in the believer a capacity to fulfil henceforth the law of God not in the letter but in the spirit—that is to say, to fulfil henceforth the ethical principles implied, if inadequately expressed, in the old Mosaic Law, to obey henceforth that higher law of which love is the fulfilling. St. Paul does teach justification by faith without the *works of the law*, but never justification by faith without *good* works. It is only the works of the law—works done in obedience to the law and apart from the new motive power supplied by Christ and the presence of His Spirit—which are excluded from any saving effects. The works of the law are excluded not because they are not good, but

[1] Rom. viii. 15-17.   [2] Gal. iv. 6.

because men can never do enough of them to satisfy
the old law's requirements. But there is a higher law
revealed to the Christian conscience by the indwelling
Spirit, to which the Christian is still subject. " So then,
I myself with the mind "—the higher part of the man
which is acted upon by the Spirit of God—" serve the
law of God." [1]   This is what St. Paul means by obeying
the law not in the oldness of the letter, but in newness
of the spirit.[2]   And such obedience is necessary for
sanctification and final salvation. Justification is sometimes thought of as a judicial sentence already passed
by God at the moment of belief, sometimes as the final
sentence of acquittal at the great judgement ; but only
when justification is followed by sanctification will the
first sentence anticipate the last.   Sanctification is thought
of as a gradual process : salvation is the completion of that
process.   Christians are not usually spoken of as persons
already saved : they are only "being saved." They
are not fully saved till the moral transformation is completed and recognized at the judgement. Primarily
salvation means acquittal at the judgement or the blessed
life with Christ which follows that acquittal ; though by
anticipation the Christian is thought of as already beginning to some extent even here the life which will be his
in completeness hereafter. Whether the process of
salvation will ever be completed, depends emphatically
upon conduct.[3]

Side by side with his doctrine of justification by faith
there is in St. Paul a very explicit doctrine of judgement
by works.[4]   " We must all be made manifest before the
judgement-seat of Christ ; that each one may receive the
things done in the body, according to what he hath done,

---

[1] Rom. vii. 25.   [2] Rom. vii. 6.

[3] St. Paul's language is still more full of "transmuted Eschatology" than his
Master's. " The eschatological living with Christ changes itself, therefore, in the
mind of the Apostle into the ethical new life of the Christian present " (Pfleiderer,
Paulinism, i. 196).

[4] Faith is thought of as both a χάρισμα or gift of God (Rom. xii. 3 ; 1 Cor. xii. 8, 9) and
a response of the individual will (" your work of faith," 1 Thess. i. 3). There is no inconsistency in this for any one who does not regard the existence of self-determination
as inconsistent with a rational Determinism. Nevertheless St. Paul would not perhaps
have used the expression " work of faith " after the complete development of his theory
of " free grace " in Romans.

whether it be good or bad." [1] Only those who have been
made really righteous can survive that judgement or " be
saved."   And thus at bottom the Catholic theory of
justification finds more support in St. Paul, and is far
nearer his real thought, than the Protestant theory in its
strict traditional form.   If grammatically and for the
purposes of his quasi-juridical argument justification
means counting righteous, practically it means for St.
Paul a making righteous as well.   Justification, in the
sense of present forgiveness, may be by faith *only*, but
not so ultimate salvation.

St. Paul's language often seems to assume that faith
in Christ will invariably have all these moral effects.
And yet it is obvious enough that if we say that faith
is to have these moral effects, faith must be something
much more than that mere intellectual assent in which,
according to his own formal statements, it ought to
consist.   The Apostle is generalizing from his own experience.   Directly we leave St. Paul's formal arguments
and treat his language as a revelation of his own personal
religious experience, our difficulties begin to disappear.
In him belief in Christ, submission to His influence,
reception into the Church and all the new spiritual
influences and experiences which followed upon that
reception, did have these transforming effects. The
effects of his new conviction were so overwhelming, in
his own case and in that of whole masses of other
Christians, that it was natural enough for him to assume
that the same effects would follow in the case of all
Christians.   And yet they did not, and do not now.
According to the logical requirements of his theory all
Christians ought to be good Christians.   But they are
not, and were not even in St. Paul's day when profession
of Christianity cost so much that baptism might well be
taken as a proof of real inward change.   Over and over
again he deplores the moral defects of his converts.
Even in his own case he contemplates the possibility
that, after having preached the Gospel to others, he
might himself be rejected. [2]   And he never falls back

[1] 2 Cor. v. 10   [2] 1 Cor. ix. 27.

upon the device of saying that such ultimate defection, in himself or in others, would show that they had never possessed true faith at all, and never were really justified.   The doctrines of "assurance" and "final perseverance" in their Calvinistic form, can derive no support from his pages.[1]

Thus, if we are to make St. Paul consistent with himself, we must say that it is not all faith which justifies, but only one particular kind of faith.   When he recognizes that there is a kind of faith so strong that it could remove mountains,[2] and which is yet worthless in the sight of God because it is unaccompanied by charity, he is unsaying all that the letter of the Epistle to the Romans logically implies.   If we would penetrate to St. Paul's deepest meaning, we must interpret the teaching of the Epistle to the Romans by that magnificent panegyric on charity which is so much dearer to the heart of modern Christendom than St. Paul's theory of justification. *I shd think* *was?* "Faith, hope, charity, these three; but the greatest of these is charity." [3]   That could not be so if faith—in the sense of the Epistle to the Romans—were the only

---

[1] Two closely connected questions about St. Paul's doctrine of Election have been much controverted :

(1) There is the question whether it is the Church that is elected or the particular persons composing it.   (This is connected with, or another form of, the more modern question whether it is the individual or the Church which is primarily the subject of justification.)   The two views are not mutually exclusive unless the suggestion is made that, while the Church was elected and predestined to glory, the particular persons who were to compose it were quite undetermined.   Of this view, often maintained by Arminians, there is no trace in St. Paul.

(2) There is the closely connected question whether election is to a certain spiritual status in this life—to be members of the Church, to possess the knowledge of Christ—or to ultimate salvation.   As to this we may say that St. Paul usually thinks primarily of the former, but he does at times assume that the first carries with it the second. "To predestinate" is clearly to St. Paul the same thing as "to elect," and the elect will be saved.   "Whom he foreordained, them he also called : and whom he called, them he also justified : and whom he justified, them he also glorified " (Rom. viii. 30). The first step carries with it all the others.   All who are called into the Church are justified, all who are justified are glorified.   As a matter of exegesis, the Calvinist is right here, except that St. Paul, unlike the Calvinist, would probably have assumed that all the baptized were converted and consequently justified.   St. Paul certainly would not have spoken of one who would be condemned at the judgement as justified.   But no less certainly he elsewhere assumes that many Christians might be finally condemned.

[2] It may be suggested that this faith is merely the faith that works miracles and that this removes the inconsistency ; but surely St. Paul would not have admitted that the faith which does this is a different faith from the faith by which a man believes in Christ.   And if it is, that involves the admission that St. Paul uses the word in different senses without explicitly distinguishing them.

[3] 1 Cor. xiii. 13.

thing wanted for justification and salvation.   Once more in this matter of justification, as in his views about the atonement, we have discovered a contradiction—a contradiction in words and in strict logic—between St. Paul's theories and his deepest spiritual convictions. It was a matter of immediate experience with him that since he had been converted, had believed, had been baptized, had shared the spiritual life of the Christian community, he had become another man, and had been enabled to fulfil—not indeed in absolute perfection but as he had never fulfilled it before—the law in its true inner meaning, that new meaning which Christ had taught him, and which he so perfectly expressed in the emphatic declaration that all the commandments " are summed up in this word, namely, ' Thou shalt love thy neighbour as thyself.' " [1]   For him faith carried with it all these moral consequences, but it did not do so for all who believed ; and yet the theory which he had adopted required that it should.   The theory required that faith should mean nothing but belief : in the real experience of the man it stood for all the effects which faith had produced in him—a passionate devotion to the doing of God's will, a sense of union and communion with God through Christ, active love for his fellow-men. Once again, as in the language which he uses about the effects of Christ's death, there is a hiatus between the formula and the deepest experience of the man.

Can we do anything to explain this contradiction between the theory of the rabbinic theologian and the real convictions of the man ? I believe that we can. St. Paul's theory of justification is to be explained, as the theory of atonement through Christ's death is to be explained, by the source from which it came, i.e. the Old Testament.   Justification by faith was no new doctrine. Whether men were to be justified by faith or by works was a standing matter of controversy among the rabbis, and each side appealed to Scripture.[2]   St. Paul's theory

[1] Rom. xiii. 9.
[2] The controversy over faith and works was an old Jewish controversy. Dr. Schechter quotes from the Talmud the words " Our father Abraham came into possession of this world and of the world to come only by the merit of his faith " (Jewish Quarterly Review,

is based upon the authority of passages in the Old Testament—the erroneous LXX. translation of Habakkuk: " The just shall live by faith ";[1] the supposed precedent of Abraham; Isaiah's declaration that " whosoever believeth on him shall not be put to shame ";[2] Joel's statement that " whosoever shall call upon the name of the Lord shall be saved," [3] and the like.[4]   He was driven into the theory by the necessity of reconciling the freedom of

---

vi. p. 413), but the contrary view was also common.   And so among Christians the same stock instances are appealed to on each side (cf. St. Paul and Heb. xi. with James ii.). Among the Jews (as, indeed, in St. Paul) we sometimes find both views taken by the same writer.   Cf. Apocalypse of Baruch xlii. 2 : " As for what thou didst say . . . ' To whom will these things be, and how many (will they be) ? '—to those who have believed there will be the good which was spoken of aforetime, and to those who despise there will be the contrary of these things."   But in li. 7 sq. we read of " those who have been saved by their works. . . . They shall be made like unto the angels, and be made equal to the stars."   In 4 (2) Esdras vi. 5 we read : " Before they were sealed that have gathered faith for a treasure " ; yet in vii. 77 the angel says to Ezra : " Thou hast a treasure of good works laid up with the Most High."   In viii. 32, 33 God is represented as " merciful, to us, namely, that have no works of righteousness " ; but " the just, which have many good works laid up with thee, shall for their own deeds receive reward," and in ix. 7 faith and works seem alternative modes of salvation : " Every one that shall be saved, and shall be able to escape by his works, or by faith, whereby he hath believed."   (Something like this seems to be implied in Acts xiii. 39.)   On the other hand, in xiii. 23 the saved are " such as have works and faith toward the Almighty."   See also Additional Note E (below, p.135).   In speaking of St. Paul as a " rabbinic theologian " I do not mean to assume that St. Paul's ideas about the burden of the law are typical of the Judaism of the Jerusalem schools.   Even those who doubt whether St. Paul was really brought up at the feet of Gamaliel do not, I suppose, doubt that his education, wherever received, and whatever type of Judaism it represented, was that of a future rabbi.

[1] Hab. ii. 4 (Rom. i. 17).   The real meaning is " by his faithfulness," i.e. to God's commands.

[2] Is. xxviii. 16, LXX. (Rom. x. 11).   This is really the decisive point of St. Paul's argument.   " On him " is not either in the Hebrew or the LXX.

[3] Joel ii. 32 (Rom. x. 13).   In Joel " the Lord " means of course God.   The use of this passage is noticeable as showing how little St. Paul had a definite theory as to the particular belief about Christ which must be entertained as a condition of salvation.

[4] Sometimes (cf. Johannes Weiss, Christ : the Beginnings of Dogma, E.T., p. 72) the Old Testament passages which St. Paul cites only prove his point by the aid of some addition, which no doubt for him was really implied, but which is not in the Old Testament at all, e.g. (1) " So also it is written, The first man Adam became a living soul.   The last Adam became a life-giving spirit " (1 Cor. xv. 45).   The first sentence is a quotation from Gen. ii. 7 (the exact words are " the man became a living soul ") ; the second is not " written " at all, unless he is quoting from an apocryphal book.   It is probable that St. Paul is here impressed by the exegesis of Philo, who made Gen. i. an account of the creation of man's body (the first Adam), while the second chapter records the creation of the second Adam, the heavenly man who was to appear at the end of history (Joh. Weiss, l.c. pp. 73-4).   (2) In Gal. ii. 16 : " For by the works of the law shall no flesh be justified " ; where Lightfoot remarks : " A quotation from the Old Testament, as appears from the Hebraism οὐ πᾶσα, and from the introductory ὅτι.   The words are therefore to be regarded as a citation of Ps. cxliii. 2 : οὐ δικαιωθήσεται ἐνώπιόν σου πᾶς ζῶν."   But the whole force of the argument turns on the " by the works of the law," which is not in the O.T. at all.   The same argument is used in Rom. iii. 20, except that there St. Paul, while introducing the quotation, makes it a conclusion from his own reasoning.

Gentiles from the law with the teaching of the Old
Testament, and the dogma of its plenary inspiration.
The hiatus is quite undeniable.   And yet after all St.
Paul had himself in his Epistle to the Galatians done much
to bridge it by the simple phrase " faith working through
love."   This amounts to the admission that it is only
when faith produces, as it does not always produce, love,
that God pronounces just the man who has it.   The
Protestant theory of justification by faith—hardly perhaps
the ultra-Protestant watchword " justification by faith
only "—has on its side the letter of St. Paul's teaching.
The scholastic distinction between an unformed faith
(*fides informis*), mere intellectual belief, which saves not,
and a perfected faith (*fides formata*) which saves because
it produces love, comes far nearer to the deepest convictions of the man and to the teaching of his Master.
Our Lord taught that God forgives the truly penitent.
In so far as St. Paul meant by faith in Christ an attitude
towards God as revealed in Christ—a devotion inspired
by the thought of God's love exhibited in Christ, an
absorption of Christ's spirit, a union or self-identification
with Christ—which actually creates penitence and love,
the difference between Master and disciple tends to
vanish away.[1]

How much modern meaning we can discover in St.
Paul's theories of atonement and justification is a question
which we shall have to consider more at length hereafter.
But perhaps in the light of the contrast which we have
discovered between the logic of St. Paul's theories and
his strongest moral and religious convictions we can
already discern a partial answer to our problem.   St.
Paul's *theories* rest mainly upon exegesis, largely mistaken
exegesis or mistranslation, of the Old Testament, and are

[1] " Ce qui permet de mieux apprécier la fidélité du paulinisme à l'enseignement de
Jésus c'est de constater la moindre fidélité d'autres théologies.   C'est ainsi que le johan-
nisme ne fait plus aucune place à l'idée si importante de l'appel des pécheurs par le Christ "
(Goguel, *L'Apôtre Paul et Jésus-Christ*, p. 378 *note*).   This is true enough, except
that the contrast between St. Paul and St. John is, I think, exaggerated.   The same
writer goes on to say : " Il enseigne qu'il n'y a pas à ce salut d'autre condition que la foi,
c'est-à-dire le don du cœur à Dieu en dehors de tout mérite propre de l'homme " (*l.c.*
p. 379).   I agree that this is the modern equivalent of what St. Paul teaches.   We
may even say that he teaches it explicitly, but it cannot be denied that he teaches much
else which is not easily reconciled with such a conception of faith.

constructed in order to reconcile his new Christian convictions with old Jewish ideas which we do not share. The premisses rest upon exegesis : the logic by which inferences are made from them is rabbinic logic : the exegesis is rabbinic exegesis. The most conservative theologian of the present day will admit that we cannot attach much meaning to the exegesis which identifies Hagar with Mount Sinai in Arabia and interprets it of the Jerusalem which now is,[1] or to the idea that the rock which Moses struck and the stream which flowed from it was Christ,[2] or to the argument which St. Paul bases upon the distinction between " seed " and " seeds " in the promise to Abraham.[3] Why should we feel bound—as even liberal theologians, especially of the Lutheran variety, often seem to assume— to accept theories which St. Paul arrives at by precisely the same kind of premisses and the same kind of logic ? We must be bold enough to admit that there is an element in St. Paul's teaching—not so prominent an element as it has sometimes been made—which the developed moral consciousness simply cannot accept. We do not and cannot share St. Paul's views about the law, his theories of inspiration, his rabbinic exegesis or his rabbinic logic. Therefore we cannot accept the conclusions which he reaches by those means—his theory of atonement through the substitutionary sacrifice of Christ or his theory of justification by belief, in the form which he actually gives to them. St. Paul's deepest moral and religious convictions on the other hand rest upon the deliverances of his conscience, upon what he had learned from Christ, upon his own religious insight, and upon his personal experience of the effects which flowed from acceptance of Christ. And these are of infinitely greater value to us, as they have been of infinitely greater value in the history of Christianity, than the rabbinic theories which even the Church of the Fathers never accepted without large, if unavowed, qualifications. At bottom St. Paul's conception of God's character was the same as our Lord's : it was from Him that he learned it.

[1] Gal. iv. 25.   [2] 1 Cor. x. 4.   [3] Gal. iii. 16.

But he could not—in a day or even in a life-time—completely rid himself of the old legalistic conceptions which he derived from the religion in which he was brought up and the school in which he was educated. In him the liberal and universalistic doctrine—the doctrine of Gentile Christianity—which he had learned from Jesus and from the Hellenistic interpretation of His teaching, contended with the rabbinic traditions and prejudices and theories which were not really consistent with the newly found idea of God. He was therefore driven into stating the new doctrine in terms of the old, defending it by arguments borrowed from the old, elaborating theories which really bring back the conception of a God who was not a loving Father but a stern, exacting, and somewhat arbitrary Judge who has threatened penalties of which in a gentler mood He repents, and yet who must still keep His word. We shall be most faithful to the spirit of St. Paul's teaching by dropping the inadequate formula in which he endeavoured to make his presentation of Christianity intelligible to the rabbinic mind, and adhering to that genuinely Christian conception of God which the formula unsuccessfully strove to express.

Interpret St. Paul according to the letter of his rabbinic theories and we must needs pronounce that his religion was a different religion from that of his Master, and a religion which cannot be that of the modern world. Interpret St. Paul in the light, not of his rabbinic arguments, but of those inmost convictions which were dictated by his own experience, and at once we begin to see the possibility of a doctrine of the atonement which is intelligible to the modern mind, and which is as much in harmony with the teaching of his Master as his theories are in contradiction to it. The world can no longer accept Jesus as Lord and Master because He fulfilled the prophecies which were supposed to point to a vicarious expiation through His death, or believe in justification by faith on the evidence of St. Paul's quotations or misquotations from Genesis and Habakkuk. But all that St. Paul says about the unchangeable love of God as exhibited in the coming of Christ, all that he says about the redeeming and regenerating effects of that supreme revelation of God's nature made once for all in Jesus, is confirmed by the experience of thousands both among those who have accepted, and among those who have been very little impressed by, the Apostle's formal theories. Look at the letter of St. Paul's theories in his most rabbinical moments, and the God of St. Paul may well seem to be a wholly different Being from the God whom Christ taught men to believe in by the Sermon on the Mount, by the parables of the returning Prodigal and the repentant Publican, by His life of toil and His death of self-sacrifice for man. Look at St. Paul in his less logical but more inspired moments—at his outbursts of praise and thankfulness to God for the love shown in Christ, at his actual teaching about the character and ultimate purposes of God, about God's love to man and willingness to forgive the penitent, about His presence in the hearts of men through the Spirit; look at his matchless words of exhortation and his application of Christ's teaching to the practical needs of the growing Church;—and there we have a Paul who is in complete harmony with his Master. When St. Paul is so understood, Christ's God is Paul's God—a God whose wrath needs not, and never needed, to be satisfied by the death of His own Son, but whose nature, whose love, whose willingness and power to save from sin, have been most fully and finally revealed by Jesus Christ, by His character and by His words, by His life and not least by that one event in which was so completely summed up the spirit of that life, His death upon the Cross. We may even add that without St. Paul's help we should hardly have understood the full significance of Christ's message and Christ's work—all that He could be to the world, and all that He may be to each one of us who tries to approach God through Him, and to accept the way of salvation which He first opened up. And above all we should not have understood to the full the additional force and persuasiveness which have been added to the Gospel which Jesus preached not only by the life of love which He lived but by the death of love

which He died.[1] The rejection of St. Paul's theory
of substitution diminishes little from the debt which is
owed to him by the Church of all ages.

ADDITIONAL NOTES TO LECTURE II

NOTE A

ST. PAUL'S USE OF THE TERMS ATONEMENT, RECONCILIATION,
JUSTIFICATION, SALVATION, REDEMPTION, SANCTIFICATION

What was the distinction between these terms?

(1) Reconciliation (καταλλαγή) or the corresponding verb is except
in one passage (2 Cor. v. 20) spoken of as something that happened in
the past : "For if, while we were enemies, we were reconciled to
God through the death of his Son, much more, being reconciled, shall
we be saved by his life ; and not only so, but we also rejoice in God
through our Lord Jesus Christ, through whom we have now received
the reconciliation" (Rom. v. 10, 11, here only translated "atonement"
in A.V. Cf. Rom. xi. 15 ; 2 Cor. v. 18, 19, 20 ; Eph. ii. 16 ; Col. i. 20).
Considering the large place which the idea has occupied in later systems,
it will surprise some people to discover that these are the only passages
in which St. Paul uses the term. It seems to imply something that takes
place in a definite time : yet it is not clear at what moment the change
of relations between God and man takes place. Sometimes the reconciliation is thought of as effected once for all by the death of Christ or
generally by His work on earth ("God was in the world reconciling"—
which suggests a gradual process) : but in 2 Cor. v. 20 he exhorts
his readers, though already Christians, "in the name of Christ" to
be "reconciled to God"). The use of the aorist (καταλλάγητε)
suggests a definite time in the future, and yet St. Paul can hardly mean
to imply that his hearers are unconverted. "Make quite sure that you
have been reconciled, and that the reconciliation is complete enough

---

[1] "If to recognize that ' morality is the nature of things ' is to turn it into religion,
and so give it an infinite access of strength ; then St. Paul's bold proclamation of the doctrine that it was through death only that Christ the Son of God could open up the gates
of life, was the most important step ever taken in the development of Christian thought ;
for it made the ethical principle of self-abnegation into a revelation of the divine order
in the government of the world " (Edward Caird, *Evolution of Religion*, ii. 201). That
St. Paul did much to develope this idea, and to stamp it upon the consciousness of Christendom, is true enough ; but I have tried to show that it was the discovery of the Apostolic
Church rather than of St. Paul alone. I will add another quotation from Pfleiderer :
" Thus, beneath the harsh dogmatic form of a vicarious expiation, there shows itself as
the true kernel, the profound thought of a re-birth of mankind through the inspiration
and renewing power of a divine-human deed of love " (*Primitive Christianity*, i. 341).
In spite of the fact that Pfleiderer was still too much influenced by a survival of the
Tübingen theories, and in spite of the progress on the critical and historical side which
has been made by others, I should like to acknowledge the value of Pfleiderer's work
which it seems the fashion with English theologians to depreciate. He was not a worse
theologian because he was also a philosopher.

to lead to ultimate salvation," would perhaps express his meaning. St. Paul nowhere sanctions the idea that "conversion" must take place at a definite moment : in fact there is no term in his vocabulary which can be identified with conversion. The Christian life begins with belief or with baptism, and though the two were in his time closely associated, they could not have been actually simultaneous : so little has he worked out a system which can be identified either with later Catholicism or with later Protestantism.

Mr. J. K. Mozley [1] quotes Dr. Driver's statement that the English word atonement formerly meant "reconciliation," while now it suggests chiefly the making amends or reparation, and remarks himself that "whereas the idea of reconciliation is implied in the word 'atonement,' however the latter be interpreted, the reverse, if atonement is not interpreted as at-one-ment, is not necessarily the case."

(2) There are passages in which justification (δικαίωσις) seems to be spoken of as still future : Rom. iii. 30 (one God who "shall justify the circumcision by faith," etc.). Cf. Rom. ii. 13, iii. 20 : but these passages are not conclusive, for St. Paul is speaking of the results which were to flow in the future from what Christ did once for all in the past. Usually at all events justification is spoken of as something past in the case of Christians, "being justified freely by his grace through the redemption that is in Christ Jesus" (Rom. iii. 24) ; so v. 1 (" being justified by faith, let us have peace with God") ; v. 9 (" being now justified by his blood, shall we be saved") ; Rom. viii. 30 (" he also justified ") ; 1 Cor. vi. 11 (" but ye were justified ").

(3) The terms "save" and "salvation" are used in such a way that it is often impossible to say whether the salvation is thought of as something past, as present and progressive, or as wholly future. But in some places it is clearly one or other of these. Normally, we may say, it is something future, and is so far something distinct from reconciliation : so in Rom. v. 9 (" Much more then, being now justified by his blood, shall we be saved from the wrath of God through him "). In the next verse (quoted on p. 124) it will be observed that, while reconciliation is attributed to the death of Christ, future salvation is said to be due to His life. This probably does not mean the influence of Christ's life on earth but the action or influence of the risen Lord. So 1 Cor. x. 33. To be saved means to be acquitted at the judgement. This appears very distinctly in 1 Cor. v. 5 (" that the spirit may be saved in the day of the Lord Jesus ") and 1 Cor. iii. 15. But in 1 Cor. i. 18 Christians are spoken of as persons who are "being saved" (σωζόμενοι). So 1 Cor. xv. 2 (" by which also ye are being saved . . . if ye hold fast "). St. Paul clearly thought of salvation as a process which begins now and is completed at the judgement. The only instance in which salvation is spoken of as something which has already taken place is in the later Epistle, Eph. ii. 8, "by grace have ye been saved (ἐστε σεσωσμένοι) through faith."

(4) The term redemption (ἀπολύτρωσις) is occasionally used in much

---

[1] *Doctrine of the Atonement*, p. 11 *note*.

the same sense as salvation, but here there is naturally a more distinct reference to the price paid by Christ rather than to the resulting state of those whom He saves. In Gal. iv. 4, 5 we are told that "God sent forth his Son . . . that he might redeem them which were under the law, that we might receive the adoption of sons." The bondage from which the Galatians had been set free is explained as the bondage "to them which by nature are no gods" (*i.e.* probably, in St. Paul's view, to evil spirits worshipped as gods). In Rom. iii. 24 Christians are said to be "justified freely by his grace through the redemption that is in Christ Jesus." In Rom. viii. 23 he speaks of them as "waiting for our adoption, the redemption of our body." Here, as in several other places, the work of Christ (nothing is said as to what part of that work) is thought of as actually producing or causing immortality by its direct action—a thought enormously emphasized and developed by later Greek theology. In these cases the redemption is clearly future : it takes place at the judgement. So in Eph. i. 7 we read "in whom we have our redemption through his blood, the forgiveness of our trespasses." Here the redemption might be thought of as something already accomplished, but it is more probable that "we have" means that it is already secured to us. In Eph. i. 14 and iv. 30 ("the day of redemption") it is undoubtedly future. In 1 Cor. i. 30 Christ is said to have been "made unto us wisdom from God, and righteousness and sanctification, and redemption" where redemption may actually be supposed to come last, and to be the consequence of the preceding justification and sanctification.

It would seem then that no very precise distinction is made between the use of all these terms : they are aspects or stages of one and the same process. Primarily they all refer to the acquittal at the judgement and entrance into the Kingdom which Christ's work will secure for believers, but all may be used to indicate the present status of believers and the moral effects of that status. These moral effects—the deliverance from actual sinfulness—are particularly prominent in the case of "salvation" : and in this case the effect of Christ's work is definitely looked upon as a gradual process but one fully completed only at the judgement. The term "sanctification" still more definitely refers to the moral effects : and here the possibility of a less or more naturally becomes most prominent. But justification and sanctification are not as sharply distinguished as in later Protestant theology. They are so closely connected that no definite distinction of time can be supposed to be made between them, although "justification" is more closely connected with immediate forgiveness, sanctification more explicitly with the continuing process. "But ye were sanctified, but ye were justified" (1 Cor. vi. 11) : here justification is put last ; in 1 Cor. i. 30 "sanctification" is mentioned before "redemption." In both cases sanctification is treated as belonging to the past. In 1 Thess. iv. 3 it is progressive and future : "This is the will of God, even your sanctification." So 1 Thess. v. 23 ("sanctify you wholly"), and Eph. v. 26 ("that he might sanctify it, having cleansed it by the washing of water with the word").

NOTE B

ST. PAUL'S CHRISTOLOGY

The question of St. Paul's Christology lies beyond the scope of these Lectures, but it will be convenient to notice a few points in it which have a bearing upon our subject. (1) St. Paul thought of Jesus as the Messiah, and therefore, in his view of what Messiahship meant, a heavenly Being, the Son of God, who existed with the Father before His manifestation on earth (Rom. viii. 32 ; more distinctly in Phil. ii. 5-7). Nothing is said as to whether the pre-existence was eternal or had a beginning. The world was made and is governed "through Him" (Rom. xi. 36 ; Col. i. 17 ; 1 Cor. viii. 6).

(2) Jesus is always very sharply distinguished from the Father. "For us there is one God, the Father, . . . and one Lord, Jesus Christ" (1 Cor. viii. 6).

(3) Christ is very closely associated with the Father e.g., in benedictions, and is altogether so exalted and supernatural a Being that we may well say with M. Goguel that for St. Paul "il y a en Christ quelque chose de divin." The strongest unquestionable statements of St. Paul on this head are that "God was in Christ, reconciling the world unto himself" (2 Cor. v. 19), and (later) that "in him dwelleth all the fulness of the Godhead bodily" (Col. ii. 9 ; cf. i. 19).

There is no place in which He is certainly called God, though it is not quite impossible that in the passage "who is over all, God blessed for ever" (Rom. ix. 5), the last words do refer to Christ and are not a separate sentence.[1]

(4) Christ is everywhere thought of as subordinate to God the Father, and St. Paul, at least at one period of his thought, looked forward to a time when "the Son shall also himself be subjected to him that did subject all things unto him, that God may be all in all" (1 Cor. xv. 28). The period during which Christ was the Vicegerent of God in the rule of the universe would have an end. This conception would be difficult to reconcile with the Christology of the later Epistles. It is impossible, however, to treat Phil. ii. 6 (οὐκ ἁρπαγμὸν ἡγήσατο τὸ εἶναι ἴσα Θεῷ) as implying divinity or equality with the Father. It is distinctly implied that He is *not* equal to the Father ; His condescension consisted just in this—that (unlike the rebellious angels) He did not aspire to this absolute equality, but on the contrary descended below His true position by voluntarily becoming man or at least appearing in the "likeness of men." It is implied that He was only just below, but not equal to, God.

(5) It is important to note the difference between St. Paul's position and that of the later fully developed Logos theology. In St. Paul Christ did not, as that theology holds, pre-exist as a Being who was God but not man, and then become a Being who was both God and

---

[1] Titus ii. 13 is probably translated rightly (by R.V.) : " Our great God and Saviour Jesus Christ." In 1 Tim. iii. 16 the right reading is certainly ὅς, not Θεός.

Man. It was "the heavenly man" that pre-existed, or (what is for him the same thing) a Spirit—perhaps with a glorious or heavenly body—a body of a fine, celestial quality. (This idea is attributed to him by Johannes Weiss, and not without probability, on the analogy of the "spiritual body" with which the redeemed are to be clothed, but there is no passage which absolutely justifies this attribution.) There is in St. Paul no distinction between the human (yet superhuman) Jesus and the pre-existent Son of God. And this implies that St. Paul could not attribute to Him such an identity with God as the later doctrine of the Trinity (*e.g.* in St. Augustine and St. Thomas Aquinas) postulated. Germs of this later theology can be detected side by side with ideas which might naturally be developed into Arianism ; but St. Paul would never have accepted, and would not have understood, the idea that the Father and the Son are but one single Consciousness —"una mens," in the language of St. Augustine. A Trinity (subject to the reserves mentioned above) we can discover in him but not an "undivided Trinity."

(6) St. Paul sometimes identifies the Son with the Spirit (1 Cor. xv. 45 ; 2 Cor. iii. 17), and practically, especially in the Epistle to Colossians and the other later Epistles, attributes to Him the functions of the Stoic or the Philonian Logos. (The word is not used, though he has the Philonian term εἰκών.) At other times the Spirit is placed side by side with God and Christ (1 Cor. xii. 3 *sq.* ; 2 Cor. xiii. 14). This shows how far his Christology is from being a completely thought-out system. The explanation of the ambiguity seems to be that where Christ is thought of as a historical Person, a human (though now glorified) Being, He is distinguished from that indwelling influence which is for him equally the Spirit of God and the Spirit of Christ (Rom. viii. 9, 11 ; Gal. iv. 6 ; Phil. i. 19). On the other hand where Christ is thought of as either a pre-existent Being or as the source of the indwelling influence in human souls, the Spirit can be absolutely identified with the Christ or Son of God. Thus he can equally speak of "Christ in us" (Rom. viii. 9), of the Spirit of God (identified in the same verse with the Spirit of Christ, Rom. viii. 9), or of "the supply of the Spirit of Jesus Christ" (Phil. i. 19). The identification of the Logos or Son with the Spirit is of course found also in some of the earlier Fathers.

(7) The clue to St. Paul's Christology is to be found in the Christology of later Judaism. "Recently, as against this view [that St. Paul arrived at his Christology by independent reflection on the appearance of the Risen Christ to himself] Wrede and Brückner have conclusively shown that Paul, before his conversion, held the belief as a Pharisee, that the Messiah existed from all eternity with God in heaven ; he looked with longing for the day when God should reveal His Son, and with passionate energy put forth his whole strength, to realize that righteousness which alone could bring down the Christ from heaven. Then, in the moment that Jesus appeared before him in the shining glory of His risen existence, Paul identified Him with his own Christ, and straightway transferred to Jesus all the conceptions

which he already had of the celestial being—for instance that he had existed before the world, and had taken part in its creation." [1] To regard these apocalyptic ideas as the main source of St. Paul's Christology, is quite consistent with recognizing that he may have been directly or indirectly influenced also (1) by Philo or other representatives of Alexandrian Judaism, (2) by the Stoic conception of the Logos which a native of Tarsus must have imbibed with the air he breathed, (3) and perhaps to some extent by the ideas embodied in the "Hermetic Literature," as to which see Reitzenstein, *Poimandres*, p. 330 *sq*.

The question that interests us here is how far St. Paul's conception of the atonement was connected with his Christology, and to this question a quite definite answer can be given. Many later atonement-theories (*e.g.* the views of St. Athanasius or St. Anselm) St. Paul could not have held, for there is in him no such absolute identification of Christ with God, and no such distinction between the human and the divine element in Him, as these theories presuppose. On the other hand the theory of pre-existence as a heavenly and glorious Being is vital to his thought. For it is the condescension of this heavenly Being in voluntarily coming down to earth and assuming human flesh, the flesh of sin—in a way which nevertheless did not involve personal sinfulness on His part—which enabled God, by allowing Him to be crucified, to condemn " sin in the flesh," *i.e.* to punish with death the flesh which in Adam and his posterity had sinned. And it is this love and humility which call forth that fervent and adoring gratitude which is the source of all the subjective effects of belief in Christ in himself and other believers.

In two directions these considerations will be of great importance when we ask how far St. Paul's doctrine of the atonement can be accepted by those whose conception of Christ and His relation to the Father is different from St. Paul's : (*a*) We must remember that there could not be such an *isolation* of Christ's *death* from other aspects of His work as is responsible for the worst features in some later theories. Even when St. Paul seems to dwell exclusively upon " the death of the cross," the thought of the voluntary descent from heaven and the whole life of obedience and humiliation is always there in the background (he became obedient *even to the point of death*, μέχρι θανατοῦ, Phil. ii. 8, but not only in death). Equally little is the thought of Christ's death ever separated from the thought of the resurrection and exaltation of Christ and all the effects of that resurrection upon the redeemed. "We shall understand Paul's thought only if we remember that when he speaks of the death of Christ, the resurrection is at the same time always in his mind. Every one of his declarations concerning the death of Christ really means death turned by the resurrection into triumph." [2] And (*b*) we must remember that orthodox dogmatic thought has not accepted, nor can any modern philosophical re-interpretation of that thought accept, such an absolute separation of the pre-existent heavenly Being from God the Father, and such a

---

[1] Johannes Weiss, *Christ : the Beginnings of Dogma*, p. 63.
[2] Johannes Weiss, *lib. cit.* p. 109.

K

subordination of Him to the Father, as we find in St. Paul. St. Paul's theology is only saved from Di-theism (in so far as he looks upon Christ as in any sense divine) by his thorough-going Subordinationism. How far this consideration requires modification in a modern inter-pretation of the atonement, I shall consider in my last Lecture.

NOTE C

ON ST. PAUL'S USE OF PROPITIATION (ἱλαστήριον) IN ROMANS III. 25

The one passage in which St. Paul uses the word ἱλαστήριον of Christ has played such a large part in controversies upon the subject that it seems desirable to deal with it in somewhat greater detail than has been possible in the Lecture.

The adjective ἱλαστήριος means "propitiatory" : the substantive ἱλαστήριον means a propitiatory sacrifice or propitiation. Attempts have been made to connect the meaning of the word in St. Paul with its use in the LXX. for the "mercy-seat." The facts about this use seem to be as follows. The word ἱλαστήριον occurs in Ex. xxv. 17, where the Hebrew has the words, "and thou shalt make a *Kappōreth* [A.V. mercy-seat] of pure gold." *Kappōreth* means a cover, and it has sometimes been supposed that it is used here to imply that this piece of ritual furniture had the effect of covering sin. It seems, however, that its real meaning was simply "the cover or lid of the Ark." The LXX. translators understood it in this way, and rendered it by ἐπίθεμα, but they added the *adjective* ἱλαστήριον as a theological explanation of the term : καὶ ποιήσεις ἱλαστήριον ἐπίθεμα χρυσίου καθαροῦ, which may be translated "a propitiatory cover" or "a cover of use for propitiation." But in other passages they use the substantive ἱλαστήριον as an equivalent for this Ark-covering. "The word is now," says Dillman,[1] "a substantive and signifies something like *propitiatory article*. It does not mean *cover*, nor even *propitiatory cover*, but for the concept *cover* it substitutes another, which only expresses the ceremonial purpose of the article. The *Kappōreth* was for the translators a 'symbol of the divine mercy,' σύμβολον τῆς ἵλεω τοῦ θεοῦ δυνάμεως, as Philo, *De Vit. Mos.* iii. 8 (ed. Cohn), speaking from the same theological standpoint, explains it, and therefore they named this symbol ἱλαστήριον." The LXX. word is the source of Luther's translation "Gnadenstuhl," whence no doubt the "mercy-seat" of Tyndale and our present English Bible.

Was this use of ἱλαστήριον consciously present to the mind of St. Paul? Ritschl vehemently asserted that it was,[2] and interprets it as meaning in St. Paul "propitiatory sacrifice." Prof. Deissmann with equal vehemence denies this, and supposes it to be used (as in many Greek inscriptions) to mean simply "votive-gift." The question does not seem to me as important as these writers make it. Deissmann does not

---

[1] *Bible Studies*, E.T., Ed. 2, p. 126.
[2] *Die Christliche Lehre von der Rechtfertigung*, ii., 1889, p. 171.

deny that votive-gifts were intended to win favours of a god. It is important to notice that no sacrifices were offered on the *Kapporeth*, and we must put away altogether the notion that in using the term St. Paul was definitely treating Christ or His death as a "cover" for the sins of men (a very favourite idea of Luther's). But the *Kapporeth* was sprinkled with blood on the great day of atonement, and this association can hardly have been altogether absent from the mind of St. Paul. It is probable that we cannot entirely get rid of the idea of "propitiation" (in its ordinary sense) from St. Paul's use of the term, and we cannot define his meaning more accurately than by the use of this term. Nevertheless Deissmann is no doubt right in insisting that the emphasis of the passage is upon the fact that God has of His free favour provided the means for enabling men to approach Him, not upon the sacrificial character of the means by which that approach is to be effected.

It may be well to quote the whole passage in which St. Paul uses the term :

"But now apart from the law a righteousness of God hath been manifested, being witnessed by the law and the prophets" [notice how St. Paul betrays the source of his theory] ; "even the righteousness of God through faith in Jesus Christ unto all them that believe ; for there is no distinction ; for all have sinned, and fall short of the glory of God ; being justified freely by his grace through the redemption that is in Christ Jesus : whom God set forth [1] to be a propitiation, through faith, by his blood, to shew his righteousness, because of the passing over of the sins done aforetime, in the forbearance of God ; for the shewing, I say, of his righteousness at this present season : that he might himself be just, and the justifier of him that hath faith in Jesus " (Rom. iii. 21-26).

No doubt the main thought here is that the goodness or righteousness of God is shown in His free forgiveness of sins, that the sentence of acquittal which God passes upon the believer, and the real goodness which He imparts to him, are due to God's mercy, not to man's merits. But it is clear that St. Paul thinks of Christ's death as the means graciously provided by God for enabling Him thus to pass over sin ; and it is therefore impossible to exclude the thought that God's righteousness is also shown in exacting the penalty for sin by sending His Son to die, and accepting His death in lieu of the deaths of those who have really sinned. The way in which this substitution could be effected, and how it was consistent with the justice of God, is not explained, simply because for St. Paul it rested upon authority—the authority of Scripture. He was content to take it as a revealed objective fact "witnessed by the law and the prophets." The following interpretation of Weinel seems to me amply justified :

"Of all the many interpretations which are rendered possible through the manifold meanings which are borne by the words and the compressed style of the sentence, it seems to me that the following

---

[1] προέθετο. Weinel, *St. Paul*, p. 306, wants to translate "purposed" ; this seems possible but not necessary.

translation is still the best: 'Whom God chose as a propitiatory (sacrifice) through his blood by means of faith.' That is to say: God's character is indeed love and compassion. He shows His love to us in that ' while we were still sinners Christ died for us.' He loves men : though, were He to regard their actual condition, they must be ' enemies ' to Him, *i.e.* hated, 'vessels of His wrath,' and not of His love. But His love wished to help them and reconcile them to Himself. Simple forgiveness of sins was not, however, possible for God. He was bound to show His justice, which mankind might begin to doubt, since for so long a time He had sent no flood upon sinners, but had apparently looked on at sin unmoved. This justice would be satisfied either by punishment or by a propitiation ; God's love could not admit of punishment ; a propitiation was therefore the only possible alternative." [1]

It seems hardly worth while to discuss (as has often been done) what particular form of sacrifice St. Paul was thinking of in the other particular passages where sacrificial language is used. Pfleiderer reminds us "that the Mosaic law provided sin-offerings and guilt-offerings for lesser offences but not for mortal sins, that there was no sacrifice within the legal order which could make atonement for, and dispense from punishment." [2] "At the same time," he adds, "it cannot be doubted that the general conception of sacrifice is in no way foreign to St. Paul's doctrine of redemption, but in some form or other underlies all passages where the blood of Christ is mentioned." The sacrificial idea which underlay St. Paul's conceptions was rather the general sacrificial idea common to the whole ancient world than any definite theory about the efficacy of sacrifice contained in the Mosaic Law. It should, I think, be added that, as soon as St. Paul begins to theorize about forgiveness, his ideas become juridical rather than sacrificial.

It is worth noticing that the middle ($\dot{\iota}\lambda\dot{\alpha}\sigma\kappa\epsilon\sigma\theta\alpha\iota$) is hardly ever in the LXX., and never in the New Testament, used with God as its accusative, but with accusative of the sin as in Heb. ii. 17 ($\tau\dot{\alpha}s\ \dot{\alpha}\mu\alpha\rho\tau\dot{\iota}\alpha s$) or of the object cleansed, or with dative of the sin or the person, or with $\pi\epsilon\rho\dot{\iota}$, etc. See additional note on 1 John ii. 2 in Westcott's *Commentary.* " Such phrases," says the Bishop, " as ' propitiating God ' and God ' being reconciled ' are foreign to the language of the N. Test. Man is reconciled (2 Cor. v. 18 ff. ; Rom. v. 10 f.)."

In conclusion I may remark that 4 Macc. (xvii. 22) speaks of the martyrs as having been made "an equivalent ($\dot{\alpha}\nu\tau\dot{\iota}\psi\nu\chi o\nu$) for the sin of the people and it is by the blood of those righteous men [the martyrs] and by their expiatory death that the divine Providence saved Israel " ($\tau o\hat{\nu}\ \dot{\iota}\lambda\alpha\sigma\tau\eta\rho\dot{\iota}o\nu\ \theta\alpha\nu\dot{\alpha}\tau o\nu\ \alpha\dot{\nu}\tau\hat{\omega}\nu\ \ldots\ \delta\iota\dot{\epsilon}\sigma\omega\sigma\epsilon\nu$). If, as is highly probable, this was the source of St. Paul's thought and expression, the questions discussed above hardly arise. The general idea of sacrifice lies behind the application of it to the death whether of the martyrs or of the Messiah, but there is no definite theory as to why there should be a need of propitiation or how this need was satisfied by the death of Christ.

[1] *St. Paul*, E.T., pp. 305-6.
[2] *Primitive Christianity*, i. 337.

NOTE D

ON ROMANS V. (THE EFFECTS OF ADAM'S SIN)

Two main views may be taken of the classical passage, Rom. v. 12 :
(1) It may be understood to mean that St. Paul holds that Adam
sinned, and as a consequence the penalty of death was inflicted both
on him and on his posterity. " For that all sinned" will then mean
" All sinned, constructively or collectively *in Adam*," and therefore all
suffered the penalty, though from Adam to Moses many (or all) did
not actually sin. Nevertheless they all suffered the penalty, just as all
obtain life through Christ, though they had personally done nothing to
deserve it. (Cf. 2 Cor. v. 14 : " One died for all, therefore all died.")
(2) It may be held that St. Paul means that, as a consequence of
Adam's transgression, all were born sinful, and consequently sinned,
though as they, unlike Adam, had not received any express command,
their sin was not so grievous : they had not sinned in the same
deliberate and wilful manner as Adam, and consequently sin could not
be imputed to them personally in the same sense as it was to Adam.

In either case ἐφ' ᾧ must certainly mean " because," and not "in
whom " referring to Adam : though the Latin mistranslation "in quo "
may almost be said to be the foundation-stone of the Augustinian
theology.[1]

As an instance of the first view I may quote Pfleiderer, who makes
the universal sinfulness purely constructive. He says (on Rom. v. 14) :
" The difficulty here lies in the juxtaposition of two apparently
contradictory reasons assigned for the universal domination of death ;
on the one hand the one transgression of the one man Adam (οὕτως),
and on the other hand the transgression of all. . . . But in this hard
and unqualified juxtaposition of these two different reasons is contained
doubtless an indication that it was the Apostle's intention that they
should be regarded, *not as two different things, but as one and the same* ;
that, consequently, the *transgression of Adam at once and as such was also
the transgression of all.* Of course it is only possible to view the
matter thus by supposing that, through a certain moral or mystic
identity with Adam as the representative head of the race, all *were
made partakers* of his act." [2]

It seems to me probable that as a matter of mere grammatical
exegesis the first of these interpretations is nearer to St. Paul's thought
than the other. He thinks of the penalty (not merely the tendency
to sin hereafter) as collectively incurred by Adam's sin and collectively
punished by the mortality of his posterity. The whole point of the

---

[1] See note in Sanday and Headlam. It is surprising to find Sir W. Ramsay translating " in proportion as " (*Teaching of St. Paul in Terms of the Present Day*, p. 153).
To think of the penalty of death as something which could be endured less or more is
surely nonsense. St. Paul certainly means physical death.

[2] *Paulinism*, Eng. trans. 2nd ed., i. 39, 40. In the Second (German) Edition he
adopts the second view.

involved sentences in verses 14 and 15 is that universal death is not accounted for by the personal sins of all individuals. The second view gives no meaning to the "Nevertheless." At the same time, looking to St. Paul's argument as a whole and to his doctrine elsewhere, I cannot believe that he thought of Adam's posterity as actually innocent. That would ruin his whole argument : he no more thought of man's sinfulness as *merely* constructive than he thought of his justification and salvation through Christ as merely "imputed"— as leaving him morally just where he was before. He is trying to establish an actual universal sinfulness. The introduction of Adam's fall would be irrelevant unless he thought of it as explaining and causing this universal sinfulness. The statement "even unto those who had not sinned," etc., may be taken (as it is by those who hold the second view) to mean that, though they may have done sinful acts, the men from Adam to Moses were not guilty in the same sense as Adam (St. Paul would in that case seem almost to have forgotten the doctrine of Natural Law expressed in the first chapter). Or he may have thought (this was a favourite idea with many Jewish writers as with the Pelagians) that some few of the virtuous patriarchs were actually sinless. The two views can easily be combined. He may have thought of the men before Moses as mostly sinning, but not having their sins imputed to them on account of the absence of positive divine command, while some few of them contrived to be relatively or even absolutely virtuous. All were sinful but in a smaller degree and a different sense than those who came after Moses. The law made obedience more difficult, and sin more guilty. This is its precise function in verse 20 : "the law came in beside, that the trespass might abound." Sin was universal in a sense even before Moses, but it was increased by the coming of the law and the disobedience to it.

In the earlier Jewish anticipations of the fall-doctrine, we find frequent traces of *exceptions* to the universal sinfulness : it was thought that sinful tendencies might be overcome by exceptional heroism or divine favour. Thus there was a Jewish story that when the angel of service asked God if Moses and Aaron had not kept the whole law, and yet had died like Adam, God answered in the words of Eccles. ix. 2, "All things come alike to all : there is one event to the righteous and to the wicked." But the authority of Rabbi Simeon b. Eleazar is then claimed by Ammi : "Moses and Aaron also died in their own sins."[1] This implies that some excepted Moses and Aaron from the universal tendency. So in 2 (4) Esdras vii. [48] the "evil heart" is said to have infected "*well-nigh* all that have been created." It must be remembered that most Jewish writers who exhibit approximations to the doctrine of original sin attempt to combine it with the theory of free-will. In St. Paul the admission of exceptions seems inconsistent with his doctrine of universal sinfulness, but after all he does not say that even the few pre-Mosaic good men did not sin at all—only they did not sin as Adam did.

---

[1] Tennant, *The Fall and Original Sin*, p. 164.

I must acknowledge great obligations to the discussion of this passage (and the whole subject) by Dr. Tennant in *The Sources of the Doctrines of the Fall and Original Sin.* I confess that I cannot quite understand the view which he ultimately attributes to St. Paul, but on all that concerns the Jewish origins of the doctrine his book is a mine of learning.

M. Goguel [1] thinks it probable that for St. Paul the narrative of the fall was "only an allegorical story of the idolatry of primitive men," but he does not deny that St. Paul thought of it as historical, and therefore the "only" seems hardly justified. In some cases a story may be historically true and yet also allegorical (M. Goguel cites the case of Hagar) ; but I cannot see how this can be so here. In Hagar's case the literal narrative has no spiritual meaning ; in Adam's case the narrative has no meaning apart from the spiritual interpretation : the disobedience, if it took place, was itself a sin. It might be taken as typical of other sins, especially idolatry ; but it could not be "only an allegorical story" except to one who believed it to be unhistorical. It is true that, in spite of the letter of Scripture, there was a strong disposition to understand the sin of Eve as sexual transgression with the serpent or (more rarely) with Adam ; but still that sin is supposed to be an historical event. There is no doubt that this was the meaning of the legends which lie at the back of the biblical story : Gen. i., ii. and vi.—another development—come from the same source.

NOTE E

JEWISH VIEWS OF THE FALL AND ORIGINAL SIN

For a full account of the Jewish antecedents of the doctrine of the fall as expounded by St. Paul and later Christian theology, the reader must be referred to Dr. Tennant's learned and profoundly interesting book on *The Fall and Original Sin*, and Thackeray's *The Relation of St. Paul to Contemporary Jewish Thought*, but a few main facts, for which I am almost wholly indebted to Dr. Tennant, may be noted here :

(1) There are passages in the Old Testament which in a quite vague and undogmatic manner suggest a universal sinful tendency in human nature. Such passages are Gen. iv. 5 *sq.*, vi. 5, 13, viii. 21, where it is said that "the imagination (*Yezer*) of man's heart is evil from his youth " ; which was perhaps the origin of the later doctrine that there was in the heart of man an inborn tendency to evil (*Yezer hara*). The idea that no one can be absolutely pure before God occurs in Job and elsewhere (Job iv. 17, "Shall mortal man be just before God," R.V. margin ; xiv. 4, xxv. 4 ; Prov. xx. 9 ; 1 Kings viii. 46 ; 2 Chron. vi. 36 ; Eccles. vii. 20 ; Ps. cxxx. 3 ; Jer. xvii. 9). And sometimes we have the idea that man is sinful from his birth (Job xv. 14, 15 ; Ps. li. 5), but this is perhaps only rhetorically meant.

---

[1] *L'Apôtre Paul et Jésus-Christ*, p. 156.

This sinful tendency is nowhere connected with the fall-story, and nowhere amounts to an incapacity for good.

(2) There are traces of the idea that the sin of man not only began with, but was caused by, the fall of Adam, in Ecclesiasticus : "From a woman was the beginning of sin ; and because of her we all die" (ἀπὸ γυναικὸς ἀρχὴ ἁμαρτίας, καὶ δι' αὐτὴν ἀποθνήσκομεν πάντες, xxv. 24). The word ἀρχή is ambiguous : it may mean "beginning" or "origin." Since the discovery of the original Hebrew, however, it appears that the original word (*teḥillah*) has a "predominantly temporal sense." [1] How far the writer traces the mortality of man to the sin of Adam is disputed ; but such seems to be the *prima facie* meaning of the above passage. In any case "he certainly believed an evil disposition to have been inherent in man from the first, and regarded this inclination, which the individual can still coerce by free-will and devotion to the law, as the source of his sinfulness." [2] This *Yezer hara* is thought of as implanted by God, and not as due to Adam's fall.

(3) In Wisdom ii. 23, 24 we read "Because God created man for incorruption, and made him an image of his own proper being : but by the envy of the devil death entered into the world." Dr. Tennant doubts whether this passage is to be accepted as an assertion of the writer's belief in pre-existence (cf. viii. 19, 20) and immortality (cf. iii. 1-4). He takes ii. 24 to mean "spiritual or eternal death." There is no doubt a difficulty in reconciling the conflicting statements ; but the simplest solution seems to be that he thought that only the good were immortal (as God intended all men to be). The Canaanites are treated as inherently bad on account of Noah's curse (xii. 1-11), which shows that the idea of hereditary sinfulness was not uncongenial to the author of "Wisdom."

(4) Philo allegorizes the fall-story : the serpent represents sensuous pleasure ; the death incurred by Adam is spiritual death. The soul is naturally immortal : the body and the animal soul are naturally mortal. There is a tendency to regard man as necessarily weak and sinful on account of his bodily nature, but this is not connected with the fall of Adam, and Philo strongly asserts free-will (παντὶ γενητῷ . . . συμφυὲς τὸ ἁμαρτάνειν, *De Vita Mosis*, iii. 17 : ἐπεὶ δ' οὐδὲν τῶν ἐν γένεσει βέβαιον, τροπὰς δὲ καὶ μεταβολὰς ἀναγκαίως τὰ θνητὰ δέχεται, ἐχρῆν καὶ τὸν πρῶτον ἄνθρωπον ἀπολαῦσαί τινος κακοπραγίας, *De Mundi Opif.* 53).

(5) The rabbinical sayings in the Talmud and Mishna contain all sorts of views and fancies about the fall of Adam, which cannot be reproduced here. The belief that the death of his posterity was due to Adam's sin is frequent. Indications of a belief in inherited sinfulness are less clear. But "in the period in which the New Testament was written, the conception of the evil inclination must have been definite and widespread, for it had been known to Ben Sira on the one hand, and it was a commonplace with the Tanaim on the other." [3]

---

[1] Tennant, p. 112.   [2] Tennant, p. 116.   [3] Tennant, p. 169.

This tendency is generally thought of as divinely implanted in Adam. It is usually unconnected with the fall of Adam, but in the second recension of Aboth di R. Nathan, c. 41 (ed. Schlechter), it is said that the seventh of the punishments decreed against Adam was : "There shall be in him the *Yezer hara*." [1] This doctrine was not interpreted in such a way as to exclude free-will.

(6) Much the same state of opinion is revealed by the various Jewish Apocalypses ; but there are rather more traces of an advance towards a definite doctrine of original sin. In the ground-work of the book of Enoch (2nd cent. B.C.) there is a doctrine of the fall of angels built up upon Gen. vi., and it adopts that explanation of the origin of evil among men (lxxxiv. 4). The Greek Apocalypse of Moses makes Eve's sin the cause not only of death but of sinfulness to her posterity (x., xiv., xxxii.) ; but the Armenian version does not necessarily mean more than Ben Sira's "from a woman was the beginning of sin." [2]

There are two versions of the Sclavonic "Secrets of Enoch." In one of them (Recension A), but not in the other, we have a quite definite doctrine of hereditary sinfulness arising from Adam's fall. In cxl. 1 *sq.* we read, "And I saw all our forefathers from the beginning with Adam and Eve, and I sighed and wept, and spake of the ruin (caused by) their wickedness : Woe is me for my infirmity and that of my forefathers. And I meditated in my heart and said : ' Blessed is the man who was not born, or, having been born, has never sinned before the face of the Lord, so that he should not come into this place, to bear the yoke of this place.' " This is, according to Dr. Tennant, the "earliest occurrence of the idea of inborn infirmity inherited from Adam, and a Jewish doctrine of Original Sin more explicit, and earlier, than the teaching of St. Paul upon the subject." [3] But it is not certain how much may be due to a Christian translator of the original Greek. The date of the work is supposed to be the first half of the first century A.D. It may be added that the writer makes the sin of Eve to be unchastity with Satan.

(7) If we put aside the Secrets of Enoch, the Jewish writings which show the most definite approach to the Christian teaching on the subject are two books both of which were written after 70 A.D. These books are the (Syriac) Apocalypse of Baruch (ed. Charles) and the Fourth (in our Apocrypha Second) Book of Esdras, extant in a Latin and various oriental translations. That Adam's sin involved death to his posterity is clearly taught in the Apocalypse of Baruch, xxiii. 4 : " Because when Adam sinned and death was decreed against those who should be born, then the multitude of those who should be born was numbered " [note the predestinarianism]. " Owing to his transgression untimely death came into being, and grief was named, and anguish was prepared, and pain was created . . ., and the begetting of children was brought about, etc." (lvi. 6 ; cf. xvii. 2-3, xlviii. 42-47). It is primarily death and misery that descend to Adam's posterity ;

---

[1] Tennant, p. 171.
[2] Tennant, p. 178. But this does not seem a natural interpretation.
[3] Tennant, p. 210.

there is no distinct statement that the general (but not universal) sinfulness of mankind is attributable to Adam, though that may be suggested. In any case the doctrine of an hereditary penalty is combined with a strong assertion of freedom and individual responsibility. "For though Adam first sinned and brought untimely death upon all, yet of those who were born from him each one of them has prepared for his own soul torment to come, and again each one of them has chosen for himself glories to come . . . Adam is therefore not the cause, save only of his own soul, but each of us has been the Adam of his own soul" (liv. 15, 19). This doctrine is probably intended as a correction of the teaching which we find in 4 (2) Esdras (iii. 4-8, vii. 11, 118, etc.) which develops a much more consistently deterministic doctrine of a fall of Adam involving original sin in his posterity, and also what looks like a Greek version of the Pharisaic belief in the *Yezer hara* or evil impulse which dwelt in man's body from the first : "For the first Adam bearing a wicked heart (*cor malignum*) transgressed and was overcome ; *and not he only*, but all they also that are born of him. Thus disease was made permanent ; and the law was in the heart of the people along with the wickedness of the root. So the good departed away, and that which was wicked abode still" (iii. 21, 22). Here then sin is increased by Adam's fall ; in the following passage the fall is itself due to *Yezer hara* : "For a grain of evil seed was sown in the heart of Adam from the beginning, and how much wickedness hath it brought forth unto this time" [iv. 30 ; cf. vii. 35, 48, 68 (in this last place universal sinfulness is definitely asserted), vii. 46, viii. 51]. So in vii. 118, "Oh, thou Adam, what hast thou done ? For though it was thou that sinned, the evil is not fallen on thee alone, but upon all of us that come of thee." In viii. 56 we have an assertion of "liberty," but there are many passages of a decidedly deterministic tone. Western philosophers would have no difficulty in reconciling the two doctrines, but it is not probable that there was any definite solution of the antinomy in the mind of the author. All we can say is that the emphasis is on the predestinarian side, as that of the Apocalypse of Baruch is on the free-will side, and this last may have been directed against the teaching of St. Paul.

The same divided attitude on the question of free-will and necessity is attributed to St. Paul by Mr. Thackeray.[1] He thinks that St. Paul simply puts together the two opposed views current in the Jewish schools (libertarian and predestinarian) without attempting to reconcile them. I cannot see any traces of a doctrine of indeterministic free-will (at least after the fall) in St. Paul except in the sense in which all libertarians discover such inconsistencies in the language of all determinists. Such exhortations as Rom. vi. 12 ("let not sin reign in your mortal bodies") could be found in the writings of every Augustinian and every modern determinist, and none of them would admit that there was any inconsistency.

Dr. Tennant[2] is disposed to deny any connexion between St.

---

[1] *The Relation of St. Paul to Contemporary Jewish Thought*, p. 33.
[2] *The Fall and Original Sin*, p. 265.

Paul's view and the *Yezer hara* on the ground that the doctrine regards this tendency as implanted in Adam by the Creator, while St. Paul seems to treat Adam's sin as wilful. But (1) St. Paul says nothing which is inconsistent with the view that such an evil impulse may have been the cause of Adam's fall, and (2) it is not suggested that St. Paul accepted the Jewish doctrine without any modification. The doctrine was extremely fluid, and assumed various forms. Originally the notion of a *Yezer hara* had nothing to do with the theory of a fall of Adam which involved the ruin of all mankind. But in later Jewish thought (especially 4 Esdras) the two theories seem to have a tendency to coalesce. 4 Esdras is the work which exhibits the closest approximation to the doctrine of St. Paul. All the materials for St. Paul's doctrine are to be found in the Jewish thought of his age, but of course *his* doctrine of original and universal sin could not—logically at all events—be held by an orthodox Jew. To hold a doctrine of absolutely universal sinfulness without a remedy would be to admit that God's promises to Israel had failed. To admit that men could be righteous otherwise than by observing the law would be to go beyond strict Judaism, though doubtless Jewish teachers often insisted on the mercifulness of God. It was just because St. Paul's opinions or his experience forced on him the conception of universal and inevitable sinfulness that he was driven to the idea of a righteousness which did not spring from such observance ; or (quite as probably) his belief in a salvation which did not come from the law left him free to push to extremes tendencies which were already at work in Judaism, but which a consistent Jewish thinker could hardly develope to the full. St. Paul could make sinfulness universal, just because he believed in a remedy which was equally open to all.

The really important matter for us is not to determine exactly how much of St. Paul's doctrine was actually to be found in any particular Jewish teacher, but to take note that all the questions which St. Paul discusses were matters of common controversy in the Jewish schools. It is probable that no feature of St. Paul's doctrine was without its supporters except so far as his faith in Christ differentiated his whole position from that of any Jew. None of the writers quoted were so decidedly anti-Pelagian and deterministic as St. Paul ; even Esdras only maintains that few are saved : the *Yezer hara* does not seem to be irresistible (vii. 92). But from the polemic of Baruch in favour of free-will it seems clear that there were some who denied it, and it is not probable that he was thinking *only* of St. Paul and his followers.

NOTE F

THE ESCHATOLOGY OF ST. PAUL

I have thought it best not to interrupt the argument of Lecture II. by dwelling upon the details of St. Paul's eschatology, since they do not really affect his attitude towards the main question here discussed, *i.e.* his doctrine of salvation through the death of Christ. Nevertheless, it may be well briefly to call attention to the nature of his doctrine of the last things, if only in order to illustrate the fact that a vast gulf is fixed between his real teaching and those who in modern times have made the loudest professions of accepting that teaching to the letter.

The details of the eschatology varied at different times. It was the belief of St. Paul, as of the Church generally, that Christ would come again in a startling, supernatural manner, deliver or save all Christian believers and admit them to a glorious immortality, while supernatural pains and penalties would fall upon the rest of the world. So much was the Christian hope of immortality associated with this personal coming of Christ that in Thessalonica some were anxious about the fate of those who had the misfortune to die before the Parousia. Hence St. Paul found it necessary to declare that those who were then alive would have no advantage or precedence over deceased Christians. The dead in Christ would rise first. Then those which were alive would be "caught up in the clouds, to meet the Lord in the air" (1 Thess. iv. 17), and would be ever with the Lord. Here nothing is said as to the fate of those who are not saved. In 2 Thessalonians it is explained that before the Parousia comes there must first be a revelation of the "lawless one, whom the Lord Jesus shall slay with the breath of his mouth" (ii. 8). His coming is declared to be "with all deceit of unrighteousness for them that are perishing ($\tau o \hat{i}s$ $\dot{a}\pi o\lambda\lambda\upsilon\mu\acute{e}\nu o\iota s$, ii. 10) ; because they received not the love of the truth, that they might be saved." It is implied that these too will be "slain," or "destroyed," *i.e.* cease to exist.

In 1 Cor. xv. it is further implied that after the judgement there is to be a reign of Christ — presumably (to judge from indications given elsewhere as to the general belief of the Church, *e.g.* the Apocalypse of St. John) upon this earth. After this comes "the end when he shall deliver up the kingdom to God, even the Father" (1 Cor. xv. 24-27). "Then shall the Son also himself be subjected to him that did subject all things unto him, that God may be all in all" (1 Cor. xv. 28). In this process of subjecting all things under Him, there would be room for some punishment of the wicked besides immediate annihilation. But it seems to be implied that the punishment, whatever its nature, would be followed by extinction, while the saved would enter upon their full life of glory, presumably in heaven. Some punishment of the wicked before extinction seems to be implied in the statement of 2 Cor. v. 10 that "we must *all* be made manifest before the judgement-seat of Christ ; that each one may receive the things done in the body, according to what he hath done, whether it be good or bad." There is only one passage in St. Paul which suggests the possibility of an ultimate salvation for those who have not heard of, or who have rejected, Christ here, and that is the passage in which he hopes that all, or at least all Jews, will ultimately be saved (Rom. xi. 32). It may be that he is thinking of the future acceptance of so much of the nation as should live to be converted and accept Jesus as Messiah, but this is difficult to reconcile with the idea of a speedy Parousia. We must not expect to find in St. Paul a completely consistent theological system. The one thing that is perfectly plain about his view as to the fate of those rejected at the judgement is that there is no room in his thought for the idea of everlasting punishment.

It is evident that his argument would be greatly improved, and far more consistent with his conviction that the ultimate purpose of God is to have mercy upon all, if we did understand him to mean that the process of salvation might be begun or continued hereafter in some at least of those to whom Christ had not brought salvation in this life. Possibly, when he wrote Rom. xi., that thought was in his mind, but we can hardly attribute that view to him as a definite doctrine. Even if we do understand "All Israel shall be saved" to include both the spiritual Israelites and at least the good among the Israelites after the flesh, it is probable that St. Paul would still think of the fate of the wicked as ultimately annihilation. It must be remembered that, while all Pharisaic Jews were agreed as to the resurrection of the just, all sorts of beliefs were held as to the fate of the wicked.

NOTE G

ON ST. PAUL'S LATER DOCTRINE OF SALVATION

The account which has been given in Lecture II. of St. Paul's view of the atonement is chiefly based on the second group of his epistles—Romans, Galatians, 1 and 2 Corinthians. It seems desirable to add a few words as to the doctrine of salvation taught or implied in his later epistles. It must not be forgotten that the doctrine of the epistles to the Romans and Galatians was intended to serve a particular controversial purpose. The doctrine that justification depended upon the death of Christ appropriated by faith was thought out in St. Paul's mind as a solution of the problems connected with the obligation of the Mosaic Law. It supplied the basis for his answer to two questions— (1) the theoretical question why the Messiah died, and (2) the practical question why it was that the law was no longer binding—no longer to be observed by Gentiles, not in any strictly religious way binding even upon Jews. On the practical question St. Paul's view triumphed : even the Jewish section of the Church conceded the admissibility of the Gentiles to the Church. In St. Paul's later days the battle may have been largely won ; and, as the stress of this controversy was less felt, the prominence of the doctrine developed in the Epistle to the Romans and the others of the same group began to diminish. Of course he never gave up the fundamental idea—salvation through Christ's death, a salvation dependent upon God's free favour and to be attained through faith. But the emphasis on it becomes less, the antagonism between faith and works less violent ; the necessity of something besides faith was more and more impressed upon St. Paul's mind by experience.

Thus in the Epistle to the Philippians the voluntary death of Christ is insisted upon partly as an example of humility and unselfishness, partly as the ground of His subsequent exaltation to the right hand of God, which was the basis of all the Christian's hope for the future (ii. 5-11). The idea that salvation demands effort becomes more prominent. "God is the cause of your good will and your exertions," he tells his readers, "and that influence of His depends on His good pleasure, but all the same you must work out your own salvation" (ii. 12, 13). He still emphasizes the fact that his own hopes of salvation depend solely upon a righteousness which proceeds from God and is founded upon faith : but God's goodness is looked upon as a motive for perseverance. "I press on, if so be that I may apprehend that for which also I was apprehended by Christ Jesus" (iii. 12). The tendency of this epistle is towards the increased identification of the "imputed" righteousness of God with its moral effects (iii. 9-11)—a fact which has quite absurdly been made a ground for disputing the genuineness of the epistle, as if there might not just as well be a development in the Apostle's thought as in that of a disciple !

In the Epistle to the Colossians there occurs one of the strongest assertions of the retrospective effects of Christ's death, the passage about Christ "having blotted out the bond written in ordinances" (ii. 14). But here greater emphasis is laid upon the pre-existent supremacy of Christ and the revelation of God in His incarnation than upon the actual death. Here the Apostle is warning his readers against a form of Judaism ; but it is not the Pharisaic Judaism which would impose the Mosaic Law as a necessity of salvation ; rather a Jewish (possibly Essene) Gnosticism which insisted upon asceticism—asceticism going far beyond the requirements of the Mosaic Law. And these things are attacked not so much because to insist on them would involve the false principle of reliance upon works, but because of their spiritual uselessness for one who has appropriated the moral and spiritual results of Christ's death and resurrection. Throughout the epistle the knowledge attainable through Christ, and the moral effects of that knowledge, are more insisted upon than the forensic theory of justification. "Let the word of Christ dwell in you richly in all wisdom" (iii. 16). The fact that St. Paul could now think of his own sufferings as filling up "that which is lacking in the afflictions of Christ" (i. 24) seems to indicate an approach to a more ethical, and less juridical, way of thinking of the effects of Christ's death.

The general tone of the Epistle to the Ephesians is much the same, though the references to an Essene-Gnostic mode of thought are less explicit. The new feature in this epistle is the increased prominence of the idealized Church. The mystical or moral union with Christ which is prominent in every one of St. Paul's epistles here becomes more distinctly thought of as realized in the Christian society. The influence of Christ is so dependent upon that of His Church that the Church is regarded not only as His body but as His "fullness" ($\pi\lambda\dot{\eta}\rho\omega\mu\alpha$)—that without which Christ Himself (or the revelation of God in Him) would not be complete (i. 23).[1]   It would be perhaps too much to say that redemption is thought of as reaching the individual only through his union with the Church ; but this idea—hereafter to be enormously developed—is distinctly suggested by the epistle.

Throughout all this quite perceptible development there is absolutely no giving up of any one Pauline idea or formula, and therefore the existence of such a development constitutes no reason whatever for questioning the genuineness of the epistles.   The whole development exhibited in these epistles may be summed up by saying that the tendency is towards an insistence upon Christ's work as revelation rather than as retrospective atonement, and upon the moral effects of that revelation rather than upon the juridical acquittal which it effected. And here St. Paul points the way towards just the development of his doctrine which is required for those who would adapt his teaching to the needs of the modern Christian.   To a large extent, as we shall see, that development was worked out in the actual teaching of the later Church.

---

[1] Cf. Armitage Robinson, *Ephesians*, pp. 42 *sq.*, 255 *sq.*

LECTURE III

THE TEACHING OF PRIMITIVE CHRISTIANITY

Hereby know we love, because he laid down his life for us ; and we ought to lay down our lives for the brethren.—1 JOHN iii. 16.

LECTURE III

IN my last lecture I tried to show that the true origin of the doctrine of atonement through the death of Christ, unknown to the teaching of our Lord Himself, is to be found in those passages of Jewish prophecy—especially the great fifty-third chapter of Isaiah—which seemed to speak of a Messiah who should suffer and die for the sins of His people. The doctrine was at first accepted simply and solely upon authority; and for that reason it was accepted without explanation. It was accepted as a fact revealed, in the strictest and most supernatural sense, to the prophets. There was no generally received theory as to the reasons which made the death of Christ a necessity, or as to the way in which that death secured forgiveness to the sinner. I have endeavoured to show that this view of its origin is supported by St. Paul's express declaration that he had received as part of the traditional creed of the Church the doctrine that "Christ died for our sins according to the scriptures," and by the fact that, in so far as he gives reasons for the belief, those · reasons are simply citations from Scripture. I shall hope in the present lecture to show you that this view is strongly confirmed by a study of the earliest Christian literature outside St. Paul.

Everywhere in that literature importance is attached to the death of Christ, though hardly that paramount importance which is ascribed to it by St. Paul and the later theology which exaggerates even the teaching of St. Paul. And as to the way in which it is spoken of we may notice three things :

147

(1) Wherever in these writings there is anything which suggests the idea of a substituted punishment or an expiatory sacrifice, the suggestion is invariably contained in the express words of prophecy—most often in quotations from the 53rd of Isaiah, or in stock traditional formulae which are so clearly based upon such passages as to be virtual quotations. They amount to the bare statement that sins are forgiven through Christ's death, through His blood, or through His Cross; that Christ was a sacrifice for sin; that He died " for " or " on behalf " of mankind and the like. The doctrine is put forward authoritatively, dogmatically—most often without defence, explanation, or theoretical development.

(2) When and where anything like a reason or theory or explanation is given, it is, for the first century and a half of the Church's history, invariably a theory of an ethical or spiritual kind. St. Paul stands absolutely alone in adopting—though even he does so doubtfully and tentatively—a theory of substitution or vicarious punishment or something very like it. Everywhere else—with one possible and partial exception of which I shall speak shortly—the efficacy attributed to Christ's death is subjective rather than objective, prospective rather than retrospective, moral rather than juridical. Invariably explanation of the traditional language is founded on some appeal made by the death of Christ to reason or conscience or emotion. We constantly feel that the theories hardly justify or account for the traditional formulae which they profess to explain—taken at their face value. These statements about the death of Christ would doubtless never have been accepted upon the basis of mere authority unless they had seemed to be confirmed by the reflection, or by the moral and spiritual experience, of believers. But at every turn one feels that there is a certain hiatus between the formula, taken literally, and the experience which is supposed to confirm it. The dogmatic formula *seems* at least to speak of some objectively valid, vicarious act of atonement: the explanation demands only some subjective and ethical effect exercised by the contemplation of

Christ's death or (much more often) of His whole life, teaching, and work. The formula demands that Christ's atoning work should be accomplished in an exclusive or at least a paramount way by His death : the experiences testify to spiritual effects derived from belief in or attachment to the incarnate Son of God, His life, His teaching, and His Church ; but not to any such exclusive efficacy of His death as the formula, on the face of it, would seem to demand.

(3) Most significant is the fact that St. Paul's theories about atonement and justification exercised almost no influence. We find, in many of these writings, abundant evidence of the impression left by St. Paul upon the Church. The great battle of St. Paul's life—the struggle for Gentile freedom—was crowned with rapid and magnificent success. Even Jewish Christianity soon abandoned the attempt to impose circumcision and the law upon Gentile converts. St. Paul's universalism, his ethical teaching, his doctrine about the sacraments and the Church, less universally and immediately his language about the Person of Christ, made a profound impression upon succeeding writers and upon the general belief of the Church. But the characteristic ideas of the Epistle to the Romans were simply left on one side —partly no doubt just because they were an innovation, and an innovation which stood apart from the main current of the Church's tradition ; partly because they did not altogether commend themselves or fit in with the pre-existing ideas and intellectual tendencies of either Jewish or Gentile converts ; but probably most of all for the simple reason that they were not understood. Even when St. Paul's language about atonement and justification is actually quoted or echoed, the language is used in a more or less altered and rationalized sense. Like the older traditional expressions, St. Paul's own words eventually, though very gradually, themselves became accepted formulae ; and then they too, like the older and vaguer formulae, were explained in a more or less non-natural manner. This was what occurred in regard to the Pauline statements about salvation by

the death of Christ, and still more unmistakably with the formula of justification by faith, which was not universally and unreservedly accepted even as a formula.

These generalizations hold good, I believe, alike of the writings included in the Canon of the New Testament and of the earliest Fathers before Irenaeus.

The Epistle to the Hebrews.

There is, however, one canonical book which might at first sight be supposed to constitute a conspicuous exception to this generalization. Later theories of atonement are based quite as much upon the Epistle to the Hebrews as upon the teaching of St. Paul. These theories have in fact resulted from a somewhat uncritical combination of the juridical language of St. Paul with the sacrificial language of the Epistle to the Hebrews. On the face of it nothing can seem more crudely, more uncompromisingly sacrificial, objective, expiatory, than the language of this writer. The principle of the old law was that without shedding of blood there can be no remission of sins ; its one deficiency was, he seems to say, that the victims were the wrong victims. Just as under the old Jewish system, or in any other sacerdotal and legalistic religion, it was of no use to slaughter a goat when the true expiation was a lamb, so the mistake of Judaism was to suppose that the blood of bulls and of goats could take away sin. A much more precious victim was required—even that Messiah or Son of God whose superiority to the angels through whom the old law was given the writer takes so much pains to exhibit. Christ was to " taste death on behalf of every man." [1] He was to make " propitiation for the sins of the people," [2] " to put away sin by the sacrifice of himself," [3] to bear, or rather " bear away," the sins of many.[4] Christ is the Highpriest who once for all offered Himself—a new and

---

[1] Heb. ii. 9.

[3] Heb. ii. 17, R.V.   (A.V. reconciliation).

[2] Heb. ix. 26.

[4] Heb. ix. 28 (ἀνενεγκεῖν)—a condensed quotation from Isa. liii. 11.   Cf. Stevens, *The Christian Doctrine of Salvation*, p. 84.

un-Pauline thought, suggested no doubt by Philo's language about the priestly function of the Logos.   The writer is fond of such words as sacrifice, purification, altar, consecrate, sprinkling, and the like, and the references to the blood of Christ are more frequent in this one Epistle than in all St. Paul's Epistles put together.

Such is the first impression, but I believe it is an erroneous, or at least a very one-sided, impression.   The full reasons for this conclusion could only be exhibited by a detailed examination of the Epistle.   Here I can only call your attention to a few of the most important points :

(1) It is quite certain that there is in this writer no trace of the idea that Christ's death was a vicarious punishment, and we must not import this idea into our own interpretation of the sacrificial language which he undoubtedly does use.[1]   It is doubtful how far to the Jewish mind sacrifice ever implied the notion that the victim was substituted for the sacrificer : certainly there is no trace of that notion in this Epistle.   Nor is there any suggestion of a sacrifice which in any way satisfied the wrath or the justice of God.   Even from the point of view of strict exegesis, we are entitled to say that to the writer, though Christ's death was a sacrifice, the sacrifice was not substitutionary, not what in ordinary modern language would naturally be understood by a propitiatory sacrifice, though the word propitiation is once used ; [2] even the word " expiatory " has associations which are foreign to the author's mind.   Wherever the writer attempts to tell us what sort of sacrifice it is which Christ offered, it would seem that it was for him a sacrifice

---

[1] " The apparatus of a juristic philosophy of atonement is not only wanting here, but is incongruous with the method and nature of the author's thought.   The efficacy of Christ's work stands connected, for his mind, with his conception of the supersensuous, archetypal world of reality, of which it is a part.   For Paul, Christ's death saves indirectly by providing a way of salvation ; for our author it saves directly through its inherent power to cleanse the life" (Stevens, *The Christian Doctrine of Salvation*, p. 88-9).

[2] Εἰς τὸ ἱλάσκεσθαι τὰς ἁμαρτίας τοῦ λαοῦ, Heb. ii. 17.   (A.V. reconciliation, R.V. propitiation.)   The verb is used in the New Testament only here and in the publican's prayer (Luke xviii. 13), where the passive (ἱλάσθητί μοι) is translated " be merciful to me."

of purification.   The effects which he attributes to it are
purification, sanctification, perfecting—not so much mere
retrospective cancelling of guilt, as the actual removal
not only of guilt but of sinfulness.   The Son, " when
he had made purification for sins, sat down on the right
hand of the Majesty on high." [1]   " By one offering he
hath perfected for ever them that are being sanctified." [2]
The only question that can fairly be argued is how far
this effect was thought of as resulting directly and
objectively from the sacrifice, and how far it was thought
of as due to the moral and subjective effect on the believer's mind.   And to this question it is probable that
no definite answer can be given.   The two things were
so closely associated together in the writer's mind that
he did not definitely distinguish them.[3]

(2) There is, indeed, one passage in which the purpose
of Christ's death is said to be " that through death
he might bring to nought ($\kappa\alpha\tau\alpha\rho\gamma\acute{\eta}\sigma\eta$) him that had
the power of death, that is, the devil; and might
deliver ($\dot{\alpha}\pi\alpha\lambda\lambda\acute{\alpha}\xi\eta$) all them who through fear of death
were all their lifetime subject to bondage." [4]   This
passage supplies the most plausible basis to be found in

---

[1] Heb. i. 3 ($\kappa\alpha\theta\alpha\rho\iota\sigma\mu\acute{o}\nu$).
[2] Heb. x. 14.   It is strange that the R.V. should retain the A.V. " are sanctified."
[3] The offering of Christ is compared, or contrasted, with many different kinds of
sacrifice.   The one High-priest is contrasted with the many Jewish priests " who
offer the gifts according to the law " (viii. 4).   In x. 11, 12 the sacrifice of Christ is treated
as the reality symbolized by the daily Temple sacrifice (which was not strictly the sin-
offering), but is here spoken of as a " sacrifice for sins " ($\mu\acute{\iota}\alpha\nu$ $\dot{\upsilon}\pi\grave{\epsilon}\rho$ $\dot{\alpha}\mu\alpha\rho\tau\iota\hat{\omega}\nu$ $\theta\upsilon\sigma\acute{\iota}\alpha\nu$)
and later as an " offering " ($\pi\rho\sigma\sigma\phi\rho\acute{\alpha}$), but the effect of Christ's sacrifice is said to be the
perfecting of those who are being sanctified ($\tau\epsilon\tau\epsilon\lambda\epsilon\acute{\iota}\omega\kappa\epsilon\nu$).   In ix. 7 Christ is compared
to the High-priest entering into the holy of holies " not without blood "—the blood of the
goat and also perhaps of the bullock slain as a sin-offering (Lev. xvi. 9 ; cf. Heb. xiii. 11).
Later (ix. 19) comes a reference to the blood of the victims slain by Moses at the
inauguration of the first Covenant with which the book and the people were sprinkled.
In the O.T. the people are sprinkled, not the book.   The only importance of these
details is that they show that (1) the author vaguely thought of all the sacrifices of the
ancient law as somehow intended to (but failing to) " take away sin," without much
distinguishing between one sort of offering and another ; (2) there is a marked absence
of any reference to the burnt offering in which the destruction of the victim is most prominent ; (3) there is a complete absence of any reference to the substitutionary idea (he
dwells upon the use of the blood of the goat slain, but not of the goat sent into the wilderness, which might be interpreted, rightly or wrongly, to mean that the sins of the people
were laid on him) ; (4) the most prominent effect of sacrifice is with him not retrospective forgiveness, but perfecting or purification (x. 1, 22)—present moral improvement.
We may remember, too, without exaggerating, the principle so much insisted upon by
Bishop Westcott—that blood in the O.T. suggests the idea of life rather than of death.
[4] Heb. ii. 14.

Scripture for the later theory of the death of Christ as
a ransom paid to the devil : but it by no means supports
that theory. Nothing is said about payment *to* the
devil, or about the satisfaction of any just claim on his
part. All that it does is to attribute efficacy to the
death of Christ in overcoming the devil's work—both
by setting men free from sin and by restoring the immortality which had been lost through the fall.[1] But
there is nothing in these words which can compel us to
adopt any particular theory as to the way in which that
work was accomplished : they are quite intelligible if we
understand this efficacy of the spiritual and ethical effect
of Christ's victory. Indeed, the language used by the
writer seems positively to suggest that he thought of
this victory as accomplished by Christ's resistance to
temptation and patient endurance of suffering, and the
encouragement which this achievement, combined with
the resurrection that followed, has given to believers.
It is by the will of God, which Christ came to fulfil, that
Christians have been sanctified through the offering of
the body of Christ once for all.[2] The atonement was
effected by the removal of fear and the sense of guilt.
On the whole, therefore, this may be set down as a
passage of the usual primitive type—an assertion of
objective atonement expressed in traditional language
followed by an ethical or subjective explanation.

(3) We must remember the general aim of the Epistle.
The writer is addressing Christians who were Jews by
birth or adoption. It was perhaps written at the moment
when the destruction of the Temple was threatened or
not long after that destruction was accomplished, though
a later date is by no means impossible. The writer's
object was not so much to combat Judaizing influences
as to counteract a tendency to a general relaxation of
confidence in their Christian faith. He seeks to con-
vince them that the promises of God made to the Jewish

---

[1] Cf. 2 Tim. i. 10, "Christ Jesus, who abolished death" (καταργήσαντος μὲν τὸν
θάνατον), and Rev. xii. 11, "They overcame him because of the blood of the Lamb."
For the later development of the idea that Christ's death weakened the power of evil
spirits, cf. below, pp. 195, 242 *sq.*, 262 *sq.*, etc.
[2] Heb. x. 10.

people had not failed, but were already fulfilled in part, and would be completely fulfilled hereafter, by Jesus. What he fears is not so much Judaizing, in the sense of continued insistence upon the law on the part of Christians, as relapse into actual Judaism through wavering faith in the superior claims of Christianity. The writer's Christianity is universalistic : so far he is the disciple of St. Paul. But his way of reconciling his hearers to a Christianity which proclaims the supersession of the law was totally different from St. Paul's.[1] The old sacrificial system never appears to have had much interest for St. Paul, though of course it was accepted as part of the law : in the Hebrews we hear little of the law except on its ritual and sacrificial side. And the writer exhibits this sacrificial system as originally intended to be merely a transitory and visible type of the new, and only effectual, mode of reconciliation with God which Christianity provided. To carry out this purpose he had to represent the death of Christ as the true sacrifice which would secure the remission of sins, symbolized, but not really secured, by the ritual sacrifices of the old law. The old ritual, as he says, was a " parable referring to the time now present." [2] To develope the parallel, to emphasize the contrast, to show the infinite superiority of the one true sacrifice which Christianity provided, he fairly revels in sacrificial language ; he makes the most of every detailed point both of outward similarity and of inward difference which he could discover between the old ritual and the one true sacrifice to which it pointed. As the sacrificial victims were slain without the camp, so Jesus suffered without the gate of Jerusalem.[3] As the High-priest entered the holy of holies with blood not his own, so the great High-priest entered into heaven by the sacrifice of Himself.[4] As the first covenant was not dedicated without blood, so the new covenant

---

[1] " For Paul, Christ has abolished the law : for our author he has fulfilled it. In this matter, as M. Ménégoz says, the writer of Hebrews is an evolutionist, while Paul is a revolutionist " (Stevens, *Christian Doctrine of Salvation*, p. 78).

[2] Heb. ix. 9 : παραβολὴ εἰς τὸν καιρὸν τὸν ἐνεστηκότα.

[3] Heb. xiii. 11, 12.

[4] Heb. ix. 24-27.

required the shedding of the Messiah's blood.[1]   And so on.   But it remains quite possible that in such passages the writer is to some extent identifying himself with the point of view of his hearers, while leading them on to the higher and more spiritual theology which he had adopted for himself.   "If you insist that a sacrifice for sin is necessary," he seems to say, "then the Christian revelation has provided such a sacrifice in the death of Jesus."   His language is quite consistent with the belief that the sacrificial terms which the writer adopted were to him largely symbolic and metaphorical—unconsciously or even consciously an adaptation to the spiritual needs of men who, as he reminds them very pointedly, were not yet on the highest religious level, spiritually babes in Christ not yet fitted for solid food.[2] That this is so, is powerfully suggested by the way in which the metaphor or symbol is so often mixed up with the reality which it symbolizes.   It is the conscience that is by the blood of Christ cleansed from dead works to serve the living God.[3]   It is the heart that must be "sprinkled"[4] with the blood of Jesus.   The blood of sprinkling "speaketh" better things than the covenant of Abel.[5]   The writer could hardly have indicated more clearly that the death of Christ operates by its moral effects.   The carnal ordinances of the old law, he tells us, could not "as touching the conscience make the worshipper perfect,"[6] and were only imposed —not till a more efficacious victim could be offered— but till a "time of moral reformation."[7]   There is no notion of the mere cancelling of guilt ; the effect of the

---

[1] Heb. ix. 15-20.   The argument here turns upon the ambiguity of the word διαθήκη, which means both "covenant" and "testament."   The Jews applied the word denoting covenant to the Roman institution of a testament or will, and the identification of language enables the writer to maintain that what is true of a "will" (*i.e.* that it only operates after the death of the testator) was true also of the new "covenant" inaugurated by the death of Jesus.   I cannot believe that ἐπὶ νέκροις actually means "when made over a slain victim," as is contended by some who try to interpret the whole argument as referring to covenants and not at all to testaments.

[2] Heb. v. 12.   [3] Heb. ix. 14.

[4] Heb. x. 22.   Cf. the "sacrifice" of praise—that only sacrifice which still remains to be offered by the Christian (Heb. xiii. 15).

[5] Heb. xii. 24.

[6] Heb. ix. 9.

[7] Heb. ix. 10 (μεχρὶ καιροῦ διορθώσεως).

death of Christ is a moral effect which could hardly be supposed to operate merely *ex opere operato*.

(4) The writer was a Jew, but he was a philosophical Jew; one whose mind had been steeped in that Alexandrian philosophy which was disposed to interpret, not merely the ritual requirements but even the historical events of the Old Testament as simply types and symbols of higher spiritual truths. His indebtedness to Philo almost beyond a doubt amounts to close literary dependence.[1] And this Philonian attitude was only a particular development or application of that Platonic philosophy which regarded the whole phenomenal Universe as merely a manifestation of supersensible, intelligible realities or " ideas." [2] From this point of view the death of Christ upon the cross, though it was in a sense the antitype to which the Mosaic sacrificial system pointed, was yet after all only a visible embodiment or representation of some deeper spiritual reality. We may not be able quite definitely to formulate what this reality was : it is likely enough that the author himself would have admitted, on the evidence of the established Christian tradition, that there was a deeper mystery about the death of Christ than he could fully express in words. But it would not perhaps be too much to say that to him that reality was Christ Himself, or the mediation of Christ—not so much the past death of Christ, or any continuing effect of that death, as the present activity of the Christ who died but who is now in heaven,[3] and who both intercedes for men and directly exercises a saving influence upon the souls of believers, purifying them from their sins and leading them to

[1] See an excellent discussion in Ménégoz, *La Théologie de l'Ép. aux Hébreux*, p. 197 *sq.* The writer may also have been influenced by the Fourth Book of Maccabees. See Mr. Emmet's Introduction to his edition of that work (*Translations of Early Documents*, Series II.), p. 20.

[2] It is possible that for the author of the epistle some of these realities, though supersensible and not exactly material, are thought of as having a concrete, local reality in Heaven—like the Ark and (for Christians) the Church, which were supposed to be pre-existent in Heaven before their manifestation in time.

[3] " La propitiation pour le péché est transportée de la terre dans le ciel. . . . Ainsi la mort du Christ sort de l'histoire et prend le caractère d'un acte métaphysique . . . une fonction sacerdotale, un acte transcendant de purification rituelle, accompli hors de l'humanité " (Sabatier, *La Doctrine de l'expiation et son évolution historique*, p. 36-7).

God—a work which is going on now and will be completed at the Parousia. In accordance with the fundamental idea of the Alexandrian philosophy, he was profoundly convinced of the necessity of a mediator to enable men to approach God. And for him that mediator was Jesus, the Son of God : but the outpoured blood was to him the symbol of the true mediation rather than the substance of it. The death was essential, because in that way alone could the incarnate Son pass through the heavens into that glorious region in which He ever lived to make intercession for men. Doubtless a highpriest must have something to offer ; but what Christ offered was " Himself." [1] The phrase is notable ; the sacrifice was not His death or His sufferings, not even His life, but Himself or His Will. And it was "through the eternal spirit," [2] be it noted, that He " offered " Himself—in some transcendental, spiritual sense far removed from the more commonplace associations of the term. In another place, after quoting the language of a very anti-sacrificial psalm (" Sacrifice and offering thou wouldest not "), he continues, " Then said I, Lo, I am come (in the roll of the book it is written of me), to fulfil thy will, O God." [3] The sacrifice was the sacrifice of perfect obedience.

(5) Whenever the writer attempts anything like an explanation of the way in which Christ's blood has a redeeming or saving effect, he immediately becomes quite ethical, rational, and spiritual. It was necessary, he teaches, that the Mediator should be in all things tempted like as we are, yet without sin.[4] And His sufferings were necessary both for the perfecting of His own character, and as making possible that sympathy with others which would enable Him spiritually to help them. " It became him . . . to make the Captain of their salvation perfect through sufferings." [5] " For in

---

[1] Heb. ix. 14.   [2] Heb. ix. 14.
[3] Heb. x. 5-7.   [4] Heb. iv. 15.
[5] Heb. ii. 10. The word ἀρχηγὸς was specially used of the leader of a Greek colony, who conducted the immigrants into the new country, showed them the way into it, and ruled them after their arrival in it. So the idea seems to be that Jesus, by His sufferings and the resistance to temptation which they involved, was the first to win salvation or perfection for Himself, and so, both by the example which He affords and the help which

that he himself hath suffered, being tempted, he is able to succour them that are tempted " ; [1] " who . . . though he was a Son, yet learned obedience by the things which he suffered ; and having been made perfect, he became to all them that obey him the cause of eternal salvation." [2] How did He do this ? The old sacrificial language is once again employed : " For by one offering he hath perfected for ever them that are being sanctified." [3] But in the very next sentence comes the ethical interpretation : " And the Holy Ghost also beareth witness to us : for after he hath said, This is the covenant that I will make with them after those days, saith the Lord ; I will put my laws on their heart, and upon their mind also will I write them ; then saith he, And their sins and their iniquities will I remember no more." A very different covenant this from the new covenant of traditional theology ! It would hardly be possible more directly to suggest that it was the new knowledge of God's Will which Christ brought with Him into the world, the increased power of doing that Will, and the consequent outpouring of the Spirit on the Church and on the individual, to which the atoning, sin-remitting, sin-removing efficacy of Christ's work was really due. The thought of Christ as the great example of faith in God and obedience to God—an obedience involving suffering and culminating through death in a glorified life—is very prominent in this Epistle. No doubt it is assumed that there was a sort of ritual necessity or appropriateness in the new covenant, like the old, being ratified with blood ; but the blood-shedding was not the covenant itself, nor is there a single trace of a covenant which assumes the form, " Believe that your sins are forgiven by the blood of Christ, and they are forgiven." The new covenant itself was simply the fuller revelation of God's Will,

---

He supplies, makes it possible for others to follow Him, as it were, into the promised land.
[1] Heb. ii. 18. No doubt this help is thought of as active help, going on now, not merely the help afforded by the present knowledge of what Christ has done in the past. For the author, as for the Philonian, the world was full of such spiritual influences, good and bad.
[2] Heb. v. 8.   [3] Heb. x. 14.

and the closer communion with God which the coming of Christ brought with it. The way for this communion was no doubt prepared by the fulfilment of the promise, "Their sins and their iniquities will I remember no more": but it is significant that, apart from this quotation, no word exactly answering to "forgiveness" occurs in the Epistle. We hear of the putting away of sin, but the idea of retrospective forgiveness is merged in the idea of present and prospective cleansing, purifying, perfecting.[1]

It is difficult in reading this Epistle to say exactly where metaphor or symbol ends and spiritual reality begins. It represents a stage in the development of thought in which types, symbols, visible embodiments of invisible and spiritual realities, parallelisms between the past and the present, were things of no small importance. We may even say that there is a tendency almost to identify or to confuse the symbol with the thing symbolized.[2] And that is because the symbol was often to him more than a symbol. The writer was full of the idea of mysterious spiritual influences exercised through

[1] Pfleiderer insists that the sacrifice of Christ is represented " as the doing away, not with the power of sin upon the will, but with the tormenting and defiling consciousness of sin (consciousness of guilt) in the conscience " (*Paulinism*, ii. 67). No doubt this is the case; but I doubt whether the writer would have distinguished the two things so sharply as his commentator. He does undoubtedly look upon the work of Christ as producing an assurance of forgiveness which no repentance or moral change would have given *by itself*, but then he thinks of the work of Christ as producing repentance and moral regeneration at the same time that it conveys the assurance of forgiveness. I should say much the same with regard to Pfleiderer's insistence (p. 68) that " the fact that this word (ix. 13 and 14) is replaced and explained by καθαρίζειν, shows that ἀγιάζειν, or the effect of the death of Christ, does not denote moral sanctification, or giving a new direction to the will . . . But the blood of sacrifices has this real significance, that it ' sanctifies ' those who were defiled with regard to external theocratic purity ; that is to say, it places them in the condition of belonging to God, according to the relations established by the theocratic covenant. Accordingly, we are compelled by analogical reasoning to understand the ἀγιάζειν, which is the effect of the death of Christ, to mean the *sanctification by which we truly belong to God* in accordance with the relations established by the new covenant " (xiii. 11, 12). No doubt all this is true enough as far as it goes, but it does not alter the underlying implication that the " sanctification " under the old covenant was merely formal and ritual, while the " sanctification " under the new covenant implies a moral change.

[2] How closely he identified the symbol with the thing symbolized and the thing symbolized with the symbol may be illustrated by the passage in which he speaks of the things in the heavens being " cleansed (καθαρίζεσθαι) with better sacrifices than these." Of course he could not have thought of any actual use of the physical blood of Christ (though I have heard this idea defended in a sermon by an eminent scholar of the last generation), but still the writer's " heavenly things " are to him something more concrete than the Platonic " ideas."

the medium of visible things. Doubtless he believed in a mysterious necessity for the death of Christ which went beyond anything which he could articulately express. But, so far as his thought is articulate, there is no effect which he attributes to the death of Christ which may not perfectly well be understood of a subjective influence exerted upon the believer by the revelation of God contained in the teaching, character, and personality of Christ, by the belief in His Resurrection and future Parousia and the immortality which it would bring with it. In the revelation which had these spiritual effects the example of perfect obedience pushed to the point of self-sacrificing death held a prominent place. But no theory of substituted punishment or of substitutionary sacrifice, of retrospective efficacy or expiation, can derive any real countenance from the language of the Epistle to the Hebrews—so long as we attend to the explanations which the author offers in his own words, and not to the traditional phrases and formulae which he dutifully repeats. In so far as he attributes salvation to any objective efficacy of Christ's work, he lays stress upon the continuous influence of the risen and glorified Christ upon the believer now, upon His continued intercession with the Father, and upon the salvation which He will accomplish for the redeemed soul hereafter, rather than upon anything already accomplished by Christ in the past. The death was rather the indispensable preparation and condition of the true sanctifying work of Christ than the work itself.

When we turn from the language used about the death of Christ to the subjective conditions of salvation, we find the difference between this writer and St. Paul hardly less striking. The writer echoes St. Paul's language, and was not uninfluenced by his teaching. But he can hardly be said to accept St. Paul's doctrine of justification by faith ; for both the word and the idea of justification are absent. The word justification belongs to the vocabulary of law, and the writer thinks in terms of ritual rather than of law. He quotes, indeed, St. Paul's favourite passage in Habakkuk : " My just one shall live by faith." [1]   Faith is no doubt for him, as often in earlier and purely Jewish thought, necessary to salvation : and faith does imply for him, as for St. Paul, belief. But it is primarily belief in God. He nowhere speaks of faith in Christ. "Without faith it is impossible to be well-pleasing unto him, for he that cometh to God must believe that he is, and that he shows himself (γίνεται) a rewarder of them that seek after him." [2]   And faith is with him, much more clearly than in the controversial passages of St. Paul, valued for its effects rather than for itself.

The magnificent panegyric upon faith in the eleventh chapter seems at first sight Pauline enough in spirit, though after all it may rather be an echo of the old Jewish doctrine and the stock Jewish examples upon which St. Paul's own teaching was unquestionably based. The faith which saved Gideon and Baruch and Rahab was no doubt belief in the promises of God, though (if the illustrations are really to prove anything) it must include, or at least carry with it, the moral energy or will-power which enabled them to act. But it will be observed that it is not said of these heroes of the old covenant and of the new (as it is in St. Paul) that their faith was imputed to them for righteousness ; or that it actually constituted by itself a new and technical kind of righteousness, entirely different from the righteousness of ordinary morality : on the contrary it was their faith which actually enabled them to do good works, and by these good works (it is implied) they were saved. "Who through faith subdued kingdoms, wrought righteousness, obtained promises, stopped the mouths of lions, quenched the power of fire, escaped the edge of the sword, from weakness were made strong, waxed mighty in war, turned

[1] Heb. x. 38. The writer inserts the μου which St. Paul omits. The MSS. of the LXX. vary between δίκαιος ἐκ πίστεώς μου and δίκαιός μου ἐκ πίστεως : the Hebrew is translated in A.V. "by his faith," i.e. constancy, endurance, faithfulness.

[2] Heb. xi. 6. Such passages seem to show that the statement of Ménégoz that faith in this Epistle means "le don du cœur à Dieu" or "la consecration de l'âme à Dieu" is much too unqualified. It is assumed that sincere belief will carry with it obedience, but the element of intellectual belief is not to be got rid of. Still, much more clearly than in the controversial passages of St. Paul, faith is more than belief ; it is practically obedience.

M

to flight armies of aliens." [1]   And so when the writer speaks directly of Christian faith, it is still primarily faith in God rather than the Pauline faith in Christ or in something which Christ has done, and a faith of so very practical a character that it is convertible with obedience. It is to those who obey Him that Christ becomes the author of eternal salvation.[2] The opposition between faith and works is altogether absent.[3] Doubtless a measure of belief is presupposed by the obedience, but there is no trace whatever of the theory that forgiveness and salvation are conditional upon the belief in any past transaction. Christ is represented rather as the great example and source of faith than as its object.[4] He is "the author and perfecter of our faith." [5]

Faith in God would include, for the Christian, faith in His revelation of Himself through Christ, but it is rather faith in what God will yet do for the Christian through Christ than faith in anything which He has done already. It is significant that, when the writer speaks of the " principles of Christ," he does not include the death of the Redeemer. Doubtless some belief about Christ is implied in baptism; but the only doctrines of Christianity explicitly mentioned are "repentance from dead works, faith towards God, the teaching of baptisms, and of laying on of hands (at or after baptism), and of resurrection of the dead, and of eternal judgement." [6] The object of faith is thus essentially something future. Faith is for him chiefly present belief in the future fulfilment of God's promises. In one place faith is actually defined as the " realization of things hoped for:" [7] The faith of our Epistle has much more in common with the faith of Philo than with

---

[1] Heb. xi. 33-4.   [2] Heb. v. 9.

[3] In Heb. vi. 1 faith is included among the " first principles of Christ " : " not laying again a foundation of repentance from dead works, and of faith toward God." Of course " dead works " mean " bad deeds," not " the works of the law." There is no disparagement of works in the Epistle—not even of " works of the law."

[4] Cf. Pfleiderer, *Paulinism*, ii. 83.

[5] Heb. xii. 2.   [6] Heb. vi. 1, 2.

[7] Heb. xi. 1.   There has been much dispute as to whether ὑπόστασις here means (1) " substance " (A.V.) or (2) " assurance " (R.V., " une assurance certaine," Ménégoz, *Ép. aux Héb.* p. 141).   I see no reason to believe that ὑπόστασις ever actually *means* a subjective state of mind, though doubtless the assertion that faith *is* the reality can only be true in the sense that a strong conviction is equivalent to the reality. " Realization " may perhaps be accepted as suggesting this.

the Pauline conception of faith in Christ.[1] It is a belief in God's promises which produces patient endurance of trial and persecution, and enables men to do the will of God and so obtain the promised reward.[2] We might perhaps infer from the writer's own procedure that the mystical significance of the death of Christ belonged for him rather to the perfection of a Christian's belief, that perfection to which he invited them to press on under his guidance, than to those " principles " or " elements " which a Christian learned at baptism, and without which he could not be a Christian. That there was this mysterious significance in the death of Christ, he undoubtedly held ; but the very fact that the teaching about it belonged to the inner mysteries of the Christian religion suggests that for him the actual pouring out of Christ's blood upon the cross was rather the outward symbol or manifestation—though doubtless a deeply important symbol —of a more spiritual reality than a sacrifice in the cruder pagan or Jewish sense. The writer would clearly have no sympathy with those who would make the doctrine of an atonement through Christ's death both the beginning and the end of all Christian teaching.

A misleading impression may be given as to the teaching of the epistle if a word is not said as to its attitude towards baptism. Its teaching is spiritual, but this by no means excludes considerable emphasis on the outward symbols of spiritual realities. The necessity for baptism is always presupposed, although the stress is laid rather upon the act of repentance which accompanied the immersion than upon the rite itself. What exactly the writer would have thought as to the efficacy of repentance without baptism it is impossible to say : he would certainly have attached none to baptism without repentance and the sincere declaration of belief which accompanied it.[3] And the one great baptismal repent-

---

[1] Ménégoz, (p. 11) refers to *De migratione Ab.* 9.

[2] " That ye be not sluggish, but imitators of them who through faith and patience inherit the promises " (Heb. vi. 12). " Ye have need of patience, that, having done the will of God, ye may receive the promise " (Heb. x. 36).

[3] Ménégoz (p. 147) seems to think that the writer thought of baptism as purifying from ritual impurities committed before the man's entrance to the Church. I see no ground for this theory.

ance was the only repentance which could be accepted. "If we sin wilfully after that we have received the knowledge of the truth, there remaineth no more a sacrifice for sins, but a certain fearful expectation of judgement and a fierceness of fire which shall devour the adversaries." [1] This appalling doctrine of the one repentance is found nowhere else in the New Testament, but there can be no doubt as to the intense earnestness with which it was believed by the early Church or that section of it by which the doctrine was accepted. It is one which, not indeed without a struggle, the voice of the later Church has happily refused to endorse.

The Petrine Epistles

In the first of the Epistles attributed—in all probability mistakenly attributed—to St. Peter,[2] there is much emphasis upon the sufferings of Christ—not exclusively, be it noted, the death. The writer emphasizes the fact that those sufferings were foretold by the prophets, and that it was through them that the promised Messianic salvation was to be accomplished.[3] He duly repeats the traditional formula about redemption through Christ's blood. His readers are those who are elected "unto obedience and sprinkling of the blood of Jesus Christ." [4] "Knowing that ye were ransomed ($\epsilon\lambda\upsilon\theta\rho\dot{\omega}\theta\eta\tau\epsilon$) not

[1] Heb. x. 26, 27 ; so in vi. 5, 6. I see nothing to warrant Pfleiderer's attempt (*Paulinism*, ii. 92) to limit the unpardonable sin here spoken of to a relapse into Judaism. Any grievous and deliberate sin would be included ; but no doubt the doctrine does practically involve something like the later distinction between venial and mortal sins.
[2] The great objection to the Petrine authorship (apart from the weak external attestation) is, to my mind, not so much the dependence upon St. Paul, which has been greatly exaggerated, as the style and language of the Epistle. It seems to be admitted by those best qualified to judge (including some who are nominally defenders of the Petrine authorship, *e.g.* Dr. Bigg who defended even 2 Peter), (1) that the work was not written in Greek by St. Peter, and (2) is not a translation. It is a fine piece of Greek rhetorical writing. To say (with Bigg) that the Epistle was written by Silvanus in the name of St. Peter is really to admit that the work is pseudonymous, and does not convey the ideas of St. Peter, but of somebody else. It is, to say the least of it, extremely difficult for one man to write a book and for another to supply the language. If the book is pseudonymous, we must impartially ask what is its probable date, and the tone is certainly much more suggestive of the post-apostolic age than of the apostolic : it is addressed to the "dispersion" in Bithynia and the neighbouring countries, which makes it extremely tempting to connect it with the persecution recorded by Pliny in A.D. 110, though it may of course be earlier than that actual date.
[3] 1 Pet. i. 10, 11.   [4] 1 Pet. i. 2.

with corruptible things, with silver or gold, from your vain manner of life handed down from your fathers ; but with precious blood, as of a lamb without blemish and without spot, even the blood of Christ." [1]   The reference to the lamb recalls Isaiah ; the language about redemption is also drawn from Isaiah and other prophets. " Christ suffered for sins once, the righteous for the unrighteous." [2]   And there is an express quotation from Is. liii. and an application of it to the death of Christ : " Who did no sin, neither was guile found in his mouth : who, when he was reviled, reviled not again ; when he suffered, threatened not . . . who his own self bare our sins in his body upon the tree . . . by whose stripes ye were healed." [3]   But except in these quotations there is nothing to suggest the idea of substitution. The redemption is, indeed, always stated as a matter of objective fact, but the explanations added are always ethical, prospective, subjective. It was not from the guilt of past sins, or the punishment that was their due, that his hearers were redeemed by the precious blood of Christ, but from a "vain manner of life." [4]   Christ suffered, not to cancel the guilt, but " to bring us to God." [5]   The whole object of the Epistle is to exhort its readers to the patient endurance of persecution, and the references to Christ's sufferings are usually introduced by way of example : it is as an example that he quotes the passage of Isaiah about the sufferings of Jesus. [6] His readers are told that they are partakers in these sufferings, [7] as they could not well be if the writer thought of them as constituting a unique, expiatory sacrifice. And the effect of Christ's death is so closely associated with that of the resurrection that it becomes doubtful whether it is not really to the hope and encouragement supplied by that event, or to some actual, objective influence attributed to it, that the saving effects of the death are ascribed. " The sufferings of Christ " were foretold by the prophets, but they are closely associated with

[1] I Pet. i. 18, 19.   [2] I Pet. iii. 18.
[3] I Pet. ii. 22-25.   [4] I Pet. i. 18.
[5] I Pet. iii. 18.   [6] I Pet. ii. 21.
[7] I Pet. iv. 13.

" the glories that should follow them." [1]   It is by
the resurrection of Jesus Christ from the dead that
Christ has " begotten us again . . . unto an inheritance
incorruptible, and undefiled, and that fadeth not away." [2]
A new feature in this Epistle is the idea of Christ's
descent into Hades, and it is important to notice that it
is by the preaching of Christ in Hades (nothing is here said
about the death) that the disobedient generation of Noah
are to be saved.[3]   Baptism is distinctly spoken of as the
source of salvation, but it is at once explained in a way
which makes it doubtful whether it is the outward rite
that is meant or the repentance and amendment which
it signifies : it is " not the putting away of the filth of
the flesh, but the interrogation of a good conscience
toward God, through the resurrection of Jesus Christ," [4]
which really has the saving effect.

Faith is much insisted upon, but the word is used rather
in the sense of the Epistle to the Hebrews than in that of
St. Paul.   It is faith in God [5]—not faith in Christ.   It is
always closely associated, on the one hand with hope, and
on the other with obedience.   It is not faith in a past
transaction but faith in a living Christ whom having not
seen they love, and in His future Parousia.   The end of
faith is salvation, but there is no notion at all that faith
will save otherwise than by the good works which it
produces.   " The truth " and " the gospel " are not so
much things to be believed, as things to be " obeyed." [6]
The influence of St. Paul upon the language of this
Epistle has seemed to some so manifest that it has
frequently been treated as the chief objection to its
genuineness.   But it is only the vaguer and wider ideas
of St. Paul which can be discovered here: the distinctively
Pauline doctrines are absent.   There is no explanation
of the death of Christ as something demanded by the
justice of God, no idea of substituted punishment, no
language suggesting expiation except in actual words

---

[1] 1 Pet. i. 11.   [2] 1 Pet. i. 3, 4.   [3] 1 Pet. iii. 19.
[4] 1 Pet. iii. 21, 22.   The " interrogation " suggests the questions put at baptism.
[5] " Who through him are believers in God, which raised him from the dead, and gave
him glory ; so that your faith and hope might be in God " (1 Pet. i. 21).
[6] 1 Pet. i. 22, iv. 17.

derived from prophecy, no disparagement of the law and its works, no insistence upon the gratuitousness of salvation so marked as to suggest that salvation is not salvation by the works which faith produces quite as much as by the faith which inspires them. After all, the doctrine of the Epistle is rather the common faith of the Church, coloured by recollection of St. Paul's language and influenced by his Universalism, than a reproduction of his characteristic tenets.[1] The Epistle testifies as much to the triumph of St. Paul's general conception of Gentile Christianity even in circles predominantly Jewish as to the limited influence of the specifically Pauline theology.

The probably later Second Epistle of St. Peter calls for little special notice except for the light which it throws upon the kind of reception which St. Paul's Epistles met with in the Church at large. St. Paul's works are reverentially treated ; but it is recognized that they are dangerous, for they have now been abused by the Gnostics and have to be explained—perhaps explained away. His writings contained " things hard to be understood, which the ignorant and unstedfast wrest, as they do also the other scriptures, unto their own destruction." [2] The writer declares that " the long-suffering of our Lord is salvation ; even as our beloved brother Paul also, according to the wisdom given to him, wrote unto you, as also in all his epistles." [3] This is a very much attenuated version of St. Paul's doctrine of salvation through faith. The tendency of the Epistle is to make the gift conveyed by Christ consist chiefly in the knowledge of God ; and practically to identify faith with obedience. God's "divine power hath granted unto us all things that pertain unto life and godliness ; " but the revelation works " through the knowledge of him that called us by his own glory and

---

[1] It would be difficult to prove for certain that the writer had read any one Epistle of St. Paul's, though of course the later the date assigned the greater becomes the probability that he had read some of them.   The influence of Hebrews is much more unmistakable, especially in the expression " unto obedience and sprinkling of the blood of Jesus Christ " (1 Pet. i. 2).

[2] 2 Pet. iii. 16.   [3] 2 Pet. iii. 15, 16.

virtue."[1] Salvation comes from the knowledge of God conveyed through Christ, especially knowledge of His promises.[2] The object of the Epistle is to keep alive the waning hope of an immediate Parousia. And the effect of the Parousia will be that Christians become " partakers of the divine nature, having escaped from the corruption that is in the world by lust." [3] This may possibly be the first appearance of this immensely influential idea—that salvation amounts to an actual deification. Here the effect is attributed to the knowledge conveyed by Christ—not so much, as afterwards, to any direct effect upon the mortal body of the incarnation or the resurrection. There is an allusion to the " cleansing from his old sins," [4] which no doubt means baptism : otherwise no saving efficacy is anywhere attributed in this Epistle to the death of Christ.

The Epistle of St. James

We must pass on to that other Catholic Epistle in which the Pauline doctrine of justification by faith is not merely ignored but explicitly contradicted. All sophistical evasions notwithstanding, it is impossible to doubt that the Epistle attributed to St. James is intended as a protest against the Pauline doctrine of justification by faith, or at least against the use which was made of it in certain circles. The author does not deny the value of faith in the sense of belief, but he attributes value to belief only in so far as belief inspires action. The case of Abraham—in St. Paul's hands the classical instance of the principle that it is belief which justifies—is turned the other way. Abraham was justified by works " in that he offered up Isaac his son upon the altar." [5] " What doth it profit, my brethren, if a man say he hath faith, but have not works ? can that faith save him ? . . . Even

---

[1] 2 Pet. i. 3.   [2] 2 Pet. i. 3, 4.

[3] " Whereby he hath granted unto us his precious and exceeding great promises ; that through these ye may become partakers of the divine nature, having escaped from the corruption that is in the world by lust " (1 Pet. i. 4). Cf. ii. 20 : " After they have escaped the defilements of the world through the knowledge of the Lord and Saviour Jesus Christ."

[4] 2 Pet. i. 9.   [5] Jas. ii. 21.

so faith, if it have not works, is dead in itself. . . . I, by my works, will show thee my faith." [1] And the illustration given of the belief which inspires love and works is simply belief in one God, and this is expressly declared to be of no value without works : " the devils also believe, and shudder." [2] The general conclusion is that " by works a man is justified and not only by faith." [3] Faith and works—not faith only—a doctrine of which we shall hear again, possibly not a very different doctrine from what St. Paul really meant, but one hardly to be reconciled with the letter of his teaching, and certainly not to be reconciled with the teaching which has made a watchword of " justification by faith only " !

Nowhere in this Epistle is there the smallest indication of any special efficacy in the death of Christ. Its teaching about the forgiveness of sins is the simple teaching of the Master Himself : " He that converteth a sinner from the error of his way, shall save a soul from death, and shall cover a multitude of sins." [4] To Luther this Epistle was a worthless " epistle of straw." And so it ought logically to be to all who hold the doctrine of the atonement to be the whole, or at least the central truth and the only possible expression, of Christianity. We cannot with certainty infer that the writer would have repudiated the simple traditional statements of the early Church about the saving efficacy of Christ's death. And yet it is not at all impossible that it does represent the teaching of that Jewish section of the Church which did not even receive the doctrine that Christ died for our sins according to the Scriptures : at all events it represents the teaching of a Church in which the Messiah was thought of chiefly as a Teacher, though He was also a Messiah who had risen from the

---

[1] Jas. ii. 14-18.   [2] Jas. ii. 19.   [3] Jas. ii. 24.

[4] Jas. v. 20. It may be suggested that the previous words, " if any among you do err [or wander, πλανηθῇ] from the truth, and one convert him," preclude such an interpretation as I have put upon the words. I do not say that " wandering from the truth " might not in the writer's view include forsaking or giving up belief in Jesus as Messiah, but the verse would be inconsistent with the whole teaching of chapter ii., unless we suppose that he was thinking primarily of practical apostasy from the moral teaching of the Gospel. The concluding words of v. 20, " and shall cover a multitude of sins," are difficult to interpret. The simplest interpretation seems to me the most probable : " Repentance will cause a multitude of sins to be forgiven."

dead, and would shortly come again in judgement.[1] The Epistle of St. James has sometimes been disparaged as a half-Jewish and but half-Christian writing. Jewish it may have been in the sense that its Christology is undeveloped : but there is no trace of Jewish opposition to Gentile liberty. Fully Christian it is not if Christianity necessarily means a doctrine about the death of Christ. But no epistle in the Canon is so full of quotations from or allusions to the teaching of Jesus, and no New Testament writing is more full of His spirit. The Pauline Universalism has been absorbed, but not any doctrine which can be regarded as distinctively Pauline. It would be rash to assume, after the manner of Baur, that the epistle represents the teaching of a Petrine party bitterly opposed to the teaching of St. Paul : but it most undoubtedly represents a Church in which his influence was at a minimum. If we had to choose between the debt which the Church owes to St. Paul and the debt which it owes to this Epistle, few would have much hesitation in acknowledging that the greater debt is due to St. Paul. If the admission of this Epistle to the Canon had involved the rejection of the Pauline Epistles, we might have put up with the exclusion of " St. James." As it is, we may welcome the ultimate decision of the Church, after long debate, to accept this epistle, though the accepted view of its authorship is probably erroneous. It represents a valuable protest against the exaggerations of St. Paul, and the far more serious exaggerations which have sprung from his teaching in later times. On two conditions only can any one who respects that decision of the Church contend that it was right in including both St. Paul and " St. James " in its Canon. In the first place, we must abandon the notion that the acceptance of all St. Paul's theories—or even of the traditional language about the death of Christ—is a necessary and vital part of Christianity : and secondly, St. Paul's doctrine of salvation by faith in Christ must be so understood as not to exclude the equal truth of St. James' doctrine of salvation by

[1] Jas. v. 8.

works—not, indeed, by the observance of all the " works of the law," but by the practice of Christ's own royal law, " Thou shalt love thy neighbour as thyself." The way to such a solution of the antinomy was, as has been already pointed out, prepared by St. Paul's own doctrine of a faith which works by love : but such a doctrine, if it is really insisted upon, must involve the admission that much of the teaching of the Epistle to the Romans requires a good deal of correction, or at least of non-literal interpretation and toning-down, before it can be harmonized with that simple teaching of Jesus Himself which is the direct and immediate source of the Christianity revealed by the Epistle of St. James. By any one who accepts the teaching of this Epistle, St. Paul's doctrine of salvation by faith can only be accepted in a sense which makes it equally permissible to speak of salvation by works.

The Apocalypse

One other writing there is in the New Testament which has sometimes been treated as a document distinctively representative of " Jewish Christianity," and that is the Apocalypse. In a sense this view of the writing is even truer than was suspected at the time when the Tübingen school attempted to portion out the New Testament writings between the supposed Petrine and Pauline parties : for most scholars would now be prepared to accept the view, if not that the " Revelation of St. John " is a single Jewish Apocalypse re-edited by the Christian hand which also prefixed to it the epistles to the Seven Churches, at least that most of its imagery is derived from the language of Jewish Apocalypses which have been adapted to Christian use or transformed into Christian Apocalypses before they were put together into this definitely Christian writing. Undoubtedly in tone and temper this book is more Jewish than any other writing of the New Testament : yet we may easily exaggerate its Judaic character. There is no trace in it of any attempt to impose the Jewish law upon Gentiles, or even to insist upon its observance by Jewish Christians. It is entirely universalistic; though the writer was no doubt more interested in the twelve thousand who were sealed from each of the twelve tribes than in the great multitude which no man can number, who stood before the throne clothed with white robes, and palms in their hands.[1] Nor does it teach a very low doctrine of the person of Christ: strangely unlike as is the martial Messiah who rides on the white horse to the Logos of Philo or the later Johannine writings, Jesus is actually called "the Word of God."[2] He sits near to the throne of God, or even on the throne,[3] and salvation is due to Him as well as to God. Honour and praise are bestowed upon Him, perhaps worship of a kind.[4] He is the Son of God, but He is not treated as God. Here, however, we are not concerned with the writer's general theology. The question for us is, "What does he teach about the death of Christ?" And the answer to this question is not difficult. He is simply full of that earlier and simpler doctrine of the atonement which was certainly pre-Pauline, and which was generally taught in churches little or not at all influenced by St. Paul. The doctrine that Christ "loveth us, and loosed us from our sins by his blood,"[5] appears in the opening verses of the book—in the first of the letters to the Churches: and the central scene of the Apocalypse itself is the praise of the Lamb, a Lamb that had been slain. "Worthy art thou to take the book, and to open the seals thereof: for thou wast slain and didst purchase unto God with thy blood men of every tribe, and tongue, and people, and nation."[6] The saints overcome the Devil "because of the blood of the Lamb."[7] The "virgin" saints were "purchased from among men, to be the first-fruits unto God and unto the Lamb."[8] These are

---

[1] Rev. vii. 9.   [2] Rev. xix. 13.
[3] Rev. xxii. 1.   [4] Rev. v. 8-14.
[5] Rev. i. 5. I accept the Revisers' reading. The allusion to the "ransom" idea will be noticed here and in the following passages.
[6] Rev. v. 9.   [7] Rev. xii. 11.
[8] Rev. xiv. 4 (cf. 3). Notice the expression, "the Lamb that hath been slain from the foundation of the world" (Rev. xiii. 8). It shows (a) the feeling of a necessity arising

the common, traditional metaphors, derived ultimately from the Jewish prophets : the influence of Is. liii. is conspicuous in the very application to Jesus of the term "lamb." [1] But of any definite answer to the question why the death of Christ was necessary, or how it operated to produce the salvation which somehow sprang from it, there is no trace. The way in which the death of Christ is spoken of in the Apocalypse is, no doubt, a significant illustration of the fact that the idea of salvation by the death of Christ lived rather in the imagination of the early Church than in its thoughts.

If there is nothing that reminds us of St. Paul in the teaching of this book about the death of Christ, still less is there anything which suggests a distinctive doctrine of salvation by faith. It is assumed that none will be saved but those whose names are written in the Lamb's book of life, and these are no doubt those who possess Christian faith. But this faith is conceived of as a very practical thing : the saints were those who " keep the commandments of God, and the faith of Jesus." [2] Salvation is not by faith but by works, though it is assumed that none but Christians can perform the works which are necessary to salvation. It is not their faith, but their works that follow the departed souls.[3] The dead will be judged " out of the things which were written in the books, according to their works." [4]

We need not believe that it is St. Paul or any associates or followers of his that are attacked in the message to the Church of Ephesus as men who " call themselves apostles, and they are not." [5] Nevertheless it remains true that the Apocalypse is almost as un-Pauline as the Epistle of St. James. If we remember its position as a Christianized version of Jewish Apocalyptic, we must not lay

---

from prophecy, (b) that the death of Christ was surrounded by a sense of mystery. The statements about it in this book must not, therefore, be accepted in a too literal and prosaic sense. The actual, visible sacrifice did not take place before the foundation of the world ; it was a symbol of something deeper and eternal and changeless.

[1] In spite of the fact that the LXX. Isaiah uses ἀμνός, and the Apocalypse ἀρνίον, Swete (on Rev. v. 6) suggests that the latter may come from Jer. xi. 19, or from a non-Septuagintal version of Isaiah.

[2] Rev. xiv. 12.   [3] Rev. xiv. 13.
[4] Rev. xx. 12.   [5] Rev. ii. 2.

too much stress upon its dogmatic silences : but we may safely say that, but for its acceptance of Gentile Christianity, it shows no trace either of the highest or of the more questionable elements in the great Apostle's teaching.

The Synoptic Gospels and Acts

This will be a convenient place to say a word about the teaching on this subject of the historical books of the New Testament—the Gospels and the Acts—or rather about the state of opinion which they represent in their authors and the Church generally, as distinct from their evidence as to the teaching of our Lord Himself. As to the Synoptic Gospels it will be enough, perhaps, to say that they all contain traces of the common belief of the Church as to the redeeming efficacy of Christ's death; but in none of them is there any definite theory, substitutionary or other, as to the source of its necessity or the nature of its efficacy. A necessity in the death is always recognized, but it is more often than not simply the necessity that prophecy should be fulfilled : and its saving effect is always expressed in the language of prophecy. If the passage about the " ransom for many " be not a genuine saying of Jesus, it must represent a current formula of the Church. It occurs, as we have seen, in the two first Gospels. Much has been written about the " Paulinism " of St. Mark; but it is doubtful how far the emphasis upon Christ's sufferings, and upon saving faith, which it exhibits was not rather due to the common belief of at least the Gentile Churches than to any distinctly Pauline doctrine. Whatever "Paulinism" there is in St. Mark is reproduced in St. Matthew, though it is there combined with much that is more Jewish in tone. St. Luke is full of the Pauline spirit in his emphasis on the love and forgivingness of God to Jew, Gentile, and Samaritan : this is shown especially in sayings which he alone reports; but there is not a trace of distinctively Pauline doctrine, or of any special significance attached to the death of Christ beyond the fact that it fulfilled the prophecies.

I have already commented on the complete absence of any allusion to the atonement in the earlier chapters of the Acts.[1] Even in the later speeches of St. Peter and St. Paul the references to any such doctrine are surprisingly slight. The Hellenistic Evangelist Philip distinctly tells the eunuch that the words of Isaiah about the sufferings and death of the Servant were fulfilled in the death of Jesus,[2] but he does not quote the passages which suggest vicarious efficacy. Only St. Paul is made to proclaim that through Jesus " every one that believeth is justified from all things from which ye (the Jews) could not be justified by the law of Moses " [3]—but not specifically through His death or through faith in that death : rather (it is implied) through the resurrection which has just been mentioned. St. Peter is made to say that the hearts of the Gentiles were cleansed by faith.[4] Everywhere the preaching of the Apostles—of St. Paul no less than of the others—is of the Messiahship of Jesus, the fulfilment of prophecy in His coming, His death,[5] His resurrection, and the outpouring of the Spirit, the judgement to come, salvation through belief in Him and obedience to His teaching, the proof of His Messiahship and hope of immortality afforded by His resurrection. In only one passage of the whole book is the forgiveness of sins distinctly connected with the death of Jesus : and that is in the farewell of St. Paul to the elders of Miletus, who are exhorted " to feed the Church of God, which he purchased with his own blood." [6] Here we have the old prophetic metaphor which underlies the use of the term "ransom " in early Christianity, but there is no trace of the Pauline insistence upon Christ's death—still less of St. Paul's characteristic theories about it.

---

[1] Above, p. 76. The expression " hanging him on a tree " (Acts v. 30 and x. 39) doubtless contains a reference to Deut. xxi. 23.

[2] Acts viii. 28-35.   [3] Acts xiii. 39.   [4] Acts xv. 9.

[5] " How that the Christ must suffer, and how that he first, by the resurrection of the dead, should proclaim light both to the people and to the Gentiles " (Acts xxvi. 23). But the light comes through the resurrection, not through the death.

[6] Acts xx. 28. In xxvi. 18 St. Paul speaks of Christ (at his conversion) as sending him to preach to the Gentiles " that they may receive forgiveness of sins, and inheritance among them which are sanctified by faith that is in me," but without reference to the death.

I do not of course dwell upon these facts to show
that the formula, " Christ died for our sins according
to the scriptures," was unknown to the early Church,
or to question the immense importance attached to it
by St. Paul—at least in the period covered by his letters.
But the evidence of the Acts probably points to the
existence of a period or of circles in which the doctrine was
unknown, and certainly to a period in which it occupied
a very subordinate place in the general belief of Christians,
especially of Jewish Christians.[1] It may seem at first
sight almost incredible that such a doctrine should have
been accepted, and yet not made a very prominent feature
in the teaching of those who accepted it. The explanation probably lies in the fact that the death of Jesus was
looked upon mainly as the necessary prelude to the
resurrection. The resurrection was valued as setting
a seal on the Messiahship of Jesus, as guaranteeing the
truth of His teaching and the certainty of salvation

---

[1] In definitely Jewish-Christian or anti-Pauline circles it continued to be unknown.
There is strong evidence of this in the pseudo-Clementine Recognitions. This work
proceeds from the anti-Pauline section of the Church ; but, whether or not owing to
judicious omissions and corrections of the translator, Rufinus, the anti-Paulinism is of a
mitigated and attenuated order. There is no insistence on the observance of the law ;
indeed the chief purpose of Christ's coming was to put a stop to animal sacrifices, which
had previously been tolerated rather than commanded by God. St. Paul's apostleship is
denied by implication (" neque Apostolus praeter nos," iv. 35), and James is regarded
as the chief of the Apostles, while the succeeding Bishops of Jerusalem are the chief
bishops (" ut nulli doctorum credatis, nisi qui Jacobi fratris domini ex Hierusalem detule-
rit testimonium, vel eius quicumque post ipsum fuerit "). From the beginning to the
end of the work there is no special insistence upon the death of Christ, nor any suggestion
that salvation comes through His death, though there is much insistence upon the fulfilment of prophecy—a fact which confirms the view that it was among Gentile Christians
that the atonement doctrine originated. Salvation is obtained by repentance and baptism (i. 39, i. 63). Belief in Christ is implied in baptism, and it is distinctly taught that
sins " cannot be purged by any other," but that is because no one else could so powerfully
persuade men to repentance and righteousness (i. 51). Belief in Christ means practically
obedience to His teaching (i. 33). He is primarily " the true prophet." The most
important articles of faith are belief in the commands of Christ and in His teaching about
the future judgement. (" Fides autem futurum esse dei iudicium credens continet
hominem a peccato," v. 3.) Justification by works is as clearly taught as in the Epistle
of St. James. (" Si bene agentes salutem consequi meruimus," ii. 21. Cf. iv. 5, v. 6.)
Great stress is throughout laid upon free-will. The teaching of the writer is everywhere
based chiefly on the Synoptic Gospels, but there are slight echoes of the fourth Gospel.
Baptism is to be in the name of the Trinity (iii. 67). The Eucharist is occasionally
mentioned side by side with baptism as necessary to salvation (i. 63). The writing
shows how largely, for many sections of the Church, Christianity consisted chiefly in
Monotheism, acceptance of the moral and religious teaching of Christ, and a strong
confidence in the efficacy of baptism ; but the worthlessness of baptism without repentance and amendment is duly insisted upon. The teaching of the Clementine
Homilies is much the same, except that the anti-Paulinism is here less veiled.

and immortality for those who believed and practised it. It was a matter of indifference therefore whether men spoke of being saved by Christ's blood or of being saved by His resurrection or more vaguely of being saved through Christ. Even as regards St. Paul himself the evidence of the Acts (upon the assumption of the Lukan authorship) must be held to show either that his characteristic and distinctive theories about the death of Christ found little expression in his ordinary teaching, or that this side of his teaching [1] was little understood and appreciated even by his immediate disciples. It is probable that both interpretations of the facts represent part of the truth. The love of God as shown by Christ's incarnation, death, and resurrection taken together must assuredly have formed part of St. Paul's habitual teaching : but the definite theory that the death was necessary to satisfy the wrath of God against sin was perhaps reserved for occasions when some controversial purpose demanded a further explanation of the Messiah's death than was supplied by the commonly accepted doctrine that it was foretold by the prophets and the necessary prelude to the resurrection. And this distinctive doctrine long exercised, as we shall see hereafter, very little influence even in those sections of the Church in which St. Paul's authority was at its highest.

The Johannine Gospel and Epistles

The influence of St. Paul upon the Gospel and Epistles of St. John is of a very different kind from any which can be traced in the rest of the New Testament. The influence of St. Paul's spirit is immense. In his high Christology, his developed Universalism, his high and spiritual conception of the Church, his intense appreciation of the Christian ethic, their author represents the culmination of Paulinism. But there is a complete

---

[1] To say " I determined not to know anything among you, save Jesus Christ, and him crucified " (1 Cor. ii. 2) is not (as is often assumed) the same thing as " I determined to preach nothing but the doctrine of the atonement." Even in his Epistles—which deal expressly with disputed matters—St. Paul has much to say about Christ besides the effects which he attributed to His death.

N

absence of St. Paul's distinctive theories or at least of his phraseology, of all that we specially associate with the Epistles to the Romans and Galatians. The Paulinism which he recalls and developes is rather the Paulinism of the later Epistles—especially the two Epistles specially addressed to the Churches of Asia Minor. The characteristically Pauline ideas about salvation are not so much either adopted or contradicted as transcended, and swallowed up in a Christianity which was remoter from ordinary Judaism than even the teaching of St. Paul. A Jew by birth the writer must have been, and a Jew not unacquainted with Palestine : but a rabbi he was not, and had never been. The Judaism which for him had been transformed into Christianity was not the rabbinic Judaism of Jerusalem, but rather the Judaism of the Hellenized and philosophical type which is best known to us in the form which it assumes in the writings of Philo and the school of Alexandria.[1] His Christianity was that of one who had been in much closer and more direct contact than St. Paul, not perhaps directly with Greek philosophy, but with an intellectual atmosphere to which Greek philosophy had contributed as much as the law and the prophets.[2] What were the effects of this atmosphere upon the writer's attitude towards the Christian doctrine of salvation ?

In the Johannine writings there is a strong underlying sense of some profound necessity for Christ's death, and occasional suggestions of some mysterious influence exercised by it. In part, here as everywhere, the necessity is at bottom the necessity that prophecy should be fulfilled. The prophecies of Christ's death are much

---

[1] Professor Percy Gardner has recently (in The Ephesian Gospel) insisted that the philosophy presupposed by the Johannine writings is not so much the Alexandrian philosophy as another and similar philosophical school at Ephesus. This may be so, but when Philo supplies such an easily intelligible explanation of the Johannine philosophy, the assumption is hardly necessary. In any case, the supposed Ephesian School must have had much in common with the Alexandrian.

[2] Many a modern religious teacher is profoundly impressed by the idea of " evolution " who has not himself read a page of Darwin, of Herbert Spencer, or any of his successors, and by the idea of development without having read Hegel or any Hegelian. Newman's book on the Development of Doctrine (written ten years before the Origin of Species) shows how much an idea may be in the air and influence those who have read none of the sources with which the ideas are associated in the minds of students.

insisted upon ; the writer sees in the details of the passion the fulfilment of predictions in the psalms and the prophets.[1]   One of the indications of the freedom with which he has departed from the synoptic tradition is to be found in the allusions to the death as the supreme purpose, or part of the supreme purpose, for which Christ came into the world, which are introduced in the earliest days of His ministry.   He is pointed out by the Baptist to his disciples as the " Lamb of God which taketh away the sin of the world " [2]—the old image of Is. liii. which had passed into the traditional Church formula.   To Nicodemus, quite early in His ministry, our Lord speaks of the necessity that " the Son of man must be lifted up, that whosoever believeth may in him have eternal life." [3]   Later on, He announces that He is the good shepherd, and lays down His life for the sheep.[4] Caiaphas is made prophetically to declare that it was expedient that one man should die for the people, and that the whole nation perish not.[5]   In the last great discourse He tells His disciples that He would lay down His life for His friends.[6]   In such passages there is a vague suggestion of some deep mystery connected with the death of Christ ; but, so far as any actual explanation or formulated doctrine is concerned, there is not a word which necessarily implies a substitutionary sacrifice or, indeed, any literal sacrifice at all : nothing that implies that Christ died for man in any sense other than that which a supreme benefactor of humanity might be said to die for men—though of course He is for the writer much more than a supreme benefactor.   And all that is said of the effects of that death may quite well be understood of its subjective effects upon the believer in Christ.

In the first of the Johannine Epistles the references

---

[1] John xix. 24 (Ps. xxii. 18) ; xix. 28 (Ps. lxix. 21) ; xix. 31 *sq.* (Ex. xii. 46, Ps. xxxiv. 20, Zech. xii. 10).

[2] John i. 29.

[3] John iii. 14 ; cf. viii. 28, xii. 32.

[4] John x. 14, 15.   It is significant that he does not say " will lay down."   The laying down is not confined to the death.   Doubtless the Evangelist had in mind the synoptic saying, " He that loseth his life for my sake shall find it."

[5] John xi. 50.   [6] John xv. 13.

to the Church's accepted formula are more frequent and
explicit : [1] " The blood of Jesus his Son cleanseth us
from all sin." [2]   Jesus is described as the " propitiation
for our sins ; and not for ours only, but also for the
whole world." [3]   But even that phrase is little more than
a variant of the traditional formula that Christ died in
some sense as a sacrifice for sin ; the association of
the word translated " propitiation " ($\iota\lambda\alpha\sigma\mu\acute{o}s$), or rather
its derivative ($\iota\lambda\alpha\sigma\tau\acute{\eta}\rho\iota\sigma\nu$), with the " mercy-seat," if
not too much to be insisted on, need not be forgotten
in this connexion : and after all the " propitiation " is
not explicitly connected with the death.   Even if such
a connexion is assumed, its use need not mean more
than that the death of Jesus is the event by which most
conspicuously God has revealed His merciful purpose
of forgiveness.   So again sins are forgiven " for His
name's sake " [4]—which certainly suggests the idea that
forgiveness was in some way earned by Christ's merits.
But however much such phrases may be held *prima facie*
to suggest some objective efficacy, the moment the writer,
whether in the Gospel or the Epistles, leaves these
traditional formulae and speaks in his own words, he
immediately begins to think of some subjective effect,
of a perfectly intelligible and ethical character, to be
exercised on the soul of the believer.   The Son of Man
is to be lifted up—not to make a vicarious expiation and
appease His Father's wrath, but " to draw all men
unto " Himself,[5] to exercise a moral attractive force.
It would be impossible to extract from the Johannine
writings (if they are to be interpreted by themselves and
not by reference to St. Paul or later theories) any other
account of the purpose of Christ's dying than this—

---

[1] A fact which suggests that the writer, though the discourses are mainly his composition, was not entirely regardless of tradition or historical probability and propriety
in putting words into our Lord's own mouth.

[2] 1 John i. 7.

[3] 1 John ii. 2 ($\iota\lambda\alpha\sigma\mu\sigma s$) : so in iv. 10.   The word for mercy-seat is $\iota\lambda\alpha\sigma\tau\acute{\eta}\rho\iota\sigma\nu$.
(See above, p. 130.)   Cf. the use of $\iota\lambda\acute{\alpha}\sigma\theta\eta\tau\iota$ in the parable of the Publican (lit. " be
propitiated," and so " be favourable "), where any idea of actual propitiation or even of
mediation is out of the question.

[4] 1 John ii. 12.   We may for ourselves explain such words as meaning " in virtue
of that character of God which Christ reveals," and much in the Johannine writings
would sanction such an interpretation.

[5] John xii. 32.

that He suffered (1) to reveal His own and the Father's love, (2) as an example to encourage His followers to lives of self-sacrifice, (3) as a necessary presupposition of the resurrection. " God so loved the world that he gave his only begotten Son " [1] to be incarnate and (no doubt) to die. " Greater love hath no man than this, that a man lay down his life for his friends." [2] " Hereby know we the love of God, because he laid down his life for us : and we ought to lay down our lives for the brethren." [3] " I lay down my life that I may take it again." [4] Outside the traditional formulae there is not a word to suggest any substitution, any vicarious efficacy, or even any objective efficacy. Nothing is said about the saving effect of Christ's work which may not be understood of the moral influence of His life and death.

Indeed, most of what is said of the saving influence which proceeds from Christ, both in the Gospel and in the Epistles, may most naturally be understood of His teaching. The water which Christ will give to the believer, and which " shall become in him a well of life springing up unto eternal life," [5] is clearly His teaching, however much the imagery of the baptismal water may be in the background. What our Lord, in the view of the Evangelist, means by the necessity of eating His body and drinking His blood, appears unmistakably from the explanation which immediately follows : " The words that I have spoken unto you are spirit and are life." [6] He is thinking, no doubt, of the eucharistic rite, but of what it symbolized, the influence of Christ's words upon the heart and the life, rather than of the rite itself. Everywhere the Evangelist spiritualizes the traditional rites and the traditional formulae of the Church : to him they are essentially symbols. It is because Christ has the words of eternal life that His true disciples adhered

---

[1] John iii. 16.　　　　　　　　[2] John xv. 13.
[3] 1 John iii. 16. The words " of God " (omitted in R.V.) are probably a gloss, but they perhaps express the real thought of the passage.
[4] John x. 17.
[5] John iv. 14. I do not deny that the symbolism of baptism may be in the background, but the saying is as little to be limited to baptism as is " the same is He that baptizeth with the Holy Spirit " (John i. 33).
[6] John vi. 63.

to Him when others went away.[1]   To believe in Christ
is primarily to believe His words : " If ye believe not
his writings, how shall ye believe my words ? "[2]   It is
because of the words which He has spoken unto them
that the disciples are clean.[3]   " If a man love me, he
will keep my word, and my Father will love him, and we
will come unto him."[4]   A Christian is one who abides
in Christ, and in whom His words abide.[5]   To abide
in Christ is to have His words abiding in one.   " He
that rejecteth me and receiveth not my sayings, hath
one that judgeth him : the word that I spake, the same
shall judge him in the last day."[6]   In what has sometimes been called the great high-priestly prayer our Lord
sets forth the very essence of His mission, as the Evangelist
understood it.   He has finished the work which the
Father has given Him to do.   And what is that work?
" The words which thou gavest me, I have given unto
them"; " I have given them thy word"; "I made known
unto them thy name."[7]   It is true that He declares that
for their sake He sanctifies or offers Himself, but only
" that they also might be sanctified."   The word used
($\dot{a}\gamma\iota\dot{a}\zeta\omega$) is sacrificial in its associations, but if a sacrifice
is pointed to, it is a sacrifice which all Christians are
called upon to offer.[8]   The absence in this prayer of
the smallest reference to any vicarious sacrifice which,
according to the conventional theology, the Saviour was
just about to offer by His death, and which He alone
could offer, is as eloquent as any positive repudiation
could be.

And if we turn to the subjective conditions of salvation, what do we find ?   Immense emphasis upon belief
in Christ, in the Gospel and still more in the Epistles,
but not specifically upon belief in the forgiveness of sins

---

[1] John vi. 68.   [2] John v. 47.
[3] John xv. 3.   [4] John xiv. 23.
[5] John xv. 7.   [6] John xii. 48.
[7] John xvii. 4, 8, 14, 26.
[8] John xvii. 19.   There is, as M. Loisy remarks, " a sort of play upon words " :
the word " consecrate " will best bear the double sense.   But we cannot suppose, as
conventional interpreters hold, that the word is used in two quite distinct senses.   The
author is consciously spiritualizing a traditional phrase.   The only difference between
the two cases is that " Christ does for Himself that which is done for the disciples "
(Westcott).

through Christ's blood.   Where the exact content of belief is formulated, it is the truth that Jesus is the Son of God or that Jesus Christ cometh in the flesh.[1]   " Whosoever shall confess that Jesus is the Son of God, God abideth in him, and he in God." [2]   More generally it is simply belief in Christ that gives eternal life.   So far the Evangelist was no doubt repeating the common faith of the Church, as well as expressing his own deepest convictions.   Belief in Christ was to him the one supreme source of spiritual life.   But he by no means makes belief by itself the cause or supreme condition of salvation. On the contrary, what he always insists upon is the moral effects of belief—so much so that we may say he practically interprets faith or belief in Christ as obedience to Christ's commandments, and especially to the supreme command of love towards the brethren.   " He that believeth on the Son hath eternal life ; but he that obeyeth not the Son shall not see life, but the wrath of God abideth on him." [3]   " The sheep hear his voice." [4] When our Lord, according to the Evangelist, speaks of Himself as " the way, and the truth, and the life," [5] He could not have been referring to any result of His death ; for He expresses surprise that Philip had been so long time with Him, and yet asked to be shown the Father. According to a certain type of teaching, no knowledge of God has any value that is not based upon faith in Christ's death.   " He that hath my commandments and keepeth them, he it is that loveth me " [6]—a sheer impossibility, according to some, till after the Crucifixion. " Already ye are clean because of the word which I have spoken unto you " [7]—through the words, not through the atoning sacrifice hereafter to be offered.   " If ye keep my commandments, ye shall abide in my love " [8] —not " if ye have faith in my atoning blood."   " To this end have I been born, and to this end am I come into the world, that I should bear witness unto the truth.   Every one that is of the truth heareth my voice." [9]   A very

---

[1] 2 John 7.   [2] 1 John iv. 15.
[3] John iii. 36.   The R.V. has substituted " obeyeth not " for " believeth not."
[4] John x. 3.   [5] John xiv. 6.   [6] John xiv. 21 ; cf. xiv. 15.
[7] John xv. 3.   [8] John xv. 10.   [9] John xviii. 37.

different purpose from that assigned to Christ's coming by those who teach that He came into the world only or chiefly to die ! " Every one that loveth is begotten of God, and knoweth God." [1]

Spiritual union with Christ and imitation of Him as shown by love toward the brethren—that, according to the fourth Evangelist, is the one condition of salvation ; nay, it constitutes salvation. Doubtless he held that love of the Christian type could be produced only by the acceptance of the revelation of God in Christ, and in that revelation a death, the self-sacrificing death for humanity, had its place. But, profoundly as the writer was influenced by the Pauline theology, there is hardly a page of the Johannine Gospels and first Epistle which does not contradict the letter of the Pauline theories : while the contradiction of later doctrines which have at times been supposed to be the very pith and marrow of the Christian religion is still more glaring and undeniable. If we think, not of the Pauline dialectic and the Pauline theories, but of the spirit of St. Paul's best teaching, doubtless the contradiction disappears. St. Paul's panegyric on charity might, in all but style, have been written by the fourth Evangelist: nor would the latter have scrupled to accept the modified theory of the Galatian Epistle about the justifying effects of a faith which works through love. But this last expression implies a very much liberalized interpretation of the formula which St. Paul developes in his more controversial passages.

I must not stay now to ask how much of the language either of St. Paul or of St. John is susceptible of modern re-statement, and I will only throw out the suggestion that, if we put out of sight everything in St. Paul which finds no echo in St. John, we shall be on the way to an appropriation of that central core of eternal truth which underlies them both. After all, the fundamental idea both of St. John and of St. Paul is simply that the death of Christ, the culminating act in a life of self-sacrifice, is the supreme manifestation of Christ's love, and therefore of the love of the Father whom He reveals ; and that the

---

[1] 1 John iv. 7.

contemplation of that life and death gives other men the power, as nothing else has done, to overcome temptation and to lead lives of love like His. That simple thought is surrounded, at times perhaps contradicted and obscured, by an intellectual environment which cannot be ours : for the ideas of a modern man about God and the Universe can never be quite those of the first century : but in that simple idea lies the central truth which they have communicated to the world. And St. John's expression of that idea can be appropriated by the modern mind with far less modification than is required by St. Paul's.

There is, indeed, only one aspect in which St. John's doctrine of salvation requires much modernization to make it possible to the modern Christian. Gospel and Epistles alike are pervaded by a strong sense of a great gulf dividing the Church from the " world " : the world is thought of as evil. Though there is no explicit statement as to the ultimate destiny of virtuous pagans, the underlying assumption is that only Christians can be saved ;[1] nor can any doctrine of degrees of salvation find explicit sanction from the teaching of these writings, though it would not be very difficult so to interpret them. Broadly speaking, the contrast between the moral condition of the Christian world and that of heathenism justifies the Johannine attitude. The Church was, indeed, the abode of spiritual light ; the heathen world was spiritually dark. But there was no doubt in the best pagan life of the time more light than the writer would have been prepared to recognize—at all events more than he actually does recognize : nor can we easily believe that the best heathen will hereafter meet with no more acceptance with God than St. John may possibly have expected for them. Nor again will the extreme bitterness with which he speaks of intellectual

---

[1] There is, indeed, no explicit doctrine of everlasting punishment in the Johannine writings. There is a general assumption that those who have not believed in Christ will be condemned at the Messianic judgement ; the exact results of that judgement are not defined. As to the backsliding Christian, the writer modified the stern doctrine of the Epistle to the Hebrews by distinguishing between sins " not unto death " and other sins : " If any man see his brother sinning a sin not unto death, he shall ask, and God will give him life for them that sin not unto death. There is a sin unto death : not concerning this do I say that he should make request " (1 John v. 16).

disbelief in Jesus, the disbelief whether of the pagan or
of the heretic, commend itself unreservedly to an age
too well acquainted with the causes which prevent
intellectual acceptance of new truth to suppose that such
rejection is always due merely to moral depravity.   The
teaching of St. John requires widening before it can be
pronounced to be perfectly in accordance either with the
spirit of Jesus, or with what the Spirit has taught to the
Church of later ages.   But we may add that after all
nothing definite is said as to the ultimate fate of either
disbeliever or heretic : no teaching in the New Testament
lends itself more readily to the expansion which we
demand.   This is naturally the case with the writer
who more than any other has got rid of the narrow
outlook associated with the expectation of an immediate
Parousia and a literal reign of the saints on the earth ;
and who more than any other taught the Christian Church
to expect the continued guidance of the indwelling
Spirit of God which should lead them progressively to
new truth—truth latent but not expressly contained in
the teaching of its Founder.   " It is expedient for you
that I go away : . . . I have yet many things to say
unto you, but ye cannot bear them now.   Howbeit
when he, the Spirit of truth, is come, he shall guide you
into all the truth : . . . he shall glorify me : for he
shall take of mine, and shall declare it unto you." [1]   No
doctrine lends itself more readily to the kind of development which all early Christian teaching requires than
that of the writer who may be said to have first formulated
for Christian readers the very idea of development.

I have laid stress upon the prominence which the
teaching of Christ occupies in the Johannine idea of
salvation.   Nothing can be further from my intention
than to suggest that the writer thought of Jesus simply
as a teacher or a prophet.   He was the supreme Teacher,
and He was so just because in a supreme degree the
Logos—the Word of God—resided in Him : but it was
primarily through His teaching that the incarnate Logos
brought the supreme healing influence to bear upon

[1] John xvi. 7, 12-14.

the world. And in his conception of the saving effect
which Christ exercised over the world the thought of
His actual present influence is as prominent as the
thought of His past teaching. And this present influence, whether on the individual soul or on the Christian
community as a whole, is not distinguished from the
work of the Holy Spirit—that other Comforter and
Helper who, though another, is not another. For St.
John the statement that the Comforter would be sent is
the equivalent of the statement, " I will come to you." [1]
In the Johannine writings the thought of atonement is
merged in the higher and more comprehensive idea of
revelation—a revelation begun by the historic Jesus,
but continued in the Church both through the influence
of the words once spoken in the past and through that
abiding and present influence of God which may be
equally spoken of as the work of the Father, of the Son,
or of the Holy Spirit. It is not too much to say that
the worst developments of the atonement doctrine arose
from the conception of a sharp separation between the
three manifestations of God (not in St. John spoken or
thought of as three " Persons ") which would have been
impossible to the author of the fourth Gospel. " He that
hath seen me hath seen the Father." [2]   " I will not leave
you desolate, I come unto you." [3]   " I say not unto you
that I will pray the Father for you, for the Father himself
loveth you, because ye have loved me, and have believed
that I came forth from the Father." [4]   With such a
conception of God, there could be no room for the
doctrine that the Father could not forgive sinners unless
He were propitiated or placated by the death and sufferings of an innocent Son. The dominant conception
of the death of Christ in the Johannine writings is simply
that it is the supreme act in that highest revelation of
God's love which is constituted by the incarnation as a
whole and by the continuing presence of the Spirit. [5]

[1] John xiv. 18.   [2] John xiv. 9.
[3] John xiv. 18.   [4] John xvi. 26, 27.
[5] It is admitted even by Dr. Denney (*The Death of Christ*, p. 182) that " if we use
the word redemption at all . . . we must say that redemption is conceived in the
Gospel as taking place through revelation."

The Pastoral Epistles

The Pastoral Epistles, which in their present form at least cannot, as I believe, with any probability be attributed to St. Paul, may be said to constitute the connecting link between the New Testament and the sub-apostolic writings. They may, indeed, contain fragments of St. Paul's own letters, and they are much influenced by Pauline language. But in spirit they belong, pretty clearly, to a later age. They represent a period in which the teaching of the Church was assuming the form of a fixed tradition, claiming apostolic origin, and rapidly becoming stereotyped in simple phrases and formulae, largely designed to counteract the wild speculations of Gnosticism which were now rampant, if they had not yet attained their fullest and most systematic development. We hear of "the faith" or "the teaching" as well as of faith : faith is faith in Christ, but it is quite as much belief in the Church's very simple teaching about Him : and the emphasis on practical morality is greater than the emphasis upon faith. Faith and love are very closely associated together.[1] In such writings we naturally find the traditional statements about the work of Christ, and sometimes about His death, but there is little of the Pauline emphasis upon the death. "Faithful is the saying, and worthy of all acceptation, that Christ Jesus came into the world to save sinners."[2] "Great is the mystery of godliness ; He who was manifested in the flesh, justified in the spirit, seen of angels, preached among the nations, believed on in the world, received up in glory."[3] It is remarkable that in this last early liturgical fragment— which may very well be spoken of as the first trace of a liturgical as distinct from a baptismal creed—there is no express mention of the death. The doctrine of the Church is identified with the actual sayings of Christ : "If any man teacheth a different doctrine, and consenteth

[1] 1 Tim. i. 14, ii. 15, iv. 12.
[2] 1 Tim. i. 15.
[3] 1 Tim. iii. 16.   It is generally recognized that the true reading here is ὅς, not θεός.

not to sound words, even the words of our Lord Jesus Christ." [1] In the first Epistle to Timothy the only doctrinal reference to the death of Christ is the statement that there is " one mediator between God and men, himself man, Christ Jesus, who gave himself a ransom for all." [2] In the second Epistle we have an echo of the Pauline doctrine of dying with Christ which seems to have passed into a Christian hymn : " If we died with him, we shall also live with him." [3] In the Epistle to Titus the writer speaks of Christ as having given " himself for us, that he might redeem us ($\lambda \upsilon \tau \rho \acute{\omega}\sigma \eta \tau \alpha \iota$) from all iniquity, and purify unto himself a people for his own possession," [4] and of God our Saviour as having saved us "not by works done in righteousness, which we did ourselves, but according to His mercy . . . through the washing of regeneration and renewing of the Holy Ghost." [5] That there should be such scanty traces of any distinctly Pauline doctrine in Epistles which were put forward in his name is good testimony to the slight influence exercised by the distinctively Pauline theology even in Churches which greatly reverenced his name. Here we have just the traditional statements and metaphors accepted by the Church, and a few traces of distinctively Pauline language ; but there is no attempt to insist upon any distinctively Pauline theory or explanation of Christ's death, or to substitute any other for it. The Pauline theories have not yet become part of the Church's really operative theology.

The Apostolic Fathers and Apologists

What has been said about the attitude of the non-Pauline Epistles towards the death of Christ holds

---

[1] 1 Tim. vi. 3.

[2] 1 Tim. ii. 5. The word is $\dot{\alpha}\nu\tau\dot{\iota}\lambda\upsilon\tau\rho\sigma\nu$, not as in Matt.-Mk. $\lambda\acute{\upsilon}\tau\rho\sigma\nu$. Hence the passage must be regarded as an independent reproduction of the traditional phrase rather than as a quotation. The substitution of " all " for " many " is noticeable : the origin of the phrase in Is. liii. has been forgotten. The historic fact of the death is mentioned in vi. 13.   [3] 2 Tim. ii. 11.

[4] Titus ii. 14. It will be noticed that here, as elsewhere in early writings, the emphasis is rather on what Christians were redeemed or purchased *for* than on what they were redeemed *from*.

[5] Titus iii. 5.

equally of the Apostolic Fathers, and of Justin and other writers up to Irenaeus. In some of them, indeed, there is nothing to connect salvation with the death of Christ. That is so in the short writings known as the *Didache* and the 2nd Epistle of Clement, and in the much longer *Shepherd of Hermas*,[1] which is entirely occupied with repentance, forgiveness, and salvation. But in most of them we find the accustomed quotations from prophecy, and the traditional formulae which are based upon them. We are told by Ignatius, for instance, that "the Cross is salvation and life eternal";[2] and by Clement of Rome that the spies promised to save Rahab and her family when they saw the scarlet wool in the window (observe how the authority for the atonement always comes from the Old Testament) "making it plain that it is through the blood of the Lord that there shall be redemption to all who believe and hope in the Lord."[3] In Clement again we read: "On account of the love which he had for us Jesus Christ our Lord gave his blood on our behalf, and his flesh for our flesh, and his life for our life."[4] Ignatius tells us that even for the angels, "if they do not believe in the blood of Christ, for them also judgement is appointed."[5]

The references to the blood of Christ are peculiarly frequent in this writer, and he is one of the very few at all early writers who ever define the belief which saves as belief in the blood or death of Christ.[6] In most of these writers the traditional phrases about the sacrificial

---

[1] " He has purified their sins at the cost of many labours and sufferings " (*Sim.* 5, vi. 2)—an echo of Hebrews—can hardly be regarded as an exception.

[2] Περίψημα τὸ ἐμὸν πνεῦμα τοῦ σταυροῦ, ὅ ἐστιν σκάνδαλον τοῖς ἀπιστοῦσιν, ἡμῖν δὲ σωτηρία καὶ ζωὴ αἰώνιος (*Eph.* xviii. 1).

[3] Πρόδηλον ποιοῦντες ὅτι διὰ τοῦ αἵματος τοῦ Κυρίου λύτρωσις ἔσται πᾶσιν τοῖς πιστεύουσιν καὶ ἐλπίζουσιν ἐπὶ τὸν Θεόν (1 *Cor.* xii. 7).

[4] Διὰ τὴν ἀγάπην, ἣν ἔσχεν πρὸς ἡμᾶς, τὸ αἷμα αὐτοῦ ἔδωκεν ὑπὲρ ἡμῶν Ἰησοῦς Χριστὸς ὁ Κύριος ἡμῶν ἐν θελήματι Θεοῦ, καὶ τὴν σάρκα ὑπὲρ τῆς σαρκὸς ἡμῶν καὶ τὴν ψυχὴν ὑπὲρ τῶν ψυχῶν ἡμῶν (1 *Cor.* xlix. 6). In 1 *Cor.* ii. 1 the παθήματα αὐτοῦ refer, according to the common reading, to God (τοῦ Θεοῦ), but there is a variant Χριστοῦ. Lightfoot reads Θεοῦ ; Loofs and others Χριστοῦ. If Θεοῦ be the right reading (as is probably the case), Clement uses language which would afterwards have been considered Sabellian.

[5] Μηδεὶς πλανάσθω· καὶ τὰ ἐπουράνια καὶ ἡ δόξα τῶν ἀγγέλων καὶ οἱ ἄρχοντες ὁρατοί τε καὶ ἀόρατοι, ἐὰν μὴ πιστεύσωσιν εἰς τὸ αἷμα Χριστοῦ [τοῦ Θεοῦ], κἀκείνοις κρίσις ἐστίν (*Smyrn.* vi.).

[6] Τὸν δι' ἡμᾶς ἀποθανόντα ἵνα πιστεύσαντες εἰς τὸν θάνατον αὐτοῦ τὸ ἀποθανεῖν ἐκφύγητε (*Trall.* ii.).

character of the death can be found.   But as soon as
they attempt to explain precisely how the death of Christ
contributes to the forgiveness of sins, it is always some
subjective, ethical, and quite intelligible effect upon the
believer to which the saving efficacy is attributed.   Here
it will be as well to enumerate the different reasons which
are given in these writings for the death of Christ. They
have for the most part already been met with in the
canonical writings which we have examined, but they
are now more definitely formulated, so as to constitute
some nearer approach to a theory on the subject.

(1) The death of Christ is treated as a necessary
element in the incarnation.   Christ would not have been
man, if He had not died.   And particularly the death
is appealed to as a refutation of that earliest of heresies,
the Docetism which denied the reality of Christ's body,
and consequently of His true humanity.   "All these
things," says Ignatius, "He suffered for our sakes; and He
truly suffered, as also He truly raised Himself." [1] Christ
died, in the words of Justin, "showing by these things
that he has become truly a man capable of suffering." [2]

(2) In so far as any further *a priori* necessity for
Christ's death is recognized, it is, as a rule, simply the
necessity that prophecy should be fulfilled.   The argument from the fulfilment of prophecy impressed Jew and
Greek alike to an extent which is startling to those who
are accustomed to read ancient writings with a critical
eye. [3]   The exact fulfilment of the prophecies by the
death of the Messiah was therefore to the ancient Church
a particularly convincing proof that He was the Messiah
or Son of God.   Allusions to the detailed accompaniments of His death were found in the most irrelevant
expressions of psalmist or historian—such as the horns

---

[1] Ταῦτα γὰρ πάντα ἔπαθεν δι᾿ ἡμᾶς [ἵνα σωθῶμεν], καὶ ἀληθῶς ἔπαθεν, ὡς καὶ
ἀληθῶς ἀνέστησεν ἑαυτόν (*Smyrn.* ii.   Cf. *Magnes.* xi. ; *Trall.* ix., x.).

[2] Δηλῶν διὰ τούτων ὅτι ἀληθῶς παθητὸς ἄνθρωπος γεγένηται (*Dial. c. Tryph.* 99.
Cf. 98 ἄνθρωπος ἀντιληπτικὸς παθῶν, and 103 *ad fin.*)

[3] Miracles were not a very convincing proof to an age in which such stories were
current in connexion with all religions : the correspondence between the prophecy and
the historical event was, as it were, a miracle which the inquirer could verify for
himself.   The importance attached to this evidence might be most fully illustrated by
the strongly anti-Jewish writer of the Epistle to Barnabas, which is chiefly occupied with
the subject.

of the unicorn or the outstretched arms of Moses. In Justin, for instance, we read : " If this [the suffering of death in accordance with prophecy] is that which characterizes him and points him out to all, how could we also have failed with confidence to believe in him?" "And as many as know the writings of the prophets," says the same writer, " will say that it is He and no other, if they only hear that He was crucified." [1]

(3) If the death was necessary to fulfil the prophecies of that death, it was still more obviously necessary to make possible the resurrection—the crowning miracle, the supreme proof both of Christ's divine Sonship and of man's immortality. All through the early history of the Church (as we have already seen in the Acts), the resurrection occupied a far more prominent place in the Church's teaching than the crucifixion. We may even suspect that, when an early Christian spoke of the blood of Christ, he was usually thinking quite as much of the triumph over death as of the death itself. This ground for the necessity for Christ's death is often closely connected with the necessity of fulfilling prophecy—the supposed prophecies of the resurrection. Thus, according to the author of the so-called Epistle of Barnabas, Christ " endured in order to destroy death and show forth the resurrection from the dead, because it was necessary for Him to be manifested in the flesh, in order that He might both fulfil the promise to the fathers and, preparing for Himself the new people, might show, while He was upon the earth, that, as He has accomplished the resurrection, so He will Himself conduct the judgement." [2]

---

[1] After Trypho has explained this difficulty (εἰ δὲ καὶ ἀτίμως οὕτως σταυρωθῆναι τὸν Χριστόν, ἀποροῦμεν), Justin replies : εἰ μὲν μὴ ἔμελλε πάσχειν ὁ Χριστός, φημὶ αὐτῷ ἐγώ, μηδὲ προεῖπον οἱ προφῆται ὅτι ἀπὸ τῶν ἀνομιῶν τοῦ λαοῦ ἀχθήσεται εἰς θάνατον καὶ ἀτιμωθήσεται καὶ μαστιχθήσεται καὶ ἐν τοῖς ἀνόμοις λογισθήσεται καὶ ὡς πρόβατον ἐπὶ σφαγὴν ἀχθήσεται . . . καλῶς εἶχε θαυμάζειν. Εἰ δὲ τοῦτό ἐστι τὸ χαρακτηρίζον αὐτὸν καὶ πᾶσι μηνύον, πῶς οὐχὶ καὶ ἡμεῖς θαρροῦντες πεπιστεύκαμεν εἰς αὐτὸν ; Καὶ ὅσοι νενοήκασι τὰ τῶν προφήτων, τοῦτον φήσουσιν, οὐκ ἄλλον, εἰ μόνον ἀκούσειαν ὅτι οὗτος ἐσταυρωμένος (Dial. c. Tryph. 89). Trypho then admits the necessity for " suffering and being led like a sheep," but asks why he should die " so disgracefully and dishonourably." Justin then enumerates the various " parallels and types " which point to crucifixion as the necessary mode of death—Moses holding up his arms, etc.

[2] Αὐτὸς δὲ ἵνα καταργήσῃ τὸν θάνατον καὶ τὴν ἐκ νεκρῶν ἀνάστασιν δείξῃ, ὅτι ἐν

(4) The death of Christ is constantly spoken of as an example of obedience to God, humility, and patient endurance of persecution. So, immediately after quoting Is. liii., Clement goes on to base upon it not an assurance of forgiveness through Christ's blood but an exhortation to humility.[1] How little the mere use of the word " sacrifice " necessarily implies any theory of unique and all-potent vicarious expiation, is shown by the fact that Ignatius speaks of his own approaching martyrdom as likewise a sacrifice to God for His flock. " Grant me nothing more than that I may be poured out as an offering to God, for there is still an altar ready."[2] Hermas does not hesitate even to declare that " the sins of all these [the Martyrs] were taken away because they suffered on account of the name of the Son of God."[3]

(5) The death of Christ is treated as a revelation of the love of God, moving the sinner to gratitude, repentance, and amendment. When the death of Christ—as distinct from His incarnation and His teaching—is brought into special connexion with the forgiveness of sins, it is (whenever explanation of any kind is given) always in this way that the death is supposed to be efficacious. " Let us look steadfastly to the blood of Christ," says Clement, " and recognize how precious it is to His Father, for being poured out for our salvation it brought to all the world the grace of repentance."[4] Only through the repentance which the thought of God's love inspires does it work. " In love were all the elect of God made perfect ; without love nothing is well-pleasing to God ; in love the Master took us unto Himself. It was on account of the love which He had towards us that

---

σαρκὶ ἔδει αὐτὸν φανερωθῆναι, ὑπέμεινεν, ἵνα καὶ τοῖς πατράσιν τὴν ἐπαγγελίαν ἀποδῷ καὶ αὐτὸς ἑαυτῷ τὸν λαὸν τὸν καινὸν ἑτοιμάζων ἐπιδείξῃ, ἐπὶ τῆς γῆς ὤν, ὅτι τὴν ἀνάστασιν αὐτὸς ποιήσας κρινεῖ (Barn. v. 6, 7).

[1] Ὁρᾶτε, ἄνδρες ἀγαπητοί, τίς ὁ ὑπογραμμὸς ὁ διδομένος ἡμῖν· εἰ γὰρ ὁ Κύριος οὕτως ἐταπεινοφρόνησεν, τί ποιήσωμεν ἡμεῖς οἱ ὑπὸ τὸν ζυγὸν τῆς χάριτος αὐτοῦ δι' αὐτοῦ ἐλθόντες ; (1 Cor. xvi. 17).

[2] Πλέον [δέ] μοι μὴ παράσχησθε τοῦ σπονδισθῆναι Θεῷ, ὡς ἔτι θυσιαστήριον ἕτοιμόν ἐστιν (Rom. ii. 2).

[3] Πάντων τούτων αἱ ἀμαρτίαι ἀφηρέθησαν ὅτι ἔπαθον διὰ τὸ ὄνομα τοῦ υἱοῦ τοῦ Θεοῦ (Sim. 9, xxviii. 3).

[4] Ἀτενίσωμεν εἰς τὸ αἷμα τοῦ Χριστοῦ καὶ γνῶμεν ὡς ἔστιν τίμιον τῷ πατρὶ αὐτοῦ, ὅτι διὰ τὴν ἡμετέραν σωτηρίαν ἐκχυθὲν παντὶ τῷ κόσμῳ μετανοίας χάριν ὑπήνεγκεν (1 Cor. vii. 4).

O

Jesus Christ our Lord gave His blood on our behalf. ., and His flesh on behalf of our flesh, and His soul on behalf of our souls."[1] Ignatius speaks of God in Christ as calling "us in His passion, since we are members of Him;" and he actually identifies the love of Christ with His blood.[2] So in Justin's words, "He excited all that fear God to praise Him in consequence of His having shown mercy to them."[3] No doctrine could be more in harmony with the teaching of our Lord Himself : such a doctrine adds nothing to the teaching of the Master Himself except that from the nature of the case He could not well have insisted Himself upon this influence of a death which had not yet taken place.

(6) Occasionally there is the thought which is prominent in the Epistle to the Hebrews—that Christ suffered that He might be able to sympathize with mankind and so save them. Justin speaks of the Logos becoming man "in order that becoming a fellow-participator even in our sufferings, He might also effect our healing."[4] Then in a Syriac work of Melito we read: "For our Lord, when He was born man, was condemned in order that He might loose, was seized upon in order that He might let go, suffered in order that He might have compassion."[5] It will be observed that here, as often, the forgiveness of sins is attributed to the direct act of Christ—not to any actual consequence of His death or to the subjective contemplation of that death.

---

[1] Ἐν τῇ ἀγάπῃ ἐτελειώθησαν πάντες οἱ ἐκλεκτοὶ τοῦ Θεοῦ· δίχα ἀγάπης οὐδὲν εὐάρεστόν ἐστιν τῷ Θεῷ· ἐν ἀγάπῃ προσελάβετο ἡμᾶς ὁ δεσπότης· διὰ τὴν ἀγάπην, ἣν ἔσχεν πρὸς ἡμᾶς, τὸ αἷμα αὐτοῦ ἔδωκεν ὑπὲρ ἡμῶν Ἰησοῦς Χριστὸς ὁ Κύριος ἡμῶν ἐν θελήματι Θεοῦ, καὶ τὴν σάρκα ὑπὲρ τῆς σαρκὸς ἡμῶν καὶ τὴν ψυχὴν ὑπὲρ τῶν ψυχῶν ἡμῶν (Clem. Rom. 1 *Cor.* xlix. 5, 6).

[2] Ἐν τῷ πάθει αὐτοῦ προσκαλεῖται ὑμᾶς, ὄντας μέλη αὐτοῦ (*Trall.* xi.) : ὑμεῖς οὖν τὴν πραϋπάθειαν ἀναλαβόντες ἀνακτήσασθε ἑαυτοὺς ἐν πίστει, ὅ ἐστι σὰρξ τοῦ Κυρίου, καὶ ἐν ἀγάπῃ ὅ ἐστιν αἷμα Ἰησοῦ Χριστοῦ (viii. 1). The passage is interesting as showing how easily the early Christian mind passed from the symbol to the thing symbolized. I may add that Ignatius adopts St. Paul's idea of a mystical dying with Christ (ἐὰν μὴ αὐθαιρέτως ἔχωμεν τὸ ἀποθανεῖν εἰς τὸ αὐτοῦ πάθος, τὸ ζῆν αὐτοῦ οὐκ ἔστιν ἐν ἡμῖν, *Magnes.* 5). This is not a common thought in the earliest Fathers.

[3] Πάντας τοὺς φοβουμένους τὸν Θεὸν προέτρεπεν αἰνεῖν τὸν Θεὸν διὰ τὸ ἐλεῆσαι (*Dial. c. Tryph.* 106). Justin goes on to explain that it was the fulfilment of prophecy and Christ's own predictions by the death and resurrection which produced repentance in the apostles.

[4] Ὅπως καὶ τῶν παθῶν τῶν ἡμετέρων συμμέτοχος γενόμενος καὶ ἴασιν ποιήσηται (2 *Apol.* 13).

[5] Cureton, *Spicilegium Syriacum*, p. 52.

(7) In the very anti-Jewish Epistle of Barnabas we find that one purpose of Christ's death was to complete the guilt of the Jews and so justify the transference of their covenanted privileges to the Christians. "He was manifested that they might have their tale of sins completed, and that we might receive the covenant through Him who inherited it." [1]

(8) Sometimes, as already in several passages in the canonical epistles, we have a vague suggestion that the death of Christ constituted a triumph over the devil and other evil spirits. It is difficult in such passages to say whether the thought is simply of a moral victory over moral evil or of a supernatural conquest of supernatural beings. At this stage the two things are not sharply distinguished, and of course this efficacy is always connected with the effect of the resurrection, without which the death could not possibly be regarded as a triumph. Here we have the germ of the theory that the death of Christ was an actual price or ransom paid to the devil. I will postpone illustration of this view until we come to study it in its developed form. [2]

There is nothing in any of these ways of treating the death of Christ which shows the influence of St. Paul's characteristic teaching.

And when we turn from the objective cause to the subjective conditions of salvation, equally little trace do we find of St. Paul's distinctive doctrine of justification by faith apart from works. Still more rarely is there any exclusive emphasis on belief in the blood of Jesus. Sometimes, but more rarely than might be expected, we find quotations or echoes of St. Paul's actual words about faith. As is natural, these are particularly frequent in the Roman Clement. He declares indeed, that, " being called by His will in Christ Jesus, we are not justified by ourselves or by our own wisdom or knowledge or piety or by works which we have performed in holiness of heart, but by faith, by which the Almighty God justified all who have been justified since the beginning of the

[1] See below, pp. 212-3.　　　　[2] See below, pp. 201, 242 sq.

world." [1] But how little he really appropriated the characteristic doctrine of St. Paul, or at least that side of St. Paul which (to the exclusion of all other sides) has been emphasized by the traditional dogmatics, is shown by his comments and interpretations. So far as actual belief is insisted on, it is not specifically belief in the atoning blood, or even belief in Christ at all. After explaining that the scarlet thread of Rahab signified that redemption from sin comes through the death of Christ, he goes on to say that this is only to " all who believe and hope in God." [2] How completely it is to the moral effects of belief that he really attributes salvation is shown by the fact that in this very chapter he declares that Rahab was saved " on account of faith *and hospitality*." [3] He even speaks of our being " justified by works and not by words." [4] It is hardly too much to say that in Clement the doctrine of justification by faith is interpreted to mean justification by works. It is a significant fact that, when Clement speaks about the necessity of Christian instruction for children, he tells us simply that they are to be taught " how humility prevaileth with God, how much pure love availeth with God, how the fear of Him is noble and great and saves all who walk holily in a pure mind." [5] There is no specific reference to the death of Christ. This of course does not imply that he thought little of Christian doctrine, but it does show how largely Christian doctrine for him consisted simply in the Christian idea of God and in Christian morality. This was all the doctrine he thought it necessary for children to learn.

[1] Καὶ ἡμεῖς οὖν, διὰ θελήματος αὐτοῦ ἐν Χριστῷ Ἰησοῦ κληθέντες, οὐ δι' ἑαυτῶν δικαιούμεθα οὐδὲ διὰ τῆς ἡμετέρας σοφίας ἢ συνέσεως ἢ εὐσεβείας ἢ ἔργων ὧν κατειργασάμεθα ἐν ὁσιότητι καρδίας, ἀλλὰ διὰ τῆς πίστεως, δι' ἧς πάντας τοὺς ἀπ' αἰῶνος ὁ παντοκράτωρ Θεὸς ἐδικαίωσεν (1 Cor. xxxii. 4).
[2] Πρόδηλον ποιοῦντες ὅτι διὰ τοῦ αἵματος τοῦ Κυρίου λύτρωσις ἔσται πᾶσιν τοῖς πιστεύουσιν καὶ ἐλπίζουσιν ἐπὶ τὸν Θεόν (1 Cor. xii. 7).
[3] Διὰ πίστιν καὶ φιλοξενίαν ἐσώθη Ῥαὰβ ἡ πόρνη (1 Cor. xii. 1). So it was " on account of faith and hospitality " that a son was given to Abraham in his old age (x. 7). He was blessed " because he wrought righteousness and truth by means of faith " (xxxi. 2).
[4] Ἔργοις δικαιούμενοι καὶ μὴ λόγοις (1 Cor. xxx. 3).
[5] Τὰ τέκνα ὑμῶν τῆς ἐν Χριστῷ παιδείας μεταλαμβανέτωσαν· μαθέτωσαν, τί ταπεινοφροσύνη παρὰ Θεῷ ἰσχύει, τί ἀγάπη ἁγνὴ παρὰ τῷ Θεῷ δύναται, πῶς ὁ φόβος αὐτοῦ καλὸς καὶ μέγας καὶ σώζων πάντας τοὺς ἐν αὐτῷ ὁσίως ἀναστρεφομένους ἐν καθαρᾷ διανοίᾳ (1 Cor. xxi. 8).

Ignatius is the most dogmatic of this whole group of writers. He is therefore the most popular with many modern theologians. He insists strenuously on the necessity of orthodox belief, as he understood it : and more than any other of the Apostolic Fathers he emphasizes the necessity of the belief in Christ's death. The death of Christ is with him one of the " three mysteries of a cry " [1]—that is, mysteries which caused men to cry out, amazing mysteries—the other two being " the virginity of Mary and her child-bearing." He tells us that even for angels the law holds that, " if they do not believe in the blood of Christ, for them too judgement is appointed." [2] Yet even for Ignatius " Faith is your guide, love is the way that leads to the Father." [3] The most formal definition of the conditions of salvation which he reaches is that " faith is the beginning of life ; love is the end thereof." [4] Ignatius may certainly be cited in defence of the formula, often accepted by later Catholic orthodoxy, that salvation is by faith *and* works. So Theophilus speaks of him who is well-pleasing to God " through faith and righteousness and the doing of good works." [5] Some writers go further. Barnabas does not hesitate even to exhort his reader either to save his soul by preaching the word " or by labouring with thy hands thou shalt work unto the ransom of thy sins." [6] Even when salvation is attributed to faith, faith is (as already in Hebrews) practically identified with obedience to the commandments of God or of Christ.

[1] Καὶ ἔλαθεν τὸν ἄρχοντα τοῦ αἰῶνος τούτου ἡ παρθενία Μαρίας, καὶ ὁ τοκετὸς αὐτῆς, ὁμοίως καὶ ὁ θάνατος τοῦ Κυρίου· τρία μυστήρια κραυγῆς, ἅτινα ἐν ἡσυχίᾳ Θεοῦ ἐπράχθη (*Eph.* xix. 1). This is the first allusion to the Virgin Birth in Christian literature apart from the present text of the prefaces to the first and third Gospels.

[2] Καὶ τὰ ἐπουράνια καὶ ἡ δόξα τῶν ἀγγέλων καὶ οἱ ἄρχοντες ὁρατοί τε καὶ ἀόρατοι, ἐὰν μὴ πιστεύωσιν εἰς τὸ αἷμα Χριστοῦ [τοῦ Θεοῦ], κἀκείνοις κρίσις ἐστίν (*Smyrn.* vi. 1. Cf. also *Trall.* ii. 1).

[3] ἡ δὲ πίστις ὑμῶν ἀναγωγεὺς ὑμῶν, ἡ δὲ ἀγάπη ὁδὸς ἡ ἀναφέρουσα εἰς Θεόν, *Eph.* ix. 1.

[4] Ὧν οὐδὲν λανθάνει ὑμᾶς, ἐὰν τελείως εἰς Ἰησοῦν Χριστὸν ἔχητε τὴν πίστιν καὶ τὴν ἀγάπην· ἥτις ἐστὶν ἀρχὴ ζωῆς καὶ τέλος· ἀρχὴ μὲν πίστις, τέλος δὲ ἀγάπη (*Eph.* xiv. 1).

[5] *Ad Autolycum* ii. 38. There is absolutely no allusion to the atonement in this Apology of three books (c. A.D. 170), while there is a fairly full account of the doctrine of the Logos.

[6] Διὰ λόγου κοπιῶν καὶ πορευχόμενος εἰς τὸ παρακαλέσαι καὶ μελετῶν εἰς τὸ σῶσαι τὴν ψυχὴν τῷ λόγῳ ἢ διὰ τῶν χειρῶν σου ἐργάσῃ εἰς λύτρον ἁμαρτιῶν σου (*Barn.* xix. 10).

Thus according to Hermas, one of the seven women who surround the tower of the Church " is called Faith : it is through her that the elect of God are saved." [1] But this does not prevent his saying that the commandments are " good and strong and glad and glorious and able to save the soul of a man " [2]—very un-Pauline teaching. The idea that a man cannot keep all the commandments of God tends to prevent their being kept.[3] Of those who have suffered " for the name " he says that their sins were forgiven because they suffered on account of the name of the Son of God.[4] Still more un-Pauline, and here we must add unevangelical, is the doctrine that it is possible for a man to earn additional glory by doing more than is commanded.[5] Works are insisted upon just as strenuously as faith : " Do thy work," he says, " and thou shalt be saved." [6] Elsewhere salvation is attributed to the fear of God which produces good works.[7] At times, in all these writers, the saving efficacy of Christ's work is made to consist mainly—sometimes wholly—in His teaching. According to the author—probably a layman or possibly a Reader [8]—of the Homily misnamed the 2nd Epistle of Clement, " Christ willed to save those who were being lost, and He saved many," but He saved simply " by

---

[1] Ἡ μὲν πρώτη αὐτῶν, ἡ κρατοῦσα τὰς χεῖρας, Πίστις καλεῖται· διὰ ταύτης σώζονται οἱ ἐκλεκτοὶ τοῦ Θεοῦ (Vis. 3, viii. 3). Self-control (ἐγκρατεία), is a daughter of faith : simplicity, knowledge, guilelessness, gravity, love (ἁπλότης, ἐπιστήμη, ἀκακία, σεμνότης, ἀγάπη) are " daughters one of the other " (Vis. 3, viii.).

[2] Συζητῶν περὶ τῶν ἐντολῶν, ὅτι καλαὶ καὶ δυναταὶ καὶ ἱλαραὶ καὶ ἔνδοξοι καὶ δυνάμεναι σῶσαι ψυχὴν ἀνθρώπου (Sim. 6, i. 1).

[3] Νῦν δέ σοι λέγω· ἐὰν ταύτας μὴ φυλάξῃς, ἀλλὰ παρενθυμηθῇς, οὐχ ἕξεις σωτηρίαν, οὔτε τὰ τέκνα σου οὔτε ὁ οἶκός σου, ἐπεὶ ἤδη σεαυτῷ κέκρικας τοῦ μὴ δύνασθαι τὰς ἐντολὰς ταύτας ὑπὸ ἀνθρώπου φυλαχθῆναι (Mand. 12, iii. 6. Cf. the rest of the chapter).

[4] Ὅσοι ποτὲ ἔπαθον διὰ τὸ ὄνομα, ἔνδοξοί εἰσι παρὰ τῷ Θεῷ, καὶ πάντων τούτων αἱ ἁμαρτίαι ἀφῃρέθησαν, ὅτι ἔπαθον διὰ τὸ ὄνομα τοῦ υἱοῦ τοῦ Θεοῦ (Sim. 9, xxviii. 3).

[5] Ἐὰν δέ τι ἀγαθὸν ποιήσῃς ἐκτὸς τῆς ἐντολῆς τοῦ Θεοῦ, σεαυτῷ περιποιήσῃ δόξαν περισσοτέραν, καὶ ἔσῃ ἐνδοξότερος παρὰ τῷ Θεῷ οὗ ἔμελλες εἶναι (Sim. 5, iii. 3).

[6] Τὸ δὲ σὸν ἔργον ἐργάζου, καὶ σωθήσῃ (Sim. i. 11). In the next chapter he shows how the rich man may procure salvation by the intercession of the poor whom he has succoured. Cf. Vis. 3, viii. 5 : ὅταν οὖν τὰ ἔργα τῆς μητρὸς αὐτῶν πάντα ποιήσῃς, δυνάσαι ζῆσαι.

[7] Οὗτος δέ ἐστιν ὁ φόβος, ὃν δεῖ σε φοβηθῆναι καὶ σωθήσῃ (Mand. 7, i. 1).

[8] Such is a possible interpretation of the words : ἀναγινώσκω ὑμῖν ἐντευξιν εἰς τὸ προσέχειν τοῖς γεγραμμένοις, ἵνα καὶ ἑαυτοὺς σώσητε καὶ τὸν ἀναγινώσκοντα ἐν ὑμῖν (2 Cor. xix. 1).

coming and calling us when we were now being lost."[1]
He insists upon the importance of faith ; but faith is
simply faith in the promises of God, and faith is valued
only for the repentance and good works to which it leads.[2]
He assumes that such faith is necessary to the service of
God, and the salvation which such service will procure
is salvation by Christ ; but salvation is nowhere in this
writing specially connected with the death of Christ.
The spirit of this charming little sermon is for the most
part entirely in accordance with the spirit of Christ's
own teaching.[3] Such simple teaching was still possible
in the Church of about 120 A.D. or later.[4]

It may be well to insist a little further upon the
special significance of the teaching of Justin in this
matter. From an early Christian writer who had been
before his conversion a professional philosopher it
would be natural to expect, in Apologies addressed to the
heathen, something like a reasoned account of so prominent a feature in Christianity as the belief in a crucified
Saviour who was at once divine and human : while in
his formal argument with Trypho the Jew he was forced
to come to close quarters with what presented itself to
Jewish minds as the most offensive feature in the new
religion—the scandal of the crucified Messiah. And
we are not altogether disappointed : he does more often
touch on the purpose of Christ's sufferings and death
than any writer we have yet examined—except, of course,
St. Paul. He repeats the usual formulae, and adds

---

[1] Οὕτως καὶ ὁ Χριστὸς ἠθέλησεν σῶσαι τὰ ἀπολλύμενα, καὶ ἔσωσεν πολλούς, ἐλθὼν
καὶ καλέσας ἡμᾶς ἤδη ἀπολλυμένους (2 Cor. ii. 7). So ποιοῦντες γὰρ τὸ θέλημα
Χριστοῦ εὑρήσομεν ἀνάπαυσιν (vi. 7). So Χριστὸς ὁ Κύριος, ὁ σώσας ἡμᾶς (ix. 5), but
this is equivalent to ἐγένετο σὰρξ καὶ οὕτως ἡμᾶς ἐκάλεσεν.

[2] Ἡμεῖς οὖν ἐν καθαρᾷ καρδίᾳ δουλεύσωμεν τῷ Θεῷ, καὶ ἐσόμεθα δίκαιοι · ἐὰν
δὲ μὴ δουλεύσωμεν διὰ τοῦ μὴ πιστεύειν ἡμᾶς τῇ ἐπαγγελίᾳ τοῦ Θεοῦ, ταλαί-
πωροι ἐσόμεθα (2 Cor. xi. 1). Οὕτως καὶ ἡμεῖς, ἕως ἐσμὲν ἐν τούτῳ τῷ κόσμῳ, ἐν
τῇ σαρκὶ ἃ ἐπράξαμεν πονηρὰ μετανοήσωμεν ἐξ ὅλης τῆς καρδίας, ἵνα σωθῶμεν ὑπὸ τοῦ
Κυρίου, ἕως ἔχομεν καρπὸν μετανοίας (viii. 2).

[3] He does, however, attach a kind of importance to almsgiving and to fasting, which
is hardly in accordance with Christ's teaching. Καλὸν οὖν ἐλεημοσύνη ὡς μετάνοια
ἁμαρτίας · κρείσσων νηστεία προσευχῆς, ἐλεημοσύνη δὲ ἀμφοτέρων · ἀγάπη δὲ
καλύπτει πλῆθος ἁμαρτιῶν · προσευχὴ δὲ ἐκ καλῆς συνειδήσεως ἐκ θανάτου ῥύεται.
μακάριος πᾶς ὁ εὑρεθεὶς ἐν τούτοις πλήρης · ἐλεημοσύνη γὰρ κούφισμα ἁμαρτίας γίνεται
(2 Cor. xvi. 4).

[4] Harnack discovers in it the letter of Pope Soter to Dionysius of Corinth (circa
170 A.D.), but the words cited in note 8, p. 198, suggest an oral discourse, and certainly
not a Pope.

prophetic proof-texts in great abundance.   He expressly
bases his assertion that in baptism the sins of the penitent
and believing are forgiven " through the blood of Christ
and His death " on the fact that Isaiah said so ; [1] and
he then quotes the whole of the great passage in Is. liii.
But he never speaks of Christ's death as being a punishment for sin, very rarely as a sacrifice.[2]   And when he
explains, his explanations are all rational and éthical.
There is not one of them which may not be brought
under one or other of the above heads.   This is all the
more remarkable because he is much more seriously
influenced by St. Paul than most of the writers who
preceded him.   He not unfrequently quotes characteristic Pauline language.   The Apostle of the Gentiles
was now beginning, in all except heretically Jewish-
Christian circles, to be recognized as an authority who
must be accepted and explained somehow.   Yet it is
only in actual quotations of Pauline formulae that he
can be said to adopt Pauline theories : the formulae are
explained in a way of his own, and frequently explained
away, or left on one side.   Thus he explains St. Paul's
doctrines of original sin and predestination in a very
libertarian or Pelagian sense.   The fall, according to
Justin, brought with it no necessity of sinning, but God
foresaw the way in which successive generations would
abuse the gift of free-will, and so foretold and fore-

---

[1] Ἐκεῖνο τὸ σωτήριον λοῦτρον ἦν ὅ εἶπε, τὸ τοῖς μεταγινώσκουσι καὶ μηκέτι αἵμασι
τράγων καὶ προβάτων ἢ σποδῷ δαμάλεως ἢ σεμιδάλεως προσφοραῖς καθαριζομένοις
ἀλλὰ πίστει διὰ τοῦ αἵματος τοῦ Χριστοῦ καὶ τοῦ θανατοῦ αὐτοῦ, ὃς διὰ τοῦτο
ἀπέθανεν, ὡς αὐτὸς Ἡσαΐας ἔφη (*Dial. c. Tryph.* 13).   So again : αἵματι σωτηρίῳ
πεπιστεύκαμεν (*op. cit.* 24).   τὸ σωτήριον τοῦτο μυστήριον, τουτέστι τὸ πάθος τοῦ
Χριστοῦ, δι' οὗ τούτους ἔσωσεν (*op. cit.* 74).   And again : ὡς καὶ ἡμᾶς βεβαπτισμένους
ταῖς βαρυτάταις ἁμαρτίαις, ἃς ἐπράξαμεν, διὰ τοῦ σταυρωθῆναι ἐπὶ τοῦ ξύλου καὶ δι'
ὕδατος ἁγνίσαι ὁ Χριστὸς ἡμῶν ἐλυτρώσατο καὶ οἶκον εὐχῆς καὶ προσκυνήσεως ἐποίησε
(*op. cit.* 86).   In Ignatius we get the idea that it was by the baptism of Christ that the
baptismal waters acquired that cleansing power (ὃς ἐγεννήθη καὶ ἐβαπτίσθη ἵνα τῷ
πάθει τὸ ὕδωρ καθαρίσῃ, *Eph.* 18), as in our own baptismal service (" didst sanctify
water to the mystical washing away of sin "), and yet this power was ultimately, it
would seem, dependent on the Passion (τῷ πάθει).   The ambiguity of the language
testifies to the difficulty which was experienced in establishing a connexion between
the two things ; for the most part the process was by the simpler-minded Christians
regarded as a piece of magic : the mysterious efficacy of Christ's death was applied to
the individual by baptism.   There was no question as to the justice or the rationale of
the arrangement.

[2] Προσφορὰ ἦν ὑπὲρ πάντων τῶν μετανοεῖν βουλομένων ἁμαρτωλῶν (*Dial. c.
Tryph.* 40) ; where he is speaking of the Paschal lamb as a type of Christ—of course
echoing St. Paul.

ordained the remedy.[1]   Like St. Paul, he several times
quotes the Deuteronomic language about the curse involved
in death by crucifixion and applies it to Christ ; but he
explains it to mean merely that Christ endured a shameful
death, and expressly denies that Christ was accursed
by God.[2]   The reason for the death in such passages
seems simply that prophecy should be fulfilled and the
resurrection made possible.   It is not exclusively by
His death that Christ saves men, but by the whole of
His work—His incarnation, His revelation of the
Father, His resurrection, and not least His teaching.
Men are saved through Christ because He has a unique
power of bringing men to repentance, and helping them
to sin no more.[3]   The Gospel is for him a new law.[4]
He prefers to think of men as " called by the Cross " of
Christ than as redeemed by it.[5]   There is, indeed, another
side to Justin's teaching : in so far as he can be said to
believe in any objective effect of Christ's coming, he
thinks of it as having taken place for the destruction of
the evil spirits : [6] as is shown by the efficacy of exorcisms
in the name of Christ.   But though in one place these
effects are attributed to the " passion of Christ," [7] this
is not so in any exclusive sense.   Elsewhere the triumph
over the Devil is distinctly referred to His birth,[8] or His

---

[1] Dial. c. Tryph. 102. Cf. 1 Apol. 28, 43. In 2 Apol. 5 he seems to explain the
origin of evil by Gen. vi. rather than by the fall of Adam.

[2] Εἰ οὖν καὶ τὸν ἑαυτοῦ Χριστὸν ὑπὲρ τῶν ἐκ παντὸς γένους ἀνθρώπων ὁ πατὴρ
τῶν ὅλων τὰς πάντων κατάρας ἀναδέξασθαι ἐβουλήθη, εἰδὼς ὅτι ἀναστήσει αὐτὸν
σταυρωθέντα καὶ ἀποθανόντα, διὰ τί ὡς κεκατηραμένου τοῦ ὑπομείναντος κατὰ τὴν τοῦ
πατρὸς βουλὴν ταῦτα παθεῖν τὸν λόγον ποιεῖτε, καὶ οὐχὶ μᾶλλον ἑαυτοὺς θρηνεῖτε ;
(Dial. c. Tryph. 95). Cf. cc. 89, 96 (οὐχ ὡς τοῦ Θεοῦ καταρωμένου τούτου τοῦ
ἐσταυρωμένου).

[3] Δι' οὗ οἱ πάλαι πόρνοι καὶ ἄδικοι ἐκ πάντων τῶν ἐθνῶν σώζονται, ἄφεσιν ἁμαρτιῶν
λάβοντες καὶ μηκέτι ἁμαρτάνοντες (Dial. c. Tryph. 111).

[4] Σαββατίζειν ὑμᾶς ὁ καινὸς νόμος διὰ παντὸς ἔθελει (Dial. c. Tryph. 12).

[5] Οἵτινες διὰ τοῦ ἐξουθενημένου καὶ ὀνείδους μέστου μυστηρίου τοῦ σταυροῦ κληθέντες
ὑπὸ τοῦ Θεοῦ (Dial. c. Tryph. 131).

[6] 2 Apol. 6.

[7] Βοηθὸν γὰρ ἐκεῖνον καὶ λυτρωτὴν καλοῦμεν, οὗ καὶ τὴν τοῦ ὀνόματος ἰσχὺν καὶ τὰ
δαιμόνια τρέμει, καὶ σήμερον ἐξορκιζόμενα κατὰ τοῦ ὀνόματος Ἰησοῦ Χριστοῦ, τοῦ
σταυρωθέντος ἐπὶ Ποντίου Πιλάτου . . ὑποτάσσεται, ὡς καὶ ἐκ τούτου πᾶσι φάνερον
εἶναι ὅτι ὁ πατὴρ αὐτοῦ τοσαύτην ἔδωκεν αὐτῷ δύναμιν, ὥστε καὶ τὰ δαιμόνια ὑποτάσ-
σεσθαι τῷ ὀνόματι αὐτοῦ καὶ τῇ τοῦ γενομένου πάθους αὐτοῦ οἰκονομίᾳ (Dial. c. Tryph.
30 ; cf. 76, 85).

[8] Καὶ γὰρ τὸ εἰπεῖν τὸν Ἡσαΐαν · Λήψεται δύναμιν Δαμασκοῦ καὶ σκῦλα Σαμαρείας,
τὴν τοῦ πονηροῦ δαίμονος, τοῦ ἐν Δαμασκῷ οἰκοῦντος, δύναμιν ἐσήμαινε νικηθήσεσθαι
τῷ Χριστῷ ἅμα τῷ γεννηθῆναι (Dial. c. Tryph. 78).

birth, death, and resurrection taken together.[1] But the wonders effected by the use of Christ's name as a charm do not include the forgiveness of sins : still less is the victory over the Devil made into a theory to explain the necessity for Christ's death. This victory over the demons is accepted as a fact, just as the forgiveness of sins through Christ's death is accepted as a fact. At present the one fact was not used to explain the other.

When we turn to his teaching about the subjective conditions of salvation, Justin more frequently than his predecessors employs the Pauline language about justification by faith. But his profound sense of the value of Christian belief does not prevent his thinking of the philosophers and poets of Paganism as well as the Jewish prophets as inspired by the Word.[2] Those who before the coming of Christ lived in accordance with the eternal principles of morality, " who lived with the word," were really " Christians, even though they were called Atheists." [3] " Those who did the things which are universally and naturally and eternally good are well-pleasing to God, and will be saved through this same Christ in the resurrection no less than the just men who lived before them, Noah and Enoch and Jacob and the rest, with those who have recognized this Christ to be the Son of God." [4] He had no doubt a confident expectation that the unbelieving Jew or Gentile would go to an everlasting hell. But we may assume from his general tenour that such a fate would be reserved for those who had enjoyed the opportunity of hearing the Gospel message : he could hardly conceive that anything but wilful resistance to the light could prevent a rightly disposed person failing to accept the teaching of the incarnate Logos. While he assumes that Christian belief is normally necessary to salvation, he is no rigid

---

[1] *Dial. c. Tryph.* 85.   [2] 2 *Apol.* 8, 10, 13.

[3] Οἱ μετὰ λόγου βιώσαντες Χριστιανοί εἰσι, κἂν ἄθεοι ἐνομίσθησαν, οἷον ἐν Ἕλλησι μὲν Σωκράτης καὶ Ἡράκλειτος καὶ οἱ ὅμοιοι αὐτοῖς, ἐν βαρβάροις δὲ Ἀβραὰμ καὶ Ἀνανίας καὶ Ἀζαρίας καὶ Μισαὴλ καὶ Ἠλίας καὶ ἄλλοι πολλοί (1 *Apol.* 46).

[4] Ἐπεὶ οἱ τὰ καθολοῦ καὶ φύσει καὶ αἰώνια καλὰ ἐποιοῦν εὐάρεστοί εἰσι τῷ Θεῷ, καὶ διὰ τοῦ Χριστοῦ τούτου ἐν τῇ ἀναστάσει ὁμοίως τοῖς προγενομένοις αὐτῶν δικαίοις, Νῶε καὶ Ἐνὼχ καὶ Ἰακὼβ καὶ εἴ τινες ἄλλοι γέγονασι, σωθήσονται σὺν τοῖς ἐπιγνοῦσι τὸν Χριστὸν τοῦτον τοῦ Θεοῦ υἱόν (*Dial. c. Tryph.* 45).

stickler for orthodoxy. He knows of Christians who disbelieved the Virgin Birth, but does not deny their claim to be Christians or doubt of their salvation.[1] It is abundantly clear that Justin values belief only on account of its effects upon the life. Faith is practically interpreted to mean obedience: " We are called and are real children of God who keep the commandments of the Christ." [2] And when Justin speaks in his own words, and is not echoing St. Paul or the prophecies, he more frequently speaks of knowledge and repentance than of faith.

We have seen that up to this point the tendency of early Christian teaching is towards a doctrine of salvation which is rational, ethical, and spiritual. This statement must not be taken as denying that there was another side to early Christian religion. Whatever may be thought of the influence of the mystery religions upon St. Paul, there can be no doubt that Christians converted from Paganism shared some of the beliefs which found expression in the mystery religions of their time, though they were probably more disposed to put an ethical and spiritual interpretation upon external rites than their pagan neighbours. It has been admitted throughout that the rational or ethical interpretation of the death of Christ does not seem fully to explain what Christians believed about it. It was undoubtedly thought of as a source of a mysterious power and spiritual influence; and so far as this influence was not simply a rational and intelligible influence on the soul of the believer, it was an influence which was supposed to work through outward and visible acts in ways closely analogous to the rites of the mystery religions. Immense importance was attached to communion with the visible Church,[3] but still more to the initiatory rite of

---

[1] *Dial. c. Tryph.* 48. His own belief in it is based upon the testimony of prophecy. On the other hand the really heretical Montanists and Gnostics are merely "people who are called Christians " (*op. cit.* 80).

[2] Θεοῦ τέκνα ἀληθινὰ καλούμεθα καὶ ἐσμέν, οἱ τὰς ἐντολὰς τοῦ Χριστοῦ φυλάσσοντες (*Dial. c. Tryph.* 123).

[3] Πᾶσιν οὖν μετανοοῦσιν ἀφίει ὁ Κύριος, ἐὰν μετανοήσωσιν εἰς ἑνότητα Θεοῦ καὶ συνέδριον τοῦ ἐπισκόπου (Ignatius, *Philadelph.* viii.). In Ignatius, of course, we have the strongest and crudest insistence upon the necessity of communion with the single

baptism. It was certainly believed that baptism carried with it an immediate and plenary remission of past sins. But this does not imply so unethical an attitude as it might seem to do at first sight. For baptism did not mean to them *mere* immersion in the baptismal waters. It included the public confession of sin, the profession of faith, the solemn turning away from evil and the resolution to obey the very exacting and practical demands which the Christian society made upon them. It was immediately followed by the laying on of hands and prayer for the outpouring of the Holy Spirit. The most mechanical view of baptism was hardly possible so long as infant baptism was either altogether unknown or a rare exception. In the days of persecution baptism almost necessarily implied some real moral change. It is, we may suppose, to the baptismal repentance rather than to baptism itself that the bestowal of forgiveness is attributed by Hermas ; since he admits that those who fall asleep in righteousness and in great holiness may be saved even " without the seal "—an exception not yet confined, as it was later, to those who had died a martyr's death.[1] Less in accordance with the teaching of Christ Himself was his denial that post-baptismal sin could be forgiven more than once—a doctrine not universally taught and ultimately rejected by the Church.[2] There was no doubt a tendency to make salvation dependent upon Church membership and its attendant rites, but a consciousness that the actual Church was not absolutely identical with the true and ideal Church was not wholly lost when the author of the 2nd Epistle of Clement could write : " So long as we do the will of God our Father we shall belong to the first Church, the spiritual Church which was created before the sun and

---

Bishop and the Bishop's Church. Other writers of this early period have a far less narrowly ecclesiastical conception of Christianity. That is doubtless why Ignatius is so often quoted, and the others so rarely.

[1] Σφραγὶς οὖν τὸ ὕδωρ ἐστίν· εἰς τὸ ὕδωρ οὖν καταβαίνουσι νεκροί, καὶ ἀναβαίνουσι ζῶντες (Hermas, *Sim.* 9, xvi. 4) : ἐκεῖνοι δὲ οἱ προκεκοιμημένοι νεκροὶ κατέβησαν, ζῶντες δὲ ἀνέβησαν . . . ἐν δικαιοσύνῃ γὰρ ἐκοιμήθησαν καὶ ἐν μεγάλῃ ἁγνείᾳ· μόνον δὲ τὴν σφραγῖδα ταύτην οὐκ εἶχον (*ib.* 6, 7).

[2] Μετὰ τὴν κλῆσιν ἐκείνην (*i.e.* after the baptismal repentance) τὴν μεγάλην καὶ σεμνὴν ἐάν τις . . . ἁμαρτήσῃ, μίαν μετάνοιαν ἔχει (*Mand.* 4, iii. 6).

the moon : but if we do not the will of God, we shall belong to the Church of which the Scripture said : ' My house has become a den of thieves.' "[1] There must, of course, have been every degree of materialism and every degree of spiritualism in the way in which these things were understood in the primitive Church. Doubtless there were simple Christians who thought of the washing away of sins in baptism in almost as mechanical a fashion as that in which the pagan devotee thought of the Tauro-bolium or the Mithraic baptism, though no Christian would have denied that real repentance was necessary to give efficacy to the rite. On the other hand the theologians who have come down to us represent naturally the views which prevailed among the more intelligent Christians : and in them the tendency, without any actual denial of traditional beliefs, is always—in this early period—towards a moralizing and spiritualizing inter-pretation both of the atonement once for all effected through Christ and of the process by which its efficacy is brought to bear upon the individual soul.

And now I will endeavour to sum up the results at which we have arrived :

(1) We have seen that the way in which the atoning effects of the death of Christ are spoken of by the early Christian writers of the first century and a half of the Church's life strongly confirms our view that the doctrine originated in the language of prophecy, and was adopted on authority, not in the first instance as the result either of reflection or of any kind of religious experience, how-ever much reflection and experience may subsequently have been called in to interpret the accepted formula.

(2) We have found that, in spite of the general acceptance from prophecy—and occasionally from St. Paul—of language which suggests some sort of vicarious punishment, sacrifice, or expiation, these writers and the Churches which they represented instinctively shrank from the substitutionary theory which St. Paul attempted

---

[1] Ὥστε, ἀδελφοί, ποιοῦντες τὸ θέλημα τοῦ πατρὸς ἡμῶν Θεοῦ ἐσόμεθα ἐκ τῆς ἐκκλησίας τῆς πρώτης, τῆς πνευματικῆς, τῆς πρὸ ἡλίου καὶ σελήνης ἐκτισμένης · ἐὰν δὲ μὴ ποιήσωμεν τὸ θέλημα Κυρίου, ἐσόμεθα ἐκ τῆς γραφῆς τῆς λεγούσης, Ἐγενήθη ὁ οἶκός μου σπήλαιον λῃστῶν (2 Cor. xiv. 1).

to work out on the basis of these prophetic passages, and adopted explanations of them inconsistent with a very literal or natural interpretation of the language which they profess to explain—explanations which agree in attributing the effects produced by the death of Christ to some subjective and purely moral influence of that death. Moreover, even the subjective effects of Christ's work are not attributed exclusively or even primarily to His death. The effects of Christ's death are merged in, or subordinated to, the general influence exercised by the whole work of the incarnation—the life of self-sacrifice, the resistance to temptation, the obedience, the fulfilment of the Messianic mission, the resurrection, and (by no means least prominent) the teaching. There is a complete absence of any definite *theory* of vicarious punishment or substitution.[1]

(3) We have seen that still more conspicuously and perhaps with a fuller consciousness of what it was doing, the Church never heartily accepted St. Paul's doctrine of justification by faith—that is, the doctrine of St. Paul in his most dogmatic moments. Sometimes it was wholly ignored : at other times, even when the formula was accepted, it was interpreted in a way which would more naturally have been expressed by saying that men are saved by the repentance, the change of heart and consequently of life, which was due to the influence of Christ and His work.

May we not take encouragement from this chapter in the history of Christian doctrine to confess that for

---

[1] There is only one passage in the writings of this period which ought perhaps to be treated as an exception to the general tendency, and that is a passage in the *Epistle to Diognetus* (ix. 2-5), in which the writer repeats the Gospel saying about the ransom, and then quotes and expands the language of the first Epistle of St. Peter (iii. 18) about the just dying for the unjust : he exclaims, " O sweet exchange ($\dot{a}\nu\tau a\lambda\lambda a\gamma\hat{\eta}s$), O inscrutable workmanship, O unexpected benefits, that the injustice of many should be hidden in One righteous, and that the righteousness of One should justify many lawless." Here the thought of substitution is certainly emphasized, but the passage is after all only a rhetorical paraphrase of the ransom passage in the Gospel, read in the light of Is. liii. and of St. Paul. There is no theory as to why a death was necessary, and the words, " what else could hide our sins except His [Christ's] righteousness " may be treated as an attempt at ethical explanation. It is significant that this early approach to a substitutionary theory grows out of the ransom passage in the Gospels, which was to exercise so enormous an influence hereafter. The date of this Epistle is later than most of the writers hitherto considered, possibly as late as A.D. 180, and, if so, contemporary with Irenaeus : for the whole passage see below, p. 215.

us too the formulae which the early Church derived firstly from the prophets and afterwards from the teaching of St. Paul can only be accepted with very considerable freedom of interpretation or re-interpretation ? We are no longer prevented, as the early Church was prevented, by belief in verbal or plenary inspiration and in the Messianic interpretation of prophecy from boldly rejecting any formulae which, taken at their face-value, seem to say that sin cannot be forgiven without a vicarious sacrifice, a vicarious punishment, or some other kind of expiation. On the other hand, when we come to the positive explanations which are given of the formulae by the earliest teachers of Christianity, we shall find that their value is for the most part quite unaffected by our refusal to accept the traditional formulae as absolutely binding authorities, and that there is very little in their teaching which we cannot heartily appropriate. These explanations were based upon the reflection, the experience, the conscience of the Church ; and they are confirmed by the experience of other ages—including our own. It remains true now that belief in Christ and in the God whom Christ reveals does, in those who respond to the appeal which it makes, lead to repentance, amendment of life, the overcoming of sin, the attainment of holiness. So understood, the doctrine of the Church does not contradict the teaching of its Founder, though it does develope and supplement it in a manner which was not unnecessary if due emphasis was to be laid upon the importance of that new and culminating revelation of God which was made to the world in Him, and which from the nature of the case He could hardly teach Himself.

We must not deny that there are some things in many of the early writers even outside St. Paul which we cannot appropriate without some modernization. Their conception of the physical Universe, their conception of historical evidence, their belief in the incessant and ubiquitous influences of evil spirits, their metaphysics and their psychology—in short the whole context of their religious thought—was different, and context must to some extent affect content. But if we concentrate our attention on the points upon which all the early Christian writers agree rather than upon those in which they differ, we should not go very far beyond the facts if we were to say that what the earliest Church really believed in was salvation by the influence of Christ and of His teaching. That this influence was enormously enhanced by the appeal made in His self-sacrificing death was true then, and it is true now. Isolate the death of Christ, as is done by many later systems, and the idea of the atonement through Christ's death becomes an unintelligibility which the conscience and reason of the modern world has practically rejected : see in Christ's death the crowning and typical act in a life devoted to the teaching, by precept and example and character, of self-sacrificing love, and the doctrine of the atonement is still full of meaning, and in perfect harmony with the spoken message of Him who died. Would that so much could be said of the later theories which have invited men to seek salvation by reliance upon the death of Christ and the deliberate repudiation of His teaching !

ADDITIONAL NOTE TO LECTURE III

OTHER REFERENCES TO THE ATONEMENT IN THE APOSTOLIC FATHERS

St. Ignatius (Bishop of Antioch : died *circa* 110)

Salvation through the Cross of Christ and belief in it

Περίψημα τὸ ἐμὸν πνεῦμα τοῦ σταυροῦ, ὅ ἐστιν σκάνδαλον τοῖς ἀπιστοῦσιν, ἡμῖν δὲ σωτηρία καὶ ζωὴ αἰώνιος. *Eph.* xviii. 1.

My spirit has become an off-scouring on account of the Cross, which is a stumbling-block to those who believe not, but to us salvation and eternal life.

The Death in close connexion with the Resurrection

Μηκέτι σαββατίζοντες ἀλλὰ κατὰ κυριακὴν ζῶντες, ἐν ᾗ καὶ ἡ ζωὴ ἡμῶν ἀνέτειλεν δι᾿ αὐτοῦ καὶ

No longer sabbatizing but living in accordance with the Lord's Day, on which also our life rose again through Him and

τοῦ θανάτου αὐτοῦ, ὅν τινες ἀρνοῦν-
ται· δι' οὗ μυστηρίου ἐλάβομεν τὸ
πιστεύειν, καὶ διὰ τοῦτο ὑπο-
μένομεν, ἵνα εὑρεθῶμεν μαθηταὶ
Ἰησοῦ Χριστοῦ τοῦ μόνου διδασκάλου ἡμῶν· πῶς ἡμεῖς δυνησόμεθα
ζῆσαι χωρὶς αὐτοῦ; *Magnes.* ix. 1, 2.

His death, which some deny, by
which mystery we received the
gift of faith, and on account of
this we endure, in order that we
may be found disciples of Jesus
Christ, our only Teacher. How
shall we be able to live without
Him?

Salvation through belief in Christ without special reference to the Death

Ἐν ᾧ καὶ πιστεύσαντες ἐσώθησαν
ἐν ἑνότητι Ἰησοῦ Χριστοῦ . . . ὑπὸ
Ἰησοῦ Χριστοῦ μεμαρτυρημένοι καὶ
συνηριθμημένοι ἐν τῷ εὐαγγελίῳ
τῆς κοινῆς ἐλπίδος.   *Philadelph.*
v. 2.

In whom also they [the Old
Testament prophets] believing
were saved in the unity of Jesus
Christ . . . having witness borne
to them by Jesus Christ, and being
numbered together in the gospel
of our common hope.

POLYCARP (Bishop of Smyrna : *died* 155)

Christ died for our sins (with quotation from Acts ii. 24)

Ἰησοῦν Χριστόν, ὃς ὑπέμεινεν
ὑπὲρ τῶν ἁμαρτιῶν ἡμῶν ἕως
θανάτου καταντῆσαι, ὃν ἤγειρεν ὁ
Θεὸς λύσας τὰς ὠδῖνας τοῦ ᾅδου.
Phil. i. 2.

Jesus Christ, who for our sins
endured to face even death, whom
God raised up, having loosed the
pains of Hades.

Salvation by grace, not works (with quotation from Eph. ii. 8)

Εἰδότες ὅτι χάριτί ἐστε σεσωσμένοι, οὐκ ἐξ ἔργων, ἀλλὰ θελήματι
Θεοῦ διὰ Ἰησοῦ Χριστοῦ. *Phil.* i. 3.

Knowing that by grace ye are
saved, not of works, but by the
will of God through Jesus Christ.

Christ died for us and as an example (with quotation from 1 Peter ii. 22, 24)

Ἀδιαλείπτως οὖν προσκαρτερῶ-
μεν τῇ ἐλπίδι ἡμῶν καὶ τῷ
ἀρραβῶνι τῆς δικαιοσύνης ἡμῶν,
ὅς ἐστι Χριστὸς Ἰησοῦς ὃς ἀνήνεγ-
κεν ἡμῶν τὰς ἁμαρτίας τῷ ἰδίῳ
σώματι ἐπὶ τὸ ξύλον, ὃς ἁμαρτίαν
οὐκ ἐποίησεν, οὐδὲ εὑρέθη δόλος ἐν
τῷ στόματι αὐτοῦ. ἀλλὰ δι' ἡ-
μᾶς ἵνα ζήσωμεν ἐν αὐτῷ πάντα
ὑπέμεινεν. μιμηταὶ οὖν γενώμεθα
τῆς ὑπομονῆς [αὐτοῦ]· καὶ ἐὰν

Unceasingly therefore let us
hold fast to our hope and to the
earnest of our righteousness, which
is Jesus Christ, who bore our sins
in His own body upon the tree,
who did no sin, neither was guile
found in His mouth. But on
account of us, in order that we
might live in Him, He endured
all. Let us then become imitators
of His endurance : and, if we

πάσχωμεν διὰ τὸ ὄνομα αὐτοῦ, δοξάζωμεν αὐτόν. τοῦτον γὰρ ἡμῖν τὸν ὑπογραμμὸν ἔθηκε δι᾽ ἑαυτοῦ, καὶ ἡμεῖς τοῦτο ἐπιστεύσαμεν. *Phil.* viii. 1, 2.

suffer for His sake, let us glorify Him. For He gave this example to us in His own person, and we believed this.

Christ died and rose on our account

Τὸν ὑπὲρ ἡμῶν ἀποθανόντα καὶ δι᾽ ἡμᾶς ὑπὸ τοῦ Θεοῦ ἀναστάντα. *Phil.* ix. 2.

Him who on our behalf died and on our account was raised up by God.

The Shephera of HERMAS (? 140–155)

Christ's work to cleanse from sin by His labours and to teach

Καὶ αὐτὸς τὰς ἁμαρτίας αὐτῶν ἐκαθάρισε πολλὰ κοπιάσας καὶ πολλοὺς κόπους ἠντληκώς. οὐδεὶς γὰρ δύναται σκαφεῦσαι ἄτερ κόπου ἢ μόχθου. αὐτὸς οὖν καθαρίσας τὰς ἁμαρτίας τοῦ λαοῦ ἔδειξεν αὐτοῖς τὰς τρίβους τῆς ζωῆς, δοὺς αὐτοῖς τὸν νόμον ὃν ἔλαβε παρὰ τοῦ πατρὸς αὐτοῦ. *Sim.* 5, vi. 2, 3.

And He Himself cleansed their sins by labouring much and enduring many toils : for no one can dig without toil or labour. Having Himself then cleansed the sins of His people, He showed them paths of life, giving to them the law which He received from His Father.

Salvation only through "the name"

Καλῶς ἐξέφυγες, φησίν, ὅτι τὴν μέριμνάν σου ἐπὶ τὸν Θεὸν ἐπέριψας καὶ τὴν καρδίαν σου ἤνοιξας πρὸς τὸν Κύριον, πιστεύσας ὅτι δι᾽ οὐδενὸς δύνῃ σωθῆναι εἰ μὴ διὰ τοῦ μεγάλου καὶ ἐνδόξου ὀνόματος. *Vis.* 4, ii. 4.

Thou didst escape [the beast] well, saith she [the Church], because thou didst cast thy care upon God, and didst open thine heart to the Lord, believing that by nothing canst thou be saved but by the great and glorious name.

Salvation through Repentance and Faith in God

Πᾶς γὰρ δίψυχος ἀνήρ, ἐὰν μὴ μετανοήθῃ, δυσκόλως σωθήσεται. καθάρισον οὖν τὴν καρδίαν σου ἀπὸ τῆς διψυχίας, ἔνδυσαι δὲ τὴν πίστιν, ὅτι ἰσχυρά ἐστι, καὶ πίστευε τῷ Θεῷ ὅτι πάντα τὰ αἰτήματά σου ἃ αἰτεῖς λήψῃ. *Mand.* ix. 6.

For every double-minded man if he do not repent, shall be saved with difficulty. Cleanse therefore thy heart from double-mindedness, and clothe thyself with faith, because it is strong, and believe in God that will receive all thy petitions which thou askest.

THE EPISTLE OF BARNABAS (? *circa* 130 A.D.)

Forgiveness through the blood of Christ

Εἰς τοῦτο γὰρ ὑπέμεινεν ὁ Κύριος παραδοῦναι τὴν σάρκα εἰς καταφθοράν, ἵνα τῇ ἀφέσει τῶν ἁμαρτιῶν ἁγνισθῶμεν, ὅ ἐστιν ἐν τῷ αἵματι τοῦ ῥαντίσματος αὐτοῦ. [Followed by quotation from Is. liii. 5, 7.] V. 1.

For to this end the Lord endured to deliver His flesh unto destruction, that by the remission of our sins we might be sanctified, which sanctification is in the blood of His sprinkling.

Christ offered His body as a sacrifice for us to fulfil the prophecy of Isaac

Εἰ οὖν ὁ υἱὸς τοῦ Θεοῦ, ὢν Κύριος καὶ μέλλων κρίνειν ζῶντας καὶ νεκρούς, ἔπαθεν ἵνα ἡ πληγὴ αὐτοῦ ζωοποιήσῃ ἡμᾶς, πιστεύσωμεν ὅτι ὁ υἱὸς τοῦ Θεοῦ οὐκ ἠδύνατο παθεῖν εἰ μὴ δι᾽ ἡμᾶς. ἀλλὰ καὶ σταυρωθεὶς ἐποτίζετο ὄξει καὶ χολῇ. ἀκούσατε πῶς περὶ τούτου πεφανέρωκαν οἱ ἱερεῖς τοῦ ναοῦ. γεγραμμένης ἐντολῆς· Ὃς ἂν μὴ νηστεύσῃ τὴν νηστείαν, θανάτῳ ἐξολεθρευθήσεται [Lev. xxiii. 29], ἐνετείλατο Κύριος, ἐπεὶ καὶ αὐτὸς ὑπὲρ τῶν ἡμετέρων ἁμαρτιῶν ἔμελλεν τὸ σκεῦος τοῦ πνεύματος προσφέρειν θυσίαν, ἵνα καὶ ὁ τύπος ὁ γενόμενος ἐπὶ Ἰσαὰκ τοῦ προσενεχθέντος ἐπὶ τὸ θυσιαστήριον τελεσθῇ. [Followed by other prophecies fulfilled by the Crucifixion, including an allusion to the scapegoat.] vii. 1-3.

If then the Son of God, being Lord and One who was hereafter to judge quick and dead, suffered in order that His wound might give us life, let us believe that the Son of God could not suffer except on our account. But moreover when He was crucified He was given vinegar and gall to drink. Hear how the priests in the temple have revealed the meaning of this. The commandment being written "Whosoever shall not keep the fast, he shall die the death," the Lord commanded when He was about to offer the vessel which contained His spirit in order that the type which was set forth in Isaac who was brought to the altar might be fulfilled.

Remission of sin and moral regeneration through Christ

Ἐπεὶ οὖν ἐκαίνισεν ἡμᾶς ἐν τῇ ἀφέσει τῶν ἁμαρτιῶν, ἐποίησεν ἡμᾶς ἄλλον τύπον, ὡς παιδίων ἔχειν τὴν ψυχήν, ὡς ἂν δὴ ἀναπλάσσοντος αὐτοῦ ἡμᾶς (vi. 11).[1]

Since then He renewed us in the remission of sins, He made us to be another type, so as to have the soul of children, as though He himself were re-creating us.

---

[1] The context refers to the incarnation generally, though both death and resurrection have been mentioned.

Purposes of the Incarnation and Death

Αὐτὸς δὲ ἵνα καταργήσῃ τὸν θάνατον καὶ τὴν ἐκ νεκρῶν ἀνάστασιν δείξῃ, ὅτι ἐν σαρκὶ ἔδει αὐτὸν φανερωθῆναι, ὑπέμεινεν ἵνα καὶ τοῖς πατράσιν τὴν ἐπαγγελίαν ἀποδῷ καὶ αὐτὸς ἑαυτῷ τὸν λαὸν τὸν καινὸν ἑτοιμάζων ἐπιδείξῃ, ἐπὶ τῆς γῆς ὤν, ὅτι τὴν ἀνάστασιν αὐτὸς ποιήσας κρινεῖ. . . . εἰ γὰρ μὴ ἦλθεν ἐν σαρκί, οὐδ᾽ ἂν πως οἱ ἄνθρωποι ἐσώθησαν βλέποντες αὐτόν· ὅτε τὸν μέλλοντα μὴ εἶναι ἥλιον, ἔργον τῶν χειρῶν αὐτοῦ ὑπάρχοντα, ἐμβλέποντες οὐκ ἰσχύουσιν εἰς τὰς ἀκτῖνας αὐτοῦ ἀντοφθαλμῆσαι. οὐκοῦν ὁ υἱὸς τοῦ Θεοῦ εἰς τοῦτο ἐν σαρκὶ ἦλθεν, ἵνα τὸ τέλειον τῶν ἁμαρτιῶν ἀνακεφαλαιώσῃ τοῖς διώξασιν ἐν θανάτῳ τοὺς προφήτας αὐτοῦ. οὐκοῦν εἰς τοῦτο πέμεινεν. λέγει γὰρ ὁ Θεὸς τὴν πλήγην τῆς σάρκος αὐτοῦ ὅτι ἐξ αὐτῶν. Ὅταν πατάξωσιν τὸν ποιμένα ἑαυτῶν τότε ἀπολεῖται τὰ πρόβητα τῆς ποιμνῆς. αὐτὸς δὲ ἠθέλησεν οὕτω παθεῖν· ἔδει γὰρ ἵνα ἐπὶ ξύλου πάθῃ. λέγει γὰρ ὁ προφητεύων ἐπὶ αὐτῳ· φεῖσαί μου τῆς ψυχῆς ἀπὸ ῥομφαίας. [Ps. xxii. 20. Here follow passages from Ps. cxix. 120; xxii. 17; Is. l. 6, 7.] (v. 6-13.)[1]

But He Himself that He might destroy death and show forth the Resurrection of the dead, because it was needful that He should be manifested in the flesh, endured [that it should be so] in order that He might both perform the promise to the fathers, and making ready to Himself the new people might demonstrate, while upon the earth, that He Himself should cause the (general) resurrection and should be the Judge. . . . For if He had not come in the flesh, neither would men ever have been saved by beholding Him. When they look upon the sun that shall one day cease to be, being the work of His hands, they are not able to look full in the face of his rays. Therefore the Son of God came in the flesh, in order that He might complete the guilt in those who persecuted the prophets to the death. Therefore He carried endurance even to this point. For God speaks of the wound of His flesh that it came from them. "When they smite their own shepherd, then the sheep of the flock shall be destroyed."[2] Now it was He Himself who willed thus to suffer : for it was needful that He should suffer upon the tree. For He that prophesieth of Him said "Deliver my life from the sword."

Purpose of the Incarnation : to complete the guilt of the Jews and to redeem from evil a new people for God

Ἐφανερώθη δὲ ἵνα κἀκεῖνοι [the Jews] τελειωθῶσιν τοῖς ἁμαρτή-

But He was manifested that they [the Jews] might have their

---

[1] In this tangled passage the purpose of the death (as distinct from the incarnation) generally appears to be (1) to complete the guilt of the Jews, (2) to prepare for the resurrection, and so destroy death, (3) to fulfil the prophecy. Men are actually saved by looking on Him. His miracles and teaching have just been mentioned.

[1] Zech. xiii. 7.

μασιν καὶ ἡμεῖς διὰ τοῦ κληρονομοῦντος διαθήκην Κυρίου Ἰησοῦ λάβωμεν, ὃς εἰς τοῦτο ἡτοιμάσθη, ἵνα αὐτὸς φανεὶς τὰς ἤδη δεδαπανημένας ἡμῶν καρδίας τῷ θανάτῳ καὶ παραδεδομένας τῇ τῆς πλάνης ἀνομίᾳ λυτρωσάμενος ἐκ τοῦ σκότους, διάθηται ἐν ἡμῖν διαθήκην λόγῳ. γέγραπται γὰρ πῶς αὐτῷ ὁ πατὴρ ἐντέλλεται, λυτρωσάμενον ἡμᾶς ἐκ τοῦ σκότους ἑτοιμάσαι ἑαυτῷ λαὸν ἅγιον . . . [After quoting Is. xlix. 6, 7]. γινώσκομεν οὖν πόθεν ἐλυτρώθημεν (xiv. 5-7).

tale of sins completed, and that we might receive the covenant through Him who inherited it, even the Lord Jesus, who was prepared beforehand for this purpose, that He might appear and redeem out of the darkness our hearts which had already been paid over unto death and delivered up to the lawlessness of error, and so might establish the covenant in us through the word. For it is written how the Father enjoineth Him to redeem us from darkness and to prepare for Himself a holy people. . . . We know then whence we were redeemed.

Forgiveness through Baptism and the Cross in accordance with Prophecy

Ζητήσωμεν δὲ εἰ ἐμέλησεν τῷ Κυρίῳ προφανερῶσαι περὶ τοῦ ὕδατος καὶ περὶ τοῦ σταυροῦ. περὶ μὲν τοῦ ὕδατος γέγραπται ἐπὶ τὸν Ἰσραήλ, πῶς τὸ βάπτισμα τὸ φέρον ἄφεσιν ἁμαρτιῶν οὐ μὴ προσδέξονται ἀλλ᾽ ἑαυτοῖς οἰκοδομήσουσιν. λέγει γὰρ ὁ προφήτης . . . ἐμὲ ἐγκατέλιπον πηγὴν ζωῆς καὶ ἑαυτοῖς ὤρυξαν βόθρον θανάτου [Jer. ii. 13; other quotations follow]. . . . αἰσθάνεσθε πῶς τὸ ὕδωρ καὶ τὸν σταυρὸν ἐπὶ τὸ αὐτὸ ὥρισεν. τοῦτο γὰρ λέγει· Μακάριοι οἳ ἐπὶ τὸν σταυρὸν ἐλπίσαντες κατέβησαν εἰς τὸ ὕδωρ. . . . τοῦτο γὰρ λέγει ὅτι ἡμεῖς μὲν καταβαίνομεν εἰς τὸ ὕδωρ γέμοντες ἁμαρτιῶν καὶ ῥύπου, καὶ ἀναβαίνομεν καρποφοροῦντες ἐν τῇ καρδίᾳ [καὶ] τὸν φόβον καὶ τὴν ἐλπίδα εἰς τὸν Ἰησοῦν ἐν τῷ πνεύματι ἔχοντες [xi. 1, 2, 8, 11].

But let us inquire whether the Lord took care to signify beforehand concerning the water and concerning the Cross. Concerning the water it is written with regard to Israel, that they will not receive the baptism that bringeth remission of sins, but will build a house for themselves. For the prophet saith, "They abandoned me, the fountain of life, and digged for themselves a pit of death. . . ." Ye perceive how He appointed the water and the Cross for the same purpose. For this is His meaning, "Blessed are they that have set their hope on the Cross and go down to the water . . ." (quoting from Ezekiel xlvii. 1, 7, 12).[1] For this He saith that we go down into the water full of sins and filth, and come up bearing fruit in our hearts and resting our fear and hope on Jesus in the spirit.

Salvation by belief in Christ: the serpent in the wilderness a type

Πάλιν Μωϋσῆς ποιεῖ τύπον τοῦ Ἰησοῦ, ὅτι δεῖ αὐτὸν παθεῖν καὶ

Again Moses makes a type of Jesus, showing that He must die

----

[1] With perhaps an echo of John vi. 51.

αὐτὸς ζωοποιήσει. . . . εἶπεν δὲ πρὸς αὐτοὺς Μωϋσῆς· Ὅταν, φησίν, δηχθῇ τις ὑμῶν, ἐλθέτω ἐπὶ τὸν ὄφιν τὸν ἐπὶ τοῦ ξύλου ἐπικείμενον, καὶ ἐλπισάτω πιστεύσας ὅτι αὐτὸς ὢν νεκρὸς δύναται ζωοποιῆσαι, καὶ παραχρῆμα σωθήσεται (xii. 5, 7).

and He must make alive. . . . And Moses spake to them: "When," saith he, "any one of you is bitten, let him come to the serpent that hangeth upon the tree, and believing hope that He being dead is able to make alive, and immediately he shall be saved."

Salvation by works

Δεῖ οὖν ἡμᾶς περὶ τῶν ἐνεστώτων ἐπιπολὺ ἐραυνῶντας ἐκζητεῖν τὰ δυνάμενα ἡμᾶς σώζειν. φύγωμεν οὖν τελείως ἀπὸ πάντων τῶν ἔργων τῆς ἀνομίας (iv. 1).

We must then inquire deeply concerning the present and seek out the things that can save us. Let us then flee altogether from all works of lawlessness.

Justification (in the future) by works

Μὴ καθ' ἑαυτοὺς ἐνδύνοντες μονάζετε ὡς ἤδη δὲ δικαιώμενοι, ἀλλ' ἐπὶ τὸ αὐτὸ συνερχόμενοι συνζητεῖτε περὶ τοῦ κοινῇ συμφέροντος. λέγει γὰρ ἡ γραφή· Οὐαὶ οἱ συνετοὶ ἑαυτοῖς καὶ ἐνώπιον ἑαυτῶν ἐπιστήμονες [Is. v. 21]. γενώμεθα πνευματικοί, γενώμεθα ναὸς τέλειος τῷ Θεῷ. ἐφ' ὅσον ἐστὶν ἐν ἡμῖν, μελετῶμεν τὸν φόβον τοῦ Θεοῦ [καὶ] φυλάσσειν ἀγωνιζώμεθα τὰς ἐντολὰς αὐτοῦ (iv. 10, 11. Cf. also xv. 7).

Do not entering in privily abide apart by yourselves, as if ye were already justified, but assembling in the same place inquire concerning the common interest. For the Scripture saith, "Woe unto them that are wise for themselves, and understanding in their own sight." Let us become spiritual, let us become a perfect temple unto God. As far as is in us, let us exercise ourselves in the fear of God [and] let us strive to keep His commandments.

Justification by faith and the word

Οὕτως οὖν καὶ ἡμεῖς τῇ πίστει τῆς ἐπαγγελίας καὶ τῷ λόγῳ ζωοποιούμενοι ζήσομεν κατακυριεύοντες τῆς γῆς (vi. 17).

Thus then we also being (continually) made alive by our faith in the promise and by the word shall live having dominion over the earth.

The Epistle to Diognetus (? circa 150 A.D.)

Christ sent to persuade and in love

Ἀλλ' ἐν ἐπιεικείᾳ [καὶ] πραΰτητι ὡς βασιλεὺς πέμπων υἱὸν βασιλέα

But it was in gentleness and meekness that He sent Him, sending Him as a King might

ἔπεμψεν, ὡς Θεὸν ἔπεμψεν, ὡς [ἄνθρωπον] πρὸς ἀνθρώπους ἔπεμψεν, ὡς σῴζων ἔπεμψεν, ὡς πείθων, οὐ βιαζόμενος· βία γὰρ οὐ πρόσεστι τῷ Θεῷ· ἔπεμψεν ὡς καλῶν, οὐ διώκων· ἔπεμψεν ὡς ἀγαπῶν, οὐ κρίνων (vii. 4).

send a Son who was also a King ; He sent Him as God ; He sent Him as a man to men ; He sent Him as saving, as using persuasion, not force ; for force is not becoming to God ; He sent Him as calling, not as persecuting ; He sent Him as loving, not judging.

Faith necessary to see God

Ἐπέδειξε δὲ διὰ πίστεως, ᾗ μόνῃ Θεὸν ἰδεῖν συγκεχώρηται (viii. 6).

And He [God] revealed Himself by faith, whereby alone it has been granted to see God.

Christ a ransom or exchange, that we might believe in the goodness of God

Ἐπεὶ δὲ πεπλήρωτο μὲν ἡ ἡμετέρα ἀδικία, καὶ τελείως πεφανέρωτο ὅτι ὁ μισθὸς αὐτῆς κόλασις καὶ θάνατος προσεδοκᾶτο, ἦλθε δὲ ὁ καιρὸς ὃν Θεὸς προέθετο λοιπὸν φανερῶσαι τὴν ἑαυτοῦ χρηστότητα καὶ δύναμιν (ὢ τῆς ὑπερβαλλούσης φιλανθρωπίας καὶ ἀγάπης τοῦ Θεοῦ), οὐκ ἐμίσησεν ἡμᾶς οὐδὲ ἀπώσατο οὐδὲ ἐμνησικάκησεν, ἀλλὰ ἐμακροθύμησεν, ἠνέσχετο, ἐλεῶν αὐτὸς τὰς ἡμετέρας ἁμαρτίας ἀνεδέξατο, αὐτὸς τὸν ἴδιον υἱὸν ἀπέδοτο λύτρον ὑπὲρ ἡμῶν, τὸν ἅγιον ὑπὲρ ἀνόμων, τὸν ἄκακον ὑπὲρ τῶν κακῶν, τὸν δίκαιον ὑπὲρ τῶν ἀδίκων [1 Peter iii. 18], τὸν ἄφθαρτον ὑπὲρ τῶν φθαρτῶν, τὸν ἀθάνατον ὑπὲρ τῶν θνητῶν. τί γὰρ ἄλλο τὰς ἁμαρτίας ἡμῶν ἠδυνήθη καλύψαι ἢ ἐκείνου δικαιοσύνη; ἐν τίνι δικαιωθῆναι δυνατὸν τοὺς ἀνόμους ἡμᾶς καὶ ἀσεβεῖς ἢ ἐν μόνῳ τῷ υἱῷ τοῦ Θεοῦ; ὢ τῆς γλυκείας ἀνταλλαγῆς, ὢ τῆς ἀνεξιχνιάστου δημιουργίας, ὢ τῶν ἀπροσδοκήτων εὐεργεσιῶν· ἵνα ἀνομία μὲν πολλῶν ἐν δικαίῳ ἑνὶ

But when our iniquity had been fully accomplished and it had been fully shown that the reward that was to be expected for it was punishment and death, and the time had come which God had ordained, the time when He should henceforth manifest His own goodness and power (O the exceeding philanthropy and love of God !), He did not hate us or reject us, nor bear us malice but was long-suffering and patient ; in pity for us He Himself took upon Him our sins ; He Himself gave up His only begotten Son as a ransom for us, the holy one for the unholy, the guiltless for the evil, the righteous for the unrighteous, the incorruptible for the corruptible, the immortal for the mortal. For what else could hide our sins but His righteousness ? In whom was it possible for us lawless and impious ones to be justified except in the Son of God alone ? O the sweet exchange ! O the inscrutable creation ! O the unexpected benefits, that the lawlessness of many should be hidden in One

κρυβῇ, δικαιοσύνη δὲ ἑνὸς πολλοὺς
ἀνόμους δικαιώσῃ. ἐλέγξας οὖν ἐν
μὲν τῷ πρόσθεν χρόνῳ τὸ ἀδύνατον
τῆς ἡμετέρας φύσεως εἰς τὸ τυχεῖν
ζωῆς, νῦν δὲ τὸν σωτῆρα δείξας
δυνατὸν σώζειν καὶ τὰ ἀδύνατα,
ἐξ ἀμφοτέρων ἐβουλήθη πιστεύειν
ἡμᾶς τῇ χρηστότητι αὐτοῦ, αὐτὸν
ἡγεῖσθαι τροφέα, πατέρα, διδάσκαλον, σύμβουλον, ἰατρόν, νοῦν,
φῶς, τιμήν, δόξαν, ἰσχύν, ζωήν
(ix. 2-6).

righteous, and that the righteousness of One should justify many
lawless ones ! Having then shown
in the former period the incapacity
of our nature to attain life, and
having now revealed the Saviour
able to save even creatures which
are thus incapable, He willed that
for both reasons we should believe
in His goodness, and should regard
Him as nurse, father, teacher,
counsellor, physician, mind, light,
honour, glory, strength, life.

THE ELDERS CITED BY IRENAEUS (? 100–150)

The Patriarchs and prophets saved by Christ

In adventu Domini nostri remissa sunt eis peccata (Irenaeus,
Haer. iv. c. 47).

In the coming of our Lord, they
(the Patriarchs) had their sins
forgiven them.

The descent into Hades : the Patriarchs saved by belief in Christ

Et propter hoc Dominum in ea
quae sunt sub terra descendisse,
evangelisantem et illis adventum
suum, remissione peccatorum ex-
sistente his qui credunt in eum.
. . . Et illis quidem curatio et
remissio peccatorum mors Domini
erat (Irenaeus, *Haer.* iv. c. 42, 3).

And on account of this [the
Presbyters testified] that the Lord
descended to the regions which
are under the earth, preaching
the good news of His advent to
them also, there being remission
of sins for those who believe in
Him. . . . And to them, indeed,
the death of Christ was the cure
and remission of sins.

Is. liii. *applied to Christ*

Καὶ ὁ Κύριος ἡμῶν Ἰησοῦς
Χριστὸς ὡς κριὸς ἐδέθη, καὶ ὡς
ἀμνὸς ἐκάρη, καὶ ὡς πρόβατον εἰς
σφαγὴν ἤχθη, καὶ ὡς ἀμνὸς ἐστ-
αυρώθη. [Then follows an
elaborate application to Jesus of
the typical story of Abraham's
attempted sacrifice of Isaac.] (Ap.
Routh, *Rel. Sac.* i. p. 122.)

And our Lord Jesus Christ was
bound as a ram, and as a lamb
was shorn, and as a sheep was led
to the slaughter, and as a lamb
was crucified.

Christ's death a ransom (with quotations from Is. liii.)

Ὑπὲρ Ἰσαὰκ τοῦ δικαίου ἐφάνη κριὸς εἰς σφαγήν, ἵνα δεσμῶν Ἰσαὰκ λύθῃ. ἐκεῖνος σφαγεὶς ἐλυτρώσατο τὸν Ἰσαάκ· οὕτω καὶ ὁ Κύριος σφαγεὶς ἔσωσεν ἡμᾶς, καὶ δεθεὶς ἔλυσε, καὶ θυθεὶς ἐλυτρώσατο. (Ap. Routh, *Rel. Sac.* i. pp. 123-4.)

On behalf of Isaac the righteous there appeared a lamb (led) to the slaughter, in order that Isaac might be loosed from bonds. He being slain ransomed Isaac : so also the Lord being slain saved us, and being bound loosed us, and being sacrificed ransomed us.

The two Baptisms (of Martyrdom and water)

Ὥσπερ δὲ φυτὸν Σιαβὲκ [the burning bush], τοῦτ᾽ ἔστιν ἀφέσεως, ἐκάλεσε τὸν ἅγιον σταυρόν, οὕτω καὶ Ἰεζεκιὴλ ἐν τῷ τέλει ὕδωρ ἀφέσεως ἐκάλεσε τὸ ἐκτυποῦν τὸ ἅγιον βάπτισμα. δύο γὰρ συνέστη τὰ ἄφεσιν ἁμαρτημάτων παρεχόμενα, πάθος διὰ Χριστόν, καὶ βάπτισμα. (Ap. Routh, *Rel. Sac.* i. p. 124.)

And as by the bush Sabek, that is (the bush) of forgiveness, he meant the Holy Cross, so also Ezekiel in the end gave the name of water of forgiveness to the water which typifies holy Baptism. For two things are brought together which afford forgiveness of sins, suffering for Christ and Baptism.

TATIAN

The only passage which could possibly be called a reference to the idea of atonement through the death of Christ is an allusion to the fact that the Jews rejected "the minister of the suffering God" (Oratio, 13). He afterwards declares that "men, after the loss of immortality, have conquered death by submitting to death in faith, and by repentance a call has been given to them, according to the word which says 'since they were made a little lower than the Angels'" (*op. cit.* 15).

LECTURE IV

PATRISTIC THEORIES

And the word became flesh and dwelt among us.—JOHN i. 14.

LECTURE IV

PATRISTIC THEORIES

WE have—in the most cursory fashion no doubt—surveyed the teaching of the Church for the first one hundred and fifty years of its existence. We have met with no distinctly formulated theory of a substitutionary type in any of these earlier writers, with the single and partial exception of St. Paul. One more theologian at least must be added to this category—a far greater writer than any of the non-canonical writers we have hitherto examined. Clement of Alexandria was the first great Christian philosopher. We have, indeed, found a Christian philosopher in Justin Martyr : and very beautiful is the result in him of a fusion between the stream of inspiration which had its origin in Judaea and that which flowed from those other great *praeparatores evangelii*—Socrates and Plato. But Justin was not a great thinker. He was one of those men, more numerous in the ancient world than in ours, who sought in philosophy rather a guide to life than a solution of speculative difficulties. Titus Flavius Clemens of Alexandria was a man of much higher calibre. Justin was a Hellenized Samaritan : Clement was not merely a Greek, but in all probability an Athenian by birth or, at least, education.[1] Here

---

[1] Epiphanius xxxii. 6. He became the head of the "Catechetical School" of Alexandria towards the close of the second century, he retired from Alexandria on the outbreak of the persecution under Severus (302-3 A.D.), and he is last heard of in 311 A.D. I have used the edition of Stählin. In all that relates to Clement and Origen I am much indebted to the late Dr. Bigg's work, *The Christian Platonists of Alexandria*. There is also an excellent and much fuller treatment of Clement's teaching in Dr. Tollinton's *Clement of Alexandria*, to which I should probably have referred more frequently had it reached me before this lecture was practically finished.

for the first time we can feel in reading the pages of a Christian writer that we are conversing with the intellectual fellow-countryman of Plato and Aristotle—with a mind to which nothing in pagan literature or philosophy that was high and noble and of good report was unknown or unwelcome; but in which the best thought of the ancient world was sweetened, purified, elevated by that crowning element in the moral ideal which had been hidden from the wise and prudent, and was now revealed to Christ, and through Him alike to the babes in Christ and to the philosophers of a new era.

Clement of Alexandria

All that has been said about the attitude of the earlier writers towards the death of Christ and the scheme of salvation holds also of Clement. Occasionally, though but rarely, we meet with the same quotations from Is. liii.[1] and other prophets, the same general statements about being saved through Christ's blood [2] or about His death being an offering or a propitiation or a ransom; [3] and there are the same ethical and subjective explanations. When the sufferings of Christ are dwelt upon, it is always either for the purpose of increasing our sense of Christ's goodness, or by way of example. " He has

---

[1] *Strom.* ii. xv. 64.

[2] Passages of this sort are particularly common in *Quis Dives Salvetur ?* e.g. 23 : τὸν σὸν ἐξέτισα θάνατον, ὃν ὤφειλες ἐπὶ τοῖς προημαρτημένοις, but even here, when emphasis is laid upon the sufferings (ἐπὶ μεγάλῳ μισθῷ), they are treated as incidental to the teaching and the whole work of Christ, and the moral is that "we should love Him equally with God " (τοῦτον οὖν ἀγαπᾶν ἴσα χρὴ τῷ Θεῷ, *Q.D.S.* 29). Cf. *Protrept.* xi. 111 ; τῶν δεσμῶν λῦσαι τοῦτον ὁ κύριος αὖθις ἠθέλησεν, καὶ σαρκὶ ἐνδεθείς (μυστήριον θεῖον τοῦτο), τὴν ὄφιν [which has just been explained allegorically as Pleasure] ἐχειρώσατο, καὶ τὸν τύραννον ἐδουλώσατο, τὸν θάνατον, καὶ τὸ παραδοξότατον, ἐκεῖνον τὸν ἄνθρωπον τὸν ἡδονῇ πεπλανημένον, τὸν τῇ φθορᾷ δεδεμένον, χερσὶν ἡπλωσμέναις ἔδειξε λελυμένον. In *Q.D.S.* 37 Christ gives Himself as a ransom: λύτρον ἑαυτὸν ἐπιδιδοὺς καινὴν ἡμῖν διαθήκην καταλιμπάνει· " ἀγάπην ὑμῖν δίδωμι τὴν ἐμήν." τίς δέ ἐστιν αὕτη καὶ πόση ; ὑπὲρ ἡμῶν ἑκάστου κατέθηκε τὴν ψυχὴν τὴν ἀνταξίαν τῶν ὅλων· ταύτην ἡμᾶς ὑπὲρ ἀλλήλων ἀνταπαιτεῖ. Such language is clearly metaphorical, but it paved the way for the theory of a ransom paid to the devil.

[3] Ἱερεῖον . . . αἵματι κυρίου λελυτρωμένους, *Paed.* i. v. 23: ὁλοκάρπωμα γὰρ ὑπὲρ ἡμῶν ἄπυρον θῦμα ὁ Χριστός (*Strom.* v. x. 70). In *Paed.* iii. xii. 98 he quotes the Johannine ἱλασμός (cf. Bigg, 2nd ed. p. 104). The most distinct statement as to Christ's dying for men is in *Strom.* iv. vii., but there is nothing substitutionary or retrospective about the language ; the Saviour died "that we might live." Clement goes on to speak of Christ's death as an example.

willed to be a brother, and He was so good (or kind), as even to die for us." [1] If Clement speaks of Christ as " laying down for us the life that was equal in value to the whole world," the meaning of such a self-surrender is that " he demands of us the same sacrifice on behalf of one another." [2] If he speaks of Christ as " loosening man from his chains " or as " slaying the serpent by putting on human flesh," such language is always used metaphorically or allegorically ; it is expressly explained that the serpent means pleasure.[3] And after all much more stress is laid upon the saving work of the Logos in guiding and healing souls by means of reward and punishment,[4] and upon the life and character, the teaching and the example of the Logos in His incarnate life, than upon any effect of His death : [5] he even explains the blood of Christ to mean knowledge.[6] The influence of St. Paul is at a minimum : the story of the fall is allegorized, and the idea of original sin is almost absent.[7] For him the history of mankind before the

---

[1] Ἀδελφὸς εἶναι βεβούληται, ὃ δὲ καὶ εἰς τοσοῦτον ἀγαθὸς ὥστε καὶ ὑπεραποθανεῖν (*Paed.* i. ix. 85). This is the more significant, as it is given in explanation of the " ransom for many." It should be observed that the sufferings of Christ are not, for Clement, limited to those attendant upon His death. " What is important to observe," says Dr. Tollinton (*Clement of Alexandria*, ii. 16), " is the fact that the Lord's πάθος meant at this stage of Christian thought something wider and more fundamental than the single experience of His death. That was the climax of His submission ; but the real problem was solved, the real condescension of the Divine made manifest, the moment it could be stated that the very God had entered into the domain of man's experience. It is in this sense we should still interpret the clause, ' He suffered,' in the Creed : εἰ παθητὸς ὁ Χριστός (Acts xxvi. 23) is a phrase of similar import in the New Testament." Sometimes Clement, with doubtful consistency, makes Christ ἀπαθής, which would naturally mean " incapable of suffering " (ἀπαθὴς περὶ ψυχήν, *Paed.* i. c. ii. 4) Dr. Tollinton defines ἀπαθής as " liable to no motive of pleasure or pain," or, perhaps, in spite of the addition "in soul," Clement meant no more than that the Logos, the Divinity in Christ, did not really suffer. There is undoubtedly a tendency towards Docetism in Clement, though he is certainly not an absolute Docetist. Cf. *Strom.* vi. lxxi. 2.

[2] See passage quoted above, p. 222, n. 2.

[3] See above, p. 222, n. 2.

[4] Ἔχετε, ὦ ἄνθρωποι, τὴν θείαν τῆς χάριτος ἐπαγγελίαν, ἀκηκόατε καὶ τὴν ἄλλην τῆς κολάσεως ἀπειλήν, δι᾽ ὧν ὁ κύριος σώζει, φόβῳ καὶ χάριτι παιδαγωγῶν τὸν ἄνθρωπον (*Protrept.* x. 95).

[5] Καθήκει δ᾽ ἡμῖν ἀνταγαπᾶν μὲν τὸν καθηγούμενον ἀγαπητικῶς ἀρίστου βίου, βιοῦν δὲ πρὸς τὰ διατάγματα τῆς δι᾽ αὐτοῦ προαιρέσεως, οὐ μόνον ἐπιτελοῦντας τὰ προστάττομενα ἢ παραφυλαττόντας τὰ ἀπαγορευόμενα, ἀλλὰ καὶ τῶν εἰκόνων τὰς μὲν ἐκτρεπομένους, τὰς δὲ ὡς ἐνὶ μάλιστα μιμουμένους ἐπιτελεῖν καθ᾽ ὁμοίωσιν τὰ ἔργα τοῦ παιδαγωγοῦ (*Paed.* i. iii. 9).

[6] *Adumbrationes in* i *Ioann.* v. 6. Only a Latin translation survives.

[7] In so far as sin is due to any external influence, it is due rather to the same tempter through whom Adam fell than to any consequence of his fall (*Protrept.* i. 7), though he does speak of Εὐὰν ἐκείνην, δι᾽ ἣν ἡ πλάνη παρηκολούθησε (*l.c.* ii. 12). It is assumed that

coming of Christ is rather a gradual ascent from a state
of ignorance, and therefore of sinfulness, to higher and
higher knowledge.

Clement is, indeed, fully impressed with the need
of salvation, and salvation comes, for him, only and
always through the Logos, and salvation in the fullest
sense only through the incarnate Logos. But that is
because what man wanted for salvation was above all
things knowledge; and both before and after the incarnation the Logos or Word of God was the great source
of knowledge. That same Word of God (not in Clement
and many other early theologians sharply distinguished
from the Spirit [1]) who "gives to the Greeks also
Philosophy through the lower angels," [2] and to the Jews
through the prophets, who had revealed God to some
extent in the reason and conscience of ordinary men,
had dwelt in Christ in an extraordinary and unique
degree. Clement is full of this Logos theology: full
of the conviction that the Logos assumed human flesh
in Christ. But with him the chief purpose of the incarnation is the communication of knowledge—fuller
knowledge of the truth about God and human life than
the world had ever known before. To Clement the
incarnation is not a mere remedy for the fall—a mere
afterthought of the Creator: there would have been,
it is suggested, an incarnation had there been no fall,
for without it, he tells us, "man would not have attained
the true end of his being," i.e. the knowledge of God. [3]

---

all men have sinned, though he will not say that the fall brought any necessity of sinning:
"peccato Adae subjacemus secundum peccati similitudinem" (*Adumbrationes in ep.
Judae*). But in quoting these last words Dr. Bigg remarks, "I doubt very much whether
this passage, which goes on to lay down the doctrine of reprobation, is from the hand of
Clement."

[1] Ὁ κύριος πνεῦμα καὶ λόγος· ἡ τροφή, τούτεστι κύριος Ἰησοῦς, τουτέστιν ὁ λόγος
τοῦ Θεοῦ, πνεῦμα σαρκούμενον (*Paed.* I. vi. 43).

[2] Οὗτός ἐστιν ὁ διδοὺς καὶ τοῖς Ἕλλησι τὴν φιλοσοφίαν διὰ τῶν ὑποδεεστέρων
ἀγγέλων (*Strom.* VII. ii. 6).

[3] Οὐκ ἄλλην αἰτίαν ἔσχε τοῦ ποιεῖν αὐτὸν ὁ Θεὸς ἢ ὡς οὐκ ἄνευ αὐτοῦ οἵου τε ὄντος
τὸν μὲν γενέσθαι δημιουργὸν ἀγαθόν, τὸν δὲ εἰς γνῶσιν ἀφικέσθαι Θεοῦ. οὐ γὰρ ἄλλως
ἂν τὸ οὗ ἕνεκεν ἄνθρωπος γέγονεν ἐποίησεν ὁ Θεός, εἰ μὴ ἄνθρωπος ἐγέγονει (*Paed.* I.
iii. 7). I assume that in the last words Θεός or ὁ κύριος is the subject of γέγονεν. His
strong tendency to Docetism prevents his insisting as much as some early Fathers on the
death of Christ as proving the reality of His human nature. Cf. *Adumbrationes in
ep.* I *Joannis*, where Clement (if it be Clement) mentions a tradition about St. John
having tried to touch the Lord's body, and having found that it did not resist his pressure,

Clement is equally fond of speaking of Christ as the Teacher and as the Saviour. And the two words mean for him much the same thing, for it is mainly by His teaching and His influence that Christ saves.[1] Only multiplied quotations from Clement and other Greek Fathers of the higher order could sufficiently emphasize the prominence in their Christianity of the idea that Christ was the great bringer of the light for which the world had been longing for so many centuries, the completer of the long course of divine self-revelation. These authors must be read in bulk if you would appreciate the intense joy and gratitude with which they were filled by their possession of that new and otherwise unattainable knowledge, and their eagerness to communicate it to others. And these men knew the best that ancient thought had to offer as to the supreme problems of human life and destiny ; and they by no means despised the measure of light which had been thus bestowed upon the world. That depreciation of our Lord's moral and religious teaching which is now common both with ultra-orthodox and with ultra-liberal theologians will find no support in Clement. For those who are bitten with this tendency—very common among our younger students of theology—I can imagine no healthier cathartic than a course of the best Greek Fathers. To realize the importance of that knowledge of God and of the moral ideal which Christ brought to the world of ancient culture may help us to appreciate what we owe to it now, and preserve us from the ignorant delusion that all religions and all philosophies have taught much the same thing with equal clearness, consistency, and persuasiveness.

Clement's emphasis upon the knowledge-giving side of Christ's work naturally brought with it increased stress —a one-sided stress undoubtedly—upon the importance of knowledge for the individual Christian. Clement was a Gnostic: his ideal Christian was "the true Gnostic."

---

[1] Ναὶ μὴν καὶ καθ' αὐτὴν ἰᾶται τὴν ψυχὴν ἐντολαῖς καὶ χαρίσμασιν, ἀλλὰ ταῖς μὲν ὑποθήκαις τάχα δὴ μέλλει · χαρίσμασι δὲ πλούσιος "ἀφέωνταί σοι αἱ ἁμαρτίαι" τοῖς ἁμαρτωλοῖς ἡμῖν λέγει (Paed. I. ii. 6). It will be observed that Clement thinks of the Logos as directly forgiving sins (especially in baptism) rather than as winning forgiveness from the Father by His death.

Q

Like those Gnostics who strayed too far from the paths of Christian tradition to be recognized by the "great Church," Clement was not content with a religion of simple faith. He believed that it was the duty of those who had the requisite leisure, the requisite education and spirituality of mind, to add to their faith knowledge. Knowledge, he declares, is greater than faith : [1] the true Gnostic is more than the simple Christian : he has a reason for what he believes. But unlike some of the heretical Gnostics, he admitted that it was possible for simple men to be saved by faith only : and even the Gnostic must begin with faith before he advances to knowledge. It is difficult to define precisely what Clement means by faith. It may perhaps be called an elementary kind of knowledge as to the truth of Christianity, resting chiefly upon the value-judgement (to use a modern phrase) by which the believer recognizes the moral perfection of Christ's teaching and character.[2] Clement expressly speaks of faith as " choosing what is best." [3] But he strongly insists also that it involves an act of the will, for knowledge implies attention : it must be sought for, and it will express itself in action, so that sometimes faith is almost identified with obedience.[4] To him that walks in accordance with reason ($\kappa a \tau \grave{a} \lambda \acute{o} \gamma o \nu$) the first thing to learn is the recognition of ignorance ($\tau \hat{\eta} s \ \grave{a} \gamma \nu o \acute{\iota} a s$

[1] Πλέον δέ ἐστι τοῦ πιστεῦσαι τὸ γνῶναι, καθάπερ ἀμέλει τοῦ σωθῆναι τὸ καὶ μετὰ τὸ σωθῆναι τιμῆς τῆς ἀνωτάτω ἀξιωθῆναι (Strom. VI. xiv. 109).

[2] It is, however, one of the characteristics of the true Gnostic that he will not ask for a demonstration of some things : to do so is among the things worthy of punishment (κολάσεως ἄξια), i.e. not only such questions as " if there is a Providence " (εἰ πρόνοιά ἐστι), but such questions as whether the whole Christian dispensation (οἰκονομία) is due to such divine Providence. This is apparently because the πρόνοια is manifest from the wisdom and order of the works of God (Strom. v. i. 6), so that after all even faith rests upon a rational inference from experience. The weakness of Clement's philosophy springs largely from the fact that he does not sufficiently recognize the distinction between Reason and reasoning. He is disposed at times to limit the idea of " what is reasonable " to " what can be demonstrated." As to how we get the ultimate premisses from which deductive reasoning starts, he is far from clear : he does not distinguish between (1) a self-evident truth, (2) a probable truth, and (3) an assumption or hypothesis provisionally adopted with a view to subsequent verification.

[3] Ἐχρῆν, μὲν ὑμᾶς, ὦ ἄνθρωποι, αὐτοῦ πέρι ἐννοουμένους τοῦ ἀγαθοῦ ἔμφυτον ἐπάγεσθαι μάρτυρα ἀξιόχρεων πίστιν αὐτόθεν οἴκοθεν περιφανῶς αἱρουμένην τὸ βέλτιστον (Protrept. X. 95).

[4] Οὐ πιστεύει δὲ ὁ μὴ ποιῶν ἃ ἐνετείλατο (Strom. IV. vii. 42). And yet he makes no sharp distinction between knowledge and faith, for baptism does convey some knowledge of God : ἐφωτίσθημεν γάρ· τὸ δὲ ἔστιν ἐπιγνῶναι Θεόν· οὔκουν ἀτελὴς ὁ ἐγνωκὼς τὸ τέλειον (Paed. I. vi. 25). This is of course against the heretical Gnostics.

ἐπίστασις). "Being ignorant a man seeks, and having sought he finds the Teacher; and having found he believes, and having believed he hopes, and loving he henceforth enters upon the process of becoming like to Him who has been loved, hastening to be that which by anticipation he loved."[1] In one place he defines faith as "the reasonable assent of a soul endowed with free-will,"[2] in another as a "voluntary anticipation of knowledge"—the Stoic "prolepsis,"[3] and compares it to the act of mind by which we accept the axioms of mathematics.

In any man of good-will, he seems to have thought, brought into contact with the Gospels and the Church, conscience would testify to the supreme goodness of Christ and of the Christian ideal, and this would lead to the conviction that Christ and the religion which He taught must come from God. Such a conviction would justify the plain man in accepting and resting content with the teaching of Christ, the Scriptures, and the Church; while for the few it would serve as the basis and starting-point of the higher knowledge (γνῶσις) or philosophy[4] and of the salvation which gnosis brings. It is hardly possible to deny that there was in Clement

---

[1] Ἡ γοῦν τῆς ἀγνοίας ἐπίστασις τὸ πρῶτόν ἐστι μάθημα τῷ κατὰ λόγον βαδίζοντι. ἀγνοήσας τις ἐζήτησεν, καὶ ζητήσας εὑρίσκει τὸν διδάσκαλον, εὑρών τε ἐπίστευσεν, καὶ πιστεύσας ἤλπισεν, ἀγαπήσας τε ἐντεῦθεν ἐξομοιοῦται τῷ ἠγαπημένῳ, τοῦτ᾽ εἶναι σπεύδων ὃ φθάσας ἠγάπησεν (Strom. v. vii. 17 ; cf. also Strom. iv. vii.).

[2] Ψυχῆς αὐτεξουσίου λογικὴν συγκατάθεσιν (Strom. v. i. 3.)

[3] Πίστις δὲ ἣν διαβάλλουσι κενὴν καὶ βάρβαρον νομίζοντες Ἕλληνες πρόληψις ἑκούσιός ἐστι, θεοσεβείας συγκατάθεσις, "ἐλπιζομένων ὑπόστασις κ.τ.λ." (Strom. ii. ii. 8). In c. iv. 17 it is a πρόληψις διάνοιας. He makes an interesting attempt to show that all knowledge begins with such a πρόληψις, by which he appears to mean that a man must begin by accepting truths from his teacher (or at all events by voluntarily attending to his teaching) because they are obvious to common sense, before he can learn the grounds of them. (Cf. Strom. ii. iv. 13, 14.) In such passages he often reminds us of Mr. A. J. Balfour's line of apologetic thought. The faith which produces repentance is sometimes said to be simply the belief in a future judgement (Strom. ii. vi. 27) ; at other times it is belief in the truths of the Christian revelation, but nowhere has it any special connexion with the death of Christ. It should be observed, too, that faith is sufficiently widely interpreted as to include the principle of goodness in Jews and Greeks as well as Christians: those who are saved are those who desire faith (οἱ τὴν πίστιν προσιέμενοι, Strom. vi. v. 42). For Clement's view of faith the whole of Strom. ii. is important, especially cc. ii.-vi.

[4] Καὶ δὴ ἡ πρώτη πρὸς σωτηρίαν νεῦσις ἡ πίστις ἡμῖν ἀποφαίνεται, μεθ᾽ ἣν φόβος τε καὶ ἐλπὶς καὶ μετάνοια σύν τε ἐγκρατείᾳ καὶ ὑπομονῇ προκόπτουσαι ἄγουσιν ἡμᾶς ἐπί τε ἀγάπην ἐπί τε γνῶσιν (Strom. ii. vi. 31). In Strom. iv. vii. 53 the stages are (1) learning with fear (διδασκαλία δι᾽ ἣν ἀπεχόμεθα τῆς ἀδικίας), (2) hope, (3) love (τελειοῖ δὲ ἡ ἀγάπη ὡς προσῆκόν ἐστι, γνωστικῶς ἤδη παιδεύουσα).

a certain over-estimation of the intellectual or rather the contemplative life ; we may discover in him the beginning of that doctrine of two moral standards—one for the religious, the other for Christians in the world—which so deeply corrupted the later Church. But he cannot be accused of any over-estimation of *mere* intellectual belief, whether of the simple or of the higher Gnostic kind. With him moral purity and intellectual insight are so closely connected that the one is unattainable without the other. The supreme ideal for him is a condition of intellectual insight which is inseparable from a certain moral condition. The ultimate purpose of the incarnation is summed up in the assertion : " The Word of God became man that you also may learn from a man how a man becomes a God."[1] The supremacy of contemplation or philosophic insight ($\theta\epsilon\omega\rho\iota\alpha$) over practical activity, and the moral qualities which are expressed in such activity, is so complete in Clement's view that he even declares that, upon the impossible supposition that salvation and the knowledge of God could be separated, the true Gnostic, if called upon to choose between them, would choose the knowledge of God.[2] Salvation is

---

[1] Ὁ λόγος ὁ τοῦ Θεοῦ ἄνθρωπος γενόμενος, ἵνα δὴ καὶ σὺ παρὰ ἀνθρώπου μάθῃς, πῇ ποτε ἄρα ἄνθρωπος γενῆται Θεός (*Protrept.* i. 8). Cf. *Protrept.* xi. 114 : οὐρανίῳ διδασκαλίᾳ θεοποιῶν τὸν ἄνθρωπον. So he who obeys the Lord and follows the prophecy given through Him is fully perfected after the image of His Teacher, and becomes a God while still walking in the flesh (οὕτως ὁ τῷ κυρίῳ πειθόμενος καὶ τῇ δοθείσῃ δι' αὐτοῦ κατακολουθήσας προφητείᾳ τελέως ἐκτελεῖται κατ' εἰκόνα τοῦ διδασκάλου ἐν σαρκὶ περιπολῶν Θεός (*Strom.* VII. xvi. 101). It will be observed that the deification is here a deification through moral progress : it practically means the attainment of moral perfection, and no doubt of immortality through that perfection ; but it is not (as with later Greek theologians) a metaphysical process of acquiring " incorruptibility." Harnack's attempt to make the Latin theology more ethical than the Greek on the ground that salvation means to the Latin forgiveness, while to the Greek it means " deification," has no ground, at least as regards the earlier Greek theologians. They are not less but more ethical because they think of goodness rather than escape from punishment. The element in Clement that may be criticized as unethical is his exaltation of contemplation over practical goodness. In one place he says that for the true Gnostic " his end through Gnostic activity in accordance with the commandments culminates in contemplation " : τὸ τέλος αὐτῷ δι' ἐνεργείας γνωστικῆς τῆς κατὰ τὰς ἐντολὰς εἰς θεωρίαν περαιοῦται (*Strom.* VII. xiii. 83). Still more strangely he declares (exaggerating Aristotle) that " the end both of him who lives the political life and of him who lives according to the law is contemplation. So a rightly conducted political life is merely a means to an end (ἀναγκαῖον), while to philosophize is the noblest thing " (*Strom.* I. xxv. 166). And yet it is the characteristic of the Gnostic that he fulfils all the commandments of God from pure love of his neighbour (*Strom.* IV. xviii. 113). Clement never quite succeeded in co-ordinating what he had learned from the ancient philosophers and what he had learned from Christ.

[2] *Strom.* IV. xxii. 136.

with him rather a means to knowledge than knowledge a means to salvation.

From this point of view it mattered little to him whether he spoke of salvation as due to faith or to knowledge or to love or to knowledge and works.[1] At times he deliberately embraces the Socratic doctrine that ignorance is the cause of sin : consequently the removal of ignorance necessarily produces repentance and so forgiveness, amendment, salvation. " To him who is put in mind of the better," he says, " there follows of necessity repentance for the worse."[2] Occasionally, however, he admits that the weakness of the flesh is a contributory cause of sin, and all that he says on this head must be qualified by his strong assertion of free-will in the popular, indeterministic sense.[3] " We needs must love the highest when we see it," thought Clement : but we are always free to choose or to reject it. His whole philosophy of salvation is brought together in this sentence : " The heavenly and truly divine love in this way comes to men, whenever the truly noble, being kindled in the man's soul by the divine Word, is enabled to shine forth, and, what is greatest of all, upon right willing salvation immediately attends, will and life being, so to speak, yoked together."[4]

---

[1] Ἡ ἄγνοια δὲ τὸ σκότος καθ' ἣν περιπίπτομεν τοῖς ἁμαρτήμασιν, ἀμβλυωποῦντες περὶ τὴν ἀλήθειαν· φωτισμὸς ἄρα ἡ γνῶσίς ἐστιν ὁ ἐξαφανίζων τὴν ἄγνοιαν καὶ τὸ διορθωτικὸν ἐντιθείς (Paed. I. vi. 29). He goes on to speak of baptism as the " one reasonable Paeonian drug " which procures forgiveness of sins, but all the emphasis is on the knowledge communicated by baptism.

[2] Ἕπεται δὲ ἐξ ἀνάγκης τῷ ὑπομνησθέντι τῶν βελτιόνων ἡ μετάνοια ἡ ἐπὶ τοῖς ἥττοσιν (Paed. I. vi. 32). κατ' ἐπίστασιν οὖν, ὡς ἔοικεν, τοῦ κακοῦ καὶ ἀγάθου βίου σώζεται ὁ γνωστικός, " πλέον τῶν γραμματέων καὶ Φαρισαίων " συνιείς τε καὶ ἐνεργῶν (Strom. VI. xv. 115). The stress laid upon free will might not seem to allow much room for " grace," though no doubt knowledge is very much due to causes beyond our control, but in fact Clement is very full of the idea of divine assistance ; τῷ πεπιστευ- κότι προσεπιπνεῖσθαι τὸ ἅγιον πνεῦμά φαμεν (Strom. v. xiii. 88).

[3] His Libertarianism is so strong that he will not speak of God as willing the death of Christ. It happened, " God not preventing it " (μὴ κωλύσαντος τοῦ Θεοῦ, Strom. IV. xii. 86) : God wills us to be saved by our own exertions (ἐξ ἡμῶν αὐτῶν βούλεται σώζεσθαι, Strom. VI. xii. 96). It is obvious that the two doctrines : (1) ignorance is the sole cause of sin, and (2) sin is wilful, are not logically combinable, unless it is held that all ignorance is wilful ; but we are not really free to disbelieve what we once see to be true, if only we see it clearly enough.

[4] Ὁ γέ τοι οὐράνιος καὶ θεῖος ὄντως ἔρως ταύτῃ προσγίνεται τοῖς ἀνθρώποις, ὅταν ἐν αὐτῇ που τῇ ψυχῇ τὸ ὄντως καλὸν ὑπὸ τοῦ θείου λόγου ἀναζωπυρούμενον ἐκλάμπειν δυνηθῇ · καὶ τὸ μέγιστον, ἅμα τῷ βουληθῆναι γνησίως τὸ σωθῆναι συντρέχει, ὁμοζυγούντων, ὡς ἔπος εἰπεῖν, προαιρέσεως καὶ ζωῆς (Protrept. xi. 117).

Normally this illumination and the response of the will to it took place at baptism. Clement does not question the common belief of the Church that baptism carried with it immediate and plenary forgiveness of sins. But baptism was to him primarily, in the stock phrase of the age, an " illumination "—a direct and immediate illumination of the mind by the divine Word or Spirit.[1] At baptism Christ as God forgives sins, and as man He educates (παιδαγωγῶν) to the avoidance of sin.[2] In one place he distinctly raises the question whether it is the act of baptism or the accompanying catechetical instruction which produces this saving illumination, and he declines to answer it. " Thou canst not tell the time," he says, " for the instruction brings the soul round to faith, and faith is educated by the Holy Spirit at the same time as the baptism." [3] In all this there is absolutely no reference to any special connexion of the death of Christ with forgiveness : with Clement, as more or less with most of the succeeding Greek Fathers, the doctrine of the atonement is completely merged in that of the incarnation, and with him at least, the main purpose and meaning of the incarnation is revelation— the disclosure of truth about God. That does not mean that he takes a light view of sin, or underestimates the need for repentance. But he is profoundly impressed with the idea that the removal of sin is a gradual process : the past cannot be cancelled ; forgiveness is only possible so far as the man has actually become better : and the process of improvement need not end in this life. From Plato Clement had learned that all " punishment "

---

[1] Οἱ βαπτιζόμενοι τὰς ἐπισκοτούσας ἁμαρτίας τῷ θείῳ πνεύματι ἀχλύος δίκην ἀποτριψάμενοι ἐλεύθερον καὶ ἐνεμπόδιστον καὶ φωτεινὸν ὄμμα τοῦ πνεύματος ἴσχομεν, ᾧ δὴ μόνῳ τὸ θεῖον ἐποπτεύομεν, οὐρανόθεν ἐπεισρέοντος ἡμῖν τοῦ ἁγίου πνεύματος (Paed. i. vi. 28). It will be observed that here sin is made the cause of ignorance rather than ignorance the cause of sin, but for Clement the intellectual and moral side of the process are inseparable.

[2] Τὰ μὲν ἁμαρτήματα ὡς Θεὸς ἀφιείς, εἰς δὲ τὸ μὴ ἁμαρτάνειν παιδαγωγῶν ὡς ἄνθρωπος (Paed. i. iii. 7).

[3] Οὐ γὰρ ἔχοις εἰπεῖν τὸν χρόνον · ἡ μὲν γὰρ κατήχησις εἰς πίστιν περιάγει, πίστις δὲ ἅμα βαπτίσματι ἁγίῳ παιδεύεται πνεύματι (Paed. i. vi. 30). He sometimes distinctly speaks of knowledge as securing forgiveness: ὁ δ᾽ ἐν γνώσει γενόμενος ἅτε μηκέτι ἁμαρτάνων παρ᾽ ἑαυτοῦ τὴν ἄφεσιν τῶν λοιπῶν κομίζεται ('Εκ τῶν προφητικῶν ἐκλογαί, § 15). He hesitates about the forgiveness of post-baptismal sin. In Strom. ii. xiii. he is inclined to limit the possibility of repentance to one occasion after baptism ; not so in Q.D.S. 39.

($\kappa \acute{o} \lambda a \sigma \iota s$)—as distinct from "vengeance" ($\tau \iota \mu \omega \rho \acute{\iota} a$) —is for the benefit of the punished or of others : [1] punishment is only justified as medicine, and the conception is directly applied to the future punishment of the wicked. It would seem to follow from this that he must necessarily reject the idea of everlasting punishment. How far can we say that he has done so ? As regards those who have lived before the coming of Christ he declares quite explicitly that virtuous Jews and pagans would hereafter have the opportunity of embracing the faith of Christ.[2] In one place he declares that all are saved who desire faith. He will even say that the Greeks were justified by philosophy, though not (he adds) to complete righteousness.[3] And the qualification was duly insisted upon : only through the knowledge of Christ, whether it came in this world or in any other, was full and complete salvation to be obtained.

This largeness of view was, we have seen, by no means an isolated phenomenon in the Church. The belief in the preaching of Christ to the spirits in prison made it possible for the early Christian to hope that both

---

[1] Ἔπεται δὲ τῷ ἀγαθῷ, ᾗ φύσει ἀγαθός ἐστιν, ἡ μισοπονηρία, διὸ καὶ κολάζειν μὲν αὐτὸν ⟨ἂν⟩ ὁμολογήσαιμι τοὺς ἀπίστους· ἡ γὰρ κόλασις ἐπ' ἀγαθῷ καὶ ἐπ' ὠφελείᾳ τοῦ κολαζομένου, ἔστι γὰρ ἐπανόρθωσις ἀντιτείνοντος· τιμωρεῖσθαι δὲ μὴ βούλεσθαι. τιμωρία δέ ἐστιν ἀνταπόδοσις| κακοῦ ἐπὶ τὸ τοῦ τιμωροῦντος σύμφερον ἀναπεμπομένη (Paed. I. viii. 70). The whole of this and the next two chapters is devoted to the question. So he speaks of the fire which Christ brought into the world as a δύναμιν . . . παιδευτικήν (Ἐκ τῶν, προφ. ἐκλογαί, § 26). In a doubtful Fragment (ed. Klotz, I. iv. p. 83) he speaks of souls as κολαζόμεναι ὑπὸ τοῦ ἀσβέστου πυρὸς ἀπεράντῳ τιμωρίᾳ, but if this is really Clement's, he directly contradicts the passage of the Paedagogus quoted above. Dr. Tollinton (Clement of Alexandria, ii. 249) remarks : " Like the Apologists, Clement held the theory of conditional immortality. The soul is not naturally immortal." Clement certainly speaks of immortality as the gift of God (as any Theist might do), but I see no reason to believe that he thought that unredeemed souls were ever extinguished.

[2] Δίκαιος τοίνυν δικαίου καθὸ δίκαιός ἐστιν οὐ διαφέρει ἐάν τε νομικὸς ᾖ ἐάν τε Ἕλλην· οὐ γὰρ Ἰουδαίων μόνων, πάντων δὲ ἀνθρώπων ὁ Θεὸς κύριος, προσεχέστερον δὲ τῶν ἐγνωκότων πατήρ. He goes on to declare that the good οἱ πρὸ νόμου εἰς πίστιν ἐλογίσθησαν καὶ δίκαιοι εἶναι ἐκρίθησαν . . . εἰ καὶ ἐν Ἅιδου ἔτυχον ὄντες καὶ ἐν φρουρᾷ, ἐπακούσαντας τῆς τοῦ κυρίου φωνῆς εἴτε τῆς αὐθεντικῆς εἴτε καὶ τῆς διὰ τῶν ἀποστόλων ἐνεργούσης, ᾖ τάχος, ἐπιστραφῆναί σε καὶ πιστεῦσαι (Strom. vi. vi. 47). The idea of the Apostles joining in the preaching to the spirits in Hades is an interesting addition, and seems to show a desire to rationalize the whole conception. The opportunities of the future were not to be limited to the few hours which Christ was supposed to have passed in Hades.

[3] Καίτοι καὶ καθ' ἑαυτὴν ἐδικαίου ποτὲ καὶ ἡ φιλοσοφία τοὺς Ἕλληνας, οὐκ εἰς τὴν καθολοῦ δὲ δικαιοσύνην, εἰς ἣν εὑρίσκεται συνεργός· καθάπερ καὶ ὁ πρῶτος καὶ ὁ δεύτερος βαθμὸς τῷ εἰς τὸ ὑπερῷον ἀνιόντι καὶ ὁ γραμματιστὴς τῷ φιλοσοφήσαντι. (Note that δικαιόω here clearly means " make righteous," not " declare righteous," and so in the Fathers generally.) Cf. Strom. I. xx. 99.

Jews and pagans who had failed to obtain salvation before death would hereafter have the opportunity of listening to Christ's teaching, repenting, and being saved. But as regards those who had had Christian truth presented to them, and who had failed to accept it—still more as regards those who had become Christians and fallen away—the general tendency of the Church's teaching was no doubt against the hope of any further opportunity. It was certainly thought that they would be condemned at the judgement; and no definite hope of their future salvation was usually entertained, though it cannot be said that the doctrine of everlasting punishment was universally taught. Clement is the first writer who definitely raises the moral difficulties connected with the idea of divine punishment. As against the Marcionites he strongly maintains that punishment is not inconsistent with love, and that therefore God may punish, as He is represented as doing both in the Old Testament and in the New; but he altogether repudiates the idea of punishment to satisfy the divine wrath or a mysterious necessity of retribution. Punishment is not vengeance. Clement did not venture to go beyond these generalities, but there can be no doubt that he would heartily have sympathized with the development subsequently given to his teaching by his pupil Origen. Clement certainly did not believe that the opportunity for repentance and moral improvement ended with death, though his intense belief in the freedom of the will might make him hesitate to adopt the confident Universalism of his disciple.[1]

No early Christian writer is more full of the spirit

[1] Dr. Bigg says : " There can, I think, be no doubt (though it has been doubted) that Clement allowed the possibility of repentance and amendment till the Last Day, but that he regards probation as ceasing then " (2nd ed. p. 147). I see no ground in the passages which he quotes (*Strom.* v. xiv. 91, VII. ii. 12) for this distinction. Indeed, they seem absolutely inconsistent with it. In the first passage (referring to Plato) he speaks of punishment as educational (τοιαῦτά τινα εἰς τὴν παίδευσιν σωφρονίζοντα παρεισάγων κολαστήρια), and in the latter he says : παιδεύσεις δὲ αἱ ἀναγκαῖαι . . . διά τε προκρίσεων ποικίλων καὶ διὰ τῆς κρίσεως τῆς παντέλους τοὺς ἐπὶ πλέον ἀπηλγηκότας ἐκβιάζονται μετανοεῖν. If the object of punishment inflicted at the last judgement is to produce repentance, it is implied that the punishment must cease when the repentance has taken place. I have understood προκρίσεις to mean punishments after death but before the judgement, rather than punishments in this life : it might include both. There are no doubt fragments of doubtful genuineness which suggest the usual view.

of Christ than Clement. The one weak point in his
practical Christianity is a tendency to exalt knowledge
above love, though after all we must remember that the
knowledge to which he attaches the most importance is
the knowledge of God, which included for him a knowledge of the moral ideal, and necessarily carried with it
the actual aiming at that ideal. It is not so much
intellectual activity as religious contemplation—a contemplation which included much intellectual activity—
which he tends to exalt above the life of practical duty.
In Clement the tendency is not carried to very anti-social
lengths : Clement was no monk, no recluse, hardly an
ascetic : but we cannot fail to see in his teaching anticipations of the spirit which was soon to fill the Egyptian
desert with wasted, and often very unlovely, lives.[1]

Irenaeus

So far we have searched in vain for any definite
theory of an objective redemption effected by the death
of Christ which goes beyond the bare repetition of the
traditional language based on the Old Testament. At
what point did any such theory first enter into the stream
of Christian theology ; or, in so far as it was already
present in St. Paul, when did St. Paul find a successor
in the attempt to build up such a theory ? The answer
is plain and certain. The first of the Fathers who holds
the theory of an objective redemption approximating
to the idea of substitution is Irenaeus,[2] though even in
him the theory is still always struggling with the older
and more philosophical modes of presentation. Irenaeus
was the first writer who may be said definitely to have
conceived the idea of a dogmatic theology as distinct
from an apologetic philosophy. Three changes in the
religious situation had made such an attempt necessary,

---

[1] This side of Clement's teaching is fully dealt with by Dr. Bigg, *Christian Platonists*
(2nd ed. pp. 126-132).
[2] Irenaeus lived originally in Asia Minor, where he tells us that as a boy he had heard
Polycarp (martyred in 155) : Bishop of Lyons in Gaul, A.D. 177. His great work,
Contra Haeresis, was probably written after this date. I have used the edition of Harvey.

and in particular had forced upon Christian writers the necessity of theorizing about the atonement in a way which had not been done before.

(1) The earlier Church had not found it necessary to construct a theology of the atonement because there were no rival theologies in the field. The extravagant and half-Christian systems of the Gnostics forced, or at least tempted, the Church into stereotyping its doctrine, into defining what had hitherto been undefined, and contracting the liberty of speculation which had hitherto been enjoyed. It has been said that the Gnostics were the first theologians : at all events it is certain that it was Gnosticism which demanded that the orthodox Church teachers should construct a rival theology, which should at least reply to the heretical objections, and give an answer to the problems which they had raised.

(2) It is true that it was the doctrine of the Trinity and the Person of Christ which was most strictly defined, and was most jealously guarded. Orthodoxy practically meant the holding of the right doctrine of the Trinity and (especially after Nicaea) of the incarnation. But though much freedom of speculation was allowed about most other subjects, some account had to be given of the atonement : the idea was too deeply embedded in the Christian tradition to be simply ignored. Marcion and the Gnostics had brought into prominence the collision between the attributes of justice and mercy in God. They had met the moral difficulties of the Old Testament —difficulties then aggravated by an extreme theory of inspiration—by boldly denying all identity between the God of the Jews and the God revealed in Christ. The God of the Jews, the God who created the world, the God of the Old Testament, was just but not merciful. Creation and the contact with matter which it involved were the source of sin. The God of the Jews was the author of the threatenings and punishments from which mankind needed deliverance : the scheme of redemption was the work of the higher and really benevolent Deity who had revealed Himself in Christ. The one point of contact between Gnosticism and the primitive Christianity of

the Church was just the doctrine of a salvation through Christ. If, as sober thought and the facts of history demanded, the God whom Jesus worshipped and revealed was to be represented as the same God as the God of the Old Testament, there was obviously a moral problem to be solved as to the relation between the divine punishments threatened in the Old Testament and that divine mercy to which the teaching of Jesus and of St. Paul bore witness. The religion of the Gnostics was essentially a religion of redemption—redemption conceived of very much in the sense of the pagan mysteries : if the Church was to hold its own against them, it must perfect its scheme of redemption. It had to explain why a God of love should not forgive sin without demanding the death of His divine Son.

(3) We have already seen how profound was the influence exercised upon the early Church by the authority of the Old Testament, and how wide was the liberty which Christian thinkers enjoyed where that authority was not involved. For good and for evil the Christian Church had taken over the Old Testament as Scripture, and for a long time the Old Testament was the only Scripture. In the earliest Christian writings only the actual sayings of the Lord are quoted with the same kind of authority as that enjoyed by the Old Testament : but gradually the earliest Christian writings came themselves to be placed in the same category of inspired Scripture. By the last quarter of the second century the New Testament canon was almost settled, and in that canon the letters of St. Paul held an undisputed place, and enjoyed an authority second, but only second, to that of the Gospels.[1]   Henceforth it became impossible for Christian speculators to ignore those elements of St. Paul's teaching which did not happen to be congenial to a particular writer or a particular circle. The characteristic theories of St. Paul had to

---

[1] It is probable that the use made of St. Paul's Epistles by the Gnostics was a contributory cause of the position which they secured as well as of the prominence now given to theories of redemption. Prof. Burkitt has even suggested that we owe to the Gnostics the collection of Epistles which has come down to us.

be explained; they had to be accepted in the letter, even when the interpretation put upon them was as arbitrary and unhistorical as the interpretation which had often been applied to the older Scriptures. The result was a theology which rested upon authority to a vastly greater extent than the theology of the prophet Hermas and of philosophers like Justin or Clement, and in which the theories of redemption and justification specially characteristic of St. Paul assumed a prominence which had never previously been given to them.

Of these tendencies Irenaeus was the most prominent exponent. He aimed at building up a system of the universe or at least a theory of salvation, not indeed without help from philosophy, but ostensibly resting upon the basis of authority or tradition, pure and simple. That aim made it necessary for him to construct for the first time a theory about the effect of Christ's death. As a matter of fact he constructed many such theories, not very easy to reconcile with one another, and yet very obviously growing out of one another. For Irenaeus, sensible enough as a defender of the Christian tradition against Gnostic extravagances, was a thinker of no very high order—not very acute and not very consistent.[1] He seems always engaged in tentative efforts at explanation which fail to satisfy even his own mind. Putting aside the old traditional phrases and the old subjective or ethical explanations of that death, such as we have already encountered in the earlier writers, we meet in Irenaeus with three or four more or less new lines of thought or modes of speech.

(1) In him the tendency, already prominent in St. Paul, to find parallels between the fall through the first Adam and the redemption through the second Adam is developed into a theory—the theory of a peculiar fitness in the method of redemption actually adopted by

---

[1] In particular we may notice : (1) The inconsistency of the theory which attributed salvation to the incarnation (which is a product of the Logos doctrine), with the idea of salvation by the cross which is accepted from St. Paul and from tradition. (2) The inconsistency between the eschatology implied by the whole theory of a deification of humanity through the incarnation with the chiliastic hopes which Irenaeus continued to assert. I do not say that in either case the reconciliation was impossible, but it was certainly not effected by Irenaeus.

God.[1] Irenaeus represents a stage of intellectual development in which it seemed natural that the whole
course of human history should be controlled and directed
with a view to the production of striking and edifying
parallelisms or symbolisms. There was a peculiar
appropriateness, he taught, in the arrangement that, as
Paradise was lost by one man's fault, so it should be
regained by one man's sufferings. He was in the
state of mind—frequently repeated in the history of
religious ideas—in which analogies do duty for reasons,
for arguments, for thought. To Irenaeus it appeared
quite a grave reason for Christ's death on the Cross to
say that, as a tree had been the cause of the fall, so it
was fitting that another tree—the tree of the Cross—
should be the cause of redemption, just as there was a
fitness in the recovery through another woman of what
had been lost through Eve.[2]

(2) By gradual and imperceptible stages the idea of
a fitness in this parallelism seems to grow into the theory
of a " recapitulation " (ἀνακεφαλαίωσις) of all things
in Christ—a theory suggested both by the language of
St. Paul and by Gnostic speculation. " That which
He appeared, that He also was : God recapitulating in
Himself the ancient creation, in order that He might

---

[1] The idea of the fall is prominent in Irenaeus (as *a* fall—not the biblical fall—is
prominent in the Gnostics). But his notion of the condition to which human nature
was reduced by the fall was a moderate one compared with much that followed. It did
not destroy man's free will—in which largely consisted his likeness to God. The whole
scheme of redemption was designed to secure that man should be persuaded, not forced,
into goodness. Man's chance of winning incorruptibility was destroyed by the fall :
death descended to Adam's posterity and apparently (though this is not emphasized)
some weakening of his will for good. The fall was allowed in order to increase man's
gratitude for salvation and his sense of his own weakness (" ut plus diligeret eum, cui enim
plus dimittitur plus diligit, cognoscat autem semetipsum, quoniam mortalis et infirmus
est." *Haer.* III. xxi. 2). Sometimes the curious notion is added that, as a Saviour pre-
existed, there must be somebody for Him to save. Cf. III. xxxii. 1 (" Cum autem prae-
existeret salvans, oportebat et quod salvaretur fieri, uti non vacuum sit salvans "). This
implies that the fall was predestined : in Irenaeus strong predestinarian statements occur
side by side with strong assertions of human freedom. Cf. *Haer.* IV. *cc.* vii. lix. lx.

[2] " Manifeste itaque in sua propria venientem Dominum, et sua propria eum bajulante
conditione, quae bajulatur ab ipso, et recapitulationem ejus quae in ligno fuit inobedientiae, per eam quae in ligno est obedientiam, facientem, et seductione illa soluta, qua
seducta est male illa, quae jam viro destinata erat virgo Eva, per veritatem evangelisata
est bene ab angelo jam sub viro Virgo Maria " (*Haer.* v. xix. 1). Cf. III. xxxi. 1.

The parallel between Eve and the Virgin is already found in Justin, *Dial. c. Tryph.*
100. Harnack remarks that " the later Mariolatry has one of its roots in the parallel
between Eve and Mary " (*Hist. of Dogma*, ii. 277),

slay sin and destroy the power of death, and give life
to men." ¹

It is difficult to find in such vague expressions an
idea capable of definite formulation. The meaning
seems to be that in Christ, the second Adam, that true
ideal of humanity, which owing to the fall the first Adam
and his posterity had failed to realize, has now at
last attained its full realization through Him in all
redeemed humanity.² The words " restoration " and
" renovation " are often used practically as synonyms
of " recapitulation." This was effected primarily by
the incarnation, and the theory is not brought into any
very close connexion with the death of Christ, except in
so far as the death was necessary to the resurrection.³
The language of Irenaeus does, indeed, occasionally
suggest the doctrine, afterwards much developed and
not yet quite extinct among us, that in Jesus the whole
of Humanity—the universal of Humanity—suffered
death, the appointed penalty of sin, that therefore every
individual man may be held to have suffered it, and that
so God, having fulfilled His threat that he who sins shall
die, is now free to pardon ; but it can hardly be said that he
definitely formulates that view.   He does hold that it was
fitting that the deliverance of mankind should be effected
by the "same thing"—Humanity—by which the fall
had been occasioned.   And this could only be done by
One who was God as well as man.   " It was necessary
that He who should begin to slay sin, and redeem man
doomed to death, should become the very thing which man
was, that is man, . . . in order that sin should be slain
by man, and man should come out of (the dominion of)
death." ⁴   " He then, as we said before, united man to

¹ " Quod autem parebat, hoc et erat ; Deus, hominis antiquam plasmationem in se recapitulans, ut occideret quidem peccatum, evacuaret autem mortem, et vivificaret hominem " (*Haer.* III. xix. 6).

² In *Haer.* v. ii. 1 he speaks of Christ as " restoring to His creation that which was
said at the beginning, that man was made in the image and likeness of God, not seizing
upon what was not His own by fraud but justly and benignantly assuming His own."

³ In one place he distinctly says that the resurrection is the real cause of the
incarnation : εἰπών γὰρ, εἰ δὲ Χριστὸς κηρύσσεται, ὅτι ἐκ νεκρῶν ἐγήγερται, ἐπιφέρει
τὴν αἰτίαν ἀποδίδους τῆς σαρκώσεως αὐτοῦ (*Haer.* III. xix. 3).

⁴ " Oportebat enim eum qui inciperet occidere peccatum, et mortis reum redimere
hominem, id ipsum fieri quod erat ille, id est hominem : qui a peccato quidem in

God. For if man's conqueror had not been man, the enemy would not have been conquered justly. And, again, if it had not been God who granted the salvation, we could not have securely held that salvation. And if man had not been united with God, he could not have participated in incorruption."[1] But it is not exclusively by His death that this triumph over man's ancient enemy is effected, though occasionally there is a special emphasis on the death. In general, it is the perfect obedience of Christ shown alike in His life and in His death,[2] His resistance to temptation[3] and His triumph over death at the Resurrection which has the redeeming effect rather than the death itself considered as penalty or as suffering. In him, as in most Greek Fathers after him, it is not so much the retrospective forgiveness of sins as the destruction of sinfulness and the consequent or concomitant restoration of that incorruptibility and immortality, that vision of God, that divine Sonship and communion with God,[4] nay, that actual deifica-

servitium tractus fuerat, ut peccatum ab homine interficeretur, et homo exiret a morte. ὥσπερ γὰρ διὰ τῆς παρακοῆς τοῦ ἑνὸς ἀνθρώπου, τοῦ πρώτως ἐκ τῆς ἀνεργάστου πεπλασμένου, ἁμαρτωλοὶ κατεστάθησαν οἱ πολλοί, καὶ ἀπέβαλον τὴν ζωήν· οὕτως ἔδει καὶ δι' ὑπακοῆς ἑνὸς ἀνθρώπου, τοῦ πρώτως ἐκ παρθένου γεγενημένου, δικαιωθῆναι πολλούς, καὶ ἀπολαβεῖν τὴν σωτηρίαν" (Haer. III. xix. 6).

[1] ἥνωσεν οὖν, καθὼς προέφαμεν, τὸν ἄνθρωπον τῷ Θεῷ. εἰ γὰρ μὴ ἄνθρωπος ἐνίκησεν τὸν ἀντίπαλον τοῦ ἀνθρώπου, οὐκ ἂν δικαίως ἐνικήθη ὁ ἐχθρός. πάλιν τε, εἰ μὴ ὁ Θεὸς ἐδωρήσατο τὴν σωτηρίαν, οὐκ ἂν βεβαίως ἔσχομεν αὐτήν. καὶ εἰ μὴ συνηνώθη ὁ ἄνθρωπος τῷ Θεῷ, οὐκ ἂν ἠδυνήθη μετασχεῖν τῆς ἀφθαρσίας. ἔδει γὰρ τὸν μεσίτην Θεοῦ τε καὶ ἀνθρώπων, διὰ τῆς ἰδίας πρὸς ἑκατέρους οἰκειότητος, εἰς φιλίαν καὶ ὁμόνοιαν τοὺς ἀμφοτέρους συναγαγεῖν· καὶ Θεῷ μὲν παραστῆσαι τὸν ἄνθρωπον, ἀνθρώποις δὲ γνωρίσαι τὸν Θεόν (Haer. III. xix. 6; cf. xxxi. 1).

[2] " Eam quae in ligno fuerat obedientiam per eam quae in ligno fuerat obedientiam sanans" (Haer. v. xvi. 2).

[3] So much stress is laid upon the successful resistance to the Devil—especially at the temptation—that this may almost be said to amount to another distinct theory of redemption (Haer. III. xix. 5)—the theory adopted by Milton in Paradise Regained. In fact, the theory of Irenaeus is rather a theory of vicarious fulfilment of God's law than of vicarious punishment. " Praeceptum ejus perfecit dominus, factus ex muliere et destruens adversarium nostrum, et perficiens hominem secundem imaginem et similitudinem Dei" (v. xxi. 2). It is generally left obscure how the resistance to temptation benefited us. Sometimes it seems to have a direct influence upon the bodies of men ; sometimes it " propitiates the Father " (v. xvii. 1) ; sometimes it destroys sin, and this destruction of sin is closely connected with the victory over the devil, the full meaning of which depends upon the transaction with him explained below. Irenaeus also (v. xxi. 2) emphasizes, as against Marcion, the fact that it was by quoting and obeying the precepts of the ancient law that Christ effected the deliverance.

[4] "Ὁ λόγος ἄνθρωπος [καὶ ὁ υἱὸς Θεοῦ υἱὸς ἀνθρώπου ἐγεννήθη], ἵνα ὁ ἄνθρωπος τὸν λόγον χωρήσας, καὶ τὴν υἱοθεσίαν λαβών, υἱὸς γένηται Θεοῦ. Non enim poteramus aliter incorruptelam et immortalitatem percipere, nisi adunati fuissemus incorruptelae et immortalitati. Quemadmodum autem adunari possemus incorruptelae et

tion,[1] for which man was created, that is the ultimate object of the scheme of salvation. And this was effected by the incarnation as a whole. Jesus Christ was made what we are, in order that we might become what He is.[2] Here we have (as in his contemporary, Clement) the characteristic thought of almost all subsequent Greek theology. God became man in order that man might become divine, become God, or rather " become *a* god "—that is the constantly repeated formula. It is seldom quite clear how far either Irenaeus or his successors thought of this restoration as effected by the moral influence of Christ's character and teaching and example, and the revelation of the Father which they contain, and how far by a sort of metaphysical or almost physical effect upon "humanity " of the one body rendered incorruptible by its union with the divine nature.[3] It is not too much

---

immortalitati, nisi prius incorruptela et immortalitas facta fuisset id quod et nos, ut absorberetur quod est corruptibile ab incorruptela, et quod erat mortale ab immortalitate, ut filiorum adoptionem perciperemus ? " (*Haer.* III. xx. 1.). It should be remembered that with Irenaeus (as with Ignatius and the Asia Minor school generally) the incarnation is thought of as the dwelling of the Logos in human *flesh* : there is no distinct idea of a human soul (or mind) in Jesus. But he comes nearer to the two-nature Chalcedonian formula than Ignatius. (See Fragment 8.) The two-nature doctrine is first found in Tertullian (in a form which would have afterwards been considered Nestorian), or rather, perhaps in a fragment of Melito (Harnack, *Texte u. Untersuch.* i. 2, p. 249 *sq.*).

[1] Πῶς δύνανται σωθῆναι, εἰ μὴ ὁ Θεὸς ἦν ὁ τὴν σωτηρίαν αὐτῶν ἐπὶ γῆς ἐργασάμενος; ἢ πῶς ἄνθρωπος χωρήσει εἰς Θεὸν, εἰ μὴ ὁ Θεὸς ἐχωρήθη εἰς ἄνθρωπον; (*Haer.* IV. lii. 1).

[2] " Propter suam immensam dilectionem factus est quod sumus nos, uti nos perficeret esse quod et ipse " (v. praef.).

[3] The higher view is predominant in such a representation as the following : " Quoniam et ipse in similitudine carnis peccati factus est, uti condemnaret peccatum, et jam quasi condemnatum projiceret illud extra carnem ; *provocaret autem in similitudinem suam hominem, imitatorem eum assignans* Deo, et in paternam imponens regulam ad videndum Deum, et capere Patrem donans; Verbum Dei quod habitavit in homine, et Filius Hominis factus est, ut assuesceret hominem percipere Deum " (*Haer.* III. xxi. 2). The lower view comes out when he speaks of immortal life as secured by eating the flesh of Christ in the Eucharist (v. ii. 2 ; see below, p. 280). Often the two points of view are inextricably intertwined. Sometimes a view slightly different from either is taken : " It was needful that the Mediator between God and man should, by virtue of his own kinship to both of them, bring the two into friendship and harmony, and should represent man to God and make God known to man " (*Haer.* III. xix. 6. For the Greek see above, p. 239). The deification theory is still in Irenaeus combined—however inconsistently—with a continued assertion of the Chiliastic Eschatology, *i.e.* the belief in a very literal reign of Christ upon earth, during which the righteous will eat and drink with Christ the produce of a miraculously fertile earth (*Haer.* v. xxxiii. 3). The Chiliastic hope remains also in Tertullian and Hippolytus. It began to disappear in the East during the third century, but survived much longer in the West. As to the meaning of " deification " in the Fathers, it must be remembered that, according to the old Greek belief, men were mortal, the gods alone were immortal (cf. Burnet, " The Socratic doctrine of the Soul," in *Proceedings of the British Academy*, vol. vii.). Only a few exceptional individuals were

to say that, in so far as they meant the former, their doctrine had in it the germ of all reasonable teaching on the subject : while, in so far as they meant the latter, we are in the region of pure myth—none the less myth because the idea comes from the corrupt following of Plato—though it is a myth of a much higher type, and much more amenable to a higher interpretation, than some of the theories which we shall hereafter encounter.

(3) Occasionally the theory of recapitulation seems to pass into a definite theory of substitution. Irenaeus speaks of the Lord as " having redeemed us by His own blood, and given His own life on behalf of our lives (ὑπέρ) and His flesh instead of (ἀντί) our flesh." [1]

(4) The above statement leaves open the question why such a substitution was necessary, how it took effect, or how it was just that one man should die for another. Elsewhere Irenaeus attempts to enlighten us. Certain passages of the Old Testament about the relation of God to Israel had already suggested the idea that Christ laid down His life as a ransom for many—an idea embodied in the saying attributed to Christ Himself by the two first Evangelists. In St. Paul and in other writers the same conception led to the application of such phrases as " redemption " (ἀπολύτρωσις, λύτρωσις), to the work of Christ, and in particular to His death : and this usage had grown into the more definite statement that Christ's death was the ransom (λύτρον), by paying

---

taken up into heaven and became immortal, and these were considered to have become gods. Thus Theophilus remarks that, if God had made Adam immortal from the beginning, " He would have made him God " (*Ad Autol.* II. 27). But the ethical interpretation was not altogether absent : at its highest, deification may be said to have meant the attainment both of likeness to God, moral and intellectual, and of the immortality which was the fitting reward (or perhaps presupposition) of such attainment. It is probable that in strictness θεοποιεῖσθαι ought to be translated to " become a god," not " to become divine," but all the same Christians would perhaps have shrunk from the bold expression but for the convenient absence of an indefinite article in Greek. Of course they would never have thought of a man becoming ὁ Θεός ; even Christ was to the early Christian writers generally Θεός.

[1] Τῷ ἰδίῳ οὖν αἵματι λυτρωσαμένου ἡμᾶς τοῦ Κυρίου, καὶ δόντος τὴν ψυχὴν ὑπὲρ τῶν ἡμετέρων ψυχῶν καὶ τὴν σάρκα τὴν ἑαυτοῦ ἀντὶ τῶν ἡμετερῶν σαρκῶν (*Haer.* v. i. 2). Except in the passage of Matthew-Mark about the ransom, this is, I think, the first trace that Christ is said to have died " instead of " us (ἀντί) and not " on behalf of " us (ὑπέρ), but the ransom idea is in the background of Irenaeus' thought. In view of this passage, Harnack's words, " Teachings as to vicarious suffering on the part of Christ are not found in Irenaeus " (*Hist. of Dogma,* ii. 291) seem to be too unqualified.

which Christ had redeemed those who believed in Him.[1]
But it had never been distinctly laid down to whom
the ransom was paid. Then there was the Lukan
passage in which our Lord beholds Satan as lightning
fallen from heaven,[2] and the parable of the strong man
armed who keepeth his palace until a stronger than he
shall come upon and overcome him.[3] Moreover, the
fourth Gospel had represented the death of Christ as
directly brought about by the Devil, had called the
Devil "the prince of this world," and had spoken
of Christ's death or His resurrection as bringing about
his judgement.[4] The redemption effected by Christ—
by His resistance to temptation and by His resurrection
—was thus naturally described as a triumph over the
Devil and other evil spirits. So in the Apocalypse the
saints overcome the Devil because of the blood of the
Lamb.[5] From this it was not a long step to the thought
of Ignatius that the incarnation brought with it the
destruction of the power of evil spirits by the extinction
of magic and the oracles as well as by the disappearance
of ignorance.[6] The idea of a literal "descent into hell"
of Christ and a preaching to the spirits in prison is as
early as the first Epistle of St. Peter;[7] and St. Paul had
spoken of the Devil as the "prince of the power of the
air."[8] We have already seen how even so philosophical
a writer as Justin had taught that the chief purpose of

---

[1] Cf. the more definite notion of purchase (ἐξαγοράσῃ) in Gal. iv. 5 ; and " Ye were
bought with a price " (τιμή) in 1 Cor. vi. 20, vii. 23.

[2] Lk. x. 18.

[3] Lk. xi. 21, 22.

[4] John xiv. 30, xvi. 11 ; cf. xii. 31, where Loisy accepts the reading " shall be cast
down " (βληθήσεται κάτω). Cf. Lk. xxii. 35 (" This is your hour and the power of
darkness "). Cf. also 1 Cor. ii. 8.

[5] Rev. xii. 11.

[6] Ὅθεν ἐλύετο πᾶσα μαγεία καὶ πᾶς δεσμός, ἠφανίζετο κακίας ἄγνοια, καθῃρεῖτο
παλαιὰ βασιλεία [διεφθείρετο], Θεοῦ ἀνθρωπίνως φανερουμένου εἰς καινότητα ἀϊδίου
ζωῆς (Eph. xix. ; cf. Milton's " The oracles are dumb "). It is to be observed that this
effect seems to follow upon the appearance of the star (in Ignatius a star of supernatural
brightness, exceeding the brightness of the sun) at Christ's birth : it is not specially
connected with His death. We get a nearer approach to the later conception in Apol-
linaris (Fr. Migne, т.v. c. 1268) : τὸ ἀληθινὸν τοῦ Κυρίου πάσχα, ἡ θυσία ἡ μεγάλη, ὁ
ἀντὶ τοῦ ἀμνοῦ παῖς Θεοῦ ὁ δεθείς, ὁ δήσας τὸν ἰσχυρόν, καὶ ὁ κριθείς, κριτὴς ζώντων
καὶ νεκρῶν. The idea of the binding the strong man or " harrowing of hell " was
largely suggested by the saying in Mk. iii. 27 (=Matt. xii. 29 ; cf. Lk. xi. 21), where
the words are of course purely proverbial or parabolic.

[7] 1 Pet. iii. 19.

[8] Eph. ii. 2 ; cf. 2 Cor. iv. 4 : " the god of this world."

Christ's coming was to weaken the power of the Devil, and how firm was his belief in the wonder-working efficacy of exorcism in the name of the Crucified.[1] Along these lines there was gradually evolved a scheme in which all the vague, confused, more or less metaphorical expressions of earlier writers are taken in grim earnest, and hardened into a definite and very astonishing theory. By the fall man had become the slave or subject of the Devil. Christ's death was the ransom paid to the Devil for his release. Why any such ransom should be paid, it is difficult to understand, since it is admitted that man really belonged to God, and that the fall by which he passed under the Devil's dominion was accomplished by a misrepresentation on the part of the Devil. Man was deceived into the belief that he would win enlightenment and immortality by eating the forbidden fruit. But apparently it was, according to Irenaeus, more suitable to the dignity and justice of God that He should effect His object by persuasion rather than by force— that is, it would seem, by persuading the Devil to bring about the death of Christ, and so making it just for God to release man from his dominion. By bringing about the death of the sinless Christ the Devil had claimed more than was his due; that made it just for God, by way of set-off or compensation, to take back from him something to which he could plead at least the title of long possession. Here is the *locus classicus* for this view :

" The potent Word and true Man rationally redeeming us by His blood, gave Himself as a redemption [or ransom] for these who were led into captivity. And, since he [the Devil] unjustly ruled over us by an apostasy [*i.e.* by exciting Adam to apostasy or rebellion],[2] and whereas we by nature belonged to Almighty God, alienated us contrary to nature, making us his own disciples, He, the Word of God powerful in all things, and not failing in His own justice, behaved justly even as against the very apostasy; redeeming [or buying back] what was His own from that apostasy, not violently [or

---

[1] See above, p. 201.
[2] Or the words may be translated " since an apostasy ruled over us."

arbitrarily], inasmuch that apostasy dominated over us from the beginning—not insatiably seizing on what was His own, but by way of persuasion, as it beseemed God to get what He wanted by persuasion and not by employing violence; so that neither should the law of justice be violated nor the ancient creation of God perish." [1]

Here is another passage :

"For if man who had been created by God that he should live, losing his life and injured by the serpent who had corrupted him, were not any more to return to life, but were wholly abandoned to death, God would have been conquered, and the wickedness of the serpent would have overcome the will of God. But since God is unconquered and magnanimous, He showed Himself magnanimous with a view to the reproof of man and the probation of all, as we have already said : but through the second Man He bound the strong and spoiled his vessels, and evacuated death by giving life to the man who had been subjected to death. For Adam was first made a vessel for his [the Devil's] possession, whom he both held under his power (that is to say, he unjustly brought transgression upon him), and by pretending to offer him immortality made him subject to death. For promising that they should be as gods, which it was not in his power to secure, he produced death in them : whence also he who had carried off man as a captive was justly recaptured by God : while man who had been led captive was loosed from the chains to which he had been condemned." [2]

---

[1] "Verbum potens, et homo verus, sanguine suo rationabiliter redimens nos, redemtionem semetipsum dedit pro his, qui in captivitatem ducti sunt. Et quoniam injuste dominabatur nobis apostasia, et cum natura essemus Dei omnipotentis, alienavit nos contra naturam, suos proprios nos faciens discipulos, potens in omnibus Dei Verbum, et non deficiens in sua justitia, juste etiam adversus ipsam conversus est apostasiam, ea quae sunt sua redimens ab ea, non cum vi, quemadmodum illa initio dominabatur nostri, ea quae non erant sua insatiabiliter rapiens, sed secundum suadelam, quemadmodum decebat Deum suadentem, et non vim inferentem, accipere quae vellet; ut neque quod est justum confringeretur, neque antiqua plasmatio Dei deperiret " (Haer. v. i. 1).   M. Rivière (Le Dogme de la Réd. p. 376) declares that Irenaeus never says to whom the ransom was paid, but I do not think it can be doubted that he means it to be paid to the devil.

[2] " Si enim qui factus fuerat a Deo homo ut viveret, hic amittens vitam laesus a serpente qui depravaverat eum, jam non reverteretur ad vitam, sed in totum projectus esset morti, victus esset Deus, et superasset serpentis nequitia voluntatem Dei.   Sed quoniam Deus invictus et magnanimis est, magnanimem quidem se exhibuit ad correptionem hominis et probationem omnium, quemadmodum praediximus : per secundum autem hominem

I may add that the doctrine of Irenaeus was probably suggested to him by the theory of redemption first put forward by Marcion.[1] It was because by bringing about the death of Jesus the God of the Jews—the generally just but not benevolent Demiurge—had violated his own laws, that it became just for the true and benevolent God to set man free from the Demiurge. Irenaeus simply substituted the Devil for the Demiurge.

It should be observed that this theory, hideous as it is, is not precisely the same theory as that which represents the death of Christ as a substitutionary, an expiatory, or a propitiatory sacrifice, nor is it really even compatible with it.   Still less is it a theory of vicarious punishment. If the Father allowed Christ to die merely that the just claims of the Devil might be satisfied, He did not die because the Father's wrath must have a victim or because an abstract justice demanded punishment.   At the same time this incompatibility was not usually seen by those who accepted the theory of a transaction with the Devil : the theory was treated as an explanation of the biblical or traditional language about the sacrificial or penal character of Christ's death, and appears side by side with such language in Irenaeus and his successors.   In some of its exponents it had at least the good effect of neutralizing conceptions of sacrifice or punishment, which, if not less childish, were grosser, more immoral, and more derogatory to the character of God.

Moreover, it would be unjust to Irenaeus not to point out once more that side by side with this extraordinary scheme, there appear other and nobler views—for the most part those with which we have already met.   Sometimes we could almost suppose that the triumph over

---

alligavit fortem, et diripuit ejus vasa, et evacuavit mortem vivificans eum hominem qui fuerat mortificatus.   Primum enim possessionis ejus vas Adam factus est, quem et tenebat sub sua potestate, hoc est praevaricationem inique inferens ei, et per occasionem immortalitatis mortificationem faciens in eum.   Etenim promittens futuros eos tanquam deos, quod ei non est omnino possibile, mortem fecit in eis : unde et juste a Deo recaptivatus, qui hominem captivum duxerat ; solutus est autem condemnationis vinculis, qui captivus ductus fuerat homo " (*Haer.* III. xxxii. 2).

[1] The Gnostic Saturninus also taught that Christ came for the destruction (κατάλυσις) of the God of the Jews and of the devils (Hippolytus, *Philosophumena* vii. 28).

the Devil consists simply in the actual moral regeneration which the example, teaching, and influence of Christ brought into the world. The dominating idea of Irenaeus is the incarnation of God in Christ, and, in spite of all his rhetorical metaphysic, the incarnation is with him primarily the self-revelation of God.[1] No one knows better how to represent the incarnation, the death, and the resurrection of Christ simply as a revelation of the character of God, moving man to gratitude and answering love—"that he might ever be grateful to God, having received the gift of incorruption from Him; that he might love Him the more, for he to whom more is forgiven loves more; and might know himself that he is mortal and weak, but might also know God . . . and further might know all the other virtues of God exhibited towards him, and that taught thereby he might feel how great is God."[2] The fact is that Irenaeus was so completely the victim of his own rhetoric that it is difficult to discover from his writings where metaphor is supposed to end, and sober fact to begin; while the language in which he expresses his real and deep appreciation of the moral and spiritual effects of Christ's work is always more or less coloured by vague and crude metaphysical theories which prevent a modern mind from adopting it without considerable translation into more intelligible equivalents.

As regards the subjective conditions of salvation the teaching of Irenaeus does not differ materially from that of his predecessors. There is the same adoption of traditional language about justification by faith, side by side with explanations which recall St. James rather than St. Paul. Sometimes it is justice (or goodness) and faith together which secure salvation; in other places justice or righteousness alone is spoken of as having power to bring about the resurrection of body and soul;

[1] " Non enim aliter nos discere poteramus quae sunt Dei, nisi magister noster, verbum existens, homo factus fuisset " (*Haer.* v. i. 1).

[2] " Haec ergo fuit magnanimitas Dei, ut per omnia pertransiens homo, et morum agnitionem percipiens, dehinc veniens ad resurrectionem quae est a mortuis, et experimento discens unde liberatus est, semper gratus exsistat Domino, munus incorruptelae consecutus ab eo, ut plus diligeret eum, cui enim plus dimittitur plus diligit, cognoscat autem semetipsum, quoniam mortalis et infirmus est; intelligat autem et Deum . . . intelligat autem et reliquas virtutes Dei omnes in semetipsum ostensas, per quas edoctus sentiat de Deo, quantus est Deus " (*Haer.* III. xxi. 2).

elsewhere love and faith.[1] Sometimes salvation and
eternal life are said to be given to "those who love God,
and believe His promises, and have been made little
children in malice";[2] or still more simply and nobly
we are told that "to follow the Saviour is to share His
salvation, and to follow the light is to receive
it."[3] Against the Gnostics Irenaeus insisted much
upon the necessity of orthodox belief; indeed, no one
early writer did so much to lay down the main lines
in the development of the theology which should
hereafter be considered orthodox; but on the whole he
still belongs to that earlier and happier period in which
orthodox belief was chiefly valued for its effects upon
life and conduct, and not as an arbitrarily imposed
"condition of salvation." The wider hopes of Clement
for the non-Christian world and for the future of souls
not fit for immediate heaven are absent; otherwise, in
His dealings with those who do profess the Christian
faith, the God of Irenaeus is still a God of righteousness
and love.

This ransom theory of Irenaeus became, and for
nearly a thousand years continued, the dominant orthodox traditional theory on the subject. The details of
the transaction with the Devil vary considerably in
different writers. In particular two new elements were
brought into prominence, which are hardly to be discovered in Irenaeus. In the first place the dominion
of the Devil over man, which Irenaeus (if not quite
consistently) treats as unjust, is now explicitly treated
as a just dominion: by sin Satan had become man's
lawful lord: deliverance without the payment of a
ransom would have been not merely unbecoming to

---

[1] " Si enim natura et substantia salvat [referring to the Gnostic belief that superior
natures were necessarily saved, irrespectively of their moral performance], omnes
salvabuntur animae; si autem justitia et fides, quare non salvet ea quae similiter cum
animabus in corruptelam [*l.* incorruptelam] cedere incipiunt corpora ? " (*Haer.* II.
xliv. 1). In the next section we read " Si quidem potens est justitia illuc transducere ea
quae participaverunt ei," etc.

[2] " Qui sunt autem qui hic salvantur, et accipiunt vitam aeternam ?   Nonne hi qui
diligunt Deum, et qui pollicitationibus ejus credunt, et malicia parvuli effecti sunt "
(*Haer.* IV. xliv. 3).

[3] " Sequi enim Salvatorem participare est salutem, et sequi lumen, percipere est
lumen " (*Haer.* IV. xxv. 1).

God, but a positive injustice, and therefore to a just God an impossibility. Secondly, a further explanation was attempted of the way in which the Devil was induced to accept this ransom or equivalent. This was effected, it now appears, by a trick on the part of God Himself : the Devil was outwitted by the use of his own tools. He was induced to bring about the death of Christ, thinking that thereby he would be enabled to add Him to the number of his lawful subjects. But there he had overreached himself. He thought he was dealing with a mortal man : he found that his captive was the Prince of life who not only could not be really killed but became the source of life to his emancipated subjects. The final touch was added to the grotesque theory by Rufinus and others when they represent Christ's humanity as the bait which the Devil was induced to swallow, and so was caught on the hook of His divinity.[1]

Tertullian

The introduction of the second of these new elements —the theory of the divine trick—was partly due to a too literal interpretation of certain unfortunate expressions of Origen : the germ of the first—the juridical justification of the transaction—is first suggested by Tertullian. But it is only by later writers that these traits are fully developed into the definite juridical theory described above. It is hardly possible to exaggerate the importance of the effects exercised upon the development of theology by the circumstance that the Greek Fathers had been trained in the schools of Greek philosophy, while the education of the Latins had been for the most part an education in Roman law,[2] and, as I should be

---

[1] Harnack attributes this embellishment to Gregory the Great, but it is found in Gregory of Nyssa (below, p. 305), Rufinus, and many other earlier writers. Rufinus says : " Sacramentum illud susceptae carnis, quod supra exposuimus, hanc habet causam, ut divina filii Dei virtus, velut hamus quidam habitu humanae carnis obtectus . . . principem mundi invitare possit ad agonem ; cui ipse carnem suam velut escam tradens, hamo eum Divinitas intrinsecus teneret insertum ex profusione immaculati sanguinis" (*In Symb. Apostol.* 16). It is also found in the *Life of Anthony* attributed to Athanasius where Christ catches the devil like a dragon on a hook, but here the Chalcedonian refinement about the two natures is absent. The idea of a trick may have been suggested by 1 Cor. ii. 8.

[2] Cf. Maine, *Ancient Law*, chap. ix. (4th ed. p. 340 *sq.*).

inclined to add, Roman rhetoric. When we compare the spirit of Irenaeus with that of Tertullian, this difference becomes very apparent. His theology is for the most part based upon Irenaeus, but it is the theology of Irenaeus latinized—that is to say coarsened and legalized.[1]

In Irenaeus the ransom theory was a piece of crude and rather puerile metaphysic. In Tertullian not merely the scheme of the atonement but all the relations between God and man put on the character of legal transactions. His pages bristle with phrases like " debt," " satisfaction," " guilt," " merit," " compensation." The idea of original sin is the root-idea of his theology : the actual term is, indeed, his invention, though it is not pushed to the length of denying free-will in man after the fall.[2] Original sin means to him both an inheritance of guilt or responsibility for the sin of Adam and also an actual corruption of nature.[3] And the prominence of this conception tends by itself to an emphasis upon the death of Christ, as distinct from the incarnation in general, which was not usual in the earlier Greek theology. Tertullian is perhaps the first Christian writer to

---

[1] I have used the edition of Oehler (Leipsic, 1853).

[2] " Vitium originis," " primordiale delictum." Loofs traces this notion and also his insistence on the need of divine grace to Stoic influence (*Dogmengeschichte*, pp. 69, 163-164), and quotes Seneca's words about a " communis insania " which prevents our following nature. Without denying this influence, I cannot but feel that there is enough in St. Paul to suggest these ideas, however little he can be made responsible for the form which they assume in Tertullian.

[3] " Sed et si benedictio patrum semini quoque eorum destinabatur sine ullo adhuc merito eius, cur non et reatus patrum in filios quoque redundaret ? " (*Adv. Marcion.* ii. 15, t. ii. p. 102). Here the notion is distinctly an inheritance of *guilt*. Elsewhere the inheritance of guilt is hardly distinguished from a corruption of nature, inclining to evil : " Satanan denique in omni vexatione et aspernatione et detestatione pronuntias, quem nos dicimus malitiae angelum, totius erroris artificem, totius saeculi interpolatorem, per quem homo a primordio circumventus, ut praeceptum Dei excederet, et propterea in mortem datus exinde totum genus de suo semine infectum, suae etiam damnationis traducem fecit " (*De testimonio animae*, 3, t. i. p. 405). So in *Adv. Marcion.* v. 17, t. ii. p. 325 : " Apparet communi naturae omnium hominum et delicta et concupiscentias carnis et incredulitatem et iracundiam reputari, diabolo tamen captante naturam, quam et ipse iam infecit delicti semine illato." Cf. *De pudicitia* 6 (t. i. p. 802), *De anima*, 41 (t. ii. p. 622), where he declares that the " malum animae . . . ex originis vitio antecedit," but adds that this corruption of nature is not complete : " Quod enim a Deo est, non tam extinguitur quam obumbratur." Man would not have suffered physical death but for the fall (t. ii. p. 638). The freedom of the will is often asserted, but no attempt is made to deal with its relation to original sin. The fullest treatment of the subject is in *Adv. Marcion.* ii., where he declares that " ita in utrumque exitum libertas patuit arbitrii " (6, t. ii. p. 92). The image of God is made to consist chiefly in this freedom. His assertion that grace can " subject " this freedom (*De anima*, 21, t. ii. p. 590) involves him in great difficulties. Cf. *De exhort. castitatis*, 2, t. i. p. 738.

represent the death of Christ as the chief purpose of
His coming, and he distinctly declares that there would
have been no incarnation but for the fall.[1] He retains
Irenaeus' theory of a direct salvation by the incarnation
apart from the death of Christ, and exhibits the old
tendency to explain its operation by the influence of
His example and teaching.[2] But, side by side with this
more primitive theology, we have theories which seem
to make salvation depend entirely upon the death. Most
of these had already appeared in Irenaeus, but in Tertullian
they all tend to assume a different and a lower form.
Sometimes the death seems to have no other purpose
than the fulfilment of prophecy;[3] at other times the
parallelisms between the fall and the atonement are
insisted upon as constituting a sort of metaphysical
necessity. The fall had been due to man : one who was
like man alone could pay the penalty.[4] It was as a
virgin that Eve sinned : therefore salvation must be
also through the fruit of a virgin.[5] Whatever exactly

[1] " Taceo quod figitur : in hoc enim venerat " (De Patientia, 3, t. i. p. 592). " Cum
Christus non alia ex causa descenderit quam peccatorum liberandorum " (De idolat. 5,
t. i. p. 72).

[2] " In filio . . . miscente in semetipso hominem et Deum, in virtutibus deum, in
pusillitatibus hominem, ut tantum homini conferat, quantum Deo detrahit. Totum
denique Dei mei penes vos dedecus sacramentum est humanae salutis. Conversabatur
Deus, ut homo divina agere doceretur " (Adv. Marcion. ii. 27, t. ii. p. 118).

[3] " Igitur non in hanc passionem Christum maledixit, sed distinctionem fecit, ut qui
in aliquo delicto iudicium mortis habuisset et moreretur suspensus in ligno, hic male-
dictus a Deo esset qui propter merita delictorum suorum suspenderetur in ligno. Alio-
quin Christus qui . . . non pro meritis suis in id genus mortis expositus est, sed ut ea
quae praedicta sunt a prophetis, per [should we read propter ?] vos ei obventura imple-
rentur, sicut in psalmis ipse spiritus Christi iam canebat dicens : Retribuebant mihi mala
pro bonis, et, Quae non rapueram, tunc exsolvebam " (Tertullian, Adv. Judaeos, 10,
t. ii. p. 727). The " non pro meritis suis " may be thought to imply that it was on
account of the " merits " of others, but the writer, as usual when the substitutionary idea
appears, does not go much beyond the actual words of Scripture. Elsewhere he does
not refuse to regard Christ as cursed by God : " qui et maledictum in se creatoris admisit
ligno suspensus " (Adv. Marcion. i. 11, t. ii. p. 60, cf. v. 3, t. ii. p. 281).

[4] " Ob hoc igitur missum filium in similitudinem carnis peccati, ut peccati carnem simili
substantia redimeret, id est, carnea, quae peccatrici carni similis esset cum peccatrix
ipsa non esset. Nam et haec erit Dei virtus, in substantia pari perficere salutem " (l.c. v.
14, t. ii. p. 315). It will be observed that Tertullian shrinks from quite adopting Irenaeus'
conception of the actual identity between the human nature which the Word assumed
with the human nature which sinned. The notion at the bottom of such theories is
really something very like the belief in " sympathetic magic."

[5] " In virginem enim adhuc Evam irrepserat verbum aedificatorium mortis. In
virginem aeque introducendum erat dei verbum extructorium vitae : ut quod per eius-
modi sexum abierat in perditionem, per eundem sexum redigeretur in salutem. Credi-
derat Eva serpenti : credidit Maria Gabrieli. Quod illa credendo deliquit, haec credendo
delevit " (Tertullian, De carne Christi, 17, t. ii. p. 454). Cf. above, p. 237.

the theory of " recapitulation " meant to Irenaeus, to
Tertullian it meant definitely the restoration of all things
to the state in which they actually were before the fall [1]
rather than the fulfilment of God's ideal for his creation.
The death of Christ is now practically treated as a punishment borne by the innocent for the guilty,[2] though the
word punishment is never used, and Tertullian abstains
from using the word "satisfaction " in connexion with the
death of Christ, fond as he is of applying it to the expiatory
sufferings of sinful man ; and even in him the idea of
substitution is usually expressed in language borrowed
from the Old Testament or from St. Paul.   Finally, the
ransom theory occasionally reveals itself in a coarser
and more definitely juridical form than in Irenaeus,
though it is only by putting together a number of separate
passages that Tertullian's meaning can be discovered.
He speaks of the Devil as having a natural—which we
may presume to mean a just—dominion over his own
subjects, *i.e.* sinners, though he has none over God's
own household.[3]   He speaks of sinners as redeemed "from
the angels that hold the power of this world." [4]   He
declares that it was reasonable that God should take
back His image and similitude which had been captured
by the Devil by an operation which was the converse
of the Devil's fraud, *i.e.* (practically) by a rival fraud.[5]

---

[1] " Cui ergo competent secundum boni existimationem, quam proposuerit in sacramento voluntatis suae, in dispensationem adimpletionis temporum (ut ixa dixerim, sicut
verbum illud in Graeco sonat) recapitulare (id est, ad initium redigere vel ab initio recen-
sere) omnia in Christum quae in coelis et quae in terris, nisi cuius erunt omnia erunt ab
initio, etiam ipsum initium, a quo et tempora et temporum adimpletionis dispensatio, ob
quam omnia ad initium recensentur in Christo ? " (Tertullian, *Adv. Marcion.* v. 17,
t. ii. p. 323). Cf. 19, p. 333 : " ipsum, in quo omnia recensentur, in Christum ad
initium revocata etiam indifferentia escarum."

[2] " Quatenus ita voluit, ut livore eius sanaremur, ut dedecore eius salus nostra
constaret. Et merito se pro suo homine deposuit, pro imagine et similitudine sua,
non aliena " (*Adv. Marcion.* iv. 21, t. ii. p. 214).

[3] " Habere videtur diabolus propriam iam potestatem, si forte, in eos qui ad Deum
non pertinent, semel in stillam situlae et in pulverem areae et in salivem nationibus depu-
tatis a Deo, ac per hoc diabolo expositis in vacuam quodammodo possessionem.   Ceterum
in domesticos Dei nihil illi licet ex propria potestate " (*De fuga in persec.* 2, t. i. p. 466).

[4] " Et dominus quidem illum redemit ab angelis munditenentibus potestatibus, a
spiritualibus nequitiae, a tenebris huius aevi, a iudicio aeterno, a morte perpetua " (*De
fuga in persec.* 12, t. ii. p. 484).

[5] " Sed et hic ratio defendit, quod Deus imaginem et similitudinem suam a diabolo
captam aemula operatione recuperavit " (*De carne Christi,* 17, t. ii. p. 454).   The meaning of " aemula operatione " (as is clear from the context) is that as the Devil seduced
man by putting into the virgin Eve the tempting word, so God redeemed man by intro-

Putting all these statements together, we are, I think, justified in saying that Tertullian means to explain and justify the redemption of man as a kind of set-off for the unjust death of the innocent brought about by the Devil, but the theory is not clearly explained till a later date.[1]

Whatever doubts there may be about Tertullian's theory as to the reasons for Christ's death, there can be none as to his conception of the way in which the atonement is appropriated. Faith and baptism are the conditions of forgiveness for pre-baptismal sin.[2] And faith with him means quite definitely belief in all the articles of the orthodox Creed. For subsequent sin—sins of a definitely mortal character, such as fornication or relapse into Paganism—he is at times prepared to allow the possibility of one subsequent forgiveness [3] after public confession, penance, and absolution; but afterwards in his Montanist days he will not hear of the restoration of such persons to Church Communion after even one fall, and roundly denounces the Church and the Bishop of Rome, no less than the Roman prophet Hermas, as guilty of condoning lust and vice by admitting of such a restoration.[4] Sometimes he does not positively exclude the possibility of divine, as distinct from ecclesiastical, forgiveness; but elsewhere he seems to insist upon a literal acceptance of the terrible doctrine of the Epistle to the Hebrews about their future except in the one case

---

ducing the redeeming Word into the womb of the virgin Mary. The words may be translated " by a converse operation." There is a hint of the idea of pious fraud, but it would be perhaps too much to translate " by an act of rival fraud."

[1] *E.g.* by Ambrosiaster ; see below, p. 329.

[2] " Proinde cum ad fidem pervenit reformata per secundam nativitatem ex aqua et superna virtute, detracto corruptionis pristinae aulaeo totam lucem suam conspicit. Excipitur etiam a Spiritu Sancto, sicut in pristina nativitate a spiritu profano " (*De anima,* 41, t. ii. p. 623). Martyrdom was equivalent to Baptism : " Dimicationem martyrii, et lavacrum sanguinis exinde securum " (*Scorpiace,* 6, t. i. p. 512). He is here dealing with the case of post-baptismal sinners, but his doctrine would no doubt extend (as with the early Church generally) to the unbaptized.

[3] " Collocavit in vestibulo poenitentiam secundam, quae pulsantibus patefaciat ; sed iam semel, quia iam secundo ; sed amplius nunquam, quia proxime frustra " (*De paen.* 7, t. i. p. 657). He goes on to urge repentance even on those who had sinned a second time, though apparently without hope of restoration to Church Communion.

[4] *De pudicitia,* 10, 21, t. i. pp. 813, 841-4 : he describes the *Pastor* of Hermas as a " scriptura quae sola moechos amat," in spite of the fact that it allows only one repentance for post-baptismal sin.

of martyrdom.¹ And there can be no doubt about the nature of the penalty for those who do not obtain forgiveness—everlasting torment both of the body and the soul (which with him is simply a subtler kind of body) in a hell of material fire which he places in the interior of the earth.² Tertullian was the first of the Fathers to enrich Christian theology with the notion that the spectacle of his persecutors in torment would heighten the joys of the persecuted believer's heaven.³

It is not only by his definite doctrine that Tertullian represents a serious lowering of level in Christian theology. His writings are, indeed, full of noble Christian eloquence, if his eloquence is a little too much that of counsel for the crown in the old state-trials. There is a fine glow of zeal for a puritanically interpreted Christian ideal, a *saeva indignatio* against the pagan vices of the outside world, a high scorn for the sophistical compromises by which timid Christians excused their lapses from Christian principle when suffering or martyrdom might be the result. But his whole conception of religion—of God, of duty, and of salvation—is poisoned by the substitution of legal for moral conceptions. Morality is for him, as for no previous Christian writer, a doing of the will of God not because what God commands is good, but because an autocratic Deity commands it—a conception quite inconsistent with his clumsy attempt to vindicate the intrinsic justice of the atonement. God is represented as an arbitrary legislator who had interdicted most of the things which make life pleasant and attractive,⁴ promising reward for obedience, and threaten-

---

¹ *De pudicitia*, 10, 20, t. i. p. 814 *sq.*, 839.

² *De anima*, 7, t. ii. p. 566, *et passim*; *Apologeticum*, 47, t. i. p. 290. There are some few traces of a Purgatory; the surviving may pray and "offer" for the "refrigerium" of deceased Christians awaiting the judgement (e.g. *De monogamia*, 10, t. i. p. 776), but in *De testimonio animae*, 4 (t. i. p. 405), the "cruciatus" and the "refrigerium" are treated as alternatives, and each is everlasting. On the other hand, in *De anima*, 58 (t. ii. p. 650), the words "till thou hast paid the uttermost farthing" are held to imply a "modicum quoque delictum mora resurrectionis illic (*sc.* in inferis) luendum."

³ *De spectaculis*, 30, t. i. p. 62. Mr. Emmet (Art. on "The Bible and Hell," in *Immortality*, pp. 178, 204) points out that the thought is found in the earlier Apocalyptic literature (Enoch xxvii. 3, lxii. 12; Assumpt. Mos. x. 10.)

⁴ Not, however, marriage. He strongly asserts the lawfulness, almost the duty, of *one* marriage.

ing direst punishment for transgression. He has, indeed, in His love for mankind (how such a being should be capable of love is not explained) contrived an arbitrary scheme of salvation by which a small, capriciously selected section of the human race may escape the inherited sentence upon Adam's misdeeds and the sins which, whether through inherited corruption or through their own free will, have been committed up to the moment of their availing themselves of that remedy. But even for pre-baptismal sin some measure of " satisfaction " is due, and after that a strict debtor and creditor account is kept of their misdeeds; and the life of the faithful Christian after baptism becomes little more than an anxious effort to escape the eternal flames which are the certain penalty of any serious transgression, and to " compensate " by constant fasting and austerity for the minor lapses which not even the utmost zeal and watchfulness can escape. It is chiefly by self-inflicted suffering that God can be " placated." With Tertullian begins the degradation of repentance into " penance,"[1] and the sharp distinction between mortal and venial sins.[2] God is represented almost entirely as a criminal judge — a criminal judge whose decisions were not unlike those of the persecuting magistrates with whom Christians of that age were too well acquainted. Fear becomes the prevailing religious motive: the attitude of a Christian is too much that of a trembling criminal at the bar of God: and, if ever his attitude rises into one of greater joy and confidence, it is only when he contemplates the day when he will reap the full reward of all his sufferings and take part in judging the evil angels and the human persecutors who have so long afflicted him. With Tertullian begins the legalism, the morose asceticism, the narrow other-worldliness, the furious zeal for orthodoxy, which Christian theology, and especially Western theology, never completely shook

---

[1] " Hoc enim pretio dominus veniam addicere instituit, hac paenitentiae compensatione redimendam proponit impunitatem " (De paen. 6, t. i. 653).

[2] De pudicitia, 2, 3 (t. i. p. 796 sq.), 12 (p. 815 sq.), 16 (p. 826 sq.). In the first of these chapters there is a definite attempt to distinguish between venial and mortal sins : a list of seven sins which " veniam non capiant " is given in 19, t. i. p. 838.

off, though the worse extravagances of his anti-social Montanism were rejected by the good sense and the more really Christian temper of the Catholic Church.[1] And yet after all it must not be supposed that Tertullian was a stranger to the love of God or of man. There is another and a tenderer side to Tertullian's character and teaching. His vindication of the Christians' doctrine and their mode of life—not only of its innocence but of its essential reasonableness and its beauty—is among the noblest that have come down to us. Though Christianity had come to mean something very different from anything taught by Jesus, it could never quite shake off the influence of His character even in a Tertullian.[2]

Origen

To turn from the pages of Tertullian to those of the next great Christian theologian—Origen—is like emerging from a dimly-lighted Roman catacomb into the brilliant sunshine of a southern noon. Once more we find ourselves in the atmosphere of the best Greek thought—the same atmosphere that was breathed by his predecessor, Clement of Alexandria. At first sight, indeed, the disciple may seem less congenial to the modern reader than his master. It appears to be uncertain whether he was by extraction a Greek of Alexandria or a Hellenized Copt. Clement was chiefly engaged in explaining and vindicating Christian Theism

[1] In justification of my estimate of Tertullian I can do little but refer to his works *passim*, but here are a few characteristic remarks : " Bonum factum Deum habet debitorem, sicuti et malum : quia judex omnis remunerator est causae " (*De paen.* 2, t. i. p. 646). " Audaciam existimo de bono divini praecepti disputare. Neque enim quia bonum est, idcirco auscultare debemus, sed quia Deus praecepit " (*lib. cit.* 4, p. 650). "Quam porro ineptum, quam poenitentiam non adimplere, ei veniam delictorum sustinere. . . . Hoc enim pretio dominus veniam addicere instituit ; hac paenitentiae compensatione redimendam proponit impunitatem " (*lib. cit.* 6, p. 653). " Delictum domino nostro confitemur, non quidem ut ignaro, sed quatenus satisfactio confessione disponitur, confessione paenitentia nascitur, paenitentia Deus mitigatur " (*lib. cit.* 9, p. 660). " Quis iam dubitabit omnium erga victum macerationum hanc fuisse rationem, qua rursus interdicto cibo et observato praecepto primordiale iam delictum expiaretur, ut homo per eandem materiam causae satis deo faciat, per quam offenderat, id est, per cibi interdictionem, atque ita salutem aemulo modo redaccenderet inedia, quam exstinxerat sagina, pro unico inlicito plura licita contemnens " (*De jejunio*, 3, t. i. p. 856). " In quantum non peperceris tibi, in tantum tibi deus, crede, parcet " (*De paen.* 9, t. i. p. 661).
[2] For a fine vindication of Tertullian see Glover, *Conflict of Religions in the Early Roman Empire*, chap. x., but I think it is overdone.

and Christian Neo-Platonism, in comparing and contrasting the Christian idea of God and His relation to the universe with various pagan systems. As regards the details of Christology he dealt for the most part in vague generalities : and he was by no means a consistent thinker. By the time of Origen it was less easy for a Christian philosopher to adopt such an attitude. The completer formation of a New Testament canon, the extreme theory of inspiration which had now been extended from the Old Testament to the New, the increasing acuteness of ecclesiastical controversy, and the increasing insistence upon ecclesiastical orthodoxy made it impossible for Origen to be content with Clement's vague theology. Clement was mainly a Christian philosopher : Origen was the founder of scientific "Dogmatic." But, just because of this difference in his position, he was forced to come to much closer quarters with the real difficulties—both the difficulties which are presented to every thorough-going attempt to "vindicate the ways of God to man" and the special difficulties of the Christian tradition which he had accepted—than had ever been done by Clement. In the attempt to reconcile a philosophical view of the universe with a very strong theory of inspiration he was driven to adopt that allegorizing method of interpretation which had already been applied by pagan moralists to explain away the ethical crudities of Homer and the poets ; and this makes much of his writing, especially his commentaries or homilies upon books of scripture, rather weary reading. His determination to evade no difficulties often drove him into theories which do not commend themselves to the modern mind ; but his resolute attempt to carry out the line of thought which his presuppositions involved make him a far greater, as well as a far bolder, thinker than the amiable, cultivated, but vague and vacillating Clement. Origen is by far the greatest mind among the Christian Fathers : indeed, no one else approached him.[1]

---

[1] I have used the text of Lommatzsch (Berlin, 1831–48), except for the *Commentary on St. John*, for which I have used the edition of Prof. Brooke (Cambridge, 1896).

In Origen the questions about the nature of the Word
and His relation to the Father which are left undetermined in the fourth Gospel and in Clement are definitely
cleared up. The Logos is to him decidedly a distinct
Mind from the Father's : equally clearly is He inferior
to the Father, " generated," or (as he does not hesitate
to say) " created," by an act of the Father's will, but the
creation is an eternal creation. So far his position
halts between the mode of thought which afterwards
became Arianism and that which was afterwards identified
with the name of Athanasius. So far we may with
equal truth say that he halts between Ditheism and true
Monotheism—a position impossible to a modern philosopher, however common in popular religious thought.
But nothing can be more intelligible or more ethical
than his doctrine of the incarnation. Like Clement,
but even more explicitly, he recognizes that Jesus was
not the only man with whose soul the Word was united.
Jewish prophets and Greek sages alike had been inspired
by Him, but the incarnation in Jesus was more complete
and perfect. His attitude towards pagan philosophy is
very much that of Clement, if he has perhaps a stronger
sense of its deficiencies. Philosophy was a propaedeutic
to Christianity as grammar is to philosophy.

Here are a few illustrations of Origen's Christology :
"We say that the Logos was united and made
one with the soul of Jesus in a far higher degree than
any other soul, seeing that He alone was able completely to receive the highest participation in the true
Word and the true Wisdom and the true Righteousness."[1]

" They see that from Him the divine and the human
nature began to be united (lit. woven together) so that
human nature might become divine by participation
in the more divine, not in Jesus alone but also in all
those who not only believe but also take up the life
which Jesus taught."[2]

---

[1] Ὅντινα τῇ Ἰησοῦ μάλιστα παρὰ πᾶσαν ψυχὴν ψυχῇ ὠκειῶσθαι καὶ ἡνῶσθαί
φαμεν, μόνῳ τελείως χωρῆσαι δεδυνημένου τὴν ἄκραν μετοχὴν τοῦ αὐτολόγου καὶ
τῆς αὐτοσοφίας καὶ τῆς αὐτοδικαιοσύνης (Contra Celsum, v. 39, Lom. xix. 241). The
ὅντινα refers to the δεύτερος Θεός, i.e. the Word.
[2] Ὁρῶσιν ὅτι ἀπ' ἐκείνου ἤρξατο θεία καὶ ἀνθρωπίνη συνυφαίνεσθαι φύσις, ἵν'

S

One supreme difference there is between the union of the Logos with Christ and His union with men. In those who have most nearly approximated to the goodness and the wisdom of Christ the best that is in them is due to Him. "On account of Him there have come to be many Christs in the world, even all who, like Him, loved righteousness and hated iniquity."[1] As might be expected with a writer who takes so philosophical a view of the incarnation, we find a doctrine of salvation which is for the most part rational, intelligible, in the highest degree ethical. There is much more stress upon the teaching and the example of Christ, and upon His revelation of the Father, than upon His death. It was chiefly by teaching and example that the incarnate Word saves from sin. The conventional phrases about the death of Christ are repeated. As a commentator upon St. Paul he, of course, repeats all the Pauline phraseology. But whenever the traditional language is explained, it is explained in the pre-Irenaean manner. The death of Christ completes the revelation begun by the life and the teaching. It fulfils the prophecies : it constitutes the supreme proof of perfect obedience, the supreme revelation of the love both of the Word and of the Father whom He reveals : it is the supreme example of self-sacrifice and humility. If he does sometimes ascribe to the death of Christ all the spiritual effects which follow from the incarnation taken as a whole, it is because the part is taken as the symbol of the whole ; and it is by a moral influence upon the believer that the work of Christ is held to justify and save. "In this way Christ also slew the enmity in his own flesh, since by undergoing death he gave an example to men of resistance to sin, and thus at length . . . reconciled men to God by his own blood."[2]

ἡ ἀνθρωπίνη τῇ πρὸς τὸ θειότερον κοινωνίᾳ γένηται θεία οὐκ ἐν μόνῳ τῷ Ἰησοῦ, ἀλλὰ καὶ πᾶσι τοῖς μετὰ τοῦ πιστεύειν ἀναλαμβάνουσι βίον, ὃν Ἰησοῦς ἐδίδαξεν (Contra Celsum, iii. 28, Lom. xviii. 287).

[1] Δι' αὐτὸν πολλοὶ Χριστοὶ γεγόνασιν ἐν τῷ κόσμῳ, οἵτινες ἀνάλογον ἐκείνῳ ἠγάπησαν δικαιοσύνην καὶ ἐμίσησαν ἀδικίαν (Contra Celsum, vi. 79, Lom. xix. 433).

[2] Hoc ergo modo Christus occidit inimicitiam in carne sua, cum morte suscepta exemplum dedit hominibus usque ad mortem resistere adversum peccatum, et ita demum resoluta inimicitia in carne sua, reconciliavit per sanguinem suum homines Deo (In Rom. iv. 12, Lom. vi. 313).

To these generalizations there is one apparent exception. In the development of Irenaeus' monstrous ransom theory a prominent place is generally attributed to the great thinker Origen. And it is probable that certain passages in his influential writings did much to stamp this theory upon the theology of both East and West. In particular he laid emphasis upon the idea of the divine stratagem by which Satan was outwitted. But considerable injustice has been done to Origen by the historians of doctrine [1] who identify his theory with the crude ideas of Irenaeus, Tertullian, and their followers. I will quote the most famous of these passages, and I think you will see that, fairly interpreted, it does not imply the theory which we have just considered :

"But to whom did He give His soul as a ransom for many ? Surely not to God. Could it be then to the evil one ? For he had us in his power, until the ransom for us should be given to him, even the life [or soul] of Jesus, since he (the evil one) had been deceived, and led to suppose that he was capable of mastering that soul, and he did not see that to hold Him involved a trial of strength (βάσανον) greater than he was equal to. Therefore also death, though he thought he had prevailed against Him, no longer lords it over Him, He (Christ) having become free among the dead, and stronger than the power of death, and so much stronger than death, that all who will amongst those who are mastered by death may also follow Him [i.e. out of Hades, out of death's domain], death no longer prevailing against them. For every one who is with Jesus is unassailable by death." [2]

---

[1] Especially Harnack. M. Rivière has the justice to recognize that " nulle part il n'exprime le principe juridique posé par saint Irénée (*Le Dogme de la Réd.* p. 381), but he still seems to make insufficient allowance for the rhetorical and metaphorical character of Origen's language. It is curious that Dr. Bigg, in the admirable lectures devoted to Origen in his *Christian Platonists of Alexandria*, only touches upon the ransom theory quite incidentally in a note.

[2] Τίνι δὲ ἔδωκε τὴν ψυχὴν αὐτοῦ λύτρον ἀντὶ πολλῶν; οὐ γὰρ δὴ τῷ Θεῷ· μή τι οὖν τῷ πονηρῷ; οὗτος γὰρ ἐκράτει ἡμῶν, ἕως δοθῇ τὸ ὑπὲρ ἡμῶν αὐτῷ λύτρον, ἡ τοῦ Ἰησοῦ ψυχή, ἀπατηθέντι, ὡς δυναμένῳ αὐτῆς κυριεῦσαι, καὶ οὐχ ὁρῶντι, ὅτι οὐ φέρει τὴν ἐπὶ τῷ κατέχειν αὐτὴν βάσανον. διὸ καὶ θάνατος αὐτοῦ δόξας κεκυριευ-κέναι, οὐκέτι κυριεύει, γενομένου ἐν νεκροῖς ἐλευθέρου, καὶ ἰσχυροτέρου τῆς τοῦ θανάτου ἐξουσίας, καὶ ἐπὶ τοσοῦτον ἰσχυροτέρου, ὥστε καὶ πάντας τοὺς βουλομένους αὐτῷ ἀκολουθεῖν τῶν κρατουμένων ὑπὸ τοῦ θανάτου ἀκολουθεῖν, οὐδὲν ἰσχύοντος κατ'

Now it will be observed that nothing whatever is said here about this ransom to Satan *justifying* the forgiveness of sins or the cancelling of the death-penalty. The theory is put forward not as an ethical defence of God's scheme of redemption, but as a mere statement of fact. The ransom—a phrase which, as it was found in the Gospels, had to be accepted and explained—represents simply the price by paying which our Lord actually effected the salvation of mankind. Man's deliverance cost Jesus that death upon the Cross. Death and many other physical evils were, according to Origen, not only in this case but in all cases, brought about by the Devil or other evil spirits. An intense belief in the activity of good or evil spirits was characteristic of Origen as of all his contemporaries, Christian or pagan alike, who had any religion at all. There is nothing metaphorical about his allusions to spirits, but what he says about the ransom is obviously metaphorical. And the metaphor is not taken from the court of justice or the civil contract in which a slave is manumitted for a just price, but from the battle-field.[1] The ransom is a ransom paid to a conqueror who has physically carried off a prisoner. Elsewhere Origen definitely calls the Devil an "unjust tyrant," and compares the work of Christ to the act of the lawful monarch's son who voluntarily disguises himself as an ordinary subject that he may the better persuade, not the Devil but the captives, to return to the dominion of their Father, their lawful Lord, as they might at any time do by an act of their own free will.[2] Moreover, you will notice that the

---

αὐτῶν ἔτι τοῦ θανάτου· πᾶς γὰρ ὁ μετὰ τοῦ Ἰησοῦ ἀνεπίληπτός ἐστι τῷ θανάτῳ (*In Matt.* xvi. 8, Lom. iv. 27). My interpretation of this passage is strongly supported by the whole of Tom. xiii. (especially cc. 8, 9), where the agency of the evil spirits in bringing about Christ's death and the φιλανθρωπία of God in allowing it are insisted upon without a word about any *just* claim of the Devil or other evil spirits against man, or any scheme for getting round these just claims.

[1] " Redemtio dicitur id quod datur hostibus pro his quos in captivitate detinent ut eos restituant pristinae libertati " (*In Rom.* iii. 7, Lom. vi. 203-4). For the whole passage see below. Cf. *Sel. in Psalmos*, 33, Lom. xii. 140.

[2] " Regem ponamus justum et nobilem, adversum injustum aliquem tyrannum ita bellum gerere volentem, ne violento videatur cruentoque vicisse conflictu, quia militantes sub tyranno sui erant, quos non perdere, sed liberare cupiebat. Consilio igitur meliore habitum sumit eorum, qui apud tyrannum erant, et specie per omnia fit similis iis, donec sub dominatione positus tyranni eos quidem, qui ei parebant, suaderet abscedere, et ad

Devil is in the passage I quoted closely associated with —almost identified with—the personified Death. To Origen the ransom is simply the price—the sufferings and death—which the Son of God had to pay to the Devil as the means of accomplishing the deliverance of man from sin and its penalty.[1] That the ransom was paid to the Devil merely means that the Devil did actually succeed in bringing about Christ's death. The whole idea is closely associated, as the context shows, with the belief that the disembodied Christ literally went down into the strong man's domain, preached to the spirits in prison, delivered them from Satan's thraldom, then rose Himself from the dead, and so assured a glorious immortality to all who would listen to His call. That in some mysterious way the bodily death of Christ (or sometimes simply His coming) prevailed over the powers of evil, Origen certainly held;[2] but not the theory of the quasi-legal transaction with the Devil, as it was represented by Irenaeus, Tertullian, and in even more grotesque forms by later theologians.

How exactly Christ's death or other self-sacrificing deaths were supposed to defeat the demons is not explained. Sometimes it is treated (as by other and less philosophical writers) as an ultimate fact : acts of self-

---

regnum legitimum repedare, ipsum vero fortem tempore opportuno alligaret, et potestates ejus ac principatus exueret, et avulsam captivitatem, quae ab eo tenebatur, abstraheret. Hoc ergo modo etiam Christus voluntate quidem exinanivit tunc semet ipsum, et formam servi accepit, passusque est dominatum tyranni, factus obediens usque ad mortem : per quam mortem dextruxit eum, qui habebat mortis imperium, id est, diabolum, ut liberaret eos, qui tenebantur a morte. Hic enim alligato forti, et in cruce sua triumphato, perrexit etiam in domum ejus, in domum mortis, in infernum, et inde vasa ejus diripuit, id est, animas, quas tenebat, abstraxit " (*In Rom.* v. 10, Lom. vi. 406). There is, indeed, one passage in which Origen, in expounding Rom. v. 17, remarks that the Apostle "ostendit, quia per delictum morti regnum datur, nec potest regnare in aliquo, nisi jus regni accipiat ex delicto " (*In Rom.* v. 3, Lom. vi. 358), but this only means that God would not have allowed the Devil to subjugate Adam, had he not deserved such a penalty. It does not imply that the Devil's dominion was a just claim as against God, or that God could not have justly freed him without an equivalent.

[1] Origen strongly emphasizes the distinction between the human soul of Jesus and the Logos—a distinction quite unknown to Ignatius and the Asia Minor School. He insists very strongly on the fact that the divine Word did not die : οὐκ ἀπέθανεν ὁ Θεὸς Λόγος. See the passage below, p. 286. According to Origen it was not the body or the spirit (πνεῦμα) of Christ, but the soul (ψυχή) which was given as a ransom (*In Matt.* xvi. 8, Lom. iv. 28). Bigg, in quoting this passage (*Christian Platonists*, 2nd ed., p. 255 *note*), adds : " The ψυχή would include the Blood, which is its οὐσία (*De Princ.* ii. 8. 2)."

[2] *In Joann.* xiii. 59, Brooke i. 320. Cf. *Sel. in Psalmos*, 17, Lom. xii. 61-2 : πρὸ τῆς ἐπιδημίας τοῦ σωτῆρος ἰσχυρότεροι ἡμῶν ἦσαν οἱ δαίμονες.

sacrifice—and particularly the supreme sacrifice of a unique personality—diffused a spiritual influence which directly acted upon the evil spirits. But he attempts to rationalize this belief. The angel-rulers of the nations were converted at the sight of Jesus, Origen suggests, and this may account for the spread of the Gospel in the regions over which they presided.[1]

There is then no attempt in Origen to explain the death of Christ as a concession to the rights of the Devil, which is the really offensive feature of the theory as expounded by Tertullian and other writers. But I am afraid it is impossible to deny that the notion of a trick on the part of God, by which the Devil was lured into compassing his own ruin, does find its origin in certain passages of Origen. It is explained, for instance, that the Devil caused Christ's death from the fear that the human race should be taken out of his hands by Christ's teaching, not knowing that His death would have greater efficacy than His teaching and His miracles.[2] But there is nothing in this idea which is really unethical or derogatory to the character of God, any more than there would be in the assertion that bad men are frequently allowed in the providence of God to compass their own ruin through under-estimating the strength of the forces opposed to them. We are very far here from the mythological representations of later and cruder writers with whom the incarnation becomes a device for concealing from the Devil the presence of a divine being beneath the outward form of humanity, as the bait is concealed by the fish-hook or the mouse-trap. Here, as in all Origen's accounts of a conflict between God and the Devil, when allowance is made for rhetorical expressions, there is nothing really grotesque or unethical, irreligious or unphilosophical, from the point of view of one to whom the universe was really the scene of a conflict between good and evil spirits, and the descent into hell a literal reality or at least a pictorial representation of an historical fact taking place in the spiritual world.

---

[1] *In Joann.* xiii. 59, Brooke i. 320.   [2] *In Matt. Comm. Series*, 75, Lom. iv. 390.

There are no doubt abundant passages in which Origen speaks of Christ's death in the conventional language as a sacrifice, or a propitiation for sin.[1] But such expressions are constantly ethicized and rationalized:[2] and where they are not so explained, they must be read in the light supplied by the explanations elsewhere given. It is a characteristic of Origen's mind and method that he never, in his attempts to construct a philosophical theology, abandons traditional modes of speech, but rather tries to raise them to a higher level by supplementing or re-interpreting them. He attributes, it is important to note, the same kind of efficacy, in an inferior degree, to the deaths of the martyrs and the good works or intercessions of other good men.[3] Sometimes he even compares the expiation effected by Christ to the acts of voluntary self-sacrifice by which ancient heroes had often been supposed to have put an end to famine or pestilence by weakening the power of the demons who caused such evils ; and goes on to contrast their limited efficacy with that sacrifice which alone could expiate the sins of the whole world, a world including for Origen the angels and perhaps the stars.[4]

---

[1] " Secundum hoc ergo, quod hostia est, propitiatio efficitur in eo, quod dat remissionem praecedentium delictorum : quae tamen propitiatio ad unumquemque credentium per viam fidei venit " (*In Rom.* iii. 8, Lom. vi. 213) ; cf. *In Lev. Hom.* i. 2, 3, Lom. ix. 177-78 ; *In lib.* I. *Sam. Hom.* ii., Lom. xi. 325 *sq.* ; *In Cant. Cantic.* iii. *ad fin.*, Lom. xv. 66.

[2] See below, pp. 285-6.

[3] " Puto sane quia sancti . . . imminuant exercitum daemonum " (*In Jesu Nave Hom.* xv. 6, Lom. xi. 141). " Videamus quomodo ipse cum filiis suis, Apostolis scilicet et martyribus, sumit peccata sanctorum " (*In Num. Hom.* x. 2, Lom. x. 96). He even goes on to suggest that the Devil has caused a remission of persecution, because he knew that the deaths of the martyrs would procure remission, and, in consequence of that cessation, " manent in nobis peccata nostra." The passage is an explanation of the statement that Aaron and his sons should take away the sins of the sanctuary (Num. xviii. 1). The absence of any reference here to Christian priests is remarkable. See *Lev. Hom.* ix. 3, Lom. ix. 345 for a still closer approximation to the idea of a treasury of merits. In Origen's *In Joan.* vi. 54, Brooke i. 174 the influence of martyrdom is rationalized, being attributed to the influence which it exercised upon the minds of the persecutors. In *Contra Celsum*, viii. 44, Lom. xx. 172 it is explained by the fear inspired in the evil spirits by their failure. Cf. *Exhort. ad Mart.* 30, Lom. xx. 275-6. At other times the influence of martyrs seems due simply to their intercession, *e.g. In Num.* xxiv. 1, Lom. x. 296, where the distinction between their work and Christ's consists in this that " ceteri precibus peccata, hic solus potestate dimisit." But only foolish people will think that they can deliver *any* soul by their prayers (*In Ezech. Hom.* iv. 8, Lom. xiv. 67). Cf. Bigg, *Christian Platonists*, 2nd ed. p. 255.

[4] *Contra Celsum*, i. 31, Lom. xviii. 64-5. It is clear here that it was by overcoming the power of Satan that he supposed the sacrifice to operate. See the passages

In one place (after an actual quotation from Isaiah liii.) he even speaks of the punishment that was due to our sins as falling upon Christ.[1] Wherever he uses language of this kind, it is always when quoting or paraphrasing the words of prophecy or of St. Paul—now of course looked upon as no less authoritative than the prophets. Doubtless he was full of belief in a mysterious efficacy radiating from the death of Christ and redounding to the spiritual benefit of men and even of angels, especially by weakening the power of the Devil and his angels.[2] At times he seems to admit the profoundly mysterious character of this influence—due, it would seem, primarily to the sinlessness of that unique soul : he was penetrated, it must be remembered, with the conviction that all Scripture was a vast treasury of mysterious meanings, into many of which he admitted himself unable to penetrate. But his passive acceptance of this great mystery on the authority of Scripture never led him into ways of thinking about the atonement which were unethical or derogatory to the character of God : for him the effect of Christ's death—whether mysterious or intelligible—is always to make men really better, not to satisfy either a divine demand or a supposed metaphysical necessity for retribution or retrospective cancelling of the past.[3]

---

below, pp. 284-6. As to the angels, see *In Joann.* i. 31, Brooke i. 40 ; for the redemption of the stars, i. 35, Brooke i. 48.

[1] *In Joann.* xxviii. 19, Brooke ii. 135. For the Greek, see below, p. 286.

[2] Cf. *In Joann.* vi. 54, Brooke i. 173 ; xxviii. 19, Brooke ii. 135 ; *Contra Celsum,* i. 31, Lom. xviii. 64 (quoted below, p. 285).

[3] The passage in which Origen most definitely adopts language which suggests the idea of vicarious sacrifice is, as might be expected, to be found in his comment upon the passage in Romans about God having set forth Christ " to be a propitiation through faith by his blood to shew forth his righteousness because of the passing over " of past sins. His exposition duly paraphrases the words. He sees in the word propitiation a reference to the mercy-seat ; and he explains that the mystical meaning of the mercy-seat is Christ, the victim by whose blood the forgiveness of past sins is effected. But after all the explanation which he gives has little reference to the death or the blood-shedding. The real antitype of the mercy-seat is the soul of Christ—that supremely excellent human soul to which the Word was united and which was the true mediator between God and man. He is called a Mediator, Origen declares, because " this sacred soul was indeed midway between the divinity of the Trinity and human fragility." (For the Latin, see below, p. 285.) Elsewhere—in a passage which more certainly reproduces Origen's thought, since here we possess the original Greek—he explains the term " propitiation " by saying that it was through the ministry of this soul of Jesus that the divine power of the Logos flows into the soul of believers, enabling them to exclaim, " I can do all

It would not be possible to state more clearly, or to repudiate more definitely, the objective or transactional explanation of the atonement than is done in the following passage : " Not without cause did he [St. Paul] say this : ' reckon (*existimate*) ye yourselves to be dead unto sin ' : which is better expressed in the Greek : ' reflect (*cogitate*) that ye are dead unto sin.' For the thing of which he speaks lies rather in thought and reason, since this sort of death must be understood to lie not in actual fact (*in effectu*) but in the region of thought. For he who reflects or reckons in his own mind that he is dead, does not sin : for example, if desire for a woman carries me away, or cupidity for silver or gold or land, and I put myself in mind that I am dead with Christ and think of that death, forthwith the desire is extinguished, and sin is put to flight." [1]   Or again, " Whence, because from this proof of so great goodness He is recognized to be good, for such a good one perhaps some one may even dare to die.   For when each one has recognized Christ's so great goodness towards him, and has had His love (*caritas*) spread abroad in his heart, he

---

things in Christ Jesus, which strengtheneth me." (Quoted below, p. 285.)   The fact seems to be that in deference to the authority of St. Paul, Origen dutifully accepts the fact that past sins were forgiven through Christ's blood ; but the real drift of his mind is towards the idea that the efficacy of Christ and His death is not retrospective but prospective—that the forgiveness is made possible by, nay, consists in, the actual moral change in the soul which is effected partly through the effect upon the believer of Christ's incarnation and partly through the direct action upon the soul of the Word Himself. He more often (like most Greek fathers) thinks of the Logos as actually Himself forgiving sin than of the Father as forgiving in consequence of anything which Christ has done : πάντων ἁμαρτημάτων ἄφεσιν παρέχει τοῖς προσφεύγουσι διὰ μετανοίας αὐτῷ (Fragm. *In Joann.* 9, Brooke ii. p. 220).   It should be remembered further that, according to Origen, the perfected Gnostic has no further need of Christ as the physician or as redemption, but only as " the Teacher of divine mysteries " (*C. Cels.* iii. 61-2, Lom. xviii. 337).

[1] " Non sine causa autem hoc dixit : ' existimate vos mortuos esse peccato ' : quod melius quidem in Graeco habetur : ' cogitate vos mortuos esse peccato.'   Res enim, de qua sermo est, in cogitatione magis et ratione subsistit, quia hujusmodi mors non in effectu, sed in cogitatione habenda est.   Qui enim cogitat vel existimat apud semet ipsum, mortuum se esse, non peccat.   Verbi gratia ; si me concupiscentia mulieris trahat, si argenti, si auri, si praedii cupiditas pulset, et ponam in corde meo, quod mortuus sim cum Christo, et de morte cogitem, exstinguitur concupiscentia, et effugatur peccatum " (*In Rom.* v. 10, Lom. vi. 412).   This is given as an explanation of the statement (which by itself might seem objective enough), " tantam esse vim crucis Christi, et mortis hujus, quam in saeculorum fine suscepit, asserimus, quae ad sanitatem et remedium non solum praesentis et futuri, sed etiam praeteritorum saeculorum, et non solum humano huic nostro ordini, sed etiam coelestibus virtutibus ordinibusque sufficiat " (*ib.* p. 409).   He then goes on to say that what will prevent men falling into sin is " caritas," which flows from the death of Christ in the way explained above.

will not only long, but even with eagerness long, to die for this good One."[1] So again St. Paul's doctrine that men are justified by Christ's righteousness is explained by the effect of Christ's example, just as it was by the example and influence of Adam and the parents descended from him that their posterity were made sinners.[2] Everywhere the effects of Christ's death are explained by its subjective or ethical influence upon the believer.

It may be remarked that these passages occur in his Commentary on St. Paul's Epistle to the Romans. Here, if anywhere, Origen might have been expected to develope a theory of substitutionary sacrifice or a just transaction between God and the Devil, had he entertained any such ideas. But no such theory is here propounded. All the texts of St. Paul which suggest any such ideas are elaborately explained away. It is a curious result of extreme theories of Biblical inspiration that the ultra-libertarian Origen can comment on every verse of this ultra-predestinarian Epistle without discovering that the thought of the Apostle and that of his libertarian commentator are poles asunder. Equally free is he from accepting St. Paul's doctrine of justification in its obvious and literal sense. The death of Christ and faith are both necessary to salvation, but neither of them avail anything without works.[3] The baptismal faith is only the beginning of salvation from evil, the

---

[1] " Unde quia ex hoc tantae bonitatis indicio ipse esse hic agnoscitur bonus, pro hoc bono forsitan quis et audeat mori. Cum enim cognoverit unusquisque tantam erga se bonitatem Christi, caritatemque ejus habuerit in corde diffusam, non solum mori pro hoc bono, sed et audacter mori desiderabit." (He goes on to speak of the Martyrs.) *In Rom.* iv. 10, Lom. vi. 303.

[2] " Hoc ergo modo etiam Christus occidit inimicitiam in carne sua, cum morte suscepta exemplum dedit hominibus usque ad mortem resistere adversum peccatum, et ita demum . . . reconciliavit per sanguinem suum homines Deo, eos duntaxat, qui inviolatum reconciliationis foedus ultra non peccando custodiunt " (*In Rom.* iv. 12, Lom. vi. 313). " Remedium dedit, ut generatio mortalis regeneratione baptismi mutaretur, et impietatis doctrinam doctrina pietatis excluderet. . . . Sed initium quidem vitae datur a Christo non invitis sed credentibus, et pervenitur ad perfectionem vitae perfectione virtutum " (*ib.* v. 2, p. 354). " Propterea enim et ipse ' obediens factus est usque ad mortem,' ut qui obedientiae ejus sequuntur exemplum, justi constituantur ab ipsa justitia, sicut illi inobedientiae formam sequentes constituti sunt peccatores " (*ib.* v. 5, p. 368). He has just explained that Christ Himself is "ipsa justitia."

[3] " Ex quo ostendit quod neque fides nostra sine Christi sanguine, neque sanguis Christi nos sine fide nostra iustificat : ex utroque tamen multo magis sanguis Christi nos quam fides nostra iustificat " (*In Rom.* iv. 11, Lom. vi. 309, on v. 8, 9).

completion of which requires works, or rather real
change of heart and life. Nothing can exceed the
clearness with which he repudiates the idea of imputed
righteousness.[1]

Origen has, indeed, a completer philosophy of
redemption than any other Christian Father. More
boldly than any of them before or since he attempts to
grapple with the problem of evil. His whole philosophy
is constructed on the basis of an extreme and uncompromising Libertarianism which is sometimes pushed
to the point of denying the divine foreknowledge.[2] He
is about the most thoroughgoing and consistent free-
willer in the whole history of human thought. Moral
evil is accounted for by the necessity of free-will for the
production of real goodness : all other evil is penal or
medicinal, a remedy for the pollution incurred by pre-
natal sin.[3] But Origen sees and admits without the
smallest attempt at evasion or concealment that even
so the existence of evil implies a limitation of the Creator's
power. God cannot produce the maximum of good,
at which He always aims, without permitting some evils

[1] " Neque enim possibile est, ut habenti in se aliquid iniustitiae possit iustitia reputari,
etiam si credat in eum, qui suscitavit Dominum Iesum a mortuis " (*In Rom.* iv. 7, Lom.
vi. 280). So *In Joann.* xix. 23, Brooke ii. 32 he elaborately traces the effects of
faith in producing works ; if they do not follow, there can be no real belief : ὁ πιστεύων
τί ἐστιν ἡ δικαιοσύνη οὐκ ἂν ἀδικήσαι· . . . εἰ ἐνδίδομεν πρὸς πόνους, οὐ πιστεύομεν
αὐτῷ, καὶ καθ' ὅ ἐστιν ὑπομονή, καὶ εἰ ἀσθενοῦμεν, οὐ πεπιστεύκαμεν αὐτῷ καθ'
ὅ ἐστιν ἰσχύς.

[2] " Non enim secundum communem vulgi opinionem putandum est bona malaque
praescire Deum, sed secundum Scripturae sanctae consuetudinem sentiendum est "
(*In Rom.* vii. 7, Lom. vii. 122), but he proceeds to explain that " praescire " means
" to love beforehand," and that God does not love evil or evil men. So again : " Vide
in quam absurdam sententiam decidant hi, qui praescientiam Dei ad hoc tantum accipiunt,
quasi qui ea quae postmodum futura sunt ante praenoscat " (*In Rom.* vii. 8, Lom. vii. 126).
Harnack denies that Origen held that God did not foreknow evil, and certainly there
are many passages which assert divine foresight strongly. The " election " of such men
as St. Paul from their mother's womb is accounted for by God's foreknowledge of their
future merits. See the original Greek of Origen's *Commentary on Rom.* i., published by
Mr. Ramsbotham in the *Journal of Theol. Studies*, vol. xiii. No. 50, pp. 210-213 : προενα-
τενίσας οὖν ὁ Θεὸς τῷ εἱρμῷ τῶν ἐσομένων, καὶ κατανοήσας ῥοπὴν τοῦ ἐφ' ἡμῖν τωνδέ
τινων ἐπὶ εὐσέβειαν καὶ ὁρμὴν ἐπὶ ταύτην μετὰ τὴν ῥοπὴν . . . προέγνω αὐτούς,
γινώσκων μὲν τὰ ἐνιστάμενα προγινώσκων δὲ τὰ μέλλοντα. Possibly Origen thought
that it was from the present but free and unnecessitated determination of the
will that God could infer how the man would act in the future—a doctrine which
would remind us of Kant's doctrine of noumenal freedom.

[3] And yet he suggests the view that temptation and even some measure of moral evil
is a necessary consequence of our bodily nature. See *De Princ.* III. iv., Lom. xxi.
329 *sq.* ; *Contra Celsum*, vii. 50, Lom. xx. 78. But the soul is sent into the body,
that by the use of freedom it may rise to a higher level. Cf. Harnack's note, *Hist. of
Dogma*, ii. 344.

and directly causing others. Even if there were no actual evil in the world, the mere fact that there is a limited amount of good excludes omnipotence in the popular sense of the word. " We must say," he tells us, " that the power of God is limited and not on the pretext of reverence deny the limitation of it. . . . He has made then as many things as He could grasp and hold under His hand and keep under the control of His providence : as He has likewise created as much matter as He could adorn."[1] Unfortunately the passage is a fragment and breaks off here. Perhaps Origen went on to say that He created as many souls as He could : more souls would have been a greater good ; had He failed to create them when He could have done so, that would argue want of love.

All the inequalities of human life are accounted for in accordance with these fundamental principles. All rational spirits were originally created free and equal [2]— equal in moral and, apparently, in intellectual capacity.[3]

[1] Πεπειρασμένην γὰρ εἶναι καὶ τὴν δύναμιν τοῦ Θεοῦ λεκτέον καὶ μὴ προφάσει εὐφημίας τὴν περιγραφὴν αὐτῆς περιαιρετέον. ἐὰν γὰρ ᾖ ἄπειρος ἡ θεία δύναμις, ἀνάγκη αὐτὴν μηδὲ ἑαυτὴν νοεῖν· τῇ γὰρ φύσει τὸ ἄπειρον ἀπερίληπτον. πεποίηκε τοίνυν τοσαῦτα ὅσων ἠδύνατο περιδράξασθαι καὶ ἔχειν ὑπὸ χεῖρα, καὶ συγκρατεῖν ὑπὸ τὴν ἑαυτοῦ πρόνοιαν· ὥσπερ καὶ τοσαύτην ὕλην κατεσκεύασεν, ὅσην ἠδύνατο κατακοσμῆσαι. Fragment in the Epistle of Justinian to Mennas, Patriarch of Constantinople, ap. Lommatzsch, xxi. 215 on De Princ. II. ix. 1.

[2] Origen was accused of holding that the souls of men might descend into animals, but this is denied in Rufinus' version of the De Princ. i. viii. 4 (Lom. xxi. 131). The fragment of the original Greek which is preserved declares that the soul which chooses evil is " bestialized by its folly and brutalized by its wickedness " : ὑπὸ τῆς ἀνοίας ἀποκτηνοῦται καὶ ὑπὸ τῆς πονηρίας ἀποθηριοῦται (Lommatzsch, l.c.) ; but this " bestialization " can hardly be understood literally, since the idea is expressly disclaimed in Contra Celsum, v. 29, Lom. xix. 217 ; viii. 30, Lom. xx. 149-150 ; In Matt. xi. 17, Lom. iii. 118. He likewise disclaims the idea of the transference of the soul into another human body on this earth, In Matt. x. 20, Lom. iii. 55 ; xiii. 1, Lom. iii. 206. Cf. In Cantic. ii., Lom. xiv. 405 ; In Joann. vi. 12, Brooke i. 125-6. The doctrine of pre-existence had been held before Plato by the Orphic brotherhoods, who thought that human souls were really gods who had fallen or sinned in a previous state, and Origen was no doubt not uninfluenced by this idea.

[3] It is not clear whether Origen thought of this creation as an eternal creation or as a creation in time, or held that time and souls were created together. Harnack (ii. 360) declares that, according to him, human souls " were created from all eternity : for God would not be almighty unless he had always produced everything." He quotes the passage in which it is said that " ne omnipotens quidem Deus dici potest, si non sint, in quos exerceat potentatum : et ideo ut omnipotens ostendatur Deus, omnia subsistere necesse est " (De Princ. i. ii. 10, Lom. xxi. 59-60), and there is much similar language in Origen. But what Origen is here immediately proving is the eternal creation or generation of the Son. It seems doubtful whether Origen means that each individual soul exists from all eternity or whether he does not mean to assert what later philosophers would have expressed by saying that God is " out of time," that time is merely sub-

They were born with ethereal bodies in a world which was free from evil. Those who used their freedom well have been promoted into angels or (if they have been less good) are born again as good men on earth : those who have abused it have become devils.[1] The evil of the world is partly the result of pre-natal sin, partly the means of purgatorial discipline. The privileges of the Jews were earned by previous good conduct, and there is nothing arbitrary about the " election " of Christians : they, too, have earned spiritual promotion in a previous state. The fall of Adam is frankly treated as allegorical. The fall of man was really a pre-natal fall. The influence of original sin is explained as meaning the evil influence exercised on Adam and other fathers by their example and bad education of their children.[2] Great moral changes—from good to evil or

---

jective, and that from the point of view of God the whole series of events which make up the world's history always exists. This is quite compatible, of course, with believing that souls began to exist at a point of time ; indeed, many of the philosophers who have taken this view have believed neither in pre-existence nor in immortality. Origen believed in the creation of this world, but there were other worlds before it (*De Princ.* III. v., Lom. xxi. 344 *sq.*). Methodius declares that he held μὴ εἶναι χρόνον, ὅτε οὐκ ἦν ταῦτα. A beginning of creation would make God changeable : οὐκ ἄρα δυνατὸν λέγειν μὴ εἶναι ἄναρχον καὶ συναΐδιον τῷ Θεῷ τὸ πᾶν (Fragment in Lommatzsch, xxi. 58, 59). Perhaps some of the difficulties may be reconciled by his doctrine that πάντα τὰ γένη καὶ τὰ εἴδη ἀεὶ ἦν. (See another fragment in Lom. xxi. 59.) The fact is that Origen has not succeeded better than more modern philosophers in transcending the antinomies involved in our ideas of time.

[1] *De Princ.* III. v. 4, Lom. xxi. 348 *sq.* But sometimes it is suggested that saints may be sent down into the world not by way of punishment, but for the benefit of other souls. *In Joann.* xiii. 43, Brooke i. 296, cf. x. 30, Brooke i. 221. So *In Joann.* ii. 31, Brooke i. 97 it is suggested that men like John the Baptist were originally angels, and may have become incarnate voluntarily. It would appear, moreover, that the abuse of freedom must sometimes produce undeserved suffering for others. So (*In Ezech. Hom.* i. 2, Lom. xiv. 8) such men as Daniel suffer not for their own sins but that they bring consolation to others.

[2] " Aut magis simpliciter accipiendum videtur . . . ut hoc sermone (Rom. v. 14) omnes, qui ex Adam praevaricatore nati sunt, indicari videantur, et habere in semet ipsis similitudinem praevaricationis ejus non solum ex semine, sed ex institutione susceptam. Omnes enim, qui in hoc mundo nascuntur, non solum nutriuntur a parentibus, sed et imbuuntur . . . Ubi vero aetas adoleverit, et agendi quae sentit libertas accesserit, ibi jam aut pergit in viam patrum suorum, sicut de nonnullis regibus scribitur, aut certe incedit in viam Domini Dei sui " (*In Rom.* v. 1, Lom. vi. 342-3). It is to be observed that in Rom. v. 14 (v. 1, Lom. vi. 316) Origen reads " in eos qui peccaverunt in similitudinem praevaricationis Adami, qui est forma futuri," omitting the " non " and thereby avoiding one most serious difficulty in St. Paul's theology. There are, indeed, passages in which the fact of original sin seems to be admitted in something more like the usual sense. He says, for instance, that as soon as a man reaches an age at which he knows the distinction between good and evil " primo omnium malitiam suscitari " (*In Rom.* iii. 2, Lom. vi. 177). He justifies child-baptism because there is " in omnibus genuinae sordes peccati " (*l.c.* v. 9, Lom. vi. 397), and holds that " omnes . . . nos homines

evil to good—take place slowly and with difficulty.
Only after a number of re-incarnations, or perhaps
rather re-births, in successive worlds or aeons will human
souls be fitted for perfect blessedness.[1] There is a
purgatorial fire through which even saints like St. Peter
and St. Paul must pass.[2] And the ultimate destiny of
the righteous is to be assigned a place in the stars.[3]
But every step in the rise of the soul must be due to its
own efforts. The whole scheme of the incarnation is
designed to aid such efforts. It is a scheme contrived
for the express purpose of persuading, without forcing,

---

qui ex semine viri cum muliere convenientis concepti sumus, illa necessario utimur voce,
qua dicit David, quoniam ' in iniquitatibus concepit me mater mea ' " (*In Rom.* vi. 12,
Lom. vii. 69). Christ, he goes on to say, owing to His miraculous conception, shared
our nature : " pollutionem tamen peccati, quae ex concupiscentiae motu conceptis tradi-
tur, omnino non habuit." Since he appears to admit that concupiscence " has the nature
of sin " (" concupiscentia hic culpabilis ponitur," vi. 8, p. 45), it is difficult to see
how Origen could reconcile such statements with his strong assertions of freedom.
According to Dr. Bigg, it was when he came to Palestine and found the usage of infant
baptism established that he came to feel the necessity of admitting the existence of
original sin. But both ways of thinking are to be found in the *Commentary on Romans*,
and there is no absolute inconsistency between them if it is admitted that the inherited
evil tendencies are due to pre-natal sin. In the above passages we are dependent upon
Rufinus, but see a strong assertion of original sin in *C. Celsum*, vii. 50, Lom. xx. 78.

[1] *De Princ.* I. vi. 3, Lom. xxi. 111 ; II. iii. 3, Lom. xxi. 151 ; III. i. 21, Lom. xxi. 301.
It is obvious that the tendency of these views is to destroy the old doctrines that no
repentance, or only one repentance, after baptism is possible. At the same time, in his
earlier life, Origen seems to have approved of the rule that certain mortal sins were not
to be forgiven by the Church. See *De Orat.* 28 *ad fin.*, Lom. xvii. 243. In *In Lev.
Hom.* ii. 4, Lom. ix. 191, however, the words " una tantummodo venia est peccatorum "
seems to be an objection which he proceeds to correct. But all this has no bearing upon
the question of divine forgiveness since the sin for which there was no forgiveness in this
aeon, or the aeon to come, might be atoned for in one of the countless aeons of the vast
hereafter (cf. Bigg, *Christ. Platonists*, 2nd ed. p. 277). Origen did much to develope the
distinction between mortal and venial sin : he admits the practical impossibility of
altogether escaping the latter. See *In Jesu Nave Hom.* xxi. 2, Lom. xi. 184.

[2] " Ut ego arbitror, omnes nos venire necesse est ad illum ignem (1 Cor. iii. 13) ;
etiamsi Paulus sit aliquis vel Petrus, venit tamen ad illum ignem" (*Sel. in Psalmos, Hom.* iii.
1, Lom. xii. 181-2). Cf. *In Luc. Hom.* xiv. Lom. v. 136 : " Ego puto, quod et post
resurrectionem ex mortuis indigeamus sacramento eluente nos atque purgante."
The " fire " in the case of the just is a testing, rather than a punitive, fire. " Quia
transeant per eum justi, et non comburantur " (*In Ezek. Hom.* v. 2, Lom. xiv. 73) ; but
there are in all or most men elements which must be destroyed by the purgatorial flames.
St. Paul could say that he desired to depart and be with Christ : Origen could not honestly
say that for himself, for he feared the purgatorial fire : οἶδα γὰρ ὅτι, ἐὰν ἐξέλθω, τὰ ἐμὰ
ξύλα καυθῆναι ἐν ἐμοὶ δεῖ. ξύλα γὰρ ἔχω τῆς λοιδορίας κ.τ.λ. (*In Ier. Hom.* xix. 3,
Lom. xv. 364). In *De Princ.* II. x. 4, Lom. xxi. 234 *sq.* the whole conception of the
" fire " is spiritualized : " quod unusquisque peccatorum flammam sibi ipse proprii
ignis accendat."

[3] *In Lib. Jesu Nave Hom.* xxv. 4, Lom. xi. 208. Elsewhere he speaks more doubtfully (*In Num. Hom.* xxviii. 2, Lom. x. 367-8). For the very refined sense in which
Origen held the resurrection of the body, see *Selecta in Psalmos*, Ps. i., Lom. xi. 384-91.
There would be an identity of " form " (εἶδος) between the present body and the spiritual
resurrection body, in which there would be no flesh or bone or skin.

souls to make that free choice of good without which
no true goodness, according to Origen, was possible.
It is only by persuasion, example, moral influence that
a soul can be made better even by the incarnate Word;
and it is only so far as it is persuaded to repent, and so
to become better, that God will or can forgive the sin
that is past.

No spirit has ever sunk so low that he cannot rise,
though, if his fall is grievous, it can only be by slow and
gradual stages.[1]   Origen was accused of holding, and
almost certainly did hold, that even the Devil can be
saved.[2]   This is the feature of Origen's philosophy
which gave the greatest scandal to his age, and which is
most sedulously concealed by his more orthodox translator Rufinus.   The great obstacle to the achievement
of this purpose is the existence of free-will, but in time
even that obstacle would be surmounted.[3]   And then
would come the day spoken of by St. Paul when the
Son himself would be subject to Him that subjected all
things to Him.   The meaning which Origen gives
to that subjection of all things to Christ is precisely
this, the salvation of all the spirits which God has created
—more than their salvation, for they will be angels,
diviner than they were before, or even "gods."[4]

[1] *De Princ.* i. vi. 3 (Lom. xxi. 110, 111).
[2] Rufinus makes Origen deny this, and Dr. Bigg seems prepared to accept the denial.
In the *Epistola ad Amicos*, Lom. xvii. 8, according to the version of Jerome, certain of
Origen's adversaries taught that the Devil could be saved (" posse salvari "), according to
that of Rufinus they affirmed that it was Origen who taught " diabolum esse salvandum."
Both translators substantially agree in making Origen say : " quod ne mente quidem quis
captus dicere potest " (cf. Dr. Bigg, *Christian Platonists*, 2nd ed. p. 278).   But I cannot see
that there can be any doubt about the meaning of this (*De Princ.* iii. vi. 5, Lom. xxi. 364-
365) : " destrui sane novissimus inimicus ita intelligendus est, non ut substantia ejus,
quae a Deo facta est, pereat, sed ut propositum, et voluntas inimica, quae non a Deo, sed
ab ipso processit, intereat.   Destructum ergo, non ut non sit, sed ut inimicus non sit et
mors.   Nihil enim omnipotenti impossibile est, nec insanabile est aliquid factori suo."
(So also *In Lev. Hom.* ix. 11, Lom. ix. 365.)   The universalistic and the non-universal-
istic passages are not strictly irreconcilable ; Origen probably held that all souls would
cease to be evil, but not that all would be good enough to attain to the very highest
bliss.   Cf. *In Num. Hom.* xi. 5, Lom. x. 116.   In *De Oratione*, 27, Lom. xvii. 226 he
has hopes for those who have sinned against the Holy Ghost ; they cannot be saved in
this age or the next, but they may be in some later age.
[3] " Manere quidem naturae rationabili semper liberum arbitrium non negamus ;
sed tantam esse vim crucis Christi et mortis hujus quam in saeculorum fine suscepit,
asserimus, quae ad sanitatem et remedium non solum praesentis et futuri sed etiam
praeteritorum saeculorum et non solum humano huic nostro ordini, sed etiam coelestibus
virtutibus ordinibusque sufficiat " (*In Rom.* v. 10, Lom. vi. 409).
[4] " Subjectionis enim nomen, qua Christo subjicimur, salutem, quae a Christo est,

Such universalism is, indeed, difficult to reconcile
with that "free-will of indifference" which will never
be beyond the possibility of a fall; but Origen thought
that he could reconcile these two apparently conflicting
views of the universe by holding that the love inspired
in rational spirits by the cross of Christ was so intense
that it must ultimately overcome the theoretical possibility
of a renewed fall. And this salvation will extend to
those who have not had the opportunity of listening to
the Gospel message in this age or aeon, but who will
have the opportunity of doing so in one of the countless
aeons that are to come.[1]

Origen is by far the greatest thinker whom the
patristic age produced, the most modern of all the fathers
in spite of the very unmodern mystical exegesis on
which much of it is based, the father from whom we
have still most to learn. I need not dwell upon those
features of his thought which have since become impossible to us. His cosmology is that of the ancient

---

indicat subjectorum" (*De Princ.* I. vi. 2, Lom. xxi. 105). *Cf. Select. Psalmos
Hom.* ii. 1, Lom. xii. 168-69. It is implied in such passages that the redemptive
effect extends to all spirits and not merely to man. Cf. fragment given by Lommatzsch,
xxi. 456-7. Ἀλλ' εὐθέως σου μεταβάλλει ἡ ψυχὴ καὶ μεταμορφοῦται, καὶ γίνεται
κρεῖττόν τι καὶ θειότερον παρ' ὃ ἦν τὸ πρότερον. (*In Jer.* Hom. xvi. 1, Lom.
xv. 290). Sometimes the theory of deification is more strongly stated : ταῦτα δὲ
παρεθέμεθα ἵνα πάσῃ δυνάμει φεύγωμεν τὸ εἶναι ἄνθρωποι καὶ σπεύδωμεν γένεσθαι
θεοί (*In Joann.* xx. 29, Brooke ii. 80). Sometimes it is said that all to whom the
Word of God comes are already gods (*In Ezech.* Hom. i. 9, Lom. xiv. 21). Cf. *De Oratione*,
27, Lom. xvii. 220 : ἵνα τρεφόμενοι τῷ ἐν ἀρχῇ πρὸς θεὸν θεῷ λόγῳ θεοποιηθῶμεν.
In Origen the meaning of deification is predominantly ethical rather than metaphysical,
though of course it implies immortality. The face of God which the redeemed are to
see is explained to mean οἱ λόγοι τῶν ἐπὶ γῆς οἱ χαρακτηρίζοντες τὸν δημιουργικὸν
αὐτοῦ λόγον (*Sel. in Psalmos*, 99, Lom. xii. 126).

[1] The virtuous Gentile who has followed the light of reason "licet alienus a vita
videatur aeterna, quia non credit Christo, et intrare non possit in regnum coelorum, quia
renatus non est ex aqua et Spiritu, videtur tamen quod per haec quae dicuntur ab Apostolo
bonorum operum gloriam et honorem et pacem perdere penitus non possit" (*In Rom.* ii.
7, Lom. vi. 98). Elsewhere (*In Matt. Comm. Series*, 39, Lom. iv. 271) he suggests that
Britons and others who have not heard the Gospel here "audituri sunt autem in ipsa
saeculi consummatione." He appeals to Matt. xxiv. 14. There are plenty of *prima
facie* inconsistencies in Origen's eschatology. It is probable that his opinion wavered, and
that in his more popular writings he uses conventional phrases which hardly represent
his deepest thoughts, *e.g.* : ἤτοι ἐν ᾅδῃ οὐδεὶς ἐξομολογήσεται ἢ πάνυ ὀλίγοι
(*Sel. in Psalmos*, 6, Lom. xii. 8). But at times he quite explicitly declares that hell
itself will have an end : "Non solum ergo peccator non erit, sed etiam locus ejus, quisque
ille est, quaeretur et non erit" (*In Psalmos Hom.* ii. 6, Lom. xii. 176). One of Origen's
quaintest notions is that, when the prophets speak of "the land" being punished, this
may be meant literally—that the "land" (or the earth) is an animal which has sinned
(*In Ezech.* Hom. iv. 1, 3, Lom. xiv. 56, 61), though in another place he treats this as
absurd (*Sel. in Ezech.* 14, Lom. xiv. 215).

world. His doctrine of pre-existence, in spite of distinguished modern imitators,[1] seems to most of us to involve more difficulties than it avoids. His extreme indeterminism can only be reconciled with the facts of heredity and the facts of human life in general by free incursions into a very speculative, and indeed somewhat mythological, region of thought ; and his assumption that all souls were originally equal and alike—so that their future is in some sense but a restoration of a previous state—often gives an unmodern tone to his eschatology.[2] But the general spirit of Origen is the spirit in which modern theology must be reconstructed ; and, apart from the pre-existence theory, there is little in his doctrine of redemption which may not be appropriated almost unaltered by the modern theologian. In particular in regard to the real meaning and justification of the divine forgiveness—a word which most modern theologians glibly use without the smallest consciousness of its difficulty—Origen has a suggestion which goes to the root of the matter. The tendency of bad acts, he tells us, is to make a man bad, and of good acts to make him good. The only way in which a bad man can justly be freed from punishment by a good and just God is by his being induced to repent and so to become actually good. Justification to Origen means simply the being made actually righteous. The incarnation of the Word, the example and teaching of Christ, the love which is shown by His incarnation and His voluntary death, the influence which He continues to exercise over the hearts of men through His Church, help to produce this effect. They tend to make him actually good, and, so far as they do so, punishment would be useless and unjust. " If there is anyone, therefore, . . . who at one time did evil, it is certain that he was then evil when he acted evilly. But if, repenting of his former sins, he corrects his mind and brings it round to good things, and acts rightly, speaks rightly, thinks

[1] The most distinguished of these is Renouvier (in *La Nouvelle Monadologie*), who adopts Origen's theory of a pre-natal fall.

[2] " Semper enim similis est finis initiis " (*De Princ.* i. vi. 2, Lom. xxi. 106). But qualifications follow.

T

rightly, wills rightly, does not he who does these things
seem to you good, and deservedly to receive good
things? Likewise also if from being good anyone is
turned about to the doing of evil, he shall not be
judged to be now the good man which he was and
is not, but be judged to be bad, as he actually is.
The good or bad acts pass away, but according to
their quality they mould and form the mind of the agent,
and leave it good or bad, to be destined either to punishment or to reward. It will therefore be unjust either
that a good mind should be punished for bad deeds, or
that a bad mind should be rewarded for good acts.
But that what we say may be made still plainer, let us
add also this : let us suppose that a soul, in which
dwells impiety, injustice, folly, luxury, and all the
multitude of evils to which it has made itself the minister
and slave—if this soul, returning to itself, again opens
the door of its mind to piety and the virtues, will
not piety entering in forthwith dethrone impiety ? . . .
How therefore will it be just to blame a soul now
full of the virtues for those things which it did
when it was not yet the friend of the virtues, and to
condemn a pious soul for impiety, a just soul for injustice,
a self-controlled soul for vice ? In this way therefore
even in those whose iniquities are forgiven, and whose
sins are covered, God must be believed to keep justice
according to truth." [1]

---

[1] " Si quis ergo sit, verbi gratia, qui egerit aliquando male, certum est quia malus
erat tunc, cum agebat male. Is vero si praeteritorum poenitens mentem suam corrigat
ad bona, et bene agat, bene loquatur, bene cogitet, bene velit ; qui haec agit, nonne tibi
videtur bonus, et merito recipere bona ? Similiter et si ex bono quis convertatur ad
malum, non jam bonus, quod fuit, et non est, sed malus judicabitur, quod est. Actus
enim sive boni, sive mali, praetereunt, sed secundum sui qualitatem agentis mentem
imaginantur, et formant, eamque vel bonam relinquunt, vel malam, seu poenae, seu prae-
miis destinandam. Erit ergo iniquum, vel bonam mentem pro malis gestis puniri, vel
malam pro bonis actibus munerari. Verum ut adhuc planius fiat, quod dicimus, addamus
etiam haec : ponamus esse animam, in qua habitet impietas, injustitia, stultitia, luxuria,
et multitudo omnis malorum, quibus scilicet ministram se famulamque subdiderit.
Quodsi in semet ipsam regressa haec anima pietati rursus et virtutibus mentis suae
januam pandat, nonne ingressa pietas impietatem depellet ? . . . Quomodo ergo jam
plenam virtutibus animam justum erit de his arguere, quae gesserit, cum nondum
esset amica virtutum, et de impietate piam, de injustitia justam, de luxuria sobriam
condemnare ? Hoc ergo modo etiam in his, quorum remissae sunt iniquitates, et
quorum tecta sunt peccata [from the context it appears that this means " per baptismi
gratiam vel per poenitentiam "], credendus est Deus secundum veritatem servare

It is only, according to Origen, because they enable and help men to repent and become really righteous that any part of Christ's work—His incarnation, His teaching, His example, His death, His resurrection, the fear and the hope inspired by the judgement which He foretold—can lead to his forgiveness. Forgiveness is for Origen no arbitrary favour of a God who might justly have punished, but a necessary result of God's character—the character most fully revealed by Christ. That God will forgive the sins of the truly penitent without any other conditions whatever was, we have seen, the teaching of our Lord Himself.[1] It is no less the doctrine of Origen, who has made to it only the quite consistent addition that Christ's coming and work are the greatest power in the world for helping men to attain that penitence and amendment upon which forgiveness depends. The best modern thought on the atonement has added little to this doctrine; not often

---

judicium " (*In Rom.* ii. 1, Lom. vi. 70-71). It follows from this view of the atonement that justification is a real making righteous : " Per hanc etenim hostiam carnis, quae oblata est pro peccato, et damnavit peccatum, hoc est, fugavit peccatum, et abstulit, ut justificatio legis impleretur in nobis, qui legem secundum spiritum custodimus, et non secundum carnem " (*In Rom.* vi. 12, Lom. vii. 70).

[1] The assumption that baptism was necessary to salvation may be held to be an exception to this principle, but Origen disclaims the idea that baptism avails without belief and repentance : " Si non consepelitur Christo, nec legitime baptizatur " (*In Rom.* v. 8, Lom. vi. 380 ; cf. p. 386) ; and, since baptism was held to be divinely commanded, refusal to be baptized would constitute a moral offence. Origen contemplates the baptism of " parvuli " (*Hom. in Luc.* xiv., Lom. v. 135) ; but this does not necessarily mean actual infants. Baptism does not always secure the gift of the spirit (*In Ezech. Hom.* vi. 5, Lom. xiv. 86). The Eucharist was also thought of as helping to procure forgiveness : " Si autem sanguis testamenti infusus est in corda nostra in remissionem peccatorum nostrorum, effuso eo potabili sanguine in corda nostra, remittuntur et delentur omnia, quae gessimus ante, peccata " (*In Matt. Comm. Series* 86, Lom. iv. 420) ; but the context shows that Origen understood such statements in no mechanical or magical sense : with Origen emphatically the sacraments are what Bishop Gore has called " moral means of salvation." They contribute to procure forgiveness only by making people who duly use them really better. Cf. *In Lev. Hom.* ii. 4 (Lom. ix. 191 *sq.*). Here seven channels of forgiveness are enumerated—baptism, martyrdom, alms, mutual forgiveness, conversion by another, charity (" per abundantiam caritatis "), " poenitentia." But this is merely to meet the objection that Christianity provided fewer means of forgiveness than Judaism with its numerous expiations : it hardly amounts to a formal doctrine. In the same book he speaks of priestly absolution (implied in poenitentia), but the efficacy of such absolution depends upon the character and spiritual power of the priest (*In Lev. Hom.* v. 3, Lom. ix. 246). Consequently, " nisi habeat pectus ex omnibus membris electum [mystical interpretation of the command that the priest is to have the right breast and right shoulder] non est sacerdos, et nisi habeat brachium dextrum non potest adscendere ad altare Dei nec sacerdos nominari " (*In Lev. Hom.* v. 12, Lom. ix. 269). There is no idea at all in Origen of duly administered sacraments being absolute guarantees of salvation.

has it ever quite attained the same level of rationality and spiritual insight.[1]

[1] In making redemption result from or consist in a real influence upon human nature exercised by the incarnation as a whole, Origen was following Irenaeus and what Loofs calls the " Asia Minor theology " ; but with him intelligible ethical influences take the place of a physical incorruptibility communicated to the soul by Christ's glorified body : " Origenes hatte die auf verkürzten kleinasiatischen Traditionen ruhende ' physische Erlösungs-lehre ' bereits nicht mehr ignorieren können, doch hatte er sie wegspiritualisiert " (Loofs, *Dogmengeschichte*, p. 203).

ADDITIONAL NOTE TO LECTURE IV

A CATENA ON THE ATONEMENT FROM IRENAEUS, ORIGEN, AND TERTULLIAN [1]

IRENAEUS

Incarnation to make God known

Verbum Dei quod habitavit in homine, et Filius Hominis factus est, ut assuesceret hominem percipere Deum, et assuesceret Deum habitare in homine, secundum placitum Patris. (*Contra Haereses* III. xxi. 2.)

Christ came as revealer and example

Non enim aliter nos discere poteramus quae sunt Dei, nisi magister noster, Verbum exsistens, homo factus fuisset. Neque enim alius poterat enarrare nobis quae sunt Patris, nisi proprium ipsius Verbum. *Quis enim* alius *cognovit sensum Domini? aut quis alius ejus consiliarius factus est?* Neque rursus nos aliter discere poteramus nisi magistrum nostrum videntes, et per auditum nostrum vocem ejus percipientes, ut, imitatores quidem operum, factores autem sermonum ejus facti, communionem habeamus cum ipso ; a perfecto, et eo qui est ante omnem conditionem, augmentum accipientes. (*Contra Haer.* v. i. i.)

The attractive, illuminating, and life-giving power of Christ's death

Et Aeon quidem passus est passionem ipse requirens Patrem, et non praevalens invenire : Dominus autem passus est, ut eos qui erraverunt a Patre, ad agnitionem, et juxta eum adduceret. Et illi quidem inquisitio magnitudinis Patris fiebat passio perditionis : nobis autem Dominus passus, agnitionem Patris conferens, salutem donavit. Et illius quidem passio fructificavit fructum foemineum, sicut dicunt, invalidum, et infirmum, et informem, et inefficacem ; istius autem passio fructificavit fortitudinem et virtutem. [Including, as the next sentence shows, the working of miracles.] . . . Et Dominus quidem per passionem mortem destruxit ; et solvit errorem, corruptionemque exterminavit, et ostendit veritatem, et incorruptionem

---

[1] Passages already quoted in full are omitted.

donavit, et ignorantiam destruxit; vitam autem manifestavit, et ostendit veritatem, et incorruptionem donavit. (*Contra Haer.* II. xxxii. 2.)

Christ's death the source of reconciliation

Qui per passionem reconciliavit nos Deo. (*Contra Haer.* III. xvii. 9.)

The theory of fitness

Primogenitus enim *mortuorum* natus Dominus, et in sinum suum recipiens pristinos patres, regeneravit eos in vitam Dei, ipse initium viventium factus, quoniam Adam initium morientium factus est. (*Contra Haer.* III. xxxii. 1.)

The theory of recapitulation

(1) Hujus verbum unigenitus, qui semper humano generi adest, unitus et consparsus suo plasmati secundum placitum Patris, et caro factus, ipse est Jesus Christus Dominus noster, qui et passus est pro nobis, et surrexit propter nos, et rursus venturus est in gloria Patris, ad resuscitandam universam carnem, et ad ostensionem salutis. . . . Unus igitur Deus Pater quemadmodum ostendimus, et unus Christus Jesus Dominus noster, veniens per universam dispositionem et omnia in semet ipsum recapitulans. In omnibus autem est et homo plasmatio Dei : et hominem ergo in semet ipsum recapitulans est, invisibilis visibilis factus, et incomprehensibilis factus comprehensibilis, et impassibilis passibilis et Verbum homo, universa in semet ipsum recapitulans : uti sicut in supercoelestibus et spiritalibus et invisibilibus princeps est Verbum Dei ; sic et in visibilibus et corporalibus principatum habeat, in semet ipsum primatum assumens, et apponens semet ipsum caput Ecclesiae, universa attrahat apto in tempore. (*Contra Haer.* III. xvii. 6.)

(2) Et antiquam plasmationem in se recapitulatus est. Quia quemadmodum per inobedientiam unius hominis introitum peccatum habuit, et per peccatum mors obtinuit ; sic et per obedientiam unius hominis justitia introducta vitam fructificet his, qui olim mortui erant, hominibus. Et quemadmodum protoplastus ille Adam de rudi terra, et de adhuc virgine (*nondum enim pluerat Deus, et homo non erat operatus terram*) habuit substantiam, et plasmatus est manu Dei, id est, Verbo Dei, *omnia enim per ipsum facta sunt*, et sumsit Dominus limum a terra, et plasmavit hominem : ita recapitulans in se Adam ipse Verbum exsistens, ex Maria quae adhuc erat virgo, recte accipiebat generationem Adae recapitulationis. (*Contra Haer.* III. xxx.)

(3) [Luke traces the genealogy to Adam] Significans quoniam ipse est qui omnes gentes exinde ab Adam dispersas, et universas linguas, et generationem hominum cum ipso Adam in semet ipso recapitulatus est. (*Contra Haer.* III. xxxii. 1.)

(4) Ταῦτα γὰρ πάντα [blood, water, etc.] σύμβολα σαρκὸς τῆς ἀπὸ γῆς εἰλημμένης, ἣν εἰς αὐτὸν ἀνεκεφαλαιώσατο, τὸ ἴδιον πλάσμα σώζων. (*Contra Haer.* III. xxxi. 2.)

(5) Οὐδὲ γὰρ ἦν ἀληθῶς σάρκα καὶ αἷμα ἐσχηκὼς, δι' ὧν ἡμᾶς ἐξηγοράσατο, εἰ μὴ τὴν ἀρχαίαν πλάσιν τοῦ Ἀδὰμ εἰς ἑαυτὸν ἀνεκεφαλαιώσατο. (*Contra Haer.* v. i. 2.)

(6) Filius Dei factus est homo, antiquam plasmationem in semet ipsum suscipiens. (*Contra Haer.* IV. lii. 1.)

(7) Quando incarnatus est [Filius Dei] et homo factus longam hominum expositionem in se ipso recapitulavit, in compendio nobis salutem praestans, ut quod perdideramus in Adam, id est secundum imaginem et similitudinem esse Dei, hoc in Christo Jesu reciperemus. (*Contra Haer.* III. xix. 1.)

(8) Quemadmodum ab initio plasmationis nostrae in Adam ea quae fuit a Deo adspiratio vitae unita plasmati animavit hominem, et animal rationabile ostendit ; sic in fine Verbum Patris et Spiritus Dei, adunitus antiquae substantiae plasmationis Adae, viventem et perfectum effecit hominem capientem perfectum patrem. (*Contra Haer.* v. i. 3.)

(9) Ad mortem descendens, et dispensationem consummans salutis nostrae. (*Contra Haer.* III. xix. 2.)

Recapitulation explained as renovation, and combined with the ransom theory

Non ergo justus adventus ejus qui secundum eos advenit in aliena [*i.e.* εἰς τὰ ἀλλότρια] ; neque vere nos redemit sanguine suo, si non vere homo factus est, restaurans suo plasmati quod dictum est in principio, factum esse hominem secundum imaginem et similitudinem Dei ; non aliena in dolo diripiens, sed sua propria juste et benigne assumens ; quantum attinet quidem ad apostasiam, juste suo sanguine redimens nos ab ea ; quantum autem ad nos, qui redemti sumus, benigne. Nihil enim illi dedimus, neque desiderat aliquid a nobis, quasi indigens ; nos autem indigemus ejus quae est ad eum communionis, et propterea benigne effudit semet ipsum, ut nos colligeret in sinum Patris. (*Contra Haer.* v. ii. 1.)

The incarnation as the source of regeneration and immortality

Filius Altissimi Dei Patris omnium, qui operatus est incarnationem ejus, et novam ostendit generationem; uti quemadmodum per priorem generationem mortem haereditavimus, sic per generationem hanc haereditaremus vitam. (*Contra Haer.* v. i. 3.)

The incarnation as source of incorruption

Εἰ μὴ συνηνώθη ὁ ἄνθρωπος τῷ Θεῷ, οὐκ ἂν ἠδυνήθη μετασχεῖν ἀφθαρσίας. (*Contra Haer.* III. xix. 6.)

Christ's conquest over the Devil

Luctatus est enim, et vicit : erat enim homo pro patribus [surely we must read 'fratribus'] certans, et per obedientiam, inobedientiam persolvens : alligavit enim fortem, et solvit infirmos, et salutem donavit plasmati suo, destruens peccatum.   (*Contra Haer.* iii. xix. 5.)

The ransom theory combined with recapitulation or reintegration

Et captivus quidem ductus est juste is qui hominem injuste captivum duxerat ; qui autem ante captivus ductus fuerat homo, extractus est a possessoris potestate, secundum misericordiam Dei Patris : qui miseratus est plasmati suo, et dedit salutem ei, per Verbum, id est per Christum redintegrans : ut experimento discat homo, quoniam non a semet ipso sed donatione Dei accipit incorruptelam. (*Contra Haer.* v. xxi. 3.)

The death of Christ as a revelation of love

Et ex hoc autem quod Dominus in cruce dixerit : *Pater, dimitte eis, non enim sciunt quod faciunt,* longanimitas, et patientia, et misericordia, et bonitas Christi ostenditur, ut et ipse pateretur, et ipse excusaret eos qui se male tractassent.   Verbum enim Dei quod nobis dixit : *Diligite inimicos vestros, et orate pro eis qui vos oderunt,* ipse hoc fecit in cruce, in tantum diligens humanum genus, ut etiam pro his qui se interficerent, postularet.   (*Contra Haer.* iii. xix. 5.)

Justification by the Advent of Christ

Omnes enim homines *egent gloria Dei,* justificantur autem non a semet ipsis, sed a Domini adventu, qui intendunt lumen ejus.   (*Contra Haer.* iv. xlii. 4.)

Immortality secured by the Eucharist

Ἐπειδὴ μέλη αὐτοῦ ἐσμεν, καὶ διὰ τῆς κτίσεως τρεφόμεθα . . . καὶ τὸν ἀπὸ τῆς κτίσεως ἄρτον ἴδιον σῶμα διεβεβαιώσατο, ἀφ᾽ οὗ τὰ ἡμέτερα αὔξει σώματα. ὁπότε οὖν καὶ τὸ κεκραμένον ποτήριον, καὶ ὁ γεγονὼς ἄρτος ἐπιδέχεται τὸν λόγον τοῦ Θεοῦ, καὶ γίνεται ἡ εὐχαρι-στία σῶμα Χριστοῦ, ἐκ τούτων δὲ αὔξει καὶ συνίσταται ἡ τῆς σαρκὸς ἡμῶν ὑπόστασις· πῶς δεκτικὴν μὴ εἶναι λέγουσι τὴν σάρκα τῆς δωρεᾶς τοῦ Θεοῦ, ἥτις ἐστὶ ζωὴ αἰώνιος, τὴν ἀπὸ τοῦ σώματος καὶ αἵματος τοῦ Κυρίου τρεφομένην, καὶ μέλος αὐτοῦ ὑπάρχουσαν ; [1]   (*Contra Haer.* v. ii. 2.)

---

[1] It will be observed that the eucharistic elements are treated as the body of Christ because they receive the Word ; there is no identification with the actual body of Christ. Mr. Bishop has pointed out that the earliest form of the ἐπίκλησις in the Liturgies was an invocation of the Logos (not as later of the Spirit).   This suggests that the Western theory that consecration is effected by recitation of the words of institution arose from an ignorant Western misunderstanding of the term Logos.   See his remarks in *Texts and Studies* (ed. Robinson), vol. viii. No. 1, p. 138 *sq.*

Tertullian

Christ as victim offered up for man

Ipse etiam effectus hostia per omnia pro omnibus nobis. (*Adv. Judaeos*, 14—Oehler ii. 740.)

The death of Christ the central doctrine of Christianity

Totum Christiani nominis et pondus et fructus, mors Christi negatur [by the Marcionites]. (*Adv. Marcionem*, iii. 8—O. ii. 132.)

Purpose of the incarnation to deliver us from the Devil's angels

Cum Christus non alia ex causa descenderit, quam peccatorum liber- andorum. . . . Si quis autem dissimulat illam effigiem aerei serpentis suspensi in modum figuram designasse dominicae crucis a serpentibus, id est ab angelis diaboli, liberaturae nos, dum per semetipsam diabolum id est serpentem interfectum suspendit, etc. (*De Idololatria*, 5— O. i. 72.)

The love of Christ shown by incarnation and death

Certe Christus dilexit hominem illum in immunditiis in utero coagulatum. . . . Propter eum descendit, propter eum praedicavit, propter eum omni se humilitate deiecit usque ad mortem, et mortem crucis ; amavit utique quem magno redemit. (*De Carne Christi*, 4— O. ii. 431.)

The fitness of redemption through incarnation

Ob hoc igitur missum filium in similitudinem carnis peccati, ut peccati carnem simili substantia redimeret, id est carnea, quae peccatrici carni similis esset, cum peccatrix ipsa non esset. Nam et haec erit dei virtus in substantia pari perficere salutem. Non enim magnum, si spiritus dei carnem remediaret, sed caro consimilis peccatrici, dum caro est, sed non peccati. (*Adv. Marcion.* v. 14— O. ii. 315.)

The theory of recapitulation

(1) Quodsi contra erit mali finis cum praeses eius diabolus abierit in ignem quem praeparavit illi deus et angelis eius, prius in puteum abyssi relegatus, cum revelatio filiorum dei redemerit conditionem a malo, utique vanitati subiectam, cum restituta innocentia et integritate conditionis pecora condixerint bestiis, et parvuli de serpentibus luserint, cum pater filio posuerit inimicos sub pedes, etc. (*Adv. Hermogenem*, 11—O. ii. 349.)

(2) Denique hanc disciplinam, Secundum praecepta, inquit, et doctrinam hominum deputavit in eos qui caput non tenerent, id est ipsum in quo omnia recensentur, in Christum ad initium revocata etiam indifferentia escarum. (*Adv. Marcion.* v. 19—O. ii. 332-3.)

Justification by faith

Et ideo ut vidit agnovisse legem illos Hierosolymis expungendam [Deus] ex fide iam iustificandos sine legis ordine remediavit. (*Adv. Marcion.* iv. 35—O. ii. 254.)

A new status conferred in Christ

Ita omnis anima eo usque in Adam censetur, donec in Christo recenseatur, tamdiu immunda, quamdiu recenseatur ; peccatrix autem, quia immunda, respuens ignominiam suam et in carnem ex societate. (*De Anima*, 40—O. ii. 621.)

Connexion of baptism with the passion of Christ

[The Apostles could not confer true Christian Baptism but only the Baptism of John] utpote non adimpleta gloria domini, nec instructa efficacia lavacri per passionem et resurrectionem, quia nec mors nostra dissolvi posset nisi domini passione, nec vita restitui sine resurrectione ipsius. (*De Baptismo*, 11—O. i. 630.)

Death the consequence of the fall

Qui autem primordia hominis novimus, audenter determinamus mortem non ex natura secutum hominem, sed ex culpa, ne ipsa quidem naturali. (*De Anima*, 52—O. ii. 638.)

Use of paenitentia

Omnis paenitentia confessio est delicti, quia locum non habet nisi in delicto. (*De Carne Christi*, 8—O. ii. 442.)

The fall

Malum igitur animae, praeter quod ex obventu spiritus nequam superstruitur, ex originis vitio antecedit, naturale quodammodo. Nam, ut diximus, naturae corruptio alia natura est, habens suum deum et patrem, ipsum scilicet corruptionis auctorem, ut tamen insit et bonum animae illud principale, illud divinum atque germanum, et proprie naturale. Quod enim a deo est, non tam extinguitur quam obumbratur. (*De Anima*, 41—O. ii. 622-3.)

ORIGEN

Christ the true Paschal Lamb

Ὁ δὲ ἀληθὴς ἁγνισμὸς οὐ πρὸ τοῦ πάσχα ἦν ἀλλ' ἐν τῷ πάσχα, ὅ τε Ἰησοῦς ἀπέθανεν ὑπὲρ τῶν ἁγνιζομένων ὡς ἀμνὸς Θεοῦ, καὶ ἦρε τὴν ἁμαρτίαν τοῦ κόσμου. (*In Johann.* xxviii. 25, Brooke ii. p. 146.)

Christ an offering for sin

Quod hostia pro peccato factus sit Christus, et oblatus sit pro purgatione peccatorum, omnes Scripturae testantur, et praecipue Paulus ad Hebraeos scribens, cum dicit : "hoc enim fecit semel, semet ipsum offerendo hostiam," etc. (*In Rom.* vi. 12, Lom. vii. 69.)[1]

The ransom theory

(1) Secundum voluntatem Patris forma servi suscepta, obtulit victimam pro universo mundo, tradens sanguinem suum principi hujus mundi, secundum sapientiam Dei, quam "nemo principum hujus mundi cognovit : si enim cognovissent, nunquam Dominum majestatis crucifixissent," nec sanguis ille, quem sitierant, non tam sitim, quam vires eorum exstingueret, regnumque destrueret : nec accideret iis illud, quod Dominus in Evangelio dicit : "ecce nunc princeps hujus mundi judicatus est " : et illud "ecce videbam Satanam sicut fulgur cadentem de coelo." (*In Rom.* iv. 11, Lom. vi. 308.)

(2) Κατανόει γάρ, ὅτι ὁ μὲν πατὴρ ὑπὲρ ἡμῶν πάντων παρέδωκεν αὐτὸν ὑπὸ φιλανθρωπίας· αἱ δὲ ἀντικείμεναι δυνάμεις, παραδοῦσαι τὸν Σωτῆρα εἰς χεῖρας ἀνθρώπων, οὐκ ἐσκόπουν τὸ ὑπέρ τινων σωτηρίας παραδιδόναι αὐτόν, ἀλλὰ τὸ ὅσον ἐπ᾽ αὐταῖς, ἐπεὶ οὐδεὶς αὐτῶν ἐγίνωσκε τὴν τοῦ Θεοῦ σοφίαν τὴν ἐν μυστηρίῳ ἀποκεκρυμμένην, παρεδίδουν αὐτὸν ἀποθανούμενον, ἵνα ὁ ἐχθρὸς αὐτοῦ θάνατος ὑποχείριον αὐτὸν λάβῃ, ὁμοίως τοῖς ἐν τῷ Ἀδὰμ ἀποθνήσκουσι. . . . οἶμαι δὲ ἀναγκαίως ἐξητᾶσθαι καὶ ταῦτα, διὰ τὸ τὸν παραδιδόμενον εἰς χεῖρας ἀνθρώπων Ἰησοῦν μὴ ὑπὸ ἀνθρώπων εἰς χεῖρας ἀνθρώπων παραδίδοσθαι, ἀλλ᾽ ὑπὸ δυνάμεων, αἷς ὑπὲρ ἡμῶν πάντων παρέδωκεν ὁ πατὴρ τὸν υἱόν, ἐν αὐτῷ τῷ παραδιδόσθαι, καὶ γίνεσθαι ὑπὸ τοὺς οἷς παρεδόθη, καταλύοντα τὸν τὸ κράτος ἔχοντα τοῦ θανάτου [a quotation from Heb. ii. 14, 15 follows]. (*In Matt.* xiii. 8, Lom. iii. p. 227.) [Origen goes on to explain that we too, when we σύμμορφοι γινόμεθα τῷ θανάτῳ τοῦ Χριστοῦ, likewise pass under the power of the Devil, and then share the triumph of His Resurrection.]

(3) Ἡ γὰρ κατ᾽ εἰκόνα θεοῦ δεδημιουργημένη τιμιωτέρα ἐστὶ πάντων. εἷς μόνος δεδύνηται δοῦναι ἀντάλλαγμα τῆς ἀπολλυμένης πρότερον ψυχῆς ἡμῶν, ὁ ὠνησάμενος ἡμᾶς τῷ ἑαυτοῦ "τιμίῳ αἵματι." (*Exhortatio ad Martyr.* 12, Lom. xx. 12.) [Cf. *In Matt.* xii. 28, Lom. xii. 175, where again the use of the term ἀντάλλαγμα is connected with the quotation of 1 Pet. i. 18, 19.]

(4) Si ergo "pretio emti sumus," ut etiam Paulus adstipulatur, ab aliquo sine dubio emti sumus, cujus eramus servi, qui et pretium poposcit quod voluit, ut de potestate dimitteret quos tenebat. Tenebat autem nos diabolus, cui distracti fueramus peccatis nostris. Poposcit ergo pretium nostrum sanguinem Christi. Verum donec Jesu sanguis daretur, qui tam preciosus fuit, ut solus pro omnium redemtione sufficeret, necessarium fuit eos, qui instituebantur in lege, unum-

---

[1] This will serve as a fair specimen of the passages about the sacrifice of Christ which are quotations or echoes of Scripture. They could of course be multiplied indefinitely.

quemque pro se, velut ad imitationem quandam futurae redemtionis, sanguinem suum dare ; et propterea nos, pro quibus completum est pretium sanguinis Christi, non necesse habemus pro nobis ipsis pretium, id est, sanguinem circumcisionis offerre. (*In Rom.* ii. 13, Lom. vi. 139, 140.)

(5) Videamus attentius, quid sibi velit redemtio quae est in Christo Jesu. Redemtio dicitur id quod datur hostibus pro his, quos in captivitate detinent, ut eos restituant pristinae libertati. Detinebatur ergo apud hostes humani generis captivitas peccato tanquam bello superata : venit Filius Dei qui " factus est nobis " non solum " sapientia a Deo, et justitia, et sanctificatio," sed " et redemtio " : et semet ipsum dedit redemtionem, id est, semet ipsum hostibus tradidit, ac sitientibus iis suum sanguinem fudit : et haec est credentibus facta redemtio, sicut et Petrus in epistola sua scribit, dicens " quia non corruptibili argento vel auro redemti estis, sed pretioso sanguine unigeniti Filii Dei." Hoc fortassis et Salomon sub mysterio designabat, dicens : " redemtio animae viri propriae divitiae ejus." Si enim requiras, quae sint animae propriae divitiae, invenies sapientiam divitias esse, et justitiam, et sanctificationem. Haec autem omnia Christum esse dicit Apostolus. Christus ergo est animae divitiae, et ideo ipse est redemtio ejus. (*In Rom.* iii. 7, Lom. vi. 203-4.)[1]

Christ's death not only an example but the beginning of the victory over devils

Καθὸ δὲ ἄνθρωπος ἦν, παντὸς μᾶλλον ἀνθρώπου κεκοσμημένος τῇ ἄκρᾳ μετοχῇ τοῦ αὐτολόγου, καὶ τῆς αὐτοσοφίας, ὑπέμεινεν, ὡς σοφὸς καὶ τέλειος, ἅπερ ἐχρῆν ὑπομεῖναι τὸν ὑπὲρ παντὸς τοῦ γένους τῶν ἀνθρώπων, ἢ καὶ τῶν λογικῶν, πάντα πράττοντα. Καὶ οὐδὲν ἄτοπον, καὶ ἀποτεθνηκέναι τὸν ἄνθρωπον, καὶ τὸν θάνατον αὐτοῦ οὐ μόνον παράδειγμα ἐκκεῖσθαι τοῦ ὑπὲρ εὐσεβείας ἀποθνήσκειν, ἀλλὰ γὰρ εἰργάσθαι ἀρχὴν καὶ προκοπὴν τῆς καταλύσεως τοῦ πονηροῦ καὶ διαβόλου, πᾶσαν τὴν γῆν νενεμημένου. (*Contra Celsum*, vii. 17, Lom. xx. 28.)

The Devil crucified by Christ's crucifixion

Visibiliter quidem filius Dei in carne crucifixus est, invisibiliter vero in ea cruce diabolus cum principibus suis et potestatibus affixus est cruci. (*In Lib. Jesu Nave Hom.* viii. 3, Lom. xi. 77.)

Propitiation explained ethically

Dicitur tamen agnus, quia voluntas et bonitas ejus, qua Deum repropitiavit hominibus et peccatorum indulgentiam dedit, talis exstitit humano generi quasi agni hostia immaculata et innocens, qua placari

---

[1] I add the last sentences because they show how easily Origen, even when using the language of the ransom theory, drops the traditional language, and passes on to what he most believed in—the moral influence of Christ upon the soul.

hominibus divina creduntur. (*In Num. Hom.* xxiv. 1, Lom. x. 293-4.)

Propitiation as strengthening

Πῶς δ' ἂν παράκλητος καὶ ἱλασμὸς καὶ ἱλαστήριον χωρὶς δυνάμεως Θεοῦ ἐξαφανιζούσης ἡμῶν τὴν ἀσθένειαν γένεσθαι οἷός τε ἦν, ἐπιρρεούσης ταῖς τῶν πιστευόντων ψυχαῖς, ὑπὸ Ἰησοῦ διακονουμένης, ἧς πρωτός ἐστιν, αὐτοδύναμις Θεοῦ, δι' ὃν εἴποι τις ἄν· Πάντα ἰσχύω ἐν τῷ ἐνδυναμοῦντί με Χριστῷ Ἰησοῦ; (*In Joann.* i. 33, Brooke i. 45.)

Meaning of propitiation

"Proposuit" enim intelligitur, quasi prius posuit, hoc est, priusquam esset. Quod enim est, ponitur, quod nondum est, proponitur. Non ergo convenit de eo, qui semper erat, id est, de verbo Dei dici, quia propositus est ; sed de anima ejus, quae, licet inseparabilis sit a Verbo Dei, creata tamen est, et Unigeniti deitate posterior. (*In Rom.* iii. 8, Lom. vi. 212.) [The word "propiatorium" is identified with the mercy-seat which typified the soul of Christ.] Anima haec sancta media quidem fuit inter divinitatem Trinitatis et fragilitatem humanitatis. Haec ergo potest intelligi propiatorium. (*Ib.* p. 209.)

Christ's death compared with cases of voluntary human sacrifice by pagans

Ἆρα γὰρ οὐχ ἑώρων οἱ τοῦ Ἰησοῦ μαθηταί, τολμῶντες οὐ μόνον Ἰουδαίοις ἐκ τῶν προφητικῶν λόγων παριστάνειν, ὅτι οὗτος ἦν ὁ προφητευθείς, ἀλλὰ καὶ τοῖς λοιποῖς ἔθνεσιν, ὅτι ὁ χθὲς καὶ πρώην σταυρωθείς, ἑκὼν τοῦτον τὸν θάνατον ὑπὲρ τῶν ἀνθρώπων γένους ἀνεδέξατο, ἀνάλογον τοῖς ἀποθανοῦσιν ὑπὲρ πατρίδων, ἐπὶ τῷ σβέσαι λοιμικὰ κρατήσαντα καταστήματα, ἢ ἀφορίας, ἢ δυσπλοίας; εἰκὸς γὰρ εἶναι ἐν τῇ φύσει τῶν πραγμάτων, κατά τινας ἀπορρήτους καὶ δυσλήπτους τοῖς πολλοῖς λόγους, φύσιν τοιαύτην, ὡς ἕνα δίκαιον, ὑπὲρ τοῦ κοινοῦ ἀποθανόντα ἑκουσίως, ἀποτροπιασμοὺς ἐμποιεῖν φαύλων δαιμονίων, ἐνεργούντων λοιμοὺς ἢ ἀφορίας, ἢ δυσπλοίας, ἤ τι τῶν παραπλησίων. λεγέτωσαν οὖν οἱ βουλόμενοι ἀπιστεῖν τῷ Ἰησοῦν ὑπὲρ ἀνθρώπων ἀποτεθνηκέναι τρόπῳ σταυροῦ, πότερον οὐδὲ τὰς Ἑλληνικὰς παραδέξονται καὶ βαρβαρικὰς πολλὰς ἱστορίας, περὶ τοῦ τινας ὑπὲρ τοῦ κοινοῦ τεθνηκέναι καθαιρετικῶς τῶν προκαταλαβόντων τὰς πόλεις καὶ τὰ ἔθνη κακῶν; ἢ ἐκεῖνα μὲν γεγένηται, οὐδὲν δὲ πιθανὸν ἔχει ὁ νομιζόμενος ἄνθρωπος πρὸς τὸ ἀποθανεῖν ἐπὶ καθαιρέσει μεγάλου δαίμονος, καὶ δαιμόνων ἄρχοντος, ὑποτάξαντος ὅλας τὰς ἐπὶ γῆν ἐληλυθυίας ἀνθρώπων ψυχάς; (*Contra Celsum*, i. 31, Lom. xviii. 64-5.)

Christ alone (unlike heathen heroes) expiated the sins of the whole world

Περὶ δὲ τοῦ πολλάκις ἐπικρατούντων τινῶν χαλεπῶν ἐν τῷ τῶν ἀνθρώπων γένει, οἷον λοιμῶν ἢ ἐπιβλαβῶν νηνεμιῶν ἢ λιμῶν, λύεσθαι τὰ τοιαῦτα, οἱονεὶ κατουργουμένου τοῦ ἐνεργοῦντος αὐτὰ πονηροῦ

πνεύματος διὰ τὸ ἑαυτόν τινα ὑπὲρ τοῦ κοινοῦ διδόναι, πολλαὶ φέρονται
Ἑλλήνων καὶ βαρβάρων ἱστορίαι, τὴν περὶ τοῦ τοιούτου ἔννοιαν οὐκ
ἀποπτυόντων οὐδὲ ἀποδοκιμαζόντων· πότερον μὲν οὖν ἀληθῆ ἐστι τὰ
τοιαῦτα, ἢ μή, οὐ τοῦ παρόντος ἐστὶ καιροῦ μετ᾽ ἐξετάσεως διαλαβεῖν·
πλὴν ὁ δυνάμενος ὑπὲρ ὅλου κόσμου, ἵνα πᾶς ὁ κόσμος καθαρθῇ,
ἀναδέξασθαι ἐπὶ καθαρσίῳ αὐτοῦ ἀπολομένου ἂν εἰ μὴ ἀνεδέξατο τὸ
ὑπὲρ αὐτοῦ ἀποθανεῖν, οὔτε ἱστόρηται πώποτε οὔτε ἱστορηθῆναι δύναται,
μόνου Ἰησοῦ τὸ πάντων τῆς ἁμαρτίας φορτίον ἐν τῷ ὑπὲρ τῶν ὅλων
χωρὶς Θεοῦ σταυρῷ ἀναλαβεῖν εἰς ἑαυτόν, καὶ βαστάσαι τῇ μεγάλῃ
ἰσχύϊ δεδυνημένου. καὶ γὰρ οὗτος μόνος ἐπιστήμων ἦν τοῦ φέρειν
μαλακίαν, ὥς φησιν ὁ προφήτης Ἡσαΐας λέγων· Ἄνθρωπος ἐν πληγῇ
ὢν καὶ εἰδὼς φέρειν μαλακίαν. καὶ οὗτός γε τὰς ἁμαρτίας ἡμῶν ἔλαβε
καὶ μεμαλάκισται διὰ τὰς ἀνομίας ἡμῶν, καὶ ἡ ὀφειλομένη ἡμῖν εἰς τὸ
παιδευθῆναι καὶ εἰρήνην ἀναλαβεῖν κόλασις ἐπ᾽ αὐτὸν γεγένηται. οὕτω
γὰρ ἀκούω τούτων· Παιδεία εἰρήνης ἡμῶν ἐπ᾽ αὐτόν, κ.τ.λ. [Is. liii. 5.
Other quotations follow from Is. liii. ; Gal. vi. 14, etc.] (*In Joann.*
xxviii. 19, Brooke ii. 135.)

The human soul of Jesus died for man, not the divine Logos

Διὸ καὶ αὐτός φησι· Νῦν δὲ ζητεῖτέ με ἀποκτεῖναι, ἄνθρωπον ὃς
τὴν ἀλήθειαν λελάληκα. καὶ ἐπεὶ ἄνθρωπος μέν ἐστιν ὁ ἀποθανών,
οὐκ ἦν δὲ ἄνθρωπος ἡ ἀλήθεια καὶ ἡ σοφία καὶ εἰρήνη καὶ δικαιοσύνη,
καὶ περὶ οὗ γέγραπται· Θεὸς ἦν ὁ λόγος· οὐκ ἀπέθανεν ὁ Θεὸς Λόγος
καὶ ἡ ἀλήθεια καὶ ἡ σοφία καὶ ἡ δικαιοσύνη· Ἀνεπίδεκτος γὰρ ἡ εἰκὼν
τοῦ Θεοῦ τοῦ ἀοράτου, ὁ πρωτότοκος πάσης κτίσεως, θανάτου. ὑπὲρ
τοῦ λαοῦ δὲ ἀπέθανεν οὗτος ὁ ἄνθρωπος, τὸ πάντων ζῴων καθαρώτερον,
ὅστις τὰς ἁμαρτίας ἡμῶν ἦρε καὶ τὰς ἀσθενείας, ἅτε δυνάμενος πᾶσαν
τὴν ὅλου τοῦ κόσμου ἁμαρτίαν εἰς ἑαυτὸν ἀναλαβὼν λῦσαι καὶ
ἐξαναλῶσαι καὶ ἐξαφανίσαι, ἐπεὶ μὴ ἁμαρτίαν ἐποίησε μηδὲ εὑρέθη
δόλος ἐν τῷ στόματι αὐτοῦ, οὐδὲ ἔγνω ἁμαρτίαν. κατὰ τοῦτο δ᾽ οἶμαι
καὶ τὸν Παῦλον εἰρηκέναι οὕτως· Τὸν μὴ γνόντα ἁμαρτίαν ὑπὲρ ἡμῶν
ἁμαρτίαν ἐποίησεν, ἵνα ἡμεῖς γενώμεθα δικαιοσύνη Θεοῦ ἐν αὐτῷ.
(*In Joann.* xxviii. 18, Brooke ii. 134.)

Christ justifies by example

Propterea enim et in sequentibus adjungit, et dicit de Domino
Jesu : "qui traditus est propter peccata nostra, et resurrexit propter
justificationem nostram" : ut ostendat, quia ea, pro quibus Christus
traditus est, etiam nos abhorrere debeamus et abjicere. . . . Justificat
ergo eos Christus tantummodo, qui novam vitam exemplo resurrectionis
ipsius susceperunt, et vetusta injustitiae atque iniquitatis indumenta vel
ut causam mortis abjiciunt. (*In Rom.* iv. 7, Lom. vi. 281-2.)

The Atonement a mystery

Οὗτος δὴ ὁ ἀμνὸς σφαγεὶς καθάρσιον γεγένηται, κατά τινας ἀπορρήτους λόγους, τοῦ ὅλου κόσμου, ὑπὲρ οὗ κατὰ τὴν τοῦ πατρὸς

φιλανθρωπίαν καὶ τὴν σφαγὴν ἀνεδέξατο, ὠνούμενος τῷ ἑαυτοῦ αἵματι ἀπὸ τοῦ ἁμαρτίαις ἡμᾶς πιπρασκομένους ἀγοράσαντος. (*In Joann.* vi. 53, Brooke i. 172-3.) [Cf. below, c. 54 : ἵν᾽ ἅμα περὶ πάντων ὡς ἀπορρητοτέρων ὄντων καὶ ὑπὲρ ἀνθρωπίνην φύσιν ἀπολογώμεθα.]

Victory over the devils

Φοβερὸς δὲ τούτοις τοῖς πνεύμασι γενόμενος ὁ σωτήρ, ἀφαιρεῖ αὐτὰ ἐνεργούντων [*forte leg.* ἐνεργουμένων] ᾧ αὐτὸς οἶδε καιρῷ, ἵνα μετανοή- σωσιν. (*Selecta in Psalmos, Ps.* lxxv., Lom. xiii. 16.)

Explanation of " slaying the enmity "

Hoc ergo modo etiam Christus occidit inimicitiam in carne sua, cum morte suscepta exemplum dedit hominibus usque ad mortem resistere adversum peccatum. (*In Rom.* iv. 12, Lom. vi. 313.)

Deification explained ethically

Κἂν γὰρ τηρῇ ὁ σωτήρ, ὅτι ὃν ἐφόρεσεν, ἄνθρωπος ἦν· ἀλλ᾽ εἰ καὶ ἦν ἄνθρωπος, ἀλλὰ νῦν οὐδαμῶς ἐστιν ἄνθρωπος. " εἰ γὰρ ἔγνωμεν Χριστὸν κατὰ σάρκα, ἀλλὰ νῦν οὐκέτι γινώσκομεν," φησὶν ὁ ἀπόστολος. ἐγὼ δι᾽ αὐτὸν οὐκέτι εἰμὶ ἄνθρωπος, ἐὰν ἀκολουθῶ αὐτοῦ τοῖς λόγοις· ἀλλὰ λέγει, "ἐγὼ εἶπα· θεοί ἐστε, καὶ υἱοὶ ὑψίστου πάντες." οὐκοῦν ὡς "πρωτότοκός ἐστιν ἐκ τῶν νεκρῶν," οὕτω γέγονε πρωτότοκος πάντων ἀνθρώπων, εἰς θεὸν μεταβαλών. (*In Ierem. Hom.* xv. 6, Lom. xv. 288.)

The ransom and deification

Dei igitur sumus, secundum quod ab eo creati sumus. Effecti vero sumus servi diaboli, secundum quod peccatis nostris venundati sumus. Veniens autem Christus redemit nos, cum serviremus illi Domino, cui nosmet ipsos peccando vendidimus. Et ita videtur tanquam suos quidem recepisse, quos creaverat, tanquam alienos autem acquisisse, quia alienum sibi dominum sive errando sive peccando quaesiverant. Et fortasse recte quidem dicitur redemisse nos Christus, qui pretium nostri sanguinem suum dedit. Quid tale autem, ut nos mercaretur etiam diabolus dedit ? Ergo, si videtur, ausculta. Homicidium pecunia diaboli est. Ille enim ab initio homicida est. Fecisti homicidium : diaboli pecuniam suscepisti. Adulterium diaboli pecunia est. Diaboli enim in eo imago est, et superscriptio. Commisisti adulterium : accepisti diaboli numisma. Furtum, falsum testimonium, rapacitas, violentia, haec omnia diaboli census est, et diaboli thesaurus. Talis enim pecunia de ejus moneta procedit. Hac igitur pecunia emit ille quos emit, et efficit sibi servos omnes qui hujuscemodi censu ejus quantulumcunque susceperint. (*In Ex. Hom.* vi. 9, Lom. ix. 68, 69.)

CONTINUATION OF LECTURE IV

LATER GREEK FATHERS

After the time of Origen there can hardly be said to have been in the East any new or original thought with regard to the atonement. The ideas already thrown out by the apostolical fathers and the apologists, by Irenaeus and Origen, are further developed and combined in various proportions. And the result is a view of the whole subject which was higher or lower very much in proportion to the extent to which the influence of Origen predominated over that of other elements, and in proportion as his teaching was really understood. The high level of Origen's theology was not continuously maintained. There is a tendency to materialize and literalize thoughts which in him were spiritually, philosophically, and ethically intended, and to relapse into the more confused and less ethical ideas of Irenaeus. Origen's metaphorical language about the transaction with the Devil was imitated, but understood with much greater literalness. The notion of an ethical restoration of humanity through the influence of Christ to that divine ideal which it was originally intended to realize was degraded into the notion of a metaphysical, or almost physical, transmutation of the human body from a corruptible into an incorruptible body through the sympathetic influence of Christ's triumph over the powers of evil, His sinlessness and His resurrection. And the channel of this regenerating influence is chiefly the sacraments, thought of in a more mechanical or, at all events, a more thaumaturgic and less ethical sense than was the case with Origen. It is chiefly through baptism that the forgiveness of sins is connected with the death of Christ, the nature of the connexion being usually quite unexplained except by hardening St. Paul's metaphors [1] into literal fact. The eucharist is the "medicine of immortality" which acts in an almost physical manner upon the soul and body of the recipient. The idea of substituted punishment or expiation, though rarely emphasized, appears occasionally. Finally, Origen's bolder and more universal-

[1] Rom. vi. 3, 4 ; Col. ii. 12.

288

istic thoughts about the future destiny of souls were reproduced only by a few writers who were definitely disciples of Origen, such as Gregory of Nyssa.   The idea of everlasting torments became the dominant, traditional, and conventional opinion, though it may be denied that the Origenistic view was ever condemned by any really general Council.[1]   This lowering of tone characterizes different writers in very different degrees; some of them were bold thinkers, others timid; some of them were men of philosophic mind, others mere exegetes, polemists, or ecclesiastical politicians.   But in all of them the nobler thoughts reappear to some extent.   In all of them Christ is thought of as the great Revealer of God.   In all of them the thought of His death is subordinate to that of His incarnation and His life as a whole. In all of them salvation is attributed to the influence of His life, teaching, and resurrection as well as to His death.   In all of them the death of Christ, whatever else it was, was a revelation of God's love.   Greek theology never descended to the level with which we have already made acquaintance in Tertullian or to the still deeper level of degradation which was eventually reached by the theology of the West.

Further than this it is scarcely possible to generalize.   One of the most instructive effects of any serious study of the subject is to exhibit the great variety of opinion which prevailed and which was tolerated upon this subject.   Orthodoxy in the patristic period (as Harnack so frequently points out) consisted in a correct belief as to the doctrine of the Trinity, to which in the later patristic age was added a correct belief as to the relations of the two natures in Christ.   As to the atonement or the conditions of justification no authoritative definitions were attempted, and wide liberty prevailed.   The bare formula, " Christ died for our sins," was binding—little more.   I propose briefly to notice the view of the leading Greek theologians of the later patristic age ; but there can be no better illustration of the way in which the doctrine of the atonement was subordinate to, and merged in, that of the incarnation than the fact that in many important and voluminous writers it is scarcely possible to find an allusion to the death of Christ which amounts to anything like a theory of the atonement.

HIPPOLYTUS, BISHOP OF ROME [2] (wrote A.D. 190–235)

The last remark is conspicuously true of Hippolytus, who, in

---

[1] See note in Bigg, *Christian Platonists*, 2nd ed. p. 325, and the authorities there referred to.

[2] It is now generally admitted that the work called *Philosophumena*, formerly attributed to Origen and edited as such by Miller, must be attributed to Hippolytus.   I have used Miller's edition ; other works and fragments are printed by Migne (*Pat. Graec.* x.).

spite of the fact that he was Bishop or Pope or (as later Roman pontiffs held) Anti-pope of Rome, may for the present purpose be treated as a Greek father. He wrote in Greek, and was a disciple of Origen : he was indeed the man who for the first time introduced the scientific theology of the Logos into the eminently unphilosophical, practical, and rhetorically minded Church of Rome, the traditions of which lay in the direction of Sabellianism. He became the orthodox rival of the legitimate but practically Sabellian Pope Callistus. In his elaborate *Philosophumena* or *Refutation of Heresies* there is hardly so much as an allusion to the atonement or the doctrine of salvation until the very last chapter. In that chapter the purpose of believing in Christ is represented to be " that you may learn from us who is the true God and what is His orderly creation," and that " by that knowledge ye may escape the threatened judgement of fire that is coming." Further, this instruction will carry with it immortality and deification.[1] He concludes with an appeal to his readers not to put off repentance. " For Christ is the God who is over all, who has commanded us to wash off sin from men, making the old man new, since he has called man an image of Himself from the beginning in figure, thus symbolizing His longing for thee, to whose holy commandments being obedient, and becoming a good imitator of the good One, thou shalt be honoured by Him and become like Him. For God hath need of thee and hath made thee a God unto His glory : " or, as he puts it in the same chapter, " thou shalt have thy body immortal and incorruptible together with thy soul, and thou shalt receive the Kingdom of Heaven, thou that hast lived on earth and known the heavenly King, and shalt be a companion (ὁμιλητής) of God, and a joint-heir with Christ, not enslaved to lusts or passions and diseases : for thou hast become a god." [2] And in the next sentence this being made a god is explained as equivalent to having become immortal.

Here it will be observed that the purpose of the incarnation (including the resurrection) is to confer on mankind, (1) the knowledge of God, (2) immortality and moral transformation. The salvation thus offered was secured by knowledge or belief, repentance, obedience, and the imitation of Christ. There is simply no allusion at all to any special efficacy of Christ's death. And the forgiveness of sins seems to be (as not unfrequently in the earlier fathers) simply the act of the Logos, rather than something which by His sufferings Christ has won from the Father. It is Christ's command that sins shall be forgiven. Salvation is the

---

[1] *Phil.* x. 34. Cf. *Discourse on the Holy Theophany*, 8 : " If then man has become immortal, he will also be a God. And if he be made a God by water and the Holy Spirit after the regeneration of the laver, he is found also a fellow-heir with Christ after the resurrection from the dead."

[2] *Phil.* x. 34.

work of Christ because of this command, and because it was dependent upon the knowledge of God which was due to the fact of the incarnation and the teaching of the Incarnate.

In a fragment of his work against Beron and Helicon, there is a passage in which he does connect the salvation of men in some special way with the death of Christ, or rather with His sufferings :

"For on this account has the God of all things become man, in order that by suffering in the flesh, which is susceptible of suffering, He might redeem (λυτρώσηται) our whole race, which was sold to death ; and that, by working wondrous things by His divinity, which was insusceptible of suffering, through the medium of the flesh, he might restore it to that undefiled and blessed life from which it fell away by yielding to the devil : and that He might harden the holy orders of intelligent existences in the heavens into immutability (εἰς ἀτρεψίαν) by the mystery of His incarnation (σωματώσεως), the purpose (ἔργον) of which is the recapitulation of all things into Himself . . . to the intent that He might be believed to be God, while working out of Himself (αὐτουργῶν) by the flesh, which is by nature weak, the salvation of the whole." [1]

It will be observed that after all salvation is mainly attributed to the incarnation : in a previous sentence of the same fragment he speaks of the "saving act of the incarnation." So far as any intelligible connexion is established between the sufferings of Christ and the redemption, it would seem that the sufferings are regarded simply as a necessary consequence of the incarnation : and perhaps a demonstration of its reality. The saving effects here seem to follow as a sort of direct metaphysical consequence from the union of deity and humanity in Christ, but in the light of other passages it is clear that the idea of salvation through knowledge and the moral effects of knowledge is more prominent with him than with Irenaeus. His doctrine of redemption is based upon Irenaeus, but upon Irenaeus interpreted in a more philosophical spirit than his own.

When Hippolytus does more directly connect salvation with the death upon the cross, it is usually in connexion with baptism. Thus in the conclusion of the *Discourse on the Holy Theophany*, he says: "He who goes down with faith to the laver of regeneration, who ranges himself against the Devil, with Christ, who renounces the enemy, and makes the confession that Christ is God ; he puts off the bondage, and puts on the adoption of a son ; he comes up from baptism brilliant as the sun," etc. [2]

---

[1] Fragment 2 in Migne, *Pat. Gr.* x. 833. There are one or two vague references to the cross in "Christ and Anti-Christ " (4, 59).
[2] *Theophan.* 10.

It is probable that Hippolytus would have said that the death of Christ was in some way the cause or source of this purifying power of baptism, but it will be observed that it is to the confession and the renunciation and the faith which resulted from previous instruction that he primarily attributes the moral transformation —not simply to the ritual act. There is no direct reference to the transaction with the Devil : it may underlie such expressions as "He is crowned victor over the Devil"[1] or "hiding the dignity of the Divinity, that He may elude the snares of the dragon";[2] but the first of these passages refers explicitly to victory at the temptation, and presumably the second also, since it follows a reference to the teaching of the Baptist.[3]

METHODIUS, BISHOP OF OLYMPUS, AFTERWARDS OF PATARA (fl. c. A.D. 300)

Methodius was an opponent of Origenism, but a philosophical opponent, being in fact much more of a Platonist, except as regards the theory of pre-existence and all that went with it, than Origen himself. As a theologian, he was in the main a follower of Irenaeus : his millenarianism is still more decided. While we can hardly attribute to him any definitely new theory of the atonement, the following points of view are noticeable :

(1) He pushes St. Paul's doctrine of the second Adam and Irenaeus' theory of recapitulation to the point of literally identifying Christ with Adam. Adam was "not only the type and image of Christ, but also the very same thing—Christ, because the eternal Word descended upon him : for it was fitting that the oldest of the aeons and the first of the archangels, when about to hold communion with men, should dwell in the oldest and the first of men, even Adam."[4] The Logos was already incarnate in Adam : the redemption was effected not merely by the same humanity which fell but by the same individual man.

(2) He develops the Pauline idea that by the act of baptism (special emphasis being laid upon the faith and the knowledge implied in baptism) Christ is spiritually born again in the believer, who thereby becomes himself a Christ.[5] There is thus a sort of

---

[1] *Contra Noetum*, 18 : στεφανοῦται κατὰ διαβόλου.

[2] *Theophan.* 4.

[3] Cf. Fragment 7, Migne c. 865 : The Word "declared Him who hung on the tree to be Lord over the conqueror, and thus through the tree He is found victor." There is another such reference in a passage quoted by Rivière from *In Cant. Magn.* frag. 2, ed. Achelis, p. 83. All these references only imply the view which we found in Origen (see above, p. 259 *sq.*), not the legal theory of Tertullian, etc.

[4] *Conviv. Virgin.* iii. 4 : οὐ μόνον τύπον αὐτὸν ἡγούμενος εἶναι καὶ εἴκονα, ἀλλὰ καὶ αὐτὸ τοῦτο Χριστὸν καὶ αὐτὸν γεγονέναι διὰ τὸ τὸν πρὸ αἰώνων εἰς αὐτὸν ἐγκατασκῆψαι λόγον, κ.τ.λ.

[5] *Conviv.* viii. 8 : ἐγὼ γὰρ τὸν ἄρσενα [Rev. xii. 5] ταύτῃ γεννᾶν εἰρῆσθαι νομίζω τὴν ἐκκλησίαν, ἐπειδὴ τοὺς χαρακτῆρας καὶ τὴν ἐκτύπωσιν καὶ τὴν ἀρρενωπίαν

fresh incarnation of the Logos in the Church and in each individual member of it. Almost equal stress is laid upon each
side of the matter—the presence of Christ in the Church and in
each individual.

(3) Methodius' doctrine, like that of Irenaeus, is in the main
salvation through the incarnation. He held that "the Word
has assumed the nature of man, in order that, having overcome
the serpent, man might by Himself reverse the condemnation unto
death which had been pronounced against him. For it was fitting
that the evil one should be overcome by no other, but by him
whom he had deceived, and whom he was boasting that he had subdued ; because no otherwise was it possible that the sin and the condemnation should be destroyed, unless that same man on whose
account it had been said, ' Dust thou art, and unto dust thou
shalt return,' should be created anew, and undo the sentence which
had gone forth against all," etc.[1] The transaction with the Devil
may lie in the background of this statement, but it is not explicitly
said in what way humanity in Christ "destroyed sin and condemnation." Since He did so by being "created anew," it is
hardly probable that the death is specially thought of. It was
rather by overcoming temptation that the conquest was effected,
and when a special efficacy is attributed to the Passion, it is chiefly
the victory over death, and so over the demons, in the resurrection
that the writer seems always to have in mind.[2]

(4) In Methodius we hear much about salvation by faith.
And yet his principal writing is an extravagant laudation of
virginity. Even the efficacy of Christ's conquest over the Devil
is largely the efficacy of His virginity : " from the time when
Christ became man, and adorned and armed His flesh with
virginity, the savage tyrant who was lord of incontinence was
taken away, and peace and faith have dominion, men no longer
turning so much as before to idolatry."[3] And salvation seems
at times to be definitely secured by obedience to Christ's
supposed command in this respect. " The law was not of itself
sufficient to free humanity from corruption, until virginity, succeeding the law, governed man by the precepts of Christ."[4]

τοῦ Χριστοῦ προσλαμβάνουσιν οἱ φωτιζόμενοι, τῆς καθ᾿ ὁμοίωσιν μορφῆς ἐν αὐτοῖς
ἐκτυπουμένης τοῦ λόγου καὶ ἐν αὐτοῖς γεννωμένης κατὰ τὴν ἀκριβῆ γνῶσιν καὶ πίστιν·
ὥστε ἐν ἑκάστῳ γεννᾶσθαι τὸν Χριστὸν νοητῶς· καὶ διὰ τοῦτο ἡ ἐκκλησία σπαργᾷ
καὶ ὠδίνει, μέχριπερ ἂν ὁ Χριστὸς ἐν ἡμῖν μορφωθῇ γεννηθείς, ὅπως ἕκαστος τῶν
ἁγίων τῷ μετέχειν Χριστοῦ Χριστὸς γεννηθῇ. Καθ᾿ ὃν λόγον καὶ ἔν τινι γραφῇ
φέρεται, "μὴ ἅψησθε τῶν Χριστῶν μου," . . οἱονεὶ Χριστῶν γεγονότων τῶν κατὰ
μετουσίαν τοῦ πνεύματος εἰς Χριστὸν βεβαπτισμένων, συμβαλλούσης ἐνταῦθα τὴν
ἐν τῷ λόγῳ τρανῶσιν αὐτῶν καὶ μεταμόρφωσιν τῆς ἐκκλησίας. The idea that all
Christians are Christs is already found in Origen ; see above, p. 258.
[1] *Conviv.* iii. 6.
[2] See the fragments from the Homily *De Sancta Cruce.*
[3] *Conviv.* x. 1. ' Cf. cap. 4.   [4] *Conviv.* x. 1.

(5) The extremely monastic (and Pelagian) tone of these doctrines is obvious. Emphasis on the death of Christ is at a minimum ; and the necessity even of the incarnation turns chiefly upon the influence of Christ's example and precepts, especially in the matter of virginity. It might be said that according to Methodius the supreme purpose of the incarnation is to make virginity possible, and thus to immortalize the human body. "Who was ever able to receive Christ or the Spirit perfectly, unless he first purified himself? For the asceticism (ἄσκησις) which exercises the soul from childhood unto desirable and delectable glory, and carries this self-restraint into the soul so that it becomes capable of resisting any temptation with ease, and at the cost of small toils achieves for itself mighty hopes, is chastity, which gains immortality to our bodies." [1]

Harnack concludes his treatment of Methodius with the following remarks : "The theology of Methodius was in the Eastern Church, like Tertullian's in the West, a prophecy of the future. His method of combining tradition and speculation was not quite attained even by the Cappadocians of the fourth century. Men like Cyril of Alexandria were the first to resemble him. *In Methodius we have already the final stage of Greek theology.*" [2]

ATHANASIUS, BISHOP OF ALEXANDRIA (*c.* A.D. 296–373)

Athanasius is sometimes spoken of as the one Greek father, or at all events the first of them, who imitated the Latins in emphasizing the idea of the atonement as distinguished from that of the incarnation.[3] It is true that there is more emphasis on the fall and on the atoning efficacy of Christ's death than in some other Greek fathers : as against the Arians he continually insists that only a really divine being could effect the work of redemption. But the spirit of his theology is on the whole the Greek spirit. It is true he was very unspeculative, very little of a thinker. His theological system is arrived at chiefly by way of exegesis, and the religious interest is stronger than the intellectual. But his view of redemption is still in great part ethical and intelligible. He is not in the habit of speaking of Christ's death as a vicarious punishment, but the idea is in the background of his thought to this extent—that he does represent the death of Christ as due to the necessity that the divine threat of death should somehow be

---

[1] *Conviv.* x. 6.
[2] *History of Dogma*, iii. p. 111.
[3] Harnack's statement that Athanasius "referred everything to the thought of redemption" seems to be only true if we give "redemption" a very much higher and wider meaning than it bears in St. Augustine or in Luther.

fulfilled.[1] For God to have restored the forfeited gift of incorruption upon mere repentance would have been inconsistent with the veracity of God.[2] Man must die, and die by the particular form of death which involved a curse.[3] That threat was somehow fulfilled by the death of Christ—that is to say, the death of His body, for Christ is to Athanasius simply the Logos inhabiting a human body. If He did possess a soul at all, that was simply the natural or animal soul which was so closely connected with the body that it might be said to be simply the life of the body : rational soul or human intellect He had none. Athanasius uses without explanation such conventional terms as " sacrifice " or " ransom," and speaks indifferently of the death as being instead (ἀντί) of all and on behalf (ὑπέρ) of all. The clearest statement that he ever makes as to the effects which flow from Christ's death is contained in the following passage : " For the Logos knowing that the corruption of men could not be undone, unless at all costs there was a death, and it was not possible for the Word to die, being immortal and the Son of the Father, for this reason He takes to Himself the body that can die, so that this body participating in the Word who is above all, may become liable to death on behalf of all, and on account of the indwelling Word, may remain immortal, and in future the corruption may cease in all by the grace of His resurrection. Whence, as a victim and a sacrifice free from all blemish, carrying unto death the body which He took unto Himself, He made death to disappear in all his likes by the offering of an equivalent. For the Word of God, being above all, presenting His own temple and His bodily organ as an equivalent for the life of all, fittingly discharged the debt which was owing to Death : and thus the incorruptible Son of God, dwelling with all through that which was like them, fittingly clothed all with incorruptibility in the promise of His resurrection."[4]

[1] De Incarnatione Verbi, vi.
[2] 'Αλλ' ἡ μετάνοια οὔτε τὸ εὔλογον τὸ πρὸς τὸν Θεὸν ἐφύλαττεν· ἔμενε γὰρ πάλιν οὐκ ἀληθής, μὴ κρατουμένων ἐν τῷ θανάτῳ τῶν ἀνθρώπων (De Incarn. vii. 3. I have used Bishop Robertson's edition of this work). Moreover, he goes on to say that forgiveness by itself would not have restored incorruptibility, and in that case God's original design in creating man would have been frustrated.
[3] Ib. xxv. 2.
[4] Συνιδὼν γὰρ ὁ Λόγος, ὅτι ἄλλως οὐκ ἂν λυθείη τῶν ἀνθρώπων ἡ φθορά, εἰ μὴ διὰ τοῦ πάντως ἀποθανεῖν, οὐχ οἷόν τε ἦν τὸν Λόγον ἀποθανεῖν ἀθάνατον ὄντα καὶ τοῦ Πατρὸς Υἱόν, τούτου ἕνεκεν τὸ δυνάμενον ἀποθανεῖν ἑαυτῷ λαμβάνει σῶμα, ἵνα τοῦτο τοῦ ἐπὶ πάντων Λόγου μεταλαβόν, ἀντὶ πάντων ἱκανὸν γένηται τῷ θανάτῳ, καὶ διὰ τὸν ἐνοικήσαντα Λόγον ἄφθαρτον διαμείνῃ, καὶ λοιπὸν ἀπὸ πάντων ἡ φθορὰ παύσηται τῇ τῆς ἀναστάσεως χάριτι. ὅθεν ὡς ἱερεῖον καὶ θῦμα παντὸς ἐλεύθερον σπίλου, ὃ αὐτὸς ἑαυτῷ ἔλαβε σῶμα προσάγων εἰς θάνατον, ἀπὸ πάντων εὐθὺς τῶν ὁμοίων ἠφάνιζε τὸν θάνατον τῇ προσφορᾷ τοῦ καταλλήλου. ὑπὲρ πάντας γὰρ ὢν ὁ Λόγος τοῦ Θεοῦ εἰκότως τὸν ἑαυτοῦ ναὸν καὶ τὸ σωματικὸν ὄργανον προσάγων ἀντίψυχον ὑπὲρ πάντων ἐπλήρου τὸ ὀφειλόμενον ἐν τῷ θανάτῳ καὶ οὕτως συνὼν διὰ τοῦ ὁμοίου τοῖς πᾶσιν ὁ ἄφθαρτος τοῦ Θεοῦ Υἱός, εἰκότως τοὺς πάντας ἐνέδυσεν ἀφθαρσίαν ἐν τῇ ἀναστάσεως ἐπαγγελίᾳ (ib. ix. 1). The following chapter should also be read, but it only expands the same idea.

This is a definite doctrine of substitutionary sacrifice, though not, in express words, of substitutionary punishment. The idea seems to be that by the death of such a victim the debt of death—incurred by Adam's sin—was satisfied, and satisfied in the case of all who shared that humanity with which in the case of the one body the Word was united. More clearly than in Irenaeus, the death of Christ is represented as not merely equivalent to, but actually identical with, the death of all:[1] all literally did die in the death of the One. The stress is, however, not upon the retrospective act of sacrifice, but upon the regenerative effects which followed, and followed from the resurrection rather than from the death.

In this passage Athanasius goes very near to the characteristic Western view that the Word became incarnate chiefly that He might be able to die, and approximates to the later view of "satisfaction" afterwards developed by Anselm. But though the death of Christ is with Athanasius the *conditio sine qua non* of redemption, it is not the real source of it. For redemption with him does not mean only or primarily forgiveness of past sin: such forgiveness, he admits, the Father might perhaps vouchsafe on man's repentance.[2] But repentance would not by itself remove the "corruption" involved in the fall. The essence of redemption is the restoration to man's body of that incorruptibility which was lost by the fall. This is the line of thought which we have already encountered in Irenaeus, but in Athanasius it is much more developed and systematized. He seeks to represent corruptibility not as an arbitrary penalty imposed by God, but as the natural and inevitable consequence of sin. Man was not by nature incorruptible or immortal. His body, and apparently even his rational soul, were by nature mortal. But man alone among the animals was made "in the image of God"; that is to say, on him alone was bestowed the gift of reason, which carried with it the chance of winning incorruption by freely acting in accordance with reason. This gift was due to participation in the Logos.[3] Had man always retained this resemblance,

---

[1] Τὸ μὲν οὖν σῶμα, ὡς καὶ αὐτὸ κοινὴν ἔχον τοῖς πᾶσι τὴν οὐσίαν· σῶμα γὰρ ἦν ἀνθρώπινον . . . ὁ πάντων θάνατος ἐν τῷ Κυριακῷ σώματι ἐπληροῦτο (*De Incarn.* xx. 4, 5).

[2] *Ib.* vii. 2, 3: though even so there remains the difficulty of the unfulfilled threat of death.

[3] Οὐχ ἁπλῶς, ὥσπερ πάντα τὰ ἐπὶ γῆς ἄλογα ζῷα, ἔκτισε τοὺς ἀνθρώπους· ἀλλὰ κατὰ τὴν ἑαυτοῦ εἰκόνα ἐποίησεν αὐτούς, μεταδοὺς αὐτοῖς καὶ τῆς τοῦ ἰδίου Λόγου δυνάμεως, ἵνα ὥσπερ σκιάς τινας ἔχοντες τοῦ Λόγου καὶ γενόμενοι λογικοί, διαμένειν ἐν μακαριότητι δυνηθῶσι (*De Incarn.* iii. 3). The following sentences seem to suggest that Athanasius supposed that after the fall man actually ceased to be immortal; the souls of men died with their bodies and remained dead till the work of Christ restored immortality to body and soul alike. Athanasius does not (like Augustine) hold that there would have been no physical death but for the fall: had man avoided sin, he had τῆς ἐν οὐρανοῖς ἀφθαρσίας . . . τὴν ἐπαγγελίαν (*ib.* 4).

the natural corruptibility would have been changed into incorruptibility.[1] By the fall this capacity of winning incorruption
was lost : " the reasonable man made after the image " was in
the process of disappearance, though it had not disappeared
altogether. And this lost image and capacity of incorruption
could only be restored by and through Him from whom it was
originally derived. Just as a portrait which has lost its resemblance
to its original through age and ill-usage can only have that resemblance restored by the man sitting again to the painter, so the
image of God, blurred and defaced by sin, could only be restored
by the renewed contact of humanity with its divine original.[2]
This renewal of contact was effected by the incarnation.

To the one body in which the Logos took up His abode incorruption was *ipso facto*, as a sort of physical consequence, restored.[3]
By some process which is never fully explained, and which perhaps
at bottom very much resembles the " sympathetic magic " of
primitive man, the effects of this contact are supposed to extend
to humanity in general.[4] But so far as the process is explained
at all, the restoration would seem to be due to ethical and intelligible consequences of Christ's work. The renewed power of
resisting sin and winning back incorruption is traced to the confidence inspired by Christ's miracles, to the effects of His teaching
and example, above all to the hope inspired by the resurrection.
So far, redemption is effected through the subjective effect of
Christ's work upon the soul ; but a sort of direct, physical, or
metaphysical effect of the incarnation upon the soul, very much in
the sense of Irenaeus, seems to be contemplated too. On any interpretation, redemption is due to the incarnation as a whole, of which
the crucifixion is only an incident, though a necessary incident.

Elaborate reasons are, indeed, given why the particular mode
of death should be a death upon the cross—some of them rather
childish reasons. It must not be death by disease, for that might
suggest that the Word was weak, and it was unbecoming that He
who was to heal the diseases of others should Himself suffer from
disease. It would be unseemly for Him who was the Life to
cause His own death : the death must be due to others. It must
be public in order that the triumph over death might be equally
so. It must be a mode of death devised by His enemies, lest it
should be supposed that the Word could only overcome a particular
kind of death chosen by Himself. The body must not be divided,
lest a divided body should supply arguments for schismatics who

---

[1] Διὰ δὲ τὴν πρὸς τὸν ὄντα ὁμοιότητα, ἣν εἰ ἐφύλαττε διὰ τῆς πρὸς αὐτὸν [God]
κατανοήσεως, ἤμβλυνεν ἂν τὴν κατὰ φύσιν φθοράν, καὶ ἔμεινεν ἄφθαρτος (*De Incarn.*
iv. 6).

[2] *Ib.* xiv.   [3] *Ib.* xx. 4, cf. xli.-xlv.

[4] It had also the effect of destroying the power of magic and producing the cessation
of the Oracles (*ib.* xxxi.).

wished to divide the mystical body of Christ. It must be the death to which a curse was specially annexed by prophecy. It must involve the lifting up of the hands in order that the Christ might seem to invite or draw all men unto Him. He must suffer in the air in order to purify it of demons.[1] But all these considerations are really subordinate to what in Athanasius is the supreme purpose both of the incarnation and of the death, *i.e.* the preparing the way for the resurrection of Christ which carried with it as a sort of physical consequence the restoration of the potential incorruptibility of man's body lost by the fall. Here again it is not clear whether the resurrection is supposed to restore incorruption simply by the hope and consequent power of right-doing inspired by it or by some sort of physical or metaphysical participation in the incorruptibility of the risen body. But it is certain that for Athanasius the resurrection is the real source of redemption.[2] For him as much as for Clement of Alexandria the supreme purpose of the incarnation, of which the death of the Saviour is but a subordinate aspect, was the deification of man. " He became man, that we might be made gods." [3]

On the whole Athanasius' scheme of redemption belongs to the higher, Hellenic type of thought about the matter. It is free from the more objectionable features of Western orthodox theories. But much of it is difficult to appropriate or to modernize, because it is so much bound up with quite unmodern notions about an essential difference between corruptible and incorruptible matter. We can attach no real meaning to the idea that all human bodies were made corruptible through the sin of one man, and had the quality of incorruptibility restored to them—as a sort of physical consequence—by the indwelling of the Logos in the body of Jesus. Moreover, on one side the appeal which the orthodox view of the atonement makes to religious feeling is conspicuously wanting in Athanasius. Athanasius does, indeed, say much about the condescension and philanthropy of the Word in submitting to become a man. Redemption is with him no act of arbitrary grace : he does not think of God as acquitting some and condemning others when He might quite justly have

---

[1] *De Incarn.* xxi.-xxv.

[2] Cf. a passage of that characteristically Greek father Apollinarius : θανάτῳ δὲ παραδοὺς τὴν σάρκα τὸν θάνατον ἔλυσε διὰ τῆς ἀναστάσεως εἰς τὴν πάντων ἡμῖν ἀνάστασιν ('Η κατὰ μέρος πίστις 35, ed. Lietzmann p. 181).

[3] Αὐτὸς γὰρ ἐνηνθρώπησεν ἵνα ἡμεῖς θεοποιηθῶμεν (*De Incarnatione Verbi*, liv. 3). The above account of Athanasius' doctrine of redemption is derived entirely from this very early treatise. In his later works the conceptions of salvation and deification through the incarnation are still more prominent, and there are few passages of a substitutionary or expiatory character. (The difference is much insisted upon by Dr. Melville Scott in his *Athanasius on the Atonement*.) But since this early treatise, in spite of its name, is really a treatise upon redemption, and we have no other work especially devoted to that subject, it would be rash to assume that Athanasius had deliberately changed his view.

condemned all.   It would have been " unseemly," and therefore impossible, for God not to have provided a way of recovery to fallen man : for that would imply the failure of God's whole purpose in making man, which was a loving design to bring into existence rational beings capable of winning incorruptibility.[1] So far he does represent the atonement as a revelation of God's love.   But after all the Word, like the Father, was incapable of suffering.   He does, indeed, speak of Christ's body as " suffering," but it seems doubtful whether this implies more than submission (for the moment) to the physical change implied in death, and reversed by the bodily resurrection.   We can only suppose the Christ of Athanasius to have felt pain, weariness, sympathy, and the like, if we attribute to that father the crude notion—so clearly exposed by Aristotle—that pain is an affection of the body and not of the mind.   It is, indeed, possible that he may have supposed that the flesh included the animal soul, but he can hardly have thought this as regards the rational soul.   There is no evidence that he believed that there was any conscious mind in Christ except the divine Logos.

The thought of Athanasius about the effect of Christ's death hovers between a vague metaphysic and a purely ethical theory of redemption.   Much of his language may be said to be modern enough and true enough if we understand it of the ethical effects of the incarnation rather than of its metaphysical influence upon an abstract, universal humanity ; much of that language was certainly meant to be, and more of it may be, understood in this purely ethical sense.   We cannot say that it was intended to be wholly ethical.   And in one respect, as we have seen, Athanasius' Christology hardly allows him to present the atonement in its most truly ethical light.   A Christ who did not really feel pain or sorrow or sympathy cannot reveal the love of God as may be done by one who is thought of as fully human, while also in a unique sense divine.   The Catholic Church had overcome Docetism so far as to believe in the reality of Christ's human body : but after all, Athanasius' Christ was not really, but only appeared to be, a man.[2]   It is true that in his later Orations

---

[1] Οὐκ ἄξιον γὰρ ἦν τῆς ἀγαθότητος τοῦ Θεοῦ τὰ ὑπ' αὐτοῦ γενόμενα διαφθείρεσθαι (De Incarn. vi. 4).

[2] The following is a very clear instance : ὅταν τοίνυν ἐσθίοντα καὶ τικτόμενον αὐτὸν λέγωσιν οἱ περὶ τούτου θεολόγοι, γίνωσκε ὅτι τὸ μὲν σῶμα, ὡς σῶμα, ἐτίκτετο καὶ καταλλήλοις ἐτρέφετο τροφαῖς, αὐτὸς δὲ ὁ συνὼν τῷ σώματι Θεὸς Λόγος τὰ πάντα διακοσμῶν, καὶ δι' ὧν εἰργάζετο ἐν σώματι οὐκ ἄνθρωπον ἑαυτόν, ἀλλὰ Θεὸν Λόγον ἐγνώριζεν (De Incarn. xviii. 1).   In the next sentence he uses the word "suffering" (πάσχον), but continues : ἔπρεπε καὶ ταῦτα ὡς περὶ ἀνθρώπου λέγεσθαι (notice the ὡς).   Πάσχον therefore does not necessarily imply consciousness of pain.   In xxi. 7 he admits that Christ hungered διὰ τὸ ἴδιον τοῦ σώματος, ἀλλ' οὐ λίμῳ διέφθαρη διὰ τὸν φοροῦντα αὐτὸ Κύριον.   Athanasius constantly denies that Christ was ἄνθρωπός. Cf. Orat. contra Arianos, iii. 34.   I assume that the treatise against Apollinarius attributed to Athanasius is not genuine.

against the Arians he often asserts the contrary, and in one place expressly explains that "body" stands for human nature in general.[1] It is possible that by this time he had to some slight extent overcome the Apollinarian tendency which is plainly manifest in the treatise on the incarnation, but later theology would certainly have branded even his maturer works as decidedly Apollinarian.

Athanasius' doctrine of redemption may be said to represent the normal teaching of Greek theology from that time to the present, interpreted in various ways—with varying shades of philosophical and spiritual insight or of unphilosophical and unspiritual crudity according to the capacity and temper of different ages and different writers. These interpretations range from the level of high philosophy in Gregory of Nyssa to that of magic or thaumaturgy in such writers as John of Damascus. Frequently, however, it must be admitted, the same writer passes from one level to the other with strange facility.[2]

EUSEBIUS, BISHOP OF CAESAREA (c. A.D. 260–339)

In none of the fathers whom we have examined—from Irenaeus onwards—is there a complete absence of the traditional statements which seem on the face of them to make the death of Christ in some very literal sense a punishment or expiation for sin. But when philosophical and ethical explanations are given in other passages, it is natural and reasonable to explain the cruder statements imposed upon the writers by tradition in the light of the passages which obviously express their own thought. In the later Greek fathers this traditional treatment grows on the whole (in spite of one notable exception)[3] more and more prominent; and in the less philosophical writers it was evidently meant to be taken quite as seriously and as literally as the older and more characteristically Greek ideas of redemption which survive side by side with them. M. Rivière is quite justified in pointing out that this side of the later Greek theology has been too much

---

[1] "'Ο Λόγος γὰρ . . . σὰρξ ἐγένετο'" τῆς γραφῆς ἔθος ἐχούσης λέγειν "σάρκα" τὸν ἄνθρωπον . . . "σάρκα" γὰρ καὶ οὗτος καὶ Ἰωὴλ τὸ τῶν ἀνθρώπων γένος λέγουσι (Or. iii. 30). But this passage, looked at in its context, does not seem to me conclusive. Cf. also a passage in which he speaks of the flesh as "ignorant" (Or. iii. 43), but his whole discussion on the limits of Christ's knowledge leaves the impression that he thought of the Incarnate as possessing no human mind at all.

[2] In the sermon De passione et cruce Domini, attributed—no doubt falsely—to Athanasius, Migne, t. xxviii., there is a very definite doctrine of vicarious punishment (which is expressly called "vengeance," τιμωρία), and much is said about the trick played upon the Devil which caused him to be the author of his own ruin. The descensus ad inferos is described with childish realism.

[3] Gregory of Nyssa. See below, p. 303.

forgotten by previous historians of dogma in their sweeping contrasts between the Eastern and Western doctrine.[1] It was largely these later Greek fathers who supplied the elements of which the Anselmian doctrine was ultimately built up, though after all there always remained a decided difference of emphasis between East and West in all that pertains to redemption.

The first Greek writer who strongly emphasized the idea of substitutionary punishment is Athanasius' older contemporary, Eusebius, Bishop of Caesarea in Palestine. He declares that Christ " being punished on our account and enduring a retribution which He did not owe but we did on account of the abundance of our offences, was constituted for us the cause of the forgiveness of our sins, having drawn upon Himself the curse which was awarded to us, becoming a curse on our behalf." [2]

In the same book he speaks of Christ's death as putting an end to God's wrath against men. The tenth book of his *Demonstration of the Gospel* is devoted to the death of Christ. Two things will probably strike the reader of that book. The first is the dependence of the whole conception upon Old Testament prophecy. Although there was no longer any unwillingness to accept Pauline ideas, it was still from Is. liii. rather than from St. Paul that substitutionary and sacrificial ideas were derived. And the other is the prominence of the idea of the conquest of the demons, the descent into Hades, and the subsequent resurrection. One main object of the *Preparation of the Gospel* is to develope the typical significance of the Mosaic law of sacrifice. It is assumed that under the old law sins were atoned for in the fullest and most literal sense by animal sacrifices. Earlier writers had been more impressed by the contrast between the old sacrifices and the new : Eusebius tries as much as possible to identify them, and this attempt reacted upon his view of the sacrifice offered by Christ, and tends to put it completely on a level in its *modus operandi* with those sacrifices of bullocks and of goats which could never take away sins.

Yet Eusebius has enough of the older Greek spirit left to ask how the sacrifice of one—even of such a one—should prevail to take away the sins of so many : and he answers it by combining the Western emphasis upon Christ's death with the usual Greek

---

[1] As regards the earlier Greek fathers he seems to me to overlook the principle insisted on above : in Clement of Alexandria, Origen, and even in Athanasius the face value of traditional statements is very much reduced by explanations and even contradictions derived from other passages. I am indebted to M. Rivière for some of the citations of which I have availed myself in the following pages.

[2] Ὑπὲρ ἡμῶν κολασθεὶς καὶ τιμωρίαν ὑποσχών, ἣν αὐτὸς μὲν οὐκ ὤφειλεν, ἀλλ' ἡμεῖς τοῦ πλήθους ἕνεκα τῶν πεπλημμένων, ἡμῖν αἴτιος τῆς τῶν ἁμαρτημάτων ἀφέσεως κατέστη . . . τὴν ἡμῖν προστετιμημένην κατάραν ἐφ' ἑαυτὸν ἑλκύσας, γενόμενος ὑπὲρ ἡμῶν κατάρα (*Demonstr. Evan.* x. 1, Migne xxii. 724). The usual quotations from Is. liii. precede and follow.

conception of an effect produced upon humanity at large by the
close connexion or identity of our humanity with that of Christ.
More distinctly even than Athanasius he has formulated the idea
that men in general have died because they shared the nature of
Him who actually did die. It is explained that this effect is
produced in accordance with the "laws of sympathy."[1]   M.
Rivière renders the Greek word by the fashionable term of modern
orthodoxy, "solidarity." Perhaps he was instinctively desirous
of avoiding the more literal translation which would too glaringly
emphasize the essential identity of the conception with the old
idea of "sympathetic magic."

It is unnecessary to illustrate further the crudity of Eusebius'
presentation: no Western, Catholic or Protestant, has ever
presented the idea either of vicarious punishment or vicarious
sacrifice in a more repulsively juridical form. It may be added
that the relation between the Father and the Son implied by such
a doctrine fits in much better with the semi-Arianism of which
Eusebius was accused, than with the Catholic doctrine. In the
Demonstration of the Gospel one is constantly reminded of *Paradise
Lost*, and it is not impossible that the great Arian poet may have
been directly influenced by Eusebius' representations of the fall
and redemption.

ADEIMANTUS OR PSEUDO-ORIGEN (4th Cent.)

The most serious protest that has come down to us against
the theory of a ransom to the Devil is contained in the dialogue
"upon right faith in God," which bears the name of Adeimantus
Origenes, but was clearly the work of another Adeimantus who
lived after the Nicaean Council in the reign of Constantine. It
occurs in the course of an attack upon the Marcionites and other
heretics, and it is interesting to see that this Catholic writer—
and with good reason—treats the theory as really a piece of
Marcionite dualism. This passage is so important that I give
the long extract from it which is printed in Harnack: I will only
add Harnack's comment: "That is an argument as acute as it is
true and victorious."[2]

"He that was sold, then, you said, was Christ? Who is the
seller? Did the simple myth come down to you that he who
sells and he who buys are brothers? If the Devil, being bad, has
sold to the good, he is not bad but good: for he that of old envied
man is now no longer impelled by envy, handing over his authority
to the good. He then who has ceased from envy and all manner

---

[1] Κατὰ τοὺς τῆς συμπαθείας λόγους.

[2] *Hist. of Dogma*, ii. 291. The whole treatise is printed in Lommatzsch's edition of
Origen, xvi. 254 *sq.*

of evil will be righteous. God then Himself is found to be the seller. The truth is rather that the men who have sinned alienated themselves on account of their sins, but were ransomed (or bought back) again on account of His lovingkindness. For this is what the prophet says : ' For your sins ye were sold and for your transgressions I sent away your mother.' And another prophet again : ' For nought were ye sold, and not with silver shall ye be ransomed.' ' Not with silver '; that is to say, ' with the blood of Christ.' For this is what the prophet says, ' He was wounded for our transgressions; with his stripes we were healed.' And reasonably, since according to you he was sold when he gave his own blood; how then did he also rise from the dead ? But if he that took the price paid for men, the blood, gave it, it can no longer be said that he sold it. And if he did not give it, how did Christ rise ? For in that case the saying, ' I have power to lay it down, and I have power to take it again,' no longer holds. The Devil then holds the blood of Christ as the price of man. What immense and blasphemous folly ! . . . He laid down that which he took. What sort of a sale was this, when the prophet says, ' Let God arise and let his enemies be scattered.' Where a resurrection is, there is death."

Gregory, Bishop of Nyssa (c. A.D. 335-395)

In the group of writers known as the " School of Cappadocia " —the two Gregories and Basil—we return to the higher traditions of Greek philosophical theology. Of these three men the boldest and most philosophical was Gregory of Nyssa, an avowed disciple of Origen. His " Great Catechism " contains an apologetic summary of Christian doctrine and is a very fine piece of work. Although the doctrine of redemption is prominent, there is much more insistence upon the necessity of a sound doctrine of the Trinity for a true conception of salvation than upon the scheme of redemption itself. Like Athanasius, Gregory argues that none could restore fallen humanity but its Creator.[1] He contends that no salvation is possible upon the Arian view, because the work of one who is not really God could not lead to that participation in God which is the ultimate goal of salvation. The ransom theory is accepted, and it is clear that with Gregory there is much less metaphor or rhetoric about it than was the case with Origen. Gregory is obviously thinking of the ransom of a slave rather than of a captive taken in war, and he labours to prove the justice of the transaction. And yet it is stated in a way which somehow

---

[1] *Oratio Catechetica Magna*, 8.

avoids the childishness of Irenaeus and the grossness of Tertullian. He does not pretend that he can demonstrate that no other method of salvation was possible.[1] It is probable that the theory has never been stated with so much intellectual clearness and definiteness as in the following passages :

" As good, then, the Deity entertains pity for him who has fallen, and as wise is not ignorant of the means for his recovery; and just judgement must also form part of that wisdom : for no one would associate true justice with the absence of wisdom. What, then, under these circumstances is justice ? It is the not exercising any arbitrary sway over him who has us in his power, not tearing us away by the superiority of force from his hold, and so leaving some colour of justification to him who had enslaved man through pleasure. For as they who have bartered away their freedom for money are the slaves of those who have purchased them ; for they have constituted themselves their own sellers, and it is not allowable either for themselves or any one else on their behalf to put in a claim to freedom for them, not even though those who have thus reduced themselves to this sad state are of noble birth ; and, if any one out of regard for the person who has so sold himself should use violence against him who has bought him, he will clearly be acting unjustly in thus tyrannically rescuing one who has legally been purchased as a slave; whereas, if he wishes to pay a price to get such a one away, there is no law to prevent that,—in the same way, now that we had voluntarily bartered away our freedom, it was requisite that not the tyrannical method of recovery, but the one consonant with justice should be adopted by Him who in His goodness had undertaken our emancipation. Now this method is something of this kind ; to make over to the master of the slave whatever ransom he may agree to accept for the person in his possession. . . . He then, who . . . shut his eyes to the good in his envy of man in his happy condition, while he generated in himself the nether darkness of wickedness, he who suffered from the disease of ambition to rule—that primary and fundamental cause of propension to the bad and the mother, so to speak, of all the wickedness that followed — what would he have accepted in exchange for the thing which he held, but something higher and better, in the way of exchange, that thus, by an exchange of the less for the greater, he might foster his own special passion of pride ? . . . [Here the writer insists on the power of Christ as shown by the miracles.] The enemy then, beholding in Him such power, saw also that what he had the opportunity of obtaining in Him was something greater than what he held. For this reason he chooses Him as a ransom for those who were shut

---

[1] *Oratio Catechetica Magna*, 17, ed. Srawley.

up in the prison of death. But it was out of his power to look on the aspect of God, face to face, except by looking at some portion of that fleshly nature which through sin he had so long held in bondage. Therefore it is that the Deity invests Himself with flesh, in order, that is, to secure that he, by looking upon something of like nature and akin to himself, might have no fears in approaching that supereminent power; and might yet by perceiving that power, exhibiting as it did, yet only by gradual stages, more and more splendour in the miracles, deem what was seen an object of desire rather than of fear. Thus, you see how goodness was united with justice, and how wisdom was not divorced from them." [1]

It will be observed that the justice of the arrangement is not made out in quite the same way as in the earlier writers. The Devil here does not have man taken out of his custody by way of set-off for his injustice in bringing about Christ's death. God and the Devil have both voluntarily consented to the transaction, and that is why the arrangement is just. Only it has not the consequences which the Devil expected: he thought that He whom he justly killed was simply of mortal nature: he found that He was not only not mortal but the source of immortality. The deception practised by the Devil is emphasized, and the hook-metaphor is introduced (possibly Gregory is the inventor of it), though he avoids the grotesque corollary which is found in others— that the Devil was left hanging on the hook:

" In order to secure that the thing offered in exchange on our behalf might be the more easily accepted by him who demanded it, the Deity was hidden under the veil of our nature, that so, as is done by greedy fish, the hook of Deity might be gulped down along with the bait of flesh, and thus, life being introduced into the house of death, and light shining in darkness, that which is the contradictory of light and life might vanish away; for it is not in the nature of darkness to remain when light is present, or of death to exist when life is active." [2]

Gregory feels some embarrassment in justifying the trick that was thus played upon the Devil. He does so partly by the principle that " by the reasonable rule of justice, he who practised deception receives in return that very treatment, the seeds of which he had himself sown of his own free-will," and partly by insisting that this disciplinary process will ultimately conduce to the good of the

---

[1] *Oratio Catechetica Magna*, 22, 23.

[2] Ὡς ἂν εὔληπτον γένοιτο τῷ ἐπιζητοῦντι ὑπὲρ ἡμῶν τὸ ἀντάλλαγμα, τῷ προ-καλύμματι τῆς φύσεως ἡμῶν ἐνεκρύφθη τὸ Θεῖον, ἵνα κατὰ τοὺς λίχνους τῶν ἰχθύων τῷ δελέατι τῆς σαρκὸς συναποσπασθῇ τὸ ἄγκιστρον τῆς Θεότητος· καὶ οὕτω τῆς ζωῆς τῷ θανάτῳ εἰσοικισθείσης, καὶ τῷ σκότει τοῦ φωτὸς ἐμφανέντος, ἐξαφανισθῇ τῷ φωτὶ καὶ τῇ ζωῇ τὸ κατὰ τὸ ἐνάντιον νοούμενον. οὐ γὰρ ἔχει φύσιν, οὔτε σκότος διαμένειν ἐν φωτὸς παρουσίᾳ, οὔτε θάνατον εἶναι ζωῆς ἐνεργούσης (*ib.* 24).

Devil himself, for (even more decidedly than Origen) Gregory believes in the salvability of the evil one.[1]

The ransom-theory is there, and it is unquestionably in Gregory to be taken seriously. Indeed it is much more carefully and—on certain premisses—more plausibly worked out by him than by any one else. But although the theory, even as presented by Gregory, is childish and absurd enough to a modern mind, Gregory's general scheme of salvation is entirely free from the features which inspire us with horror and disgust in the pages of Tertullian and Augustine. There is much less of the idea of substitutionary or vicarious sacrifice than there is in Athanasius.[2] His view of the fall and its consequences is sane and moderate. Indeed it is the extreme " liberty of indifference " which he assigns to the human will rather than any over-emphasis on the idea of hereditary corruption which creates difficulties for the modern mind—a liberty so uncompromising that one does not quite see how there is any room for the idea of original sin considered even as a liability or tendency to actual sin, especially as we hear nothing of Origen's theory of pre-existence and pre-natal sin. But above all, it is the absence of the gloomy Western eschatology that makes the difference. He feels, no less than Origen, the difficulty of re-conciling absolute freedom of the will with a confident prediction of the ultimate restoration of all rational souls to their original perfection ; yet there can be no doubt about the universalism of the following passage. After defending the principle that the avoidance of a greater evil may justify the infliction of a smaller, and insisting on the Platonic analogies of medicine and cautery, he proceeds :

" In like manner, when in the course of long periods of time, the evil of our nature which now is mixed up with it and has grown with its growth has been expelled, and when there has been a restoration of those who are now lying in sin to their primal state, a harmony of thanksgiving will arise from all creation, as well from those who in the process of purgation have suffered chastisement as from those [i.e. baptized and right-living Christians] who needed not any purgation at all. These and the like benefits the great mystery of the divine incarnation bestows. For having passed through all those properties of our nature in respect of which He was mixed with humanity, such as birth, rearing, growth, even to the tasting of death, He accomplished all the results above mentioned, both freeing man from evil, and healing even

---

[1] *Oratio Catechetica Magna*, 26.

[2] In *De Occursu Domini*, Migne xlvi. 1165, he makes Christ offer his body to Christ in place of (ἀντί) humanity; but, as Mr. J. K. Mozley points out, this humanity is spoken of as " purified by faith in Christ," so that the sacrifice is not expiatory. M. Rivière adds a few other instances of conventional language about the death of Christ, *e.g.* ἀντάλλαγμα τοῦ ἡμετέρου θανάτου (*Contra Eunom.* v., Migne xlv. 693, etc.).

the introducer of evil himself.   For the purging of moral disease, however painful it be, is a healing of its weakness." [1]

Elsewhere he distinctly declares that Scripture "teaches the complete annihilation of evil." [2]

The necessity which Gregory attributes to the death of Christ is a very objective necessity indeed.   It was demanded to satisfy the claims of justice, and Gregory repeats the traditional notion that even the death on the cross was required so that its four arms " might bind all things to Himself—things in the heavens, in the earth, and below the earth."   But there is absolutely no trace of anything like substitution or expiation or vicarious punishment.   The saving effect of Christ's work springs not so much from His death as from the triumph over death.   The resurrection restores the natural incorruptibility of the human body, dissolving that temporary liability of the soul to be separated from the body which was the consequence of the fall.   This takes place as a sort of physical or metaphysical consequence of the influence of the indwelling Word upon human nature through its effect upon our human body and soul.   " Now, indeed [*i.e.* at the creation], He who keeps Nature in being was transfused into us ; but then [at the incarnation] He was mixed with our nature, in order that by intermixture with the divine it might become divine, being delivered from death and freed from the tyranny of the enemy.   For His return from death becomes to the mortal race the beginning of the return to immortal life." [3]   This effect was produced not specifically by Christ's death but rather by the incarnate life as a whole, culminating in the resurrection.

Redemption reaches the individual primarily through baptism. Gregory has no doubt of the absolute necessity of the baptismal waters.   But he does not treat the efficacy as a mechanical result of the physical washing and the appropriate words : " It is prayer to God and the invocation of the heavenly grace, and water and faith by which the mystery of regeneration is effected." [4]   But if no change of will and change of life accompany baptism—as he assumes to be frequently the case—baptism will avail nothing. " It may be a bold thing to say," he declares, " yet I will say it, and will not admit that in these cases the water is anything but

---

[1] *Cat. Magn.* 26. Cf. *De Anima*, p. 211.   In this passage Gregory questions the notion that Hades is a place, since disembodied spirits are out of space.   In the same way he regards the purgatorial " fire " as a metaphor.

[2] Ἐν τούτῳ δέ μοι δοκεῖ τὸν παντελῆ τῆς κακίας ἀφανισμὸν δογματίζειν ὁ Λόγος (*De Anima*, p. 229 b).   Cf. the beautiful treatise *De Mortuis*, Migne xlvi. 526 *sq.*

[3] Νῦν μὲν οὖν ἐγκέκραται ἡμῖν ὁ συνέχων ἐν τῷ εἶναι τὴν φύσιν· τότε δὲ κατεμίχθη πρὸς τὸ ἡμέτερον, ἵνα τὸ ἡμέτερον τῇ πρὸς τὸ Θεῖον ἐπιμιξίᾳ γίνηται θεῖον, ἐξαιρεθὲν τοῦ θανάτου, καὶ τῆς τοῦ ἀντικειμένου τυραννίδος ἔξω γενόμενον. ἡ γὰρ ἐκείνου ἀπὸ τοῦ θανάτου ἐπάνοδος ἀρχὴ τῷ θνητῷ γένει τῆς εἰς τὴν ἀθάνατον ζωὴν ἐπανόδου γίγνεται (*Cat. Magn.* 25).

[4] *Ib.* 33.

water, for the gift of the Holy Spirit in no way appears in him who is thus baptismally born." [1] And one thing further is necessary —the eucharist. The soul is saved by means of baptism, but the restoration of incorruptibility to the body can come only from the actual absorption of the eucharistic elements—the " Word transmuted into body." [2] For this is with Gregory, even more decidedly than with Athanasius, the final end of the whole process of salvation—the restoration of " incorruptibility " which was forfeited by the fall, the " deification " not only of the soul but of the body. The idea of forgiveness is altogether merged in the idea of this " deification." Indeed, the word forgiveness rarely occurs in Gregory : so fully has he grasped Origen's fundamental idea that forgiveness is made possible only by actual moral change. That the " deification " can result only from moral change, no one is more convinced.

So far Gregory's conception of redemption is an eminently ethical one. But there is little emphasis on the moral influence of Christ's teaching or character. The emphasis is all upon the free-will of the individual on the one hand, and on the quasi-physical influence of the incarnation and the resurrection upon " human nature " in general, operating directly or through the sacraments. That the sacraments operate through the actual and personal influence of the Word Himself is an idea constantly insisted upon by Gregory : and that being so, we ought not to speak of materialism in connection with his doctrine. But the increased emphasis upon the quasi-magical influence of the incarnation upon " human nature " in general and the much smaller insistence upon the influence of teaching and character do put Gregory's theology upon a somewhat lower level than that of the great Alexandrians. Gregory was a real philosopher : but he lived in an age in which metaphysic was showing a strong tendency to degenerate into a mixture of mysticism and thaumaturgy. The great service to Christian theology rendered by Gregory was to keep alive the Origenistic protest against the horrible eschatology which was already becoming dominant in the Western Church, and to re-affirm with even increased emphasis the fundamental truth that the only way in which sins can be forgiven is by the sinner being made really better.[3]

GREGORY OF NAZIANZUS, BISHOP OF CONSTANTINOPLE
(c. A.D. 325–389)

Another member of the same Cappadocian School was the contemporary Gregory of Nazianzus. In him we do not meet

---

[1] *Cat. Magn.* 40.   [2] *Cat. Magn.* 37.
[3] Other writers in whom there are traces of the same universalistic eschatology are Diodorus of Tarsus, Didymus, and Theodore of Mopsuestia.

with the definitively Origenistic eschatology of his namesake of Nyssa, but on the other hand he has the merit of distinctly protesting against the transaction with the Devil. In one place his protest is veiled in the rather obscure language of a theological poem : here are the words somewhat literally translated :

I enquire to whom was the blood of God poured out ?
If to the evil one—alas ! that the blood of Christ should be offered to the wicked one !
But if you say " To God "—how shall that be, when it is to another (than God) that we were enslaved ?
The ransom ever belongs to him who holds (the captive).
Can this be true, that He should offer a sacrifice to God,
In order that God Himself should snatch us away from the dominion of him that held us captive,
And receive as an equivalent for him who had fallen
The Christ ? For the Anointer of that Christ is not capable of being taken captive.
This is what we think. But we respect the (accepted) types (of heavenly things).[1]

The last words are highly significant. The traditional language about the transaction with the evil one had become a part of the universally accepted doctrine of the Church : if it was absent from creeds and conciliar canons, it was the very pith and marrow of popular theology. Gregory therefore suggests that the " myth " had better be re-explained in an allegorical manner rather than be positively abandoned. Possibly his meaning is that we must keep the traditional language of the " ransom," but explain that it was paid to God, not to the Devil. But in the Oration specially devoted to the doctrine of redemption, he denies that it is a ransom at all : it is an outrage to suppose that " the robber " could receive God Himself in payment for us ; and he asks, " If it is paid to the Father ; firstly, one may ask : ' how ' ? for it is not He who held us prisoners. And secondly, how can the Father reasonably take pleasure in the blood of the Only-begotten, He who did not accept Isaac when offered by his father, but put a ram in place of the reasonable victim. It is thus evident that if the Father accepts the blood of His Son, it is not because He had

[1] Ζητῶ τὸ αἷμα τῷ προσερρύη Θεοῦ ;
Εἰ μὲν πονηρῷ · φεῦ, τὸ Χριστοῦ τῷ κακῷ ·
Εἰ τῷ Θεῷ δέ, πῶς ἑτέρῳ κρατουμένων
Ἡμῶν ; ἐπὶ κρατοῦντός ἐστ' ἀεὶ λύτρον.
Ἦ τοῦτ' ἀληθές, αὐτὸν προσφέρειν Θεῷ,
Ἵν' αὐτὸς ἡμᾶς τοῦ κρατοῦντος ἁρπάσῃ,
Λάβῃ τε ἀντάλλαγμα τοῦ πεπτωκότος
Τὸν Χριστόν ; ὁ χρίσας γὰρ οὐχ ἁλώσιμος.
Οὕτω φρονοῦμεν · τοὺς τύπους δ' αἰδούμεθα.
(Poemata Dogmatica, i. viii. 65-69, Migne xxxvii. 470).

demanded or had need of it, but by reason of the economy of salvation, and because man needed to be sanctified by that which was human in God ; in order that He might deliver us Himself, having triumphed over the tyrant by force, and might bring us back to Himself by the mediation of His Son, who has done all things for the glory of the Father, to whom He is seen in all things to yield." [1]

Elsewhere he more explicitly declares that it is outrageous to suppose that " the robber " could receive God Himself in payment for us.[2] In the same spirit Gregory Nazianzen denies that Christ could really have become a curse for us : he explains St. Paul's language to mean merely that he " was called a curse " by others, was treated as if he were accursed without really being so.[3] The real thought of Gregory comes out in a passage in which he declares that Christ being God could have saved us by a mere word of command, but preferred to do it in a way which would exhibit His love and sympathy, and excite men to imitate Him by showing the same love to their fellows. Unlike some of the fathers, he is not afraid to use that word " sympathy " for fear of admitting the theological enormity of a " suffering " Deity.[4] More conventional language about the atonement may here and there be found in Gregory as in all Greek fathers ; but no one has taken a more fundamentally ethical view of the subject.

BASIL, BISHOP OF CAESAREA (A.D. 329–379)

The small part which theories about the death of Christ played in most Greek theology is well illustrated by the difficulty which we experience in extracting from the bulky writings of Basil, an even more famous member of the Cappadocian School, and brother of the Nyssene Gregory, any definite thoughts upon the subject. He uses the conventional language about expiation and the ransom. No *man* can ransom his own soul ; and, since Christ did give His life as an equivalent for all men, that shows that he

---

[1] *Oratio* xlv. 22, Migne xxxvi. 654. Elsewhere he uses language which implies the trick upon the Devil. See *Oratio* xxxix. 13, Migne xxxvi. 349. But the ransom is not actually paid to the Devil.

[2] *Oratio* xlv. 22, Migne xxxvi. 654.

[3] Οὐκ ἔστι μὲν [ἁμαρτία], ἀκούει δέ. πῶς γὰρ ἁμαρτία, ὁ καὶ ἡμᾶς τῆς ἁμαρτίας ἐλευθερῶν ; πῶς δὲ κατάρα, ὁ ἐξαγοράζων ἡμᾶς ἐκ τῆς κατάρας τοῦ νόμου ; ἀλλ' ἵνα καὶ μέχρι τούτων τὸ ταπεινὸν ἐπιδείξηται, τυπῶν ἡμᾶς εἰς ταπείνωσιν τὴν ὕψους πρόξενον (*Oratio* xxxvii. 1, Migne xxxvi. 284).

[4] Ταῦτα μὲν ὁ Σωτήρ, καὶ τῷ θελήματι μόνον, ὡς Θεός, σῶσαι δυνάμενος, ἐπεὶ καὶ τὰ πάντα προστάγματι συνεστήσατο· μεῖζον δὲ καὶ δυσωπητικώτερον εἰσήνεγκεν ἡμῖν, τὴν συμπαθείαν καὶ τὸ ὁμότιμον. τί δὲ ἡμεῖς οἱ Χριστοῦ μαθηταὶ τοῦ πράου καὶ φιλανθρώπου, καὶ τοσοῦτον ἡμῖν λειτουργήσαντος ; οὐ μιμησόμεθα τοῦ Δεσπότου τὴν εὐσπλαγχνίαν ; οὐκ ἐσόμεθα χρηστοῦ τοῖς ὁμοδούλοις ; κ.τ.λ. (*Oratio* xix. 13, Migne xxxv. 1060).

was not merely man.[1] And there are passages in which he speaks in the usual way of the trick by which the Devil was deceived into compassing the death of Christ and so bringing about his own ruin. Basil accepts the traditional language without apology or explanation,[2] but there is less emphasis upon the rights of the Devil than upon the supreme value or merit of Him who was offered to him as a ransom. The ransom is little more than a way of stating the necessity of Christ's death for the forgiveness of sins, which Basil like other Greek fathers formally admitted, though their general disposition is to make salvation depend upon the incarnation as a whole. The incidental way in which the idea of the ransom paid to the Devil is touched upon by such writers seems to show that it played a larger part in the popular religion than in the minds of the learned. It belonged to the uniformly accepted tradition, and probably, just because it was so universally accepted, was not the subject of discussion or the basis of speculation.

CYRIL, BISHOP OF JERUSALEM (A.D. 315–386)

From the Catecheses of Cyril of Jerusalem we are able to construct a vivid picture of the kind of instruction commonly received by the catechumens in the ancient Church. Cyril was not a philosophical theologian, and he was speaking to a popular audience: he was full of belief in the magical influence of exorcisms and the like. It is not surprising, therefore, that in his writings we meet with little but conventional language about the atonement. We have the usual account of the trick played upon the Devil; and, though the word " punishment " is not used, the death of Christ is explained as a device by which God's threat of death was fulfilled, and yet in a way which was consistent with the " philanthropy " of God. Christ took " our sins in his own body upon the tree." [3] The Bishop concludes by thus

---

[1] Τί γὰρ δύναται ἄνθρωπος εὑρεῖν τηλικοῦτον, ἵνα δῷ ὑπὲρ λυτρώσεως τῆς ψυχῆς αὑτοῦ; ἀλλ' εὑρέθη ἐν ὑμῖν πάντων ἀνθρώπων ἀντάξιον, ὃ ἐδόθη εἰς τιμὴν λυτρώσεως τῆς ψυχῆς ἡμῶν, τὸ ἅγιον καὶ πολυτίμητον αἷμα τοῦ Κυρίου ἡμῶν Ἰησοῦ Χριστοῦ, ὃ ὑπὲρ ἡμῶν ἐξέχεε πάντων· διόπερ καὶ τιμῆς ἠγοράσθημεν. εἰ οὖν ἀδελφὸς οὐ λυτροῦται, λυτρώσεται ἄνθρωπος; εἰ δὲ ἄνθρωπος λυτρώσασθαι ἡμᾶς οὐ δύναται, ὁ λυτρωσάμενος ἡμᾶς οὐκ ἄνθρωπος. In Psalm. xlviii. 4.

[2] Παντὶ δὲ αἰχμαλώτῳ λύτρων χρεία πρὸς τὴν ἐλευθερίαν. Οὔτε οὖν ἀδελφὸς τὸν ἑαυτοῦ ἀδελφὸν δύναται λυτρώσασθαι, οὔτε αὐτὸς ἕκαστος ἑαυτόν· διότι πολλῷ βελτίονα δεῖ εἶναι τὸν λυτρούμενον τοῦ κεκρατημένου καὶ δουλεύοντος ἤδη. In Psalm. lxviii. 3. Cf. Ep. cclxi. 2 and De Spir. Sancto. viii. 18.

[3] Ἐχθροὶ γὰρ ἦμεν Θεοῦ δι' ἁμαρτίας· καὶ ὥρισεν ὁ Θεὸς τὸν ἁμαρτάνοντα ἀποθνήσκειν. Ἔδει οὖν ἓν ἐκ τῶν δύο γενέσθαι, ἢ ἀληθεύοντα Θεὸν πάντας ἀνελῖν· ἢ φιλανθρωπούμενον παραλῦσαι τὴν ἀπόφασιν. ἀλλὰ βλέπε Θεοῦ σοφίαν· ἐτήρησεν καὶ τῇ ἀποφάσει τὴν ἀλήθειαν, καὶ τῇ φιλανθρωπίᾳ τὴν ἐνέργειαν. ἀνέλαβε

addressing the catechumens : " As Jesus taking upon Him the
sins of the whole world died, that having died as regards sin, He
might raise thee up in righteousness, so do thou also, descending
into the water, and in a manner buried in the waters, as He was
buried in the rocky tomb, rise again, walking in newness of life." [1]
Piety or salvation with him depended upon belief in orthodox
dogma and in good works: the best works would be useless without
the pious dogmas. [2]

In his answer to the question why this one death should have
had so mighty an efficacy, Cyril may be credited with having
taken one step further than any previous writer towards anticipat-
ing the Anselmian doctrine of satisfaction by the superabundant
merits of Christ : " the iniquity of our sins was not so great as
the righteousness of Him who died for us : we did not sin so much
as He who laid down His soul for us did righteously." [3]   It may
be added that Cyril—and herein is a noticeable difference from
Anselm—absolutely repudiates the idea of original sin. [4]

CHRYSOSTOM, BISHOP OF CONSTANTINOPLE
(c. A.D. 347–407)

The school of Antioch exhibits certain tendencies which
differentiate it strongly from the rest of the Greek-speaking
world.   It resisted both what was best and what was worst in
the school of Alexandria—both its philosophy and that mystical
interpretation of Scripture by which it was able to reconcile philosophy with the dogma of plenary biblical inspiration.   Chrysostom
perfectly represents the tendencies of his school : he was essentially
a rhetorician incapable of philosophical thought; but he has all
the good sense and good taste which were undermined by the habit
of seeking for profound mysteries in every word of the Old Testament.   In such a writer we should not expect a serious theory of

---

Χριστὸς τὰς ἁμαρτίας ἐν τῷ σώματι ἐπὶ τὸ ξύλον κ.τ.λ. (Cat. xiii. 33). The
transaction with the Devil seems to be implied in iii. 11, xii. 15. In the last chapter
he introduces the fish-hook metaphor, with the addition that the Devil, in trying to
swallow it, was compelled to vomit forth those whom he had already devoured.

[1] Cat. iii. 12.

[2] Ὁ γὰρ τῆς θεοσεβείας τρόπος ἐκ δύο τούτων συνέστηκε, δογμάτων εὐσεβῶν καὶ
πράξεων ἀγαθῶν. καὶ οὔτε τὰ δόγματα χωρὶς ἔργων ἀγαθῶν εὐπρόσδεκτα τῷ Θεῷ,
οὔτε τὰ μὴ μετ' εὐσεβῶν δογμάτων ἔργα τελούμενα προσδέχεται ὁ Θεός· . . . μέγιστον
τοίνυν κτῆμά ἐστι τὸ τῶν δογμάτων μάθημα (Cat. iv. 2).

[3] Cat. xiii. 33. M. Rivière is hardly justified in saying that this amounts to the
doctrine of an *infinite* superabundance of merit. A still closer approach to the Anselmian
doctrine is to be found in a later Greek writer, Proclus, Patriarch of Constantinople
from 434 to 466, from whom M. Rivière (Le Dogme de la Réd. pp. 202-3) gives a long
citation.

[4] Μάνθανε δὲ καὶ τοῦτο, ὅτι πρὶν παραγένηται εἰς τόνδε τὸν κόσμον ἡ ψυχή, οὐδὲν
ἥμαρτεν, ἀλλ' ἐλθόντες ἀναμάρτητοι, νῦν ἐκ προαιρέσεως ἁμαρτάνομεν (Cat. iv. 19).

the atonement, and we do not find one—unless that name is to be given to a mere repetition of commonplaces. He accepts the doctrine on authority. Sometimes he will admit its apparent unreasonableness, and declaim, after the manner of modern preachers, against too much confidence in reason. Or again he will admit the unreasonableness of part of the scheme, and contend that the doctrine may be true because other parts of it are more reasonable or less unreasonable. " For that one man should be punished on account of another does not seem to be much in accordance with reason. But for one man to be saved on account of another is at once more suitable and more reasonable." [1] And, especially in his comments upon St. Paul and the Epistle to the Hebrews, he accepts in a literal and positive manner the language of expiation and substitution. But his tone is generally as ethical as his literalism could allow it to be. Given the mysterious necessity for the death of Christ, he dwells chiefly on the love which it shows both in the Father and in the Son. He was saved from the worst features of the substitutionary view by his strong belief in free-will, carrying with it a very moderate interpretation of original sin, and by the strength of his conviction that justification is a making righteous, not a mere counting righteous. Thus he explains St. Paul's statement that " by one man's disobedience many were made sinners " as meaning merely that they became liable to the punishment of death, *i.e.* mortality, which he exhibits rather as a necessary consequence than as a punishment strictly so called : and he goes on to show that humanity has gained more than it lost by the fall on account of the moral discipline supplied by our present life and the restoration of immortality in Christ.[2] It is generally in echoing the words of St. Paul or the Epistle to the Hebrews or in rhetorical outbursts that he falls into language of a substitutionary or expiatory type. " For Christ hath paid down far more than we owe, as much as the illimitable ocean is more than a little drop." [3] Christ's death was "equivalent to the death of all." [4] In one place he definitely compares the atonement to the act of a king who gives his son to die in the place of a bandit, and " together with the death transfers the liability (αἰτία) from the one to the other " : [5] but even here there is no emphasis on the substitutionary idea, no attempt to explain or justify the arrangement ; it occurs simply as part of an appeal for gratitude towards the Father and the Son who had shown so much love for us. The point of the appeal would be just the same if the death were supposed to operate only through the gratitude which it excites. In general Chrysostom reminds us of a good deal of modern preaching and

---

[1] *In Rom. Hom.* x. 1.   [2] *In Rom. Hom.* x. 3.   [3] *In Rom. Hom.* x. 2.
[4] Ἀντίρροπος ἦν ὁ θάνατος ἐκεῖνος τῆς πάντων ἀπωλείας. *In Heb. Hom.* xvii. 2.
[5] *In 2 Cor. Hom.* xi. 4.

writing about the atonement. He is not thinker enough even to grasp the difficulties, and therefore he has no definite solution of them : he accepts the traditional statements, but only falls into what is unethical or irrational so far as deference to authority compels him to do. In Chrysostom's time the transaction with the Devil was part of the established tradition : he accepts it with his usual literalness. The only way in which his exposition is an improvement upon some of those we have met with lies in the fact that the great preacher knows how to put things clearly, if the result is scarcely edifying. This is the way in which he expounds the saying, " Now is the judgement of this world : now shall the Prince of this world be cast out " :

" It is as if He said, There shall be a court and a justification (ἐκδίκησις). How and in what manner ? He slew the first man, having found him liable to sin (for it was through sin that death entered in). In me he did not find this. Wherefore then did he leap upon me and give me over unto death ? Wherefore did he put it into the soul of Judas to slay me ? For do not tell me *now* that God so ordained : for such a dispensation belongs not to the Devil but to His own wisdom : at present let us enquire what is the intention of that wicked one. How then is the world judged in me ? It is as if when a court was sitting it should be said to the Devil : ' Be it so, Thou didst slay them all because thou didst find them guilty of sin : why didst thou slay the Christ ? Is it not clear that thou didst so unjustly ? Therefore through him shall all the world be justified.' But that this may be made yet clearer, I will also make the matter manifest by an example. Suppose that there is a certain violent tyrant, afflicting with innumerable evils all that fall into his hands. If he were to meet with a king or a king's son and were unjustly to slay him, his death will be able to involve justification for the others also. [Or again], let us suppose that there is one who exacts a debt of his debtors, and beats them, and throws them into prison. Then let us suppose that with the same recklessness he puts into the same prison one who owes him nothing. Such a man will pay the penalty also for what he did to the others. For he (the man unjustly imprisoned) will slay him. That is what has occurred also in the case of the Son. For the things which he did against you, the Devil will incur punishment in consequence of the things which he presumed to do against the Christ." [1]

---

[1] *In Joann. Hom.* lxvii. 2, 3. The word ἐκδίκησις is best translated " justification " : here it is used in the old Scotch sense of punishment ; later on the corresponding verb is used in the sense of acquittal, the punishment being transferred to another. For another account of the transaction see *In Rom. Hom.* xiii. 5. There is a passage in Theodoret where the thought is much the same, but the unfortunate illustrations are absent (*De Providentia*, Sermo x., Migne lxxxiii. 748).

It is scarcely worth while to point out the outrageous character of this theodicy. God is in the first parallel compared to a king who will not punish offences against the law or procure the release of unjustly imprisoned subjects until a personal affront is offered to his own dignity ; or (if it is supposed that the detention is just) releases justly detained prisoners without punishment merely because the gaoler happens to have incurred his displeasure. As to the second case, one asks under what civilized system of juris-diction is a just debt wiped out because the creditor has brought a vexatious action against some one else ? Such were the shifts to which eminently Christian-minded divines were driven by the assumption that every doctrine which had found a place in the Church's tradition must be vindicated at all costs.

CYRIL, BISHOP OF ALEXANDRIA (BISHOP A.D. 412–444)

Cyril's general point of view is that of the earlier Greek fathers, especially that of his great predecessor in the see of Alexandria, Athanasius. But there is an increased tendency to emphasize the death of Christ as distinct from the incarnation : a further consideration of the matter was forced upon these later fathers by the controversies as to the relation between the two natures in Christ. When Cyril declares that the death of Christ is the " root " from which sprang a new race, when he understands Christ's saying about the grain of wheat not bearing fruit except it die to mean that His death, in a way totally unexplained, " multi-plied and bore fruit in such wise that the whole human race was reformed in Him according to the original image in which the first man was made,"[1] he is expressing the characteristically Greek point of view, except that the effect is seldom so exclusively attributed to the death ; but this did not prevent him upon occasion lapsing into decidedly substitutionary ways of thinking. He insists much upon the idea that " One died for all," but it is because they were all in some sense contained in Him that His death sufficed for all ; " since all things in Him, and He is better than all " [2]—thus combining the old Greek view with the idea (already noticed in Cyril of Jerusalem) that the overwhelming merit of such a death could win redemption for all. At times he speaks of the death

---

[1] Ὅτε τοίνυν πέπτωκεν οἷά τις κόκκος εἰς γῆν, ἀστάχυος δίκην, πολλοστὸς ἀνέφυ, τῆς ἀνθρώπου φύσεως ἀναπλαττομένης ἐν αὐτῷ, πρὸς τὴν ἐν ἀρχαῖς εἰκόνα, καθ' ἣν ὁ πρῶτος γέγονεν ἄνθρωπος (In Gen. i. p. 21, De Cain et Abel 3, Migne lxix. 44).

[2] Δέδωκεν ἀντίλυτρον ὑπὲρ ἡμῶν, τὸν Υἱὸν ὁ Πατὴρ ἕνα ὑπὲρ πάντων, ἐπεὶ καὶ πάντα ἐν αὐτῷ, καὶ πάντων κρείττων ἐστίν. In Joann. ii. i. 29, Migne lxxiii. 192. But what follows shows that even here he is thinking more of the conquest of death in the resurrection than of the endurance of a penalty for sin: "Death having devoured the Lamb on behalf of all, vomited forth (ἐξήμεσεν) all in Him and with Him."

as a punishment.[1] The point which Cyril chiefly aims at establishing in connexion with the death of Christ is that it was really God the Word who died (while remaining impassible and unchangeable), and not any mere man, however closely connected with the Word ; but he equally insists that He assumed human nature as a whole, mind as well as body, since the Devil could justly have complained if he had been defeated by one who was not man at all but God in a human body.[2] He insists much that only the death of God could have a redemptive effect: as to how even such a death could redeem, he has little to say, and is content to describe its effect in scriptural or other traditional language. In the famous letter of Cyril, "On the right faith," addressed to the Emperor Theodosius II.,[3] he speaks of Christ as "making His own flesh a repayment for the flesh of all, a gift which was truly of equivalent value." Here we can again trace the tendency towards the ideas which were to receive their fullest development in Anselm. Elsewhere the triumph of Christ over the Devil is described in the usual way, but without any attempt at juridical explanation or justification.[4]

JOHN OF DAMASCUS (c. A.D. 680–c. 760)

John of Damascus occupies the same sort of position in Eastern theology that is occupied by St. Thomas Aquinas in the West. He sums up, in scholastic form, the general doctrine of the Greek fathers. He represents, however, rather the decadence of patristic theology than the beginning or the culmination of a new movement in the history of thought. And this is characteristic

---

[1] De Incarnatione Domini, 27, Migne lxxv. 1466. Cf. De Adorat. in Spir. et ver. iii., Migne lxviii. 296.

[2] De Incarn. Dom. 16, Migne lxxv. 1443.

[3] Σάρκα μὲν τὴν ἰδίαν, τῆς ἁπάντων σαρκὸς ἀνταποτιννύς, δῶρον ἀληθῶς ἀντάξιον (De recta fide ad Theodos. 21, Migne lxxvi. 1164).

[4] In Joann. IV. viii. 42, Migne lxxiii. 894 ; De Incarn. Dom. 14, Migne lxxv. 1439-1442. The view of the atonement taken by Cyril's great opponent Nestorius was just as substitutionary as his, though his grasp upon the true humanity of Christ puts his whole treatment of the subject on to a much higher level. " Since many were overcome by fear of death, He bore even death itself, and paid for us the penalty justly due by substitution for our death—the death which unjustly came upon Himself." He died " that He might pay the penalty for us." The context implies the transaction with the Devil. (Translated from the Syriac in Bethune-Baker, Nestorius and his Teaching, p. 135.)
 The most elaborate development of the conflict between Christ and the Devil quoted in M. Rivière's wonderful collection is to be found in three homilies published in 1829 by Augusti, and attributed by him to Eusebius of Emesa. It takes the form of a drama or dialogue between the two combatants, which has much in common with the Gospel of Nicodemus (fifth century). Another very lurid account of the descensus ad inferos is to be found in a Homily attributed to Epiphanius (Hom. ii. In Sabbato Magno). Another very elaborate development of the idea of an armed conflict between Christ and the Devil is in Gregory the Great, who applies to this encounter every detail of the passage in Job about Leviathan (Moralia xxxii. 12-xxxiii. 6) : it is here that the hook metaphor is introduced.

of the contrast presented by the doctrinal history of the two churches. In the East the patristic era was not separated from medievalism by a " dark age " : but neither was there any such epoch of brilliant re-awakening as the twelfth century introduced in the West. Nor did the East recognize an authority which raised new dogmas to the level of those sanctioned by the great Councils. It continued to live upon the patristic theology : perhaps it may be said upon the dregs of it. The *Exposition of the Orthodox Faith* by John of Damascus still constitutes, we are told, the accepted theological text-book of the orthodox Eastern Churches.

We have noticed in all the Eastern fathers a perpetual struggle between an ethical and a metaphysical way of interpreting the doctrine of salvation through Christ. We have traced the increasing predominance of the metaphysical over the ethical interpretation. This predominance reaches its culmination in John of Damascus. His doctrine of salvation is mainly a metaphysic, but a metaphysic of a kind which shows a strong tendency to degenerate into mere myth or mere magic.

He does, indeed, recognize that the object of the incarnation was in part to teach the right way of life; [1] but this purpose is completely subordinate to the direct and supernatural communication of power to resist and overcome the Devil and to reach immortality, which was brought into existence—in an unintelligible and in the strictest sense supernatural manner—by the incarnation, death, and passion of Christ. The idea that Christ's death was a punishment is happily absent from this treatise; it is merely recognized, in accordance with tradition, that Christ offered Himself as a sacrifice to the Father for us. [2] The sacrifice is not exactly vicarious, because in Christ each human being has actually suffered. The theory which runs through almost all previous Greek thought on the subject is now stated with scholastic precision, and (we may add) in a way in which the logical fallacy comes out with startling clearness : " Common and universal predicates are applied to the subjects which form the particulars of the class. The essence then is common, as constituting the species, but the individual (being part of it) is particular. And it is particular, not because it has in it a part of the nature ; it has not a part of it, but it is a particular numerically as being an indivisible particular. For individuals are said to differ in number and not in nature. Essence ($o\dot{v}\sigma\acute{\iota}a$) is predicated of the individual : [3]

---

[1] *Expositio Fidei Orthodoxae*, iv. 4, 5.

[2] *Ib.* iii. 27. More decidedly substitutionary language is used in *In Tim.* i. 5, Migne xcv. 1004, and elsewhere (as is usual with Greek fathers) in his commentaries on St. Paul.

[3] I have translated the word hypostasis " individual " rather than " person," because the whole argument turns upon the application to the " person " of Christ of what is

therefore in each individual of the species the essence is perfect. Therefore neither do the individuals differ from one another in essence, but only in respect of their accidents which are their characteristic properties. For they define the individual as 'essence together with accidents.' So that the individual has what is common together with that which individualizes it besides existing substantially in itself. But the essence does not exist substantially in itself, but is only seen in the individuals. When then one of the individuals suffers, all the essence in respect of which the individual has suffered, being capable of suffering, is said to have suffered in one of its individuals : without, however, its being necessary that all the individuals of the same species should suffer too with the individual that does (actually) suffer." [1]

Here we have the old thought as to the effects which were produced upon human nature at large by its union with the divine nature in Christ developed into a doctrine of so decidedly scholastic and metaphysical a kind that it is now impossible to understand the phrases used in any ethical or really spiritual sense. The salvation of mankind flows as a direct consequence from the " hypostatic union " of the whole essence " of humanity with the whole essence of Divinity " in a single individual. The emphasis is still mainly upon the " hypostatic union " of the two natures in the incarnation, which transfers the qualities of the divine nature to the human, and thereby restores incorruptibility and secures " deification " to the human soul and body ; but there is, as compared with earlier expressions of the idea, more insistence upon the principle that the threat and penalty of death may be actually considered to have been borne by every individual united with Christ by baptism because it was borne by Him. Marvellous effects directly flow from the death itself : " the creature has been sanctified by the divine blood " : the demons become afraid of men, and so on.[2] It may be well to point out definitely the logical fallacy which is involved in this theory. It is clear of

---

supposed to be the true relation of every individual to the universal or class-name of the species to which it belongs.

[1] Τὰ κοινὰ καὶ καθολικὰ κατηγοροῦνται τῶν αὐτοῖς ὑποκειμένων μερικῶν. κοινὸν τοίνυν ἡ οὐσία, ὡς εἶδος, μερικὸν δὲ ἡ ὑπόστασις. μερικὸν δέ, οὐχ ὅτι μέρος τῆς φύσεως ἔχει, μέρος δὲ οὐκ ἔχει, ἀλλὰ μερικὸν τῷ ἀριθμῷ ὡς ἄτομον· ἀριθμῷ γὰρ καὶ οὐ φύσει διαφέρειν λέγονται αἱ ὑποστάσεις. κατηγορεῖται δὲ ἡ οὐσία τῆς ὑποστάσεως, διότι ἐν ἑκάστῃ τῶν ὁμοειδῶν ὑποστάσεων τελεία ἡ οὐσία ἐστί. διὸ οὐδὲ διαφέρουσιν ἀλλήλων αἱ ὑποστάσεις κατ᾽ οὐσίαν, ἀλλὰ κατὰ τὰ συμβεβηκότα, ἅτινά εἰσι τὰ χαρακτηριστικὰ ἰδιώματα· χαρακτηριστικὰ δὲ ὑποστάσεως καὶ οὐ φύσεως. καὶ γὰρ τὴν ὑπόστασιν ὁρίζονται οὐσίαν μετὰ συμβεβηκότων. ὥστε τὸ κοινὸν μετὰ τοῦ ἰδεάζοντος ἔχει ἡ ὑπόστασις, καὶ τὸ καθ᾽ ἑαυτὴν ὑπάρξαι· ἡ οὐσία δὲ καθ᾽ ἑαυτὴν οὐχ ὑφίσταται, ἀλλ᾽ ἐν ταῖς ὑποστάσεσι θεωρεῖται. πασχούσης τοίνυν μιᾶς τῶν ὑποστάσεων, πᾶσα ἡ οὐσία παθητὴ οὖσα, καθ᾽ ἣν ἡ ὑπόστασις πέπονθε, πεπονθέναι λέγεται ἐν μιᾷ τῶν αὐτῆς ὑποστάσεων· οὐ μέντοιγε ἀνάγκη καὶ πάσας τὰς ὁμοειδεῖς ὑποστάσεις συμπάσχειν τῇ πασχούσῃ ὑποστάσει (*Expositio Fidei Orthodoxae*, iii. 6).

[2] *Ib.* iv. 4.

course that the death of Christ (if by that is meant the particular kind of death, the penal death, suffered by Christ) is really an accident, not a universal predicate or part of the essence of "humanity." To be "passible" no doubt belongs to the essence of humanity but not this particular death : it is no more true that all men suffered punishment for sin because Christ suffered it, than it is true that all men are Jews because Christ was a Jew.

Side by side with this theory appears the transaction with the Devil in a very slightly modified form. John will not, indeed, admit that "the blood of the Lord was *offered to* the tyrant " ; it was offered to God: [1] but this does not prevent his speaking of "death" as eagerly swallowing the "bait of His body" which left Him "hanging upon the hook of His Divinity." The distinction between the Devil and death is a fine one, and elsewhere language is used which really implies the whole monstrous scheme,[2] except that, though the death of Christ is conceded to the Devil, it is not called an "offering." "He was made man, in order that that which had been conquered might conquer. For He who can do all things was not so weak that He could not also by His almighty power and strength deliver mankind from the domination of the tyrant. But the tyrant would have had grounds for complaint, if, after he had conquered man, he had in turn been forcibly compelled by God (to give him up). Wherefore God who sympathizes with and loves mankind, wishing to proclaim the fallen as victor, becomes man, appealing to the like by means of the like " [3]—an expression which once again reminds us of primitive man's philosophy of "sympathetic magic."

The connexion with Christ which was necessary to enable the individual to reap the benefits brought into the world by the union of the two natures in Christ and the consequent payment of the debt owed by humanity are thought of as effected primarily by the sacraments, which operate in the most strictly mechanical or rather physiological manner.[4] Faith is, of course, required, and no writer more definitely identifies faith with belief—belief in the whole elaborate system of Christian doctrine, including the decrees of Chalcedon and much else. He not only expects but prays for the damnation of Julius of Halicarnassus, Gaius, Patriarch of Alexandria, and their followers who believed the body of Christ to be incorruptible before the resurrection, although he has just explained with much subtlety that in a certain sense

---

[1] *Expositio Fidei Orthodoxae*, iii. 27.

[2] *Ib.* iii. 27.

[3] Τῷ ὁμοίῳ τὸ ὅμοιον ἀνακαλούμενος (*ib.* iii. 18).

[4] *Ib.* iv. 9, 13. The body of Christ actually passes "into our essence" or substance (εἰς τὴν ἡμῶν οὐσίαν), and removes the cause of disease and death. The relics of the saints were similarly valuable for the expulsion of demons and the cure of disease (*ib.* iv. 15).

this was true.[1] By this time all that was liberal in the teaching of such men as Origen and Gregory of Nyssa was forgotten. No purgatory or any other of the humane expedients of Western schoolmen was any longer allowed in the Eastern Church to mitigate the horrors of hell for imperfect Christians, pagans, or heretics. The greater prominence in his pages of the death of Christ, as distinct from the incarnation, in contrast with some of the earlier Greeks, is closely connected with his strong belief in the wonder-working efficacy of the cross as a charm against evil spirits, and his desire to vindicate the actual worship of the material cross.[2] The Eastern Church of this period did, indeed, preserve a nobler tradition than that of the West, and traces of its nobler features remain even in John of Damascus, but in so degraded a form that one almost feels inclined to exclaim, "Corruptio optimi pessima!"

---

[1] *Expositio Fidei Orthodoxae*, iii. 28.
[2] *Ib.* iv. 11. John insists indeed that it is not the wood but the "shape" of the cross which is adored (τὸν τύπον ὡς Χριστοῦ σύμβολον).

LECTURE V

LATIN THEOLOGY—AUGUSTINE, ANSELM, ABELARD

Herein was the love of God manifested in us, that God hath sent his only begotten Son into the world, that we might live through him.— 1 John iv. 9.

LECTURE V

WE have seen that the earliest Christian writers, while they repeat the traditional formulae based upon Isaiah liii., are for the most part quite free from any substitutionary or expiatory theory of the Atonement, and give explanations of it which are essentially ethical, intelligible, spiritual. The redeeming work of Christ is almost invariably explained as due to the subjective effect produced upon the believer by His death, or (more usually) by His teaching and work as a whole. Clement and Origen, we have seen, likewise maintain the same high level in their teaching on the subject. We have seen how the teaching of the Church on this matter deteriorated in Irenaeus, who—amid much speculation of a higher character—introduced the theory that the death of Christ was a ransom paid to the Devil, a ransom without which it would have been inconsistent with the justice of God to release mankind from the bondage to the Devil incurred by the sin of Adam. This theory ultimately became the generally accepted doctrine upon the subject. It prevailed almost everywhere in East and West. We find it expressed or implied, more or less definitely, in nearly all the great fathers and theological writers down to the twelfth century.[1] Some are silent, but there are few definite protests. One comes from the able fourth-century writer Adeimantus, whose work has been mistakenly attributed to his greater

---

[1] St. Bernard, *De erroribus Abelardi*, c. 5.

namesake, Adeimantus Origenes,[1] another from Gregory of Nazianzus,[2] followed in a more hesitating fashion by John of Damascus.[3]

The theory of the ransom was accepted by philosophical Greek fathers, but its real influence was very different in the East and in the West. In the East it was little more than an excrescence—a formula repeated and accepted in obedience to tradition, largely perhaps in deference to those unfortunate passages in which Origen used the language about the ransom in a metaphorical sense. With the Eastern fathers—and I may add the Eastern liturgies—the habitual way of thinking and speaking about the death of Christ was the nobler way marked out by such writers as Justin and Clement, the real thought of Origen, and, to some extent, in spite of inconsistent ideas, even by Irenaeus. Their theology centres round the incarnation rather than the atonement. The death of Christ is to them part of the divine process for getting rid of sin, but their theory is not concentrated upon the idea of sin and its punishment. The incarnation is to them no mere device for getting rid of the consequences of a fall which unexpectedly threatened to ruin the work of God, and so saving a small fragment of humanity from the awful doom which awaited the vast majority. It was—such at least is the implied tendency of their teaching—part of the original world-plan by which God designed from all eternity to bring into existence rational beings, made in His own image, whom He would educate into that participation in His own perfection which they described as the knowledge of God, or even as an actual deification. Many of us will perhaps in this matter take the liberty to disagree with Harnack and the Ritschlian theologians, who imagine that they are treading in the footsteps of Luther by extolling the Latin theology at the expense of the Greek. A very large proportion of English theologians would perhaps agree that the Greek theology, rather than the Latin, has marked out the lines which any modern, philosophical

---

[1] See the passage quoted above, p. 302.
[2] See above, p. 309.   [3] See above, p. 319.

reconstruction of Christian doctrine must follow.   It is a gross misrepresentation to say that the Western theology is more ethical than the Eastern.   The characteristically Western view of sin and the Western idea of God are juridical rather than ethical, unphilosophical rather than spiritual.   To speak broadly, the Eastern theologians based their conception of God upon a respect for the deliverances of conscience and for the moral teaching of Christ much more consistently than the Western.   And in their interpretation of the atonement the best of them at least seldom lost sight of that conception.   The one great compensating merit of Western theology is its much greater hold upon the humanity of Christ : the Greeks rarely escaped an Apollinarian tendency.[1]   With many of them it was an abstract " humanity " that the Logos assumed.   So far as the Latins emphasized the reality not merely of Christ's " flesh " but of His human soul, so far as they made Christ really share the " passions " and the sufferings of humanity, their view of redemption was a deeper one than the Greek.   Unfortunately the emphasis on Christ's humanity often only tended to increase the contrast between the Father who received, and the Son who offered, a sacrifice thought of as " placating " or " satisfying " God.[2]

With what degree of literalness the ransom doctrine and the substitutionary ideas which were, perhaps not very logically, associated with it, were accepted by philosophically minded Greek fathers, it would be hard to say.   It was, as we have seen, when the theory got into the hands of legally minded Westerns like Tertullian and his successors that it bore its bitterest fruit, and became the parent of many other views which have continued to blacken the character of God long after the formal abandonment of the ransom theory itself.   These tendencies reach their culmination in the writings of St. Augustine.

[1] The Antiochian school is of course an exception, and so was Origen himself, if the same cannot be said of his followers.
[2] Cf. Harnack, *Hist. of Dogma*, v. 54.

It must not, indeed, be supposed that we can draw an absolutely hard and fast line between the East and West in this matter, or that all the Western fathers exhibit the tendencies which we have already observed in Tertullian, and which culminate in St. Augustine. Hippolytus, the greatest of early Roman theologians, wrote in Greek, and must be looked upon as practically a Greek : his theology is the Origenistic theology of the Logos, and he tells us very little about the death of Christ.[1] Many of the early Latin writers treat the death of Christ very much in the spirit of the Apostolic fathers and the Apologists, though they are still simpler and less philosophical, and even the traditional statements about the death of Christ rarely occur. For Arnobius, Christ is the Teacher, the bringer of immortality, the Son of God who saves, but not specially by His death. When apologizing for the shameful death of the Christ, he has nothing to say but that His miracles show that the death was voluntary, and that He would not have endured it, were it not that " the inscrutable plan of fate had to be brought to light in hidden mysteries " — mysteries which none can understand " except those on whom He Himself has thought fit to bestow the blessing of so great knowledge " [2] — and Arnobius makes no claim to be one of these. From the writings of Lactantius it would be difficult to discover — but for the stock quotation from Isaiah liii. and the bare statement that Christ was " slain for the sins of many " — that there had ever been supposed to be any connexion between the death of Christ and the forgiveness of sins. The death of Christ is still treated simply, after the fashion of the earlier writers, as an example, a demonstration of His real Humanity, the indispensable prelude to the resurrection and the harrying of hell. There is much about the magical efficacy of the sign of the cross in the overcoming of demons, but nothing

---

[1] The much later Hilary of Poitiers is another Origenist in the West, but that does not prevent his speaking of Christ's suffering as penal (*In Psalm.* liii. 12) ; yet in the same passage he denies that Christ really felt the pain of the suffering ! Cf. *In Psalm.* lviii. 8, where the transaction with the Devil also appears.

[2] *Contra Gentes*, i. 62, 63.

about the expiatory value of the cross itself. Sometimes the whole philosophy of the incarnation consists in the doctrine that only God could be a perfect Teacher, and that only One who was a man could show men how to practise what He preached.[1]

But these Latin writers were apologists rather than theologians : they wrote for pagan readers, and did not attempt to unfold the more mysterious doctrines of their newly adopted faith. The more theological Latins carried on and exaggerated the legalizing tendencies of Tertullian. The two most influential of them, Cyprian and Ambrose, were lawyers. Cyprian, like Tertullian a native of Carthage, was a man of milder temperament or at all events more of a statesman and a man of the world. If he may be looked upon as in some sense the father of Sacerdotalism, it must be remembered that the system of ecclesiastical discipline grew up as a means of overcoming the harsh severity of those who would allow no forgiveness of grave post-baptismal sin. There can be no doubt, however, of the unfortunate effect which the penitential system exercised upon Western ideas about sin and salvation. Cyprian is full of the idea that post-baptismal sin must be " satisfied for," that God must be " placated " by prayers and tears, by fasting, by self-inflicted sufferings and almsgiving; and there emerges in his writings—distinctly, though faintly—the notion that saints and confessors are capable of earning more " merit " than is required for their own salvation, and that this merit can be transferred by the Church to the credit of others.[2] Generally speaking, it may be said that the tendency of Cyprianic views was to make salvation more than ever dependent upon the machinery of a single ecclesiastical organization. He is the author of the fatal saying that " outside the Church

---

[1] See Book iv. of his *Institutiones Divinae*, especially cc. 24, 25, where we find a very full discussion of the objections made to the shameful death of Christ, elaborate reasons for the particular form of death, and many wonderful stories of the wonder-working efficacy of the sign of the cross.

[2] See *De Lapsis* and *De Oper. et Eleemosyn., passim*. For a collection of passages illustrating these conceptions in Tertullian and Cyprian see Wirth, *Der Verdienst-Begriff* (Leipzig, 1892 and 1901). Cf. Bethune-Baker, *Introduction to the History of Christian Doctrine*, p. 353, and his article in *Church Quarterly Review*, Oct. 1902, p. 207.

there is no salvation " ; [1] and with him the test of being inside the Church is communion with the properly constituted Bishop.[2]

In Cyprian there is no new thought about the death of Christ.[3] He is fond of applying sacrificial language to that death, and he makes all redemption depend upon it. The one hope of a Christian is " in the wood." [4] The sacrifice offered by Christ upon the Cross, though admitted to be necessary to the forgiveness of original sin and the source of all sacramental efficacy, is, indeed, completely overshadowed by the prominence of ecclesiastical " satisfaction." That is not the case with St. Ambrose, who is much more distinctly the predecessor and master of St. Augustine; he fairly revels in the ransom theory, which he developes with much picturesque detail,[5] and he still further emphasizes the idea of substitution. The idea of substitutionary punishment has never yet found a more definite expression than in his doctrine that Christ died in order that, "since the divine decrees cannot be broken, the person rather than the sentence should be changed." [6] And, generally speaking, there is an increasing use of sacrificial language in speaking of Christ's death, and an increasing emphasis upon the ideas which form the characteristic element in the teaching of St.

[1] " Salus extra ecclesiam non est " (*Ep.* lxxiii. 21). Cf. *de Unitate Eccles.* 6 : " Habere jam non potest Deum patrem qui ecclesiam non habet matrem."

[2] *Ep.* lxvi. 8.

[3] The idea of the transaction with the Devil perhaps underlies the expression " quid vero astutius quidve subtilius quam ut Christi adventu detectus ac prostratus inimicus, etc." (*De Unitate Eccles.* 3). Harnack declares that Cyprian applied the idea of " satisfaction " to the sacrifice of Christ, but he gives no quotation or reference. The one clear instance of the idea of satisfaction being applied to the work of Christ before Anselm discovered by M. Rivière is in a passage of Radulphus Ardens, who was, however, a contemporary of his. *In Dom.* p. i. *Hom.* x. (Migne, T. clv. 1700).

[4] *Ep.* lxxvi. 2.

[5] He gives the theory a turn of his own by taking very seriously rhetorical metaphors of Origen. He states the transaction in terms of civil rather than of criminal justice. Adam incurred a debt to the Devil which had descended like a burdened estate, with ever accumulating interest, to his posterity. Christ by His death wiped out the interest, but transferred the debt to Himself, and He is a " bonus creditor " (*In Ps.* xxxvi. 46). Another original idea of Ambrose is that the marriage of the Virgin was part of the trickery by which the Devil was deceived, as also our Lord's silence as to His own divine nature (*In Luc. Exp.* ii. 3).

[6] " Ut quia solvi non queunt divina decreta, persona magis quam sententia mutaretur " (*In Luc. Exp.* iv. 7). Cf. *De fuga Saeculi*, vii. 44. For the trick on the Devil see *In Luc. Exp.* iv. 12 : " Oportuit igitur hanc fraudem diabolo fieri, ut susciperet corpus dominus Jesus et corpus hoc corruptibile. . . . Et ideo fames Domini pia fraus est," etc. (16).

Augustine—the fall, original sin, free grace, justification by faith;[1] although the freedom of the will is not yet definitely abandoned.

Another predecessor of St. Augustine deserves a brief mention—the unknown writer whose commentary on the whole of St. Paul's Epistles was formerly attributed to St. Ambrose, and who is now commonly spoken of as Ambrosiaster.[2] He states with peculiar distinctness the theory that the ransom scheme is justified by way of set-off for the unjust usurpation of authority of which the Devil or the devils had been guilty in bringing about the death of Christ. This idea is, I think, implied by Tertullian and other earlier writers, but it had never yet been so clearly stated as in the following sentences : "They [the evil spirits] became guilty, because, while they held the souls by the authority derived from the fact that they had sinned, they were themselves found sinners in a higher degree, inasmuch as they slew Him who had conquered them by not sinning. And so they were justly despoiled, as he [St. Paul] has said 'publicly,' that is on the cross."[3] This is precisely, as we shall see, the form of the theory adopted by St. Augustine. But I do not propose to dwell further upon the approximations to the Augustinian theology in other Latin writers :

[1] " Deus enim maluit ut salus homini fide potius quam operibus quaereretur ; ne quis gloriaretur in suis factis, et peccatum incurreret " (In Ps. xliii. Enarratio 14).

The tone of Ambrose is far less severe than that of St. Augustine, especially in three ways : (1) He retained the belief in freewill. (2) The horror of the fall and its consequence is mitigated by a strong insistence upon the idea afterwards embodied in the Church's hymn, " O felix culpa " (" Amplius nobis profuit culpa quam nocuit." De Inst. Virg. xvii. 104). (3) He played a leading part in developing the idea of Purgatory for " peccata non voluntaria, sed fortuita," a doctrine upon which he insists much more strongly than Augustine : " Iusti urentur donec impleant tempora inter primam et secundam resurrectionem ; aut si non impleverint, diutius in supplicio permanebunt " (In Psalm. i. Enarr. 54). For a collection of eschatological passages cf. Förster, Ambrosius Bischof von Mailand, pp. 172-5.

[2] From a passage in the book it seems that the author lived in the pontificate of Damasus (366–384), but it is probable that there are later insertions.

[3] " Rei enim facti sunt : quia, cum hac auctoritate animas tenerent quia peccaverant, ipsi inventi sunt amplius peccatores, dum illum qui eos non peccando vicerat occiderunt. Et sic iuste exspoliati sunt, sicut dixit, publice, id est in cruce " (In Col. ii. 15). It will be observed that the actual victory here lies in the resistance to temptation, and is quite independent of the cross : the cross has the effect of justifying the loss of power in the demons and the release of man, but the moral effect is independent of the cross. The writer makes St. Paul teach that it was decreed by God " ut, cessante lege, solam fidem gratia Dei posceret ad salutem " (Com. in Rom. iv. 5), but when he comes to Gal. v. 6 he remembers that " fides charitate fraterna debet muniri, ut perfectio sit credentis "—practically the doctrine of " fides formata."

we will pass at once to the great father who has dominated
Western theology — Catholic, Medieval, Protestant—
to an extent which has thrown into the background the
influence of all his Western predecessors.[1]

Augustine

The whole theology of St. Augustine centred round
the idea of redemption : all else is subordinate to it :
he tells us explicitly that if there had been no fall, Christ
would never have come.[2]   And redemption was, according to him, effected not merely by Christ, but mainly or
solely by His death.   And yet, when we consider the
central place which the death of Christ occupies in his
theology, it is astonishing to find how inadequately the
explanation of its necessity and efficacy is worked out.
He accepts the traditional scheme, and adds little to
it.   Just because the ransom theory, originally intended
to explain received dogmas, has by this time become itself
a dogma, it is accepted without thought or explanation or
defence.   It is constantly referred to in an allusive manner
as a truth which every one received, and which scarcely
needed exposition.   Anxious to save the omnipotence
of God, St. Augustine does, indeed, insist that, when mankind for the sin of the first man were handed over to the
power of the Devil, they did not cease to be the subjects of
God.   The falling of man under the power of the Devil
thus becomes rather a judicial sentence on the part of
God than an act of conquest on the part of the evil one.
But the dominion of the Devil is distinctly spoken of as
just, and it could not have been justly ended, it would
seem, unless the Devil had forfeited his rights by his own
injustice towards Christ.   St. Augustine does not dwell
so much as Ambrose and other predecessors upon the
idea that the death of Christ was a gain or advantage to
the Devil; but he does sometimes distinctly treat the blood
of Christ as a ransom which was given to the Devil and

---

[1] I do not propose to trace the growth of St. Augustine's mind.   What follows must
be taken as an account of his fully developed system, exhibited especially by the anti-
pelagian treatises.

[2] " Si homo non perisset, filius hominis non venisset " (*Serm.* clxxiv. 2).

which the Devil received.[1] More usually Christ's death is treated as a penal infliction endured by Christ instead of man ; but still it is endured because justice requires that it should be endured.[2] The Devil thus becomes rather the executioner of God's justice than the creditor who demands dominion over man as his due, though the other thought is not wholly absent. It is sometimes suggested in recent controversy that the idea of vicarious punishment as distinguished from vicarious satisfaction is a purely Protestant notion. The distinction, whatever be its worth, cannot be admitted in the case of St. Augustine. If he more frequently speaks of Christ as paying a debt than as suffering a punishment, the word " punishment " is distinctly used,[3] but not (any more than in other fathers) the characteristic term of later Catholicism " satisfaction."[4] And such vicarious punishment was perfectly just, since the sin of Adam passed by direct inheritance to all Adam's descendants, and so all men might justly have been doomed to eternal torments. But God chose arbitrarily to remit some part of the penalty which He might justly have claimed. The Father was content to accept the death of His innocent Son as the equivalent of that punishment in the case of some small minority of those who had inherited the guilt. St. Augustine, indeed, will not say that God could not

---

[1] " In hac redemptione tamquam pretium pro nobis datus est sanguis Christi, quo accepto diabolus non ditatus est, sed ligatus : ut nos ab eius nexibus solveremur, nec quenquam secum eorum quos Christus, ab omni debito liber, indebite fuso suo sanguine redemisset, peccatorum retibus involutum traheret ad secundae ac sempiternae mortis exitium " (De Trin. xiii. c. 15). M. Rivière, who is anxious to distinguish St. Augustine's theory from that of the ransom, admits that here, " une fois au moins," he uses the word and the idea. To my mind the idea is just as clearly implied in other passages, whether or not the actual word may be used. On this matter see the additional note at the end of this chapter (p. 364).

[2] " Quadam justitia Dei in potestatem diaboli traditum est genus humanum, peccato primi hominis in omnes utriusque sexus commixtione nascentes originaliter transeunte, et parentum primorum debito universos posteros obligante " (De Trin. l. xiii. c. 12). So elsewhere he speaks of " hominum genus per consensum seductum tamquam iure integro possidebat," and says that " iure aequissimo " Christ conquered him and freed him " a captivitate propter peccatum justa " (ib. l. iv. c. 13).

[3] " Confitere suscepisse poenam peccati nostri sine peccato nostro " (Contra Faust. xiv. 7). " Solus pro nobis suscepit sine malis meritis poenam " (Contra duas Epp. Pelagianorum, iv. 4).

[4] Loofs makes the statement of Augustine : Rivière (Le Dogme de la Réd. p. 105) extends it to all the fathers before Anselm. That Roman theologians should be wedded to this non-patristic conception is not a matter for surprise. It is occasionally defended by Anglicans who repudiate the idea of substituted punishment as " protestant." I cannot myself see much difference between the two ideas.

have redeemed men by some other means.   But he holds
that the arrangement actually adopted was just, and was
peculiarly " convenient " or congruous to the nature
and character of God, because no other method of redemption would have exhibited so much love.[1]   Man
was justly redeemed from the power of the Devil because
it was through the justice or goodness of Christ that
the emancipation was effected, because the punishment
was really paid by man, because the worth or merit of
the voluntary death of One who was not only sinless,
but God as well as man, was so enormous that the Devil
who had brought about that death could not, after so
immense a payment, justly be allowed to retain man in
his dominion, or to inflict upon him that spiritual death
which was the most important part of the penalty incurred
by sin.   " The Devil," says St. Augustine, " held our
sins " (as the title-deed, so to speak, of his dominion
over us), " and through them deservedly planted us in
death.   He, who had no sins of His own, dismissed
them, and yet was undeservedly conducted by him [the
Devil] to death.   That blood was of so great worth,
that no one clothed with Christ ought to be detained in
the eternal death which was his due by him who, even
for a time, slew Christ with undeserved death."[2]   "What
is therefore," he continues, " the justice wherewith the
Devil was conquered ?   What but the justice of Jesus
Christ ?   And how was he conquered ?   Because he
found nothing worthy of death in Him ; yet he slew Him.
And surely it was just that the debtors whom he held
should be dismissed free, on believing in Him whom,
without any debt incurred, he slew.   This is why we

---

[1] " Eos ita qui dicunt : Itane defuit Deo modus alius, quo liberaret homines . . .
parum est sic refellere ut istum modum quo nos per mediatorem Dei et hominum Christum Jesum Deus liberare dignatur, asseramus bonum et divinae congruum dignitati :
verum etiam ut ostendamus non alium modum possibilem Deo defuisse, cujus potestati
cuncta aequaliter subjacent, sed sanandae nostrae miseriae convenientiorem modum
alium non fuisse, nec esse opportuisse.   Quid enim tam necessarium fuit ad erigendam
spem nostram mentesque mortalium conditione ipsius mortalitatis abjectas ab immortalitatis desperatione liberandas, quam ut demonstraretur nobis, quanti nos penderet Deus
quantumque diligeret ? " (De Trin. xiii. c. 10).

[2] " Peccata nostra diabolus tenebat, et per illa nos merito figebat in morte.   Dimisit
ea ille, qui sua non habebat, et ab illo immerito est perductus ad mortem.   Tanti valuit
sanguis ille, ut neminem Christo indutum in aeterna morte debite detinere debuerit, qui
Christum morte indebita vel ad tempus occidit " (De Trin. xiii. c. 16).

are said to be justified in Christ's blood. Thus, that
is to say, that innocent blood was poured out for the
remission of our sins."[1] Augustine goes on to insist
on the peculiar justice of the debt being paid by one
who was man as well as God—the old thought of
Irenaeus. If He had not been man, He could not
have been killed : had He not been God, the voluntariness of His death would not have been so apparent.[2]
In another passage he compares the humanity of Christ
to the bait in a mouse-trap which the Devil inadvertently
swallowed, and so brought about his own ruin and the
deliverance of mankind.[3]

St. Augustine has many other ways of representing
the death of Christ.[4] He discovers all sorts of congruities
or advantages in the particular mode of redemption
actually adopted by the providence of God—those which
we have already met with and others. Sometimes he
represents it as a sacrifice of unique expiatory value :
Christ is the victim offered for our sins. At other times
he insists (very much in the vein of Irenaeus) on the
peculiar suitability of the sacrificer and the victim being
the same ; on the sacrifice being a sacrifice of mortal
human flesh, the very flesh that had sinned ; and, above
all, upon the cleansing power of a body born otherwise
than of carnal desire, and therefore sinless.[5] At times

---

[1] " Quae est igitur justitia qua victus est diabolus ? Quae nisi justitia Jesu Christi ?
Et quomodo victus est ? Quia in eo nihil morte dignum inveniret, occidit eum tamen.
Et utique justum est ut debitores quos tenebat liberi dimittantur in eum credentes
quem sine ullo debito occidit. Hoc est quod justificari dicimur in Christi sanguine.
Sic quippe in remissionem peccatorum nostrorum innocens sanguis ille effusus est " (De
Trin. xiii. c. 14).

[2] " Ideo autem illum esse opus erat et hominem et Deum. Nisi enim homo esset,
non posset occidi : nisi Deus esset, non crederetur noluisse quod potuit, sed non potuisse
quod voluit ; nec ab eo justitiam potentiae praelatam fuisse, sed ei defuisse potentiam
putaremus. . . . Et justitia ergo prius et potentia postea diabolum vicit : justitia scilicet,
quia nullum peccatum habuit, et ab illo injustissime est occisus ; potentia vero quia
revixit mortuus, nunquam postea moriturus " (ib.).

[3] " Exultavit diabolus quando mortuus est Christus, et ipsa morte Christi est diabolus
victus : tamquam in muscipula escam accepit. Gaudebat ad mortem quasi praepositus
mortis. Ad quod gaudebat, inde illi tensum est. Muscipula diaboli, crux Domini ;
esca qua caperetur, mors Domini (Serm. cclxiii. 1. So in Serm. cxxx. 2).

[4] " Nos enim ad mortem per peccatum venimus, ille per justitiam : et ideo cum sit
mors nostra poena peccati, mors illius facta est hostia pro peccato " (De Trin. l. iv.
c. 12).

[5] " Et quid tam mundum pro mundandis vitiis mortalium quam sine ulla contagione
carnalis concupiscentiae caro nata in utero et ex utero virginali ? Et quid tam grate offerri
et suscipi posset, quam caro sacrificii nostri corpus effectum sacerdotis nostri ? Ut . . .

he descends to the most childish conceits. Like his avowed but little understood philosophical master, Plato, he delights in the mystical properties of numbers. There is a peculiar beauty or harmony in the relation of two to one : therefore it was intrinsically fitting that the one death of Christ (death of the body only) should be accepted in place of the double death (the death of body and soul) incurred by man,[1] and so on. But, on the whole, in St. Augustine the idea of substituted or vicarious punishment is the central one. It stands out in his pages naked and unabashed. And St. Augustine's doctrine on this subject and no other was accounted orthodox doctrine in the Western Church until the advent of medieval Scholasticism.

We have noticed the extraordinarily small influence which was exercised over the theology of the early Church by the more distinctive ideas of St. Paul. That influence had, indeed, become strong in Tertullian, Ambrose, Victorinus, Optatus and other Latins—though combined with much that had other origins. In St. Augustine we find for the first time a theologian in whom the influence of St. Paul is overwhelmingly predominant. And yet it is not too much to say that the whole tone and spirit of the two are different. This is accounted for partly by the fact that the authority of St. Paul and his plenary inspiration turned every passing phrase, every metaphor, every momentary exaggeration of his into a hard and rigid dogma, followed out to its logical consequences with remorseless consistency, and partly by the enormous mass of doctrinal and ecclesiastical

---

idem ipse unus verusque Mediator, per sacrificium pacis reconcilians nos Deo, unum cum illo maneret cui offerebat, unum in se faceret pro quibus offerebat, unus ipse esset qui offerebat et quod offerebat" (*De Trin.* L. iv. c. 14). He retains, too, the old Greek thought that Christ took our mortal body to make us participate in His Divinity.

[1] " Merito quippe mors peccatoris veniens ex damnationis necessitate soluta est per mortem justi venientem ex misericordiae voluntate, dum simplum ejus congruit duplo nostro. Haec enim congruentia sive convenientia vel concinentia vel consonantia vel si quod commodius dicitur, quod unum est ad duo, in omni compaginatione vel, si melius dicitur, coaptatione creaturae, valet plurimum. Hanc enim coaptationem, sicut mihi nunc occurrit, dicere volui quam Graeci ἁρμονίαν vocant" (*De Trin.* iv. c. 2). As to Christ's intercession, cf. iv. 8 : " Patrem interpellans pro nobis per id quod homo erat . . . ita loquitur : ' Non pro his autem rogo,' " etc.

development which had taken place since St. Paul's time, and in accordance with which he had now to be interpreted. The result was a system and a view of the character of God at which St. Paul himself, it is probable, would have stood aghast. It may be well to point out as clearly as possible how far the teaching of St. Augustine agreed with and how far it differed from that of St. Paul.

(1) The doctrine of original sin is undoubtedly Pauline; and it is a doctrine which in itself, taken apart from its connexion with a supposed historical fall of Adam, might well ground itself simply upon the experienced facts of human nature. Modern ideas about evolution and heredity have only emphasized its truth. But with St. Augustine this doctrine receives an enormous development. His whole theology is based upon it. Everything in St. Paul which is left vague and indefinite is hardened and defined. According to St. Augustine, man was originally endowed with free-will in the popular sense of the term.[1] By the fall that freedom was lost for ever. Adam's posterity were born not merely (as the earlier fathers had taught) with a hereditary sinfulness of nature or tendency to sin, but actual sinners.[2] There was an inheritance both of guilt and of sin. None can escape that entail of sin except possibly the Mother of Christ.[3] Original sin, even before it has manifested itself in actual sinful desire or act, is an act of will and

---

[1] " Potuit enim non peccare primus homo, potuit non mori, potuit bonum non deserere " (*De correptione et gratia*, 12). " Homo quamdiu stetit in bona voluntate liberi arbitrii, non opus habebat ea gratia qua leuaretur cum surgere ipse non potest : nunc vero in ruina sua, liber est iustitiae servusque peccati : nec potest servus esse justitiae, et liber a dominante peccato, nisi eum filius liberaverit " (*Contra Julianum, opus imperfect.* i. 81). But it did require a divine " assistance," which was always forthcoming, as a *sine qua non* : " Datum est ei adiutorium perseverantiae " (*De corrept.* 12).

[2] Just as a man who by previous sins has formed a bad habit, and so placed himself under the necessity of sinning, is justly held responsible for his present sins, because he is responsible for their cause, so, it was explained, the human race is responsible for the sins of Adam because the sin of Adam is the cause of its present viciousness. " Cur ergo non creditis tantum saltem valuisse illud primi hominis ineffabiliter grande peccatum, ut eo vitiaretur humana universa natura, quantum valet nunc in homine uno secunda natura " (*Contra Julianum, opus imperfect.* i. i. 104). He assumes that the fact that infants suffer shows that they are sinful : " Propter quid ergo affliguntur parvuli, si nullum habent omnino peccatum ? " (*Op. imperfect.* ii. 81). All disease and pain as well as physical death are for St. Augustine consequences of the fall : this was denied by the Pelagians.

[3] " Excepta itaque sancta Maria Virgine, de qua propter honorem Domini nullam prorsus, cum de peccatis agitur, habere volo questionem ; unde enim scimus quid ei plus gratiae collatum fuerit ad vincendum omni ex parte peccatum " (*De Natura et Gratia*, 36).

is justly punishable. Sometimes the point is insisted upon that all his posterity was in the loins of Adam when he sinned, and so did actually sin ; original sin is therefore actual sin.[1]

St. Augustine would doubtless have accepted that saying of Calderon which Schopenhauer quotes with so much approval : " The greatest crime of man is that ever he was born." [2] For that sin God might justly have doomed the youngest infant dying a few minutes after birth to eternal torments, and He has so doomed enormously the greater part of the human race. And in the case of those who grow up, the natural badness of the human heart is such that it is absolutely incapable— apart from the supernatural grace of God, which is vouchsafed only to believers—of a single good desire or good action.[3] Hitherto, the doctrine of original sin had been taught in a way that was quite consistent with the admission that much of the image of God remained in the human soul after the fall. Such admissions are to be found in St. Augustine, but they are perfunctory. Later Protestant theory only a little exaggerated St. Augustine's teaching when it converted the " total depravity " of human nature into a dogma. For St. Augustine the *guilt* of original sin was remitted by baptism, but the badness itself remained. St. Augustine cannot quite say, without qualification, that all concupiscence is sin, for that would be to deny the efficacy of baptism. The guilt is removed, but the thing itself— the concupiscence—remains, and concupiscence is always evil, even when the will does not assent to it or allow it to culminate in actual sin : he will even say that " in a certain sense " it *is* sin,[4] and it is certain to result in actual

---

[1] He approves of Ambrose's statement that " in illo [Adam] fuisse omnes, perisse Adam et in illo perisse omnes " (*Contra Julianum*, i. 7).

[2] *The World as Will and Idea* (translated by Haldane and Hunt), i. pp. 328, 458.

[3] " Humana hic merita conticescant, quae perierunt per Adam " (*De Predestinatione*, 15). Of course St. Augustine is not merely denying that any human goodness can really imply merit in the sense of a right to demand reward of God as a matter of right, but that there is any real goodness at all before justification.

[4] " Quod concupiscentia maneat actu, et praetereat reatu " (*Contra Julian.* VI. 19. 60 : elsewhere the guilt is said to be removed, while the infirmity remains (*l.c.* ii. 1). But " modo quodam loquendi [concupiscentia] peccatum vocatur, quod et peccato facta est, et peccatum si vicerit, facit reum " (*De nuptiis et concupiscentia*, I. 23). St. Augustine

sin. By concupiscence St. Augustine means all natural
desire, but especially sexual desire, the existence of which
is to him a consequence of the fall and the chief evidence
for the reality of original sin : in fact the two things are
all but identified. The prominence of this idea in St.
Augustine amounts to an obsession. Every human
being born as the result of such desire is naturally and
necessarily sinful. Original sin *is* actual sin—to be
imputed to the free-will of the unborn infant. His
antipathy to marriage only just stops short of actual
condemnation.[1] In all this he goes much beyond anything which is to be found in St. Paul. The Pelagians
were not far wrong when they declared that at the bottom
of his heart Augustine remained a Manichee to the end
of his days.

(2) There have been different interpretations of St.
Paul's doctrines of election, grace, predestination. Only
one interpretation is possible in the case of St. Augustine.
As regards man's condition after the fall, he is an absolute
predestinarian or determinist. There is nothing in that
doctrine, taken by itself, which is inconsistent with the
doctrine of human free-will—understood in the sense
of what modern philosophers call self-determination, and
in such self-determination St. Augustine undoubtedly
believed.[2] On the other hand the popular doctrine of

---

sometimes admits an abstract possibility of avoiding sin after baptism : " Utrum quisque hoc munus acceperit, quamdiu hanc vitam ducit, incertum est " (*De dono Perseverantiae*, 1).

[1] " Ex originali peccato quod est commissum libero arbitrio " (*De Nat. et Grat.* 3 ;
cf. *De nuptiis et concupiscentia, passim*). The guilt of concupiscence is remitted by
baptism, but the thing itself remains and is always evil, though in marriage, when subordinate to the procreation of children, good use may be made of the evil thing : " Imputat vero non iam aliena sed propria. Aliena quippe erant quando hi qui ea propagata
portarent nondum erant : nunc vero carnali generatione iam eorum sunt, quibus nondum spiritali regeneratione dimissa sunt " (*De pecc. meritis*, iii. 8). The logic of St.
Augustine's thought implies that the soul as well as the body came by inheritance rather
than by a new creation, and he was strongly inclined to Traducianism, but the subject
puzzled him (see *e.g. lib. cit.* ii. 35, iii. 10). But for the fall the species would have
propagated by sexual intercourse, indeed, but without the necessity of sexual desire.
See *De Grat. et pecc. orig.* ii. 35 *sq.* The Pelagians treated concupiscence without the
consent of the will to any evil desire as innocent, and consequently attributed it to Christ.

[2] " Liberum ergo arbitrium euacuamus per gratiam ? Absit, sed magis liberum
arbitrium statuimus . . . quia gratia sanat voluntatem qua justitia libere diligatur "
(*De Spir. et Lit.* c. 30). It is clear that here the will is said to be free only when it
loves justice for its own sake (an equivocal use of the term which Kant has perpetuated),
and this is only possible to those who are already justified. Archdeacon Cunningham's
account of St. Augustine's view of predestination (*St. Austin*, Lect. iii.) seems to me

free-will in the sense of indeterminism—the real possibility of two alternative courses (*possibilitas utriusque partis*)
—the doctrine, accepted by most Anglican theologians of
all dates, was to him Pelagianism.   Now there is nothing
in such a view which is necessarily inconsistent with the
justice or the goodness of God.   Whether the idea of predestination can or cannot be reconciled with the idea of a
just and a loving God depends entirely upon our idea of
the end for which men of evil character are brought into
the world.   St. Paul is silent as to the fate of those who
are not elected to receive the grace which causes them to
believe, and to receive a moral regeneration qualifying
them for ultimate salvation.   Generally he assumes
that the fate of those who have died before the coming
of Christ or who are rejected at the judgement will be
" destruction," by which we may most naturally understand extinction of consciousness.   With St. Augustine
mercy is for the very few.   All human beings who lived
before the coming of Christ are doomed to everlasting
torments, except the pious Jews, and a few exceptional
Gentiles like Job and the Sybil, who believed in the
future coming of Christ, as well as those who, since the
coming of Christ, have failed to satisfy the Christian
conditions of salvation, though the possibility of purgatory for imperfect Christians is suggested.[1]   No doubt
St. Augustine assures us that in this tremendous sentence
God is perfectly just, and by means of the old philosophic
sophism about the purely negative nature of evil (" malum
est privatio boni ") he can still say that God is not the

---

wholly misleading.   He fails to see, or at least to recognize with sufficient candour, that
St. Augustine only escapes the conclusion that God causes evil (i.) by the sophism that
evil has no positive existence (" malum est privatio boni "), but is merely a " defect,"
which cannot be said to be created ; (ii.) by the assumption that all evil in the sub-human
world springs from the fall of man or from some similar " spontaneus defectus a bono "
(*Contra Julianum*, i. 8), thus allowing for the possibility of an uncaused event ; (iii.) by
his doctrine that the whole as a whole is good, and that so it is good that evil should
exist.   The last doctrine might be accepted if we admitted the presupposition that the
omnipotence of God must be understood as not excluding some limitation, but this
Augustine never cordially does.   As it stands, it is impossible to defend Augustine's
view without practically admitting that " good " for God means something quite different
from what it does for us, and so denying the validity of the moral judgement.   It is
impossible to make out that Augustine's predestinarianism is one whit less uncompromising than that of Calvin, though no doubt his view of human nature is a shade
less untrue to facts.

[1] *Encheiridion*, c. 69.

cause of evil. But the unsophisticated reason and conscience of mankind will refuse to recognize a Being who brings such an overwhelming balance of sin and misery into the world as a just, a righteous, or a loving God. According to any reasonable computation of the value of the blessedness enjoyed by the few as compared with the sin and the everlasting misery of the many, the evil must enormously predominate. And for the existence of that evil St. Augustine cannot (like Origen) plead any intrinsic necessity of things, for his idea of the arbitrary omnipotence of God is absolutely unqualified. If St. Augustine is asked why God creates so much misery and sin and so little goodness and happiness, why He gives grace to one and withholds it from another, he can only answer : Some are saved to show God's mercy, others damned to show the truth of His vengeance.[1]

(3) As to what the conditions are under which some small portion of the human race is to be saved from the appalling doom that is to overtake the vast majority, there can also be no doubt. They are baptism, repentance, faith, reception of the eucharist, communion with the true visible Church.[2] In the case of infants, baptism alone is necessary. For unbaptized infants there is no hope, though theirs is the "mildest punishment" (*mitissima poena*). All who are not with Christ are with the Devil.[3] Equally little hope is there for the best of pagans. For St. Augustine their virtues are but "splendid vices," for their good deeds cannot be done from right motives, and so are not really virtues. Denifle has indeed pointed out that the famous phrase "splendid vices" is not found in St. Augustine, but it correctly

---

[1] " Neque enim utrumque demonstratur in omnibus, quia, si omnes remanerent in poenis iustae damnationis, in nullo appareret misericors gratia ; rursus si omnes a tenebris transferrentur in lucem, in nullo appareret veritas ultionis " (*De Civ. Dei*, xxi. 12).

[2] " Nec salus nec vita aeterna sine baptismo et corpore et sanguine Domini cuiquam speranda est " (*De peccatorum meritis*, i. 24). Perhaps penance should be added, since its necessity is often dwelt upon. It is unnecessary to quote passages in which the necessity of faith is insisted on, but faith will not avail without baptism : in commenting on Matt. xix. 14 he explains that "to believe " in the case of infants means " to be baptized " (*De peccatorum meritis*, i. 19).

[3] " Potest proinde recte dici parvulos sine baptismo de corpore exeuntes in damnatione omnium mitissima futuros. Multum autem fallit et fallitur qui eos in damnatione praedicat non futuros " (*De pecc. meritis*, i. 16). There can be no intermediate region, " ut possit esse nisi cum diabolo qui non est cum Christo " (*ib. c.* 28).

expresses his teaching. He does actually declare that in a heathen pity is a vice.[1] I need not say that there is nothing of all this in St. Paul. On the least universal-istic interpretation of St. Paul, the heathen or the un-baptized infant simply perish.

(4) In his insistence upon faith, St. Augustine has St. Paul on his side. And St. Paul does formally in some passages treat faith as meaning merely intellectual belief, though elsewhere he seems to make it include much more. Nowhere does he value faith without love. But, after all, the belief which St. Paul required was very simple—a general belief in the Messiahship of Jesus and in the revelation of God through Him. He never suggests that his opponents (extreme as were their differences) would be lost at the judgement : on the contrary many of them would be saved as through fire. St. Augustine meant by faith belief[2]—intellectual belief—in the enormously complicated mass of dogmatic statements, chiefly about the doctrine of the Holy Trinity, which the creed of the Church had come to embrace.

[1] The fourth book of *Contra Julianum Pelagianum* is devoted to the virtues of the heathen ; see especially cap. 3.   Augustine admits that the heathen might do the acts which justice, charity, etc., required (humility being the only kind of virtuous action which is denied them), but they are not true virtues but rather " base and ugly . . . though to you they seem so true and beautiful," because (1) not done from right motives, *i.e.* because commanded by God (" propter illum ") ; (2) because they are not ac-companied by faith, the absence of which by itself makes the will bad, however good the motive. Thus in a heathen pity is a vice : " vitium est infideliter misereri." As to exactly what the true motive is, Augustine is by no means verbally consistent. " Caritas " is constantly spoken of as the true motive ; yet sometimes the " caritas " is explained as being the " caritas felicitatis aeternae " (*De Civ. Dei*, v. 24), which comes very near the frank egoism of Paley, who maintained that virtue consisted in " doing good to man-kind in obedience to the will of God and for the sake of everlasting happiness." He can hardly mean " desire of eternal felicity for others."

[2] He expressly disclaims the identification of faith with " trust " : " De hac enim fide nunc loquimur quam adhibemus cum aliquid credimus, non quam damus cum aliquid pollicemur" (*De Spir. et Lit.* c. 31). His habitual synonym for " to have faith" is "credere." He insists strongly upon the doctrine that belief is an act of the will, but we must not suppose that the " will to believe " is any the less due to grace and nothing else. We must not be misled by such a statement as " ipsum velle credere Deus operatur in homine . . . ; consentire autem vocationi Dei, vel ab ea dissentire, . . . propriae voluntatis est " (*De Spir. et Lit.* c. 34). If the context is attended to, it will be seen that St. Augustine is merely distinguishing between the kind of belief which is forced upon the mind, *e.g.* by the presentation of outward objects, and that which requires an effort of will ; but the act of will itself is the necessary result of " prevenient " and " co-operating " grace. The libertarian interpretation given to such passages by Denifle (as against Luther) and most modern Roman Catholics is quite unjustified. As a really scholarly and trust-worthy statement of St. Augustine's doctrine, Mozley's *Augustinian Doctrine of Pre-destination* may still be recommended as the best English book on the subject.

Without correct belief charity would avail nothing.[1]
Heretics and schismatics were as little capable of salvation
as pagans. At the same time it is important to observe
that no one could state more clearly the uselessness of
faith without love. Heretics and schismatics were lost
because they had no love. " Faith," he declares, " can
exist indeed without love, but it avails not." At times
he will even say : " To believe in Christ is to love Christ."
So far he is quite Pauline : not so in his extreme emphasis
on doctrinal orthodoxy.

(5) A word must be said as to St. Augustine's use of
the term " grace." There is a tendency even in St.
Paul to a technical conception of grace ; yet in him it
never lost its primary meaning, which was simply the
" favour " or " mercy " of God. To St. Augustine the
term grace means a divine influence upon the soul
without which it is incapable of the smallest good action.[2]
So far there is nothing to criticize : the meaning of the
word has changed, but there is no harm in the change.
Certainly no modern theistic philosopher will quarrel
with St. Augustine for saying that neither right belief nor
right action is possible without a divine activity in the
soul. Few modern philosophers will defend the semi-
Pelagian evasion which suggests that one and the same
human will has (independently of the divine energy)
that " free-will of indifference " which enables it to
co-operate or not to co-operate with the promptings of
the divine Spirit, and which makes all the man's conduct

---

[1] " Eadem quippe Trinitate fruendum est, ut beate vivamus ; si autem falsum de
illa crediderimus, inanis erit spes et non casta charitas : quomodo igitur Trinitatem quam
non novimus credendo diligimus ? " (De Trin. viii. 5). Elsewhere he declares that there
are many who call themselves martyrs, but who on account of their errors are outside
the Church (" praeter ecclesiam tuam "), and therefore are not " sons of thine hand-
maid " (In Psalm. cxv.).

[2] " In the doctrine of grace two different conceptions are manifestly combined,
namely, the thought of grace through (per, propter) Christ, and that of grace emanating
independently of Christ from the essential nature of God as the supreme good and supreme
being (' summum bonum, summum esse '). The latter inconsistency was of greatest importance for Augustine's own Theology, and for the attitude of Western Theology after
him " (Harnack, Hist. of Dogma, v. 101-2). It is true that from the point of view of
orthodox Christology the " combination " may be defended, since the influence comes
equally from Son and Father : but it had undoubtedly the disastrous consequence of
enabling the medieval Church to adopt the language of St. Paul, and yet practically to
ascribe salvation almost entirely to the operation of sacraments which had only a nominal
connexion with the historical Christ without any consciously experienced influence of
the historical Personality revealed in the Gospels. Cf. below, p. 377 sq.

essentially " undetermined," incalculable, and independent of his previous character. St. Augustine's later followers were right enough in contending that, when the response is made by the human will, that response is itself due to grace. The real complaint against St. Augustine is not that he conceded too much to grace, but that he too sharply and arbitrarily differentiated between the divine influence which is shown by the good works of the pagan and those of the baptized believer— between what are called merely " natural " virtues and those which are the effect of grace ; [1] and that he at least gave a powerful impetus to the tendency which almost identified this divine influence with a quasi-magical operation of the sacraments. The modern theologian who wishes to tread in the steps of Justin and Clement and Origen will not ascribe the good works of a Socrates or a Marcus Aurelius or a modern agnostic, in Pelagian fashion, to the use which they have made of a free-will with which the divine will and action have nothing to do. They will rather say that whatever measure of goodness there was in such men was due, no less than the virtues of a St. Paul or a St. Francis of Assisi, to different kinds and different measures of the same divine influence.

(6) The word " justification " in St. Augustine means a making righteous, not (as in St. Paul) a declaring righteous.[2] This change in the meaning of the term corresponds with the real thought, though not with the actual usage, of St. Paul. And it is one which had at least the advantage that it made quite impossible any disparagement of the necessity for good works. There could not be justification without a measure of real

---

[1] Cf. Harnack, v. 65 : " He was the first to separate *nature* and *grace*." How Harnack can go on to say that " by this means he connected religion and morality " I fail to see. I should have said that the distinction, when made sharp and absolute, tends in precisely the opposite direction.

[2] " Ut iustificetur, id est iustus fiat " (*De Spir. et Lit.* 10). The " justitia Dei " spoken of by St. Paul is so called because " impertiendo eam iustos facit " (*ib.* c. 11). St. Paul's " the doers of the law shall be justified " is explained to mean that good works can only be done by believers in Christ : " iustificationem opera non praecedunt " (c. 26). He goes on to interpret " justified " as " iusti deputabuntur," but, as he adds, (unlike later Protestants), only those can be thus " held just " who have actually been made just.

goodness, and consequently, when the opportunity is given, good works. There is nothing fictitious in the righteousness which is given to the justified; it is no mere "imputation" of an unreal goodness. Augustine has no objection even to saying that there is a "merit" in these good works: only the merit is itself a gift of God.[1] St. Augustine would have done still better perhaps if he had banished the word "merit" altogether from these controversies, as belonging rather to the half-thought-out conventions of human life than to the real deliverances of the moral consciousness. Had he done so, some of the worst features of his own and subsequent justification theories would have been avoided. The idea of intrinsic worth represents much better all that is true in the idea: the notion that the intrinsic value of one man's act or character can be transferred to another and quite different character would be too absurd to occur to any one; nor could the most unethical of theologians well suppose that, where there is real goodness, however much it may be due to the influence of another, that goodness is worthless.[2]

(7) But the greatest of all differences between St. Paul and St. Augustine remains to be mentioned—the difference of moral ideal. Whatever may be thought of the relation between the theology of Christ Himself and that of His great disciple, there can be no doubt as to the marvellous identity in their ethical ideal—an identity which, as I have already contended, is accounted

---

[1] "Justitiam quippe dare sibi non potest quam perditam non habet. . . . Accipit ergo iustitiam, propter quam beatitudinem accipere mereatur" (*De Trin.* xiv. 15).

[2] It may be observed that, though St. Augustine's is often treated as the typical or classical instance of sudden conversion, he never dogmatizes about the necessity of a sudden conversion, nor does he show any disposition to hold that a complete change of character is effected either by conversion or by baptism: he insists very much on the gradualness of the resulting changes. "Sane ista renovatio non momento uno fit ipsius conversionis, sicut momento uno fit illa in baptismo renovatio remissione omnium peccatorum: neque enim vel unum quantulumcunque remanet quod non remittatur. Sed quemadmodum aliud est carere febribus, aliud ab infirmitate, quae febribus facta est, revalescere, etc.," (*De Trin.* xiv. 17). "Resuscitatur enim anima per poenitentiam, et in corpore adhuc mortali renovatio vitae inchoatur a fide, qua creditur in eum qui justificat impium, bonisque moribus augetur et roboratur de die in diem, cum magis magisque renovatur interior homo" (*ib.* iv. 3; cf. *De pecc. meritis*, ii. 27). Moreover, grace may always be lost: in this life no one can ever be certain of election. See *De dono Perseverantiae, passim.* On this point extreme Calvinism can get no support from St. Augustine.

for by a much closer and more direct influence of the historical Christ and His teaching than it is fashionable at the present moment to recognize. We cannot say the same of St. Augustine. He acknowledges as fully as St. Paul the supremacy of charity, and he was no less devoted to the extension of the Kingdom of God, as he understood it. But he falls short of the ideally Christian "enthusiasm of Humanity." His tendency, especially in his later days, to identify the Kingdom of God with the external ecclesiastical organization was not without its practical consequences. The temper of the prelate and the ecclesiastical disciplinarian more and more asserts itself at the expense of his Christianity. Further, in his moral ideal and his practical judgements Asceticism tends to take the place of Christian charity, and even of common humanity. It would hardly be possible to worship the God of St. Augustine without contracting some of His indifference to human suffering. And St. Augustine certainly did show on many occasions an appalling indifference to ordinary human claims—the claims, for instance, of the woman with whom he had lived as his wife for fourteen years and who was the mother of his son.[1] One would have supposed that the first effect of a genuine "conversion" would have been to induce him to marry her : what he actually did was to abandon her, and to tear away from her the son whom she had borne him. I will mention another instance of his moral callousness. One of the greatest crimes of St. Augustine's age—the introduction of the Vandals into Africa — was perpetrated by a statesman and general much under his spiritual influence. That calamity, bringing with it the ultimate extinction of Christianity in those regions, was the work of Boniface, Count of Africa, and was inspired by a personal rivalry. Recent events have enabled us to realize more distinctly than we could have done a few years ago something of what that invasion meant for the unhappy provincials.

[1] It is true that they appear to have separated before the conversion was complete. It is not clear to what the separation was due. At all events Augustine made no effort to atone to her for the past.

St. Augustine rebukes him with the utmost mildness ; he treats the act as a regrettable necessity of political life rather than as a crime. He only reminds him that it would not have happened if he had not mixed in politics, but had become a monk and devoted himself to the good of his own soul.[1] When the same Boniface contracted a second marriage in spite of a vow of continence, which but for St. Augustine's teaching he would never have taken, the Saint treats the offence as a crime far more grievous than the treachery, treason, and massacre laid to his charge. Miss Julia Wedgewood has had the courage to write of him : " Holiness has eclipsed virtue." [2] I should prefer to say, " Asceticism and ecclesiasticism have extinguished morality "—even that morality of ordinary human loyalty and patriotism which constituted the most " splendid vice " of the heathen. The crime was one which would have been impossible to a Socrates, to a M. Aurelius, or even to a Cicero.

That force should be used against pagans is a proposition which had been defended, for instance, by Julius Firmicus Maternus ; but St. Augustine was the first Christian theologian to advocate its employment against heretics and schismatics ; and it is hardly possible to exaggerate the deterioration in the Christian temper which resulted from the new doctrine. How much the war against the Donatists encouraged by St. Augustine prepared the way for the eventual extinction of African Christianity under the Mahommedan sword, I forbear to enquire. There are not many pagans, even among the best, to whom we could very naturally or suitably apply the term " Christ-like " : but there are some of them to whom such a term would be more applicable than to St. Augustine.

In justice to St. Augustine a word must be said as to his great enemy. The most conspicuous adversary of the characteristic Augustinian doctrine was, of course, Pelagius ; although it must be remembered that historically Pelagianism was a reaction against Augustinianism

---

[1] *Ep.* ccxx.
[2] *The Moral Ideals*, p. 420.

rather than Augustinianism a reaction against Pelagianism. Pelagius held that every human soul was created exactly in the same state as Adam—as capable of falling, but as capable also, not merely of not sinning, but of attaining the absolute perfection of the " Evangelical counsels." Original sin was altogether denied : the fall left Adam's posterity just as it would have been if Adam had not sinned ; and—what was just as offensive in Augustine's eyes—Adam would have died even if he had not sinned.[1] All that St. Paul says about the consequences of Adam's fall is explained merely of the effects which the bad example and bad influences of parents and environment might have on the child after he was born.[2] Difficult as was the achievement of absolute sinlessness, doubtful as it was whether any but Christ had ever attained it, the difficulty never amounted for the Pelagian to an impossibility, even apart from the influence of " grace." Valuable and useful as was the assistance which Christ supplied by teaching and example in the quest of righteousness, the human will could at least take the first steps towards goodness by its own efforts. I need not stay to point out how ill such a system accords with modern knowledge—with the facts of heredity, with the dependence of morality upon the social environment, with the limited

---

[1] See Augustine, *De gestis Pelagii*, passim. At the Council of Carthage, which acquitted him, Pelagius explained that, when he maintained that a man might not sin (" posse non peccare "), he did not exclude the need of divine assistance. Such assistance was given through the knowledge of God's law, and was implied in the very " possibility " itself which was given by God—that is to say, in the free-will which is God's gift (cc. 1, 6). He even repudiated the statement attributed to Caelestius that " gratiam Dei et adjutorium non ad singulos actus dari sed in libero arbitrio esse vel in lege ac doctrina " (c. 14). By this he appears to have meant the necessity of the continual contemplation of Christ's example (*De Gratia et pecc. orig.* i. 2). Pelagius further agreed to anathematize those who taught that grace was given in accordance with merits ("gratiam Dei secundum merita nostra dari ") ; but this would appear to have meant that the teaching by which a man originally became a Christian was not merited, and was consistent with the position that " God gives all graces to him who has deserved them " (*De gestis Pelag.* c. 14), and that " by doing the divine will we merit divine grace " (*De Gratia et pecc. orig.* i. 22). Augustine in the last-quoted passage accuses Pelagius of having gone back upon his denial that grace was given " according to merit " ; but the two statements can be reconciled if we suppose that a different kind of grace is meant in each case. Grace to know God's will and the help afforded by the example of Christ, he might contend, are given without any merit on our part : grace to act upon the knowledge is given where it is deserved.

[2] Augustine, *De pecc. meritis*, i. 9. *De Gratia et pecc. orig.* ii. 15 : " non propagine, sed exemplo."

range of human freedom even in the view of those who do not accept philosophical determinism. Pelagianism represents the appeal to reason and conscience against theories which blackened the character of God, and we must be grateful to the men who made that protest, even if it was not made in the right way. The reason and conscience of later ages have not accepted all their theories. Theirs was a crude way of reconciling the ways of God to man—a way made more than ever impossible by modern thought and modern science: but, after all, the utterances and the characters of men like Pelagius and Julian of Eclanum, even as exhibited in the pages of their great enemy, often exhibit far more of the spirit of Christ and of the best early Christianity than the writings of St. Augustine himself.[1] Undoubtedly the Pelagians were quite unphilosophical in attempting to find a sphere in which the human mind could be supposed to act alone, and quite independently of divine assistance or " grace ": they enormously underestimated the extent to which the individual is dependent for such goodness as he possesses upon the influences of his environment. Undoubtedly they had an inadequate sense of the supreme and unique value of the influence exercised by Christ and the revelation of God, not merely in disclosing what goodness is but in helping men to approximate to the ideal. St. Augustine's knowledge of the human heart was far deeper than that of the honest, spiritually ambitious, innocent-minded British monk, Pelagius, or the rationalistically-minded Julian. It is because he so faithfully exhibits—albeit in an exaggerated and unhealthy form—one side or type, though it is by no means the only type, of religious experience that he appeals with so much power to so many religious minds in all ages. And yet it must not be assumed that the horrible theories with which St. Augustine identified Christ's Gospel, though they may not

---

[1] It is remarkable that, in the dialogue between himself and Julian, Augustine, who apparently compiled Julian's speeches from his writings, makes him, not indeed exactly a model of good manners, but still a comparatively decent controversialist, while he fills his own speeches with the rudest and coarsest vituperation. He evidently thought that by so doing he was exhibiting superior piety and zeal for Christian truth.

have destroyed the subjective peace of his soul, did nothing to mar the moral effects of his conversion, or of other conversions produced by the influence of such an interpretation of Christ's Gospel as his. Much that is the worst as well as much that is best in Western Christianity is due to his influence.

To a marvellous extent the theology of St. Augustine both dominated the traditional teaching of the medieval Church and inspired those revivals and the attempts at reform which broke out in its bosom, and which culminated in the great reformation of the sixteenth century. Yet after all it must be remembered that St. Augustine's teaching was never wholly accepted even by the Western Church. The Councils which condemned Pelagius and Pelagianism never approved the extreme Augustinian positions, and in all sorts of ways later developments of theology and of the ecclesiastical system counteracted, and to a large extent neutralized in practice, the harshness of St. Augustine's dogmas, if much that was best and most spiritual in his teaching disappeared also. Even in the dark ages there were minds which could not be satisfied with St. Augustine's assurance that the divine decrees which seemed to average consciences to be so arbitrary and unjust were really governed by perfect justice; and that, since evil was the mere privation of good, a mere negation or non-entity, the Author of these decrees had never been the Author of evil. Such men insisted on reserving to the human mind a little power to accept or to reject the divine grace which was offered, and on maintaining that enough divine grace was offered to every Christian to secure his salvation. The orthodoxy of the dark ages, though it nominally accepted most of the Augustinian formulae, was always tending in a direction which St. Augustine would have identified with semi-Pelagianism — a creed which was perhaps less philosophical than that of St. Augustine; but it was the only way of avoiding the awful consequences of the Augustinian theories, so long as nobody was bold enough to reject the Augustinian eschatology, and keep open the door of hope for men who died unbaptized, in ignorance, or in sin. So far was the Augustinian pre-destinarianism from being universally accepted that the monk Gotteschalk was persecuted for being too faithful an Augustinian. Still more signal was the departure from Augustinianism taken by the great scholastics of the age which followed.[1] Indeed, from one point of view the whole history of Western theology from that day to the present may be described as one long effort—with many checks and reactions no doubt—to escape from the influence of St. Augustine.[2] To one of the first great battles in that long campaign I must now pass on.

The theory which converted the death of Christ into

[1] It is to be remembered that the Commentary on the Epistle to the Romans which circulated in the Middle Ages under the name of Jerome is now generally regarded as being really the work of Pelagius himself. This is one of the facts which help to explain the way in which during the later patristic and medieval periods the language of St. Augustine was retained, but was frequently explained in a Pelagian sense. Jerome's name stood almost as high as St. Augustine's, and under cover of that name a good deal of Pelagianism could be taught.

[2] A word may be said as to St. Augustine's two greatest successors in the West. St. Leo, as is perhaps natural in the theologian whose famous " Tome " is regarded as the authoritative formulation of the " two natures " theory, gives considerable prominence to the old Greek view of the restoration of man by the mere fact of the incarnation—the union of humanity and divinity in Christ, but still he insists on the effect of the Passion, and here he formulates with legal precision the principle of the " set-off " : " Chirographum quo nitebatur excedit, ab illo iniquitatis exigens poenam, in quo nullam reperit culpam. Solvitur itaque letiferae pactionis malesuasa conscriptio, et per iniusticiam plus petendi, totius debiti summa vacuatur" (*Serm.* xxii. 4 ; Migne liv. c. 197). A still neater formulation is quoted by M. Rivière from Fulgentius Ferrandus, Deacon of Carthage : " Per indebitam exactionem quidquid ei debebatur amisit, iuste victus et iuste punitus " (*Ep.* iii. *ad Anatol.* 5).

Gregory the Great, who was a practical teacher and organizer of religion for a people rapidly sinking into barbarism rather than a theologian, dwells much upon the value of Christ's work as teacher and example, but he is an uncompromising assertor of vicarious sacrifice and vicarious punishment (" poenam culpae nostrae sine culpa suscepit," *Moral.* XIII. xxx. 34 ; " eum qui sine peccato est pro peccatoribus damnat," III. xiv. 27) ; and no one revels more heartily in depicting with picturesque and grotesque detail the defeat of Christ by the Devil. Gregory falls, as might be expected in such a writer, into a very crude antithesis between the justice of the Father and the compassion of the Son : " Deo obstitit ne feriret " (*Moral.* IX. xxxviii. 61). The ransom theory receives in his hands a flamboyant development. See *Moralia*, XVII. xxx. Cf. above, p. 316, n. 4.

Of the one really original writer who intervenes between the close of the patristic age and the great intellectual Renaissance of the twelfth century—John Scotus Erigena— I will only say that he combines the Greek idea of deification through the incarnation (which we might expect to find in such a writer) with the ordinary traditional ways of speaking about the death of Christ as a deliverance from the Devil, but he makes some attempt to moralize the idea of victory over the evil one. The Devil is already partly conquered on the earth because he can no longer injure men as much as he would like to do. That is the only chain with which the Devil is now bound, and that will be broken at the general resurrection of the last day (*De Divis. Nat.* v. 29), which he under-stood in the Origenistic manner as involving universal redemption (v. 26, 27). He quotes long passages from both Origen and Gregory of Nyssa.

a ransom paid to the Devil was generally accepted for
nearly a thousand years. During this period reason,
common-sense, reverence were not, indeed, left quite
without witnesses. The ransom theory was, as we have
seen, questioned by a few Easterns. But in the West its
ascendancy was undisputed till the twelfth century. It
can be discovered more or less explicitly in nearly every
writer of whose works there are any considerable remains.

Anselm

The emancipation of the Church from this hideous
theory was the work of two great minds—Anselm and
Abelard, two writers of whom the first may be described
as the precursor, the second as the actual founder, of the
scholastic theology. Both of them are the products of
that great intellectual revival by which Europe emerged
out of the darkness of the Dark Ages into the period
of high medieval culture and civilization. Unlike as
they were in other respects, they were alike in this—that
both of them were genuine thinkers and men of too fine
a nature to feel themselves at home in the coarse
mythology of the ransom theory.

Anselm was, it is needless to say, much the more
conservative theologian of the two. Few men have
succeeded to the same extent in combining the temper
of the saint with that of the philosopher. For such a
man the ransom theory was discredited, not only by its
intellectual absurdity but by its irreverence. To say
that man after the fall was lawfully or justly the servant
of Satan instead of the servant of God, to say that God
owed the Devil a debt which He could not justly repudiate, seemed, on the face of it, sheer blasphemy; and
Anselm absolutely denied that the Devil ever had any
lawful authority over man or any rights which God was
bound to respect. Man had never ceased to be the
servant of God. God owed the Devil nothing but
punishment: in so far as he was allowed any authority
over men, he was a mere instrument of punishment in

God's hands.[1] For the rest, the old Augustinian conceptions were for the most part retained by Anselm with
just this difference—that he made a serious attempt to
vindicate the whole scheme from the point of view of
justice instead of falling back at every turn upon the
arbitrary will of God and the declarations of Scripture.
An impersonal justice was substituted for a personal
Devil. By Anselm an attempt was made—with more
seriousness than ever before—to demonstrate *a priori*,
without reference to actual history or to authority, the
thesis that by the voluntary sacrifice of a God-man, and
in no other way, could sins justly be forgiven.

Anselm's early education at the School of Pavia had
been partly an education in law—especially Lombard
law; and, in spite of all his real metaphysical power,
legal conceptions were as prominent in his theology as they
are in the teaching of Tertullian or St. Augustine. His
theory of the atonement is based upon the assumption that
by an eternal necessity sin must be followed either by satisfaction or by punishment. Sin was to Anselm essentially
the subtraction of honour from God involved in disobedience to His commands. Consequently justice requires
either that God shall be paid an equivalent for what
He has lost or that punishment shall be inflicted. This
payment of an equivalent constitutes satisfaction—a conception which was for the first time by Anselm transferred
from the region of ecclesiastical jurisprudence, which
had long held that post-baptismal sin must be " satisfied
for " by penance or good works, to the relations between
the Father and the Son. Satisfaction is treated by Anselm
rather as a substitute for punishment than as itself
constituting punishment.[2] Punishment is something
involuntarily suffered by one who has injured another
and refuses him satisfaction. Satisfaction is something
voluntarily offered by the injurer as a substitute to the
injured for what he has lost, the loss in the case of God
being simply the loss of honour—in fact, what a modern
lawyer would call civil damages as distinguished from

---

[1] *Cur Deus Homo*, i. 7.
[2] *Ibid.* i. 13. The " Cur Deus Homo " has become the classical exposition of the
theory; it is also dealt with in his *Meditationes*.

the endurance of criminal punishment. At the same time we must not make too much of this distinction, since after all in the case of Christ the satisfaction actually consisted in the vicarious endurance of a death which, if man had endured it, would have been punishment, and the term punishment is constantly applied to that death by Anselm himself.[1] Anselm's ideas about original sin and the inheritance of Adam's guilt are the traditional Augustinian ideas. Every rational creature owes to God the debt of perfect obedience to His will. He who fails in this obedience takes from God something which is justly His. Not only must something of equivalent value be repaid, but something more must be added as a satisfaction for God's injured honour.[2] This satisfaction must comply with two conditions. In the first place the sin of Adam is infinite: that is shown by the fact, supposed to be affirmed by the moral consciousness, that it would be better that the whole world, other than God, should perish than that the smallest of God's commandments should be disobeyed.[3] God can only be satisfied by something whose value exceeds that of all the world besides God. Secondly, what must be given back to God must be, or rather must include,

---

[1] Prof. Harnack (*Hist. of Dogma*, vi. 68 *sq.*) seems to me to attach too much importance to the distinction between "satisfaction" and "punishment." The use of the first term does perhaps suggest a reverent reluctance to represent God as actually "punishing" His innocent Son. At the same time I do not think the idea of satisfaction is really on a higher plane than that of punishment, but on a lower. Punishment at least suggests the idea of some objective ethical demand, whereas satisfaction represents simply the demand for reparation to personal honour. "Sic ergo debet omnis qui peccat honorem quem rapuit Deo solvere; et haec est satisfactio" (*Cur Deus Homo*, i. 11). The origin of the idea is no doubt to be found in the penitential system and the theology which grew up around it (Tertullian, Cyprian, etc.), but no doubt the idea of the Wergild was not without its influence on the Lombard lawyer's mind. I see little ground for Harnack's discovery of an incompatibility between the idea of satisfaction and that of merit, except in so far as the first suggests the notions connected with the civil and the latter with those of the criminal tribunal —both quite inadequate to the moral reality.

[2] "Quamdiu autem non solvit quod rapuit, manet in culpa; nec sufficit solummodo reddere quod ablatum est, sed pro contumelia illata plus debet reddere, quam abstulit" (i. 11). This extra something is further defined by the words, "hoc debet dare, quod ab illo non posset exigi, si alienum [*i.e.* something of God's] non rapuisset." He then establishes the impossibility of God's remitting punishment without satisfaction, for God has threatened to punish and He must keep His word (c. 12): "necesse est ergo, ut aut oblatus honor solvatur, aut poena sequatur" (c. 13). Cf. c. 15: "ipsa namque perversitatis spontanea satisfactio vel a non satisfaciente poenae exactio . . . in eadem universitate [*i.e.* the world] locum tenent suum et ordinis pulchritudinem."

[3] *Cur Deus Homo*, i. 21.

the very thing which God has lost.   Now God, in creating
man, had proposed to Himself to create a human nature
which would conduce to His honour.   Man had taken
away from God's honour by allowing himself to be conquered by the Devil : what must be restored must consist,
therefore, in the conquest of the Devil,[1] and that implies
that in the " heavenly Commonwealth " which God had
purposed so many souls must be justified or made
righteous as would be sufficient to take the place of the
fallen angels.[2]   Neither of these conditions could be satisfied except by God ; for no life could be worth more than all
the world besides God, except the life of God Himself.
And yet the debt must be paid by man ; for it was man
who had incurred it.   Moreover, one who was only
God could not die.   Consequently the debt could only
be discharged by one in whom humanity and divinity
were united.[3]   Here, as in so many of the Fathers, we
have, of course, the old bastard Platonism which makes
the universal " human nature " into an entity separable
from any and all individual men, which can contract
and discharge obligations—the obligations of humanity
and not of any particular man.   " Humanity " is supposed to have contracted the debt in the first Adam and
to have discharged it in the second.   Moreover, no
sinful man could discharge the debt, for in every man
who inherited Adam's guilt there was the infinite demerit
which no finite performance of duty could outweigh.
All the service that man could perform toward God was
already owed : no ordinary man infected with original
sin could perform even that ; still less could he have
anything over, beyond what was required to discharge
his own debt, so as both to give back to God the very
thing which He had lost, the full tale of justified men,
and to make the additional satisfaction that was demanded by the wounded honour of God.[4]   Only the

---

[1] *Cur Deus Homo*, i. 22–3, ii. 6.   [2] i. 18.   [3] ii. 6, 7.

[4] The point that the very thing must be given back which God had lost is not worked
out quite clearly : it keeps appearing as a side-issue to the main contention that the
satisfaction must be a sufficient equivalent and more.   Sometimes this identity seems
to be established by the ultimate sanctity of the saved, sometimes simply by the appearance in Christ Himself of a perfected humanity.   When Anselm contends that " Si
nihil pretiosius agnoscitur Deus fecisse quam rationalem naturam ad gaudendum de se,

God-man who through birth of a virgin took upon Him
human nature without its entail of original sin could do
that; for only such a being could earn a superfluity of
merit beyond what was required to save Himself. The
life of perfect obedience He, as a creature, owed to God;
but—it is startling to learn, when we remember that we
are speaking of Christ as man—a voluntary death was
something more than He owed. This could only be
due as a punishment, and He had done nothing to
deserve punishment:[1] moreover God had not actually
demanded it of Him, having put it into His own power
to die or to be immortal.[2] By His voluntary death,
then, Christ acquired an infinite merit which was more
than sufficient to discharge the infinite debt.[3] And this
infinite merit must in justice be rewarded. The Father
must give the Son something of equivalent value. But
for Himself the Son wanted nothing. As man He was
sinless, and in no need of pardon: as God He already
possessed all things. Hence He had a right to transfer
the merit and its recompense—like a commercial asset—
to the account of sinful men who did want something;
and nothing could be more just or "convenient," since
men were His "kinsmen and brethren." In this way
God gets again the justified humanity which He had lost
by the fall; and, since the merit exceeded the recompense,
there is still that overplus of satisfaction which justice
demands.[4]

I must not dwell upon Anselm's views as to the positive
effects of Christ's death upon the sinner even after the

---

valde alienum est ab eo, ut ullam rationalem naturam penitus perire sinat" (ii. 4),
he would be logically committing himself to Universalism but for the false Platonism by
which it is supposed that "humanity" can be saved while the majority of men are
damned.
　[1] ii. 6-10. A further objection to the possibility of men being redeemed by a mere
man is that in that case they would have become servants of men instead of God (i. 5).
　[2] ii. 11, 18.
　[3] ii. 11, 14. Anselm's position involves the awkward consequence that one infinite
would be greater—infinitely greater—than another infinite; but such is his contention.
He speaks of the sin as "tam infinitum, etc." (ii. 14), and yet contends that "bonum
tam amabile potest sufficere ad solvendum quod debetur pro peccatis totius mundi. Immo
plus potest in infinitum" (c. 14). Perhaps he may be held to save himself by
explaining the infinity of the sin incurred by the destruction of such a life to mean
that it "incomparably exceeds" all other possible sins.
　[4] ii. 19, 20.

remission of the penalty. The necessity of grace is much less insisted on by Anselm than it is by St. Augustine. Anselm heartily accepted the doctrine of free-will in the popular sense. The arrears of satisfaction due for the past having been wiped out at baptism, pardoned man could now resume the battle against temptation with a chance of victory. By his own exertions he must now earn merit enough for his own salvation. But the work of the Saviour still contributes to help him in his struggles— first by way of example, and secondly because it is part of the pact by which God agreed to forgive sin through Christ that post-baptismal sin is to be forgiven, but not till after due satisfaction by penance.[1]

The objections to the old Augustinian scheme of redemption are no less valid against Anselm's : they stand out in even blacker outline on account of the greater intellectual keenness and sincerity of the new presentation. Anselm appeals to justice, and that in all good faith : but his notions of justice are the barbaric ideas of an ancient Lombard king or the technicalities of a Lombard lawyer rather than the ideas which would have satisfied such a man as Anselm in ordinary human life.

I need not dwell upon the tendency to confuse the conception of criminal and of civil justice, to identify moral transgression with personal affront; the debt, which according to ordinary legal ideas can be forgiven by the creditor, with the penalty due to wrong-doing which must be supposed to rest upon some moral ground and cannot therefore be arbitrarily remitted. The fundamental defect of Anselm's attempt to reconcile the traditional scheme with ordinary ideas of justice is that no civilized system of law permits the attribution of guilt to all humanity for the sin of one ; nor can the payment of a penalty by the sinless Christ rationally or morally be considered to make any easier or any juster the remission of the penalty which man owes for his own sin. So much the ordinary moral consciousness affirms unhesitatingly, even if we refuse to analyse further such

[1] ii. 16.

terms as guilt and merit, honour and debt, satisfaction
and punishment, in dealing with which Anselm never
gets beyond the most confused and superficial idols of
the market-place. After all it is only through the metaphorical treatment of Christ's death as the offering of
something valuable to the Father that Anselm can make
out that something of infinite worth is offered to God in
compensation for the infinite sin.[1] A God who really
thought that His honour was increased by millions of
men suffering eternal torments,[2] or that it was a satisfactory compensation to Himself that in lieu thereof an
innocent God-man should suffer upon the cross, would
not be the God whom Anselm in his heart of hearts
really worshipped.[3]

The theory of Anselm has the merit of recognizing
that God must act according to the highest ideas of justice,
and of acknowledging that we have no right to pronounce
just in God what would have seemed the highest injustice
among men. . Unfortunately, in working out his scheme,
the theologian allows himself to be satisfied with conceptions of justice among men which would never for
one moment have been acted upon by Anselm the humane
and enlightened Master of Novices at Bec, or by Anselm
sitting as judge in the provincial Court of Canterbury.
Even his insistence upon the intrinsic righteousness of

[1] Anselm seems to feel this difficulty, and seeks to remove it by urging that " nulla-
tenus seipsum potest homo magis dare Deo, quam cum se morti tradit ad honorem
illius " (ii. 11). That is really an argument in a circle. If the giving Himself to death
were really to the honour of God, such a death might be a set-off to the infinite sin, but
it is only by assuming that it is such a set-off that it can be shown to be to the honour
of God.

[2] See the chapter (i. 14) headed " Cujusmodi honor Dei sit poena peccantis."

[3] Harnack notices the difficulty that according to Anselm it was as man that Christ
died, while it is only by treating the death as really God's that it could be held to have
infinite worth, and talks about " a quite Nestorian diremption of the person " (History
of Dogma, vi. p. 74). But I do not know that the difficulty can be got over by simply
giving up that favourite bugbear of all Ritschlians—the doctrine of the two natures.
Harnack is on firmer ground when he complains of the purely abstract character of
the scheme, which is really quite independent of everything in the historical Christ
except His death—and, he should have added, His sinlessness. " Everything is conceived of quite abstractly, very much in the way in which a clever child thinks and speaks
of such things. This theory manages to describe the work of redemption by Jesus
Christ without adducing a single saying of His. . . . The death of Christ is entirely
severed from His life-work on earth, and isolated. This God-man need not have preached,
and founded a Kingdom, and gathered disciples ; he only required to die " (Hist. of
Dogma, vi. pp. 75-6). The same criticism applies to many modern theories less defined
and less logically worked out than Anselm's, and to none more than to Luther's.

God is marred by his tendency to treat sin simply as a personal insult to God, and the satisfaction of it as a tyrant's delight in feeling that His honour has been vindicated and His rebellious subjects compelled to lick the dust beneath His feet.   On the other hand, Anselm is always careful to exhibit the Father as fully co-operating in the scheme of redemption.   The atonement is the work of the Holy Trinity.[1]   Though the efficacy of Christ's death is not made to depend wholly upon its actual moral effects, those effects are frequently insisted upon.   Part of the infinite merit acquired by the atonement appears to consist in the superlative example of a death incurred by loyalty to justice—such as could only be afforded by one who chose to die, though He might, had He pleased, have escaped physical death altogether. And yet in one respect the abandonment of the compact with the Devil brought with it a new danger.   Since it was no longer from the Devil that man was delivered but from God Himself, since the evil one had now become merely God's gaoler and "torturer" instead of a rival sovereign, it was difficult for Anselm to escape that opposition between the justice of the Father and the love or mercy of the Son which was to become so prominent a feature in popular religious thought.[2]   If Anselm himself explicitly protests against such a view, the tendency of his thought remains.

Abelard

Very different and very much simpler is the teaching which the far bolder, if less saintly, thinker Abelard substitutes for the ransom theory.   Abelard was specially

---

[1] ii. 19.

[2] It may be doubted whether Anselm himself does actually fall into "a quite Gnostic antagonism between justice and goodness, the Father being the just one, and the Son the good" (Harnack, *Hist. of Dogma*, vi. p. 76), but the tendency of his theory was in this direction.   It is interesting to trace the possible influence of Anselm's theory in Bracton's *De legibus Angliae*, i. 8. 5 (quoted by Carlyle, *Hist. of Mediaeval Political Theory*, iii. 38), where, in proof of the doctrine that the King should be "under the law," it is maintained that Christ "cum ad recuperandum humanum genus ineffabiliter ei multa suppeterent, hanc potissimam elegit viam qua ad destruendum opera diaboli non virtute uteretur potentie, sed iustitie ratione": but Bracton does not admit an actual "necessity," and the idea might be taken from other writers.

interested in the theoretical study of morality: his *Scito te ipsum* represents a really original treatise on moral philosophy, written before the recovery of the Aristotelian writings made originality in ethics almost impossible to the medieval mind. His study of morality, combined with the task of commenting upon the Epistle to the Romans, forced upon him the problem of the atonement and its justice. In Abelard not only the ransom theory but any kind of substitutionary or expiatory atonement is explicitly denied. We get rid altogether of the notion of a mysterious guilt which, by an abstract necessity of things, required to be extinguished by death or suffering, no matter whose, and of all pseudo-Platonic hypostasizing of the universal "Humanity." The efficacy of Christ's death is now quite definitely and explicitly explained by its subjective influence upon the mind of the sinner. The voluntary death of the innocent Son of God on man's behalf moves the sinner to gratitude and answering love—and so to consciousness of sin, repentance, amendment. His position is succinctly expressed in one of the propositions condemned by the Council of Sens in 1141 and by Pope Innocent II. After stating with remorseless clearness the objections to the common ideas upon the subject, he proceeds: "I think, therefore, that the purpose and cause of the incarnation was that He might illuminate the world by His wisdom and excite it to the love of Himself." [1]

Here is a fuller explanation:

"Every man is also made juster, that is to say, becomes more loving to the Lord after the passion of Christ than he was before, because a benefit actually received kindles the soul into love more than one merely hoped for. Our redemption, therefore, is that supreme love of Christ shown to us by His passion, which not only frees us from slavery to sin, but acquires for us the true liberty of the sons of God, so that we fulfil all things not so much from fear as from love of Him who exhibited so great favour towards us, that favour than which, as He Himself attests, none greater can be found: 'Greater love,' He

[1] In *Epist. ad Rom.*, *Opera*, ed. Cousin, ii. p. 207. The Latin is given below, p. 363.

says, 'hath no man than this, that he lay down his life for his friends.'" [1]

Here is another fine passage :

" To us it appears that we are none the less justified in the blood of Christ and reconciled to God by this singular grace exhibited to us in that His Son took our nature, and in it took upon Himself to instruct us alike by word and example even unto death, (and so) bound us to Himself by love; so that kindled by so great a benefit of divine grace, charity should not be afraid to endure anything for His sake : which benefit indeed we do not doubt kindled the ancient fathers also, who expected this by faith, unto a supreme love of God no less than the men of (this) time." [2]

Abelard, inspired no doubt by Origen, sees more clearly than most who have written upon the subject, the immorality of anything which makes forgiveness arbitrary : he sees that God can only be supposed to forgive by making the sinner better, and thereby removing any demand for punishment.[3] Such was the teaching which roused St. Bernard and the older theologians of their day to fury,[4] and brought upon Abelard the sentence of perpetual imprisonment.[5] But it is important to note that the

[1] For the Latin, see below, p. 363.

[2] For the Latin, see below, p. 363. There are of course passages in Abelard in which the death of Christ is treated in the conventional way as a " sacrifice," a punishment, etc. There is no cause of surprise in this, since Abelard was professing to explain the doctrine of the New Testament (including St. Paul) and of the Church and not to supersede it.

[3] " Condonari a Deo peccatum, hoc est, eum talem fieri quem jam non sit dignum sicut antea propter illud quod praecessit peccatum, aeternaliter a Deo puniri " (Scito te ipsum, c. xix. ed. Cousin, ii. p. 628). He goes on to say that it is only eternal punishment that is thus remitted—not necessarily all punishment. He boldly defended eternal punishment on utilitarian grounds. It was good for the greater number that some should be punished eternally.

[4] " An non iustius os loquens talia fustibus tunderetur quam rationibus refelleretur ? " (Epist. de erroribus Abaelardi, v. 11). I will not attempt to expound Bernard's own doctrine, which has in it nothing novel except indeed the Anselmian doctrine of satisfaction. It is interesting to see this champion of tradition adopting quite unconsciously a formula which was really much more of an innovation than Abelard's : "Homo siquidem," inquit, " qui debuit, homo qui solvit. Nam si ' unus pro omnibus mortuus est, ergo omnes mortui sunt ' : ut videlicet satisfactio unius omnibus imputetur, sicut omnium peccata unus ille portavit ; nec alter jam inveniatur qui forefecit, alter qui satisfecit ; quia caput et corpus unus est Christus. Satisfecit ergo caput pro membris, Christus pro visceribus suis " (vi. 15).

[5] He was eventually, on the intercession of Peter the Venerable, Abbot of Cluny, allowed to find a more honourable asylum in that illustrious house. The persecution of Abelard was chiefly got up by St. Bernard, the mortal enemy of Cluny.

Council did not confine themselves to the condemnation of Abelard's positive doctrine. They condemned also the negative part of his system—his denial that Christ delivered man from the yoke of the Devil, and that this dominion of the Devil was just. The Synod does not seem to have appreciated the fact that in condemning Abelard they were condemning Anselm also.[1]

At last we have found a theory of the atonement which thoroughly appeals to reason and to conscience. There is of course nothing absolutely original in the idea. St. Paul is full of the thought. It is set forth in its simplest and purest form in the Johannine writings. It occurs over and over again in the fathers. Whatever else they teach about the death of Christ, they all with one consent teach this—that it was a revelation of the love of God, intended to call forth answering love in man. But intellectual, and still more religious, progress often consists simply in setting an idea free from a context which is really inconsistent with it. In the history of the atonement doctrine this task was accomplished by Abelard. For the first time—or rather for the first time since the days of the earliest and most philosophical Greek fathers—the doctrine of the atonement was stated in a way which had nothing unintelligible, arbitrary, illogical, or immoral about it ; in a way which appeals to the most unsophisticated intellect, to the most unsophisticated conscience, and to the simplest piety. The theory of Abelard does but isolate and emphasize that element in the preaching of the atonement to which in all ages it has owed its moving and saving power. Whatever were men's theories about the grounds on which the death of Christ became necessary, it was the love exhibited by Christ in submitting to that death which has really moved the heart, touched the conscience, and regenerated the life of believers. Men's theories about the source of that necessity have varied with their views about the Universe in general, about the nature of

---

[1] It is curious to notice how little immediate effect was produced by the criticism of Anselm. Most of Anselm's contemporaries and of the writers and successors up to the age of Abelard's pupils clung, more or less decidedly, to the older view. See the account of these writers in Rivière, *Le Dogme de la Réd.* pp. 453-460.

justice, about the authority of the Scriptures and many
other things. Some of those theories have become to
us intellectually and morally impossible. But, given
the necessity for the death, the submission to such a
death became to those who accepted the necessity the
typical, characteristic act of self-sacrificing love. " Greater
love hath no man than this, that a man lay down his life
for his friends." And, if He who so lays down His
life is taken as representing and revealing the character
of God, then no other way of ending the earthly life of
Him in whom God made this supreme self-revelation
could so fully embody and symbolize the fundamental
thought of Christianity that God is love, nor is any event
in the history of the world so calculated to awaken and
stimulate that repentance for sin upon which the possibility of forgiveness depends. Gratitude is the last spark
of the divine image to disappear from the soul of man.
Gratitude towards a human benefactor is the motive
which is most likely to appeal to the soul in which least
remains of that image. And when the human benefactor
is thought of as the supreme Incarnation of God, gratitude
to Christ passes into and becomes indistinguishable from
gratitude to the Father whom He reveals.

I will not deny that there are some difficulties even in
Abelard's view of the atonement. They will be dealt
with more fully in my concluding lecture. Meanwhile,
I will leave with you the suggestion that the difficulties
are chiefly due to the isolation of Christ's death from
His life, teaching, and work as a whole. No Latin
writer really does this so little as Abelard ; at bottom
he, like the Greek fathers, makes salvation to be due
to the work of Christ as a whole ; but, when the theory
is criticized, it is often presented as though those who
uphold it regarded or were bound to regard it as a
defence of the traditional modes of speech which do
attribute this exclusive influence and importance to the
death of Christ. When we see in the death of Christ
the most striking expression and symbol of the spirit
which dominated His whole life, our recognition of the
divine love which shines forth in that death ceases to be

dependent upon our accepting any of those always difficult and sometimes repulsive theories of substitutive or expiative or objective efficacy which were once connected with it. Abelard's theory merely sums up what is common to all the theories of the atonement, ancient and modern, and is unaffected by our rejection of the discordant impossibilities in all of them.

To see a living and permanent meaning in the doctrine of the atonement, it is not necessary for us to enter into elaborate *a priori* reasons for the death of Christ. It is enough to recognize that that death came to Him in the discharge of His Messianic task, and that He faced it from the motive which inspired the whole of His life— love to His Father and to His brethren. That is enough to enable us to say with Abelard that the death of Christ upon the cross was an essential part of an incarnation, "the purpose and cause of which was that He might illuminate the world by His Wisdom and excite it to the love of Himself."[1]

ADDITIONAL NOTES TO LECTURE V

NOTE A

ABELARD ON THE ATONEMENT

It will be well to give in full the whole article in the charges against Abelard which deals with the Atonement. It is found in the *Capitula errorum*, drawn up by St. Bernard and transmitted to the Pope.

" 'Sciendum est quod omnes nostri Doctores qui post Apostolos fuere, in hoc conveniunt quod Diabolus dominium et potestatem habebat super hominem, et jure eum possidebat.' Et post pauca : 'Nec Diabolus unquam jus aliquod habuit super hominem, sed jure eum possidebat permittente, ut carcerarius, nec [ut eum] Filius Dei a jugo Diaboli liberaret, carnem assumpsit.' Et post pauca : 'Quomodo nos justificari vel reconciliari per mortem Filii ejus dicit Apostolus, qui tanto amplius adversus hominem irasci debuit, quanto amplius in crucifigendo Filium suum deliquerit, quam in transgrediendo primum praeceptum suum unius pomi gustu ; quomodo enim amplius justum fuerit ? Quod si tantum fuerat Adae peccatum, ut expiari non posset

---

[1] For the Latin, see below, p. 363.

nisi ex morte Christi ; quam expiationem habebit ipsum homicidium, quod in Christo commissum est, tot et tanta scelera in ipsum vel suos commissa ? Numquid mors innocentis Filii tantum Deo placuit ut per ipsam reconciliaretur nobis, qui hoc peccando commisimus, propter quod innocens Dominus est occisus, nec nisi hoc maximum fieret peccatum, etiam levius potuit ignoscere multo ? Nec nisi multiplicatis malis tam ["tantum" should be read] bonum facere in quo et justiores facti sumus per mortem Filii Dei quam ante eramus, ut a peccatis jam liberari debeamus ?' Item : 'Cui vero non crudele et iniquum videtur, ut sanguinem innocentis et pretium aliquod quis requisierit, aut ullo modo ei placuerit innocentem interfici ? Nedum Deus tam acceptam mortem Filii habuit, ut per ipsam universo reconciliatus sit mundo. Haec et his similia non mediocrem movent quaestionem, non solum de redemptione sed etiam de justificatione nostra per mortem Domini nostri Jesu Christi. Nobis autem videtur quod nihilo minus sumus justificati in sanguine Christi, et Deo reconciliati per hanc singularem gratiam nobis exhibitam, quod Filius suus nostram suscepit naturam, et in ipsa nos tam verbo quam exemplo instituendo usque ad mortem praestitit, nos sibi amplius per amorem astrinxit : ut tanto divinae gratiae accensi beneficio, nulla tolerare propter ipsum vestra reformidet caritas, quod quidem beneficium antiquos etiam patres, hoc per fidem expectantes, in summum amorem Dei tanquam homines temporis,[1] non dubitamus accendisse.' Et infra : 'Puto ergo quod consilium et causa incarnationis fuit, ut mundum luce suae sapientiae illuminaret, et ad amorem suum accenderet'" (*Opera*, ed. Cousin, ii. pp. 766-7).

I add another quotation : "Justior quoque, id est amplius Dominum diligens quisque fit post passionem Christi quam ante, quia amplius in amorem accendit completum beneficium quam speratum. Redemptio itaque nostra est illa summa in nobis per passionem Christi dilectio, quae nos non solum a servitudine peccati liberat, sed veram nobis filiorum Dei libertatem acquirit ; ut amore ejus potius quam timore cuncta impleamus, qui nobis tantam exhibuit gratiam, qua major inveniri, ipso attestante, non potest : Majorem hac, inquit, dilectionem nemo habet, quam ut animam suam ponat pro amicis suis " (*Opp.*, ed. Cousin, pp. 207).

It must be admitted that Abelard sometimes shows a tendency to relapse into views hardly consistent with this position, *e.g.* "Summa vero ejus justitia exigebat, ut in nullo ejus oratio sustineret, quem nihil nisi quod oportebat velle vel facere unita ei divinitas permittebat"; and there are expressions about the earning of merit and the temporal "satisfaction" due for sin which remind us of Anselm and anticipate some of the worst features of the later medieval theology. In the *Epitome Theologiae Christianae* side by side with the nobler doctrine appears the strange notion that the goodness of Christ would increase the "invidia" of the Devil, and so his condemnation ! (*l.c.* p. 570). Abelard's Commentary on the Romans is by far the most philosophical and original of medieval Commentaries. I cannot agree with the

---

[1] Some word like "hujus" or "post Christum" seems to have dropped out.

estimate of it given in Sanday and Headlam's *International Critical Commentary* on Romans (p. cii.) : "So far as we have consulted it, we have found it based partly on Origen, partly on Augustine, and rather weak and indecisive in character."

NOTE B

M. RIVIÈRE ON THE RANSOM THEORY

M. Rivière in the work to which I have already often referred, *Le Dogme de la Rédemption*, attempts to draw a sharp distinction between (1) the theory of the ransom, which he regards as especially the theory of Origen, and (2) what he calls the "theory of abuse of power"—the theory which explains the death of Christ on the principle that the Devil's attempt to extend his sovereignty to the case of Christ, against whom as innocent he had no rights, justifies the withdrawal of guilty man from his sway. M. Rivière certainly does well to call attention to the different forms which the theory assumes in different writers, and such a learned and elaborate history of the theory has surely never been written before ; but I cannot regard the difference between the two forms of the theory as so fundamental as he supposes it to be : I should regard the second as merely an outgrowth of the first. Nor do I see on what ground he treats the first theory with so much more severity than the last. The mere fact that some of those writers who have adopted the last theory do not happen actually to speak of Christ's death as a ransom paid to the Devil does not seem to me to improve their theology. The objectionable feature in the whole system is not the mere use of the term " ransom " or of the expression " paid " or " offered " or " given " to the Devil, but the treatment of the Devil's supposed dominion over man as an assertion of just rights and a lawful jurisdiction, and the childish and immoral theory as to the way in which these rights were satisfied or bought out by Christ's death. This view of the atonement is really implied in most of the writers who have adopted the ransom theory, and is still more explicitly set forth and developed by the maintainers of the "abuse of power" theory.

In Origen I have already tried to show that this attempt at justification is absent, and therefore his language about the ransom is really free from the ethical objection which may be justly urged against his successors.

The fact that some of the language associated with the "abuse of power" theory is used by writers who have protested against the idea of a ransom paid *to* Satan does not really disprove the substantial identity of the two schemes : it merely shows that the writers could not completely throw off the tradition against which they had intellectually revolted : in the case of one of them—Gregory of Nazianzus—nothing is left of the theory but the *word* "ransom," which of course in some sense all who believed that the ransom passage in the first two gospels was a genuine saying of Christ had to accept and explain in some way : in the case of the other writer mentioned by M. Rivière, John of Damascus, all the absurdity and immorality of the theory really remain in spite of the fact that he will not say that the " ransom " was " offered *to* " the Devil.

It may be convenient to add a list of the writers to whom he attributes the two theories together with a third class composed of those who develope the idea of the victory of Christ over the Devil—often with an accumulation of extremely imaginative and realistic detail—in a rhetorical or poetical manner.

(1) Theory of Ransom : Irenaeus, Origen, Basil, Gregory of Nyssa, St. Ambrose, Jerome.

(2) Theory of "Abuse of Power" : Chrysostom, Cyril of Alexandria, Dionysius the Areopagite, Theodoret, John of Damascus, Hilary of Poitiers, Ambrosiaster, St. Augustine, Leo the Great, Fulgentius Ferrandus, Caesarius of Arles, Gregory the Great.

(3) Cassian, Eusebius of Caesarea, the author of the Life of St. Antony attributed to Athanasius, Proclus, Bishop of Constantinople, St. Pacian, Bishop of Barcelona, Eusebius of Alexandria, Eusebius of Emesa, the Gospel of Nicodemus, pseudo-Epiphanius.[1]

To these he adds the following later writers who uphold this general view of the atonement in one or other of its forms : Isidore of Seville, Rabanus Maurus, Walafrid Strabo (author of the *Glossa Ordinaria*), John Scotus Erigena, Atto of Vercelli, St. Bruno, Radulphus Ardens, Hildebert of Lavardin, Honorius of Autun.

---

[1] The classification involves a cross-division. Some of the writers mentioned under this head by M. Rivière have already appeared in one of the two first categories ; these I have omitted. I have already indicated that in my opinion Tertullian ought to be added to the first group.

LECTURE VI

SCHOLASTIC THEORIES

In Christ Jesus neither circumcision availeth anything nor uncircumcision, but faith working through love.—GAL. v. 6.

LECTURE VI

SCHOLASTIC THEORIES

In our last lecture we traced the rise and fall of the theory which represented the atonement in the light of a quasi-juridical transaction between God and the Devil—a transaction in which the just rights of the Devil, acquired by the fall, were, so to speak, bought out by the transcendent merit of Christ's death. We have seen how that theory was attacked and routed by the joint influence of St. Anselm and of Abelard, but especially of Abelard. Alike to those who insist that orthodoxy must always imply an unquestioning acceptance of past tradition and to those who despair of traditional Christianity ever adapting itself to the intellectual requirements of a new age, the fate of the ransom theory is full of instruction. Never perhaps was a theory which was once accepted as an essential part of the gospel of Christ so rapidly or so decisively abandoned.[1]

We seem to see the old theory making its last stand in the pages of Abelard's more cautious and authority-loving pupil, Peter the Lombard, Bishop of Paris, the Master of the *Sentences*, the author of that one of all the many collections of " Sententiae " or patristic opinions which was destined to become the authorized theological text-book of the now rising Universities. But his recognition of the traditional theory is little more than verbal. The Lombard uses the old language about Christ's deliverance of mankind from the power of the Devil, supported by the old quotation about the strong man

---

[1] The last uncompromising defender of the old theory mentioned by M. Rivière is Peter de la Celle, Bishop of Chartres (*Liber de panibus*, i., *Sermo* xlii.).

2 B

armed, but it is explained metaphorically. The strong
man's defeat is interpreted to mean that we are now able
to resist the temptations to which we yielded once. Side
by side with this doctrine there is something like the
Anselmic idea of a satisfaction due for sin and paid
for us by Christ; but here again the old language is
used in quite a new sense, and the actual formula of
" satisfaction " is not employed. There is nothing about
a satisfaction so great that it required a victim of greater
worth than all the world besides : it is simply laid down
dogmatically that " the punishment with which the
Church visits penitents would not suffice unless the
punishment of Christ co-operated."[1] And then an
ingenious attempt is made verbally to save the old
doctrine of the Devil's just dominion : it is admitted that
the dominion was unjust so far as the Devil's action was
concerned, but it was just in so far as it was deserved by
the sin of man, and therefore permitted by God. There
was, therefore, a sort of justice in the mode of redemption
actually adopted by God. Unlike Anselm, Peter maintains
that God might have redeemed us by the mere fiat of
divine power, but it was more " convenient " that He
should do so by justice. The Lombard dutifully quotes
a peculiarly tasteless passage from St. Augustine in which
the cross is spoken of as the mouse-trap in which the
Devil is caught by the bait of Christ's blood.[2] But he
interprets the doctrine in a new and spiritualized manner.
" By Christ's death," he declares, " we are delivered
from the chains of the Devil—that is, from our sins, and
we are in such sense set free from the Devil that neither
after this life can he find in us anything that he can
punish." The old leaven can just be detected, but it
is clear that the whole transaction with the Devil has now
become largely metaphorical. This is made quite clear
by the explanation which immediately follows. " That
is to say, by His death, the one truest sacrifice, whatever
fault there was in consequence whereof the Devil
detained us before (His coming), Christ extinguished, in

[1] For the idea of merit in Christ's death and life, see *Sent*. iii. Dist. xviii. 2.
[2] *Sermo* cxxx. 2.   Cf. the passage quoted above, p. 331, note 3.

order that in this life he should not prevail by tempting us. For though he tempts us after the death of Christ as he tempted us before, yet he cannot conquer, as he used to conquer before." [1] Nothing could be more explicit than this disciple's adoption of Abelard's central doctrine : " So great a pledge of love having been given us we too are moved and kindled to love God who did such great things for us ; and by this we are justified, that is, being loosened from our sins we are made just. The death of Christ therefore justifies us, inasmuch as through it charity is excited in our hearts." [2]

Still more explicit and unqualified is the adoption of Abelard's theory in another and somewhat earlier " Sententiarius," Robert Pullus or Pullen. Pullus vehemently denies that the Devil's dominion was just, or that Christ's death was a ransom paid to him. [3] Christ, he tells us, suffered and died " not because He could not redeem us in any other way, but that by the greatness of the price He might make known to us the greatness of His love and of our sin." [4] That is his simple theory, and he has no other. Robert Pullus was our first great Oxford theologian—with one exception the first known Oxford

---

[1] " A vinculis diaboli solvimur, id est a peccatis : et ita a diabolo liberamur, ut nec post hanc vitam in nobis inveniat quod puniat. Morte quippe sua, uno verissimo sacrificio, quidquid culparum erat unde nos diabolus detinebat, Christus extinxit, ut in hac vita nos tentando non praevaleat. Licet enim nos tentet, post Christi mortem, quibus modis ante tentabat, non tamen vincere potest, sicut ante vincebat " (*Sent.* iii. Dist. xix. 1). In the prominence of the idea of merit—not really consistent with this thought—the Lombard perhaps shows the influence of Anselm, and there are other expressions about the death of Christ (apart from the ransom theory) which it would not be difficult to interpret in a purely Abelardian sense.

[2] " Exhibita autem tantae erga nos dilectionis arrha, et nos movemur accendimurque ad diligendum Deum qui pro nobis tanta fecit ; et per hoc justificamur, id est, soluti a peccatis justi efficimur. Mors ergo Christi nos justificat, dum per eam charitas excitatur in cordibus nostris " (*ib.*).

[3] *Sentent. Libri Octo*, iv. 13 : " Quippe diabolus in homine, quem malo dono deceperat, nihil juris habebat, tanquam alienum in servum invasionem faciens merito spoliandus, iure etiam ex invasione judicandus."

[4] " Non quod aliter redimere non poterat ; verum ut quantitate pretii, quantitatem nobis sui innotesceret amoris, nostrique peccati; passus in natura hominis, quoniam divinitas intacta permansit " (iv. 13). In the thought that the sacrifice illustrated the gravity of our sin, an idea is introduced which is often insisted on by modern preachers. The idea is not without value; but, if the theory of expiation is not to be reintroduced in an attenuated form, this effect must be held to be produced not by the death, nor indeed by the work of Christ *exclusively*. The death of Christ represents part of the undeserved suffering which sin has caused. The contemplation of that undeserved suffering has done more to arouse repentance and to redeem the world than that excited by any other death, but it is not the only tragedy that sin has caused, nor the only one that has in it *some* redemptive effect.

teacher.[1] He taught in Oxford in the year 1133; and afterwards at Paris. His Abelardian doctrine of the atonement did not prevent his becoming a Cardinal and the Chancellor of the Holy Roman Church. For Abelardianism had now mounted the papal throne in the person of Guido, the pupil of Abelard, the protector of Arnold of Brescia, who as Celestine II. succeeded St. Bernard's obedient tool, Innocent II. Another famous writer of this period, Roland Bandinelli (who has sometimes been identified with Pope Alexander III.), has left behind him a book in which the atonement is treated in a completely Abelardian spirit.[2] As one reads these early scholastics on the atonement, one can only exclaim, " O si sic omnes ! "

Before I leave this group of twelfth-century schoolmen, I may add that Pullus has an admirable account of justification which contains the whole principle of the later scholastic doctrine on the subject. According to him—as according to St. Paul when he explains himself fully—the only faith which saves is the faith which works by love. It is only because it is the source of love that faith saves ; but salvation may be said to be due to faith only without works, because, if the right sort of faith is there, the love must be there too, and so the man will be saved even though, from lack of time and opportunity, he may not actually do good works ; and so in his case faith will be reckoned for works.[3]

The Abelardian doctrine of the atonement was far too simple, too rational, too oblivious of tradition to be at once accepted as the authorized theory of the Church to the exclusion of all others. It exercised considerable

---

[1] See my *Universities of Europe in the Middle Age*, vol. ii. p. 333 *sq.* The doctrine of Pullus is all the more remarkable as in other matters he is reckoned an opponent of Abelard.

[2] " Hac itaque de causa hoc modo humanum genus voluit redimere, ut ad humilitatem et sui venerationem homines magis provocaret " (*Die Sentenzen Rolands*, ed. Gietl, p. 158).

[3] " Fides, inquam, etiam ante opera justum facit. Unde ante tempus operandi de medio raptus solam salvatur per fidem : nec immerito, quoniam bonum opus necessitas excludit, sed voluntas optat et expetit. Et perfecta voluntas faciendi reputatur pro opere. Unde Apostolus fidem asserit per dilectionem operari (Gal. v. 6). Fides namque per se mortua (quoniam otiosa) per dilectionem semper operatur, dum aut si tempus habet suasu ac virtute dilectionis bona multa facit ; aut si tempore careat, dilectio pro opere computatur " (*Sentent.* iv. 15).

influence ; but after a short period of triumphant Abelard-
ism, the less revolutionary and the much more elaborate
theory of Anselm prevailed, but by no means without a
good deal of modification and combination with other
ideas. Later Protestant theory came in some respects
much nearer to Anselm's position. But in one respect
the influence of Anselm has never been shaken off:
his formula of " satisfaction "—unknown to the fathers
—has ever since remained the favourite mode of representing the work of Christ in the medieval and the
modern Roman Church. I must, however, pass over all
intermediate stages in the development of the scholastic
theology and pass on to the work of St. Thomas Aquinas,
the scholastic theologian *par excellence*.

It is impossible now to dwell upon the origin and
the nature of the mighty intellectual movement which
St. Thomas represents. I must be content with remind-
ing you of the great fact which differentiates the full-
blown scholasticism of the Middle Ages from the
scholasticism of the twelfth century—the re-discovery
of Aristotle. The earlier scholastics possessed only
a fragment of the writings of Aristotle ; they knew only
his Logic. St. Thomas had before him nearly the whole
great corpus in Latin translations made direct from the
Greek. The result of this recovery was the reconstitution
of the Church's theology upon an Aristotelian basis.
The earlier theology of the Church, so far as it was
philosophical, was for the most part based upon Platonism
or Neo-Platonism. St. Augustine was of course very
much of a Platonist. St. Thomas Aquinas was as strict
an Aristotelian as it was possible for any thinker to be
who was at the same time an orthodox Christian and
professed to accept almost *en bloc* a theology already
steeped in Platonism. This Aristotelian tendency
brought with it, among other things, a passion for definition, lucidity, precision of statement.

In St. Thomas' treatment of the atonement no new
idea emerges. In this matter, as in so many others, he
does little more than give definite form and outline to
the traditional theology of the past. St. Thomas was a

great systematizer of other men's thoughts rather than a great original thinker. Views which had given offence are slightly toned down rather than definitely abandoned. There is no single leading thought in the Thomist doctrine on this subject : he enumerates a long list of distinct reasons for the death of Christ. He touches lightly upon some of the old early patristic reasons—the necessity of showing the reality of Christ's death, its value as an example, and so on. But the points chiefly insisted upon are these :

(1) Christ merited the remission of our sins by the superabundant merit of His voluntary death. This was one of Anselm's leading ideas. Unlike Anselm, Thomas does not undertake to demonstrate that no other mode of salvation could possibly have met the requirements of justice. It is enough for him to show the justice or " conveniency " of the mode actually provided by God.[1] Bringing down the more high-flown, Platonically-minded metaphysic of Anselm to the level of Aristotelian common-sense, he will not say that the guilt of man was an infinite guilt or the merit of Christ an infinite merit. He simply insists that in His submission to a death which was in His case undeserved, Christ earned a store of merit which was much greater than was required to outweigh all the de-merit of original sin and all the actual sins of humanity.[2]

(2) For the pseudo-Platonic idea of an abstract universal humanity which sinned in Adam and his posterity and paid the penalty in Christ, Thomas substitutes the simpler Pauline thought of the Head and its members.

---

[1] In P. i. Q. xlvi. he shows (Art. 2) that another mode of liberation was " possible," but (Art. 3) that no other mode was more " convenient."

[2] " Christo data est gratia non solum sicut singulari personae, sed in quantum est caput Ecclesiae, ut scilicet et ipso redundaret ad membra ; et ideo opera Christi hoc modo se habent tam ad se quam ad sua membra, sicut se habent opera alterius hominis in gratia constituti ad ipsum. Manifestum est autem quod quicunque in gratia con-stitutus propter justitiam patitur, ex hoc ipso meretur sibi salutem, secundum illud (Matt. v. 10) : ' Beati qui persecutionem patiuntur propter justitiam.' Unde Christus per suam passionem non solum sibi, sed etiam omnibus membris suis meruit salutem " (*Summa Theol.* P. iii. Q. xlviii. Art. 1). In Art. 2 we read : " Christus autem ex charitate et obedientia patiendo, majus aliquid Deo exhibuit quam exigeret recompensatio totius offensae humani generis. [The reasons for this follow.] . . . Et ideo passio Christi non solum sufficiens, sed etiam superabundans satisfactio fuit pro peccatis humani generis."

The merit which Christ won is transferred to the soul through the mystical union of believers with the Church and of the Church with its Head.[1] This modification of the old theory does much to bring it more nearly into accordance with normal Christian experience.

(3) Not very easy to distinguish from the idea that Christ won salvation for us by the superabundant merit of His death is the thought that He caused our salvation by way of satisfaction.[2] " The Passion of Christ," we are told, " was not only a sufficient but even a super-abundant satisfaction for the sins of the human race." The idea of satisfaction has perhaps the merit of being vaguer, and so less ill-sounding, than that of vicarious punishment; but, as there is a disposition to exaggerate the difference between the Catholic idea of satisfaction and what is sometimes alleged to be the Protestant doctrine of substituted punishment, it must be pointed out that Thomas (like Anselm) expressly treats this idea of satisfaction as equivalent to the idea of punishment. " It is a convenient mode of satisfying for another," says St. Thomas, " when any one subjects himself to the punishment which another merited."

(4) The death of Christ is treated in the most un-compromising and the crudest way as a sacrifice by which God was "placated":[3] that is St. Thomas' word. At the same time he wholly disclaims the idea that the love of

---

[1] See last note. Cf. also the following succinct statement from the second Article : " Caput et membra sunt quasi una persona mystica, et ideo satisfactio Christi ad omnes fideles pertinet sicut ad sua membra." The idea comes perhaps originally from Leo the Great : " ut virtus quae inerat capiti inesset etiam et corpori " (Serm. lxvi. 4), but Leo is speaking of the effects of Christ's work as a whole. There was of course much in earlier writers to suggest the thought. It is also found in St. Bernard. (Cf. above, p. 359, n. 4).

[2] In Q. l. Art. 1 we read : " Est autem conveniens satisfaciendi pro alio modus cum aliquis se subjicit poenae quam alius meruit. Et ideo Christus mori voluit. . . . Christus per suam mortem nos perduxit ad vitam, dum sua morte mortem nostram destruxit ; sicut ille qui poenam pro alio sustinet removet poenam ejus."

[3] See the passage about satisfaction quoted in the above note. In Q. xlix. Art. 4 it is laid down that " Est hoc proprie sacrificii effectus ut per ipsum placetur Deus ; sicut etiam homo offensam in se commissam remittit propter aliquod obsequium acceptum quod ei exhibetur."

In the face of such passages I am at a loss to understand what Harnack can mean when he writes : " A vicarious penal suffering, in the strict sense of the terms, is not recognized even by Thomas, because on the whole question he allowed only a limited range to the justitia dei " (History of Dogma, E.T. vol. vi. p. 193). He himself quotes from Q. xlvii. Art. 3 : " In quo ostenditur et dei severitas, qui peccatum sine poena dimittere noluit."

God for man was caused for the first time by the death of Christ; its effect was simply to remove the obstacle to a continuance of that love which sin had created.[1]

(5) There is the Abelardian idea that we are freed from sin because we are provoked to charity by the exhibition of God's love in the death of Christ.[2]

(6) There is the old idea of redemption from the power of the Devil. Here St. Thomas goes very near indeed to the old ransom theory, actually quoting from St. Augustine words which in him implied the whole theory of the transaction. But the most grotesque and objectionable features of the theory are skilfully eliminated. The trick practised by God on the Devil disappears. The death of Christ is, indeed, treated as a ransom, or a "kind of price";[3] it is not, however, paid to the Devil but to God, and this paying of a price is treated as identical with satisfaction. The dominion which the Devil had wielded over man, which St. Bernard, Pope Innocent II., and the Council of Sens had solemnly pronounced to be just, was to St. Thomas essentially an unjust power: man was justly allowed to incur the penalty of servitude to the Devil, but only as a man is subjected by a just judge to a torturer—without prejudice to his continued allegiance to God the supreme Judge. Justice therefore demanded that man should be redeemed, but only in respect to God, not in respect to the Devil.[4] By this ingenious distinction (already made by the Lombard) the idea of God paying a ransom to, or acknowledging rights in, the Devil is avoided: and now he tries to retain the old

[1] Q. xlviii. Art. 1.   Christ had already "merited" our salvation by His love from the first moment of His conception.

[2] The "passio Christi est propria causa remissionis peccatorum tripliciter (1) per modum provocantis ad charitatem . . . (2) per modum redemptionis . . . (3) per modum efficientiae, in quantum caro secundum quam Christus passionem sustinuit, est instrumentum divinitatis ex quo ejus passiones et actiones offerantur in virtute divina ad expellendum peccatum" (Q. xlix. Art. 1).

[3] "Eius passio fuit quasi quoddam pretium, per quod liberati sumus ab utraque obligatione [i.e. peccati et poenae].   Nam ipsa satisfactio, qua quis satisfecit sive pro se sive pro alio, pretium quoddam dicitur" (Q. xlviii. Art. 4).

[4] "Quamvis igitur diabolus injuste, quantum in ipso erat, hominem sua fraude deceptum sub servitute teneret et quantum ad culpam, et quantum ad poenam; justum tamen erat hoc hominem pati, Deo permittente hoc quantum ad culpam, et ordinante quantum ad poenam. Et ideo per respectum ad Deum justitia exigebat quod homo redimeretur, non autem per respectum ad diabolum" (Q. xlviii. Art. 4).

language which really implies that, but for his machinations against Christ, the Devil would have had some sort of quasi-rights which could not justly have been ignored. As it was, he " exceeded the measure of the power entrusted to him by God by devising the death of Christ, who did not deserve death." [1]

(7) One more effect of the death of Christ is recognized by St. Thomas: and this is perhaps the predominant thought. He speaks incidentally and obscurely of Christ's passion as causing the remission of sins " by way of efficiency." [2]   " The flesh of Christ in respect of which He suffered is the instrument of His Divinity from which passions and actions operate (*operantur*) in a divine virtue for the expulsion of sins." [3]   The nature of this efficiency is not further indicated when St. Thomas is speaking of the objective effects of Christ's passion, but we can hardly be wrong in supposing that he is already thinking of that doctrine of grace and of the sacraments which is subsequently worked out in great detail. The passion of Christ is, as it were, a fountain from which flows a healing stream of grace by which sin is forgiven and justification effected. It is probable too that there is some connexion between this doctrine of the " efficiency " of Christ's death and the crude philosophical theory of a resemblance between cause and effect—that theory that like produces like, upon which so many savage taboos and so many philosophical theories at bottom depend. [4]   The parallelism insisted upon by St.

---

[1] " Excessit modum potestatis sibi traditae a Deo, machinando in mortem Christi, qui non habebat meritum mortis " (Q. xlix. Art. 2).   Cf. Q. xlvi. Art. 3 : " Conveniens fuit ut per iustitiam homo a servitute diaboli liberaretur, Christo satisfaciente pro ipso per suam passionem."   The justice is no longer justice to the Devil ; but if so, why does the Devil's abuse of power make any difference ?

[2] See above, p. 376, note 2.   It should be observed that in all the above cases it is the " passion " of Christ to which the various effects are attributed—to all the sufferings which preceded physical death.   At the same time a special efficacy is attributed to the actual death : " Effectus mortis Christi attenditur circa remotionem eorum quae contrariantur nostrae saluti ; quae quidem sunt mors animae, et mors corporis " (Q. l. Art. 6).   This actual death was " salutiferum virtute divinitatis unitae " ; whereas it was the humanity of Christ which *suffered*, and it was this suffering which earned merit.   Foley (*Anselm's Theory of the Atonement*, p. 215) refers to a decree of Innocent III. which describes Christ's bearing of punishment as the means whereby He might satisfy mercy and justice.

[3] See above, p. 376, note 2.

[4] Thus, after showing that what happened to the flesh of Christ at death was " salutiferum virtute divinitatis unitae," he proceeds : " Consideratur autem proprie alicujus

Paul between the physical death of Christ and our death unto sin, between His resurrection and ours, is converted into a metaphysical theory of direct and quasi-physical causation.

There is much more novelty in the Thomist doctrine as to the way in which the effects of Christ's passion are made available for the individual. Here we see the curious consequences which resulted from the collision between the theology of St. Augustine and the philosophy of Aristotle in the mind of one who implicitly believed in both. Thomas adhered rigidly to the Augustinian doctrine of predestination, of original sin, of the necessity for divine grace at every stage in the process of justification and sanctification. On the other hand, he was profoundly influenced by the ethics and psychology of Aristotle. From Aristotle he had learned to regard a moral act as essentially the work of the man himself, and as in that sense free. This Aristotelian doctrine, when combined with the by no means Aristotelian doctrine of future reward and punishment, led to an immense emphasis on the idea of merit. St. Thomas is so far in earnest with the doctrine that a man's sins must be his own that he denies that the sin of Adam can descend to his posterity in such wise as to deserve actual pain. No one can merit damnation by original sin alone. Here he directly contradicts St. Augustine. A "limbus puerorum" is accordingly provided for unbaptized infants instead of a place of torment.[1] At bottom St. Thomas' doctrine about human freedom was, I believe, the same as St. Augustine's—not the popular doctrine of free-will which has commonly been attributed to him

---

causae effectus secundum similitudinem causae. . . . Et ideo per mortem Christi dicitur esse destructa in nobis et mors animae, . . . et mors corporis " (Q. l. Art. 6). So the resurrection of Christ is the " efficient cause " of our resurrection (Q. lvi. Art. 1), a position supported by a citation from the metaphysics of Aristotle, " Illud quod est primum in quolibet genere est causa omnium quae sunt post " (*Met.* L. ii. text. 4), and from the pseudo-Dionysius, " Ipse Deus primo illuminat substantias sib imagis propin-quas, per quas illuminat magis remotas," after which he continues : " Et ideo Verbum Dei primo tribuit vitam immortalem corpori sibi naturaliter unito, et per ipsum operatur resurrectionem in omnibus aliis." The ascension is likewise shown to be " directly the cause of our ascension " (Q. lvii. Art. 6).

[1] *Summa Theol.* pt. iii. Suppl. Q. lxix. Art. 6. Cf. *De conceptu Virg.* c. 22 (quoted by Harnack vi. p. 302).

by modern Scholastics since the condemnation of Jansenism.[1] Both of them were consistent predestinarians
and determinists. If Thomas seems to waver for a
moment by suggesting that the individual is able to
prepare himself for grace by doing good acts, it soon
appears that in this preparatory step too the will must
be moved by God : the man must receive help which
is due to first or prevenient grace. Then comes the
grace which justifies and the co-operating grace which
enables the man to do good works and so earn merit. It
is admitted that since the fall man has been naturally
incapable of earning merit after the strictest sense of
desert (even before the fall he could not do so without
divine assistance or grace) : but by a divine arrangement
he is made capable of merit. In so far as the meritorious acts proceed from his free will, he may be said to
earn merit " of congruity." It is congruous that the
man who does virtuous acts should be rewarded by
God, though it is only God that has given him the
formed faith or charity which enables him to do them ;
while, in so far as the meritorious work proceeds from
the Holy Spirit, the man who is in a state of grace may
even be said to do good works which can really earn
merit " ex condigno " ;[2] that is to say, he may be looked
upon as jointly with God causing the good works and
meriting their reward. The rights of faith are as it
were technically saved. It is the faith that justifies,
but then faith without love is merely unformed faith

---

[1] See *Summa Theol.* P. ii. 1. QQ. cix.-cxiv. In modern times it has been usual to understand Thomas as teaching the doctrine of free-will in the sense of popular Indeterminism,
but this is opposed to his clearest utterances and to the earlier Dominican tradition. One
of Pascal's stock line of arguments against the Jesuits was to show the impossibility of
condemning Jansenism in a way which would save the position of the Dominicans. See
especially Q. cix. Art. 2. The following passage is particularly clear : " In eo, qui habet
usum liberi arbitrii non fit motio a deo ad justitiam absque motu liberi arbitrii, sed ita
infundit donum gratiae justificantis, quod etiam simul cum hoc movet liberum arbitrium
ad donum gratiae acceptandum in his qui sunt hujus motionis capaces " (Q. cxiii. Art. 3).
The acceptance of grace by the will is (ultimately) as much due to the divine action as
the offer or first movement towards good in the soul. The real meaning of " free-will,"
when used by a Determinist, is well brought out in the saying which Denifle quotes
from Matthew de Aquasparta (*Quaestiones disputatae selectae*, t. i. p. 210): "Liberum
arbitrium est essentialiter ipsa voluntas."

[2] Q. cxiv. Art. 3. Cf. *In Sent.* ii. Dist. xxvii. Q. i. Art. 4 : " Deus dat gratiam
indignis, quia his qui non sunt sufficienter ad hoc digni : sed tamen habent aliquam
dispositionem ad recipiendum, ex quo dicuntur quodammodo ex congruo gratiam mereri,
nec ex hoc sequitur quod sit invitus sed liberalis."

("fides informis")—the raw material, so to speak, out of which true saving faith is formed, but not the real thing: it only passes into the formed faith ("fides formata") which alone justifies when it produces love, and the good works to which love prompts.[1] This formula after all only stereotypes the clear teaching of St. Augustine, though perhaps the emphasis is here inverted. There is more stress on love and works and the reality of human merit, and less upon faith and the arbitrariness and gratuitous bestowal of grace. As to which comes first—the remission of sins or the infusion of that divine grace which enables the man to do good works and so merit eternal life—there is perhaps some confusion;[2] but one thing is clear: justification is, with St. Thomas, the actual making of the man good through the virtue which is infused into him by God. In some vague and undefined sense this bestowal of grace is connected with the "passion of Christ."

But what is the channel through which grace is communicated to the individual? If Thomas' Aristotelianism exercised a moralizing influence upon the Augustinian doctrine of justification, the advantage is to a considerable extent neutralized by his doctrine of sacraments.

The sacraments were not strictly the only channel by which divine grace may reach the human soul, for a heathen could not experience the faith demanded for baptism without prevenient grace. But the emphasis laid by St. Thomas upon the sacraments and the semimagical way in which they are supposed to operate goes beyond the general trend of patristic teaching as regards any sacrament except perhaps baptism. St. Thomas stereotyped the doctrine of seven and only seven sacraments:[3] and all the sacraments are now definitely pronounced to be founded by Christ Himself. Immense

---

[1] *Summa Theol.* P. ii. 2, Q. iv. Art. 3, 4, 5.

[2] This point is elaborately criticized by Harnack, *History of Dogma*, vol. vi. p. 289 *sq.* It is interesting to notice that Ritschl admits that the scholastic doctrine on this point does not "contradict the Evangelical idea of faith" if it means that faith is the turning of the will towards God as to the highest end (*Justification*, iii. 102).

[3] So already in Peter the Lombard, but divergent views were held. Cf. Harnack, *Hist. of Doctrine*, vi. 202.

importance is attributed to all of them, but the most prominent is penance. Writing half a century after the Council which for the first time established the necessity of annual confession and absolution, St. Thomas was the great exponent of the almost physical efficacy of the sacrament of penance. Penance was, as Harnack has pointed out, the medieval sacrament *par excellence*. It is absolutely essential to salvation for any one who has committed any actual mortal sin :[1] though this doctrine was not universally taught. The absolving priest is the "instrument" of the divine forgiveness. Salvation is made to depend mainly, not upon any direct effects, objective or subjective, of Christ's atonement upon the soul, but upon a mysterious influence which acts upon it in a semi-physical manner through wholly physical channels. No doubt a certain interior "disposition" is required to secure the efficacy of the outward acts. The penitent must be contrite, but no contrition can dispense with the necessity for sacramental penance after mortal sin. Venial sins may, indeed, if repented of, be remitted without priestly absolution, but the sprinkling of holy water conduces to their remission. Good works are insisted on, and must be done from a motive of love ; but the performance of penance and conformity to ecclesiastical regulations are the good works generally contemplated : while the deficiency of works in the penitent can always be supplied by the application to him of the merits of others. For him who aims at "perfection" the monastery is open : for the secular, who is content with the observance of the evangelical precepts as distinct from the evangelical counsels, the whole stress of the Thomist teaching is laid upon the sacraments.[2] Only in this somewhat external and mechanical way is the salvation of the individual connected with the work of Christ. The sacraments, we are told, "have their virtue from the passion of Christ,

---

[1] " Et ideo confessio est de necessitate salutis ejus, qui in peccatum mortale actuale cecidit " (*Summa Theol.* P. iii. Suppl. Q. vi. Art. 1).   The reason given is that without confession the priest cannot apply the " congruum remedium." The " Supplementum " of the *Summa* is not by St. Thomas, but it is based upon the views expressed in hi Commentary on the *Sentences* of Peter the Lombard.

[2] P. iii. QQ. lxxxvii., xc. ; Suppl. QQ. i.-xx.

the virtue of which is applied in some way to us by the reception of the sacraments." [1]

The lowest depth of unspirituality or (as we might call it) religious commercialism is reached in that doctrine of indulgences which Thomas had a chief hand in formulating. Sin even in the man who is forgiven had to be satisfied for by the personal sufferings or good works of the sinner. This necessity was due to the intrinsic justice of such satisfaction, and was also required for the sake of its deterrent influence. These "temporal" penalties of sin consisted partly in penalties enjoined by the Church, partly in the pains of Purgatory, except for the saints or others who had satisfied sufficiently in this life. But the merits of Christ were more than sufficient for the redemption of mankind : they were sufficient to be allowed to compensate even for those temporal penalties. And the Saints, by their works of supererogation, had added to these merits. The Pope or Bishop had therefore the power to apply this "treasury of merits" to the remission of those penalties on any conditions he pleased. [2] These conditions might be comparatively onerous. In early days a plenary indulgence might cost a crusade. Later on they became more and more trifling. In the later Middle Ages indulgence might be earned by attending particular mass or a university sermon. Even plenary indulgences were commonly bestowed for a mere payment of money.

On the whole the theology of St. Thomas has retained the position of highest authority in the Roman Church down to our own day. But his reign was by no means unquestioned. Particularly in the matter of the atonement and justification there was a disposition throughout the later Middle Ages to carry still further that mitigation of rigid Augustinianism which he had begun. This tendency developed into the system which is associated with the name of Duns Scotus. The attempt of the

[1] "Operantur in virtute passionis Christi, et passio Christi quodammodo applicatur hominibus per sacramenta" (P. iii. Q. lxi. Art. 1. Cf. also Suppl. Q. xvii. Art. 1 : "Et quia ex latere Christi dormientis in cruce sacramenta fluxerunt, ex quibus ecclesia fabricatur, ideo in sacramentis ecclesiae efficacia passionis manet."

[2] *Summa Theol.* P. iii. Suppl. QQ. xxv.-xxvii.

great Dominicans, Albert the Great, and St. Thomas, to reconstruct theology on an Aristotelian instead of a Platonic-Augustinian basis met with a conservative resistance. Of this resistance the chief organs were the University of Oxford, which was not disposed to accept Parisian innovations without a struggle, and the Franciscan Order, jealous of their great rivals, the Dominicans. In England the Franciscans were perhaps more influential than the Dominicans : and both oppositions centred in the Franciscan convent or college near Paradise Square in Oxford. On the philosophical side —in respect of the reality of universals and the innumerable questions connected therewith—the Scotist doctrine represents a more Platonic and a more Augustinian realism than that of St. Thomas. On the questions with which we are now concerned it is, however, difficult to discover anything particularly Platonic in the Franciscan tendencies.[1] On the contrary there is a weakening of the intellectualism which St. Thomas derived both from Aristotle and from at least one side of Augustine. Little as there is in common between the teaching of the Franciscan doctors and that of the " little poor man " of Assisi who knew and cared as little for Plato as he did for Aristotle, we can just recognize one genuinely Franciscan tendency in the Scotist theology. It endeavoured by a still further departure from St. Augustine to moralize and soften the harsh features of the Augustinianism which St. Thomas retained. The leading characteristic of the Franciscan ethics and theology is that it laid increased emphasis upon the will as compared with the intellect, upon love as compared with knowledge. The Scotists, unlike Thomas, actually identified " grace " with love.[2] The Franciscan Heaven

---

[1] The first great Franciscan doctor, Alexander of Hales, was earlier than Thomas Aquinas, and may be considered the connecting link between Anselm and the great Dominican. He qualifies the Anselmian doctrine of the necessity of the satisfaction offered by Christ. This line of thought was carried further by St. Bonaventura. But it is not for the most part in the early Parisian Franciscans that the beginnings of the tendencies which culminated in Duns Scotus are to be looked for, but rather in the atmosphere of Oxford.

[2] " Omnis gratia est charitas " (*In Sentent.* ii. Dist. xxvii. 4). But some fine distinctions follow.

consisted in the plenitude of love rather than in the intellectual vision of God.[1]

This change in the centre of gravity, as it were, of theology might perhaps have been expected to exercise a moralizing influence upon the doctrine of the atonement. And to some extent it has done so. In so far as he exalts the idea of the love of God, in so far as he insists on the revelation of that love by Christ, Scotus does indeed escape the moral difficulties of the older theories : so far we can trace in him the voice alike of the older Scholasticism and of Franciscan piety. It is a great improvement upon the general Western tradition that the incarnation is represented as part of the eternal purpose of God, which would have occurred whether there had been a fall or not.[2] For Scotus the death of Christ was not a punishment and was not demanded by justice. So much he explicitly teaches. He speaks of Christ's death as a satisfaction for sin, and as a sacrifice, but not as a substitutionary sacrifice. It was accepted because God willed to accept it. And God was moved to accept it simply by love. So far Scotus is the disciple of Abelard—the critic of Anselm and the Thomists. But there is another side to the matter. The Franciscan emphasis upon the will at the expense of intellect resulted in an increased insistence upon the arbitrariness of the divine volition. Morality is not yet, indeed, made to depend wholly upon the arbitrary will of God : for the first table of the decalogue is still regarded as springing from the essential nature of God ;[3] God therefore could not command men to hate

[1] "The will is superior to the intellect" was the Scotist maxim. So it was held that the "synderesis," by which a man is naturally inclined to good, is in the will and not (as Jerome and the Lombard held) in the reason (*In Sentent.* ii. Dist. xxxix. Q. 1.) Scotus takes a similar view of "Conscientia" (Q. 2). Yet we find the Franciscan Roger Bacon speaking of the truth (of the Real Presence) as that " qua deificamur et assumimur in vitam aeternam " (*Opus Majus*, ed. Bridges, vol. ii. p. 400). And even in this life " ex participatione Dei et Christi deificamur et christificamur et fimus Dei " (as an authority for this he quotes Boethius) : " ideo participatione Christi fimus Christi " (*l.c.* p. 403). This is noticeable as showing that the language about deification was not, as is sometimes assumed, exclusively Eastern. But (as with later Greeks) the deification seems to be attained chiefly by reception of the Eucharist rather than by knowledge.

[2] " Dico quod incarnatio Christi non fuit occasionaliter praevisa, sed sicut finis immediate videbatur a Deo ab aeterno " (*In Sentent.* iii. Dist. xix. 6). This was, as we have seen, the general tendency of Greek theology. For the history of this controversy, see the dissertation on the " Gospel of Creation " in Bishop Westcott's *Epistles of St. John*, p. 273 *sq.*   [3] *In Sentent.* iii. Dist. xxxvii. Q. i. 8, Q. ii. 16.

Himself. But " Everything other than God is good because it is willed by God." [1] Thus the essential goodness of God Himself is nominally saved. But human morality is made to depend solely upon the arbitrary will and pleasure of God. If God had willed men to murder or steal, it would have been forthwith right to murder or steal. This attitude towards morality dispensed the Scotist from elaborate attempts to establish the justice of the atonement. He simply declared that the merits of Christ were sufficient to atone for the sins of the whole world because God has willed to receive them as having such an efficacy. Thus Scotus at least paved the way for the idea that the connexion of the work of Christ with forgiveness and justification is wholly arbitrary and irrational.

When we come to the human conditions of justification, Duns Scotus makes an attempt—doubtless in the wrong way—to mitigate the rigours of the Augustinian scheme by reviving the old pre-Augustinian doctrine of free will in the full, popular sense. Henry of Ghent and his followers had already maintained that the heathen " in puris naturalibus "—without any grace at all—may keep the commandments of the moral law sufficiently to earn grace *ex congruo* ; and when grace is given, the human will retains the power of freely co-operating or refusing to co-operate with the moving of the divine Spirit.[2] Scotus still more decidedly maintained the possibility of a heathen doing really good acts and earning merit by his own free will. At the same time he throws out the much better and more pregnant suggestion that the Gentiles spoken of by St. Paul who by nature did the things contained in the law " did not live well without all grace "; and that nobody ever was

---

[1] " Sicut omne aliud a deo ideo est bonum, quia a deo volitum, et non e converso, sic meritum illud tantum bonum erat, pro quanto acceptabatur et ideo meritum quia acceptatum, non autem e converso, quia meritum, et bonum, ideo acceptatum " (*In Sentent.* iii. Dist. xix. 7). In Dist. xx. he goes on to maintain that an adequate satisfaction might have been offered by " unus bonus angelus " or (by divine grace) " unus purus homo."

[2] " Respondetur quod existenti in peccato mortali possibile est servare praeceptum, non autem ut manet in peccato ; sed possibile est praeparare et disponere se ad gratiam, qua data potest servare praeceptum " (Scotus, *In Sentent.* ii. Dist. xxviii. 3).

actually " in a pure state of nature (*in puris naturalibus*), since God always conducts to his true end every natural creature whom He has made, if there is no impediment or defect on his part." [1]

But if concessions are made to what seemed to be the requirements of natural morality in dealing with man's share in the process of salvation, all that relates to God's share in it—to the connexion of Christ's work with the forgiveness of sins—becomes more arbitrary than ever, though the arbitrariness may be supposed to spring from a leaning to mercy. Christ's merits are not strictly infinite. They are accepted because God wills to accept them, though there is a certain " congruity " in their being accepted as if they were infinite. In this sense Christ has merited the " first grace " which is given to every one who receives baptism, but, if an adult, he must co-operate with that grace by his own free-will.[2] The requirement of faith is reduced to an "implicit" belief in the teaching of the Church; from which any positive moral efforts can hardly be expected, since the layman is not bound to know in detail what the Church does believe. Any moral effect which may follow becomes merely the reward of this arbitrary condition of faith. If there is much insistence on love as the supreme condition of salvation, love comes to be interpreted as simple obedience to the commands of the Church. If the rigidity of the Augustinian conditions of salvation is mitigated, this is not

---

[1] He cannot, however, attain " the end," since, though he can perform good acts, he cannot do them " from charity " without grace; but this absence of charity does not involve mortal sin (*Ib.* 3). By doing the acts he " disponit se de congruo ad gratiam gratificantem sibi oblatam vel resistet." The Gentiles might, according to St. Paul, be justified by keeping the laws of nature, " sed isti non bene vixerunt sine omni gratia. . . . Si enim non resistat gratiae, justificabitur " (*ib.* 8). Against Henry of Ghent he denies that original justice in Adam was a supernatural gift; Adam possessed freedom to keep the law of nature or to disobey it. Original sin is not strictly a sin, but a natural defect (" defectus naturalis qui intrat ab origine non est defectus culpabilis sed poenalis." *In Sentent.* ii. Dist. xxx. Q. 1). " Tamen de facto nunquam erit aliquis in puris naturalibus, quia Deus naturam rationalem quam fecit semper producit ad finem, si non fuerit ex parte illius impedimentum vel defectus " (Dist. xxxiii. 5).

[2] After denying (against Anselm) that the merit of Christ could " de condigno " be treated as infinite, Scotus continues : " Tamen ex circumstantia suppositi [*sc.* Christi] et de congruo ratione suppositi habuit quamdam rationem extrinsecam, quare Deus potuit acceptare illud in infinitum, scilicet extensive, pro infinitis. . . . Sed quid et quibus meruit ? Dico quod Christus meruit omnibus, qui primam gratiam accipiunt, collationem illius, ita quod ibi non cooperatur voluntas nostra, nisi in adultis baptizatis, ubi requiritur aliquis bona dispositio voluntatis " (*In Sentent.* iii. Dist. xix. 7, 8.)

to make the goodness which wins heaven correspond more completely with goodness as understood by the ordinary moral consciousness, but for the purpose of substituting mere "attrition" for genuine "contrition" as the one interior disposition without which even St. Thomas admitted that all the machinery of Church and sacrament must prove unavailing. Attrition is defined as the kind of sorrow for sin or "servile fear," which may be inspired by anticipation of punishment;[1] and it is conveniently assumed that the sacrament of penance by the grace which it bestows turns the attrition into perfect or formed contrition.[2] That is all the personal morality that a man wants to go to heaven : all the rest may be secured by the due use of outward observances—the sacraments, indulgences, vicarious masses and so on. That cheapening of the conditions of salvation which can be traced progressively at work since the early days in which it was doubted whether a single mortal sin after baptism could ever be forgiven has now reached a point at which even the most enormous sins can be pardoned without a moment of real sorrow for their guilt. From a severity so extreme as to shock the ordinary moral consciousness the ethics of the Church have descended to a laxity which would have scandalized an average pagan.

From the purely philosophical point of view Nominalism was a revolt against Scotism. But in theology William of Occam was the successor, rather than the opponent, of Duns. Both systems were born in the Franciscan Convent of Oxford. The Occamists put the finishing touch to the downward tendency of scholastic ethics. Some of them made even the first table of the decalogue dependent upon the arbitrary will of God, and frankly admitted that God might just as well have commanded man to hate Himself as to hate his neighbour,

---

[1] In the Franciscan Alexander of Hales, who wrote before St. Thomas (*Summa*, iv. Q. xvii. m. V. Art. 2), attrition is treated as normally preceding contrition.

[2] "Dico quod bonus motus praecedens sacramentum paenitentiae tantum est attritio et dispositio de congruo ad deletionem culpae et infusionem gratiae, quae remissio culpae et collatio gratiae sunt in virtute sacramenti paenitentiae et non in virtute attritionis tantum, nisi dispositive. Sed haec attritio post collationem gratiae, quae confertur in susceptione sacramenti, fit contritio formata" (*Reportt. Paris.* iv. Dist. 15, Q. 4; Schol. 2).

and then it would have been right to hate God.[1] The
" perseitas boni " (as the Schoolmen expressively called
it)—the " in-itselfness of good "—was denied. It was
not only constructive moral philosophy that was assailed
by the Nominalism of Occam and his followers. The
same unsparing criticism was bestowed upon natural
theology, and even revealed theology, as it was understood
by St. Augustine and St. Thomas. Nominalism, when
really thought out, always means in the long run pure
scepticism. Some of the later medieval Nominalists
literally revelled in exhibiting as philosophers the speculative absurdity of the dogmas which, as theologians, they
were prepared to swallow with dutiful avidity. It was
formally maintained that a proposition might be true
in philosophy which was false in theology.[2] Authority
completely took the place alike of reason and morality.
From such a point of view it was quite unnecessary to
moralize or to rationalize the scheme of salvation. God
had willed that salvation should be attained by the death
of Christ, the merit of which could be secured for the
sinner by acceptance of the Church's doctrine, a dutiful
compliance with the rules of life which it enjoined, or a
dutiful use of those means of evading the consequences
of non-observance which the Church had so abundantly
supplied.

There is much in these later medieval theories of
justification, and still more in their practical application,
from which the modern student is tempted to turn away
either with indignation or with undiscriminating con-

---

[1] In his *Centiloquium Theologicum* (Conclusio v.) Occam maintains " quod Deus
potest facere omne quod non includit contradictionem." He admits the consequence
" Deus potest facere peccatum," but contends that " faciendo peccatum Deus non
peccat," and that " Deus posset damnare beatam Virginem et omnem multitudinem
angelorum seu beatorum," and that " aliquis possit Deum odire meritorie." It is
objected that on ordinary theological principles a man who was commanded to hate God
would have to do so from the love of God, and that this would involve a contradiction.
I will not reproduce the subtle distinctions of Occam's reply except the statement that
some do not admit that there is any contradiction.   Petrus Alliacus and Andreas de Novo
Castro were conspicuous defenders of these theses.

[2] It was maintained that in theology everything that involved no actual contradiction
might be accepted on authority, *e.g.* that God might as well have become incarnate in an
ass, a stone, or a stick as in man: "Non includit contradictionem Deum assumere naturam
asininam.   Ergo Deus potest facere ". . . . " Pari ratione potest assumere lapidem
et lignum, etc." (Occam, *Centil. Theol.* Conclusio vi.).

VI   MEDIEVAL SCHOLASTICISM   389

tempt. But it is fair to recognize that the medieval
Schoolmen (all but the latest of them), even when they
declined to follow the splendid lead of Abelard, really
did make honest and not wholly unsuccessful attempts
to reconcile the doctrines which they had inherited
(chiefly from Augustine) with the demands of the moral
consciousness, and with a conception of God which should
be in harmony with those demands. Let us summarize
the points on which these medieval theories had in them
elements of progress :

(1) The medieval eschatology was much less appalling
than that of Tertullian and Augustine, of Luther and
Calvin. The Schoolmen elaborated—from hints of
St. Augustine worked out by Gregory the Great—the
idea of a Purgatory, which made their conception of the
divine justice less of a mockery than the lip-service of
those who called God just, but represented Him as doom-
ing to everlasting torments all but the small minority
of the human race to whom He had given the grace which
was required for a full measure of faith and love. And
then even for the unbaptized there was the "limbus
puerorum," a region said to be in Hell geographically
("quantum ad situm loci"), but not qualitatively
("secundum locorum qualitatem").[1] The virtuous
pagans are equally free from any pain of sense (*poena
sensus*) or even sadness (*tristitia*). In the great poem of
Dante, it will be remembered, his beloved Virgil and his
revered Aristotle were not actually in Heaven, since they
were for ever excluded from the vision of God ; but they
were only technically in Hell. In the *Inferno* the wise
men of the ancient world are described as being "of
semblance neither sorrowful nor glad." Scotus can even
assure us that they may attain to "a knowledge of all
things naturally cognizable," and so to a "certain natural
beatitude."[2]

---

[1] St. Thomas Aquinas, *Summa Theol.* P. i. iii. Suppl. Q. lxix. Art. 5. Cf. App. Q. i.

[2] Those unbaptized persons who are only guilty of original sin suffer no "pain of
sense" or even "sadness" but only the "pain of loss" (*poena damni*) : "videtur pro-
babile concedere quod omnium naturaliter cognoscibilium possunt naturaliter cogni-
tionem habere . . . et ita aliqualem beatitudinem naturalem de Deo cognito in universali
poterunt attingere" (*In Sentent.* ii. Dist. xxxii. 3).

(2) It was something to have it definitely asserted that justification meant a real making just, not a fictitious counting just. There is value in the formula that the only faith which saves is "formed faith" (*fides formata*), a faith which produces love from which (where opportunity is given) good works must result. The weak point of the medieval theories about grace is that they tried to represent the saving effects of Christ's work as a wholly extraneous and miraculous influence which flows into the soul quite independently of any effect produced upon the believer by the thought of Christ and His work. Still, it was all to the good that the Middle Age was disposed to insist so strongly upon the love of God and man, and to make obedience the best proof of love.

(3) Nor is it at all to their discredit that the Schoolmen do insist on the necessity of good works. This side of their teaching was, as we have seen, spoilt by the tendency practically to confine the idea of good works to austerities and ecclesiastical observances of one kind or another— many of them quite useless and some of them socially pernicious. Still, it is something that the Schoolmen should have made the simple effort to do one's duty take so large a place in the conditions of salvation. Even the prominence which they give to the sacraments as the channels through which divine grace normally reaches the soul of man has its good side in so far as it can be separated from the mechanical manner in which the sacraments were supposed to operate. It at least implied that salvation was not beyond the reach of the plain man who, with little theological knowledge and no great capacity for the highest religious emotion or experience, was desirous to do his duty and ready to avail himself of all the means which the Church had provided for helping him to do it. The later Scholasticism expressly maintained that to him who does his best there is always given sufficient grace to enable him to be saved. There is no Pelagianism there (whatever Luther may say to the contrary), for without the divine grace he would not be doing his best. The weak point of all these scholastic theories of grace is that there is so little emphasis on

that conscious union and communion with Christ of which St. Paul is so full.   Nominally all grace somehow flows from Christ and His passion : actually the historical personality and character of Christ count—I will not say for nothing—but for too little.

It must be remembered that as regards this matter of justification a grave injustice has been done to the Schoolmen by Luther.   Protestant historians of doctrine, especially in Germany, have been much too ready to base their estimates of Scholasticism upon the fierce diatribes of Luther.

A great storm has recently been created in Protestant Germany by the violent attack made upon the Reformer by the learned German Friar Denifle.   No impartial historian is likely to accept Denifle's view of Luther as a licentious person who deserted his order to marry and live comfortably, who systematically told lies about the religion which he had forsaken, and whose doctrine was especially constructed for the purpose of condoning his personal vices.   But, though the book is written in the worst possible spirit, Denifle has, I think, shown conclusively that Luther's representations as to the formal and official teaching of the medieval Church are grossly misleading.   In so far as they are true at all, they are true only of the later Scholasticism—and especially of the Nominalism in which Luther himself was brought up. But even the later Scholasticism did not teach that men could be saved by their own exertions—by prayers and fastings, asceticism, taking the cowl, and so on—without the grace of God.   What the learned Dominican fails to realize is that, in spite of all the formulae which the Church had inherited from an earlier theology, the crude ideas against which Luther protested may, nevertheless, represent fairly enough the impression made by the medieval Church system upon the average monk and still more upon the average layman.   He conveniently overlooks all the scholastic doctrines which, to say the least of it, encouraged such ideas—the doctrine of attrition; the idea that, even where repentance was most complete, sins had to be satisfied for by penance;

the enormous emphasis upon asceticism, and in particular the whole atrocious system of indulgences which was the immediate cause of Luther's revolt. That a protest against these immoral and anti-Christian ideas was urgently called for, it is impossible for any serious student of Church History to deny; and I am not one of those who believe that a milder attempt to reform the Church without a rebellion against the authority of Rome could have been successful, though, it may be, much that was valuable was swept away with the rubbish. At the same time the recognition of this fact must not lead us to assume that, in the quarrel between Luther and the Scholastics, all the truth was on the side of Luther. Nor must the real defects of the later and very degenerate Scholasticism which Luther knew best blind us to the elements of real truth and value which were contained in the earlier, nobler, more robust Scholasticism of Abelard and the Lombard and St. Thomas, and even in the well-intentioned Scotist attempts to reconcile the theology of the Church with a serious belief in the divine justice and the divine mercy.

Looked at as a whole, Scholasticism was after all a noble attempt to vindicate the rights of reason in religion, to fuse into the very fabric of the Church's doctrine the best elements of ancient thought, and, above all, to assert that fundamental truth of Christianity—never perhaps up to the age of the Reformation formally denied, but often obscured—that the only faith which saves is the faith that produces love. Would, indeed, that the Church of our own day could produce and could accept a systematic and philosophical reinterpretation of Christianity which should do as much justice alike to the Christian tradition of the past and to the new knowledge of the present as was done to both, from the point of view of the thirteenth century, by St. Thomas and his successors!

ADDITIONAL NOTE TO LECTURE VI

ON THE LATER REALISM

Though in the late Middle Age Nominalism had won its way back from persecution to a position of ascendancy, the Realist opposition was never abandoned. And this later Realism was much more than a continuation of the polemics of St. Thomas or of Duns. It involved a complete abandonment of the tendency imparted to theology by the Thomist Aristotelianism, and a going back not merely to the letter but to the spirit of St. Augustine. The originator of this tendency was Thomas Bradwardine, who began life as a Fellow of Balliol and ended it as Archbishop of Canterbury. From him the tendency passed to Wycliffe—once, no doubt, a Fellow, subsequently Master, of Balliol—and from him to John Huss. The same tendency is seen in all those theologians of the late Middle Age, such men as John of Wesel and John of Goch, who are sometimes described as " Reformers before the Reformation." Deeply interesting and in many respects original as are the ideas both of Bradwardine and Wycliffe, I must pass them over. They contain little that is new as to the actual effects of the death of Christ, though, at least in Wycliffe's case, much that is new as to the way of applying them to the spiritual life of the individual, and as to the individual's relation to the ecclesiastical system and the ecclesiastical means of grace.

There is surprisingly little in the way of theory about the atonement in Wycliffe, but he holds a very definitely substitutionary view. Nobody can be punished for the sins of another except Christ, he tells us, " qui summe voluntarie et gratissime pro suorum fratrum criminibus est punitus. Hoc tamen fuit justissime, cum factus est humana species et sic genus hominum, quod peccavit "—the old pseudo-Platonic theory of the Greek fathers (*De novis ordinibus* cap. 2 in " Polemical Works," Wycliffe Soc., i. p. 330). All the conclusions reached by the Reformers as to the individual's independence of priestly mediation are anticipated in the later writings of Wycliffe, who shows, at the same time, a remarkable freedom from some of the harsher and more unethical tendencies of Reformation theology. Wycliffe and Huss are full of the idea, so abhorrent to Luther, of the Gospel as a " new law." But the return to Augustine which began in the later Middle Age can best be studied in connexion with the movement to which it ultimately led—the Reformation of the Sixteenth Century.

LECTURE VII

LUTHER AND THE REFORMATION

What doth it profit, my brethren, if a man say he hath faith, but have not works? can that faith save him?—JAMES ii. 14.

Yea, a man will say, Thou hast faith, and I have works: shew me thy faith without thy works, and I will shew thee my faith by my works.—JAMES ii. 18.

LECTURE VII

The Reformation introduced little that was really new into the theology of the atonement and much less than is commonly supposed into the doctrine of justification. The basis of the Reformation theology is, of course, the theology of St. Augustine. St. Augustine's own theology may be described as a hardening, a formulation, an exaggeration of one particular side in the many-sided theology of St. Paul. The theology of Luther represents a one-sided and exaggerated version of St. Augustine. If we compare Luther's teaching with the theology of the Middle Ages, especially of the nominalistic Scholasticism in which he was brought up, the contrast is, no doubt, from some points of view, glaring enough. But even here the difference is much less than is often supposed if we judge the Schoolmen by their own writings and not by Luther's wild and random statements about them. Like many revolutionaries, Luther was much more under the influence of tradition than he supposed. Much that he says in condemnation of the Schoolmen is not true at all of the earlier Scholasticism, with which he was very imperfectly acquainted ; while, on the other hand, some of his own most characteristic ideas—some of the ideas which most differentiate him from St. Augustine and from St. Thomas—can be definitely traced to later Nominalists such as William of Occam or Gabriel Biel, the Schoolman with whom he was most familiar. I must endeavour to justify this statement in somewhat greater detail ; and this will best be done if I endeavour to enumerate as clearly as possible the points in which the theology of the Reformation differed from that of St. Augustine or of the earlier Middle Age. I shall dwell chiefly on the teaching of Luther, but shall occasionally compare it with that of Calvin.[1]

(1) The theology of Luther, more even than that of St. Augustine, is concentrated upon the death of Christ to the neglect, absolute or relative, of all other aspects of His Person, work, and teaching. And yet it is surprising how difficult it is to extract from Luther any definite account as to why Christ's death was necessary. There is no new thought in Luther about the death of Christ. The compact with the Devil is not formally asserted, though Luther's language about the subjection of man to the Devil often reminds us of that older view which the Schoolmen had discarded. Sometimes he seems to presuppose some such theory as Anselm's.[2] At other times he makes the whole scheme of salvation quite arbitrary. Anselm insisted on an absolute, demonstrable necessity for Christ's death, and thought he could prove it on ethical or rational grounds. Luther insists so passionately upon the completely gratuitous character of the means provided by God for man's salvation, that the Father's arbitrary will and pleasure becomes for him the sole reason for His acceptance of the sacrifice offered by the Son. So far from wishing to rationalize or moralize the scheme of redemption, he exults in its irrationality. Over and over again he declares that the

---

[1] I have quoted Luther, wherever possible, from the great Weimar edition, which will eventually extend to more than fifty quarto volumes, but is at present incomplete. I have been much indebted to the late Father Denifle's *Luther und Luthertum*, which exhibits a vast knowledge both of the Schoolmen and of Luther's writings, though inspired by violent anti-Protestant prejudice. A French translation of this work by M. Paquier has been published which includes certain replies to Denifle's Protestant critics, and contains valuable additions and corrections. Denifle often quotes from an unprinted Commentary on the Romans : this has since been published by Ficker ; the references to this edition are given by the French translator. I have occasionally borrowed these quotations, but I have not been able to verify the references.

[2] This is as clear a passage as I can find on the subject : " Nos sumus offendentes. Deus cum lege sua est offensus. Et offensio talis est, ut Deus eam non possit remittere nec nos possimus solvere. Ideo inter Deum qui per se Unus est, et nos maximum est dissidium. Denique non potest Deus revocare legem suam, sed vult servari eam " (*In Gal.* iii. 20 ; Weimar XL. i. 503-4). Even here it is not clear whether the impossibility of God forgiving without satisfaction arises from His intrinsic justice or from His arbitrary will and pleasure.

scheme of redemption was something not merely beyond reason, but contrary to reason. Here he was simply treading in the footsteps of the later medieval Nominalists. It is true that it was only in theology that these later Schoolmen were anti-rationalistic : in philosophy they were excessively rationalistic. None of them blasphemed against God's gift of reason as did Luther. Philosophy and rational theology were things for which Luther frankly confessed that he had no use.

The tendency to an arbitrary view of the atonement was carried still further by Calvin, whose central doctrine was the absolute sovereignty of God. The necessity for Christ's death, according to Calvin, was not an "absolute necessity, but flowed from the divine decree upon which depended the salvation of men."[1] Even Calvin (however difficult it may be to reconcile the two views) strongly asserts that the whole arrangement sprang from the love of God—the love not only of the Son but of the Father also ; why love demanded such a sacrifice he does not explain. Whatever the ground of its necessity, there can be no doubt about the substitutionary character of the sacrifice made by Christ either in Luther or in Calvin.[2] Indeed, the idea of substitution—the idea that the Son was treated by the Father exactly as if He were guilty humanity—is now pushed further than it had ever been pushed before. Luther declares that Christ was the greatest of all sinners " because He assumed in His body the sins we had committed, to make satisfaction for them by His own blood."[3] " He was crucified and died for thee, and offered up thy sins in His own body."[4]

---

[1] *Inst.* (Genev. 1602) II. xii. 1.

[2] " Correctionem pacis nostrae illi impositam fuisse, ex Propheta nuper retulimus : fuisse propter scelera nostra a patre percussum, attritum propter nostras infirmitates. Quibus significat in locum, adeoque instar rei submissum, sceleratorum sponsorem vademque qui dependeret ac persolveret omnes, quae ab illis expetendae erant poenas : uno hoc duntaxat excepto, quod doloribus mortis non poterat detineri " (*Instit.* II. xvi. 1).

[3] " Et hoc viderunt omnes Prophetae, quod Christus futurus esset omnium maximus latro, homicida, adulter, fur, sacrilegus, blasphemus, etc., quo nullus maior unquam in mundo fuerit . . . Non quod ipse commiserit ea, sed quod ea a nobis commissa susceperit in corpus suum, pro illis sanguine proprio satisfacturus " (*In Gal.* iii. 13 ; Weimar XL. i. 433-4).

[4] " Is crucifixus, mortuus est pro te et obtulit peccata tua in corpore suo " (*In Gal.* ii. 16 ; Weimar XL. i. 224). Cf. *In Gal.* ii. 19 (*ib.* XL. i. 274) : " Jesus Christus Dei filius moritur in cruce et portat meum peccatum, legem, mortem, diabolum, infernum in corpore suo."

Luther even goes the length of saying that Christ "really and truly offered Himself to the Father for eternal punishment on our behalf. His human nature behaved ('non aliter se habuit') as if He were a man to be eternally condemned to Hell." [1] In Calvin we do not find quite such extravagant statements; but he speaks of Christ as experiencing "all the signs of an angry and punishing God," [2] and held that "Christ has taken upon Himself and paid the penalty which by the just judgement of God threatened all sinners." [3]

(2) The doctrines of original sin, of arbitrary election, and of predestination had assumed in St. Augustine a form sufficiently extreme, and yet we find in Luther (so far as such a thing is possible) a strengthening and emphasizing of these Augustinian doctrines. St. Augustine had admitted that man was free, in the ordinary popular sense, before the fall: this practically not very important reservation disappears in Luther. The fall itself and the awful penalties which it brought with it were all predestined and necessary. Strong as is the language which St. Augustine uses about the condition of man after the fall, he did not entirely abandon the earlier patristic belief that traces and relics of the divine image survived: this concession disappears when the "total depravity of human nature" came to be a formal tenet of Lutheran no less than of Calvinistic Protestantism.

(3) St. Augustine had used the term "free will"

---

[1] Denifle quotes from the *Commentary on Romans* (Ficker ii. 218): "Realiter et vere se in aeternam damnationem obtulit patri pro nobis. Et humana ejus natura non aliter se habuit quam homo aeternaliter damnandus ad infernum." We are not surprised at Luther's Dominican critic Denifle describing this as a "revolting and blasphemous doctrine." Yet Catholic preachers had indulged in very similar extravagances : see the extracts in Rivière, *Le Dogme de la Rédemption*, p. 9 : he quotes from Bossuet the statement that God "le regarde enfin comme un pécheur et marche contre lui avec tout l'attirail de justice," and from Bourdaloue the words "la justice de Dieu l'envisage comme un objet digne de toutes ses vengeances," and again, "cet abandon de Dieu est en quelque sorte la peine du dam qu'il fallait que Jésus-Christ éprouvât pour nous tous." Western Catholicism and Protestantism can neither of them afford to reproach the other with immoral doctrines of the atonement : the real difference between them is that extreme dogmatic Protestantism has made a particular view of the atonement the whole of Christianity ; if this is taken away there is nothing left ; Catholicism can part with such aberrations, and fall back upon healthier views which have never been left without witnesses.

[2] *Inst.* (1553), vii. 29 (somewhat toned down in later editions).

[3] *Inst.* (1602), II. xvi. 2.

in the sense in which it might be employed by a modern
determinist : to Luther free will—nay, all willing—is a
mere fiction. In his extremer moments he denies the
very existence of the human will.[1] His predestinarianism is not merely absolute, but of the most mechanical
and least philosophical kind. He pushed his contempt
for the human nature which God had created and redeemed to the extent of holding that, even after grace,
a man ought to hate himself and desire his own damnation.[2]
Christ was content to hold that a man should love his
neighbour as he loves himself. The doctrine that a man
should love himself better than his neighbour had been
condemned by medieval councils : [3] the doctrine that
he should hate himself is so utterly extravagant and
opposed to the plain teaching of Christ that the necessity
for condemning it had never arisen.

(4) As regards the impossibility of either faith or
good works without the divine grace, Luther was entirely
in agreement with St. Augustine; and between St.
Augustine and the Schoolmen the difference was (as we
have seen) smaller than Luther himself represents.
None of the Schoolmen thought that salvation was possible
without faith, and none of them maintained that faith
was possible without grace. But both St. Augustine
and the Schoolmen—nay, all previous theologians—

---

[1] " Male enim dixi, quod liberum arbitrium ante gratiam sit res de solo titulo, sed
simpliciter debui dicere ' liberum arbitrium est figmentum in rebus seu titulus sine re.'
Quia nulli est in manu sua quippiam cogitare mali aut boni, sed omnia (ut Viglephi
articulus Constantiae damnatus recte docet) de necessitate absoluta eveniunt. Quod
et poeta [Manilius] voluit, quando dixit ' certa stant omnia lege,' et Christus Matth.
x. ' Folium arboris non cadit in terram sine voluntate patris,' etc." (Weimar vii. 146).
So " Nondum vides spiritum et liberum arbitrium esse contraria ? " (ib. 144). St.
Augustine never denied the existence of the will, but only that there could be any *good*
will in man without grace. " Nam neque liberum arbitrium quicquam non nisi ad
peccandum valet : si latet veritatis via." Denifle is very indignant with Luther and
other Protestants for quoting the passage without the last clause, and this does make a
difference : with Augustine grace can restore something of the will's capacity for good.
[2] The Christian ought to hate himself " non voce tantum, et ficto corde sed pleno
affectu confiteri, et optare nos perdi et damnari. Quia sicut agit, qui alium odit, ita et
nos in nos agere oportet. Qui odit enim, non ficte, sed serio cupit perdere et occidere
et damnare eum quem odit " (*In Rom.* c. 9 : Ficker ii. 220). Luther here flatly contradicts St. Paul, Eph. v. 29. He might reasonably hold that each man ought to hate
himself so far as he is really hateworthy, but then, according to him, that bad self is
the whole self : there is, even after grace, no better self to love.
[3] In 1346 Nicholas de Ultricuria was condemned for maintaining even that a man
ought to love better than himself a man who is better than himself. See Denifle and
Chatelain, *Chartularium Universitatis Parisiensis*, t. ii. No. 1124.

had taught that *after* justification, with the assistance of divine grace and of the divine spirit, the Christian really did become capable of good works, works really good and well-pleasing to God.   And this was just what Luther in his more dogmatic moments categorically denied.   Not only did he deny all the ideas associated with the merit of " congruity " and " condignity " ;[1] he formally denied that, whether before justification or after justification, any human being born in original sin ever could do anything really good in the sight of God.   " The just man sins in every good work."   " Our best good work is a venial sin."   These were among the famous ninety-five theses nailed by Luther on the church door at Wittenberg.   In his explanation the last thesis is withdrawn in favour of the more uncompromising assertion that " every good work of the just man is a damnable and a mortal sin if it were judged by the judgement of God."[2]   Sometimes he pushes his insistence upon faith, and faith only, to the point of disparaging repentance.   " Priests," he declares, " err and are mad, not to absolve people, unless they are contrite, and they ask, ' Son, do you grieve for your sins ? . . .' He should only ask, ' Dost thou believe ?   Believe and have confidence.' Thus Christ said to the sinful woman, ' Thy sins are forgiven thee.'   I absolve thee, go in peace, because thou believest."[3]   " Believe firmly that thou

---

[1] " Ego enim peccatum assero quicquid ante gratiam fit in homine, tantum abest ut praeparet ad gratiam " (Weimar vii. 114) ; and of course there is for Luther no grace before or independently of full Christian belief.   No doubt all this might be qualified by taking into consideration the goodness which the Christian derives from Christ, but in Luther the distinction between the man himself and the man as worked on by Christ is so absolute that the man himself cannot properly be said to do anything even with the help of Christ.   Denifle quotes from *Com. on Romans* (Ficker iii. 114) : " Ideo recte dixi quod extrinsicum nobis est omne bonum nostrum quod est Christus "—a quite impossible psychology.   Cf. *de servo arbitrio* (Wittembergae, 1526, p. 56) : " Sic humana voluntas in medio posita est, ceu iumentum ; si insederit Deus, vult et vadit quo vult Deus. . . . Si insederit Satan, vult et vadit quo vult Satan, nec est in eius arbitrio ad utrum sessorem currere, aut eum quaerere, sed ipsi sessores certant ob ipsum obtinendum et possidendum."   Luther could never see that to ascribe an act to the will of man did not exclude the action of divine agency or " grace "—just the same mistake, at bottom, which was made by the Pelagians, who supposed that acts which they rightly regard as willed by man are quite independent of the will or the grace of God.

[2] " In omni opere bono iustus peccat."   " Opus bonum optimum factum est veniale peccatum."   " Omne opus iusti damnabile est et peccatum mortale, si iudicio dei iudicetur " (Weimar vii. 136, 138).   [3] Weimar iv. 658.

art absolved, and thou shalt be truly absolved, whatever
become of thy repentance." [1]   His sense of the radical
corruption of human nature is so profound that there
is no room for such a thing as real repentance.   Really
to repent and to hate the sin for its own sake would, as
he saw, by itself imply a certain amount of actual righteousness.   At times he goes very near to the assertion that
no repentance is possible except that which is produced
by terror of God's wrath,[2] which would be exactly the
" attrition " of his Nominalist instructors.   Sometimes
it would appear that all that he really means is that true
contrition is difficult and usually very imperfect—a
truth which probably few of his opponents would have
denied.   But elsewhere his actual assertions go far
beyond this.   According to Luther the sense of guilt
is appeased by the assurance of pardon, but the sinfulness
remains just what it was before.   The righteousness of
Christ is " imputed " to the sinner, but none of it is really
transferred to him.   For him justification means not a
making righteous but an accounting righteous and a
falsely accounting righteous.   The righteousness which
God freely bestows upon man through Christ is not,
as the Schoolmen held, a real righteousness, a righteous-

---

[1]   " Crede fortiter te absolutum, et absolutus vere eris, quicquid venerit de contritione."
This was the article condemned by Leo X. : what Luther says in his explanation amounts
to this—that the penitent's confession may well be imperfect, and yet he will be forgiven.
" Cave, cave, frater Christiane, ne unquam super tua contritione confidas : non huic sed
fidei tuae promisit deus remissionem peccatorum " (Weimar vii. 119-120).   In the
next article he explains that there cannot be faith without *some* contrition, " cum gratia
non infundatur sine magna concussione animae," and later (*l.c.* p. 122) the penitent (in
confession) is exhorted " confiteri se non esse digne contritum ac pro hoc ipso gemere."
Occasionally he will admit that contrition is the " causa sine qua non " of forgiveness
(*On Ps.* li. 5, Weimar xl. ii. 359) ; but there can be no contrition without grace, and grace
comes only with Christian faith : there is no such thing as an " amor naturalis legis et
odium peccati " (Weimar vii. 115).

[2]   He declares, indeed, in 1518, that " poenitentia vera non est nisi quae ab amore
justitiae et Dei incipit " (Weimar i. 525).   Cf. Thomas Aquinas, *Summa Theol.*
P. ii. 1, Q. 113, A. 5.   But such penitence he treats as all but impossible : " Si vere ac
libere velis confiteri, remoto Deo, praecepto, poena, gaudio, scio dices ' Si nullus esset
Deus, nullus infernus, certe vix peniterem ' " (Weimar i. 321).   True penitence (" contritio in charitate facta ") he declares that no one in this world possesses," vel saltem
paucissimos."   If all that he meant was that an absolutely perfect penitence was as
difficult as a perfect righteousness, Luther would no doubt be right.   And this is perhaps
all that Luther really means if the sermon be read as a whole.   His advice is (1) to culti-
vate hatred of sin by trying to love goodness in living examples (especially Christ) ;
(2) not to let the imperfection of our penitence prevent our praying for more penitence
and for forgiveness.   Still there is an extreme emphasis upon confident belief.

ness infused into the soul of man by God's free grace. After justification, as before it, man continues really unrighteous—incapable of any real righteousness. His righteousness is a merely imputed—that is, a fictitious, juridical, pretended—righteousness. Here we reach the one really new thing in the doctrine of Luther and of the Reformation—the doctrine of imputation,[1] though even this was only carrying a little further the later nominalistic doctrine of arbitrary divine "acceptance." St. Paul, too, held that justification meant a counting righteous, and a counting righteous of those who were not as yet righteous. But he never supposed for one moment that God counted any one righteous without also making him really righteous—more righteous at least than he was before : still less St. Augustine, with whom justification is explicitly a making righteous. Luther, in his dogmatic moments, really did hold that doctrine.[2] For Christ's sake the Father, he thought, imputes to man the righteousness of the Son, but lets him remain just as unrighteous as he was before—not merely imperfectly righteous, but incapable of any real righteousness at all.[3]

This doctrine is closely connected with his view about the nature of concupiscence. After justification, as before it, all concupiscence was to Luther sinful.[4] And

[1] " Manifestum est quomodo fiamus iusti, scilicet mera imputatione iusticiae " (In Ps. li. 1 ; Weimar xl. ii. 350).

[2] " Non quod non habeam peccatum sicut Sophistae docuerunt . . . sed absconditum est peccatum, non vult sehen, obstat Christus quem apprehendi fide, et propter illum apprehensum debent omnia peccata non esse peccata " (In Gal. ii. 16 ; Weimar xl. i. 234). Luther here (p. 233) uses the word " acceptatio " or " reputatio." So " Purificare cor est imputare cordi purificationem " (Disputationen, ed. Drews, p. 50).

[3] The word " imputation " is not used in our Articles. Hooker uses it, but he adds that we do also participate in Christ " by habitual and real infusion "—the scholastic doctrine so abhorrent to Luther (Eccles. Polity, chap. lvi.).

[4] See Weimar vii. 103 sq. This is, according to Denifle, Luther's fundamental theological error ; he adopted it, according to that critic, in the year 1515—in the middle of his Commentary on Romans, which was written between April 1515 and October 1516 (Luther und Lutherthum, i. 447). Luther was no doubt right in denying that baptism extinguished original sin in the only sense in which the term can be properly used, i.e. inherited tendencies to evil : he is clearly (as Denifle contends) wrong in treating all natural desire as in itself sinful, and the consent of the will as unavoidable. And yet, after all, Luther admits that the man who is justified does begin to be better. It is strange to find Denifle quarrelling with Luther for saying that original sin is never completely effaced, and that the remission of it in baptism is only the beginning of its disappearance ; but later Scholastics tend to make original sin a mere fiction. Some of Luther's sanest sayings are those which speak of the conquest of sin as a gradual process, e.g.: " Sic justus vocatur, non quia est, sed quia fit " (Weimar iv. 665), and again, " Chris-

concupiscence was, as he had discovered by his own
bitter experience, invincible.[1] He does not distinguish,
as the Schoolmen had done, between mere natural desire
and the consent of the will thereto. Consequently,
since no one can altogether extinguish concupiscence, no
amount of faith and no amount of grace can make a man
really righteous. Christ is not a source of real righteousness to men. He is merely, in Luther's language, " a
garment to cover their shame in the sight of God "
(Schanddeckel).[2] " We thank God," he exclaims, " that
the sin which in reality is not removed is held to be
removed, and is absorbed through the goodness of God
who dissimulates it." [3] Here Luther's German Protestant editor is so much scandalized that he has actually

---

tianus non est in facto sed in fieri" (quoted by Denifle from "Annotationes in aliquot
capita Matthaei," Jen., Opp. Lat. iv. 343), words at which Denifle is greatly shocked.
Bishop Westcott holds with Luther that a man never is, but always is becoming a Christian. In one place Luther quotes St. Bernard's " Ubi incipis nolle fieri melior, ipsa
mora peccatum est." At the same time Luther tends—in part, no doubt, generalizing
from the personal experiences of one in whom the animal nature was strong—greatly
to underestimate the extent to which in the best men evil tendencies could not merely
be resisted, but cease to be felt. He minimizes the virtues of the Saints, and thereby
really disparages the very " grace " which he pretends to extol. Cf. " Sancti intrinsice
sunt peccatores semper, illico extrinsice justificantur semper " (Ficker ii. 104).

[1] "Quod nullis consiliis, nullis auxiliis nostris concupiscentia ex nobis possit
auferri, et haec contra legem est quae dixit ' non concupisces,' et experimur omnes
invincibilem esse concupiscentiam penitus " (Weimar i. 35). Denifle is very indignant
with Luther for falsifying the teaching of St. Augustine in this matter ; but, if
Augustine escapes his criticism, it is by the finest of distinctions, especially that distinction between mortal and venial sins which Luther will not admit. St. Augustine
does sometimes recognize that concupiscence is not sin unless there is a consent of
the will (Contra Julianum Pelag. vi. 23). The Confession of Augsburg (Art. iv.) expressly identifies original sin with concupiscence, and declares that all who are not
regenerated by baptism and the Holy Spirit suffer eternal death. Our Anglican article
declares that " the Apostle doth confess that concupiscence and lust hath itself the
nature of sin" (cf. St. Augustine's "modo quodam loquendi peccatum vocatur "), but
says nothing about the fate of the unbaptized.

[2] Weimar vii. 344. Earlier he had (in the usual scholastic way) treated concupiscence
not as identical with original sin, but as a relic of it (Weimar iii. 215, 453).

[3] " Non magni pendunt, quod Deus possit hoc facere, ut manente peccato reputet
nos tamen iustos et puros esse, et ut ita absolvatur homo, quasi nullum habeat peccatum,
propter Christum. Nos vero agimus Deo gratias, quod sua imputatio maior sit quam
nostra impuritas, et peccatum, quod re vera non tollitur, sublatum reputetur et absorbeatur
bonitate Dei dissimulantis propter Christum obumbrantem, quamquam naturale illud
et substantiale maneat " (Disputationen, ed. Drews, p. 48). The text adopted by Drews
runs : " Peccatum quod re vera cum tollitur, sublatum non imputetur." But this is
quite inconsistent with the context. The Confession of Augsburg declares that " hanc
fidem imputat Deus pro iusticia coram ipso." Our Article xi. declares that " we are
accounted righteous before God, only for the merit of our Lord and Saviour Jesus
Christ by Faith," but Article xii. recognizes that good works, done after justification,
are really " pleasing and acceptable to God in Christ," which is opposed to Luther's
extremer statements.

adopted an obviously garbled text, but the doctrine is unfortunately quite what Luther habitually maintained. Sometimes, no doubt, he explains that he only means that in this life no one ever becomes *perfectly* righteous ; and he admits that through the sanctifying work of the Holy Spirit God does *begin* really to make men better ; [1] but if that is all that he meant, many of his diatribes against the Schoolmen would lose their point. For this is what few of them would have denied.

Luther carries the idea of substitution to such a point that he represents Christ as not merely dying instead of us, but as keeping the law instead of us. Christian theology had hitherto represented Christ as keeping the law perfectly that He might help His brethren to keep it less imperfectly : according to Luther He kept it in order to save us from the necessity of keeping it at all. These are his very words : " This is the Gospel . . . that the law has been fulfilled, that is, by Christ, so that it is not necessary to fulfil it, but only to adhere and be conformed to Him who fulfils it." [2] On such a view it is clear that justification comes to mean nothing but a remission of guilt and the penalties of guilt—a remission which can only be regarded as arbitrary, unintelligible, and, indeed, immoral. Well may St. Thomas declare that " remission of guilt could not be understood unless infusion of grace followed." [3]

(5) Parallel to and implied in this altered meaning of justification, there was a change in the meaning of faith. If the good works against which Luther raged

---

[1] " Incipit enim realiter purgare. Primum enim purificat imputative, deinde dat Spiritum sanctum, per quem etiam substantialiter purgamur. Fides purgat per remissionem peccatorum, spiritus sanctus purgat per effectum " (*Disputationen*, p. 50). It is interesting to note that Denifle quarrels with Luther for maintaining that for perfect justification man must wait till the last Judgement.

[2] Weimar i. 105.

[3] " Non posset intelligi remissio culpae, si non adesset infusio gratiae " (*Summa Theol.* P. ii. 1, Q. cxiii. Art. 2). In his later writings Luther denies the very notion of " infused grace " (even here he had late scholastic predecessors). " Gratiam accipio hic proprie pro favore Dei, sicut debet, non pro qualitate animi ut nostri recentiores docuerunt " (Weimar viii. 106). He was no doubt largely right as to the exegesis of St. Paul, and yet, even as regards St. Paul, this was only half the truth. When St. Paul speaks of grace as being " given " or " bestowed," and that in various measures, he does not mean that the person is, indeed, differently treated, but left as he was before. See above, p. 111.

had been merely ecclesiastical good works, if all that he had meant to deny was the doctrine that men could earn salvation by the merit of fastings, austerities, monasticism, masses, and the like, or even by more useful outward acts, and that even after forgiveness such works were necessary to expiate past sin, few modern theologians would have withheld their sympathy. Still more universal would be the agreement with his denunciation of the practical abuses to which the medieval doctrine of merit had given birth—the reliance upon mechanical penances, indulgences, and the like. But unfortunately he did not stop there. It was not only external good works which, for him, had nothing to do with salvation, but even the love from which they sprang. We have seen how the Schoolmen, developing the hint contained in St. Paul's expression "faith working by love," had distinguished between an "unformed" faith—a mere intellectual belief—and a "formed faith" which includes love, and which alone justifies and saves. And this was only a formulation of what was implied in St. Augustine. This doctrine really removed most of what was dangerous in the formula, "justification by faith." Luther will have none of this distinction. For him faith meant mere intellectual belief—that and nothing else. He expressly declares, "Faith is a kind of knowledge which sees nothing."[1] Not quite consistently with this doctrine, he elsewhere expressly identifies it with "confidence" or "trust": "fides" is identified with "fiducia." "Confidence" or "trust" might be supposed to have something to do with the will, but to allow that the will (quite apart from any question about "free will") had anything to do with salvation would have been to Luther flat Pelagianism. He constantly and vehemently denies the doctrine that it is the love or any other moral quality implied in or produced by belief which is the important thing. The doctrine that we are saved by faith formed by charity is an abominable blasphemy.[2] He complains that "even

---

[1] "Fides est quaedam cognitio quae nihil videt ; in istis nubibus sedet, nisi Christus apprehensus " (*In Gal.* xvi. 16; Weimar xl. i. p. 228-9).

[2] " 'Fides,' inquiunt, 'infusa (quam proprie vocant fidem in Christum) non liberat a

some who would be thought evangelical doctors . . . teach faith in such a way that they attribute more to charity than to faith." He definitely denies that saving faith includes any love at all.[1] "Charity may be neglected in time and place without any danger, but so cannot the word and faith be."[2] The watchword "Salvation by faith only," it is sometimes forgotten, meant to Luther salvation by faith without love. "We can be saved without charity towards and concord with the Sacramentarians, but not so without pure doctrine and faith."[3] There is absolutely no comparison between the importance of life and that of faith, any more than between heaven and earth.[4] "One little point of doctrine is of more value than heaven and earth; therefore we do not suffer it [*i.e.* doctrine] to be injured in the smallest particular. But at errors of life we may very well connive."[5] He is full of the idea that in the whole process of salvation from first to last the will is to be purely passive: when the man has been justified, then no doubt good works are to be done, but it is not he that does them, but God. "To sleep and to do nothing is the work of Christians," he exclaims in a sermon on Jacob's dream;[6] though, quite inconsistently with this doctrine,

---

peccatis, sed fides formata charitate.' . . . Profundae sunt abominationes blasphemae huius doctrinae" (*In Gal.* ii. 17; Weimar xl. i. 254). According to Luther the wedding-garment of Matthew xx. 11, 12 is faith without love. He had once held a healthier doctrine: "Fidem ego iustificantem a charitate non separo," he wrote in 1519: "Imo ideo creditur, quia placet et diligitur is in quem creditur" (E. L. Enders, *Dr. Martin Luther's Briefwechsel*, i. 408). Denifle points out that some of the late Schoolmen, the Scotist Francis Mayron and Occam, had held that God might accept us through faith alone without any infusion of love.

So, too, he storms against the scholastic doctrine (which in earlier times he had approved) that "homini facienti quod in se est, Deus infallibiliter dat graciam. Nemo dum facit quod in se est, peccat mortaliter" (Weimar vii. 142). Of course if the "quod in se est" is meant to exclude "grace," Luther might have had something to say for himself, but then Luther will not admit that there can be any grace before Christian faith. Zwingli saw that some "grace" might very well be given to a heathen.

[1] *In Gal.* iv. 8 (Weimar xl. i. 605-6).

[2] *In Gal.* v. 9 (Weimar xl. ii. 48).

[3] "Nos sine charitate et concordia cum sacramentariis possumus salvi fieri, non item sine pura doctrina et fide" (*In Gal.* v. 10; Weimar xl. ii. 51).

[4] "Nulla igitur penitus comparatio doctrinae et vitae, nec satis coelum et terra" (*ib.* 52).

[5] "Unus apex doctrinae plus valet quam coelum et terra; ideo in minimo non patimur eam laedi. Ad errores vitae autem egregie possumus connivere" (*ib.* p. 52).

[6] "Schlaffen und nigst wircken seyn der Christen werck" (Weimar ix. 407). Denifle says nothing about the context, and so makes the words seem worse than they are, but

he often urges men to make the most zealous efforts to attain the faith which he demands, and even admits that he has not fully attained it himself.   If to insist on the necessity of effort is Pelagian, Luther, too, is a Pelagian.

Faith, then, meant to Luther simply belief.   In his teaching the doctrine that salvation is by faith *alone* received an emphasis which it had never received before, even in the writings of St. Augustine.[1]   As to the exact extent of the credenda he is quite vague and inconsistent. Sometimes he includes the main articles of the Creeds : at other times belief in the atoning efficacy of Christ's substitutionary death becomes the sole article of faith : elsewhere he insists upon an equal acceptance of all the articles of his own new Protestant creed, including the doctrine of " Consubstantiation." [2]   Luther further insists that a man must believe not merely that Christ died for men in general, but for himself in particular, and that in his particular case the death has been effectual.   If there is any new article in the Reformation theology besides the doctrine of imputation, it is the doctrine of assurance—the doctrine that the believer should feel an absolute confidence in his own personal and complete salvation.[3]   " Believe that you are saved, and you are

---

they are bad enough (cf. *In Gal.* i. 2 : " Christiana sanctitas non est activa sed passiva," Weimar xl. i. 70).   The same critic points out the difficulty in which Luther finds himself as to what it is which believes.   Sometimes he is driven to say that it is faith which has faith ; sometimes he denies that there is in the Christian soul any quality called faith or charity, but only Christ.   If so, it is of course nonsense to talk, as he does elsewhere, of " fiducia cordis per Christum in Deum."

[1] One of the theses which Luther defended in 1520 was " Etiam sola fides infusa satis est ad iustificationem impii.   Imo, nisi fides sit sine ullis operibus, nihil est nequiter [*sic*] iustificat " (Weimar vi. 85-6).   It is noticeable that when Luther wants to base this teaching upon words of Christ, he has to cite the spurious ending of St. Mark's gospel.

[2] " Simili modo nos hodie pro excommunicatis et damnatis habemus, qui articulum de Sacramento corporis et sanguinis Domini incertum esse dicunt aut Christi verbis in coena vim faciunt.   Nos summo rigore omnes articulos doctrinae Christianae, magnos et parvos (quanquam nullus sit nobis parvus) volumus habere puros et certos " (Weimar xl. ii. 51).   He goes on to declare that he will have concord only with those "qui pie nobiscum sentiant de omnibus articulis Christianae doctrinae."   He will even have peace with the Papists and pray for them, but not with those who deliberately deny " one or more articles of Christian doctrine."

[3] " Fides autem esse nullo modo potest, nisi sit vivax quaedam et indubitata opinio qua homo certus est super omnem certitudinem sese placere Deo, se habere propitium et ignoscentem Deum " (*Operationes in Psalmos*, Weimar v. 395).   Yet earlier he used very different language : " Unde verus iustus confidit omnes salvari et sese timet solummodo damnari " (Weimar iv. 664).   And even in his later period he often warns his readers against " security."

saved " would be a caricature of the doctrine of St. Paul or of St. Augustine. Luther constantly uses practically those very words.[1] How different from St. Paul's " I count not myself to have apprehended. . . . I press toward the mark." . . . " Lest that by any means, when I have preached to others, I myself should become a castaway." [2] Luther did not, however, hold those doctrines of " indefectible grace " and " final perseverance " which became the note of the later Calvinism as formulated at the Synod of Dort. So long as the believer was confident in his own salvation, the sinner would certainly be saved, but the confidence might be lost, and with it the reality. The Confession of Augsburg expressly condemns those who deny that men once justified may lose the Spirit of God.[3]

(6) Among the unedifying features of popular Protestant theology which cannot justly be attributed to St. Augustine is the tendency to contrast the mercy and loving-kindness of the Son with the sternness, severity, and unrelenting justice of the Father. The anger of the just Father is propitiated because His anger and resentment is satisfied by the death of His innocent Son. The Augustinian view of the Holy Trinity implied far too strong a sense of the divine Unity for such a representation to be possible. When Father, Son, and Spirit are represented as the Power and Wisdom and the Love of " one Mind," it is clearly impossible that the Power should be thought of as angry when the Wisdom is forgiving. It is a cardinal doctrine of St. Augustine that whatever one Person of the Trinity does, the other Persons co-operate with Him in doing it. The whole work of redemption is the work of God, of the Father and of the Holy Spirit as much as the Son. How far can Luther be accused of contrasting the mercy of the

---

[1] " Quantumlibet incertus sit tam sacerdos quam peccator de contritione, rata est absolutio, si credit esse absolutum. . . . Certum est ergo remissa esse peccata si credis remissa, quia certa est Christi salvatoris promissio " (Weimar i. 631).

[2] Phil. iii. 13.

[3] Art. xii. The discouragement of " assurance " has always been a note of the sterner Catholicism. See the account given by Renan of the teaching at the Seminary of Saint Nicolas du Chardonnet in his *Souvenirs d'enfance et de jeunesse* (p.193). The Westminster Confession denies that assurance is necessary to salvation.

Son with the justice and severity of the Father ? Doubtless Luther's works are full of passages in which the work
of Christ is treated as so much testimony to the Father's
love ; and an explicit formulation of the contrary doctrine
could hardly be produced from the works of any authoritative theologian of the Reformation. But so much is
said by Luther about the Father's wrath, wrath against
all who approach Him in any way except through the
Son, about God being propitiated by the death of the
Son, and the like, that he can hardly be regarded as
without responsibility for the notion which has become
deeply engrained in popular religion, and probably not
in popular religion only. The God of Luther would
have turned away sternly and coldly and angrily from
the publican of our Lord's parable, because, though he
repented, he came to God without the name of the Son
upon his lips or the dogma of justification by faith in his
mind. Even when he speaks most definitely of the
Father's love in sending Christ, he speaks also of His
being " placated " by the Son.[1] The same may be said
still more unquestionably of Calvin. In Calvin we are
expressly told that Christ was sent as "a Mediator to
satisfy God by the effusion of His blood. . . . He offered
Himself to the Father as obedient unto death, by which
obedience He abolished the disobedience of man, which
had provoked the indignation of God."[2]

It is impossible to read the more extravagant utterances of Luther without feeling that in him that breach
between theology and morality which many previous
doctrines of justification had threatened has now reached
the point of formal divorce. For the Fathers (for St.
Augustine as much as for Origen), for the Schoolmen,
for such Augustinians as Wycliffe and Huss no less than
for the Scotists and the Nominalists, the Gospel of Christ,
whatever else it might be, was emphatically the pro-
pagation of a new and higher morality : to Luther the

---

[1] "Deus, cuius cogitatio et voluntas est, ut remissionem peccatorum et vitam aeternam consequamur per Iesum Christum filium suum, quem ad hoc misit in mundum,
ut esset propitiatio pro peccatis nostris, imo totius mundi, ut per hunc filium agnoscamus
eum esse placatum et clementem nostrum Patrem " (*In Gal.* iv. 19 ; Weimar xl. i. 650).

[2] *Inst.* (1602), xiv. 21.

doctrine that the Gospel was a new or higher law was anathema.[1] His words sometimes amount to a formal contradiction of the Gospel : the assertion that our Lord had given a new commandment was rejected by Luther as a Popish blasphemy. "A new commandment I give unto you," says the Gospel. "Christ came not to set forth a new law," says Luther.[2] The difference is irreconcilable : the question whether the Church will side with Christ or with Luther on this fundamental question is one of the largest of the religious problems on which the Church of to-day has to make up its mind.

Of course neither Luther nor any other Christian man could be consistent with such doctrines. Of course Luther taught that normally, after the man had been justified by faith, the sanctifying grace is given which enables him to do good works. The tree is known by its fruits.[3] When, for instance, he tells us that the merciful God does not impute sin after justification " on account of the cure which has already begun," [4] he writes quite in the spirit of St. Paul or St. Thomas. One of the healthiest features of Luther's practical teaching is his appreciation of the idea that to be a Christian is a lofty and difficult ideal, which can be only gradually attained. "The Christian is never made, but always in the process of being made." [5] I do not understand why Denifle, even from his own point of view, should be scandalized

---

[1] " Tanta fuit Papistarum dementia et caecitas, ut ex Evangelio legem caritatis, ex Christo legislatorem fecerint, qui graviora praecepta tulerit quam Moses ipse. Sed Evangelium docet [where ?] Christum non venisse, ut ferret novam legem et traderet praecepta de moribus, set ideo venisse dicit, ut hostia fieret pro peccatis totius mundi " (*In Gal.* i. 16; Weimar xl. i. 141).

[2] " Post legem Mosi nullam statuit novam legem. Ista pestilens opinio Ier[onymi, Orig]enis, qui pingunt Christum novum legislatorem, sicut Mahometes facit se post Christum, Papa similiter. Illi omnes pingunt Christum mendaciter. Christus—hic Paulus—non venit, ut abrogaret veterem legem, novam statueret " (*In Gal.* iv. 5 ; Weimar xl. i. 560).

[3] " In theologia vera igitur, ut homo fiat bonus per regenerationem spiritus, qui spiritus est certus, sanctus et animosus. Deinde fit, ut ceu ex arbore etiam fructus boni enascantur " (*In Ps.* li.; Weimar xl. ii. 433). But he goes on to disparage all good works except " agere gratias deo : hoc suum donum amplificare et erudire per hoc omnes homines ad eandem gratiam."

[4] " Propter incoeptam curationem " (*In Rom.* xiv., Ficker ii. 332).

[5] " Christianus non est in facto sed in fieri." The first of Luther's famous 95 theses asserted that Christ in " Penitentiam agite, etc." "omnem vitam fidelium penitentiam esse voluit " (Weimar i. 233). The second denies that " penitentia " means the sacrament of Penance.

at that expression. There is, indeed, hardly one of
Luther's more extravagant statements which may not
be balanced by more moderate statements or by counter-
assertions, though I am afraid the best of these are to
be found in his early works. And these, duly emphasized,
will generally supply most or all of the correction which
is required. Thus Luther can declare : " If thou
believest, good works will necessarily follow thy faith," [1]
and even " he believeth not truly if works of charity
follow not his faith." [2] But if by belief he really means
intellectual belief and nothing else, the statement is
opposed to obvious fact. If he means that intellectual
belief which does not tend to good works is not the faith
which justifies, he is asserting in other words exactly
the doctrine which he denounced in the Schoolmen—
the doctrine of *fides formata.* By all means, if we like,
let us say that these admissions represent the true Luther,
and put aside all the expressions that strike us as anti-
nomian or extravagant as so many temporary aberrations
provoked by the heat of controversy ; but if we do so,
we cannot at the same time—as is so often done by the
modern German theologian, whether orthodox or liberal—
maintain that the doctrine of the Reformation (on this
matter) was a new and blessed discovery, and that the
Christian world had been wrapped in darkness for the
previous five hundred, one thousand, or even fourteen
hundred years. It is not too much to say that there
was nothing in Luther's positive (as distinct from his
negative) teaching that was at once new and true ; though
doubtless he reasserted much that had been obscured or
forgotten, and denied much that very much needed to
be denied.

(7) One point more as to the relation of Luther's
teaching to medieval theology. Horrible as was the
theology of St. Augustine, the horror was a little mitigated by faint suggestions of a possible purgatorial

---

[1] Weimar xii. 559 (1523) : " Glaubstu, so mussen auch dem glauben eytel gutte
werck volgen."

[2] *In Gal.* v. 6 (Weimar xl. ii. 37). He continues : " Paul therefore in this place
setteth forth the whole life of a Christian man, namely, that inwardly it consisteth in
faith towards God, and outwardly in charity or works towards our neighbour."

suffering for those who died unfit for immediate heaven [1]—
suggestions developed, largely through the influence of
Gregory the Great, into the medieval doctrine of purgatory. And the later Schoolmen had in various ways
admitted some degree of hope for the virtuous pagan.
All this was swept away by Luther.[2] On the moral
side he was, indeed, indulgent enough in his requirements.
He admitted the possibility of a saving faith which was
accompanied by little or no moral improvement. But
on the side of dogmatic belief his demands were more
rigid than those of the severest Fathers. Never before
had the credenda been so almost completely limited to
the one article of salvation by faith in Christ's atoning
blood as they are in some of Luther's utterances ; but
in that one article such a confident belief, such an emphasis
on the " only," was demanded, that it became doubtful
whether any medieval or Roman Catholic Christian
could be saved. His language on this matter vacillates,
but at times he seems prepared to accept the position
that only Lutherans can be saved. " Now when they "
—that is to say, the Papists—" cannot tell what faith
is, they cannot have faith : much less can they teach it
to others." [3] Certainly his insistence on correctness of
doctrine and his contempt for " mere morality " would
be difficult to parallel from any previous Christian
writer. In his comment on St. Paul's words as to what
was to be done with the man overtaken in a fault, he
explains that the Apostle speaketh not of " heresies or
sins against doctrine, but of far lesser sins." [4] It is only
a logical consequence of this view when Luther declares

---

[1] E.g. *De Civ. Dei*, xxi. 13.

[2] In 1520 he does not absolutely deny the existence of Purgatory, but only denies
(1) that it is an article of faith, (2) that it can be proved by canonical scripture (here he
is undoubtedly right), (3) that the Pope can let souls out of it (Weimar vii. 149 *sq*.).
But his later utterances ignore or deny it altogether.

[3] *In Gal.* ii. 4, 5 (Weimar xl. i. 165). He admits that in the old days " Some there
were whom God called simply by the text of the Gospel (which, in spite of all, remained
in the sermon) and by baptism, and they walked in the simplicity and humility of their
heart, thinking that only monks and those ordained by bishops were holy and religious,
while they themselves were profane and secular persons in no wise to be compared with
them. They, finding in themselves no good works or merits to set up against the
wrath and judgement of God, did fly to the passion and death of Christ, and were saved
in that simplicity " (*In Gal.* ii. 16, Weimar xl. i. 245).

[4] *In Gal.* vi. i. (Weimar xl. ii. 138).

that there is in reality only one sin which can cause
damnation—the sin of incredulity.[1] He does not quite
say that there is only one virtue, the virtue of credulity.
But assuredly Luther did nothing whatever to emancipate
religious thought from the idea—still, alas, too prevalent
among religious people—that all serious enquiry into
religious truth is presumptuous and wicked. The idea
of justification by faith in all its forms had always con-
duced to the prevalence of that notion. Luther's exaggerated emphasis upon it riveted still more firmly that
paralysing chain upon European thought just at the
moment when the world seemed ready to throw it off.
If orthodox and consistent Roman Catholics had but a
precarious hope for the future, non-Christians had none.
Luther agreed with St. Augustine's view that the virtues
of the heathen were but vices. If the virtues even of
the best Christians were in the sight of God but mortal
sins, clearly there was nothing in the best virtues of a
heathen which could save him from everlasting torments.
Calvin is equally emphatic about the non-salvability of
the best heathen. The only one of the great Reformers
who allowed the possibility of a heathen being among the
elect was Zwingli, who pronounces that all true and
virtuous men will be in heaven—somewhat grotesquely
(for modern minds) including in that category not
merely such men as Socrates and Aristotle, but Hercules
and Theseus.[2]

I have not conducted this examination into Luther's
doctrine for the purpose of disparaging Luther as a man
or as a reformer. Doubtless he was not the impeccable

---

[1] " Nulla peccata eum possunt damnare, nisi sola incredulitas : caetera omnia, si
redeat vel stet fides in promissionem divinam baptizato factam, in momento absorbentur
per eandem fidem." *De captiv. Babylon.* (Weimar vi. 529).

[2] " Deinde sperandum est tibi fore ut videas sanctorum, prudentium, fidelium, con-
stantium, fortium virtuosorum omnium, quicunque a condito mundo fuerunt, sodalitatem,
coetum et contubernium. Hic duos Adamos ; . . . hic Herculem, Theseum, Socratem,
Aristidem, Antigonum, Numam, Camillum, Catones, Scipiones. . . . Denique non fuit
vir bonus, non erit mens sancta, non fidelis anima, ab ipso mundi exordio usque ad eius
consummationem, quem non sis isthic cum Deo visurus " (*Fidei Christianae Expositio,*
Opera iv., 1841, p. 65). So he regarded the salvation of the unbaptized children of
Christians as certain, while he hoped apparently for the salvation of all infants (*De
providentia Dei, ib.* pp. 125-7). Zwingli, as strict in his adhesion to predestination and
justification by faith as Luther or Calvin, was a far more philosophical thinker than
either, and there is far more of the spirit of Christ in his writings.

being of modern Lutheran hagiology. And his faults of character as a man had something to do with his defects as a teacher—his violence, his unfairness in controversy, his too indulgent attitude towards sins of the flesh, his depreciation of moral effort, his low view of the possibilities and capacities of human nature. The famous advice to Melanchthon, "Sin boldly" (*pecca fortiter*), is unhappily no isolated outburst. But no impartial student of history with a grain of psychological insight can doubt his perfect sincerity or his fundamental goodness. He was, above all, a man of heroic courage, and such a man was needed to inaugurate that great breach with corrupt tradition which is due primarily to him. Still less are these reflections intended to suggest the conclusion that the Reformation was a mistake. The conclusion which I would suggest, and which I believe could be supported by a more extended study, is rather this—that the connexion of the Reformation and its blessings with the new doctrine of justification is little more than an accident of history, and that the real work of the Reformation was almost independent of this dogma. I would even go a step further, and say that the least valuable part of the inheritance which modern Christendom owes to the Reformation of the sixteenth century is its distinctive dogmatic theology, which was in truth very largely moulded upon the traditions and ideas of medieval Scholasticism in its last and most degenerate phase. From one point of view Lutheran doctrine is simply the last, and not the best, product of an expiring Scholasticism. That some of Luther's extremer views were a little toned down in the Confession of Augsburg and the other official Lutheran standards is happily true : but the more they approximate to the older teaching of the Church, the less is it possible to recognize in them any great and beneficent doctrinal revolution.

How far the doctrine of justification by faith *only*—with the new and extreme emphasis on the "only"—has in practice exercised a demoralizing influence, is a large question, on which it is hardly possible even to touch.

I do not myself doubt the enormous practical advantages which have resulted from the Reformation, not merely in the way of intellectual emancipation and of progress, political and social, but in respect of actual morality and religion.   And yet there is another side to the matter. False speculative dogmas may sometimes be believed without practical consequences, but doctrines which affect the moral ideal or which lower the character of God are never altogether without their nemesis.   It would be possible to quote abundant testimony from Luther's own writings as to the cooling of religious ardour and charitable effort, the decline in good works— even of the works which Luther would have admitted to be really good—which actually resulted from that doctrine which Luther identified with the Gospel.   Not only do " the more part of men," he tells us, " understand the doctrine of faith carnally and turn the liberty of the Spirit into the liberty of the flesh," but " even we ourselves who teach the word, do not do our duty with so great zeal and diligence now in the light of the truth as we did afore in the darkness of ignorance.   For the more certain we are of the freedom won for us by Christ, so much the more cold and negligent are we in handling the word, in prayer, in well-doing, in suffering adversities." [1]

If we would do justice to the teaching of Luther, we must remember what was the system, what were the practices, and what were the ideas against which the new theology was a protest.   There was, indeed, much in the Reformation movement besides the new doctrines of total depravity, justification by faith only, and imputed righteousness—much which had no direct connexion with those doctrines.   And yet after all there is one point of view from which Luther's actual doctrine may well be regarded as the source of all the progress—social and intellectual, moral and religious — which directly or indirectly resulted from the Reformation of the sixteenth

---

[1] *In Gal.* v. 13 (Weimar xl. ii. 60, 61).   Cf. *In Gal.* vi. 6 (*ib.* 155-6), where he complains of the meanness of the laity in robbing the Church and not supporting their pastors, and contrasts this with the liberality of pre-Reformation times.

century. I tried to show you last Sunday how much there was that was good, healthful, and progressive in the teaching of the Schoolmen. But there is one feature of the scholastic teaching which deserves all the indignant denunciations hurled against it by Luther ; and that is the notion that sin, however sincerely repented of, however completely forgiven, must yet be " satisfied for " by the endurance of penalties or the earning of merit, and that the clergy possessed a practically un-limited power of dispensing with the penalties and distributing the merit. On these two beliefs turned nearly all the practical abuses of the medieval Church and the worst defects of its moral ideal—both its exagger-ated austerity in some directions and its extreme laxity in others : the emphasis on asceticism, the exaltation of monasticism at the expense of civil duty and family life, the excessive stress upon external religious observances, the whole system of indulgences, the employment of spiritual power for political purposes and for sheer greed of gain. In so far as justification by good works meant justification by ascetic observances on the part of some and by compounding for them on the part of others, it is impossible to exaggerate the beneficent effect of Luther's counter-formula, "justification by faith only." So far the connexion of the Reformation with the new doctrine was no mere accident. It was the very life and breath of the whole movement. To have overthrown that doctrine for one-half of Christendom and seriously weakened its hold over the other half was the enduring part of Luther's work.[1]

With all its defects, the moral ideal which the Reforma-tion practically brought into being was saner, whole-somer, more Christ-like than the ideal which it superseded. The greatest achievement of the Reformation was to put the ordinary duties of the husband and the parent, the magistrate and the citizen, the trader and the crafts-

[1] This is brought out by many passages in the Augsburg Confession. The works which the reforming preachers disparage are " certas feras, certa jejunia, fraternitates, peregrinationes, cultus Sanctorum, rosaria, monachatum et similia " (Art. xx.) ; and the Article goes on to say that even " our adversaries " no longer preach such " useless works " as formerly.

man, back into the forefront of the moral ideal in place of the anti-social uselessness of the monk, the austerities of the pious, and the pecuniary compensations for personal piety and morality which constituted too largely the religion of the average medieval layman.   Immoral as some of its theories may have been, the Reformation did involve a practical reassertion of the true relations between religion and morality ; and the good works which it encouraged were much more like the good works of Christ and the purest early Christianity than the good works of the Middle Ages.   The new ideal did largely spring out of Luther's teaching.   There is no doubt considerable exaggeration about what Luther tells us as to the current belief in the possibility of winning salvation by a monastic profession or by other austerities— considerable exaggeration, I may add, about Luther's statements in later years with regard to his own personal efforts to win salvation by his own strivings and merits. But there can be no doubt that the popular religious ideas of the Middle Ages and the moral ideal which was connected with them were steeped in a practical Pelagianism which called for a revolutionary protest.[1]

And the beneficent effect of the formula which became the watchword of the protest was not wholly negative. It did insist on the necessity, for the highest moral and religious life, of a conscious, personal relation to Christ, and through Christ to God—a necessity which was, to say the least of it, obscured by medieval theories and still more by the vast ecclesiastical machinery of the medieval Church.   Unfortunately the phrase, " faith only," taken in its natural sense, is a quite inadequate expression for this personal relation.   It is probable that many of those who have talked most about salvation by faith in the one article of forgiveness through Christ's blood have meant, at the bottom of their minds, salvation

---

[1] " Ut sperent sese per votum Deo placituros, justos et salvos fieri.   Quid alioqui, inquiunt, facerem in monasterio ? . . . quia vovent sese bonos fore per opera illa, ne cogitata semel fide justificante" (Enders iii. 224).   Denifle has done his best to vindicate medieval religion from the charges brought against it by Luther, and yet he cannot deny that very extravagant assertions were sometimes made even in serious books : he himself quotes the statement of Bartholomew of Pisa in his *Liber conformitatum* : " Nullus frater in habitu minorum est damnatus."

through spiritual union with Christ, devotion to Christ, the influence of Christ, the following of Christ, that Christ who had shown His love to men by dying for them, but not by His death alone. And in practice—perhaps to an extent unintended by the Reformers themselves—the Christ whom the Reformation set up before men's eyes was (more at least than had usually been the case in the Middle Ages) the historical Christ whose character and teaching the Gospels reveal. If in their confessions of faith the Reformers were disposed to set up a dogma about Christ in the place of Christ Himself, Luther's translation of the New Testament supplied the required corrective. It is not any new dogma about Christ, least of all anything that was new in the Reformation theory of justification, so much as the placing of Christ Himself in the centre of the religious life that has been the source of all that is best in Protestantism. The influence of Christ—His teaching, His character, His personality—wherever He is known, is so overwhelming and so life-giving that it has been able largely to neutralize the effects of the demoralizing theories which have too often been taught in His name.

The theology of Luther represents the most exaggerated expression of that substitutionary view of the atonement which, in less naked and exaggerated forms, was not originated by him. I have assumed, without much formal argument, that it is a view which, when once its nature is thoroughly appreciated, neither reason nor conscience can accept. It may be well, however, at this point, to formulate definitely the reasons on account of which perhaps few modern Christians—certainly few modern theologians—really accept that view, even among those who are still unwilling frankly to admit that they have abandoned it.

(1) It should not be forgotten that the Lutheran, and even the Augustinian, doctrines of the fall and the divine remedy for the fall imply the literal truth of the Old Testament story concerning the origin of the human

race, the sin of Adam and the penalty imposed upon him and his posterity, and indeed of many assumptions of a historical character which have been grafted upon the narrative without being really contained in it. How far the modification of the Augustinian system which is involved in the acceptance of a more modern Anthropology would necessarily extend, I will not now enquire, but it is certain that it would be very extensive. And the modification would have seemed to St. Augustine or to Luther to upset the whole scheme. I have already insisted that the rejection of the belief in Old Testament infallibility entertained by St. Paul and the early Church deprives the doctrine of the foundation upon which it was actually erected; while if we give up the belief in the infallibility of St. Paul himself, we shall be giving up the premises from which the Augustinian and Lutheran doctrine has generally been deduced in more modern times. It is clear that if God never threatened to punish disobedience to His commands, either by forfeiture of immortality or by everlasting torments, no scheme is required for reconciling forgiveness with the veracity of God. And if we deny the absolute and final authority of St. Paul, we have really no ground left for believing the theory to be true.[1] I will not insist further on these considerations, but will assume, for the sake of argument, that the doctrine may be re-stated in a way which renders it independent of the enormous changes which have taken place in our conceptions of the universe, of the early history of mankind, and of biblical inspiration since the age of the Reformation, and that grounds may be found for accepting it independently of the *ipse dixit* of St. Paul; and ask whether, even upon that assumption, anything like a penal or expiatory view of the atonement is tenable.

(2) The substitutionary doctrine, or, indeed, any doctrine which regards the death of Christ as expiatory, implies at bottom the retributive theory of punishment.[2]

---

[1] Unless it is based wholly upon the testimony of " Christian Experience," as to which see below, Appendix I., p. 467.

[2] This assumption underlies all recent defences of the traditional view. That this view of punishment is necessary to the position is admitted very frankly by the best and

That theory is still maintained by a few philosophers of distinction, though, I think, by very few. It is impossible now to discuss that theory at length. I can only say that to my own mind the retributive theory is at bottom a survival of primitive modes of thought. Punishment undoubtedly originated in the instinct of revenge. With the progress of morality it was recognized that this instinct should be controlled by a rational principle ; but there still lingered the notion that, when authorized and entitled to punish for real wrong-doing, the just ruler ought still to punish, as primitive man in his anger had punished, as though vengeance or punishment were an end in itself. The demand of the wronged individual for vengeance was transferred to an impersonal but objective "justice." From the time of Socrates and Plato, however, thoughtful men began to feel that it cannot be rational to inflict an evil except as a means to a good—the good of the offender or of others. And the same principle was fully accepted by such Christian teachers as Clement of Alexandria, Origen, Gregory of Nyssa, and Abelard. On this view of punishment, the notion that suffering or death could do away the guilt of sin, except in so far as it produces repentance or change of character, becomes impossible. The theory, moreover, is quite inconsistent with that Christian ethic which sums up the whole moral law in the requirement of universal love, and with that Christian theology which regards love as the most adequate expression of the character of God. Love cannot inflict pain or other evil except as a means to some good. If such evil ought to be inflicted, it would not be true that love is the fulfilling of the law.

(3) Even on the retributive view of punishment it is impossible to defend the punishment of the innocent in place of the guilty. Whether the cry, " the guilty man must be punished for punishment's sake " be a survival of primitive superstition or a dictate of the " pure practical

---

most moderate of its recent champions, the Rev. J. K. Mozley (*The Doctrine of the Atonement*, p. 207).   I have fully discussed the question in *The Theory of Good and Evil*, book i. chap. ix.

reason," the very principle which underlies that cry demands that the punishment should fall on the offender himself and on him only. We cannot admit it to be just that "since the divine decrees cannot be broken, the person rather than the sentence should be changed ; " [1] that, though it is a matter of indispensable justice to punish sin, it is immaterial whether it is the guilty person who is punished or some one else.[2] And the idea of vicarious punishment is not made more rational when vaguer terms like "expiation" or "satisfaction" are substituted for the plainer, more brutal, more straightforward "punishment." The term "satisfaction" may no doubt more easily be explained in some non-natural or attenuated sense which does not involve the idea of " expiation." But, as actually employed by medieval or Reformation theology, it does at bottom involve the same fundamental immorality. I may add that few of those philosophers who have held the retributive theory of punishment have ever made a serious attempt to reconcile it with the Christian ideal of forgiveness. Some of them would frankly admit the impossibility of that task, and avow that the Christian doctrine of forgiveness—the doctrine taught by Christ Himself—is, in fact, immoral.

(4) The same objections apply to the theory according to which in some constructive sense the sinner is supposed to have really suffered the penalty of his sins when Christ suffered it, because the humanity which was incarnate in Christ suffered it. This theory, which, as we have seen, was the characteristically Greek theory of the atonement, and which has been much more widely held both in East and West than the franker theory of

---

[1] Ambrose (see above, p. 328, n. 6).

[2] Sometimes the recognition of this is avoided by an ingenious use of the fallacy of equivocation. Thus Dale (*The Theory of the Atonement*, p. 392) speaks of the atonement as fulfilling " the principle that suffering—suffering of the most terrible kind—is the just desert of sin." If this principle means that " one man's suffering is the just desert of another's sin," the principle is immoral and untrue. If it means " the sinner's suffering is the just desert of the sinner's sin," such a principle is not asserted or fulfilled by a substitutionary sacrifice or punishment. Much the same evasion underlies the statement that God is under a " moral necessity of ' asserting the principle ' that sin deserves to suffer. The atonement is, in fact, in its primary aspect the manifest embodiment of God's judgment against human sin " (Ottley, *The Doctrine of the Incarnation*, ii. p. 310).

vicarious punishment, involves at bottom the same erroneous theory of punishment.   It implies that justice requires
the enduring of a penalty for sin quite independently
of any moral or spiritual effect to be produced upon
the sinner by that endurance.   When the theory is put
into a philosophical form, it further involves an abuse
of the Platonic doctrine of universals.   The universal
" humanity " is supposed to have a concrete existence so
independent of its individual manifestations that the
" universal " can be credited with the guilt of one of its
particulars and can endure the punishment which all
but one of the particulars do not endure, and yet to be
so far inseparable from those manifestations that the
endurance of the penalty can nevertheless be credited to
each and every particular.[1]   It is clear we cannot have
it both ways.   If the universal is so real and independent
that it can be punished without each particular being
punished, it cannot also be true that such a punishment
endured by the universal can imply and involve its endurance by each and every particular : no juggling with
universals will make it true to say that an individual
who has in point of fact not been punished may nevertheless be deemed to have been punished.   It is a logical
fallacy to hold that everything which is true of one
particular is true of each ; while as to the theory that
Christ is Himself " the universal of humanity " and not
merely a particular man, that is surely a form of words to
which no intelligible meaning can be attached.   A particular man cannot also *be* a universal.[2]   If it be said frankly

---

[1] " Guilt is corporate ; it implies a dislocation of the moral order for which humanity
as a whole is responsible " (J. K. Mozley, *The Doctrine of the Atonement*, p. 71).   In
many other modern works what is at bottom the same notion is concealed beneath vague
language about " the solidarity of the race," " the solidarity of Christ with the race,"
and the like.

[2] " Christ is Man—not generically, but identically, . . . Christ is not only *a* man,
but Man " (Moberly, *Atonement and Personality*, p. xx.).   On p. 87 the statement is
varied : " He was not generically, but inclusively, man."   On p. 88 we have the astounding statement that Adam too was " in a real sense Humanity."   The only way of reconciling these statements would be to proclaim (with some fathers) the personal identity
of the first and second Adam, a difficult position for a generation which has ceased to
think of the first Adam as an historical personage at all.   Philosophers will recall Aristotle's τρίτος ἄνθρωπος argument against the theory of separable universals (χωριστὰ
εἴδη), which he, rightly or wrongly, attributed to Plato.   If by the " universal of
humanity " is meant merely what ordinary people would call the ideal of humanity,

that Jesus was not a particular man at all, but merely
a Person in whom a generic " humanity " was united
with Divinity, that theory, I venture to say, no matter
how strong the authority for it, is one which, if it meant
anything at all, would be inconsistent with the recognition, in any intelligible sense, of the real humanity of
our Lord Jesus Christ.[1]

(5) Sometimes the attempt to justify an objective
theory of the atonement is made by substituting a sort
of emotional identification of the Christian with Christ
for the metaphysical identity of the earlier theories.
Thus Dr. Dale insists upon the closeness of the union of
the Christian with Christ, upon the fact that Christ is
the source of the change in his will, of his best qualities
and his best actions, in a word, of his spiritual life ; and
contends that this union turns St. Paul's assertion that
" if one died for all, then all died " from a metaphor into
a matter of hard, literal, objective fact. Repentant sinners have literally suffered the penalty because Christ
suffered it. In all that Dr. Dale says on the subject
there is a continual oscillation between statements
practically amounting to the old theories of substitution
or metaphysical identification, which are unintelligible
and immoral, and statements as to the subjective effects
of Christ's death upon the sinner which are irrelevant
to his formal argument and do not tend to establish an
objective atonement. But even if we admitted that the
closeness of the union between Christ and the race or
the redeemed part of it justifies the statement that in
Christ's death sinners have really paid the penalty of

---

the identification of Christ with the " ideal man " is intelligible enough : but then no
explanation is offered as to why it is that the sufferings of an ideal man can benefit very
unideal men, except in so far as they tend, by their moral effect, to move them to penitence and amendment. Dr. Temple, in *Foundations*, pp. 252-8, uses similar language.
Much the same theory is implied by Prof. Ottley's statement that " in Him humanity
is comprised ; His acts are ours ; His submission, His acceptance of death, His exaltation are ours " (*Doctrine of the Incarnation*, ii. p. 311).

[1] This thesis is defended by Prof. Ottley (*The Doctrine of the Incarnation*, ii. p. 282).
The Professor's statement, that " the Church has ever taught that His manhood was
impersonal," is, I venture to think, quite unhistorical. It is true that this became in
time the established tradition, especially with the later Greek theologians. The notion
of a manhood which is inherent in a Being who was not *a* man at all is one which it is
impossible to reconcile either with logic or with history.

their sins, we should still have to ask, " Wherein is the Christian the better for this suffering or this death ? " If the suffering of the penalty in this mysterious sense is supposed to cancel the guilt of sin apart from any repentance or moral change which the suffering may cause, we are still thinking on the basis of the retributive theory which supposes that punishment is an end in itself. And this theory is explicitly accepted by Dr. Dale.[1] But in so far as he means merely that Christ is the source of the Christian's spiritual life, he is really doing one of two things. Either he is adopting the subjective theory, and the effects which he attributes to the death of Christ are effects which really flow from the contemplation of that death ; or he is simply substituting in an arbitrary and quite unintelligible way "the death of Christ" for Christ's whole work and influence, and assuming that whatever moral and spiritual effects flow in any sense from Christ may be said to flow from His death, and to justify the traditional language which is used about that death. This is a device which has played a large part in the theoretical treatment of the atonement doctrine : it is assumed that salvation through a crucified Saviour is the same theory as salvation through the crucifixion of that Saviour. The facility of the transition from one conception to the other probably does much to explain the genesis of the doctrine, but the transition is one which, though psychologically intelligible, is not logically defensible.[2]

(6) The rejection of all substitutionary ideas about the atonement will necessarily modify the sense in which we can accept the formula "justification by faith," whether with or without the Protestant "only." In the first place, it will modify the content of what is believed in. In so far as faith has been understood to mean the belief that God has forgiven sin in general, or the believer's own sins, on account of the expiatory effect of Christ's blood, or (what comes to much the same thing) the merit acquired by His great act of self-sacrifice, such

---

[1] *The Atonement*, p. 373 sq.
[2] For a further examination of Dr. Dale's view, see below, Appendix III. (p. 493).

faith will clearly become impossible for one who rejects these ideas about the atonement.   When we think of Christ's death as saving from sin only because it reveals the love of God and awakens love in the sinner, the *exclusive* preoccupation with the death of Christ as distinct from His character, His teaching, and His life as a whole becomes impossible.   Faith will then mean rather belief in the whole self-revelation of God in Christ.   And this view represents, as we have seen, the general tendency of the Church's teaching down to the time of the Reformation even in the West, but still more so in the greatest Greek fathers.   Further, it will follow that faith cannot be treated (as it has too often been treated) as an arbitrarily imposed condition of salvation, or as involving a supreme kind of merit which God will reward above, or to the exclusion of, every other kind of merit.   We have seen with what unanimity, from the time of St. Paul down to that of the Reformation, the Church taught that God holds no man just except in so far as He makes him really just.   If that is so, faith can be a condition of salvation only because, and in so far as, it makes a man really better, in so far as it awakens repentance and produces good moral effects.   And if this be the attitude adopted we must accept unreservedly two corollaries :

(*a*) No value or efficacy whatever can be attributed to the intellectual belief when it does not lead to such moral regeneration.   So much is fully recognized by the medieval and Tridentine doctrine—that it is only faith " formed " or completed by love that can justify or save. Luther's denial of this fundamental Catholic truth is the most regrettable feature of his teaching, even if he did sometimes say the same thing in other words.   It is satisfactory to notice that our Anglican homily on " faith," which is specially endorsed by the Articles,[1] explicitly teaches that the faith which justifies and saves is not *fides informis*, but *fides formata*, not " unformed " or " un-completed " faith but faith " formed " or completed by love—a faith which includes love.

---

[1] If we may assume that this is the homily on justification mentioned in Art. xi.

(*b*) The other consequence is one which has not been so generally recognized by orthodox theology, at least since the days of Gregory of Nyssa; and that is that, where we do find these moral qualities, where and in proportion as we do find that genuine goodness which includes repentance or hatred of past sin, we must suppose that, there and to that extent, the man is already justified, no matter what may be the state of his intellectual belief. If his ideal be not the highest or if his repentance and amendment be incomplete, his justification will be incomplete also. We can call even Luther as a witness to the truth that justification is a gradual process so far as this life is concerned, though he seems to have recognized nothing intermediate between complete justification and absolute damnation in the next. And the moment we recognize that justification is a gradual process of making better which cannot be sharply distinguished from sanctification, it becomes impossible to suppose that humanity is divided by God into two sharply contrasted classes, of which one is wholly justified and the other wholly "reprobated." Let us assert confidently and clearly the supreme value of belief in Christ as an aid to goodness, both because the revelation of God in Him sets before us the highest exhibition of what goodness is, and because of the assurance which it gives that the divine Love is aiding our efforts now, and will hereafter complete the process of salvation already begun in all who in any heartfelt way have accepted Christ as their Lord and Master. But let us equally avoid any mode of statement which suggests that those who have not heard the name of Christ, or who have, from intellectual causes, been unable to accept the creed of His Church, are not also objects of that divine Love which received its most signal manifestation in Him. The most deadly result of the doctrine of justification by faith—whether in its extreme Reformation expressions or any other of its cruder forms—is that it has fostered the belief that honest thinking is sinful, and that there is a merit in blind credulity. The idea of justification by faith *only* in anything like the sense of the rigid Lutheran or the

rigid Calvinist is practically dead.   But the belief in the
meritoriousness of credulity and the sinfulness of honest
doubt still remains the most serious blemish in the
conventional Christianity of the Churches.   And this is
no merely speculative error which has no practical results.
Its deadly fruit still poisons the religious life of the average
parish or congregation.   It deters the clergy from study,
from thought, and from openly teaching what they
themselves really believe.   It prevents the co-operation of Christians with one another and with others,
who without fully sharing the Christians' belief, to
a large extent share the same practical aims.   The
religious newspapers abound with evidence of its continued vitality.   On every side it fosters bitter personal hatred of theological opponents, pharisaic self-
complacency, and active hostility to all intellectual
enlightenment or progress.   It is impossible for Christians really to believe that the " greatest of these is charity "
while they continue to attach so much importance to
mere belief.   The most serious " wound of the Church "
at the present moment is the disposition to think that
certain beliefs, especially if held without rational grounds
or regard to evidence, are creditable and well-pleasing to
God, apart from any moral good effects which may flow
from them, and to disparage the value or deny the existence of any moral goodness which may be found where
these beliefs are not.

(7) This last consideration naturally suggests a last
objection to the traditional doctrine which has already
been insisted on—that it is absolutely inconsistent with
the teaching of the Founder of Christianity Himself.[1]
His teaching, as we have seen, was that no condition
is required for forgiveness but sincere repentance or
change of heart.   No theory of justification can possibly
be reconciled with that teaching of our Master which
does not fully recognize that faith has no value except,
and in so far as, it actually tends to real change of heart,

---

[1] Well may Steinhart exclaim: " Did Christ, who came out of the bosom of the
Father, know Him less than Anselm of Canterbury ? " (quoted by Franks, *Hist. of the
Doctrine of the Work of Christ*, ii. p. 201).

and the amendment of life which necessarily (so far as opportunity is given) results from real change of heart. Just in so far as belief in Christ leads to and promotes that change of heart, St. Paul's doctrine of justification by faith is reconcilable with the Master's own doctrine of justification by repentance and love— so far and no further. That belief in Christ forms the most powerful of all the influences which exist or have ever existed in this world of ours for producing that repentance and amendment, that death to sin and new life unto righteousness, upon which forgiveness and reconciliation with God depend, is a conviction which can be supported by a vast accumulation of Christian experience. But that much real goodness, much real disinterested love does exist in this world which is not due to any conscious and deliberate acceptance of Christ is no less a fact, and a fact which most educated modern Christians admit, if too grudgingly and inadequately ; and, if they do admit that fact, they have already introduced an enormous modification into the system of Luther and some modification even into the far more tolerant and enlightened eschatology of the Schoolmen. We must not, indeed, speak of the goodness of the best non-Christians as if it owed nothing to Christ. Much of that goodness—most of the highest goodness which we know in the modern world—is by no means independent of the influence which Christ has exercised upon human society. Many a modern Agnostic and many an enlightened Hindoo owe the best that is in them to Christ ; and, so far as that is so, such persons are really being saved through Christ : but there has been, and is, very much real goodness in those who have never even heard the name of Christ ; and so far as their goodness is the goodness which Christ approved, they are and will be justified. Imperfect their repentance and their goodness may be : much room may be left for far deeper repentance and further progress in holiness here or hereafter. But, after all, is not that the case with the vast majority of those who live and die with conscious and sincere belief in Christ in their hearts and His name upon their lips ?

We are not told that the repentant publican was completely penitent or was pronounced wholly righteous.[1] And the teaching of that parable is completed by those other memorable words of the Saviour : " Forasmuch as ye did it unto the least of these my brethren, ye did it unto Me."

[1] " Non simpliciter justificatus ; sed justificatus comparatione Pharisaei " (Origen, *In Ezek. Hom.* ix. 2, Lom. xiv. 122).

LECTURE VIII

THE TRUTH OF THE ATONEMENT

God was in Christ reconciling the world to himself.—2 COR. v. 19.

LECTURE VIII

THE TRUTH OF THE ATONEMENT

WE have completed our historical enquiry—necessarily brief and summary—into the origin and growth of the atonement doctrine. I have tried to show that even in its simplest form the doctrine was in all probability no part of our Master's own teaching, that it originated in the necessity for explaining the scandal of a crucified Messiah, and in the prophetic utterances which seemed to solve that fundamental problem for primitive Christianity. But that explanation leaves open the question of its permanent truth and value. The historical origin of a doctrine determines little or nothing as to its validity. The belief in human immortality may have been first suggested by the phenomena of dreams. Perhaps it would never have occurred to the human mind without them : yet the modern philosopher may hold it to be true for quite other reasons than those which commended it to the mind of primitive man. The discovery that historically the doctrine of the atonement is based upon an untenable interpretation of the Old Testament may, indeed, prevent our making it, as it has sometimes been made, the beginning and end of Christianity, unless we are prepared to embrace the astounding paradox that what the Founder of Christianity taught to His disciples was not Christianity at all. It may even suggest a probability that, for those who cannot fully share the theories of Old Testament interpretation and infallibility by which the doctrine was originally dictated, its meaning and the place which it holds in Christian thought will be somewhat different from those which have been assigned to it in the past. But the doctrine would never have taken root had it not responded to something real and vital in the experience of Christians, and satisfied profound spiritual needs. At the same time it is important to bear in mind that religious experience is to a large extent affected and determined by intellectual belief. Christian experience has in point of fact varied almost as much as Christian theory; while still more frequently the same sort of experience may be interpreted and explained in a great variety of ways. We have seen how varied have been the modes in which the doctrine of an atonement through the death of Christ, originally taken over from Jewish prophecy, has been interpreted at different times in the history of the Christian Church, beginning with the period in which the canonical New Testament itself was in course of composition. It is time for us to ask which (if any) of these interpretations will most commend itself to the knowledge and experience of the present day; or how far each and all of them require to be modified in view of any clearer light which our changed knowledge of the Universe or the Christian thought and experience of later centuries may have shed upon the character of God and His relations to men. The possibility that such further light may have been bestowed upon the Christian Church cannot be excluded by those who really believe in the doctrine of a Holy Spirit working in the heart of the Church and of its individual members. And yet it may after all be found that a little selection among the rich materials accumulated by previous Christian thought may be all that is required to present us with an interpretation of the doctrine which fully meets the demands of the most modern spirit, if a certain allowance be made for the difference in the presuppositions about the Universe with which such problems must inevitably be approached by any ancient and by any modern thinker.

I have already suggested that this is actually the case. I have tried to make it plain that, if we put aside certain views of St. Paul which were not generally accepted, the ways of thinking about the atonement which prevailed in the early Church down to the time of Irenaeus, and in some Christian circles much later than that, involved no definite theory of substitution or expiation. The only suggestion which we find of any such theories is contained in traditional phrases which were originally based upon a misinterpretation of Jewish prophecy. The explanations which are given of these phrases invariably make the atoning efficacy of Christ's work depend upon subjective and ethical effects produced by the contemplation of that work upon the mind of the believer. And such explanations involve little which may not commend itself to the most modern mind. None of them limit that atoning work in any exclusive way to His death. The death of Christ is looked upon as completing that revelation of the nature and character of God which it was the object of Christ's whole mission to set forth. If the heart of that revelation is to be found pre-eminently in the self-sacrificing death of Christ, it is because the character of God as revealed by Christ may be summed up in the statement that God is love. " Greater love hath no man than this, that a man lay down his life for his friends."

The most definite and systematic expression which this subjective view of the atonement has found is in the writings of Abelard and of those Schoolmen who wrote under his immediate influence. But it is, as we have seen, much older than Abelard. It represents, on the whole, in spite of the intrusion of some heterogeneous elements, the dominant view of the best Greek theology upon the subject, and pre-eminently of Origen. In recent times there has been a great and very general return to this Origenistic or Abelardian view of the atonement. If time allowed, I believe I could show you that nearly all the more modern theories upon the subject represent one of two things—either a reassertion, whether avowed and explicit or in some more or less disguised and attenuated form, of one or other of the old substitutionary or expiatory theories, or else a view which is in principle the same as Abelard's. An examination of these theories would show that in recent theological thought the Abelardian view has more and more superseded the older substitutionary modes of representation. I should like to dwell upon the work of those writers who have contributed, in various ways and various degrees, to bring about this transformation—such men as the non-juror William Law, Coleridge, Schleiermacher, Ritschl and a whole succession of his followers in Germany, Julius Hare, Frederick Denison Maurice, Rowland Williams, M'Leod Campbell, Bucknell, Bishop Colenso, Bishop Westcott.[1] I should delight to dwell upon the work of such men and of many others, but time would fail me. The present lecture must be devoted to meeting some of the objections and difficulties which may be urged against that general view of the atonement in which they are substantially agreed.

Let me begin by setting down clearly what the theory is. That cannot be done better than by repeating once more the formulation of it which is due to Peter the Lombard: " So great a pledge of love having been given us, we are both moved and kindled to love God who did such great things for us ; and by this we are justified, that is, being loosed from our sins we are made just. The death of Christ therefore justifies us, inasmuch as through it charity is stirred up in our hearts." [2]

This is a view which, as far as it goes, would be disputed by few. It would be difficult to find the theologian by whom it would be explicitly repudiated. Assuredly Abelard's bitter opponent St. Bernard is full of that thought; though, when put forward by Abelard as the sole explanation of the doctrine, he treats it as one of his opponent's worst heresies. It is not so much the truth as the sufficiency of the Origenistic or Abelardian view which has been and is disputed.

[1] The first protest against the immoralities of the traditional doctrine came from Socinus, who, however, was much influenced by the Scotist tendency to solve all difficulties by appealing to the arbitrary will of God. Modern Unitarianism, too, was originally quite as much a protest against the traditional doctrine of the atonement as against the traditional view of the Trinity. The value of these protests must be acknowledged by all who feel how deeply the traditional views have libelled the view of God's character which finds its highest expression in the teaching of Christ and in a truly Christian doctrine of the incarnation.　　　　[2] See above, p. 371.

It may be urged that the gratitude which the thought of God's love awakens is after all based upon the assumption that there was some sort of objective necessity for the death of Christ independently of its effects upon the believer ; and that it is only because of such an objective and intrinsic effect of the death in taking away sin that reflection upon it tends to awaken gratitude, and consequently repentance, in the believing soul.   Apart from such an objective efficacy, it may be contended, the death of Christ becomes unintelligible ; and when once this unintelligibility is admitted and clearly seen, the subjective effect will no longer be produced.   This line of objection has been put with unusual directness by Dr. Denney, one of the very few scholarly theologians who in quite recent years have attempted to defend the old substitutionary view in a thoroughgoing and un-compromising manner.   I have more respect for such an attempt than I have for the attitude of those who repudiate with indignation all that strikes most modern minds as immoral or irrational in the older schemes, and then re-introduce them in attenuated or surreptitious forms, and condemn or scornfully disparage each and every intelligible alternative.   After recapitulating what he takes to be St. Paul's teaching on the subject, Dr. Denney continues :

" I do not know any word which conveys the truth of this if ' vicarious ' or ' substitutionary ' does not, nor do I know any interpretation of Christ's death which enables us to regard it as a demonstration of love to sinners, if this vicarious or substitutionary character is denied.

" There is much preaching *about* Christ's death which fails to be a preaching of Christ's death, and therefore in the full sense of the term Gospel preaching, because it ignores this.   The simplest hearer feels that there is something irrational in saying that the death of Christ is a great proof of love to the sinful, unless there is shown at the same time a rational connexion between that death and the responsibilities which sin involves, and from which that death delivers.   Perhaps one should beg pardon for using so simple an illustration, but the point is a vital one, and it is necessary to be clear. If I were sitting on the end of the pier, on a summer day, enjoying the sunshine and the air, and some one came along and jumped into the water and got drowned "to prove his love for me," I should find it quite unintelligible. I might be much in need of love, but an act in no rational relation to any of my necessities could not prove it. But if I had fallen over the pier and were drowning, and some one sprang into the water, and, at the cost of making my peril, or what but for him would be my fate, his own, saved me from death, then I should say, ' Greater love hath no man than this.' I should say it intelligibly, because there would be an intelligible relation between the sacrifice which love made and the necessity from which it redeemed. Is it making any rash assumption to say that there must be such an intelligible relation between the death of Christ — the great act in which His love to sinners is demonstrated— and the sin of the world for which in His blood He is the propitiation ? I do not think so. Nor have I yet seen any intelligible relation established between them except that which is the key to the whole of New Testament teaching, and which bids us say, as we look at the Cross, *He* bore *our* sins, *He* died *our* death. It is *so* His love constrains us." [1]

I will try to meet this objection as directly and plainly as I can.

Dr. Denney's illustration completely misrepresents not merely the theory which he is criticizing, but even the theory which he professes to defend. Our Lord did not, according to any orthodox representation, simply of His own free will, mount upon the Cross and crucify Himself. It is not too much to say that Dr. Denney makes our Lord actually commit suicide. Even according to the strictest orthodoxy the Son of God did not show His love to mankind simply by submitting as a kind of ritual act to the process of dying. The death was an incident in a real human life.

[1] *The Death of Christ*, pp. 126-7.

Some sort of death, as the earliest Fathers often insisted, was a necessary element in any really human life. And the particular mode of death was the outcome and culmination of the mode of life which He had chosen. The death was not His act, but the act of the Jewish priests, the Roman magistrate, and the Roman soldiers. The acts of all these were as much their own free acts as any other human acts ever have been or can be, though theistic thought will not deny the co-operating activity of God in all such acts. And the death came to Him as the direct and necessary consequence of His faithfulness to His Messianic calling, of a life devoted to the doing of God's will and the service of His fellow-men.[1] To the very last, according to the Synoptists, our Lord conceived it as possible that He might accomplish that task without the necessity of dying a violent death. In fact, many conservative representations of the atonement have insisted very strongly that it was not so much the mere act of dying as the complete obedience to the Father's will which it implied, the obedience shown alike by His life and His death, the obedience pushed to the point of death, that gave His passion its supreme value : " Non mors sed voluntas placuit sponte morientis " says St. Bernard.[2] " It was not the death but the will of Him who freely died " which pleased the Father. It was in becoming incarnate and in submitting to a death which others brought about, but which He could have escaped if He had wished to do so, that His love to mankind was shown. So much will be admitted by the most conservative theology : still more will that side of the matter be insisted on by

---

[1] Duns Scotus, after denying that there was any objective necessity for Christ's death, proceeds : " Christus igitur volens eos ab errore illo revocare, per opera et sermones, maluit mori quam tacere, quia tunc erat veritas dicenda Judaeis, et ideo pro justitia mortuus est, tamen de facto sua gratia passionem suam ordinavit et obtulit Patri pro nobis, et ideo multum tenemur ei. Ex quo enim aliter potuisset homo redimi, et tamen ex sua libera voluntate sic redemit, multum ei tenemur, et amplius quam si sic necessario, et non aliter potuissemus fuisse redempti ; ideo ad alliciendum nos ad amorem suum, ut credo, hoc praecipue fecit, et quia voluit hominem amplius teneri Deo, sicut si aliquis genuisset primo hominem, et postea instruxisset eum in disciplina et sanctitate, amplius obligaretur ei, quam si tantum genuisset eum, et alius instruxisset, et haec est congruitas, non necessitas " (In Sentent. iii., Dist. xx. 10). An excellent reply to Dr. Denney !

[2] De erroribus Abelardi (=Ep. cxc.), viii. 21.

those who believe that Jesus Himself had no thought of offering an expiatory sacrifice for the sins of the whole world—that He conceived Himself rather to be persisting unto death in His task of announcing and preparing the way for a Messianic Kingdom which God in His own way and at His own time would set up through Him whom He had chosen to be the Messiah. If we are to use a parallel from which some of us might have shrunk had not Dr. Denney forced it upon us, the truer representation of the matter would be not to picture Christ as saying, " To show my love for you, I will jump into the sea," but, " To show my love for you, I will allow myself to be thrown into the sea by those who have threatened to do so unless I abandon my work of preaching what I believe to be the truth of God, of preparing the way for His Kingdom and for your admission thereto." [1]   We, from the point of view of retrospective reflection, may recognize that in the eternal counsels of God the death of Christ was allowed because it was foreseen that a life ending in a violent and self-sacrificing death would be a better proof and pledge of the Messiah's love than any other kind of life ; but the death showed no less love because, from the point of view of Him who died, He was dying for His disciples in the same sense in which all His ministry was *for* them : " The Son of Man came not to be ministered unto but to minister."   His death has been more to Christendom than other martyr-deaths, just because He was so much more than other martyrs, because His life was more than other lives ; because His Messianic calling was a unique calling ; because, in fact, of all that has led Christendom to see in that life the fullest revelation or incarnation of God.   There is nothing in the fact that the necessity for the death did not arise from any objective demand for expiation which can diminish the gratitude and the love which such a death, taken in connexion with such a life, was calculated to awaken towards the Sufferer.   And if the character

---

[1] " He did not accept His sufferings as an independent task, the meaning of which was to be sought in an idea of sin as a whole, but bore them as the accident of His positive fidelity to His vocation " (Ritschl, *Justification and Reconciliation*, E.T. p. 566).

which is revealed by that Sufferer be the character of
God Himself, then the love that is awakened towards
Christ will also be love of the Father whom in a supreme
and unique way Christ reveals. And that love will
express itself in repentance and regeneration of life.
When the efficacy of Christ's death is attributed (as we
have seen it was practically attributed by so many of
the earliest and greatest fathers of the Church) to the
moral effects which it produces, that does, indeed, tend
to remove the one-sided and exclusive emphasis upon
the death which is laid upon it by Lutheran or Calvinistic theory, though not by the main stream of Catholic
theology ; it does nothing to diminish the love which
the contemplation of such a death is calculated to awaken
in the mind of him who believes that the whole life and
death of Christ was one of love for His fellows, and that
in Him who so lived and died the love of God was
uniquely and supremely manifested. Such a view of
the matter does tend, no doubt, to attribute the saving
efficacy of Christ's work not *merely* to the death, but to
the teaching, the character, the life of Him who died.
It tends, in short, to represent Christ's death as only a
part, though a necessary part, of that whole incarnation
or self-revelation of God, the object of which was to
make known God's nature and His will, to instruct men
in the way of salvation, and to excite in them that love
which would inspire sorrow for past sin and give the power
to avoid sin in the future. And that, as we have seen,
was the way in which the atonement was most frequently
viewed by the great fathers of the Church, especially in
the East. They did, indeed, teach that the death was
a necessary part of the atoning or saving work of Christ.
They never taught that it was the whole.

So far the Abelardian theory was entirely in harmony with the earlier tradition of the Church. But it
may be contended that there is an element in the doctrine
as taught by the early fathers, or even by Abelard, which
it is difficult to reconcile with modern ideas of Christ's
Person and work. Though, according to this view,
Christ showed His love by submitting to a death which

was brought about by the act of others, the incarnation itself—Christ's entrance upon the human life which made such a death necessary—was, according to the traditional representations, the voluntary act of the pre-existent Son of God.   In popular representations of the atonement it is usually presupposed that the Son who undertook the task of man's redemption was a separate Being who had existed from all eternity side by side with the Father; and who, by an act of voluntary choice, distinct from the volition of His Father, consented to become man, and as man to suffer death on behalf of those whose nature He assumed.   Such is undoubtedly the popular conception.   But that is a theory which is open to insuperable objections, and it is not really orthodox. Catholic doctrine does not, it must be remembered, make the human Jesus pre-exist, nor (unless we take a view of the fourth Gospel which criticism is almost unanimous in repudiating) did our Lord Himself ever claim such pre-existence for Himself.   It was the divine Logos that pre-existed, not the human Jesus.   Much early theology did undoubtedly represent the Son as a separate consciousness; sometimes it even called Him a " second God," but this was always in connexion with a theory of the subordination of the Son to the Father, which later theology rejected when it pronounced Arius a heretic: and, if the subordination be rejected, the theory passes from Arianism into sheer Tritheism.   Monotheism was saved by Athanasius and the Council of Nicaea; and more and more, since that turning-point in the development of doctrine, Christian thought has abandoned this way of looking at the Persons of the Trinity as distinct Minds acting in co-operation.   The Catholic theory of the Holy Trinity—as formulated by St. Augustine,[1] and in a still clearer and more philosophical form by St. Thomas Aquinas—represents that God is one Consciousness, one Mind—a Trinity of Power, Wisdom, and Will or Love—which together constitute one self-

---

[1] It should be remembered that the *Quicumque vult* is a bald and bad epitome of St. Augustine's *De Trinitate*—a bad epitome, because it leaves out everything in that work which tends to make the doctrine rational and intelligible.

conscious Being.[1] Such a view of the Holy Trinity
must, if it is thought out, involve some modification in
popular representations of the atonement, though it
implies no abandonment of any theory which can claim
to be essential to Catholic orthodoxy. It is the Arian
representation of the atonement which probably corresponds most closely to the secret thoughts of thousands
who have hardly heard of Arianism as well as of other
thousands who would be ready to denounce Arianism
in language of great severity. Many Englishmen probably derive their mental representations of the matter
very largely from the great poem of the avowedly Arian
Milton, in which the Father and the Son are represented
as holding dialogues or discussions as to the way in which
man could be delivered. If, however, we accept the
representation of the Trinity which we find in St. Augustine and (more clearly and consistently) in St. Thomas
Aquinas, we cannot regard the not yet incarnate Logos
or Son of God as having separate thoughts and a separate
will of this kind. Such a representation clearly implies
two minds, not one, and Catholic orthodoxy says that
God is One Mind, not two or three. If the pre-existent
Son be really (as St. Augustine taught) the Wisdom of
God, we cannot ascribe to Him in His pre-existent state
a Will distinct from that of the Father. If the Holy
Spirit *is* the Will or the Love of the Father, we cannot
attribute another Will or another Love to the Son. We
cannot think or talk of the atonement as involving any
kind of transaction between the Father and the Son.
The juridical, forensic view of the atonement has become
impossible to modern thought, not merely because of
the immoral or childish ideas of justice upon which it is
based, but also because it treats the relation between

---

[1] In St. Augustine the Triad is Mind (*Ipsa Mens*) or Memory, Wisdom (*Notitia*
or *Intelligentia*), Will or Love ; in St. Thomas, the Father is Principium (equivalent
to the Greek πηγὴ θεότητος, which he himself explains as " Potentia generandi
Filium ") ; the " generation " of the Word is compared to the generation of thought
by the human intellect ; the Holy Spirit is Love. Abelard uses the word " Potentia "
for the Father. In St. Augustine the human Trinity comes in rather as an illustration
of the relations between the Divine Persons than as an actual identification ; in St.
Thomas the analogy is carried out more thoroughly and consistently. But how little
even St. Augustine thought of the " Persons " as " persons " in the modern sense is
shown by his doctrine that the Love of the Father for the Son *is* the Holy Spirit.

the Father and the pre-existent Son as the relation between
distinct juridical Persons, one of whom could offer and
the other receive a sacrifice, one of whom could impose
and the other endure a punishment.   Such a conception
is part of the *damnosa hereditas* which Tertullian bequeathed to the Church when he applied the term
" Person " to denote the distinctions within the Godhead, and which later theology admitted to be totally
inapplicable if the word Person is understood in anything
like its ordinary, human acceptation.[1]

The Catholic doctrine of the Holy Trinity represents
the incarnation as due to the loving will of God, that
is to say, of the " undivided " Trinity.   Christ reveals
God because the Word or Logos of God was completely
united to His human soul, and the human soul freely
co-operated with the divine purposes.   The love which
Christ showed by dying reveals the love of God both
because the whole Self-revelation of God in Christ is due
to God's loving purpose to redeem mankind, and because
the love shown in the human life and character of Christ
is the highest revelation of the divine character.   The
Abelardian view of the atonement is entirely reconcilable
with the fully developed doctrine of the Trinity, as it is
found in St. Thomas Aquinas.   In fact that formulation
of the doctrine which reached its final form in St. Thomas
was largely due to Abelard himself.   And I may remind
you that it is a view which has been held by a general
consensus of orthodox theologians, however much some
of them may have endeavoured to combine it with other,
in some cases incompatible, views upon the subject.

I am aware that to many these scholastic ways of
expressing the idea of Christ's divinity will seem difficult,
technical, perhaps even repellent; and therefore I will
try to express what I believe to be their permanent
meaning in simpler modern language.   The love exhibited by Christ in life and in death might well be a
source of spiritual life and death apart from all theories

---

[1] " Si quis velit personae nomen sub communi et propria acceptatione intelligere,
nullo modo putet plures personas sub ea acceptione posse subsistere in unitate substantiae " (Richard of St. Victor, *de Trin.* iv. 1, quoted by Ottley, *Doctrine of the
Incarnation,* ii. p. 252).

about Christ's nature. Love is essentially contagious. The character of Jesus Christ might well inspire the desire to imitate, and move to sorrow for the sins which He hated, even if He were looked upon merely as a great teacher; and, for those who think of all great teachers as sent by God, it would also excite to the love of God. But undoubtedly the full significance of the doctrine of the atonement can only be appreciated if we can find some real meaning in the idea of a unique or supreme incarnation of the Divine Logos in Jesus Christ. An adequate discussion of that great problem would of course demand a separate and a very elaborate enquiry, but I feel bound to say something on the subject in order that we may clear up the meaning which ought to be attached to the statement : " The death of Christ saves from sin because it is a revelation of the love of God."

For most modern minds it will probably be found that the best and easiest way of translating the ancient patristic and scholastic thought about the divinity of Christ into present-day language is to think of the revelation of God in Christ as much as possible after the analogy of the imperfect but progressive revelation of God in other men—in the expanding, developing mind of man, in the reason and conscience of the best men, and in their wills or characters, so far as they have conformed themselves to the ideal set up by conscience. If God and man are thought of—in the way which is sometimes called deistic—as two wholly separate and unlike kinds of being; or if (from a quite opposite point of view) God is thought of as a super-moral Absolute to whom we cannot attribute any of the moral qualities which are more or less recognized by the conscience of all men, and which are realized in the characters and lives of the best men and women, then indeed we could attach no meaning to the idea of an incarnation of God in one human being. But, if we can say that in humanity generally there is *some* revelation of God—a growing, developing, progressive revelation, and a higher degree of such a revelation in the heroes, the saints, the prophets, the founders and reformers of great religions, then the idea of an incarnation becomes possible. If we can say that God is to some extent revealed in all men, then it becomes possible to think of Him as making a supreme, culminating, unique revelation of Himself in one human character and life. And such a crowning revelation I believe that the conscience and reason of mankind do discover in the historical Jesus of Nazareth.

So much is recognized by many modern Christians who would hesitate to adopt the traditional language of creeds and councils and theologians about Him; but none the less it may be the true and permanent meaning of that language, when due allowance is made for the difference between our philosophical terminology and that of the fourth century or the thirteenth. In Jesus Christ there is the completest, fullest, most central revelation of God that has ever been made, both because of the unique perfection of the moral and religious ideal which disclose themselves in His words, His character, and His life, and because from Him proceeds the fullest stream of further self-revelation which God has bestowed upon the world since that typical life of Sonship was lived. Such a mode of representation is in harmony alike with the best thought of the past, especially the best Greek thought of Catholic antiquity, and with the best religious philosophy of the present day.[1]

[1] Cf. the words of Edward Caird : " The infinite pitifulness of Jesus to the sorrows and evils of humanity, his absolute confidence in the possibility and even the necessity of their being remedied, and the way in which he bases his confidence in the love of God to man, and in His own unity as man with God—these taken together make up a faith beyond which religion cannot go, except in two ways, namely in the way of understanding them more adequately, and of realizing them more fully " (*The Evolution of Religion*, ii. 320-1). Cf. the recent words of Prof. Pringle-Pattison : " We are far too apt to limit and mechanise the great doctrine of the Incarnation, which forms the centre of the Christian faith. Whatever it may mean, it means at least this—that in the conditions of human life we have access, as nowhere else, to the inmost nature of the divine. ' God manifest in the flesh ' is a more profound, philosophical truth than the loftiest flights of speculation that outsoars all predicates and, for the greater glory of God, declares Him unknowable " (*The Idea of God*, p. 157. See also his remarks on the Trinitarian doctrine, p. 409). Professor Pringle-Pattison has not further developed his views of the Person of Christ. Hegelian philosophers and theologians have done much to help us to appreciate the true meaning of the incarnation. Some of them (notably Hegel himself) have, however, taken the human Christ as a *mere* symbol of this union between the divine and human nature, and have made little of the historical Jesus. Hegel insists, indeed, on the necessity of this union being attributed by Christian doctrine to a single historical individual, but speaks as if it were a matter

Of course any summary statement of this kind must fail to express all that the Christian consciousness recognizes in Christ. The full meaning of saying that God is revealed in Christ, and the grounds of the assertion, could only be exhibited by a detailed examination of our Lord's teaching, character, and religious consciousness, and a comparison of them with what we know of other teachers and other religions.[1] I must assume that you have the Gospel picture of Christ before your minds. It is on the appeal to the mind and religious consciousness of mankind which is made by that picture that any valid doctrine about Christ's Person must be grounded. If Christ is looked upon in this light as the supreme Self-revelation of God, His death may well be regarded as the typical and consummating act in that self-revelation of God. That death will be regarded as a voluntary act on the part of the incarnate Son because He could have escaped it if He had chosen to be unfaithful to His calling ; and it will be a voluntary act on the part of God because we believe that in that death, as in Christ's whole life, God was designing to reveal His love towards man. " God was in Christ "—supremely and uniquely —"reconciling the world unto Himself." [2] All human love, all human self-sacrifice is in its way and degree a revelation of God ; " Every one that loveth is begotten of God, and knoweth God." [3] It is only through human love at its highest that we can understand the divine love. Gratitude for ordinary human love —love pushed to the point of self-sacrifice—is the strongest power that exists in this world for attract-

---

almost of indifference, which historical personality was selected as a material embodiment of the universal truth. But surely the whole value of the idea of a unique incarnation depends upon the character of the human being who is selected as the supreme illustration of the revelation of God in humanity. I believe that it is of equal importance to assert the general principle that all humanity reveals God more or less or (to put it as Origen puts it) that the Word has been united in greater or less degree with more than one human personality (see above, p. 257), and to assert that there was something supreme and unique about the self-revelation of God in the historical Jesus. The supremacy of the incarnation carries with it the supreme influence of his self-sacrificing life and death in taking away the sins of the world, and so gives a meaning to the doctrine of an atonement through this particular life and death.

[1] I have to some extent attempted to do this—on the ethical side—in *Conscience and Christ*.

[2] 2 Cor. v. 19.   [3] 1 John iv. 7.

ing to that goodness of which love is the supreme element the soul that has it not, and for producing repentance for that lack of love in which sin essentially consists. In proportion as it is felt that human love reveals the love of God, the answering love which the self-sacrifice awakens will be love to God as well as love to man. The love shown by Christ will have this regenerating effect in a supreme degree in proportion as it is felt that the love of Christ supremely reveals the character of God. After all, the whole philosophy of the atonement is best summed up in those simple words of St. John : " Herein was the love of God manifested in us that God hath sent his only-begotten Son into the world that we might live through Him." [1] " Hereby know we love, because He laid down His life for us." [2]

But it may be urged in some quarters " this does not go far enough," though after all that is as far as St. John went. " What we want, some will urge, is that God Himself should die for man. We do not reach the real heart of the atonement doctrine unless we can see in the death of Christ without evasion or circumlocution the suffering and the death of God." [3] " Does your representation," it may be asked, "allow us to say this ? You cannot logically regard the atonement as a revelation of the love of God unless you are prepared to say that He who hung upon the cross was really a suffering God."

Such a problem cannot even be suggested without raising for minds acquainted with the history of doctrine the ghosts of not one but a whole host of almost forgotten controversies. I cannot enter into those controversies at length. I will only remind you that it is not orthodox to say that the divinity in Christ suffered. Western

[1] 1 John iv. 9.   [2] 1 John iii. 16.
[3] The question is often put from a point of view which claims to be ultra-orthodox. When so urged, it is meant to support some substitutionary or transactional theory of the atonement. But it is often asked also by those who hold precisely the view for which I am contending. The idea of a " passible " God has recently been favoured by some quite unorthodox thinkers, notably Mr. H. G. Wells in *God the Invisible King* and other works ; but, of course, Mr. Wells' God is merely a second God, not the Creator or Ruler of the world, a God who had a beginning in time, and the sufferings of Christ are not regarded as in any way the sufferings even of this God.

theology has always asserted the reality of Christ's humanity more heartily and consistently than Eastern theology, and has been less inclined to the Apollinarian view which, to avoid the implication that a spiritual being who was really divine could suffer, denied the existence in Christ of a rational, human soul, and treated Him simply as the Logos inhabiting a human body.[1] But even in the West it has not been held orthodox to say that the Divine nature was "passible." The idea is repudiated by St. Augustine and by St. Thomas, and, in fact, all orthodox theologians. It is only in a very technical sense that the Church has allowed phrases which imply that God suffered or died.

The more exact statement of its teaching would be rather something of this kind : "The man to whose human soul and flesh the Godhead became perfectly united suffered and died, and in virtue of that union [2] we are allowed to ascribe to the man Jesus what is strictly and primarily true of the divinity which was united with His human nature, and to the Son of God what is strictly and primarily true only of the manhood in Christ." If in the light of this principle we like to speak of God as actually suffering all that Christ suffered, there is no objection to our doing so. But I confess I do not think that modern Christians will much delight in such fine-drawn distinctions. The medieval language about God's blood and God's wounds has already become distasteful to modern Christians, and the language of not a few familiar hymns still sung in our churches is at least less popular than it was. Many will prefer to think and speak more simply. They may well be content to say, "The sufferings of Christ reveal to us the love of Christ, and the love of Christ reveals the love of God."

[1] See above on Athanasius, p. 299 *sq.*
[2] In accordance with the principle known as the *communicatio idiomatum* (ἀντίδοσις ἰδιωμάτων). As to the different meanings in which this formula may be used see Bethune-Baker's *Introduction to the Early History of Christian Doctrine*, p. 293. The doctrine has been carried further by Lutheran theologians than by Catholic orthodoxy. It must be remembered that even with this explanation the theologian who would be orthodox must confine himself to saying that Christ or the Son suffered. To say that God the Father or the Holy Trinity suffered is pure Sabellianism or Patripassianism. Yet to hold that God the Father did not feel pains which His Wisdom felt is difficult for those who hold that Father, Son, and Spirit are "One Mind."

And yet after all we may perhaps be justified in trying to find some fuller meaning than this in the idea that in Christ God has actually suffered. We need not be debarred from doing so by the extreme aversion of the patristic and scholastic theologians to think of divinity as "passible"; for it must be confessed that this aversion of theirs, which the Church took over from Greek thought rather than from Christ or St. Paul, is hard to reconcile with the essential Christian conception of God as a loving Father. The Christian God is not the pure Intelligence —cold, passionless, and loveless, "Himself unmoved, all motion's source"—that He was to Aristotle; though even the author of the Breviary hymn has borrowed this language without seeing its inconsistency with the Christian conception of a God who is essentially Love, and must therefore be moved by the sins and the sorrows and the sufferings of humanity.

Fully to discuss this subject would involve a discussion of the whole problem of evil, that is to say, of the most difficult and perplexing of all the riddles of this mysterious universe. It must suffice to say here that the only way in which the existence of so much evil of all kinds—moral evil or sin, intellectual error or ignorance, sensible evil or pain—is reconcilable with the goodness of God is (as it seems to me) to suppose that the evil is in some way a necessary means to the utmost attainable good. That is in principle the basis of all the theodicies. But if our moral consciousness reveals to us any objective truth, evil remains evil still; and if evil, it must be evil for God as well as for man. And therefore, if God loves mankind, He must needs sorrow over human sin and human pain. That much we should be entitled to say if we only accept the principle that God must be interpreted in the light of the moral consciousness; still more so if we accept the idea of Christ's divinity, and see in His character the supreme incarnation or self-manifestation of God. We may not, without a pantheistic and unintelligible confusion between God and man or a Sabellian identification of one human mind with the supreme Mind of the universe, think of this or that man's pain as actually *being* the pain of the divine consciousness. We cannot think *that* even of Christ's sufferings ; still less can we think of the eternal God as actually dying. So far the orthodox distinction is right. But we may reverently say that if God is good, if He is loving, if He looks upon men as His children—in a word, if He is like Christ—He *must* in some sense suffer in or with His creatures, and the more intensely in proportion to their nearness and dearness and likeness to Himself. A God who could contemplate such a world as ours without suffering would not be a loving God, nor would He be in the least like Christ.[1] God must suffer with and in the sufferings of all His creatures. And if there has been a supreme manifestation of God in one human Being, in one human Personality who once lived on earth and now lives eternally in a supreme union and communion with God, then we may find a special meaning— at least a symbolical meaning—in the language which treats His sufferings as being, or at least in a pre-eminent sense representing, the sufferings of God Himself. If there is some revelation of God in every human soul, and a supreme revelation in the personality of Christ, then we may certainly say that the sufferings which love imposed upon Christ represent in a supreme or unique way that sympathy or *suffering with* humanity which must needs be felt by a God of love. If as regards the sufferings of humanity in general we can say that in all our affliction God was afflicted,[2] then surely we may say the same in a pre-eminent sense of the sufferings of Him whom " the Father sanctified and sent into the world." If we cannot intelligibly say that the actual sufferings of Christ — sufferings

---

[1] Modern philosophers in general have been much more strongly opposed to the idea of a suffering God than modern theologians. It is therefore satisfactory to find Prof. Pringle-Pattison expressing his approval of a paper by Canon Streeter on " The Suffering of God " (*The Idea of God*, p. 409). He quotes also the words of Erdmann (with regard to Aristotle) : " The time had not yet come when God would be known as the God that took on himself πόνος, labour, without which the life of God were one of heartless ease, troubled with nothing, while with it alone he is Love and Creator." I have myself dealt with this question and the closely connected problem of evil in *The Theory of Good and Evil*, vol. ii. pp. 235-44, 286 *sq.*, and in a paper published in the volume of essays called *The Faith and the War*, ed. Foakes-Jackson.

[2] Is. lxiii. 9.

of a kind which necessarily imply humanity—are literally the sufferings of God, we may in quite sober
earnest say that the suffering Christ reveals a suffering God.   It is, indeed, a fact of profound
significance that Christianity sees at once the ideal of
humanity and the fullest revelation of God in One who
was a man of sorrows and acquainted with grief.   The
whole character of the Christian religion would be
different had it not done so : in that sense traditional
theology is right in regarding the idea of an atonement
through the death of Christ as the central truth of
Christianity.   Some death was, as the earliest fathers
so often insisted, necessary to any real humanity in the
Revealer.   No kind of death could have revealed the
sympathy of God so impressively as a death of suffering,
voluntarily submitted to from love of the brethren.
The atonement is the very central doctrine of Christianity
in so far as it proclaims, and brings home to the heart
of man, the supreme Christian truth that God is
love, and that love is the most precious thing in human
life.

I have tried to show how much truth and meaning
may be found in the doctrine of an atonement or redemption of the world through Christ, and in a special manner
through His death, even when we have in the fullest and
frankest manner given up all expiatory, transactional,
or objective theories of redemption.   And yet I think
it ought not merely to be admitted, but to be proclaimed
upon the housetops, that we can only find this meaning
in the doctrine if we may add that the saving influence
which we attribute to Christ is not confined to His death.
The tendency of all Greek theology was to merge the
idea of the atonement in that of the incarnation.   It is not
too much to say that for the best of them, as for the late
Dr. Illingworth, "the incarnation is the atonement."   And
that is a healthy tendency, with which we shall do well
to identify ourselves explicitly and emphatically.   Christ's
whole life was a sacrifice which takes away sin in the only
way in which sin can really be taken away, and that is by
making the sinner actually better.   Much popular lan-

guage on the subject has become quite unreal to ordinary modern minds, because it so completely isolates the death, or the sufferings which immediately preceded the death. The insistence of popular religious teaching upon the atoning efficacy of Christ's death loses all ethical value in proportion as it isolates and disconnects the atoning efficacy of that death from the saving influence of Christ's life, His teaching, His character, the visions of the risen Lord, and the hopes of immortality which those visions inspired.

And here I would particularly insist upon the importance in this connexion of our Lord's *teaching*—that is to say, of the moral ideal which it represents and the corresponding belief as to the character of the God whose nature is revealed by that moral ideal. For many of the earlier fathers, it is not too much to say, it was *primarily* by His teaching that Christ became the Saviour of the world. It was upon the appeal which this teaching made to the reason, the heart, the conscience of mankind that they based their conviction that in Him the Logos was supremely revealed : it was precisely in and through His teaching that His " Divinity " was manifested. In recent years the discovery that our Lord may have shared some of the eschatological ideas of His time to a greater extent than was once supposed has produced a tendency, even in conservative theologians, to disparage the value of His religious and moral teaching. To yield to such a tendency is simply suicidal. If it be not true that never man spake like this man, there is simply no foundation for any theory of Christ's Person which shall take Him out of the category of the prophets whose destiny it is to be superseded when a greater or a more modern prophet appears.[1]

I must not attempt now to discuss the problem which inevitably arises as to the finality of our Lord's ethical teaching and the possibility of reconciling such a finality with that indefinite development which is an obvious

[1] I have dealt more fully with this matter and with the whole question of our Lord's ethical teaching in *Conscience and Christ*.

requirement of enlightened ethical thought. I can only say here that the recognition of the supreme importance of Christ's teaching about God and human life, and a profound veneration for the character which that teaching exhibits, are an absolutely essential condition of our being able to discover any permanent meaning in the traditional doctrines of the atonement and the incarnation. It is upon the appeal which that ideal, embodied in the teaching and character of Christ, has made and still makes to the conscience of mankind that any intelligible modern interpretation of the Catholic doctrine of His divinity must depend. Here I can only assume that the force of this appeal is admitted and felt.

Of course we must not expect to find detailed guidance with regard to each perplexing problem of modern life in the teaching of Christ. The moral teaching of Christ is not a code or a system, but the enunciation of a few great principles, principles which reveal a harmonious ideal, a character, a personality. Doubtless in a sense the character is more than the words, and yet after all it is in the words that the character is chiefly expressed. If the fundamental principles embodied in these words be not true, I really do not see that there is any sense in which the religion that has made such a discovery can any longer be regarded as Christian, or that there is any reasonable basis for such fragments of Catholic doctrine as it may still repeat. Doctrines about the Church and the sacraments can have little meaning—certainly not the Christian meaning—for those to whom Christ is *nothing* but the utterer of eschatological prophecies which have not been fulfilled and the preacher of a provisional ethic—an " interims-ethik "—which was never very important or original, and which has lost what little truth or meaning it once possessed. Development, expansion, new application, fresh deduction there must be in ethics as in theology —more perhaps in ethics than in theology just because the detailed problems of conduct necessarily change with every change in the social environment. Belief in the Holy Spirit's continued work in the Church is as important an element of Christianity as belief in the historic

Christ, and it is doubtless part of the Spirit's work to appropriate and to " baptize into Christ " much spiritual treasure which is not of directly Christian origin. But unless the teaching of Christ does present itself to us as containing the eternally true pith and marrow of the moral ideal, and a true representation of the essential character of God, we have no basis for any theory of Christ's divinity, or even for exalting Him to that central and supreme position among the prophets which would be assigned to Him by most Unitarians. Reverence for Christ as a teacher must be the foundation of any Christology which can find a meaning for the idea of a divine incarnation in Jesus. And it may, with equal truth, be said that it is only in the light of Christ's teaching that we can find any present meaning in a theology which makes much of His death : for it is only in the light of His teaching about the love of God and the supreme place of love in the ethical ideal for man that the cross can be given its true meaning as the symbol of self-sacrifice— not of mere negative self-renunciation or self-denial for self-denial's sake, but of self-sacrifice inspired and directed by love of that moral ideal which is fully realized in God, and by love of the men who are made in the image of God. It is because it is the typical expression of that spirit of self-sacrifice which dominated His life that the death of Christ has played, and will continue to play, a large part in its saving efficacy. When most of the theories about Christ's death have become obsolete and unintelligible, the cross will still be the symbol, known and understood by all, of this central feature in Christ's character and in the ideal for which He lived and died.

There is one more condition under which alone the doctrine of salvation by Christ, purged of immoral and irrational accretions, can continue to be a part of modern Christianity. It must become *in a sense* less exclusive than it has sometimes been. We have seen that even of St. Paul's doctrine the theory that all but those who have believed in Christ will be tormented everlastingly formed no part ; and it was several centuries before that dark and horrible eschatology became a generally accepted

doctrine of the Church.   It is a doctrine which is plainly
inconsistent with the deepest message of the atonement
itself.   If God be the sort of Being whose nature is best
expressed by a self-sacrificing life and death, He could
not have designed everlasting, meaningless, useless
torments as the sole destiny in store for the great bulk
of His creatures.   That doctrine is dead, though much
of the language which really implies it is still repeated
in the church, the school, and the theological class-
room.   The eschatology of the future will not perhaps
be the dogmatic and confident universalism of Origen.
It will not assume that all souls will ever become
equally good and perfect.   It will not, indeed, profess
so much knowledge about the eternal future of souls
as has been sometimes claimed both by theological
optimists and by theological pessimists in the past.
But it will believe that the universe is realizing an end
which is good not only on the whole but *for* the whole.
It will find it impossible to think of the world as due to
a righteous and loving Will, and yet to suppose that
Will to care only for the whole and nothing for the
individual; to care much about the sum of good but
nothing at all about its distribution; to be benevolent to
humanity but unjust to vast numbers of individual human
beings.   It will hope that in the end there is some kind
and some measure of good reserved for each individual
human soul which God has brought into this world—
enough good to make it well on the whole for that soul
to have lived.   It will certainly not be at all ashamed
or afraid of the doctrine that in the life for which it hopes,
as in this earthly life, much painful purgatorial discipline
may form part of the remedy for sin both for those who
have not known Christ at all in this life and for those
who have imperfectly responded to His call.   But it
will not deny that some measure of salvation from sin
has resulted from many religions and teachings besides
those which come from the lips or in the name of Christ.
And in doing so it will appeal not merely to the general
teaching of the Master about the universal Fatherhood of
God but to His express words : " Inasmuch as ye did it

unto one of these my brethren, even these least, ye have done it unto me." [1]

We must not, indeed, allow ourselves to treat salvation as wholly belonging to a world beyond the grave. Salvation means primarily being saved from sin and becoming better : and goodness is an end in itself whether it is to last for a few years or for all eternity. But it is impossible to reconcile the belief that the universe is governed by a righteous Will with the amount and the distribution of evil which we see around us unless we suppose that, for the higher of God's creatures at least, life here is a training-ground for a better and richer life of infinite possibilities beyond the grave, a place for the " making of souls," a life in which the training and education begun here will be continued and lead to higher achievement, both in the way of happiness and of holiness, than that which, in the vast majority of cases, crowns the struggles of humanity here on earth, even with all the help and support which, as a matter of experience, is afforded by the belief in Christ and the God whom He reveals. Salvation means the attainment of spiritual life, and spiritual life is always worth having, no matter how short be its duration. But it is meaningless to assert that the value of such life is quite independent of its duration. The hope of salvation would be a comparatively poor thing if it meant only such emancipation from the evil of the world as is attainable for a few short years in the existing conditions of human life, and so imperfect a holiness as is possible to the vast majority of human beings whom the world-process has brought into existence. It would be the pursuit of an ideal that is not only incapable of attainment but which can only be approximated to by very few, and which even for them is doomed to ultimate frustration. It needs no argument to show that Christianity will be completely de-natured if it is interpreted as expressing a hope for the world that now is but none for the world that is to be. Christianity is not inextricably bound up with " eschatological " hopes if by that is meant that it regards with contempt the life

[1] Matt. xxv. 40.

that is possible to men on earth, or that it has no hope for the future improvement of life on this planet. It is, and it is probable that it will always remain, eschatological in the sense that it regards salvation as something which begins here but is to be completed hereafter. And of this hope the recorded and well-attested visions of the risen Lord (whatever view may be taken of their nature) will be the symbol, or the corroboration; though it is probable that the belief that those visions constituted a real manifestation of a still living Christ is more likely—for minds even a little affected by historical criticism—to be accepted because there is already a belief, or a predisposition to belief, in immortality than immortality to be accepted mainly or entirely on account of the historical evidence for the resurrection of Jesus Christ.[1]

If salvation be what Christ has taught that it is, Christianity cannot, and must not, deny the hope of it to those who have not known, or who have not professed the Christian religion here, or been united to any society of Christ's followers. That is a conception of Christianity which will now hardly be defended by enlightened theologians of any school, however little the wider conception and the "larger hope" associated therewith have yet modified the language habitually

[1] It would be out of place here to discuss the historical evidence for the resurrection. It is enough to say that the evidence for the occurrence of visions of the risen Lord to some of the disciples shortly after the crucifixion is strong. That evidence rests chiefly upon 1 Cor. xv., which was written some twenty-five years after the event, and records St. Paul's own personal experience on the road to Damascus, together with his recollections of what was generally believed in the Christian community a few years after the Crucifixion. The evidence for the resuscitation of the actual body laid in the tomb is very much weaker, resting solely upon documents probably none of them written by eye-witnesses, not written till fifty or more years after the events recorded, and inconsistent with one another in many important particulars. It is in no way necessary to a theory of the atonement that we should commit ourselves to any particular theory as to the nature of the resurrection vision, even if we had sufficient data for doing so. To minds at all affected by modern critical ideas it is impossible that the resurrection of Christ should be the triumphant and incontrovertible proof of Christ's Messiahship—perhaps of His divinity—and of our own immortality that it was to the earliest Christians ; but if we share their hope of immortality and regard the visions of the risen Lord as pointing to the immortality both of Himself and of humanity in general ("Christ the first-fruits, afterward they that are Christ's"), our view of all that is implied in the words "atonement," "salvation," "justification" will not be affected by any conclusion to which we may arrive as to the probable nature of the visions, except so far as we may be prevented from accepting the ancient theory of an actual, physical influence of the resurrection-body of Christ upon the bodily organism of every Christian man or woman.

employed in conventional religious teaching.   If repentance be, according to the Master's own teaching, the one
condition of forgiveness, repentance cannot be said to be
impossible for the non-Christian, while even the Christian's repentance is seldom perfect in this life.

And yet there is a sense in which we may, if we like,
find a meaning in the traditional doctrine that salvation
is through Christ alone.   In one sense it is of the essence
of any moral or religious doctrine to be exclusive.   Truth
must always be exclusive.   If it is true that the highest
revelation of God was made in Christ, no system which
refuses to recognize that fact can be wholly true.   There
can be in the end only one true way of salvation, for
there can be only one true moral ideal.[1]   If Christ was
right in teaching men that to repent, to think of God as
a Father who will forgive men their sins if and in proportion as they have repented of them, and with His help
to love one's neighbour as one's self is the true way to
be saved, the very meaning of what salvation is, then no
other religion or system can be wholly true which does
not teach these things.   At the same time it equally
follows that in so far as they have taught what Christ
taught, such systems are true, and *so far* men can be
saved by their means, here and hereafter.   If we
recognize that salvation from sin is a gradual process,
it is clear that there may be many degrees of salvation.
We must, indeed, reject the childish and utterly unhistorical suggestion that all religions or even all the
higher religions have, as a matter of fact, taught the
same way of salvation.   Some essentially Christian
teaching is to be found in many non-Christian
philosophies and many non-Christian religions, or
perhaps it would be truer to say in a very few of the
highest.   But history does not countenance the notion
that the Christian way of salvation, or even that any
religion except the religion historically known as Christianity, ever has taught this same way of salvation with

---

[1] And yet there is a sense in which there may be different vocations, and therefore
different ideals, for different persons—ideals which exhibit difference in identity.   See
my *Theory of Good and Evil*, vol. ii. pp. 107-148.

anything like equal purity, emphasis, and freedom from inconsistent precepts and ideas. The nearest approximations to such teaching are to be found in modern attempts at the reform of ancient religions, and these have been for the most part affected by the direct or indirect influence of Christianity. It may well be that the gradual leavening of old religions, or new reforms of old religions, by the influence of Christ and Christianity is part of the process by which the kingdoms of the world are destined in God's providence to be transformed into the Kingdom of our God and of His Christ. At the same time we must not under-estimate the enormous value of that personal, conscious following of Christ and belief in Him which is possible to him who acknowledges Christ as the one Lord and Master—the one supreme Revealer of God—and associates himself with the organized, historical body of His followers. When any of such half-Christianized religious societies shall have fully absorbed the eternal truth of Christ's revelation, they will, we may expect, themselves desire to profess the name of Him whom they will have discovered to be the supreme Redeemer. Christian life in its intensest form implies a personal devotion to Christ which cannot be shared with any other Lord or Master.

The true meaning of the incarnation or the divinity of Jesus Christ is not indeed the assertion that God is revealed in the historical Christ and in none other, but rather that the long, progressive self-revelation of God in humanity has reached its culminating moment in Christ and in the continuous revelation through the Holy Spirit in the society of His followers. The Christian may quite well acknowledge a measure of divine Self-revelation in other religions, provided that he recognizes the Christian religion as the supreme religion. Such a mode of representation is entirely in harmony with the teaching of Greek theology at its best. In the words of Origen : " The Logos was united and made one with the soul of Jesus in a far higher degree than with any other soul, seeing that He alone was enabled completely to receive the highest participation in the true Word and the true Wisdom and the true Righteousness." [1]

The eternal meaning of the Christian doctrine of salvation through Christ alone is that in the acceptance of this supreme revelation lies the true way of being saved from sin and attaining the fullest deliverance from sin, and the highest perfection, of which human nature is capable. Translated into still more modern language the meaning of the Church's early creed, " There is none other name given among men by which we may be saved," will be something of this kind: " There is none other ideal given among men by which we may be saved except the moral ideal which Christ taught by His words, and illustrated by His life and death of love: and there is none other help so great in the attainment of that ideal as the belief in God as He has been supremely revealed in Him who so taught and lived and died." So understood, the self-sacrificing life which was consummated by the death upon the Cross has indeed power to take away the sins of the whole world.

More and more, I believe, the great spiritual dividing line between men will be the line between those who really accept Christ's ideal of life and those who do not. Those who heartily believe in that ideal will probably in most cases find it possible to accept also Christ's outlook upon the universe as a universe guided and controlled by a conscious Will the nature and purposes of which may best be understood in the light of that same ideal. Those who believe that love is the thing of highest value in human life will generally believe also that " God is love indeed, and love Creation's highest law." But even if through intellectual perplexity they fail to do so, such persons may be placed among those of whom Christ said, " He that is not against us is for us," though they follow not with the great army of Christ's professed disciples. Many, doubtless, are being saved by this ideal who do not call themselves by Christ's name or formally associate themselves with those who do. And

[1] See above, p. 257.

such men are in a very real sense being saved through
Christ. And even among professing Christians by no
means uninfluenced by the Christian ideal, there are
probably millions whose highest spiritual life has been
due more to the influence of the Christian community in
which they have lived than to the conscious and deliberate
following of Christ. And so far there is a profound
meaning in the doctrine that it is the Church rather
than the individual which is the immediate " subject of
redemption." In all cases it is through the Church that
the influence of Christ first reaches the individual. And
yet on the whole it will doubtless be found that the
fullest, most efficacious, most contagious living of
Christ's life will be reserved for those who are not only
influenced by Christ and His teaching, but are consciously
and supremely influenced by it. The highest loyalty is
an exclusive loyalty. Of all the saving forces that live
and work in this world of ours the strongest is still the
influence of Christ, and that influence is at its highest
in those who know Him as their Saviour, and try to
live as He lived. The best way to lead the life of
Christ is consciously and deliberately to accept Christ
as supreme Lord and Master, and to come to the Father
through Him. There is eternal truth in the message
which answers the question, " What must I do to
be saved ? " with " Believe on the Lord Jesus Christ
and thou shalt be saved " [1]—provided only that we
interpret the language of the disciple by the still truer
and more fundamental saying of the Master Himself :
" Not every one that saith unto me, Lord, Lord, shall
enter into the kingdom of heaven ; but he that doeth
the will of my Father which is in heaven." [2]

[1] Acts xvi. 30.   [2] Matt. vii. 21.

APPENDICES

APPENDIX I

I AM aware that in many quarters, and in quarters which must be treated with deep respect, the objections which I have urged against certain traditional representations of the atonement will all be met by an appeal to what is called " Christian experience." It will be said that, no matter what difficulties the logical understanding, or even the moral consciousness, may discover in the statement, the Christian has an immediate consciousness that as a matter of objective fact, and quite independently of any influence exercised upon the believer, the sins of men have been forgiven on account of the death of Christ, and on the sole condition of faith in that death. The Christian knows immediately that such is the case. He is conscious of forgiveness and reconciliation with God, and he knows that the cause of what he feels is the objective fact of the sacrifice upon the Cross and that alone.

The recent tendency to rest the truth of Christianity upon " Christian experience " is to be welcomed in so far as it implies that the primary appeal is no longer to the external authority of Church or Bible or to historical evidence, but to something in the consciousness of mankind. But as to what that something is, there is unfortunately much deplorable vagueness. The use of the term " experience " to cover all sorts of psychical activity is calculated to lead to much confusion. It often involves a sheer refusal to think at all, and means at bottom the substitution of subjective emotion or blind reliance upon tradition for the honest effort to think rationally upon religious problems. As regards the doctrine of the atonement in particular, this tendency is to be observed not merely in religious persons who avowedly dislike and distrust any attempt at a systematic theology or religious philosophy, but in philosophers and theologians of high and deserved reputation. The Archbishop of Dublin (Dr. D'Arcy), for instance, is far too good a philosopher not to see the impossibility of such theories as those which have been examined and rejected in the preceding pages; and yet he attempts to defend the traditional view (or, as he would say, the "fact") of the atonement by a vague assertion that it is affirmed by "Christian experience,"[1] and that no subjective theory of the atonement is sufficient to justify or explain what the believer knows to be true. A critique of religious experience in general is one of the most urgent desiderata of religious Philosophy at the present moment. Such a critique would lead us far beyond the limits possible in an appendix to these lectures. I think it desirable, however, to make a few brief remarks upon this attitude of mind :

(1) The term "experience" is vague. Sometimes it appears to include all that is usually meant by philosophers when they speak of "the moral and religious consciousness." This is a very misleading use of the term. As employed by philosophers "experience" is commonly opposed to reason, and by reason is meant much besides the "discursive understanding," e.g. the power of apprehending general truths immediately or a priori—such truths as "two and two make four" or "two straight lines cannot enclose a space" or "every effect must have a cause." And reason so understood includes the power of giving moral judgements—judgements which possess objective validity. If any one deliberately rejects the authority of the moral consciousness, he rejects, as it appears to me, the only basis upon which the Christian conception of God can be defended; and I for one must ally myself on this matter with the main stream of patristic, scholastic, and Anglican theology, against what seems to me a fatal modern innovation. But some of those who appeal to religious experience would apparently admit that the judgements of our moral reason are a most important part of "religious experience," or, in the old traditional language, that "the voice of conscience is the voice of God." And in that case I should urge that they are surrendering their own position when they attempt to defend a theory which the moral consciousness condemns by an appeal to any other kind of consciousness—whether bare emotion, or "faith," or some non-rational kind of "intuition." If conscience be valid and the theories of substitution or of objective atonement are rejected by conscience, they cannot rest

---

[1] *Christianity and the Supernatural*, p. 66 *sq.* The Archbishop distinctly speaks of Christ's death as a "penalty"—a doctrine which must surely rest upon authority—for no one can well be supposed to know by immediate experience that God threatened to punish the sin of Adam by his own death and that of his posterity, and then agreed to accept the death of Christ as the equivalent of all their deaths. Apart from the statements to this effect in St. Paul, mere experience could hardly supply a basis for such assertions. And yet the Archbishop is so far from accepting St. Paul as a final authority that he feels himself free to accuse even his theories of self-contradiction. The assertion that Christ's death is not only a source of salvation but a "penalty" belongs to theory rather than to experienced fact.

upon an "experience" which includes the testimony of conscience.[1]

(2) When "experience" is at all strictly used, when it implies some kind of subjective feeling or emotion, it is clear that such emotion never gives us a knowledge of objective fact—any objective fact except the fact that such and such a person actually experiences such and such feelings or emotions. Subjective emotion may enable a man to say that he no longer feels the guilt or the power of sin since he believed such and such things, that he feels at peace with God, or that he is able to resist temptation as he could not resist it before : but, when he declares that this experience of his is due to the objective fact that God has forgiven the sins of those who entertain such and such beliefs, this is something which he could not possibly know by immediate experience. And till recently Christians never for one moment pretended to any such immediate knowledge. They declared that they so believed because it was written in the word of God. Would even a modern Christian pretend that he can know *a priori* the fact of Christ's death, or know that it has earned forgiveness for him apart from the historical testimony to the words of Christ and the writings of St. Paul ? If such knowledge is possible, why are missionaries to the heathen required ? There is always an element of inference and of theory in such statements, and the theory is derived from other sources than the immediate experience of the individual. The way in which each individual interprets his experience is determined by his other beliefs. It constantly happens that two individuals may have the same religious experiences and interpret them differently. And that has been notoriously the case with this particular doctrine of the atonement. We have met with abundant illustration of that fact in studying the history of the doctrine. There is no reason to doubt that the early Christian writers before Irenaeus had much the same experiences of forgiveness and reconciliation after they had accepted Christianity and undergone baptism as those after Irenaeus. And yet most of them, as we have seen, were content to explain their own experience, and the formal statements about the cause of that experience which they accepted on authority, by "subjective" interpretations of the Church's traditional language, while those who lived after Irenaeus explained them as due to an objective atonement effected by the death of Christ. Still more obviously there was an element of theory, due to a difference of intellectual presupposition, when a Catholic Christian supposed that he was saved by faith and works,

[1] I pass over the more technical metaphysical difficulty of making knowledge depend upon any *isolated* experience, or any *isolated* intuition, though this is an objection which presses seriously upon Dr. D'Arcy as a philosophical disciple of Mr. Herbert Bradley.

while an early Lutheran declared that salvation was due to faith alone.

(3) It sounds plausible to separate the " fact of the atonement " from theories about the atonement, and to declare that the fact rests upon experience, while it is admitted that the theories involve further processes of inference and may be more or less erroneous. But the distinction cannot be made in this hard and fast manner. What claims to be a simple statement of the atonement as a fact usually involves an element of theory, and the theory is palpably influenced by the different intellectual constitution, education, temperament, environment of individual Christians.[1] There are differences in the very simplest accounts which the simplest individuals give of the atonement. An early Christian would say, " I know I am saved by baptism in the name of Jesus," and (he might add) " by what Jesus taught." A little later he would have said, " I am saved by baptism in the name of the Holy Trinity and by believing in the orthodox doctrine of the Trinity." A medieval Christian would say, " I know that I am forgiven because I have been absolved by a Priest who has received his authority from Christ." Extreme Protestants would say : " I know that I am saved because I believe in the atoning efficacy of Christ's blood, although I remain just as sinful as before I believed." No doubt it may be urged that in all cases the work of Christ lies at the back of the theory, and so there is a common element in all of them. But (a) the individual claims as much immediate certainty for the part of his statement which differs from that of other Christians as for the part of it which is common to all, and (b) the part which is common to all these immediate certainties is shared also by those who believe in an atoning efficacy due to the subjective effects produced by Christ's life and work as a whole, and not to the objective effect of the death. In so far as we can at all distinguish between the experienced fact of the atonement and the theory of it, the follower of Justin or Origen, of Abelard or the Lombard, of Maurice or Ritschl may claim to rest his theory upon the testimony of experience quite as much as the most rigid disciple of St. Augustine or of Luther.

(4) Let us suppose these difficulties surmounted ; let us suppose that a man is entitled to say, " I know immediately that as a matter of objective fact my sins have been forgiven because Christ died upon the Cross, and for no other reason, and because I believe that they are so forgiven." Even so, the most that any one can claim on the basis of religious experience is that he knows *his* sins

---

[1] " The life and death of the Saviour we take to be facts : the recovery of men and women from lives of shame and folly, as far as this can be observed, may also be set down in the category of facts. But the connection between these two series traverses a vast expanse of theory " (Prof. Adeney in the Symposium called *The Atonement in Modern Religious Thought*, p. 144).

have been forgiven in this way : he cannot say that this is the only way in which the sins of others have been forgiven, or the only way in which such an experience of forgiveness can be attained. Universal truths cannot be known by the experience of one or even of many in any proper sense of " experience," and yet this is what the traditional doctrine of the atonement proclaims—that sins are forgiven in this way and in this way only. If the appeal is made to the general consensus of Christians, we may accept the fact that Christianity does give an experience of relief from sin and a power of resisting sin greater than seems to result from any other religion. But it is quite contrary to experience to say that such a sense of relief is *never* experienced in some degree by good Jews or Buddhists who would not describe themselves as reconciled with God through the blood of Christ, or by Unitarians, or by Trinitarians who would not ascribe it to any objective effect of Christ's death, or by those who would ascribe it not to the death of Christ so much as to the influence of Christ's teaching and character. No experience of his own can entitle any one to deny that as a matter of objective fact such persons are or will be forgiven by God, or that they may have a subjective experience of reconciliation.

And even if we confine ourselves to more traditional Christians, the appeal to experience does not seem to confirm the theory which attributes the saving efficacy of Christ and the knowledge of Him *in an exclusive manner* either to the objective or even to the subjective effects of His death. We have seen that on the whole the testimony of the Church is against that view. Both in the ancient Church and in modern times Christians who have not consciously abandoned traditional doctrines will no doubt upon occasion use traditional formulae which seem on the face of them to imply that the sense of reconciliation and the power to resist temptation spring entirely from the death of Christ :, but side by side with such statements we find in Christian literature and biography much that does not confirm that interpretation of their language. Just as good Christian lives have been led by those who would have repudiated the idea of an " objective " atonement as by those who have believed in it. There is, indeed, an enormous amount of testimony to the fact that the voluntary death of Christ has added to the saving power of Christ's life and teaching ; but, even when we think of the saving effects of that death as operating only through its subjective effects upon the believer, history and experience do not confirm the claim that the salvation which flows from Christ flows from His death only. Surely even in the case of those whose theories would assert this exclusive influence, it is obvious that their thoughts and their lives have been influenced by many other sides of Christ's work besides His death—by His teaching, by His character, by the influences which reach them through the society of other believers. It may be doubted whether His death apart from these influences would have had any effect at all. There are probably many very Christian lives in the production of which the words of Christ, His character, His example have counted for much more than His death, so far as the two kinds of influence can be distinguished : that is so even in the case of evangelically brought-up persons, who would feel bound dutifully to respect the accepted formulae. But in truth, on a reasonable view of the atonement, it is really impossible to distinguish the influence of Christ's death from the influence of His words and of His life. The influence of the character and words which explain the meaning of the death cannot be separated from the death itself, while the character and example would not have been all that they are but for the death by which the revelation of character was completed.

(5) It has so far been contended that we find the same religious experiences among Christians whose theories and explanations—about the death of Christ and other things—have differed very widely. To a certain extent that is undoubtedly the case. But it must not be assumed, as is frequently done, that the experience will always be just the same apart from the theory. The notion that religious experience is always the same, and that different "religions" or doctrinal systems are merely different ways of expressing it, is one of the most absurd suppositions that a sane man ever maintained. It is refuted on every side by history, by psychology, by any serious study of that very science of " Comparative Religion " on which it is sometimes supposed to rest. When the difference of religions is wide, the extravagance of the theory is glaring. How can it be supposed that the experience of the Hindoo mystic who thinks of the Absolute as impersonal, super-moral, sublimely indifferent to the weal and woe of mankind can be the same as that of the Christian mystic who thinks of God as a loving Father grieving over his sins and rejoicing only in righteousness ? [1] How can a Mahommedan who thinks of morality as dependent upon the arbitrary will of God experience the emotion which a Christian feels towards a God whom he thinks of as intrinsically righteous and loving towards all men ? To a certain extent no doubt religious systems are theories invented to account for experiences which are more or less the same ; but it is quite equally true that the character of a religious experience is determined in great part by the intellectual theories which have previously been accepted whether from conscious reflection or tradition, from instruction or environment, from emotional or temperamental attraction. That this is so with religions which

---

[1] I do not, of course, suggest that this is the only type of Hindoo mysticism.

differ widely is obvious. To suppose that a savage who has
conceived an admiration for the character of Christ, and worships
a God whom he thinks of as like Christ, really had the same
religious experience when he worshipped a deity whose chief
delight was human sacrifice or the smell of roast-pig is too ludicrous
a supposition to be entertained by any one for whom " religious
experience " is more than something which he has read about
in works upon religious philosophy. Savage priests or medicine-
men who have been converted to Christianity have often declared
that they did really believe themselves possessed by the god or the
devil during their religious ecstasies or wild dervish-dances and
felt the corresponding emotions; but they could no more experience them again than an Anglican archbishop. There is a
germ of truth beneath Renan's huge exaggeration that no one can
really understand a religion but one who has believed in it but
believes in it no longer. The paradox at least testifies to the fact
that religious emotion is dependent upon intellectual conviction,
and cannot be felt by those who lack the requisite conviction.
And the same principle holds with smaller religious differences.
That there is much in common between the religious experience
or, as I should prefer to say in less ambiguous language, the religious emotions and the moral life of all Christians, and especially
of the best Christians, I do not doubt. But it is undeniable that
there are considerable differences, and the differences are partly
determined by the beliefs about God and the universe which
have been acquired before the experiences come and without
which they would not occur. It is probable that no Protestant
ever experiences exactly the emotion which a Roman Catholic
enjoys as he kneels before the wafer which for him is the body of
Christ. It is equally improbable that a conventional Roman
Catholic whose religious ideas are inextricably associated with
priests and sacraments and consecrated places could ever experience
exactly what goes on in the mind of a devout Quaker as he sits
silent for an hour together in some bare meeting-house. They
have different theories about the " presence of God," and these
theories cause them to experience decidedly different feelings
though each of them might speak of those feelings as a " sense of
God's presence."

Among the differences which determine the nature of religious
experience, different modes of thinking about the sacrifice upon
the cross assuredly have an important place. When an Evangelical Christian declares that the feeling he experiences from the
belief that his sins have once for all been blotted out by an expiatory sacrifice is one which is impossible to those who have no such
belief in the atoning Blood, it is quite conceivable that he is right.
In some cases no doubt the profession of different formulae will

imply no difference at all in the " experiences " or the resulting life, because the formulae have become mere formulae : but in others, when the formulae represent profound personal convictions, their acceptance or rejection may make a very great difference. It is pretty certain that the religious experiences of Origen were different from those of St. Augustine. Which was the more valuable kind of religious experience, which represents the higher kind of religious life, may be open to question. To a certain extent we can compare and contrast the effects which different types of religious experience produce upon the life. And the result of that comparison is to show that very different kinds of religious emotion may be equally productive of good life : but it is equally certain that they do not lead to exactly the same kind of good life. To a certain extent those who believe in Christ's own criterion, " By their works ye shall know them," may estimate the relative value of different kinds of religious experience by observing the influence of the theories upon life ; but only to a certain extent. For the very point in which religious experiences differ most widely is in respect of their moral ideals—a difference which is partly produced by, and partly occasions, or reacts upon the differences in religious belief. St. Augustine's theories produced St. Augustine's life—a life which seems to some Christians a near approach to the true Christian ideal, to others a wide departure from it. It is not probable that Kant had much sympathy with the kind of life led by St. Francis and his disciples, and how unprofitable would the life led by the philosopher of Königsburg have seemed to St. Francis !

While, therefore, we may contend that our interpretation of the doctrine of the atonement is quite sufficient to account for the saving effects which theories like those of Tertullian and St. Augustine, of Luther and of Wesley, have claimed for the death of Christ, we need not maintain that the different explanations of the atonement which have been offered at various periods in the history of the Church will have no effect at all upon the religious and moral life of those who hold them. The differences in the lives led by the best representatives of different presentations of Christian doctrine are likely to be the smallest : but even in the best men differences there will be. It is abundantly proved by experience that theories about salvation which St. Augustine or St. Bernard or Luther would have anathematized are capable of producing lives of which all three of them could not but have approved. But we need not deny that, in some ways, a Christianity which lays more stress upon the life of Christ, upon His teaching and upon His example, and attaches less exclusive importance to the isolated fact of His death, is likely to produce a different kind of life from that which has generally resulted from the most complete appropriation of the older and traditional theories. In so far as we feel that the moral ideals associated with that teaching and more or less attained by its adherents are defective and one-sided, we shall regard the appeal to experience as confirming rather than refuting the more modern way of stating and explaining the doctrine of the atonement. The lives and characters of such men as St. Augustine, Luther, and even John Wesley are not incontrovertible testimony to the truth of their theology: in many ways the lives of such men exhibit the defects of their theories. In so far as we think the kind of life which a different type of theology encourages to be more in accordance with the mind of Christ as exhibited by His teaching, we shall regard that fact as confirming our view that a "subjective" theory of the atonement is more in accordance with the mind of the Master than any theory of substitution or expiation. We may reverently recognize the intense beauty of the lives which have been inspired very largely by the mode of thought which concentrates attention upon the death of Christ and interprets that death as an expiation for sin. But we need not deny that other types of religious experience may inspire lives of equal goodness—it may be goodness of the same type, or it may be goodness of another, but not less valuable, type. The "sense of sin" which makes a Christian of the more modern type revolt against the social iniquities of modern Capitalism may perhaps be something deeper and more Christ-like than the "sense of sin" which leads to an intense and sometimes selfish pre-occupation with one's own personal salvation. For my own part I believe that the best lives lived under the influence of a more modern interpretation of the atonement, and of Christianity generally, will compare very favourably with the best lives under the influence of Augustinian or Anselmic or Lutheran presentations of Christianity. If some of the most Christ-like lives are even now nurtured by the older theories, it is largely because the persons are less influenced by these ideas, and more by Christ's own example and by what the Holy Spirit has taught to the modern world, than they are themselves aware. Many ostensibly orthodox and traditional Christians are really very modern Christians indeed.

And here I should like to quote a valuable piece of testimony which I take from an interesting work by a writer who himself defends the substitutionary view of the atonement : "The Rev. Campbell Moody, a Chinese missionary, in an interesting psychological analysis of ' the heathen heart,' points out that the Chinese convert's faith is largely legalistic. It more resembles the faith of the sub-Apostolic than of the Apostolic Church; for it is interesting to note that though the earliest Christian Church was strongly 'evangelical' in its view of faith, the later Christians of the ante-Nicene period went back to the Christ of the Gospels and drew their inspiration for a holy life from an imitation of Him in His life and death. It is so specially with the 'Teaching of the Twelve Apostles' and St. Clement. ' If you ask a Chinese Christian,' says Mr. Moody, ' how one is saved, the usual answer is that a man cannot be good of himself ; he must trust in Christ for strength to lead a good life, and in that way hope to be saved or have his sins forgiven.' If we enquire further, 'What did Christ come to do ? ' some one rises to answer, ' He came to teach us.' ' To teach us what ? ' ' To teach us to worship God,' is the prompt reply. Some other Christian is able to tell us that Christ came to save us. ' How does He save ? ' ' By His almighty power.' Or perhaps we can extort the answer, ' He died for our sins '; but the meaning of these words remains unexplained. There is no clear idea of justification by faith alone. The idea is as foreign to Chinese Christians as it was to Christians of the first three centuries." [1]

When we remember the lives led, and the deaths died, in attestation of their faith both by ante-Nicene Christians and by modern Chinese converts, I do not think it is necessary to apologize for the belief which led to such a result. On the whole I should venture to say that both classes represent a higher level than was reached by the most typical Augustinian Christians of the fifth century or of the sixteenth or of the nineteenth.

(6) Two further remarks may be made on the attempt to " prove " any of those theories of the atonement which are commonly associated with what is called in the narrower sense " evangelical " teaching by the appeal to experience : (a) Marvellous as has undoubtedly been the effect of that sort of teaching, beautiful as have been the lives that it has produced, it has always been only on a comparatively small number of persons—persons of a certain temperament or brought up in a certain environment—that it has had this effect, while there are a much larger number of people who are inaccessible to such appeals but quite capable of being influenced by other representations of Christ's work ; and (b) there seems reason to believe that teaching based upon some substitutionary or " objective " theory of the atonement has largely lost its power to attract, to influence, and to " save " souls

---

[1] *The Disease and Remedy of Sin*, by the Rev. W. Mackintosh Mackay, B.D., p. 126. Of course I do not accept the few words put into the mouth of the Chinese Christian as a full and completely satisfactory account of the Christian faith. Perhaps the Chinese Christian would have benefited by some of the explanations of Christ's work so abundantly provided by the ante-Nicene theologians, insufficient as they may seem, though both of them are large-minded and tolerant, to Mr. Moody and Mr. Mackintosh Mackay. Still less should I accept Mr. Moody's identification of the " Apostolic " faith with that of orthodox Protestantism.

affected by modern ways of thinking. That is found to be so even with the least educated classes. Still more is that the case with the more cultivated. The doctrine always owed its power to the fact that the expiation was a supreme proof of the love of God. It is just because, so long as the death of Christ is considered as a punishment or expiation, it seems to the modern mind to disprove both the love and the holiness of God that the modern mind has rejected that doctrine.

(7) I have been contending that the experience of Christians does not confirm the theory that salvation is due to the death of Christ alone, but that it does confirm the theory that the greatest source of salvation in this world is the work of Christ taken as a whole—the sum total of influences that flow from His life and death, His teaching and example, His revelation of God. I think it is important to add that this influence is not always direct. Not only has the saving influence of Christ extended in some measure to many who do not " profess and call themselves Christians " ; but even over Christians the influence is not always or exclusively exercised through the individual's personal contemplation of Christ's work, or conscious imitation of His life, or conscious effort to obey His actual words. Always in the first instance, and to a large extent with many individuals throughout life, the influence reaches them through a social environment already penetrated by the influence of Christ—in other words through His Church. Whether we think of a child growing up in a Christian family, of a pagan's first contact with Christian ideas, or of the first serious aspirations after a more definitely Christian life in the mind of an individual living in a society at the most half-Christian, the beginning of the process which results in salvation is always the influence exercised by some other individual or some society of more seriously Christian people. That is the case even when the first definite influence of Christian ideas is due to a study of the New Testament, for the New Testament is a collection of writings made and circulated by a Christian society. It is important to recognize this ; for, when salvation is supposed to be due necessarily and exclusively to the individual's conscious feeling towards the personal Christ, there is a tendency either really to think of it as the prerogative of some exceedingly small number of persons whose religious experiences conform to some very definite psychological norm, or else to use language which seems hardly to correspond with the realities of life. I should myself strongly contend that the highest type of Christian life does involve personal belief in, conscious attachment to, deliberate following of Christ. And yet many are in a very real sense followers of Christ, and may be included among those who are " being saved " by His work, to whom we could not apply

with much naturalness and reality the kind of language which we properly do use to describe the attitude towards the personal Christ of Christians whose Christianity is of a more deliberate and self-conscious order.   Countless numbers of men have absorbed much of the spirit of Christ without much conscious devotion to Christ Himself.   Sometimes the ideal which really influenced them had more of Christ in it than the conventional Christ of their Church or their age.

The question whether it is the Church or the individual that is primarily " the subject of salvation " may seem a rather barren and technical controversy ; but the doctrine that it is the Church which is the primary subject of salvation (so strongly insisted on by Ritschl if not always practically remembered by his followers) has the advantage of recognizing the fact that the saving influence exercised by Christ is always at the beginning, and often to the end of earthly life, in great part an indirect influence.   A man who strives earnestly to realize an ideal of goodness historically created by Christ, and kept alive by those upon whom His influence is conscious and paramount, is really " being saved " by Christ, though (as after all is the case even with the most conscious Christians) salvation may remain in this life very incomplete. And this is the element of truth contained in those medieval theories of salvation according to which the death of Christ is thought of as causing salvation almost entirely because it is the source of the stream of " grace " which reaches the individual chiefly through the Church and the sacraments.   The Middle Age thought of that influence and of the channels through which it was exercised too mechanically : it tended to attribute salvation too much to the man's own efforts in the case of the few, and to make it too cheap, too easy, and too much dependent upon external mediation in the case of the many.   Protestantism was justified in insisting upon the privilege and the duty of personal contact with Christ on the part of the individual.   But Catholic teaching has been right in insisting upon the part which is played in the saving process, for the normal individual, by the Christian society, its influences, and its institutions.   The stress which is laid by Catholic teaching upon the sacraments corresponds with the realities of the moral and religious life if these are thought of as symbols and channels of the spiritual influence exercised by the Christian society, and not as magical rites which confer grace *ex opere operato.*

APPENDIX II

THE closer study of the mystery-religions and their history has opened up a large field of enquiry which is of great value for the understanding of early Christianity. It would be impossible here to give the reader even an outline of the enormously complicated facts, and the various theories which have been based upon them, or to enter upon any independent discussion of the questions at issue. I can only refer him to the main sources of information such as: Cumont, *Les Religions orientales* (E.T., *Oriental Religions in Roman Paganism*, by Showerman) and *Mythraïsme*; Norden, *Agnostos Theos*; Reitzenstein, *Poimandres*, and *Die hellenistische Mysterienreligionen*; Dietrich, *Eine Mithrasliturgie*; Frazer, *The Golden Bough*—an immense work, the successive volumes of which, appearing under separate titles, have taken the place of the original shorter work in two volumes: Glover, *The Conflict of Religions in the Roman Empire*; Clemen, *Primitive Christianity and its non-Jewish Sources*; Lake, *Encyclopaedia of Religion and Ethics*, Art. "Baptism," ii. 379; Estlin Carpenter, *Phases of Early Christianity*. A very judicial summing up of the whole matter (as regards St. Paul) is given in Professor H. A. A. Kennedy's *St. Paul and the Mystery Religions*; for the more detailed questions Clemen's book may be especially recommended.

A scientific discussion of these questions is here impossible, but I think it may be well to justify the general statement made in the Lectures [1] by a short account of the main facts and to state (without much argument) the impressions which a perusal of the main works on the subject has left upon my mind, in so far as they have a bearing upon the Christian doctrine of atonement.

In many of the cults of antiquity—the cults of Isis and Osiris, of Attis and Cybele, and others—a god or divine hero was

---

[1] See above, pp. 74-5.

represented as dying and coming to life again.[1]   The origin of
these religions is beyond all doubt to be found in the phenomena
of the seasons—the dying of vegetation in the autumn and its
revival in the spring.   Many ancient worships included a mourn-
ing over the dying god and a rejoicing over his resurrection.
Moreover, sacrifices of animals and sometimes of men were
offered, and the victims were supposed to be in some measure
identified with, or representative of, the deity.   Such sacrifices
were (in accordance with the widespread theory of sympathetic
magic) thought (1) to help the process of Nature's revival and so
to stimulate the growth of crops and the reproduction of animals ;
(2) to benefit the worshipper who ate of the sacrifice by the infusion into him of the divine energy which flowed from the
victim's blood.   In the three centuries before and after the
Christian era there was a great revival of these ancient religions
all through the Roman Empire, and a great development both
in their theology and in their worship.   The grosser practices
in them—such as human sacrifice—in most cases disappeared, and
the grosser ideas with them.   The oriental worships were transferred to the West, even to Rome itself, and attracted large numbers
of worshippers for whose religious needs the elementary Roman
state-religion provided no satisfaction.

" There are special strains of religious thought and feeling
more or less common to all the mystery-religions, such as that
of regeneration (in some sense) and union or communion
with deity." [2]   Moreover, the worship of the deity usually had
connected with it a brotherhood or secret society, admission to
which involved elaborate ceremonies of initiation.   Sometimes
there were many stages or degrees of initiation : and in many
cases the initiation admitted the worshipper to some kind of dramatic
representation, and included the communication of certain religious
doctrines or formulae.   One of the most remarkable of these
initiatory ceremonies was the famous Taurobolium which was
connected with the worship of the Great Mother, a deity identified
with Cybele, in which the worshipper stood in a pit and was
drenched with the blood of a bull, after which he was wrapped
in its skin, and was said to be " born again to eternity " (in
aeternum renatus).   This rite is, however, not known to have
existed before the middle of the second century A.D.

In the worship of Mithra—the Persian god or hero (originally
a god of light, in spite of his humanity closely associated with and
eventually in some sense identified with the Sun), and who had

---

[1] It is important to notice, however, that in Mithraism (the religion which seems,
superficially at least, most to resemble Christianity) the hero triumphs over his enemy—
the bull—but does not die.

[2] Kennedy, St. Paul and the Mystery Religions, pp. 69, 70.

slain a bull (more or less identified with or symbolical of the power of darkness or evil), there was both a baptism and a communion of bread and water.[1] It was by some sort of sympathy or identification with the dying god that the benefits of the initiation were supposed to be secured. Originally the object of such initiations seems to have been to escape the power of Fate ($\epsilon i \mu \alpha \rho \mu \acute{\epsilon} \nu \eta$): but a more ethical element was gradually introduced into them. In some cases the initiation required moral purification, often accompanied by fasting or other ascetic practices, and was supposed both (1) to symbolize or to procure purification from sin, and (2) to secure the gift of a blessed and immortal life after death. In many cases (as in the earlier and purely Hellenic mysteries of Eleusis) the scenes represented in the mysteries were in some ways symbolic of the judgement and the deliverance which awaited the soul after death. In Apuleius there is an account of the initiation of Lucius into the religion of Isis at Cenchreae, in which the initiated thus describes his experience : " I penetrated to the boundaries of death. I trod the threshold of Proserpine, and after being borne through the elements I returned to earth : at midnight I beheld the sun radiating white light ; I came into the presence of the gods below and the gods above, and did them reverence close at hand." [2] Those who had gone through the initiation were said to be " born again." [3]

That there was a certain resemblance between such ideas and those of early Christianity is obvious. How far can the origin and development of the Christian ideas and practices be connected with the pagan ? I must be content with a very short statement of the conclusions to which I have personally come, without much defence of them :

(1) There is no good ground for supposing that the doctrine of the atonement held by the earliest Christians was in any direct way due to the primitive pagan ideas about dying gods. It is very doubtful whether in civilized paganism the sacrificer ever supposed that the victim sacrificed was in any literal sense identical with the god or that the worshipper who ate the victim or partook in the sacred meal was really eating the god.[4] He thought of himself as sitting at the table of the god, as the recipient of a direct influence from the god, as entering into communion with him ; but there is no good evidence that he regarded himself as actually eating the flesh of the god. Such an idea would have filled any Jewish-born

---

[1] It must be remembered that our knowledge of these ceremonies relates to the period long after the beginnings of Christianity : according to Cumont, the mysteries of Mithra did not possess any importance in the time of St. Paul.

[2] *Metamorphoses*, xi. 23. [3] " Quoquo modo renatus," *ib.* xi. 16.

[4] Dr. Estlin Carpenter accepts the view that such was the belief of those who took part in the " Omophagy " in honour of Dionysius, but he only quotes modern scholars in support of it (*Phases of Early Christianity*, p. 273).

Christian, or even a pagan at all influenced by Jewish ideas, with sheer horror.   Moreover, in the earliest Jewish Christian theology, and even that of St. Paul, Christ was rarely called God, and certainly not identified with the One God, and none of the very earliest conceptions of the atonement necessarily imply the actual divinity of Him who died.   Among non-Jewish Christians the operation of these ideas about eating the god cannot be denied *a priori*; it is enough to say that nothing in the language of the earliest Christian writers about either the atonement or the eucharist is in any way suggestive of such notions, even if they were at this time entertained by civilized pagans, of which the evidence is far from sufficient.

(2) How far did the more refined ideas about the mysteries have an influence upon early Christianity ?   The *origin* of the atonement theory cannot be directly attributed to any such influence for the simple reason that it can be traced historically to a purely Jewish source—the letter of prophecy.   But it is quite possible, and even probable,[1] that it originated in Hellenistic circles ; that is to say, in minds familiar with the ritual, the language, and the ideas connected with the mysteries.   It is impossible to deny that this knowledge *may* have combined with their desire to account in some way for the death of Christ, and have helped them to discover in Isaiah liii. and elsewhere in the Jewish prophets the idea of salvation through the death of Christ : though, after all, the idea of forgiveness or reconciliation through the efficacy of a sacrifice was one which was common to all ancient religions, and in no way confined to the mystery - religions.   Still more may the analogies of the mystery-religions have helped the further development and formulation of the doctrine, and the emphasis laid upon it.   It is scarcely possible to distinguish sharply between what was due to unconscious influence and what was due simply to the fact that the idea satisfied, much more fully and on a much higher level, the same religious needs which the mysteries attempted to satisfy, and perhaps in some imperfect way succeeded in satisfying.

(3) St. Paul undoubtedly makes frequent use of the more or less technical language employed in the mystery-religions—such terms as mystery (μυστήριον, which, however, in the LXX. means simply "secret"), wisdom (σοφία, as the special higher wisdom of the τέλειοι), perfect (τέλειος), knowledge (γνῶσις), fullness (πλήρωμα), the contrast between spirit and the flesh, the contrast between spiritual (πνευματικός) and natural (ψυχικός), enlighten (φωτίζειν), rebirth (παλλιγγενεσία), salvation (σωτηρία), to put on (ἐνδύεσθαι), to be conformed to (σύμφυτος γίνεσθαι). But it is possible to contend that his use of all such terms

---

[1] See above, p. 78.

can be sufficiently explained by the LXX. or the literature of Hellenistic Judaism. Some of them were used by philosophers who had nothing to do with the mysteries : [1] and it is constantly forgotten in these discussions that most of the terms were terms which did not disappear from the language of common life and of religion in general because they were specially used in the mysteries. No modern missionary can avoid, in setting the ideas of his own religion before a people of alien race, terms employed in the non-Christian religions which he wishes to supplant. But his use of such terms does not necessarily imply that he is influenced by, or accepts, the ideas which in their non-Christian context they represent, except in so far as the fact that the same term more or less naturally translates the other implies *some* identity or analogy between them. Many of the terms employed by St. Paul might have been used without a thought of the mysteries : but it would be difficult for one who habitually spoke Greek, who lived, both before and after his conversion, in a Greek world, and in constant association with men who were or had been pagans, to have used such terms without being more or less conscious of the associations which the terms would certainly possess for his hearers. St. Paul may very conceivably have had such associations in mind, just as he often uses metaphors which were certainly derived from the games and from the civic life of towns like Philippi. The basis of St. Paul's ideas is Jewish, though it may be that they were derived rather from the Hellenistic Judaism of Tarsus already not a little tinged by a universalistic and non-Jewish Philosophy [2] (especially the Stoicism of which Tarsus was a famous centre) rather than from the Judaism of Jerusalem, and that his Judaism was apocalyptic rather than strictly " rabbinic." [3] His *theories* owe nothing to the mystery-religions : his theory of justification was, as I have tried to show, juridical rather than sacrificial. Nevertheless, it is highly probable that in the emphasis

---

[1] So Diogenes of Oinoanda (Glover, *Conflict of Religions*, p. 219). Dr. Estlin Carpenter (*Phases*, p. 21) notices Porphyry's statement that the object of philosophy was the " salvation of the soul," which is none the less significant because of its lateness. I have passed over altogether the question how far the ideas connected with the mysteries may not, at the period with which we are best acquainted, have been influenced by Christianity.

[2] *E.g.* the idea of Natural Law in Rom. ii. 14, 15, the contrast between the natural and the spiritual man (1 Cor. ii. 14), the " all things are yours " (1 Cor. iii. 22), the comparison of society with the body and its members, etc. But Stoicism had too many points of contact with Judaism for a sharp differentiation between Jewish and Stoic influence to be possible.

[3] On this subject see Mr. Claude Montefiore's most instructive book, *Judaism and St. Paul*. His conclusion is that St. Paul's " knowledge of the mystery-religions made him ready and eager to discover a universal method of salvation, suited and predestined for all men, whether Gentile or Jew " (p. 127). This is a moderate statement, to which I should not demur, but I should like to amend it by saying that it may have contributed with much else in his intellectual and religious environment to make him ready for such a religion of redemption.

he gave to the idea of a divine or quasi-divine Saviour, to the idea of a mystical communion with Him and with His death, he was unconsciously influenced by the religious atmosphere created by the mystery-religions.   Christ seemed to him the Bringer of precisely the kind of salvation which the Gentiles were vainly seeking in the mystery-religions.   It must not be supposed that there was conscious imitation, or that the influence involved the bringing down of Christianity to the pagan level.   " St. Paul has transformed these ideas in the process of assimilating them ; " [1] and even so the influence may easily be exaggerated.

(4) It is probable that much more influence was exercised by the mystery-religions upon the early Christian ideas about the Church and the sacraments, which were closely connected with, and in time reacted upon, the Church's conception of the atonement, than upon that doctrine itself.   Here, too, the *origin* of the institutions must be sought on Jewish soil.   Baptism, whether actually practised and commanded by Christ Himself or not, was clearly taken over from the practice of John the Baptist— and perhaps from the Jewish baptism of proselytes.   The symbolism of lustration is, indeed, so obvious that it is found all over the world :   here there need be no thought of borrowing.   The eucharist probably had its origin in a purely Jewish rite.[2] The idea of the Church, too, grew out of the Jewish conception of the people of God, while the individual Church was organized in imitation of the Synagogue.   But it was scarcely possible that, when pagans came to form Christian societies and to practise in them rites resembling to some extent those which the initiated practised in their mystery-fraternities, their ideas about them should not have influenced their conception both of the Christian Society and of its usages. It is clear that there were gradually imported into them many ideas which were almost absent from these institutions in their primitive Jewish-Christian form—the elaborate preparation for baptism, the idea of initiation into an organized society, the extreme insistence upon the secrecy of the doctrine and formulae communicated at baptism, the jealous exclusion of all but fully initiated persons from the eucharistic service, the different stages of the catechumenate leading up to the full admission to the Christian society, the tendency to attribute a quasi-magical efficacy to the sacramental rites, and especially to connect the actual attainment of immortality with the due performance of them, the theory which looked upon the eucharist as the " medicine of immortality " (the germ of which is found in Ignatius) in the sense that it actually transformed the gross and mortal body into a body which was

[1] Loisy in an article reproduced by Mr. Montefiore (*Judaism and St. Paul*, p. 238).
[2] See above, p. 59.

essentially incorruptible, many of the ideas ultimately connected
with the hierarchy—in all these developments it is impossible not
to trace the influence of the mystery-religions, their doctrine and
practices, and the religious philosophy connected with them.
The very application of the term " mysteries " to the eucharist
obviously implies such a transference of ideas; and these ideas
did ultimately exercise a powerful influence upon the conceptions
entertained about the atonement itself: for (as we have seen)
the death of Christ came to be looked upon as the objective source
of the mysterious influence by which the Christian attained to
immortality or " deification " — a term freely used in connection with the mystery-religions.   It is impossible to read,
for instance, the " Catecheses " of Cyril of Jerusalem or the
explanation of the atonement given by such a writer as Gregory
of Nyssa [1] without feeling at every turn the strength of this
influence, or at least the influence of the atmosphere which the
mystery-religions created.   If any one likes to say that Christianity had *by this time* become a mystery-religion, he is entitled
to do so; but he should add that it was a mystery-religion which
stood on a much higher ethical and spiritual level than (so far as
the historical evidence enables us to compare them) was ever
reached by the mystery-religions at their highest.

(5) How far can any such ideas about the sacraments and
Church (as distinct from the atonement) be discovered in the
writings of St. Paul ?   A generation or two ago the disposition
of all Protestant interpreters, whether liberal or orthodox, was to
minimize the prominence of all outward rites and observances in
St. Paul's teaching: the fashion of the moment in some quarters
is to emphasize this side of his teaching to the extent of making
them as important matters for St. Paul as they were in the mystery-
religions.   It must not be forgotten that among the votaries of
the mystery-religions themselves there was probably every degree
of spirituality and unspirituality, of literalism and symbolism, in
their ideas about the initiatory and other rites of these cults.   How
far we can institute any comparison between St. Paul's state of
mind and theirs will depend largely upon the question whether
we compare him to the higher or to the lower kind of initiator
or initiate.   And then it is most important to remember that,
while his elaboration of the doctrine about Christ's death and the
faith which appropriated it, was to a large extent his own, the rites
of the Church and the belief in their necessity were simply found
by him existing in the Church.   This is obviously so in the case
of baptism, and there is no reason to assume that it was otherwise
in the case of the eucharist.   There is to my mind not even plausi-
bility in the theory that the eucharist was in any sense an invention

---

[1] See above, pp. 307-8, 312.   Cf. pp. 280, 287, 319, etc.

of St. Paul's; since we find the same rite established, and much the same ideas attached to it, in the most Jewish as in the most Pauline, Churches. (See, *e.g.*, the anti-Pauline pseudo-Clementine writings.) The most in the way of innovation which can be attributed to him is that there may be in his allusions to the eucharist, in accordance with his general doctrine, an increased emphasis upon the idea of participating in the *death* of Christ, and of entering into communion with that death—ideas which are not prominent in the earliest liturgies or accounts of the eucharist.

But how far did he regard these rites as necessary to salvation ? We are left to conjecture, for the question is never raised : but we may be fairly safe in making the following assertions : (*a*) St. Paul attached immense importance to membership in the Christian community; he could not have understood any Christianity that did not involve membership in such a community, for it was only by treating the Ecclesia as the spiritual Israel that he could recognize Gentiles as inheritors of the prophecies. Membership in the Church involved submission to its authority : and he accepted as a matter of course the rites which the community accepted. (*b*) On the other hand, any interpretation of St. Paul's teaching is forced and unintelligible which does not make salvation depend primarily upon faith in Christ, spiritual communion with Him, and the moral condition which resulted from that communion. His teaching leaves no room for attributing any but a subordinate importance to the external rites. Preaching the Gospel was clearly to him a far more important matter than baptizing : when he dwells on the analogy between the Christian communion and similar rites in Paganism, it is rather to show the inconsistency of partaking in both than to emphasize the importance of the former. In the words of Mr. Montefiore, St. Paul's doctrine " was allied to the doctrine of the mystery-religions, but it was much more thoroughly moralised." [1] (*c*) At the same time he probably could not have understood the sort of disparagement of the sacraments which is characteristic of a certain type of Protestantism. If any one had raised the question whether it was not possible to be saved without the sacraments, he would doubtless have asked how any one could expect to be saved who neglected what he regarded as an express command of Christ. He would perhaps have denied that the faith of such a man could be a real faith. Any interpretation which makes of them more than obligatory and divinely appointed signs or symbols, or aids to moral and spiritual processes, would be inconsistent with his fundamental doctrine : on the other hand, to speak of " mere " symbols would equally fail to express his mind. He might not have accepted such a

---

[1] *Judaism and St. Paul*, p. 195. Clemen's treatment of this subject may be specially commended (*Primitive Christianity*, p. 238 *sq.*).

formula as "efficacious signs" because that might have seemed to isolate the sacramental acts from the direct influence exercised by Christ upon the soul quite independently of the sacraments, and from the faith without which they could not have the smallest value (there is, of course, no trace in his writings of infant baptism or infant communion). But such a phrase would not, perhaps, be a bad expression of his belief so far as any formula could express an attitude of mind which was essentially undefined, unformulated, or (as some would call it) "mystical." Still less would he have understood the position of one who wished to be saved by a life of isolation from the Christian community. To isolate oneself from a Christian community (the question of the relation between the many local or "house" communities and the Church at large is never discussed) would have been to aim at being saved without the moral effects which naturally flowed from true faith and membership in the Christian community : it was essentially in the life of the Christian community that the presence of the Spirit manifested itself. To aim at salvation without the Church would have implied (for St. Paul) a desire to be saved without love of the brethren.

(6) Such were the ideas of St. Paul about the sacraments, and there is no reason to believe that fundamentally these ideas were different from those which would have been accepted by other Christians, Jewish or Gentile, though the actual expression which he gave to them was due to the working of a very original mind. If that is so, we are dispensed from answering the question how far they were originally derived from the mysteries. The Gentile Churches took over the sacraments and the elementary ideas about them from the Judaeo-Christian Church. At the same time it was scarcely possible for one who had been a pagan not to be consciously or unconsciously influenced by the analogy—amid however much difference—between the usages of the Church and those of the mystery-cults ; and such an influence could hardly have failed to betray itself in his language. Nor could such an analogy fail to strike one who was in daily intercourse with Gentile Churches, and in a state of constant controversy with non-Christian Gentiles whom he was seeking to win over to the faith. St. Paul's language seems to betray a consciousness of this analogy, *e.g.* in what he says about the impossibility of being a partaker of the table of the Lord and the table of devils. And more vaguely the development given to the idea of the Church in the writings of St. Paul may perhaps be said to have been helped by the existence of the religious associations to which the early Christian Churches unconsciously assimilated themselves. For any deeper and more definite influence of the mystery-religions we must look to later ages than that of St. Paul.

(7) The general result to which, as it seems to me, the facts point is that Schweitzer is too absolute in saying that " Paulinism and Hellenism have in common their religious terminology, but, in respect of ideas, nothing " (*St. Paul and his Interpreters*, p. 238) ; if only because it is impossible to say that Judaism itself, especially the extra-Palestinian Judaism in which St. Paul was brought up, had *nothing* in common with the Hellenism of the same period, or, again, that the more religious Paganism was wholly uninfluenced by Judaism.   On the other hand, Professor Lake (in *The Earlier Epistles of St. Paul*) seems to me to exaggerate the resemblance of St. Paul's Christianity to the mystery-religions, particularly in respect of the place which the sacraments occupied in the Apostle's own mind.   What Professor Lake does most convincingly show is the influence of the mysteries upon the minds of St. Paul's converts, especially at Corinth, where many of the notions which St. Paul combats are clearly due to this source. There was certainly a tendency to make salvation independent of personal morality and to spiritualize the conception of resurrection in such a way as (without probably denying the immortality of the soul) to deny the resurrection of the body, and to make it independent of the resurrection of Christ.   And in spite of St. Paul's protests, these tendencies did ultimately produce a profound effect upon orthodox Christian thought.   The most extreme influence of the mysteries, and still more of that " Hermetic " literature and theosophy which were to some extent connected with the mysteries, is to be found in the Gnostics who ultimately drifted quite away from the Church and the Christianity of the Church ; but to a lesser degree they influenced the ideas of the Church itself, especially in Greek-speaking communities.   Even here the influence of the mystery-religions may be exaggerated. It is not only the mystery-religions but Greek philosophy which accounts for the development of the belief in an eschatological Messiah into a belief in an actual incarnation of Deity; which turned the doctrine of salvation through the Messiah into a doctrine of a " deification " through the God-man mediated by the sacraments; and which (in the Greek-speaking world) practically tended to identify the resurrection of the body with the Greek conception of the immortality of the soul.   It is chiefly (from the nature of the case) in all that relates to the Church and the sacraments that we may trace the influence of the mysteries as distinct from that of philosophy.   The philosophers had a theology and a religion, but they had, as philosophers, nothing to do with religious rites or religious communities.

If there is a certain want of definiteness about these conclusions, it may, I believe, be said that any more precise statement would be essentially misleading.   It is impossible to draw a sharp line between the assertion that such and such results were due to the influence of the mystery-religions, and the assertion that they were due to that state of religious thought and feeling out of which the mystery-religions had grown, and which they in turn fostered and kept alive. To say that, even in their developed form, the doctrine of the atonement or the sacramental doctrine associated therewith was due to the influence of the mystery-religions would be false, because the origin and substance of those doctrines are essentially Jewish. To say that these doctrines grew out of the reflection and religious experience of men who were influenced by the cycle of religious ideas which centred round the mysteries, as well as by the ideas which they derived from Judaism and the Old Testament, is true. The formula which most nearly hits the mark is perhaps to say that these doctrines, in the form which they finally attained, especially in the teaching of the Greek Fathers, were developed out of Jewish material by minds steeped in the ideas of the mystery-religions.

(8) In all comparisons between Christianity and the mystery-religions we must never forget the enormous difference which is implied by the contrast between the personality of Him through whom the Christian thought to obtain salvation and the gods or heroes of the mystery-religions. The " Saviours " of the mystery-religions were mythical personages ; there was little in the stories about them which could be made edifying except by treating them in the most purely symbolical manner ; and no ethical or religious teaching was even attributed to them. Jesus was a historical Person, whose moral and religious teaching was preserved in the Church, and occupied an enormously prominent place in the religion of that Church—a Person whose character and moral ideal still appeals to us as the highest which the world has known. The resemblances between Christianity and the mystery-religions are of a kind which can neither drag down early Christianity to the level of the mysteries, nor elevate the mysteries to the level of Christianity. In many interpretations of the Christian idea of salvation (especially the earliest), we have seen that salvation means primarily salvation by the teaching and influence of Christ : and to the last this idea was never absent, at least from Greek theology. The mystery-religions had, so far as we know, no ethical teaching which could be even compared to this : for real non-Christian approximations to the teaching of Christ we must look to quite a different quarter. None of the great Stoic philosophers would have had anything to do with the mystery-religions. And the moral influence actually exercised by the mysteries could equally little be compared with that exercised by Christianity.

That the mystery-religions did *to some extent* satisfy religious needs and produce an elevating effect upon character, I for one

have no wish to deny : but most of what is said on this head is
pure surmise.   There is hardly any evidence as to the extent to
which men were made better by the mystery-religions : the most
that is known is that *at their best* they did insist upon the necessity
of moral purification as well as upon ritual observances : in what
(besides ascetic observances) such purification consisted, or with
what success it was urged, we simply do not know.   And we do
know that there was another side—an obscene and disgusting side
—to the mysteries, which is very prominent in many of the
accounts which we have of them.   If we suppose that among
St. Paul's converts (*e.g.* at Corinth) there were many who had been
initiates of the Mysteries, his Epistles supply us with little ground
for suspecting that they were freer from the ordinary pagan vices
than other pagans.   In his view the average morality of a world
in which these mysteries (we are sometimes told) exercised such
enormous influence, was of the lowest—much lower than
anything which St. Paul attributes to his unconverted Jewish
fellow-countrymen.   St. Paul's testimony may of course be
attributed to bias : but the fact remains that, in writing to a number
of Gentile Churches, he shows himself quite unaware of the existence
of any body of men who even professed such a moral standard as
was at least aimed at by Christians and even by Jews.   Doubtless
St. Paul may have exaggerated the blackness of the pagan world.
We should hardly suspect from his writings how high was the
ideal proposed, and partially practised, by the best men of Stoicism.
We have evidence as to the excellent influence exercised by
philosophy upon certain limited and cultivated circles : we have
little such evidence as to the mysteries.   Tatian had been initiated
into some of the mysteries, and was certainly not edified by them.[1]
Writers like Professor Lake seem to me wholly oblivious of the
enormous contrast between the ideal of the Gospels and any which
could conceivably be associated with the names of Mithra or of
Osiris.

(9) The extent of the resemblance or of the contrast presented
by Christianity and the mystery-religions must obviously depend
in part upon the interpretation which we put upon Christianity.
The fundamental point of difference was, as it seems to me, the
indefinitely more ethical character of Christianity : but this is
a view which can only be taken where the ethical element in
Christianity is regarded as central and dominant.   In so far as
redemption is thought of as a moral regeneration effected by the
influence of Christ's character, and by that love of God of which
His death was the accepted symbol, there is little resemblance
between such a mode of redemption and that supplied by the mystery-
religions : there is, indeed, little in common between them besides

[1] *Oratio,* c. 29.

the bare idea of redemption. When redemption comes to be thought of as flowing in some mysterious and magical way from the crucified God-man, chiefly through the mechanical channel of the sacraments, then the resemblance of Christianity to the mystery-religions becomes very much closer. The strongest influence which can be attributed to the mystery-religions in Christianity was a tendency to substitute this latter conception of it for the former. And yet happily that transformation of Christianity was never complete. An intensely ethical conception of redemption is found even in the writers whose language about the Church and the sacraments sometimes most forcibly suggests a comparison with the ideas of the mystery-religions. It is on its lower rather than on its higher side that the Christianity of the ancient Church may be said to exhibit the influence of the mystery-religions. On the whole their influence was a deteriorating influence, and this influence did not become conspicuous till a period later than that of the New Testament writings. That this influence is at its highest, not in the Christianity of the great Church but in the Gnosticism which the Church rejected, has already been remarked.

And here it may be convenient to add a word about the distinction, of which so much is made in some quarters, between religions of redemption and legalistic religions. The common point in Christianity and the mystery-religions was that both of them were eminently religions of redemption : both of them promised to deliver men from the guilt, the dominion, and the punishment of sin, and to overcome that alienation from God which was the necessary consequence of sin. And there was *some* resemblance in the methods of redemption which were prescribed. It is probable that the mystery-religions strengthened the tendency to make of Christianity a religion of redemption— more so than it had been in its more primitive and more Jewish form. So long and so far as redemption was conceived of in an ethical manner, this was on the whole a progressive tendency. But it would have been a very pernicious tendency, had it made Christianity a religion of redemption pure and simple. The worst forms of Gnosticism may suffice to show what would become of a religion which had no legalistic element in it. The truth is that this distinction between redemptive and legalistic religions, though convenient for some purposes, becomes misleading and mischievous if treated as an absolute distinction. Every religion is both legalistic and redemptive, though one element may be stronger than the other in a particular faith. Judaism is usually taken as the typically legalistic religion : but Judaism always—and increasingly in its higher forms—recognized the need for repentance, and the willingness of God to forgive—

to say nothing of that Messianic hope which prepared the way for the distinctively Christian doctrine of redemption. And Christianity retained the idea of divine commandments, without some measure of obedience to which salvation was impossible ; in obedience to which, made possible by redemption through Christ, salvation actually consisted.[1] It is not too much to say that, while a religion which was *purely* legalistic would hardly be a religion, a religion which was purely a religion of redemption would be totally non-moral. A religion which knows of no divine law would be *ex vi termini* an anti-nomian religion.

[1] The same may be said of Buddhism, usually treated as a religion of redemption. Probably the nearest approach to a *purely* legalistic religion would be Confucianism in its learned, esoteric form, but in that form Confucianism is practically a system of secular ethics rather than what is ordinarily meant by a religion.

APPENDIX III

DR. DALE'S *Theory of the Atonement* is still regarded in many quarters with so much respect that it may be desirable to quote the paragraphs in which he sums up his position (pp. 430 *sq.*) with a few comments.

1. "The death of Christ is the objective ground on which the sins of men are remitted, because it was an act of submission to the righteous authority of the Law by which the human race was condemned (1)—a submission by One from whom on various grounds the act of submission derived transcendent moral significance (2), and because in consequence of the relation between Him and us—His Life being our own—His submission is the expression of ours (3), and carries ours with it (4). He was not our Representative in a sense which would imply that because He submitted to the just authority by which the penalties of sin are inflicted we are released from the obligations of submission. The sufferings, indeed, were His, that they might not be ours; He endured them, that we might escape from them (5). But the moral act of Christ in submitting to those sufferings while it remains for ever alone in its unique and awful grandeur, involves a similar moral act on the part of all who have ' access ' to God through Him (6).

" A real submission to the righteousness of God in condemning us was necessary before the penalties of sin could be remitted (7). This submission was made by Christ; it was made for us, on our behalf, in our name (8). But we have a part in it. In a real and not merely a technical sense the act is ours (9). It is ours because through our relation to Him it has made possible to us, though in an inferior form, a similar consent to the righteousness of the penalties which we have deserved (10). It is ours, for it is the transcendent expression and act of that eternal life in which we live, and which is perpetually revealed in our own character and history."

On this passage I should like to make the following remarks.

The numbers in the following notes correspond to the numbers which I have inserted in the text :

(1) When was the human race thus condemned ? The sentence clearly implies the literal historical truth of the story in Genesis, together with the Augustinian additions to the story, and all that follows rests at bottom upon the same assumption.

(2) A piece of vague rhetoric.

(3) This makes the Atonement a piece of play-acting. It was a dramatic representation by Christ of a punishment which might have been, but was not, inflicted upon those who had deserved it.

(4) Only true in so far as it actually causes repentance and amendment ; otherwise a fiction.

(5) This is ambiguous. It implies *either* substitution *or* the subjective, Abelardian view. The first interpretation is the one against which this book is chiefly directed : the second is that for which I have contended.

(6) The same equivocation disguised by the skilful use of the ambiguous term " involves." On the objective interpretation, the statement is a fiction. So far as " involves " means " causes or assists," it is true.

(7) If God had condemned us in the way implied by Dr. Dale's thesis, He would not be righteous. The retributive theory of punishment is clearly implied, and also the view that punishment can rightly be inflicted upon the innocent.

(8) " On our behalf " is true, if it means " that we might be made better " : if it means " that we might be supposed to have suffered a penalty which in point of fact we have not suffered," it is meaningless or immoral.

(9) A mere assertion—a fiction or at best a metaphor.

(10) If this means " be brought to acknowledge that we might justly have been punished," it is difficult to see how the endurance of a penalty by the innocent should have this effect : but if it did, the effect would be prospective and subjective, not retrospective and objective.

2. " The Death of Christ is the objective ground on which the sins of men are remitted, because it rendered possible the retention or the recovery of our original and ideal relation to God through Christ which sin had dissolved, and the loss of which was the supreme penalty of transgression " (p. 431).

How " rendered possible " ? If the answer is " because of a law which declares that the endurance of a penalty by the innocent justifies the remission of penalty in the guilty apart from the effects of the vicarious suffering," the assertion is immoral and untrue. If it means " because the death of Christ produces moral effects which make punishment unnecessary," this is the Abelardian theory.

3. "The Death of Christ is the objective ground on which the sins of men are remitted, because it involved the actual destruction of sin in all those who through faith recover their union with Him" (p. 431).

It is difficult to see how the atoning death of Christ should "involve" this actual destruction except by awakening repentance and amendment, which is the Abelardian theory : otherwise it involves a conception which is really a survival of the savage theory of "sympathetic magic."

4. "The Death of Christ is the objective ground on which the sins of men are remitted, because in His submission to the awful Penalty of Sin, in order to preserve or to restore our relations to the Father through Him, there was a revelation of the righteousness of God, which must otherwise have been revealed in the infliction of the penalties of sin on the human race. He endured the penalty instead of inflicting it" (p. 431).

If the penalty was borne by the sinless instead of the guilty, this would reveal the unrighteousness of God and not His righteousness. If it means that "the death of Christ" (in conjunction with the whole influence of His life and teaching) tends to "preserve or to restore our relations with the Father," this is a true statement, but then the death cannot properly be described as a penalty.

The constant succession of ambiguities and verbal juggleries in Dr. Dale's book produce a very painful impression—all the more so on account of the high Christian character and the tolerant disposition which the author's writings everywhere reveal. In fairness to Dr. Dale it must be remembered that the real ground of his belief, as he would no doubt have fully admitted, is the authority of Scripture. His theory is based on a view of the plenary inspiration of St. Paul's Epistles which few modern theologians would accept, and which brought with it the necessity of an uncritical reading of St. Paul's theories into the Gospel record of our Lord's own teaching. Modern theologians often repeat the same sophistries, though they have really abandoned Dr. Dale's premisses.

As it is sometimes suggested that the ideas against which this book has been largely directed are now obsolete, I may also refer to Dr. Forsyth, who explicitly regards the death of Christ as expiatory, substitutionary, and sometimes as penal, though as to this he is more hesitating. (See his Essay in *The Atonement in*

Modern Religious Thought, The Cruciality of the Cross, and other works.) In *Le Dogme de la Rédemption*, by the Abbé Rivière (Professor in the Seminary of Albi—a seminary which has a reputation for Modernism), the ideas of substitution, expiation, vicarious punishment are defended no less explicitly from the Catholic point of view, though the chief emphasis is on the idea of " satisfaction." Professor Ottley explicitly defends the proposition that Christ died as a " substitute," but combines it with the characteristically Greek theoryt hat all humanity suffered in Christ (*Doctrine of the Incarnation*, ii. p. 315). He regards Christ's death as bringing about an " objective change in the relation between God and sinful man " (*ib.* p. 319). Even the Rev. J. K. Mozley, after a very sympathetic and tolerant review of previous theories, ends by saying, " I do not therefore think that we need shrink from saying that Christ bore penal suffering for us and in our stead " (*The Doctrine of the Atonement*, p. 216). Mr. Mozley's book, I may add, contains a very full bibliography of the subject, and a classification of the theories which the various writers represent. Another recent defender of the substitutionary theory is the Rev. John Scott Lidgett in *The Spiritual Principle of the Atonement*.

I had originally intended to deal more fully with modern theories on the subject, but found that to do so with any fullness would require a second volume or a separate work.

An apology is perhaps due for the neglect of so important a work as the late Prof. R. C. Moberly's *Atonement and Personality* (1901), but the position taken up is not easy to describe or to criticize in a short space. I can only say that it seems to me an attempt to combine modern or liberal with traditional theories which, in spite of all his subtlety, still stand apart in his pages like oil and water. I have criticized the Professor's views in an article in the *Journal of Theological Studies*, iii. 178-211.

INDEX

(Figures are printed with an asterisk when the reference is exclusively to the Notes)

INDEX

y

THE END

Printed by R. & R. CLARK, LIMITED, *Edinburgh.*

NEW THEOLOGICAL WORKS

THE BEGINNINGS OF CHRISTIANITY. A Series
of Volumes by various Writers. Edited by Dr. F. J. FOAKES
JACKSON and Prof. KIRSOPP LAKE.

PART I.—THE ACTS OF THE APOSTLES

VOL. I.—PROLEGOMENA I. The Jewish, Gentile, and
Christian Backgrounds. [*Autumn* 1919.

VOL. II.—PROLEGOMENA II. Criticism. [*In the Press.*

VOL. III.—TEXT AND COMMENTARY. [*In Preparation.*

LANDMARKS IN THE HISTORY OF EARLY
CHRISTIANITY. Haskell Lectures. By the Rev. Professor
KIRSOPP LAKE, D.D. 8vo.

THE TESTING OF A NATION : Sermons Preached
on Special Occasions during the War. By RANDALL T. DAVIDSON,
Archbishop of Canterbury. Crown 8vo.

THE SPIRIT : God and His Relation to Man considered
from the standpoint of Philosophy, Psychology, and Art. By
various Writers. Edited by Canon BURNETT H. STREETER. 8vo.

CHRISTIAN FREEDOM. Hulsean Lectures, 1918–
1919. By the Rev. FRANCIS E. HUTCHINSON, M.A., Vicar of
Leyland, Preston. Crown 8vo.

CHRIST'S HISTORIC HOPE : Sermons Preached
before the University of Oxford. By the Ven. W. H. Hutton,
B.D., Archdeacon of Northampton and Canon of Peterborough.
Crown 8vo.

LONDON : MACMILLAN AND CO., LTD.

I

NEW THEOLOGICAL WORKS

THE ARMY AND RELIGION. An Enquiry: and its bearing upon the Religious Life of the Nation. With Preface by the Bishop of Winchester. Crown 8vo. 6s. net.

PATHWAYS TO CHRISTIAN UNITY: A Free Church View. A volume of Essays by members of the Swanwick Free Church Fellowship. Edited by MALCOLM SPENCER. Crown 8vo.

AN INTRODUCTION TO OLD TESTAMENT STUDY. By Rev. E. BASIL REDLICH, M.A. With Foreword by the Dean of Westminster. Crown 8vo.

THE POWER OF PRAYER. Being a Selection of Walker Trust Essays on Prayer, together with a Study of the Essays as a Religious and Theological Document, by the Rev. W. P. PATERSON, D.D., Professor of Divinity in the University of Edinburgh. 8vo.

THE REALM OF PRAYER. By the Rev. R. H. COATS, M.A., B.D., author of "Types of English Piety," "The Christian Life," etc. Crown 8vo.

BUILDING THE WALLS: A Book of Prayer and Thanksgiving for Family and Private Use. With Introduction, and new Preface, by the Archbishop of Canterbury. Third Edition. Pott 8vo.

SIR HOBBARD DE HOY. A Study of Adolescence. By the Rev. E. F. BRALEY. Crown 8vo.

The subject of this book is the religion and the religious training of the adolescent.

LONDON : MACMILLAN AND CO., LTD.